BUILDING AN AMERICAN PEDIGREE

A Study in Genealogy

NORMAN EDGAR WRIGHT, M.S., A.G.

BRIGHAM YOUNG UNIVERSITY PRESS
Provo, Utah

MULTILITH SERIES
Library of Congress Catalog Card Number: 74-9887
International Standard Book Number: 0-8425-0899-6
Brigham Young University Press, Provo, Utah 84602
Sixth printing 1980
Printed in the United States of America
          11/80   1Mp   49417

CONTENTS

APPENDIXES

LIST OF FIGURES

PREFACE AND ACKNOWLEDGMENTS

This book is designed for the person who desires to get right to work confirming and extending his genealogy records without studying theory and background information. It is a practical book based on the training and experience of the author; it provides an outline of selected sources which are essential to American genealogy, covering their time period, content, and availability.

The first sections cover the "survey phase" during which the beginner gets a proper start in genealogical record keeping and begins to determine the extent of previous research in his areas of interest. Methods, procedures, and sources which help build a solid foundation for research in original records are introduced. In later sections a worker who has reached the so-called "research phase" will find help in investigating selected major sources to confirm survey data and add new facts to his pedigree. These chapters will lead the worker--with many illustrations and examples and much bibliographic detail--to vital, church, and cemetery records, to census, probate, civil-court, land, military records, and to selected miscellaneous records where new facts can be located to confirm survey data and extend the pedigree. Additional material covering regional aspects of American genealogy is planned for later publication.

This work has been several years in planning and preparation, beginning while I was a researcher at the LDS Genealogical Society from 1957 to 1962 and continuing after that at Brigham Young University where I came to teach. A sabbatical leave in 1971 provided the time to arrange and draft the manuscript, but it has taken two additional years to refine the form and find a satisfactory publisher. BUILDING AN AMERICAN PEDIGREE has been produced because American genealogy requires unusual treatment, and a "sure cure" for all the problems associated with it has not yet been found.

To be certain, Val Greenwood's THE RESEARCHER'S GUIDE
TO AMERICAN GENEALOGY (Baltimore: Genealogical Publishing
Company, 1973) fills a real need in American genealogy. My work
and Greenwood's follow a similar approach. But while his book is
primarily a reference volume, BUILDING AN AMERICAN PEDIGREE
provides, in addition to extensive reference material, instructions
in using references, as well as profuse illustrations and examples to
guide the researcher in his work.

Ernest L. Olson of Brigham Young University Press was very
kind in reviewing the work and accepting it for publication. I express
special appreciation to Dean Martin B. Hickman of the College of
Social Science for his cooperation in seeing the work was published.
I also extend appreciation to the many students who have taken genealogy courses at Brigham Young University, because their challenge
motivated me to this work.

My lovely wife Carolyn and our children Preston, Craig, Joel,
Jerry, Diane, Suzanne, Kathryn and Nathan have also helped me in
this work and are responsible for making genealogy a living subject
with me.

N.E.W.

INTRODUCTION

A renewed interest in genealogy, especially among laymen, has created the need for the direct approach taken in this work. Modern microfilming techniques and enlarged programs of record acquisition by genealogical and historical societies have opened an entirely new world of source material to the genealogist. Many original records which have heretofore been restricted are now available and are inviting the researcher to seek and investigate. Genealogical organizations, including the Genealogical Society of The Church of Jesus Christ of Latter-day Saints, are involved in gathering and microfilming these materials for public use.

Genealogical research can provide much personal satisfaction if one will undertake it with determination and a desire to perform well. It is history at its best, with the family and the individual paramount. Nothing is more interesting than man, God's greatest creation. And genealogy is a study of man and his offspring.

Research methods and procedures in genealogy are similar to those in other fields which use the historical method. Information is gathered from historical sources, analyzed, classified, and recorded in an appropriate manner. The information is then verified and can be published for others to use.

The genealogist usually begins his work by gathering names, dates, places, and kinship information from family and home sources. He then attempts to determine the extent of information already in print which might pertain to the problem and checks this information through certain general collections of the LDS Genealogical Society in Salt Lake City. This is often referred to as the "survey phase" of research. After the researcher has gathered his survey data, he analyzes it and defines his research objectives. He decides what information he is lacking or notes any conflicts; then he outlines steps to solve the problem. To accomplish his objectives, the worker usually moves into primary sources of the various jurisdictions where the family or individual of interest resided.

The "research phase" of genealogical investigation includes searches of major records created by the towns, counties, states, and the nation where the family lived, including vital, church, cemetery, census, probate, civil-criminal court, land, military, and miscellaneous social-commercial records.

Building an American pedigree is much like trying to work a jigsaw puzzle. A person does not usually recognize where each piece fits at a single glance but follows some plan to put them in their proper place. Perhaps by gathering pieces with straight edges he can put the outside border together, and then by observing color combinations and individual outlines he may be able to place each piece in its correct position until the entire puzzle is assembled.

Some genealogical problems are solved with very little effort, while others require considerable time and study. Some may seem to defy solution so that it may be necessary to secure professional help. Most persons can perform to a fair degree in genealogical research if they are willing to put forth a little effort. It is important to recognize, however, that the specialist who has worked and studied has a definite advantage over the novice in working difficult genealogical puzzles. An experienced and qualified mechanic can diagnose an engine failure quickly, while the amateur may spend needless hours trying to locate the trouble. Likewise, a competent genealogist can evaluate a particular pedigree problem and know just what to do to solve it, while a novice might plod along in the records for days without coming close to the solution. Of course, some problems may prove impossible for even the expert. In such cases, it may be necessary to lay the work aside for a time until additional records become available or until financial help can be obtained.

But whether he is novice or professional, a researcher does well to remember the widely accepted genealogical axiom that a survey should be conducted on each genealogical problem before moving into original sources. The survey is designed to determine the extent of previous research and often provides useful information for continued research. It helps to lay a solid foundation upon which to build and, if properly conducted, can save valuable time and resources. Solutions to many genealogical problems are already near but are not recognized by the average person. A well-conducted survey can bring them to light. This is not to suggest that a researcher will not succeed if he goes directly into original sources, but a good survey will allow him to do a better job. For this reason, this volume offers instruction in survey procedures for those interested in building American pedigrees.

Genealogical research can be interesting and enlightening. It can even be fun, if you know what you are doing. So dig in and enjoy yourself!

SECTION ONE - GETTING A PROPER START

CHAPTER 1

USING SOURCES FROM THE FAMILY AND HOME

A beginning genealogical researcher starts his search for information with himself, his relatives, and family associates. The knowledge of living persons, as well as the variety of records that may be kept at home, are his first good sources of basic information, the names, dates, and places he will need to begin his records. Once he has learned to evaluate these home and family sources and has tabulated the basic facts in some sort of pedigree and family group form, he is on his way in genealogical research.

Personal Knowledge and Memory

The beginning researcher starts with what he knows already. He lists himself as parent or child on a family group sheet or pedigree chart and fills in the names, dates, and locality information that he can recall (figs. 1 and 2). A variety of genealogical charts and forms are available from commercial houses to meet the ordinary researcher's needs. Or he can, if he wants, design his own. The pedigree chart shown provides a handy view of ancestral lines, and the family group record allows for some detail about each family member.[1]

Recording facts from personal knowledge and memory is a starting point, but other sources must also be investigated to confirm information recorded and to extend the pedigree. Some people have excellent memories and are able to list many facts with little effort, but most are able to recall only limited genealogical information from memory. It is therefore necessary to turn to the testimony of others and to the recorded word for additional information.

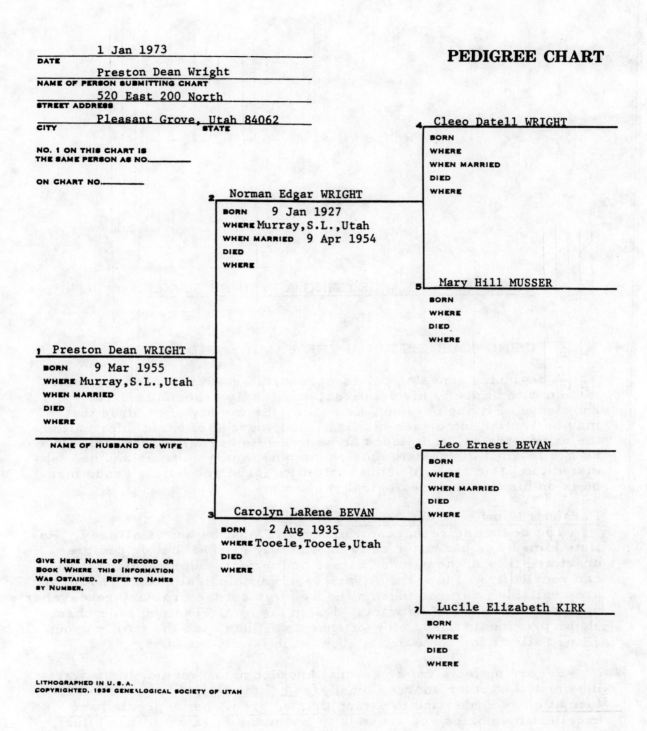

PEDIGREE CHART

DATE: 1 Jan 1973

NAME OF PERSON SUBMITTING CHART: Preston Dean Wright

STREET ADDRESS: 520 East 200 North

CITY: Pleasant Grove, Utah 84062   STATE:

NO. 1 ON THIS CHART IS THE SAME PERSON AS NO._____

ON CHART NO._____

4 Cleeo Datell WRIGHT
BORN
WHERE
WHEN MARRIED
DIED
WHERE

2 Norman Edgar WRIGHT
BORN   9 Jan 1927
WHERE Murray, S.L., Utah
WHEN MARRIED 9 Apr 1954
DIED
WHERE

5 Mary Hill MUSSER
BORN
WHERE
DIED
WHERE

1 Preston Dean WRIGHT
BORN   9 Mar 1955
WHERE Murray, S.L., Utah
WHEN MARRIED
DIED
WHERE

NAME OF HUSBAND OR WIFE

6 Leo Ernest BEVAN
BORN
WHERE
WHEN MARRIED
DIED
WHERE

3 Carolyn LaRene BEVAN
BORN   2 Aug 1935
WHERE Tooele, Tooele, Utah
DIED
WHERE

GIVE HERE NAME OF RECORD OR BOOK WHERE THIS INFORMATION WAS OBTAINED. REFER TO NAMES BY NUMBER.

7 Lucile Elizabeth KIRK
BORN
WHERE
DIED
WHERE

LITHOGRAPHED IN U.S.A.
COPYRIGHTED, 1936 GENEALOGICAL SOCIETY OF UTAH

Fig. 1.   Basic facts recorded in pedigree form

2

HUSBAND Norman Edgar WRIGHT

Born 9 Jan 1927 Place Murray, Salt Lake, Utah
Chr. Place
Marr. 9 Apr 1954 Place Salt Lake City, Salt Lake, Utah
Died Place
Bur. Place
HUSBAND'S FATHER Cleeo Datell WRIGHT
HUSBAND'S MOTHER Mary Hill MUSSER
HUSBAND'S OTHER WIVES

WIFE Carolyn LaRene BEVAN

Born 2 Aug 1935 Place Tooele, Tooele, Utah
Chr. Place
Died Place
Bur. Place
WIFE'S FATHER Leo Ernest BEVAN
WIFE'S MOTHER Lucile Elizabeth KIRK
WIFE'S OTHER HUSBANDS

	SEX M/F	CHILDREN — List each child (whether living or dead) in order of birth — Given Names — SURNAME	WHEN BORN — DAY MONTH YEAR	WHERE BORN — TOWN	WHERE BORN — COUNTY	WHERE BORN — STATE OR COUNTRY	DATE OF FIRST MARRIAGE — TO WHOM	WHEN DIED — DAY MONTH — YEAR
1 X	M	Preston Dean WRIGHT	9 Mar 1955	Murray	S. L.	Utah		
2	M	Craig Jeromy WRIGHT	22 Aug 1956	"	"	"		
3	M	Joel Kirk WRIGHT	7 May 1956	"	"	"		
4	M	Jerry Bevan WRIGHT	26 Jan 1960	"	"	"		
5	F	Diane Lucile WRIGHT	17 Oct 1961	"	"	"		
6	F	Suzanne Marie WRIGHT	15 Nov 1963	"	"	"		
7	F	Kathryn Anne WRIGHT	28 Oct 1965	American Fork	Utah	"		
8	M	Nathan Mark WRIGHT	18 Oct 1967	American Fork				
9								
10								
11								

OTHER MARRIAGES

SOURCES OF INFORMATION
1. Personal knowledge and memory of Preston D. Wright.
2. Family record of Norman E. and Carolyn B. Wright, Pleasant Grove, Utah.

Fig. 2. Basic facts recorded in family group form

3

The Testimony of Others[2]

Immediate and distant relatives as well as family associates and old-timers can often provide helpful information. It is surprising what genealogical facts some old-timers have at their fingertips. The information may of course be secondary and often must be taken with a grain of salt, but it can be very useful in directing the course of research. One should not be too concerned with the accuracy of the information at this point but should be more interested in determining what the family knows. Later research and applied techniques in source analysis and record evaluation will help determine the accuracy and completeness of the information.

Sometimes oral testimony provides the only available evidence about a particular event. (This is particularly true when it comes to such things as modern illegitimate births for which no court or church records are made.) Moreover, a living relative or an old-timer may be able to give clues which will help in searching official sources. Jesse Hulse, the informant on the death certificate of Kindness Ann Hanes, was living until just a few years ago, and even though he was over 90 years old, he could relate important facts about her family-- exact dates of settlement in various areas of the state, and accurate vital statistics on some members of the family. Information like this can save a great deal of time that might be spent in futile search in the records.

Sometimes an old-timer can provide helpful information concerning an earlier family residence or the location of cemeteries where family members have been buried. In Greene County, Tennessee, Judge Samuel Willard Doty (sixth-great-grandson to Edward Doty of Mayflower fame) had taken personal charge of the Doty Chapel Cemetery in Greene County and could give detail on nearly every person buried there. He also had documents in his possession relating to the old "Doty Homestead," which has been in the family since 1783.

Family members are sometimes reluctant to reveal or discuss certain family information for fear it might have an adverse effect on the family name or image. I think, however, that nearly every family has a skeleton or two in its closet. The researcher should be tactful and considerate in his searches when he meets such resistance, of course, but he should not be afraid to make the truth known when he finds it.

If considerately and tactfully approached, contact with old-timers can foster warm associations, as well as providing information and clues. While conducting research in Yates County, New York, my wife located a relative on her Kelsey line of whom the family had no previous knowledge. During a cordial visit at her home in Pen Yan, this relative was able to produce interesting traditions about the immigrant Kelsey family in Connecticut, as well as family letters, photographs, a family Bible, and a long-out-of-print history of Yates

4

County which included family information. Personal friendship and close kinship was engendered by the visit, and a much closer family tie now exists.

All family sources are not of equal value. For instance, the researcher must be careful in accepting family tradition at face value, for it can be deceptive. Most American families have traditions, and nearly every family has tradition which is subject to question. Perhaps "three brothers came to America in an early day from the old country" and all persons by that surname in America descend from them, or perhaps an ancestor was of "royal birth" and was "disowned for marrying a commoner." Then likely the person "fled the old country as a stowaway" or "changed his name"; hence, records cannot be found to document the story. Nearly every adult Mormon male living in the Nauvoo period was a "personal friend" or a "bodyguard" of Joseph Smith or Brigham Young, and nearly every Revolutionary soldier was a "bodyguard" to George Washington. Some of the traditions may be correct, or at least based upon truth, but many are nothing more than romantic hope or imagination.

Family tradition should not be ignored, however. Sometimes a grain of truth in family tradition can provide valuable clues for research in original sources. This was the case with an Idaho family. A family tradition held that their ancestor "Abram Montey" came to America from France with General Lafayette in 1777 and helped save America in the Revolution. Research in original sources for New York and Canada indicated that the family was in America much earlier than 1777; in fact, the immigrant, Jacque Montee, was in Canada at least one hundred years before the American Revolution. His descendants later moved from Quebec to Clinton County, New York, where several joined the Continental Army and "did help save America in the Revolution." But they did not come over with Lafayette in 1777. Abram Montey was actually born in Plattsburg, New York, sixteen years after the Revolution was over. It is interesting to note that one of his ancestors had married a Mary Lafayette who may well have been a relative of the famous French General. Was this the basis for the earlier family tradition?

Documentary Testimony[3]

In addition to oral testimony and tradition, printed and manuscript records in possession of family members are helpful sources. Most any type of record or document might be found with the family or in the home--Bibles, diaries, journals, family record books, letters, clippings, certificates, photographs, and other materials. Land and estate records might also be found among family possessions as might military and pension documents (fig. 3).

A woman recently visited her uncle in Salt Lake City and obtained her grandfather's personal journals which dated to the 1840s. Amos Milton Musser had been active in early LDS history and was a Mennonite from Lancaster County, Pennsylvania, before becoming a

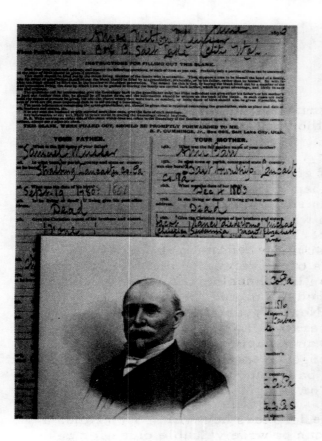

Fig. 3. Documents and photographs from the home

Mormon. Amos had recorded important genealogical facts pertaining to his family in Pennsylvania in his journals, and entries have been useful in correlating family information with original research. These journals have since been microfilmed, and copies have been deposited with the Church Historian, because they also contain information of early historical interest to the LDS Church (fig. **4**).

In cases of Mormon ancestry, LDS Family Record Books and Temple Ordinance Books compiled by family members should be given special consideration. There was a time when members were encouraged to keep special books showing ordinance work completed, and these records sometimes contain helpful genealogical facts relating to earlier periods. They are especially valuable to give or confirm place-name information and death dates (fig. **5**).

Old letters, photographs, and newspaper clippings are some of the more interesting home sources which can sometimes be used to solve unusual genealogical problems. On one occasion, a genealogist was able to locate a family in the Staunton, Virginia, 1850 census without knowing the surname of the family. The given names of several relatives were known from family letters, but the original envelopes had been destroyed and the persons writing the letters had not listed surnames. By noting the addresses and the given names mentioned, the searcher was able to find the family (Herndon) in the census schedules.

Correspondence between family members has also been responsible for the preservation of family and individual characteristics. Old letters and photographs seem to make ancestors live again, and this is one of the most satisfying rewards of genealogical research (figs. 6 and 7).

More often than not, original land and estate documents are in the home and not in the county courthouse or town hall. The courthouse entry is often a copy of the original in possession of the family. The same is true of other records. Judge S. W. Doty had the original 1783 deed to land owned in Greene County, Tennessee, until his death in 1969, and it is now in possession of his son Lyle. The land was deeded to Samuel's great-grandfather Azariah Doty in 1783, and the family, in a direct line, has retained possession and title ever since.

Cases are known where several families have lived on a particular tract or parcel of land for several generations without officially transferring title to the land. Some of these transactions remain unrecorded, while others are recorded several years after the event took place. Family records are often the only source for such information.

Military and pension documents often remain hidden among personal effects or packed away in an attic or basement, but their discovery is well worth the time and effort necessary to locate them. These

Fig. 4.   Amos Milton Musser Journals held by his son
Burton W. Musser

Fig. 5.   LDS family record and ordinance books

October The fourth 1855

Dear And Mutch Respected Children I Gladly embrace The preasant opperternity of Wrighting you Afew Laines to let you Know That wee are all well at preasant thanks Bee to god for His Mercies bestoed on us hoping These few Laines May find you all enjoying The Lik blessing wee Received your Letter Dated Augus the twentyfirst on the first day of this Month which gaue us A greadeal of satturfaction eaven to Hear that you were A living And dooing well I wish you to excuse Mee for Not wrighting you Ansunser to your Last Letter for I thought I Had Don so till Afew Days past Mother told Mee I Had not And in Afeue days wee got yours Again you said your Crops was Light on the Account of drauth And Hares is very Light this yeas on the Account Wet wheat is wourth one Dallar and fifty Cent pr bushel pork is worth five Dallars pr Hundred weight I Have sold thirty bushels of wheate And one Hundred and ten Dallars worth of Stock Hogs one Cow and Caff at twentyfive Dallars wee have yet on Hands thre Hed of Horses Nine Hed of Cattel thirty Hed of sheep And five Breading sows one Eight Hed of Killing Hogs

Fig. 6. Extract from letter of Azariah Haines, 4 October 1855

Fig. 7. Very early photographs (Azariah Haines and Sarah Tucker)

cannot always be found when they are first needed but each researcher can undertake a continuing program to locate and investigate family sources.

Certain limitations are evident in family and home sources, and careful discrimination must be used in accepting information as true. Much of it is highly unreliable and subject to misinterpretation. Some information from "memory" is based upon hearsay while some represents personal knowledge and results in quality research. The worker should use caution and should confirm his information from official public documents when he can, but he should certainly not disregard family and home sources.

For some families, collecting information from family sources is aided by family genealogical organizations which are effective in locating, preserving, and distributing genealogical information. Some have professional researchers in their employ and have correlated programs to acquire and disseminate information and to provide research direction to interested family members. More families should organize and correlate their work so that less duplication of research takes place.[4] The Genealogical Society Library in Salt Lake City maintains a special file for registration of family organizations interested in genealogy, and all families engaged in genealogical research are encouraged to register with that organization.

Problems exist in family organizations as they now operate. In some families, certain good-hearted members do most of the genealogical work, and then others move in for the results without offering adequate compensation. Sometimes an interested family member wants a copy of "all family information" without considering the time and effort which went into its compilation. Family members should be aware of this and should be more considerate in this respect.

In addition, there is a need for a general information storage and retrieval system correlated with each family organization. Much time and money are wasted in the duplication of research among family members who do not correlate their work. A Utah family may be spending time and money searching out facts on their pedigree while relatives in California are doing the same work without knowing it. Some families have developed limited central clearinghouses, but there is need for much broader work. The LDS Genealogical Society is providing some correlation for persons who are processing names through its facilities, but very little is being done to correlate original research. At the present time the individual beginning research must surge forward as if no others are working on his pedigree, and if he happens to locate others doing similar work, it is a matter of luck rather than good planning.

The genealogist should take the necessary steps to determine which other persons are working on his lines and should correlate his work with theirs. Investigation of family and home sources is an excellent way to begin accomplishing that objective.

---

1. For detailed procedure on pedigree chart numbering systems, see chapter 7 of Wright and Pratt's GENEALOGICAL RESEARCH ESSENTIALS (Salt Lake City: Bookcraft, 1967) or chapter 5 of Jaussi and Chaston's FUNDAMENTALS OF GENEALOGICAL RESEARCH, 2nd ed. rev. (Salt Lake City: Deseret Book Co., 1972).

2. For an interesting article on "Tradition and Family History," see Wright and Pratt, pp. 149-152.

3. For an interesting article on "A Few Odd Ways by which Family Records Have Been Preserved," see Wright and Pratt, pp. 153-157.

4. For excellent articles on family organization, see Theodore M. Burton, "With Whom Will We Share Exaltation?" ENSIGN, August 1971, pp. 33-35 and W. Dean Belnap, "How to Start a Family Organization and Keep It Going," ENSIGN, August 1972, pp. 81-83.

CHAPTER 2

KEEPING NOTES AND CORRESPONDING

Before the genealogist has done much practical searching, he begins to realize that some organized plan for keeping research notes is necessary if he is to correctly analyze and evaluate his work. Of course, some facts are assimilated immediately and can be transferred directly to a permanent record, but much of the data gathered must be analyzed and evaluated in connection with other material, often at a later date. Hence, some system to organize research findings while conducting research is helpful.

Failure to organize from the beginning of research can lead to confusion and unnecessary work later. One researcher recently spent over $1500 traveling to Wisconsin seeking genealogical information on his Ferris and Benson lines of Iowa County. He returned with twenty-six spiral notebooks filled with genealogical information. Each book contained information from various sources and localities. As he attempted to construct family group records from his notes, it became apparent that he had followed no organized plan in extracting facts from land, court, cemetery, and family records. Actually, he had followed no system at all, and every question required his thumbing through one or more notebooks for the answer. Before he could effectively use the material gathered, he had to spend several hours reorganizing the facts into some logical pattern. His research would have been much more effective had he kept his notes organized according to surname, record source, or locality. Of course all research is not conducted at one time, and few are able to spend several weeks filling twenty-six notebooks on a single genealogical problem, but it is easy to accumulate large amounts of unorganized research material.

All genealogical research should be considered permanent, so a good notekeeping system should be developed by every researcher from the outset. An acceptable system should clearly indicate the facts that have been located, and documentations should be detailed enough so that someone else could locate the sources of information without difficulty.

Every genealogist has his own notekeeping system; no two persons seem to follow exactly the same plan for extracting and filing research information. Some genealogists identify each source investigated on individual cards or slips of paper, while others list details on regular theme paper. Some use spiral notebooks to file their findings, while others use looseleaf ring binders or manila folders. No "best" system can be outlined because each person's objectives may differ. However, those who have workable systems usually follow similar procedures.

Documentation
But before considering specific procedures for extracting and compiling genealogical information, a word about the proper documentation that is so essential to competent research is in order. The genealogist should identify each source he investigates and should be able to distinguish research findings by their source. Published material should be identified by author, title, and publishing information, and by page or section number, when appropriate. Sources from a library should also be identified by call number or reference number, or by film or reel number if the information was taken from microfilm.

When searching census, land, probate, or similar records, a researcher should include the name of the jurisdiction which created the record: "1850 FEDERAL CENSUS OF GREENE COUNTY, TENNESSEE; Household #146/147, page 72" or "GREENE COUNTY, TENNESSEE, DEED BOOK #1 (1787-1824), page 395."

When information is obtained through personal interview, the name and address of the informant should be recorded. When information is from family tradition, that fact should be clearly stated in the notes. Genealogical information obtained through correspondence should be identified by the source, with the informant's report or letter identified. (One should, by the way, take care not to read additional information into a report or to take responsibility for its accuracy.)

Extracting and Compiling Information
Many genealogists find it helpful to take notes according to ancestral names in a certain jurisdiction. These researchers keep "research calendars" to coordinate their work. A simple research calendar would keep track of all the searches made in connection with a particular surname in a single locality, for instance. Each source investigated and all letters written for this research area would be listed on the calendar chronologically. The research findings themselves would be listed on separate numbered sheets which are cross-

referenced to the calendar.

Research calendars might be initiated for various kinds of sources--Family and Home Sources, General LDS Sources, Special LDS Sources, Compiled Sources--as well as for each state, county, or town of interest to the surname or group of surnames (fig. 8).

Another useful coordinating device is the summary form. When several persons with the same name appear in the records at the same time, it may be necessary to use summary forms to distinguish between them (figs. 9 and 9a). On such a form pertinent genealogical facts which apply to a particular individual are brought together. More complete detail can be found in the cross-referenced extracts or originals from which the information came. Actually, the family group record is a summary form, but it is much more general than a formal summary sheet and does not provide space for detailed source listings.

Successful American research usually requires evaluation of all facts gathered which pertain to a particular problem, and a notekeeping system which makes this possible is desirable. When a researcher has direct evidence from a primary source, he may not need to do much evaluating, but when he has only circumstantial evidence, he must support his statements with as much documentation as possible.

For instance, sometimes the searcher gathers information which seems to apply to the problem; however, he cannot prove that it applies without additional supporting information. He must have a notekeeping system which enables him to recall that information when supporting facts are later found. Perhaps a worker finds information in a census record that he thinks pertains to his problem. He copies the information and files it according to the system he has devised, likely either by locality or surname. Now and again, it is necessary to copy information verbatim or to make a photocopy of it, but in most cases, an extract of pertinent information will do (fig. 10).

In making genealogical extracts it is good to remember that facts should be recorded exactly as they appear and should not be abridged or changed as in an abstract and facts from different sources should be listed on separate forms; that is, extracts from census records should not be combined with those from land or probate records. When extracts are kept separate, better evaluation and analysis can be made.

In some foreign research situations, it is possible to establish good genealogical connections from one or two sources; in such cases, elaborate notekeeping systems may not be required. Regular family group records may be the only notes necessary. References can be listed at the bottom of each sheet or on the back. However, on most American problems, researchers usually copy all information which has even a remote possibility of being relevant, and then

RESEARCH CALENDAR

RESEARCHER: N. E. Wright DATE: 29 Dec 1958 REPOSITORY: G.S. SLC, Utah

JURISDICTION OF INTEREST: Greene County, Tennessee

NAMES OF INTEREST: Doty, Drane, Haines, Newman

SOURCE DESCRIPTION	DATE SEARCHED	EXTR. No.
Tax Records 1809-1817 (GS F#5636)	29 Dec 58	1
Wills and Inventories 1802-1810 (GS F#5637)	"	2
Court Minutes 1810-1832 (GS F#5633 pts 2-4)	10 Jan 59	3
Inventories and Sales 1828-1843 (GS F#5636)	"	4
1830 Census (GS F#5557 pt 7)	1 Mar 59	8
1840 Census (GS F#5559 pt 5)	2 Mar 59	9
1850 Census (GS F#5561 pt 3)	1 Mar 59	5
1860 Census (GS F#5560 pt 3)	"	6
1870 Census (GS F#5563 pt 6)	"	7
Index to Court Records Prior to 1810 (GS F#5556)	29 Dec 58	nil
North Carolina Land Grants in Greene County, Tennessee (GS F#5558)	10 Mar 59	nil
Tennessee Pensioners in Greene County (GS F#5553)	10 Mar 59	10

Fig. 8. A research calendar

GENEALOGICAL INFORMATION SHEET

DATA RELATING TO: ___Azariah DOTY_____ BIRTH DATE: _18 Feb 1745_
BIRTH PLACE: ___Piscataway, Middlesex, New Jersey_____
FATHER: ___Isaac DOTY_____ MOTHER: ___Miss RENO_____
MARRIAGE DATE: _____ PLACE: _____Virginia_____
SPOUSE: ___Sarah TUCKER_____
DEATH DATE: ___7 June 1851_____ PLACE: _Greene County, Tennessee_____
BURIAL DATE: _____ PLACE: _Doty Chapel cemetery, Greene Co, Tenn.____
BAPTIZED: _20 Oct 1931_____ ENDOWED: _19 Nov 1931_____ SEALED: _____
PATRON: ___Norman Edgar Wright_____ RELATIONSHIP: 2 gg son_____

HISTORICAL INFORMATION AND DOCUMENTATION

_____1 - DOTY-DOTEN FAMILY by Ethan Allen Doty (GS B6A24)_____

_____"3359. iii. Azariah, b. Feb. 18, 1745" (page 294)_____

_____"...Azariah Doty of Greene Co., Tenn., wrote to his brother, John Doty,____

_____in Garrard Co., Ky., giving news of the family, and requested John to write__

_____to his brother, Ephraim..." (page 294)_____

_____BROTHERS AND SISTERS:_____ #3357. i. Esther, b. about 1738_____

_____ #3358. ii. John, b. Jan. 16, 1740_____

_____ #3359. iii. Azariah, b. Feb. 18, 1745 (as above)_

_____ #3360. iv. Ann, (q. v.)_____

_____ #3361. v. Keziah, b. prob. Jan. 21, 1755._

_____ #3362 vi. Peter._____

_____ #3363 vii. Isaac md a Baxter_____

_____ #3364 viii. Francis (of Va. Ky. & Indn.)__

_____ #3365 ix. Ephraim (of Mo. in 1820)_____

_____ #3366 x. Henry (of Ohio)_____

_____ #3367 xi. Stephen b. prob. 1770._____

_____2 - Tombstone in Doty Chapel Cemetery, Greene Co, Tenn:_____

_____"Azariah Doty 1745--1851" his wife's tombstone reads:_____

_____"Sarah T. Doty 1755-1839" (see photographs in poss. of N. E. Wright)_____

_____3 - 1850 Federal Census of Greene County, Tenn. (GS F#5561 pt 3, page 268) lists:_

_____"Azariah Doty (age) 105 M Farmer (born) N. J. blind (living with his son Ephraim_

_____and grandson William C. Doty)_____

_____4 - LDS Endowment Cards lists:_____

_____"Azariah Doty b. 18 Feb 1745, Piscataway, Mddx, N. J. ;father: Isaac Doty;__

_____mother: Miss Reyno; md. to Sarah Tucker; (work at instance of Austin C. Brown)_

_____baptized: 20 Oct 1931; endowed: 19 Nov 1931" (Salt Lake Temple)_____

_____(additional information might be carried forward on continuation sheets)_____

Fig. 9. Individual summary forms

INDIVIDUAL SUMMARY SHEET

NAME: Silas PACE   BIRTHDATE: abt 1730-40

BIRTHPLACE: probably Virginia

FATHER: Richard PACE   MOTHER: Elizabeth CAIN

Search Number	Listing of Genealogical and Historical Facts
8	page 1 (PACE FAMILY HISTORY by Barnabas Pace 1844-50, a typescript)
	"second son of Richard Pace and Elizabeth Cain...
	"married Miss Mary Newsome, a Tory's daughter...
	"raised a numerous family of sons and daughters...
	"died in good old age...buried in Edgefield District, South
	Carolina near the Savannah River 25 miles from Augusta...
	"died in 1796...sons were John, William, Silas and David--all
	dead by 1850
12	Richmond County, Georgia Superior Court minutes Book 1 (GS F#276,363)
	Bill of Sale to SOLOMON NEWSOME JR. for slave named FILLIS --Solomon
	Newsome Sr. and Hezekiah Bussey testified--Proved Wilkes County,
	Georgia 14 April 1789 - dated 26 Mar 1777
13	page 33 (WILKES COUNTY, GA. RECORDS Vol. 1 GS 975.6)
	Administrator to estate of DREADZIL PACE - Indian Trader 15 Sept
	1777 Wilkes County, Georgia.
15	(Richmond County, Georgia Deeds)
	27 Feb 1787 listed of Ninety Six District, South Carolina--
	sells 100 acres in Richmond County on Germany Creek to Ambrose
	Holliday for 50 pounds Sterling--it being land originally granted
	to KNOWLES PACE Sept 1769 - Drury Pace witness.
18	(South Carolina Memorials GS 5405 pt 8)
	20 Jan 1773 - granted 100 acres in Granville County, South Carolina
	on Savannah River near Paces Island.
	(additional information might be carried forward on continuation sheets)

BYU - GRC 10/69

Fig. 9a.

RESEARCH FINDINGS EXTRACT NUMBER: 5

RESEARCHER: NEW DATE: 1 Mar 1959 REPOSITORY: Genea. Soc SLC.

SOURCE DESCRIPTION: 1850 Census of Greene County, Tennessee (GS F#5561 pt 3)

page 268 - enumerated 17 Dec 1850				
#1908-1908	William C. Doty	34 M	Farmer $1000	Tenn.
	Malvina	30 F		Tenn.
	Sarah J.	2 F		Tenn.
	Ephraim	55 M	Farmer	Tenn.
	Sarah	56 F		Va.
	Azariah Doty	105 M	Farmer	N. J. (Blind)
page 271				
#1955-1955	Abraham Haynes	30 M	Cabinet Maker $200	Tenn.
	Mary J.	26 F		Tenn.
	David A.	5 M		Tenn.
	Jesse J.	3 M		Tenn.
	Mary A.	2 F		Tenn.
	Samuel Doty	19 M		Tenn.
page 288				
#2221-2221	Jesse Doty	52 M	Tenant	Tenn.
	Tempy	35 F		Tenn.
	Nathan	10 M		Tenn.
	Elizabeth	6 F		Tenn.
	Mary A.	5 F		Tenn.
	Sarah	2 F		Tenn.
	Charles Doty	16 M	Farmer	Tenn.
	Joseph	14 M		Tenn

Fig. 10. Extract from a census record

as research continues, some facts are discarded while others are assimilated. In this system, the worker approaches his own notes much as he does actual research, i.e., by considering names, places, sources, and time periods.

Special effort should be made to copy information accurately and neatly. This will make evaluation easier and will help others who may review the work later. A researcher should not skimp on paper, thinking he will quickly jot the facts down and then record them later in better form. "Later" usually never comes, and there is a good chance error may result from the additional copywork if it does.

Occasionally, a brief extract from a genealogical source is not enough. When a document is ancestral and has been used as the basis for a direct connection, or where it has special historical significance to the pedigree problem, a researcher should make a verbatim copy. Or, when copying information from census or cemetery records for instance, it may be necessary to copy several pages of material at one time. All the facts copied may not apply at the moment, but further research may disclose a relevancy. The next-door-neighbor with the same surname may turn out to be a brother or even the father to the person of interest. Likewise, the surrounding plots to an ancestor's grave might belong to other close relatives, even though the surnames may be different, and any abridgment or rearrangement of the facts might destroy genealogical information. When a great deal of this kind of copying must be done, perhaps the time and money involved in becoming an amateur records photographer is worth it.

Photography and Notekeeping

Valuable research time can be saved if a camera is used to capture information from some genealogical records, especially in field research where travel time is an important factor. This is an excellent way to get accurate and rather inexpensive copies of original records and documents. And it is surprising how cooperative many public officials are about allowing photocopy work. Of course some documents are restricted and cannot be copied, and some officials are reluctant to authorize such activity. Most records, however, are public, and many officials are cooperative.

I have traveled extensively using my camera to make document copies, and only one official has refused me access to the records. His explanation was: "I won't make any money if I let you do the copywork!"

Experience has shown that acceptable copies can be made without elaborate lamps, light, or lenses. A 35 mm camera with a closeup lens will do the job. Regular black and white film (Plus-X or Tri-X Panchromatic) will provide excellent copies for genealogical purposes, and clear copies can be made without a tripod or flood lamps if one has a fairly steady hand. Lighting is more than adequate in most county offices to handle regular film with ASA speed of 125. However, Tri-X provides an ASA speed of 400, which is more than adequate unless one has to copy in a dark vault or attic. Good copies of marriage records and probate documents were obtained in the basement of the Harrison County, Iowa, courthouse with only a 75-watt light globe as a light source.

Documents and books can be placed at chair level for convenient copying in most instances, or large books can be placed upright against the wall or counter for copying. Sometimes it is necessary to take half-page exposures when the pages or documents are large.

There is some risk in using the camera as the sole extract medium, and caution must be used when copying records while traveling. One cannot be sure of the copywork until the film has been developed and printed, and if mistakes are made in exposure, or if the copy is blurred, the prints may not be readable. It is best to get a little experience at home or in a local library where retakes can be made before copying records in the courthouse.

It is usually necessary to do some copywork in longhand, even when using the camera. Indexes and references should be checked and copied before photos of the actual documents are made. This helps in locating documents to copy while in the courthouse or library and also allows for proper arrangement after films have been developed and printed. The usual procedure is to copy names as well as book and page references from the index in longhand and then move to the actual records for camera work. Sometimes it is necessary to refer from one document to another while doing research, and the longhand list makes this easier.

Appendix 1 of this work offers detailed information about photography for genealogy researchers.

Filing in the Research Work Folder

Most genealogists accumulate considerable material before compiling permanent records, and a filing system for work materials is useful. Regular manila folders are handy for this, and one might be initiated for each family unit of interest to the pedigree. A work pedigree chart and supporting family group records can be placed in the folder along with certificates, clippings, and other items which pertain to the family. The folder should not be considered a final resting place for such information but a convenient repository while conducting research. After work has been completed on a particular problem, document copies and certificates can be mounted or published for the benefit of others who may be interested. Permanent pedigree and family group records could also be compiled from the information, or a family history could be written.

Research calendars should be kept together, perhaps in a ring binder rather than in the work folder, and extracts might also be filed in a single series. Pertinent facts should be posted to family group records and pedigree charts as they are recognized, and summary sheets can be constructed and placed in appropriate family unit folders as they are needed.

Most LDS researchers compile permanent family group records and pedigree charts after they have completed work on a particular line. The above notekeeping system is compatible with that practice. The system is also useful when writing a family history or compiling a genealogy.

Genealogical Correspondence

Successful genealogical research requires some correspondence, and a few suggestions might be appropriate at this point.

Not all records are in a central repository, so agents or record searchers must be used to get at some desired information. Correspondence is usually the most convenient and least expensive method of obtaining such information, although it is not always the most effective.

When writing for genealogical information, the researcher should make a carbon copy of each letter and file it for future reference. A brief summary listing the addressee, purpose, date written, and the date a reply was received might be entered on the research calendar. A special calendar of correspondence could be made if desired. Such a checklist would enable the researcher to follow through on important points which otherwise might be forgotten.

Special attention should be given letters and reports which contain genealogical information such as birth dates and death dates. This information should be "lifted" from the correspondence and posted to the appropriate charts and forms; otherwise, important facts might be lost in the researcher's own files.

Judgment should be used when writing to libraries and public officials for genealogical information. Many cannot or will not make genealogical searches because of their regular duties or because they have little interest in genealogy. Some will provide detail on official record holdings, and a few will search an index or two, but deep study and investigation should not be expected of them. It is a waste of time to outline extensive family history when corresponding with such persons. The correspondence should be kept brief and courteous but specific, with the request stated exactly. If an index is to be searched, the researcher should say so; if a statement about official record holdings is desired, the request should be to the point. Rambling in vague generalities will seldom get results. Librarians and public officials are seldom qualified to evaluate the research problem or define research objectives. It is, by the way, a good practice to indicate a willingness to remit the required fee for copywork when necessary.

When officials or librarians are not able to search the records, it may be necessary and advisable to employ an agent or record searcher. Such professionals should be tested, however, before large sums of money are sent. It is better to outline a limited search, of say $15 or $25, before using an agent whose reputation is not known. Usually county or town officials can provide a list of competent researchers.

The agent should be informed which records are to be searched and, if possible, should be given a priority sequence so he may plan his work efficiently. The agent should be instructed to provide accurate copies of documents and other information located and should give complete information on the source of his material. A real problem can develop when the agent presents findings in his own words rather than as the source indicated, in other words, when he writes abstracts rather than taking complete copies or extracts. A good extract contains facts copied as they appeared in the original while an abstract suggests an abridgment or a change from the original (fig. 11).

Of course it is better to have the original or a photocopy of the original at hand for evaluation or analysis, but this cannot always be done. The researcher should notice whether the agent he has hired takes care to extract all important facts when copying the records, especially when making copies of deeds, wills, and census records. All names, dates, and places as well as other facts which may help in evaluation should be copied. It is usually better to copy too much than too little. The copier should be expected to make his own comments from time to time, but he should indicate the words are his by placing them in brackets or parentheses.

No two researchers, professional or amateur, will extract information in exactly the same way, but any two researchers should be able to reach the same conclusions from the same information, if it has been copied correctly. It is suggested that the format is not as important as the facts which are actually contained in the record, and the copier might take the liberty of changing the format without altering the meaning if he lists the facts as they were actually recorded.

Researchers who become proficient enough to be interested in writing genealogical reports for others might find helpful suggestions in appendix 2.

It is impossible to list every eventuality which might face the genealogist in notekeeping and correspondence, but these few suggestions should assist in improving research. Perhaps a little instruction, coupled with a lot of experience, will be the best teacher. It may be that much of the information in this chapter as well as the next one will be new to the beginner, but they are presented here to help him get a proper start and let him know where he can come for further assistance as he progresses.

NORTHAMPTON COUNTY, NORTH CAROLINA WILLS 1762-1791
(GS F#4847)

VERBATIM COPY OF WILLIAM PACE'S WILL, DATED 18 Nov 1788

In the name of God Amen. I William Pace of the County of Northampton in the State of North Carolina, being not in a perfect state of health and thinking it best to settle my affairs when my mind and memory are sound, thanks to my God for his mercies to me, do make and ordain this my last will and testament in manner and form following:

I give bequeath and devise unto my Brother Solomon Pace all my lands together with all my negroes named as follows: Beck, Pompey, Phillip, Randol, Austis, Boston, Young Beck, Anna, Hester, Cherry, Andrew. Likewise I give him all my goods and chattels and all and every part of my real and personal estate to him, his heirs, and assigns forever.

I do hereby constitute, ordain, and appoint my said Brother Solomon Pace to be whole and sole Executor of this my last will and testament, hereby revoking, disallowing, and negating all former wills by me made. This being my last will and testament, I have hereunto set my hand and seal this 18th Day of November 1788.

Signed, Sealed and pronounced in the presence of us, Samuel Bell, William Bell, James Bell.

William Pace (Seal)

AN ABSTRACT OF WILLIAM PACE'S WILL, DATED 18 Nov 1788

William Pace, of Northampton County, North Carolina
Will dated 18 Nov 1788
Bequeaths entire estate to his Brother Solomon Pace
Lists slaves Beck, Pompey, Phillip, Randol, Austis, Boston, Young Beck, Anna, Hester, Cherry, and Andrew
Samuel, William, and James Bell are witnesses.

AN EXTRACT FROM WILLIAM PACE'S WILL, DATED 18 Nov 1788

"...William Pace of the County of Northampton in the State of North Carolina...last will and testament...bequeath and devise unto my Brother Solomon Pace all my lands together with all my negroes named as follows: Beck, Pompey, Phillip, Randol, Austis, Boston, Young Beck, Anna, Hester, Cherry, Andrew...this 18th Day of November 1788...in the presence of us, Samuel Bell, William Bell, James Bell..."

Fig. 11. Abstract and extract of William Pace's will

CHAPTER 3

USING THE LIBRARY

After locating and compiling basic genealogical facts from home and family sources, and after establishing a workable notekeeping system, the researcher is ready to investigate selected "outside" sources which may help him confirm and extend his pedigree. Since a good portion of the genealogist's time from here on is spent in library research, he should become acquainted with general library policies and procedures as well as important library holdings at the very beginning of his work.

Some libraries provide a flyer or brochure outlining their policies and procedures, but since many do not, the researcher often must familiarize himself with the facility through personal research and consultation with reference personnel.

The card catalog is the key to the library. It includes reference cards to the library's holdings, usually by AUTHOR, TITLE, and SUBJECT. The Genealogical Society Library in Salt Lake City includes a LOCALITY category as well, but most libraries consider this a subject entry. Sometimes the library has special handlists or registers to provide reference information--the LDS Genealogical Society's registers on census, land, and probate record holdings for instance.

A genealogical researcher must use imagination and ingenuity when visiting libraries and archives, because information may be classified differently in each. Most libraries are general in scope and must consider all fields of knowledge. A few specialize in genealogy or have special genealogical sections, but most classify genealogical material right along with other historical subject materials.

References to vital statistics might be arranged according to the general subject matter and not according to names listed in the records. Census records might be classified according to locality as "population enumerations," or they may have some other designation and be filed under "social science." Court or military records may be filed in special "law sections," or they may be listed with historical material. References pertaining to religion might be listed either according to denomination or to the subject in general. Manuscript collections and rare works may be restricted, with special catalogs or handlists outlining their location and use. Important genealogical material may also be combined with unrelated subject material, and the catalogers may not have considered the genealogist when classifying the record.

Locality collections may also be deposited far from their places of origin, and correspondence or travel may be necessary to investigate them. For example, the DRAPER COLLECTION OF EARLY KENTUCKY HISTORY AND GENEALOGY is deposited with the University of Wisconsin at Madison. Likewise, many original Mormon works are located in the Huntington Library at San Marino, California, while many non-Mormon documents are found at the LDS Genealogical Society Library in Salt Lake City or at Brigham Young University.

The genealogist is usually not able to solve all his problems from a single repository, so he should plan to use several facilities before he has finished his work. Most libraries are not staffed to conduct research for the inquiring genealogist, and time-consuming requests should not be sent them. Genealogical research becomes a personal task; discretion should be used when requesting help from any library or archives.

Classification Systems

It is not the purpose of this work to explain all library classification and cataloging systems, but certain important characteristics of the LDS Genealogical Society Library in Salt Lake City and the Harold B. Lee Library at Brigham Young University are given.

Both libraries use the Dewey Decimal System or an adaptation of it. All information is classified in ten major number groups as follows:

000 - GENERAL WORKS	500 - PURE SCIENCE
100 - PHILOSOPHY	600 - TECHNOLOGY
200 - RELIGION	700 - THE ARTS
300 - SOCIAL SCIENCE	800 - LITERATURE
400 - LANGUAGE	900 - HISTORY AND GEOGRAPHY

The American genealogist might find helpful information under any of the general subject groups, but most of his help comes from "900." Encyclopedia and other general guide books are identified in the "000" series. Works on religion found in the "200" series often contain valuable genealogical information. Guides to public and vital records are located in the "300" series.

Genealogical works themselves are classified in the history series and carry a "929" number or a decimal subdivision of it:

929   - Genealogy and Heraldry
929.1 - Genealogical tools, charts, forms, methods, etc.
929.2 - Family history
929.3 - Source materials
929.4 - Personal names
929.5 - Epitaphs
929.6 - Heraldry
929.7 - Royalty
929.8 - Armorial bearings
929.9 - Flags

Under the Dewey system, a locality feature can be included with the subject (or source) feature so that certain source materials which pertain to a particular locality might be identified in the decimal number. As an example, "920" in the decimal system system pertains to "Biography," but by including additional numbers a geographical designation can also be made. The general subject and geographical designations for the "900" series follow:

900 - History	950 - Asia
910 - Geography, travels	960 - Africa
920 - Biography	970 - North America
930 - Ancient History	980 - South America
940 - Europe	990 - Pacific Ocean Islands

The above numbers may be further divided and subdivided to include a breakdown of the general geographical region. A further subdivision for North America follows:

970 - North America	975.3 - District of Columbia
971 - Canada	975.4 - West Virginia
972 - Mexico	975.5 - Virginia
973 - United States	975.6 - North Carolina
974 - Northeastern States	975.7 - South Carolina
974.1 - Maine	975.8 - Georgia
974.2 - New Hampshire	975.9 - Florida
974.3 - Vermont	976 - South Central States
974.4 - Massachusetts	976.1 - Alabama
974.5 - Rhode Island	976.2 - Mississippi
974.6 - Connecticut	976.3 - Louisiana
974.7 - New York	976.4 - Texas
974.8 - Pennsylvania	976.5 - Oklahoma
974.9 - New Jersey	976.6 - (reserved)
975 - Southern States	976.7 - Arkansas
975.1 - Delaware	976.8 - Tennessee
975.2 - Maryland	976.9 - Kentucky

977 - North Central States	978.5 - (reserved)
977.1 - Ohio	978.6 - Montana
977.2 - Indiana	978.7 - Wyoming
977.3 - Illinois	978.8 - Colorado
977.4 - Michigan	978.9 - New Mexico
977.5 - Wisconsin	979 - Far Western States
977.6 - Minnesota	979.1 - Arizona
977.7 - Iowa	979.2 - Utah
977.8 - Missouri	979.3 - Nevada
977.9 - (reserved)	979.4 - California
978 - Western States	979.5 - Oregon
978.1 - Kansas	979.6 - Idaho
978.2 - Nebraska	979.7 - Washington
978.3 - South Dakota	979.8 - Alaska
978.4 - North Dakota	979.9 - (reserved)

A book dealing with United States History would have "973" as the first part of its book number but would also have an additional symbol to facilitate an orderly arrangement on the shelf. This symbol consists of the first letter or two of the author's last name and a number derived from a special printed list. Furthermore, if an author writes more than one book on the same subject, the books are distinguished by adding a work letter to the book number, as follows:

973
B38a Beard, Charles A.
       AMERICA IN MIDPASSAGE

973
B38b Beard, Charles A.
       BASIC HISTORY OF THE U.S.

When more than one volume exists for a particular series, the volume number may also be listed as part of the book number or the year may be included on annual publications. Special location symbols may also be listed on the books to show they are to be shelved in a special location. As an example, the term "Ref. 4" is listed on special reference books in the BYU library which are shelved on the fourth level reference shelves. The LDS Genealogical Society also has several special location symbols which are currently of special significance.

E.S.	Extra Surveillance in film vaults
Q.	Oversized book in "Q" section of stacks
Folio.	Extra oversized book in "Folio" section of stacks
Ref.	Reference shelves by geographic region
P.	Parish Register Print Out in special section
P.B.	Pamphlet Box in "P.B." section of stacks
P.B.A.	Small Pamphlet Box in "P.B.A." section of stacks
P.B.Q.	Large Pamphlet Box in "P.B.Q." section of stacks
F.	A microfilm

Map.   A "Map" in special map cases
Ped.   A "Pedigree" in special pedigree files
M.S.   A "Manuscript" in special file cabinets
Reg.   A "Register" in reference section

Each library has special files and indexes to assist the researcher, but these are constantly changing. An inquiry at the reference counter or information desk is always in order in this regard. Detail on special indexes and files at the LDS Genealogical Society is presented in chapter 6.

Even though cards are filed in the main catalog in alphabetical order, sometimes the large number of entries make it necessary to have special filing rules. The following are of special interest to the genealogist:

1. When the first word of a title is an article ("a", "an" or "the"), it is disregarded in the filing.

2. Names beginning with "M'" and "Mc" are filed as though they were spelled "Mac."

3. Common abbreviations are arranged as though they were spelled out.

4. Author cards precede subject cards; that is, works by an author are filed before works about him.

5. When the same word is used for several kinds of headings, it is arranged in the following order: person, place, subject, title.

6. An author may be an organization, a government, an institution, or a society. If so, the author card may be filed by the name of the organization.

7. Books are listed under the author's real name with a cross reference from his pseudonym, if he has one.

8. Publications of societies, institutions, etc., are under the name of that organization and not under Bulletin, Proceedings, Transactions, etc.

9. Numerals are filed as if spelled out--1 as "one"; 40,000 as "forty thousand."

10. Cards are filed in the catalog alphabetically under a word-by-word arrangement. Many dictionaries, periodical indexes, and other reference books use a letter-by-letter arrangement. The difference between the two systems is quite significant and may be illustrated by the following examples:

Word-by-word Filing	Letter-by-letter Filing
New Jersey	Newark
New York	New Jersey
Newark	Newspapers
Newspapers	Newton
Newton	New York
Next to Valour	Next to Valour

Research Procedure in the Library

The arrangement of genealogical material may differ in each library, but basic research procedure remains the same. It is primarily a Surname, Locality, and Record Category approach.

1. Check the catalog for references to each name shown on the pedigree and investigate appropriate genealogies and family histories for a connection.

2. Investigate references to all pertinent surnames, including allied lines, but investigate only those which pertain to localities of known residence when the surname is common, such as "Jones" or "Smith."

3. Check existing genealogical indexes, dictionaries, compendia, periodicals, and biographical collections which relate to the region of interest.

4. Investigate local and regional histories for genealogical and biographical information which might pertain to the problem.

5. Using the locality approach, investigate vital, church, cemetery, census, probate, land, military, emigration, and social-commercial records which might pertain to the problem.

Special care and concern for the records of the library should be shown. Though libraries recognize the importance of genealogical collections, genealogists often have unfavorable reputations with librarians, as pointed out in the following article:

Genealogy . . . is a subject which does not always meet with enthusiasm among librarians. At the 1962 ALA Conference, the History Section of the Reference Services Division devoted a session to Heraldry and Genealogy. Mrs. Abbie Moran, late of Fort Worth Public Library, and an expert genealogist, had circularized librarians in twenty-six states, including Arizona, with a questionnaire regarding their attitude toward Genealogy and the facilities and staff available to handle specific research questions from patrons. In some states other than Arizona, there is a definite hostility by librarians toward genealogists. Among the topics covered by Mrs. Moran in her questionnaire were: "What are the disadvantages or reasons you and/or your library may

oppose Genealogy?" Some of the answers to this question were:
"The Subject is too special to justify the budget or staff" . . .
"Patrons misuse and mutilate the expensive books" . . . "I detest
clubs of all sorts, especially the D.A.R." . . . "Amateur genealogists are irritating" . . . "It takes too much time in training
staff members or in aiding patrons." The ALA panelist then
asked, "What are the advantages of having a genealogical collection?" Among the answers were: "It builds prestige for our
library" . . . "Genealogy is history, a type of Americana"
. . . "It has religious fulfillment for some" . . . "A good reference library must have genealogy--it is a type of historical
record which can yield facts not found elsewhere" . . . "If the
use of a book six times justifies its cost then genealogical books
are more than justified." [George W. Macko, "The Generations
of Men Shall Be Numbered," ARIZONA LIBRARIAN 22 (Summer
1965):11.]

Reference Materials

Before making searches in original records, it is often necessary
to consult special guide books and reference works for direction. The
library is the place to locate such items, though some genealogists
purchase copies of often-used reference books for their personal
libraries.

A selected list of American textbooks and manuals follows, and
special reference works essential to American genealogy are listed
and explained.

Bennett, Archibald F. ADVANCED GENEALOGICAL RESEARCH.
    Salt Lake City: Bookcraft, 1959.
    Presently out of print, but an excellent volume using actual
    research examples to show what genealogical information might
    be located from major sources.
_____. FINDING YOUR FOREFATHERS IN AMERICA.
    Salt Lake City: Bookcraft, 1957.
    Also out of print at the present time, but an excellent book giving
    a regional approach toward solving American genealogical
    problems.
_____. A GUIDE FOR GENEALOGICAL RESEARCH.
    Salt Lake City: Deseret News Press, 1951.
    An excellent text on beginning genealogy with an American view.
    Facts in this text have been used by many other authors in later
    publications, especially with respect to evaluation of evidence and
    search procedures.
Canada Public Archives. TRACING YOUR ANCESTORS IN CANADA.
    Ottawa: The Dominion Archives, 1966.
    A pamphlet dealing with the major genealogical sources available
    for Canadian research. Brief but good detail is given on major
    record sources in each of the provinces of Canada.
Colket, Meredith B. and Frank E. Bridgers. GUIDE TO GENEALOG-
    ICAL RECORDS IN THE NATIONAL ARCHIVES. Washington:

G.P.P., 1964. An excellent handbook of 145 pages dealing with sources at the National Archives. It is especially strong on military, land, census, and passenger-shipping lists.

Doane, Gilbert H. SEARCHING FOR YOUR ANCESTORS. Minneapolis: University Press, 1960.
A well written text by an authority which takes the reader through a series of genealogical experiences.

Greenwood, Val D. THE RESEARCHER'S GUIDE TO AMERICAN GENEALOGY. Baltimore: The Genealogical Publishing Co., 1973.
The most comprehensive guide to American genealogy that has yet been published, providing detailed examination of major record sources and techniques for determining objectives and evaluating evidence.

Jacobus, Donald Lines. GENEALOGY AS PASTIME AND PROFESSION. 2nd ed., rev. Baltimore: The Genealogical Publishing Co., 1968.
A superior text, written by one of the fathers of American genealogy, dealing with important ideas and concepts relating to research.

Jaussi, Laureen R. and Gloria D. Chaston. FUNDAMENTALS OF GENEALOGICAL RESEARCH. 2nd ed., rev. Salt Lake City: Deseret Book Co., 1972.
A good beginning text, nicely written and well organized, dealing primarily with survey sources and emphasizing LDS research.

Jones, Vincent L., et al. GENEALOGICAL RESEARCH: A JURISDICTIONAL APPROACH. Rev. ed. Salt Lake City: Publishers Press, 1972.
An analytical approach to genealogy with good information concerning methods, procedures, and sources. Notekeeping is emphasized, and an excellent bibliography is provided for other genealogical works.

Kirkham, E. Kay. RESEARCH IN AMERICAN GENEALOGY. Salt Lake City: Deseret Book Co., 1956.
A good text dealing with basic research methods and sources but presently out of print. The vital statistics detail is much out of date.

_____. SIMPLIFIED GENEALOGICAL RESEARCH. Salt Lake City: Deseret Book Co., 1969.
A revision of his Research in American Genealogy with new material added; including helpful information on photography in genealogy.

Pine, Leslie G. AMERICAN ORIGINS. Baltimore: The Genealogical Publishing Co., 1967.
Brief but a good text dealing with major American sources.

Rubincam, Milton, ed. GENEALOGICAL RESEARCH METHODS AND SOURCES. Washington: The American Society of Genealogists, 1960.
One of the best texts available dealing with methods and sources in American genealogy. A regionalized work with chapters on selected British countries. (See Kenn Stryker-Rodda for volume 2 of this work which deals with western states.)

Stevenson, Noel C., ed. THE GENEALOGICAL READER. Salt
Lake City: Deseret Book Co., 1958.
Presently out of print but a good reader to show the value of
various American genealogical sources. A compilation of genealogical articles written by others.

_____. SEARCH AND RESEARCH. Rev. ed. Salt Lake
City: Deseret Book Co., 1959.
An excellent guide to sources on a state basis.

Vallentine, John F., ed. HANDBOOK FOR GENEALOGICAL CORRE-
SPONDENCE. Salt Lake City: Bookcraft, 1963.
Not a genealogical text but an excellent guide for genealogical
correspondence. Sponsored by the Cache Genealogical Library
at Logan, Utah.

Williams, Ethel W. KNOW YOUR ANCESTORS. Rutland, Vermont:
C. E. Tuttle Co., 1961.
A valuable text with a regional approach to a few of the Middle
Atlantic States and a few in the Midwest.

Wright, Norman E. GENEALOGY IN AMERICA, vol. 1. Salt Lake
City: Deseret Book Co., 1968.
A comprehensive work on the states of Massachusetts, Maine,
and Connecticut with historical background information and
exhaustive detail on major genealogical source materials and
their use.

_____, comp. NORTH AMERICAN GENEALOGICAL
SOURCES. 4 vols. Southern States; Midwestern States;
Midatlantic States and Canada; and Southwestern States. Provo,
Utah: BYU Press, 1968.
Listings of source material by state with historical background
information. Mistakes are evident in references and call numbers
given.

_____. GENEALOGICAL READER, NORTHEASTERN
UNITED STATES AND CANADA. Provo, Utah: BYU Press,
1973.
A compiled collection of regional genealogical information for
Home Study courses in American genealogy at Brigham Young
University.

Wright, Norman E. and David H. Pratt. GENEALOGICAL RESEARCH
ESSENTIALS. Salt Lake City: Bookcraft, 1967.
A basic text dealing with methods and sources for America and
Britain.

Zabriskie, George O. CLIMBING OUR FAMILY TREE SYSTEMAT-
ICALLY. Salt Lake City: Parliment Press, 1969.
A basic text dealing with theory and research procedure.

Before searching the records of a particular jurisdiction, it is
advisable to check on that jurisdiction's correct designation and location. This can be done by consulting a good atlas, marketing guide,
gazetteer, geographical dictionary, or postal guide. Is the town of
interest really in the county and state proposed, or is there a chance
the basic place-name information is incorrect? Much time and
effort can be wasted searching records of the wrong locality.

RAND MCNALLY COMMERCIAL ATLAS AND MARKETING
GUIDE is an excellent reference to determine the correct city, town,
township, county, and state designation. Many towns now out of existence are included in the guide, and many township boundaries are
shown. Smaller atlases by Hammond, Collier, and other publishing
firms may also give the necessary facts, but the McNally Guide is
unusually inclusive for American localities.

Brigham Young University and the Genealogical Society in Salt
Lake City have excellent early gazetteers pertaining to the United
States. The following have been microfilmed and are available
through any of the Society's Branch Libraries:

Colange, Leo de. THE NATIONAL GAZETTEER: A GEOGRAPH-
ICAL DICTIONARY OF THE UNITED STATES. Hamilton,
Adams, and Co., 1884. (GS FILM #845, 264)

FANNING'S ILLUSTRATED GAZETTEER OF THE UNITED
STATES. Ensign, Bridgman, and Fanning, New York, 1855.
(GS #599, 773)

Hayward, John. A GAZETTEER OF THE UNITED STATES OF
AMERICA. Hartford: Case, Tiffany, and Co., 1853.
(GS #599, 735)

Mitchell, Samuel Augustus. AN ACCOMPANIMENT TO MITCHELL'S
REFERENCE AND DISTANCE MAP OF THE UNITED STATES.
Philadelphia: Mitchell and Hinman, 1834. (GS #845, 264)

Scott, Joseph. THE UNITED STATES GAZETTEER. Philadelphia: F. and R. Bailey, 1795. (GS #570, 810)

BULLINGER'S POSTAL GUIDE or any U.S. OFFICIAL POSTAL
GUIDE may be consulted to determine the county in which a particular
town or city is located, but they refer to towns with post offices, and
many smaller localities are not included. Also, they are annuals and
those published near the time of the event are the most useful. The
postal guides often contain other helpful information, including the
location of the county seat.

After determining the correct place-name designations, other
references should be consulted for more historical detail about the
localities of interest. The researcher should determine and list the
date of organization or creation of each town and county and should
list similar information for parent towns and counties. This will
help in locating and investigating source materials for those localities.

George B. Everton, Sr.'s THE HANDY BOOK FOR GENEALO-
GISTS, 6th ed., rev. and enl. (Logan, Utah: Everton Publishers,
1971) or E. Kay Kirkham's THE COUNTIES OF THE UNITED STATES
AND THEIR GENEALOGICAL VALUE (Salt Lake City: Deseret Book Co.,

1965) will provide county formation detail. They also give additional information on source materials for American counties and give the location of county seats.

Local and regional histories are also useful in determining historical and statistical information on towns and counties. Some provide graphic detail on township and county boundaries and give excellent historical information. Clarence Stewart Peterson's CONSOLIDATED BIBLIOGRAPHY OF COUNTY HISTORIES IN FIFTY STATES in 1961, 2nd ed. reprint (Baltimore: The Genealogical Publishing Co., 1963) gives good listings of American county histories in print and P. William Filby's AMERICAN & BRITISH GENEALOGY & HERALDRY: A SELECTED LIST OF BOOKS (Chicago: American Library Association, 1970) includes many locality references. The searcher can take the standard "locality approach" in the card catalog at each library he visits to locate additional material.

Sometimes records in more than one county must be searched for a single residence because it is possible an ancestor lived in one geographical location for several years but came under the jurisdiction of two or more counties. As an example, Thomas Anderson Brady was born in the western part of Virginia in 1774. The area was then under control of Augusta County and partially under Fincastle County after 1772. In 1776, Fincastle County was dissolved and Kentucky County was created. In 1780, Kentucky County was dissolved and the District of Kentucky was established with Fayette, Jefferson, and Lincoln counties organized. In 1790, nine counties were organized from the original three--including Fayette, Jefferson, Lincoln, Bourbon, Madison, Mason, Mercer, Nelson, and Woodford. Thomas Anderson Brady and/or members of his immediate family have been located in records of every one of these counties except Mason and Woodford. Because each county maintained its own marriage, probate, and deed books, each county's records should be investigated.

The following place-name guide books are found at Brigham Young University or the LDS Genealogical Society:

GENERAL

    Sealock, Richard B. A BIBLIOGRAPHY OF PLACE-NAME
        LITERATURE: UNITED STATES AND CANADA. 2nd ed.
        Chicago: American Library Association, 1967. (BYU Ref. 4
        910.016 Sel5b)

ARIZONA

    Baker, Simon and Thomas J. McCleneghan, eds. ARIZONA

ECONOMIC AND HISTORIC ATLAS. Tucson, Arizona: The
University of Arizona, College of Business and Public Administration, 1966. (BYU Map 912.791 B177a)

Barnes, Will C. ARIZONA PLACE NAMES. Tucson, Arizona:
The University of Arizona Press, 1960. (BYU Map 917.91
B26a)

Sherman, James E. and Barbara H. GHOST TOWNS OF ARIZONA.
Norman, Oklahoma: University of Oklahoma Press, 1969.
(BYU 979.104 Sh55g)

CALIFORNIA

Gudde, Erwin G. CALIFORNIA PLACE NAMES. 3rd ed.
Berkeley: University of California Press, 1969. (BYU Map
917.94 G93)

_____. 1000 CALIFORNIA PLACE NAMES. Rev. ed.
Berkeley: University of California Press, 1949. (BYU Map
917.94 G93)

COLORADO

Dawson, J. Frank. PLACE NAMES IN COLORADO. Denver:
The J. Frank Dawson Publishing Co., 1954. (BYU Map
917.88 D32p)

CONNECTICUT

Roberts, George Simon. HISTORIC TOWNS OF THE CONNECTICUT
RIVER VALLEY. Schenectady, N.Y.: Robson & Adee, 1906.
(BYU 974.6 R542h)

DELAWARE

Heck, L. W., et al. DELAWARE PLACE NAMES. Washington:
U. S. Government Printing Office, 1966. (BYU Map 917.51
H355d)

GEORGIA

Jones, Charles Colcok, Jr. THE DEAD TOWNS OF GEORGIA.
Savannah: Morning News Steam Printing House, 1878.
(BYU 975.8 J71)

White, George. STATISTICS OF THE STATE OF GEORGIA.
Savannah: W. Thorne Williams, 1849. (BYU 975.8 W583s)

IDAHO

Idaho Department of Highways, Highway Planning Survey.
GAZETTEER OF CITIES, VILLAGES, UNINCORPORATED
COMMUNITIES, AND LANDMARK SITES IN THE STATE OF
IDAHO. n. p.: n. p., n. d. (BYU Map 917.96 Idlg)

ILLINOIS

Adams, James N. ILLINOIS PLACE NAMES. Edited by William
E. Keller. Springfield: John N. Adams, 1968. (BYU 977.3006
I16t #54)

Illinois Secretary of State. COUNTIES OF ILLINOIS; THEIR
ORIGIN AND EVOLUTION. Springfield: Edward J. Hughes,
1934. (BYU 977.3 I16c)

INDIANA

Goodrich, De Witt C. AN ILLUSTRATED HISTORY OF THE
STATE OF INDIANA. Indianapolis: Richard S. Peale & Co.
1875. (BYU 977.2 G625s)

Scott, John. THE INDIANA GAZETTEER OR TOPOGRAPHICAL
DICTIONARY. Indianapolis: Indiana Historical Society,
1954. (BYU 977.2006 In2p V.18 #1)

Smith, O. H. EARLY INDIANA TRAILS; AND SKETCHES.
Cincinnati: Moore, Wilstach, Keys & Co., 1858. (BYU
977.203 Sm63e)

NOTE: The State Library at 124 North Senate Avenue, Downtown
Indianapolis, has an excellent card file on Indiana place
names.

LOUISIANA

Read, William A. LOUISIANA PLACE-NAMES OF INDIAN
ORIGIN. Baton Rouge, Louisiana: Louisiana State
University, 1927. (BYU Map 917.63 R221)

MAINE

Chadbourne, Ava Harriet. MAINE PLACE NAMES AND THE
PEOPLING OF ITS TOWNS. Portland, Maine: The Bond
Wheelwright Company, 1955. (BYU Map 917.41 C34m and
BYU 974.1 C34m)

Varney, Geo. J. A GAZETTEER OF THE STATE OF MAINE.
Boston: B. B. Russell, 1881. (BYU Map 917.41 Va43g)

MISSOURI

Ramsay, Robert L. OUR STOREHOUSE OF MISSOURI PLACE
NAMES. Columbia, Missouri: University of Missouri,
1952. (BYU Map 917.78 R148o)

NEBRASKA

The Federal Writers' Project of Nebraska. ORIGIN OF NEBRASKA
PLACE NAMES. Lincoln, Nebraska: Stephenson School
Supply Company, 1938. (BYU Map 917.82 F317o)

Fitzpatrick, Lillian Linder, A. M. NEBRASKA PLACE-NAMES,
Lincoln, Nebraska: n.p., 1925. (BYU Map 917.82 F582n)

Link, J.T. THE ORIGIN OF THE PLACE NAMES OF NEBRASKA.
Lincoln, Nebraska: University of Nebraska, 1933. (BYU
917.82 L648o)

NEVADA

Averett, Walter R. DIRECTORY OF SOUTHERN NEVADA PLACE
NAMES. Rev. ed. Las Vegas: Walter R. Averett, 1963.
(BYU Map 917.93 Av35)

Kelley, J. Wells. FIRST DIRECTORY OF NEVADA TERRITORY.
San Francisco: Valentine & Co., 1862. (BYU 917.93 K29f)

Leigh, Rufus Wood. NEVADA PLACE NAMES. Salt Lake City:
Deseret News Press, 1964. (BYU 917.93 L533m)

McVaugh, Rogers and F. R. Fosberg. INDEX TO THE GEO-
GRAPHICAL NAMES OF NEVADA. Washington: U. S.
Government Printing Office, 1941. (BYU Map 917.93 M25i)

NEW HAMPSHIRE

Charleton, Edwin A. NEW HAMPSHIRE AS IT IS. Claremont,
N. H.: Tracy and Sandford, 1855. (BYU 974.2 C381)

Farmer, John and Jacob B. Moore. A GAZETTEER OF THE
STATE OF NEW HAMPSHIRE. Concord, New Hampshire:
Jacob B. Moore, 1823. (BYU 917.42 F229g)

Fogg, Alonzo J. THE STATISTICS AND GAZETTEER OF NEW
HAMPSHIRE. Concord, N. H.: n. p., 1874.

NEW JERSEY

NEW JERSEY ROAD MAPS OF THE 18TH CENTURY. Princeton,
New Jersey: Princeton University Library, 1970 (BYU Map
912.749 P935n)

NEW MEXICO

Pearce, T. M., ed. NEW MEXICO PLACE NAMES, A GEO-
GRAPHICAL DICTIONARY. Albuquerque: The University
of New Mexico Press, 1965. (BYU Map 917.89003 P315n)

NEW YORK

French, J. H. GAZETTEER OF THE STATE OF NEW YORK.
Syracuse, N. Y.: R. Pearsall Smith, 1860. (BYU Map
917.47 F88 and BYU Ref. 4 917.47 F88)

_____. INDEX OF PERSONAL NAMES IN J. H. FRENCH'S
GAZETTEER OF THE STATE OF NEW YORK. Cortland,
New York: The Cortland County Historical Society, 1962.
(BYU Map 917.47 F88g)

NORTH CAROLINA

Powell, William S. THE NORTH CAROLINA GAZETTEER.
Chapel Hill: University of North Carolina Press, 1968.
(BYU 917.56 P871n)

OHIO

Jenkins, Warren. THE OHIO GAZETTEER, AND TRAVELER'S
GUIDE. Columbus: Isaac N. Whiting, 1837. (BYU Mor.
917.71 J419o)

Overman, William D. OHIO TOWN NAMES. Akron, Ohio:
Atlantic Press, 1958. (BYU Map 917.71 Ov2o)

OKLAHOMA

Gould, Charles Newton. OKLAHOMA PLACE NAMES. Norman,
Oklahoma: University of Oklahoma Press, 1933. (BYU
917.66 G731c)

Shirk, George H. OKLAHOMA PLACE NAMES. Norman,
Oklahoma: University of Oklahoma Press, 1965. (BYU
917.66 Sh65o)

OREGON

McArthur, Lewis A. OREGON GEOGRAPHIC NAMES. 3rd ed.
Portland: Binsfords & Mort, 1952. (BYU Map 917.95 M11)

_____. OREGON PLACE NAMES. Portland: Binsfords
and Mort, 1944. (BYU Map 917.95 M11o)

PENNSYLVANIA

Espenshade, Abraham Howry. PENNSYLVANIA PLACE NAMES. Philadelphia: The Pennsylvania State College, 1925. (BYU Map 917.48 Es64p)

SOUTH DAKOTA

Writers' Program of the Work Projects' Administration. SOUTH DAKOTA PLACE NAMES. Rev. ed. Vermillion, South Dakota: University of South Dakota, 1941. (BYU Map 917.83 W939s)

TEXAS

Madison, Virginia and Hallie Stillwell. HOW COME IT'S CALLED THAT? PLACE NAMES IN THE BIG BEND COUNTRY. Albuquerque, New Mexico: University of New Mexico Press, 1958. (BYU 917.64 M26h)

UTAH

Leigh, Rufus Wood. FIVE HUNDRED UTAH PLACE NAMES. Salt Lake City: Deseret News Press, 1961. (BYU Map 979.2 L53f)

VERMONT

Hemenway, Abby Maria. THE VERMONT HISTORICAL GAZETTEER. 4 vols. Burlington, Vt.: Miss A. M. Hemenway, 1867+. (BYU 974.3 Ve59h)

WASHINGTON

Meany, Edmond S. ORIGIN OF WASHINGTON GEOGRAPHIC NAMES. Seattle: University of Washington Press, 1923. (BYU Map 917.97 M462w 1968)

WISCONSIN

Walling, H. F., C. E. ATLAS OF THE STATE OF WISCONSIN. Boston, Mass.: Walling, Tackabury & Co., 1876. (BYU f912.775 W15)

WYOMING

Christiansen, Cleo. SAGEBRUSH SETTLEMENTS. Lovell, Wyoming: n. p., 1967. (BYU 917.87003 C462s)

Pence, Mary Lou and Lola M. Homsher. THE GHOST TOWNS OF WYOMING. New York: Hastings House, 1956. (BYU 978.7 P37)

Urbanek, Mae. WYOMING PLACE NAMES. Boulder, Colorado: Johnson Publishing Company, 1967. (BYU 917.87 Urlw)

Another valuable collection for American researchers is that of the HISTORICAL RECORDS SURVEY PROGRAMS, WORKS PROGRESS ADMINISTRATION. Guides to Public Vital and Church Records were created, Inventories of County and Town Court Houses were conducted, and various indexing and copying programs were undertaken under the program. Not all localities were included because some officials did not desire to participate, and projects initiated were not all completed because of World War II.

The GUIDES TO PUBLIC VITAL AND CHURCH RECORDS include detail on state and church vital statistics programs with historical material included. Records are identified by time-period, content, and location.

The INVENTORIES give historical information for the towns or counties covered and include specific information about records which have been kept by the respective jurisdictions. Historical facts concerning towns and counties which have been abolished are listed and unusual jurisdictional problems are explained. As an example, few people know that "Shambip" County, Utah, once included all of Rush Valley west of Utah County and an area west to Nevada. Luke S. Johnson was its first and only probate judge, presiding during the years 1852-54. According to the Tooele, Utah, HRS INVENTORY, Shambip's records are in custody of Tooele and Iron Counties.

Newspapers contain valuable genealogical information and can be used to good advantage in research if they can be located. They have not always been preserved, but it is surprising the number that are available for research. Obituary and death notices are probably two of the more important genealogical records in newspapers, but others are helpful also. Birth and marriage notices, particularly in more recent editions, as well as probate court information have also been reported in various newspapers. (Newspapers can also be used in advertising for genealogical purposes.)

The following newspaper guides and directories contain useful information on the existence and location of newspapers in America and Canada:

Brigham, Clarence S. HISTORY AND BIBLIOGRAPHY OF AMERICAN NEWSPAPERS 1690-1820. 2 vols. Worcester, Mass.: American Antiquarian Society, 1947.

This is an excellent reference for the early American period and provides detail on the location of existing newspapers through 1820. It lists information by state, giving the name of the paper, whether it was a daily or weekly, the time-period it was published, and the location of existing copies.

> Gregory, Winifred. AMERICAN NEWSPAPERS 1821-1936: A UNION LIST OF FILES AVAILABLE IN THE UNITED STATES AND CANADA. New York: The H. W. Wilson Company, 1937.

Gregory's work lists bibliographic information about newspapers which have been published in the United States and Canada after 1820 and through 1936. Information is arranged by state and province with newspapers listed under each jurisdiction, showing the title first with publishing information following.

> Ayer, N. W. & Sons. DIRECTORY, NEWSPAPERS AND PERIODICALS. Philadelphia: N. W. Ayer & Son, 1880+.

This work is a guide to publications printed in the United States and its territories, the Dominion of Canada, Bermuda, and the Republics of Panama and the Philippines. It describes the states, provinces, cities, and towns which have publications and provides maps. Details on the title, publisher, and circulation are given for each publication.

> U.S. Library of Congress. A CHECK LIST OF AMERICAN EIGHTEENTH CENTURY NEWSPAPERS IN THE LIBRARY OF CONGRESS. New ed. Washington: U.S. Government Printing Office, 1936.

> U.S. Library of Congress. A CHECK LIST OF FOREIGN NEWSPAPERS IN THE LIBRARY OF CONGRESS. Washington: U.S. Government Printing Office, 1929.

> U.S. Library of Congress, Union Catalog Division. NEWSPAPERS ON MICROFILM. 6th ed. Washington: Government Printing Office, 1967.

The Brigham Young University, the University of Utah, and the Genealogical Society libraries each have excellent collections of newspapers and periodicals. The majority are on microfilm, but some are on microcard or microfish. The Genealogical Society's collection covers a much broader geographical base than the university libraries, but each may have copies and issues which the others do not have.

Local libraries, historical societies, archives, and even county courthouses have collections of newspapers pertaining to their geographical areas. Correspondence is often effective in getting at these. When the general guides do not list newspapers for the appropriate time and place, a letter to a local repository may bring results. In a few cases, special indexes have been created for vital entries, but in most instances it is necessary to provide officials with exact dates if they are to search for information. A researcher should always remember that searching in records organized by date are time consuming and often unproductive unless the exact date of the event is known. For instance, one researcher knew that Margaret Fitzgerald of New York died in 1911. But since the exact death date was not known, he wasted three hours trying to locate her obituary notice in issues of the GOUVERNEUR FREE PRESS. Through records of St. James Catholic Church in Gouverneur, the exact date of death and burial were determined. The obituary notice was then located in the FREE PRESS in less than three minutes.

CHAPTER 4

USING GENERAL LDS SOURCES

After gathering basic genealogical information from family and
home sources, the researcher should investigate selected sources
to determine the extent of previous research on his pedigree lines.
This should include certain general collections of the LDS Genealogical Society in Salt Lake City as well as various compiled genealogical
records in other places.

The Genealogical Society of The Church of Jesus Christ of Latter-
day Saints has created certain record collections of general interest
to the entire field of genealogy because of its special name processing
procedures. One need not be a "Mormon" or a descendant of LDS
ancestors to find useful genealogical information in these collections.
Facts have been gathered and filed from several different countries
over very broad time periods, resulting in files of great magnitude.
These general collections should be investigated at the beginning of
any research program and should be rechecked from time to time as
new information is located.

The TEMPLE RECORDS INDEX BUREAU and the CHURCH
RECORDS ARCHIVES are two of the more important general collections to be considered, and both are located at the Genealogical
Society's new library in downtown Salt Lake City (fig. 12). An interested
person may obtain information from the two collections through correspondence or by a personal visit to the library. Special request
forms are currently in use to aid those who must work through correspondence, and copies may be obtained from the library or any of
its branches (fig. 13). The request forms need not be used when

Fig. 12.   New home of the LDS Genealogical Society

THE GENEALOGICAL SOCIETY   50 E. NORTH TEMPLE STREET, SALT LAKE CITY, UTAH 84150

REQUEST FOR COPY OF INDEX CARD OR ARCHIVE RECORD
(TIB REQUEST FORM)

Please PRINT your name, mailing address, and zip code in the box on each form submitted.

(Name)
(Street)
(City)   (State)   (Zip)

Enter below as much information as you have about the individual whose name is to be checked. You must have surname, given name(s), at least the year of birth or christening, and at least the state or country of birth or christening. Do not inquire about more than one individual on this form.

Surname (PLEASE PRINT)	Given name (s)	
Birth date (day, month, year)	Birthplace (parish or town, county, state or country)	
Christening date (day, mo., year)	Christening place (parish, county, state or country)	
Marriage date	Marriage place (parish, or town, county, state or country)	
Spouse Surname	Spouse Given name (s)	
Father's surname	Father's given name (s)	
Mother's surname	Mother's given name (s)	
Death date (day, month, year)	LDS baptism date	Endowment date
Your relationship to this person	(Your relationship must be given when this person was born less than 95 years ago).	

Names processed under the Name Tabulation Program and names for endowments for the living since January, 1970 will not be found in the TIB files, but are in the computer mass file. Please do not use this request form for such names.

PLEASE CHECK THE TYPE OF RECORD YOU WISH COPIED (see information on reverse side):

☐ INDEX CARD (includes LDS baptism and endowment dates)
☐ ARCHIVE RECORD SHOWING THIS PERSON AS A PARENT (includes LDS date of sealing to spouse and baptism and endowment dates)
☐ ARCHIVE RECORD SHOWING THIS PERSON AS A CHILD (includes LDS date of sealing to parents, and baptism and endowment dates)

IF YOU REQUEST A COPY OF AN INDEX CARD, PLEASE CHECK BELOW:

☐ CALL BACK   I will call for the results of this search.
☐ MAIL   Please mail the results of this search to me.

CHARGES will be made only on volume orders. Please do not send money, you will be billed if necessary after your order has been filled.

PFGS0073 2/73 1MM Printed in U.S.A. by Carr Printing Co.

Fig. 13. TIB request form

47

searching the archives in person but must be used to gain information from the Temple Records Index Bureau, whether visiting the library in person or using its facilities through correspondence. When it can be found in the files, limited information will be provided by the Society at no charge, but a reasonable charge may be assessed when copies of Archive records are located and returned with the request.

The Temple Records Index Bureau

The Index Bureau is primarily an index to LDS endowment work which has been performed since 1842, but it also includes other ordinance information such as LDS baptism dates and sealing information. The Bureau came into being during 1922-1927 to help prevent duplication of ordinance work in temples of the Church. It has existed as a card file since that time (fig. 14).

The first cards added to the file were copied from original temple ordinance books which have since been microfilmed, but later cards were made concurrently with the actual temple records. Reference to the original temple record is given on each card, and microfilm copies of the ordinance books may be searched at the Genealogical Society Library in Salt Lake City by members of the LDS Church.

Cards in the Bureau were arranged in one special alphabetical system (soundex) for many years, but a recent change resulted in their being filed according to the country of birth of the principal person shown on the card. Over 126 countries are presently represented by the more than 38 million cards in the file.

Most names submitted to the Genealogical Society for processing have been cleared through the Bureau, and identifying facts for each person whose name was cleared have been retained in the file. There are some cards on file for persons whose names have not been cleared for LDS ordinance work, but they are in the minority. (Information which pertains to living persons is confidential and will only be released to immediate family members.) Facts listed on the cards vary with each card filed, and the facts are no better than their source. Some are inaccurate and incomplete, while others are the result of personal knowledge or competent research and provide genealogical information of the highest quality. Some facts listed cannot be found in any other place (fig. 15).

Since many cards have been cross-referenced, it may be possible for a beginning researcher, using the data gathered from family and home sources, to extend an ancestral line several generations by requesting information from the Index Bureau files. However, file clerks at the Bureau may not be able to locate the desired information when insufficient identifying facts are given, so one should include as much detail as possible when submitting requests. The name, date of birth, and place of birth are minimum identifying elements for a successful search of the files, but when the name is common, exact and complete dates and places are necessary. When parentage or

Fig. 14.   Temple Records Index Bureau files

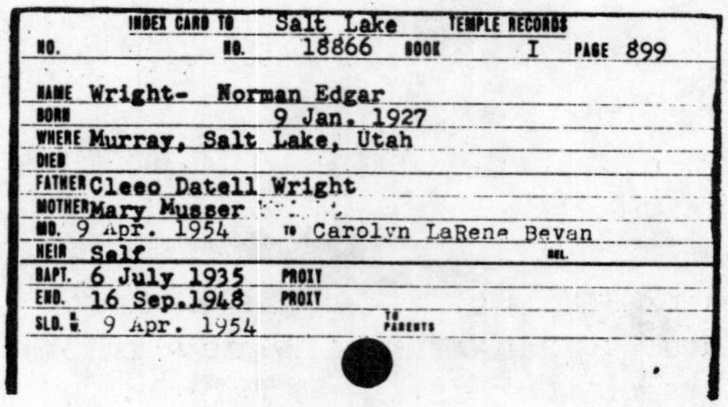

Card 1 (top left):

```
INDEX CARD TO  Salt Lake   TEMPLE RECORDS
NO.        NO.    18866   BOOK      I   PAGE 899
NAME Wright-  Norman Edgar
BORN           9 Jan. 1927
WHERE Murray, Salt Lake, Utah
DIED
FATHER Cleeo Datell Wright
MOTHER Mary Musser
NO. 9 Apr. 1954    " Carolyn LaRene Bevan
HEIR Self                           REL.
BAPT. 6 July 1935    PROXY
END. 16 Sep.1948    PROXY
SLD. 9 Apr. 1954          To PARENTS
```

Card 2 (top right):

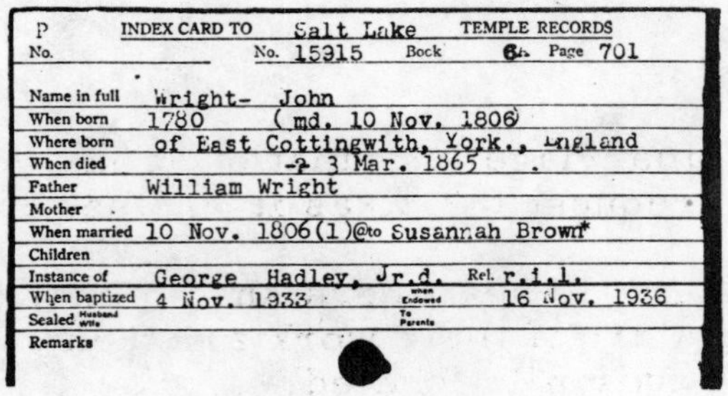

```
P        INDEX CARD TO  Salt Lake   TEMPLE RECORDS
No.              No.   15315   Book  6   Page 701
Name in full  Wright-  John
When born    1780    ( md. 10 Nov. 1806)
Where born   of East Cottingwith, York., England
When died         -? 3 Mar. 1865
Father       William Wright
Mother
When married 10 Nov. 1806(1)@to Susannah Brown
Children
Instance of  George Hadley, Jr.d.  Rel. r.i.l.
When baptized  4 Nov. 1333   Endowed   16 Nov. 1936
Sealed Husband   To Parents
Remarks
```

Card 3 (middle left):

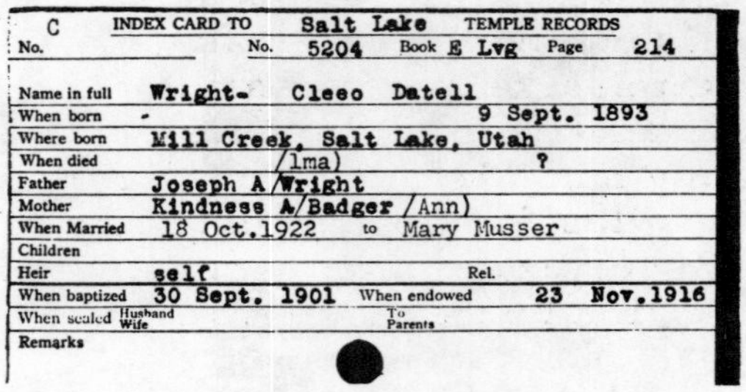

```
C        INDEX CARD TO  Salt Lake   TEMPLE RECORDS
No.              No.    5204   Book E Lvg  Page   214
Name in full  Wright-  Cleeo Datell
When born            9 Sept. 1893
Where born   Mill Creek, Salt Lake, Utah
When died        /lma/          ?
Father       Joseph A/Wright
Mother       Kindness A/Badger /Ann)
When Married 18 Oct.1922  to  Mary Musser
Children
Heir         self            Rel.
When baptized 30 Sept. 1901  When endowed  23 Nov.1916
When sealed Husband Wife      To Parents
Remarks
```

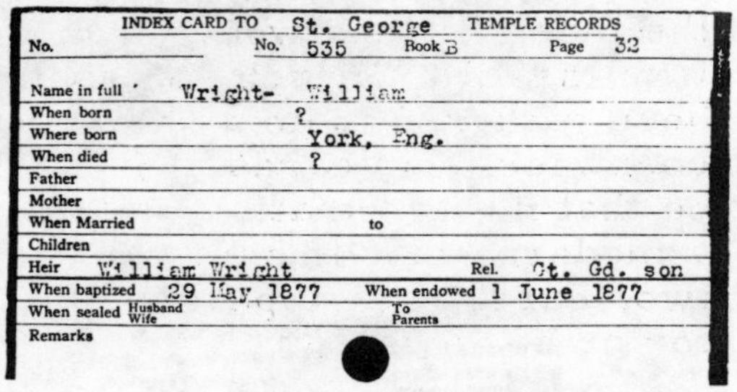

Card 4 (middle right):

```
         INDEX CARD TO  St. George  TEMPLE RECORDS
No.              No.    535   Book B   Page  32
Name in full  Wright-  William
When born            ?
Where born   York, Eng.
When died            ?
Father
Mother
When Married          to
Children
Heir         William Wright        Rel.  Gt. Gd. son
When baptized 29 May 1877  When endowed  1 June 1877
When sealed Husband Wife      To Parents
Remarks
```

Card 5 (bottom left):

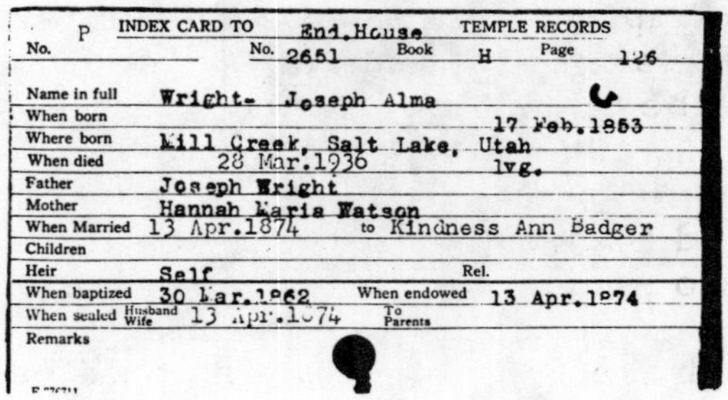

```
    P    INDEX CARD TO  End.House  TEMPLE RECORDS
No.              No.    2651   Book  H   Page  126
Name in full  Wright-  Joseph Alma
When born            17 Feb. 1853
Where born   Mill Creek, Salt Lake, Utah
When died    28 Mar.1936       lvg.
Father       Joseph Wright
Mother       Hannah Maria Watson
When Married 13 Apr.1874  to Kindness Ann Badger
Children
Heir         Self            Rel.
When baptized 30 Mar.1862  When endowed  13 Apr.1874
When sealed Husband Wife 13 Apr.1874   To Parents
Remarks
```

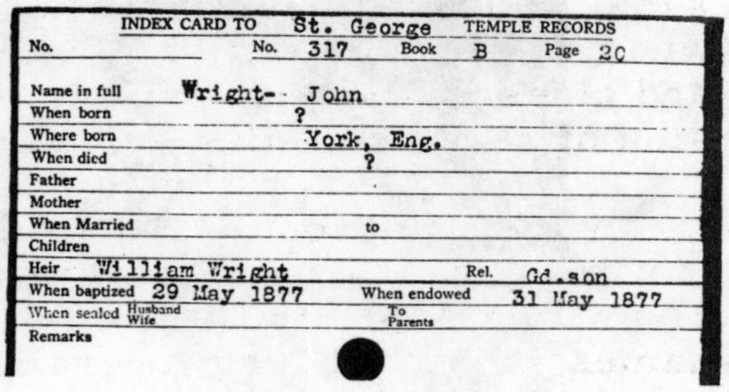

Card 6 (bottom right):

```
         INDEX CARD TO  St. George  TEMPLE RECORDS
No.              No.    317   Book  B   Page  20
Name in full  Wright-  John
When born            ?
Where born   York, Eng.
When died            ?
Father
Mother
When Married          to
Children
Heir         William Wright        Rel.  Gd.son
When baptized 29 May 1877  When endowed  31 May 1877
When sealed Husband Wife      To Parents
Remarks
```

Fig. 15.   Six generations shown on Index Bureau cards

marriage information is known, it should also be included on the request form, as it will better help identify the person.

Researchers should check each name through the files at the start of their work and then recheck them again when any new information is located. It may also be advisable to resubmit requests periodically when negative results are received because cards may be misfiled or may have been removed for processing when the search was made, or new information may have been added by others since the first request was submitted. A researcher should never assume that everything has been obtained from the files after one of the clerks has made a search. It may even be necessary to employ an accredited researcher who can search the files in person.[1] Access to the Bureau is limited to authorized employees of the Genealogical Society and to accredited researchers.

Some researchers may feel it is a waste of time to check cards in the Index Bureau when their ancestral lines have not been associated with the LDS Church, but this is often a mistake. Information has been gathered from a variety of sources and from many different countries, and cards are on file for many non-Mormon lines. It may be that no information will appear in the files for a particular line in a modern period, but after the line has been extended a generation or two, cards may appear which extend the line to the immigrant ancestor or beyond.

A few years ago, a check was made in the Bureau for facts about Nelson Hills of Hayward and Sawyer counties, Wisconsin, but no card could be located for him. Continued research disclosed his father to be Sylvester Hills who was also of Wisconsin. After making this one connection, a search of Bureau cards disclosed information for Sylvester which extended the line to the immigrant ancestor through New York and Connecticut.

The Index Bureau is of special value to early LDS Church pedigrees, and they should be checked through it without fail. Under such circumstances it may be wise to employ an accredited researcher who can search the files in person and make deductions from leads and clues on the cards which might not be made through the submission of regular request forms.

With the advent of the computer and the growth of the Index Bureau, it was logical that a marriage of the two should take place. With over 38 million cards on file, it became quite a task to clear the many names submitted for processing through the Bureau. Cards could be overlooked or misfiled and incomplete identifying information could result in mistaken identity. Also, the physical area required to house the files was becoming too large, and steps had to be taken to make the Bureau more manageable.

There will undoubtedly be many more changes affecting the Index

Bureau, and it might be that the file is microfilmed. Whatever its future might be, it will remain a valuable survey source for the American genealogist and should be used by him when possible.

Name Tabulation

No new cards are currently being added to the Temple Records Index Bureau. The Name Tabulation Program, put into full operation in October of 1969, has affected all names submitted to the Genealogical Society for processing since that time. Under the new program information is submitted on special entry and marriage entry forms.

Special rules and procedures are to be followed in copying information onto these forms.[2] When they are received by the Society, the forms are microfilmed, and the information from them is computerized. When information submitted is already on file in the Temple Records Index Bureau, it is transferred to the computer and the Index card is marked and refiled. (The information received is also checked against certain Archive records.) The program is operating successfully; several million names have already been submitted under it. Information already on file will gradually be transferred to the computer. It is expected that the transfer of information from the Index Bureau files to computer language will take considerable time, and it may be that all facts are never transferred. However, it would be hoped that genealogical information from both the computer and the Index Bureau cards would continue to be made available for research purposes.

The Controlled Extraction Program

Cards from a special computer program ("R-Tab," now called "Controlled Extraction Program") were filed in the Index Bureau for a time but have since been removed to the Church Records Archives area (fig. 16). Under this program, several thousand names were copied from several hundred English and Welsh parish registers. Index cards were printed by the computer (fig. 17). Print-out lists were also created with genealogical information arranged alphabetically for each parish whose records were copied. These lists have been bound and are shelved in the Library of the Genealogical Society at Salt Lake City. They have also been microfilmed, and copies are found in most Branch Libraries.[3]

Sometimes a check of the cards or lists from the Controlled Extraction Program can help locate the English or Welsh parish of origin for an American family. A few years ago, a student attending a genealogy class at BYU had occasion to use the computer cards and was able to solve an unusual English place-name problem from them. Regular Index Bureau cards were located for his great-grandparents Joseph Barrow and Maria Beswick, who emigrated from England as Mormon converts. However, the birthplaces shown could not be reconciled with existing localities and known family information. One card listed the birthplace of Joseph as "Bolton, Lancashire, England" while his sealing card listed "Halliday, Lancashire, England." Searches in parish registers for Bolton failed to produce information

Fig. 16. "R-Tab" files in archives area

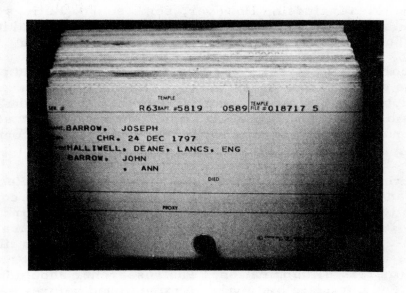

Fig. 17. An "R-Tab" card

53

on him, and no such locality as "Halliday" could be located in English reference books. It was interesting that a computer R-Tab card was on file for a Joseph Barrow who was christened at the right time to be ancestral. The christening date was 19 December 1797, and the place was listed as "Hallowell, Deane, Lancashire, England." The young man was convinced he had found his ancestor.

The Church Records Archives

A companion source to the Temple Records Index Bureau is the Church Records Archives. It consists of an estimated eight million family group records which have been filed at the Genealogical Society over the years (fig. 18).

Family group records of differing styles and content make up the collection and constitute an excellent survey source for the genealogist. Records have been submitted under different programs since the early 1920s and some early collections have been on microfilm for more than ten years. Beginning in January of 1942, all names submitted to the Genealogical Society for processing were listed on authorized family group forms, and thousands of these records have been filed in the main section of the Society's Archives (fig. 19).

Some records are incomplete and unreliable, but many are the result of original research and include information from personal knowledge. The name and address of the person who submitted the record is listed on most sheets, and the sources used to compile them are often included. However, some source listings are incomplete and represent poor documentation, sometimes making it impossible to locate the original reference.

Records in the Archives are open to the public, and photocopy facilities are available in the library. Archive records are filed in strict alphabetical sequence according to the name of the husband. All possible name variations should be considered when searching the records, and imagination should be used to locate connecting records.

There is a close relationship between the Temple Records Index Bureau and the Church Records Archives, with the two complimenting each other as a genealogical source. Ordinance work completed prior to 1942 may be recorded in the Index Bureau but may not be listed in the Archives. Likewise, some information on file in the Archives may not be recorded on the Index Bureau cards, especially sealing (marriage) information. The researcher should use both sources and correlate his work. As mentioned before, request for Index Bureau records and Archive records can be made on the same form for those who must perform research by correspondence.

An ancestral line can sometimes be extended several generations in the Archives, the same as in the Index Bureau, but a worker must be careful in accepting the facts at face value. Some of the sources

Fig. 18. Church Records Archives

HUSBAND RALPH SHEPARD *

Birth	1603 or 1606	Place Prob London, Eng
Chr.		Place
Death	20 Aug 1693	Place
Burial		Place Old Bell Rock Cem, Malden, Middx,/Eng
Father Isaac Shepard *		Mother‡

WIFE THANKS LORD *

Birth	abt 1612	Place Prob London, Eng
Chr.		Place
Death	1693	Place Malden, Middx, Mass
Burial		Place
Father Thomas Lord *		Mother‡ Dorothy Bird

Where was information shown on this family record obtained?
Charlestown Rec p 216 "Ancestry of Edward Wales Blake & Clarissa Matilda Glidden" by Edith B. Sumner; Littleton Hist Society #1 (Mass Ill);

Family Representative:
Raymond Franklin Farr
Name and address of person submitting this sheet.
Lois S. Wickers
5317 W 116 St.
Los Angeles 45, California

Sex M F	CHILDREN list each child (whether living or dead) in order of birth	WHEN BORN Day Mo. Yr.	WHERE BORN Town	County	State or Country	DIED Day Mo. Yr.	MARRIED (First Husband or Wife) List Additional Marriages with Dates on Reverse Side of Sheet	Date To
F	1 Sarah Shepard	1633			Eng	W.P. 22 Dec 1719		
M	2 Thomas Shepard *	1635	Dedham,	Norflk,	Mass	17 Sep 1719	1) Hannah Ensign *	19 Nov 1658
M	3 John Shepard *	1637	prob "	"	"	15 Dec 1699	Sarah Gable	1660
M	4 Isaac Shepard *	20 Jun 1639	Weymouth,		"	12 Feb 1676	Mary Smedley	10 Dec 1667
F	5 X Trial Shepard *	19 Dec 1641			"		Walter Power	11 Mar 1660
M	6 Walter Shepard	abt 1643	of Sudbury, Middx,		"	1719		
M	7 Abraham Shepard *	abt 1648	of Concord,		"	22 Feb 1716	Judith Filbrook	2 Jan 1672
F	8 Thanks Shepard *	10 Feb 1650	Malden,	"	"		Peter Dill	13 Dec 1669
M	9 Jacob Shepard *	8/16 Jun 1653	"	"	"	1676 (ae 56)		
M	10 Ralph Shepard	abt 1656	of Dedham,	Norflk,	"	26 Jun 1712		
M	11 Daniel Shepard	abt 1659	Malden,	Middx,	"			
F	12 Mary Shepard	abt 1660/2	"	"	"		Thomas Harris	17 Sep 1688
	13							

HUSBAND'S
Name (in full) Ralph Shepard 1606
Wife Thanks Lord

TEMPLE ORDINANCE DATA

HUSBAND	
Baptized	11 Dec 1883
Endowed	8 May 1923
	6 gg son (Relationship of Family Representative to Husband)
WIFE	
Baptized	26 May 1928
Endowed	9 Jan 1929
Sealed to Husband	4 Jan 1945 SL
	6 gg son (Relationship of Family Representative to Wife)

BAPTIZED (Date)	ENDOWED (Date)	SEALED To Parents Date & Temple
26 May 1928	16 Jan 1929	4 Jan 1945 SL
24 Oct 1921	23 Feb 1922	4 Jan 1945 SL
13 Dec 1930	24 Dec 1930	4 Jan 1945 SL
11 Dec 1883	26 Jun 1890	4 Jan 1945 SL
11 Dec 1883	21 Feb 1928	4 Jan 1945 SL
26 May 1928	9 Jan 1931	2 Feb 1951 SL
13 Dec 1930	7 Jan 1931	4 Jan 1945 SL
26 May 1928	17 Jan 1929	4 Jan 1945 SL
13 Dec 1930	8 Jan 1931	4 Jan 1945 SL
14 May 1938	19 Nov 1942	4 Jan 1945 SL
14 May 1938	19 Nov 1942	25 Oct 1954 SL
1 Apr 1954	19 May 1954	25 Oct 1954 SL

Fig. 19. Family group record from Church Records Archives

listed are vague, and much information is from family tradition or hearsay. Sometimes the persons who submitted records can be located through addresses shown and can verify information in the Archives, but in many cases these persons have moved or are deceased.

Church Records Archives collections have been arranged in various groupings over the years and will probably see many more changes. There has been a Patron's Section with family group records and pedigree charts, a Main Section with finished and unfinished ordinance work, a Sealing Section with records held in suspension while ordinance work was in process, as well as a Miscellaneous Section and the recently added Four-Generation Family Group Record Collection. With exception of the Main Section, each collection has been microfilmed, and recent indications are that the Main Section will be filmed in the near future.[4]

The Four-Generation Program

The Four-Generation Program of the LDS Church has created a group of records which are a helpful survey source applying mainly to a modern period and to LDS connected families. Since October 1969, family group records have not been added to the Archives, though "Four-Generation" sheets are still being received and filed. (Publications dealing with this program and other aspects of Priesthood Genealogy in the Church are constantly going through revision and updating. Researchers who are concerned with submitting names to the Society for clearance for temple work should consult the most recent publications about the Continuing Priesthood Program for Family Exaltation.)

---

1. A list of name and addresses of accredited researchers may be obtained from the Genealogical Society without charge (50 East North Temple Street, Salt Lake City, Utah 84150).

2. For the mechanics of the Name Tabulation Program, see the LDS Genealogical Society's RECORDS SUBMISSION MANUAL, 4th ed. (1973).

3. For more detail about Controlled Extraction Program see the Genealogical Society's RESEARCH PAPERS, series F, no. 3.

4. For additional information concerning the Church Records Archives, see Jaussi and Chaston's FUNDAMENTALS OF GENEALOGICAL RESEARCH and Wright and Pratt's GENEALOGICAL RESEARCH ESSENTIALS.

CHAPTER 5

USING SELECTED LDS AND EARLY UTAH SOURCES

If a person descends from early LDS ancestry, he should investigate certain early Church and Utah collections before searching records of the localities pertaining to his pedigree. Important facts can often be located which will guide and assist him in future research. These special collections are in custody of the Genealogical Society and the Church Historian in Salt Lake City.

Collections of special importance include various membership and ordinance records, emigration records, and miscellaneous biographical and historical works. The REGISTER OF LDS RECORDS by Laureen R. Jaussi and Gloria D. Chaston (Salt Lake City: Deseret Book Co., 1968) lists most of them and also includes current film numbers for collections which have been microfilmed. The reader should also consult Jaussi and Chaston's FUNDAMENTALS OF GENEALOGICAL RESEARCH, 2nd ed. rev. (Salt Lake City: Deseret Book Co., 1972) and Wright and Pratt's GENEALOGICAL RESEARCH ESSENTIALS (Salt Lake City: Bookcraft, 1967) for background information on the records and sources listed. This section deals primarily with methods and procedures in their use and does not cover historical background to any great length.

Ward and Branch Records

An attempt should first be made to locate the ancestor in early ward and branch records, because they contain birth, death, and marriage information as well as ordinance and historical data. An early Cache Valley, Utah, record included excommunication information on a member who "purchased goods at the store of a Gentile" while another outlined actions taken to disfellowship a member for "refusing to follow the advise of his Bishop." An early Quincy,

Illinois, branch record included historical information about baptism for the dead performed in Illinois streams. It is the opinion of the writer that few genealogists have exhausted the potential of these records when it comes to their early LDS pedigree problems.

Many early membership records (1830-1837) were lost or destroyed during early struggles of the Church, and some modern records have been lost through neglect or destructive forces. The earliest extant membership records are English branch records beginning about 1837 and a few American ward and branch records which date from the Nauvoo period (1840-1846). Wright and Pratt's GENEALOGICAL RESEARCH ESSENTIALS lists records which have been preserved for the early Illinois, Iowa, and Missouri periods on pages 184-85. A few early Nauvoo ward records and some for Winter Quarters (Florence, Nebraska) have also been preserved and are included in microfilm copies of early Salt Lake City wards. One reel of microfilm relating to Nauvoo wards is on file at BYU. Some genealogical facts from Nauvoo and early Utah Territory records have also been card indexed in various early Church collections which will be explained later in the chapter.

Existing ward and branch records (1840-1948) for the stakes, and branch records (1837-1951) for the missions have been microfilmed and are available at the Genealogical Society Library in Salt Lake City. Jaussi's REGISTER contains geographical and alphabetical lists of them on pages 73-339.

A program to transfer stake membership information to individual certificates was completed during 1941-1948, and mission membership data was transferred 1948-1951. Since those dates, individual certificates of membership have been filed in the respective wards and branches where the member resided, and duplicate copies have been kept at the central Church membership office in Salt Lake City. The Church recently completed a program to computerize membership information which will make the transfer of membership data more efficient and provide bishops and branch presidents with more detailed information about their members.

ANNUAL or FORM "E" REPORTS were kept after 1906 in all wards and branches and should be considered part of the membership records. They include statistics and information about births and blessings, baptisms and confirmations, marriages and divorces, priesthood ordinations, missionary calls, excommunications, and deaths; records made after 1938 also contain information about ward and branch officers and teachers. The information was recorded on special forms on a quarterly basis and was submitted annually to the Church Historian in Salt Lake City. The records have been microfilmed and are included with microfilmed copies of the ward and branch records, usually comprising the last roll or two of microfilm. They are an excellent source of statistical information recorded after 1906.

A great deal of patience must be exercised in searching the early records. Many are unindexed and incomplete, and sometimes it is necessary to search each section page by page and line by line to locate the desired information. The title page may or may not include complete details about the organization dates, and the index, if it exists, may or may not include the names of all persons who were actually members of the unit.

Search in these records is further complicated by the fact that it is entirely possible that a person lived in a ward or branch for some time and yet did not actually become a member of record. If an ordinance or some other event did not affect him, the clerk may not have made an entry for him in the records. It may also be necessary to search records for a time period beyond the known period of residence, because the clerk may have initiated new books or carried information about earlier members forward to new books.

If the place of residence (ward or branch) is known, the researcher may merely consult the alphabetical and geographical ward and branch lists in Jaussi's REGISTER, but if the unit of residence is not known, two or three other approaches may be necessary to locate the individual in the proper record.

Biographies, Directories, and Census Records

Frank Esshom's PIONEERS AND PROMINENT MEN OF UTAH (Salt Lake City: Utah Pioneers Book Publishing Company, 1913) lists hundreds of biographies and includes ward residence information. When the ancestor of interest was a polygamist, the record also gives details about each family. In addition, excellent portrait information is included for some individuals. But the record as a whole must be used with caution for it contains errors.

Andrew Jenson's four-volume LATTER-DAY SAINT BIOGRAPHICAL ENCYCLOPEDIA (Salt Lake City: The Andrew Jenson History Company, 1901-1936) is also good for its lists of ward or branch of residence for members, but it pertains mostly to officers in the Church such as bishops and branch presidents. When an ancestor is located, there is generally listed excellent vital information and interesting historical information concerning him.

Kate B. Carter's HEART THROBS OF THE WEST (Salt Lake City: Daughters of Utah Pioneers, 1939-1951), in twelve volumes, contains considerable genealogical and historical information about early pioneers of the West, including residence information. This work has been indexed by Beth Oyler in her INDEX TO HEART THROBS OF THE WEST (Salt Lake City: Free Public Library, 1948), and copies are on file in several Intermountain libraries (BYU Ref. 979.2 C24).

Carter's TREASURES OF PIONEER HISTORY (Salt Lake City: Daughters of Utah Pioneers, 1947-1950), in five volumes, also lists biographical and historical information about early LDS Church members, particularly those of the early Utah Territory period (1847-1896).

Another interesting historical collection is THE UTAH GENEALOGICAL AND HISTORICAL MAGAZINE, edited by the late Archibald F. Bennett (Salt Lake City: The Genealogical Society of Utah, 1910-1940). It was published in thirty-one volumes and contains much genealogical information about early Church members. (See volumes 20 and 21 for pedigree information about Brigham Young and Joseph Smith, for instance.)

Several special biographical collections have been acquired by the Genealogical Society Library, including group and regional biographies. The interested researcher should consult that library's card catalog for current listings.

Several hundred references to names found in books and pamphlets have been included in the Genealogical Society's main card catalog. These should also be consulted for early LDS Church membership information. For several years a special index file included such references, but cards from the collection have recently been incorporated in the main card catalog.

If an ancestor was a member of the LDS Church in its earliest period (1830-1850), Andrew Jenson's HISTORICAL RECORD AND CHURCH CHRONOLOGY is helpful (especially volumes 5-8). They outline many events in early LDS history and include personal facts about people who were involved in such events as Zion's Camp, the Haun's Mill Massacre, or the martyrdom of the Prophet Joseph Smith.

The JOURNAL HISTORY OF THE CHURCH, a manuscript collection in several hundred volumes, also contains helpful information about early Church members and includes much interesting historical material. It was compiled from private journals and diaries for the earlier period but has been a contemporary record since the Saints came west. The collection has been microfilmed but currently must be consulted in the Church Historian's Library. The collection has been card indexed, and it too has been filmed, but currently must be consulted through the Church Historian's Offices.

If an ancestor lived in an early Utah period (1847-1880), the 1850 federal census index for Utah should be consulted and also the 1880 index which was recently completed by genealogy students at BYU. The index to the 1880 census of Utah is on microfilm, but the 1850 is in book form at the Genealogical Society Library. The 1860 and 1870 federal census schedules have not been indexed at this writing, but with the 1850 and 1880 indexes, one should be able to locate a Utah resident without much difficulty if he actually resided in the state during that period. Also, MIGRATION SOURCES OF GREAT BRITAIN AND NORTH AMERICA by Wright and Pratt (Provo: BYU Press, 1968) should be consulted, because it is an index to Bishop's

Reports for 1852-1853 and indexes the 1850 federal census of Pottowattami County, Iowa, where many Latter-day Saints resided.

If an LDS member lived to the twentieth century, or if his descendants were living at that time, the LDS CHURCH CENSUS RECORDS for 1914-1960 should be consulted. Each record includes genealogical facts about members and includes information about their ward or branch of residence. Records for 1914, 1920, 1925, 1930, and 1935 have been arranged in one alphabet and microfilmed. So have those for 1950, 1955, and 1960, but they constitute a separate collection. The 1940 Church census was filmed separately, and none was taken in 1945, a war year. Supplements have been filmed for certain years and film numbers for each collection are listed on pages 341-52 of Jaussi's REGISTER.

UTAH DIRECTORIES, dating from 1869, and various CITY DIRECTORIES, dating from 1884, are available at the Genealogical Society Library and contain address information for Utah residents. Some directories prior to 1900 list the ward or branch of residence as well as the street address, but most of those after that period list only the street address. By consulting several directories in a series it is often possible to gain additional helpful facts about the individual or the family, including death dates and spouses names.

The Reference Department at the Genealogical Society Library in Salt Lake City has a WARD BOUNDARY MAP, showing early Salt Lake Valley wards, which can be used to determine an individual's ward of residence from a street address. Andrew Jenson's ENCYCLO-PEDIC HISTORY OF THE CHURCH OF JESUS CHRIST OF LATTER-DAY SAINTS (Salt Lake City: Deseret News Publishing Co., 1941) is also useful in that regard. It is an alphabetical listing of stakes, missions, conferences, wards, and branches to 1941.

Miscellaneous Indexes

The MEMBERSHIP CARD INDEX (also known as the Minnie Margett's File) can be used as a partial index to some early American ward and branch records, though it is primarily an index to those of the British Mission. It consists of index cards from over four hundred wards and branches, and it has been microfilmed. Jaussi's REGISTER lists film numbers for American units on pages 66-67.

The EARLY CHURCH INFORMATION CARD INDEX (also known as the Early Church Information File) can also be used as an index to certain early Utah ward records and to some historical records of the Nauvoo period (1840-1846). The file originally consisted of 150,000 index cards showing vital and statistical information about individuals connected with early LDS Church history. It was recently arranged in three files with cards showing (1) miscellaneous marriages of Utah, Idaho, and Wyoming (The Miscellaneous Marriage File), (2) Nauvoo baptisms for the dead (The Nauvoo Baptisms for the Dead File), and (3) miscellaneous events and circumstances of early Church history (The Early Church Information File).

The EARLY CHURCH INFORMATION FILE (fig. 20) includes the following information:

1 - All deaths, marriages, and related events carried in the FRONTIER GUARDIAN, published in Kanesville, Iowa, 1849-1852.

2 - Inscriptions on the Mt. Pisgah Monument at Mt. Pisgah, Union County, Iowa, covering deaths during 1846-1848.

3 - Old Nauvoo cemetery inscriptions.

4 - Genealogical facts taken from early high priest and seventies records.

5 - Genealogical facts taken from Springville, Payson, and Spanish Fork (Utah) wards for a period after 1851.

6 - Genealogical facts from the Salt Lake City 17th Ward for the period 1851-1888 and from the Union Branch of Pottowattami County, Iowa, for the period 1853-1855.

7 - Extracts from the EVENING AND MORNING STAR, the LDS MESSENGER AND ADVOCATE, the ELDER'S JOURNAL, the TIMES AND SEASONS, the WASP, and the NAUVOO NEIGHBOR.

8 - Genealogical facts from the first forty volumes of early patriarchal blessings.

The CARD INDEX TO PATRIARCHAL BLESSINGS can also provide place-name information as well as important vital statistics about LDS Church members. Index cards have been compiled from blessings given by various patriarchs of the Church and were microfilmed in 1963. (The actual blessings are in custody of the Church Historian and are confidential.) The index cards generally include the name of the person blessed, his birth date and birthplace, his parentage, his lineage (the name of one of the tribes of Israel through which he descends), the date and place of blessing, and the name of the patriarch. Reference is also given to the book and page where the original blessing is recorded. Some persons have had more than one blessing and one card may provide information which another might omit. Film numbers for the card index are listed on page 355 of Jaussi's REGISTER.

The CARD INDEX TO PEDIGREE CHARTS is an index of only fair importance, but in some instances it can provide useful kinship and locality information. Several thousand charts were submitted to the Society by Church members in the 1920s. All charts submitted were microfilmed, but only the first 18,000 were indexed for every name on the chart. The remainder were microfilmed after being

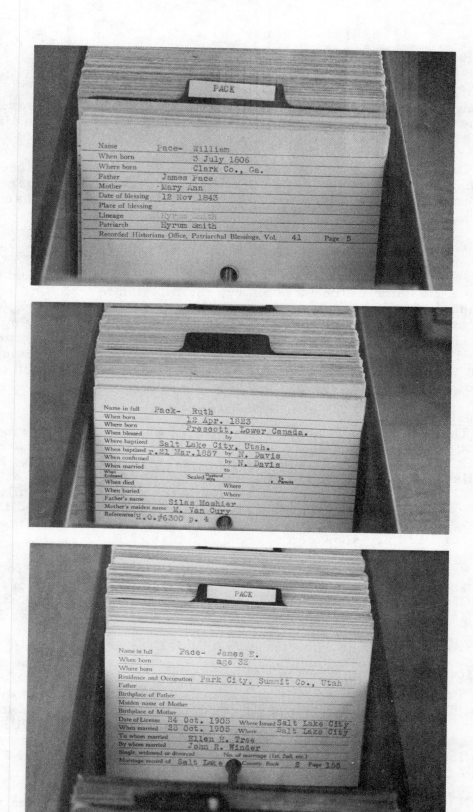

Fig. 20. Cards from ERCI file

65

arranged in alphabetical order by the name of the first person shown on the chart. Film numbers for the microfilmed charts are listed on pages 3-6 of Jaussi's REGISTER.

Cards in the Pedigree Index File have recently been microfilmed and can be borrowed by branch libraries. (Reference numbers at the bottom of each card refer to the original book, page, and chart number.)

The MISSIONARY INDEX (also known as the Missionary File) is a card index listing individuals who filled missions for the LDS Church between 1830 and 1963. The file was microfilmed in 1963 and cards include the name of the missionary, the mission to which he was called, the date of his call or departure, and sometimes even biographical information about him, though this is usually for those serving between 1830-1896 only. Facts on the index cards may also lead to microfilmed mission records which might contain additional information about the missionary. Film numbers for the index are listed on page 356 of Jaussi's REGISTER.

Emigration Records

The CROSSING THE PLAINS INDEX is a card file covering the period 1847-1869 and lists the names of individuals who crossed the plains to Utah Territory prior to the coming of the railroad. Names are listed by household and indexed by the name of the head of house. Not all persons in a particular grouping are necessarily family members, and all persons who crossed the plains are not indexed in the file. The cards were compiled from several different sources, and film numbers are shown on page 59 of Jaussi's REGISTER.

Printed lists of emigrants to the Great Salt Lake Basin for the years 1847-1850 have been published in centennial editions of the DAUGHTERS OF UTAH PIONEER MAGAZINE (Kate B. Carter, ed. Salt Lake City: Daughters of Utah Pioneers, 1847-1850) (fig. 21).

Lists of persons who died en route to Utah during the same period (1846-1848) have also been published. Some lists include the individual's year of death and sometimes his birth date and place. the DESERET NEWS for 21 December 1918 published a list of persons who died in Ohio, Illinois, Missouri, and on the Plains, and the list was later copied and filed at the Genealogical Society Library as MANUSCRIPT #844. A list of persons who died on their journey to Utah has also been included on pages 466-84 of the DAUGHTERS OF UTAH PIONEER MAGAZINE for 1956.

If the ancestor was an immigrant from Europe during the period 1849-1935, certain European emigration records should be investigated. The EUROPEAN EMIGRATION CARD INDEX (also known as the Crossing the Ocean Index) was compiled by the Church Historian's Office and includes the names of individuals who were listed in shipping registers and other early emigration records of the Church.

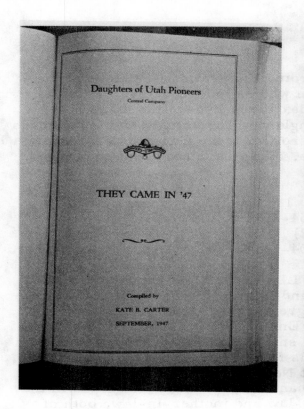

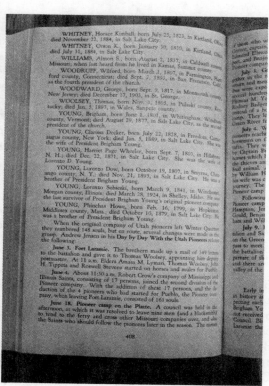

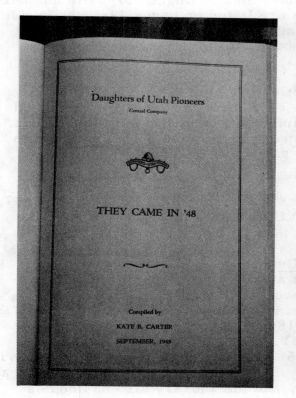

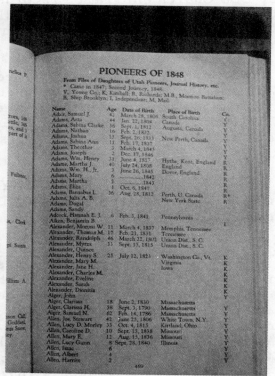

Fig. 21. Entries from Daughters of Utah Pioneers Magazine

Most of the names indexed were from "Emigration Registers of the British Mission" and were of those who sailed from Liverpool under LDS Church sponsorship. The index cards include the name of each ship and the date it sailed from England. The actual shipping records (Emigration Registers) are on microfilm at the Genealogical Society Library for the following missions. They have not been indexed, except for the British registers.

BRITISH MISSION (1849-1885; 1899-1925)
SCANDINAVIAN MISSION (1854-1896; 1901-1920)
SWEDISH MISSION (1905-1932)
NETHERLANDS MISSION (1904-1914)

The records were kept by the LDS Church and should not be confused with official U.S. Customs and Immigration records which have also been microfilmed. (My own great-grandfather--Joseph Wright, born 1817 in Bubwith, Yorkshire, England--left Liverpool in an LDS company in January of 1849 on the ship Zetland but does not appear in British mission emigration records for 1849. He does appear in U.S. customs lists for ships arriving at New Orleans [GS F#26816 pt 33]. The entry was dated 3 April 1849, and a bonus entry was found in the record showing Joseph's father-in-law and mother-in-law, both of whom were previously assumed to have died in England.) Film numbers for LDS Church emigration records are listed on pages 49-63 of Jaussi's REGISTER. A list of ships providing LDS Church emigration from Europe and a list of "Overland Companies to Utah" is also shown on pages 126-34.

The names of persons and sureties indebted to the PERPETUAL EMIGRATING FUND have also been card indexed and microfilmed and may provide additional emigration information on early LDS members. The index includes the names of persons involved with the fund for the period 1840-1877 and film numbers are listed on pages 49-63 of the REGISTER.

Andrew Jenson's DAY BY DAY WITH THE UTAH PIONEERS, 1847, and his HISTORICAL RECORD AND CHURCH CHRONOLOGY can also be useful on emigration problems.

Early Birth, Marriage, and Death Records

Early ward and branch records are the best place to locate birth, marriage, and death information about early Church members, but a few vital record collections have been kept which include them. SALT LAKE CITY DEATH RECORDS for 1848-1950 have been microfilmed and are available at the Genealogical Society Library as are SALT LAKE COUNTY DEATHS (1897-1905) and SALT LAKE COUNTY CORONERS RECORDS (1858-1881). BIRTH RECORDS FOR SALT LAKE CITY were first kept in 1897, and the Library also has copies of them for 1897-1905. Unfortunately, the early marriage records for Salt Lake County (which includes Salt Lake City) are missing for the period 1847-1886, but those for 1887-1965 are available on film at the Society Library. If an ancestor married in a county other than Salt Lake, it may be necessary to consult that county's records which may or may not be on file at the Library. Film numbers for the vital records mentioned above are listed on pages 357-63 of Jaussi's REGISTER.

Birth, marriage, and death records may also have been kept in other localities where the Saints resided before their trek West, and it may be advisable to search them also. The Genealogical Society has done extensive filming in the eastern states and is currently filming in the midwestern and southwestern states. Details about vital statistics registration in the various states are contained in appendix 4.

Incidentally, when consulting vital records, it is a good practice to locate the death or burial record first and follow with marriage and birth records. Working from the more modern event often helps to locate other facts which will be useful in later research. It is also a good practice to locate an obituary notice or newspaper account of the death when it occurred in a modern period, because the information often supplements that from the death certificate.

An OBITUARY CARD INDEX to Salt Lake City newspapers and to a few other miscellaneous periodicals has been compiled by the Church Historian's Office. A microfilm copy is available at the Genealogical Society Library and at BYU. On 31 December 1970, the Church Historian's Office completed its project of indexing the obituaries reported in the SALT LAKE TRIBUNE and the DESERET NEWS. The collection was first microfilmed in 1963 and then refilmed in April 1971 to include the latest entries. The index includes entries from the SALT LAKE TRIBUNE, the DESERET NEWS, the JOURNAL HISTORY OF THE CHURCH, the TIMES AND SEASONS, the IMPROVEMENT ERA, the ELDER'S JOURNAL, and a few other publications. With exception of the TRIBUNE and NEWS, none of the periodicals has been completely indexed. Over 100,000 cards are in the collection. Each card includes the name of the deceased, his death date, the name and date of the periodical, the page or section number where the obituary appeared, and sometimes some historical information. Film numbers for the 1971 copy follow:

A - 821636 - 821638			L - 821668 - 821671
B - 821638 - 821644			M - 821671 - 821675
C - 821644 - 821649			N - 821675 - 821677
D - 821649 - 821652			O - 821677 - 821678
E - 821652 - 821653			P - 821678 - 821682
F - 821653 - 821655			Q - 821682
G - 821655 - 821658			R - 821682 - 821685
H - 821658 - 821663			S - 821685 - 821691
I - 821663			T - 821691 - 821693
J - 821663 - 821666			U - 821693 - 821694
K - 821666 - 821668			V - 821694

```
W - 821694 - 821698
X - 821698
Y - 821698 - 821699
Z - 821699
```

An addendum "A-Z" appears on the last roll of microfilm.

The Genealogical Society Library has film copies of issues of the DESERET NEWS, but at this writing it does not have the SALT LAKE TRIBUNE. The TRIBUNE is on microfilm at BYU and the University of Utah Libraries, and they, along with the Church Historian, have copies of the other early periodicals mentioned. Film numbers for the obituary index (1963 copy) and microfilm copies of the DESERET NEWS (daily and weekly) are listed on pages 49-58 of Jaussi's REGISTER.

When an ancestor died in the Intermountain area and no reference to his death can be located in the obituary index, it might be advisable and necessary for the researcher to search issues of the appropriate newspapers himself. It should also be remembered that many death notices were carried in the two major Salt Lake papers, even when the individual died in an outlying area. And of course local papers, particularly weeklies, very frequently include family information.

The Genealogical Society Library in Salt Lake City also has several excellent cemetery and sextons' record collections which can be used in conjunction with vital and newspaper records (fig. 22).

UTAH CEMETERY RECORDS 1848-1952 have been published in thirteen volumes and are also indexed. The first five volumes are the index, and the remaining eight contain death and burial information. SALT LAKE CITY CEMETERY RECORDS 1848-1909 have also been published and are indexed in six volumes at the GS Library. RECORDS OF INTERMENTS IN THE NAUVOO CITY CEMETERY 1849-1931 are included in GS F#186550 and some are also indexed in the EARLY CHURCH INFORMATION INDEX, which has been identified previously.

Cemetery and sextons' records from many other localities are also on file at the Genealogical Society Library, but the researcher must consult the card catalog under the respective locality for their current listings.

Special Ordinance Collections

LDS ordinance records also provide valuable genealogical facts about early Church members and should not be overlooked when working LDS problems. Many early Saints were baptized for their deceased relatives and friends beginning in 1840, and the records contain excellent kinship information. Many were also endowed and sealed after baptismal work was completed, and some of the records resulting from these ordinances contain excellent birth, marriage, and death information.

Fig. 22. Cemetery records at the Genealogical Society Library

71

Original temple ordinance books were microfilmed in 1961 and copies are filed at the Genealogical Society Library in Salt Lake City. With the exception of a few early collections, they must be searched at the Library and may be used only by members of the Church. The original books remain in the respective temples.

The worker should consult pages 365-368 of Jaussi's REGISTER for detail on the types of ordinances performed, their arrangement, and indexing. The chart on pages 366-367 shows which ordinances were performed in the various temples and indicates the dates they were first recorded.

Elder Howard W. Hunter, of the Council of Twelve Apostles, gave a most informative address regarding ordinance work at the FOURTH ANNUAL PRIESTHOOD GENEALOGICAL RESEARCH SEMINAR (Brigham Young University, 12 August 1969). He not only provided pertinent doctrinal information about ordinances in general but also outlined procedures in performing certain ordinances. It was published by Brigham Young University in GENEALOGICAL DEVOTIONAL ADDRESSES--1969 and is reproduced as appendix 3 because of its significance to the subject discussed.

If the family of concern resided in or near Nauvoo between 1840 and 1846, the NAUVOO BAPTISMS FOR THE DEAD INDEX should be consulted. The file is in custody of the Genealogical Society, but the originals from which it was made are on microfilm and the call numbers are listed on page 369 of Jaussi's REGISTER (fig. 23).

For this index, cards were made giving reference to proxy names (the persons who performed the ordinances) as well as to the deceased (the persons whose work was done). The index can give valuable kinship information and can provide facts which will help in future research. Members of the Church at Nauvoo and surrounding areas were baptized as proxies for their deceased friends as early as 1840. Sometimes their "friends" turn out to be relatives, and the information can be used to extend a pedigree.

When the first proxy work for the dead was done, males did work for females and vice-versa, but this practice was not continued, and most of that early work was done again. Moreover, additional ordinance work, such as endowments and sealings, were not always performed for those whose baptism work was done at Nauvoo. So the records for some persons listed in the Nauvoo Index may not be on file in the Temple Records Index Bureau or in the Church Records Archives. For this reason, information from the Nauvoo Index can sometimes provide solution to difficult problems and can recall family information from the past which has long since been forgotten.

A Utah Jones family descends from Moses Jones who was an elder in the LDS Church in the early Nauvoo period. According to

Fig. 23. Cards from Nauvoo index

family information, he was born about 1789 in Washington County, Pennsylvania, the son of Stephen Jones (born 1763 in Sussex County, New Jersey) and Keziah Strong. Stephen was a Revolutionary War veteran; he was also a member of the LDS Church in 1842 (fig. 24).

Research in early ward and branch records indicated Moses was not born in Washington County but in Chestnut Hill, Bucks County-- across the whole state of Pennsylvania from Washington County. The Nauvoo Index to Baptisms for the Dead disclosed that Moses Jones did work for his mother as Keziah "Strawn," not "Strong" as family information suggested. Research in Bucks County records located a family which certainly could be ancestral. The records indicated one "John Straughan," son of Jacob (who was the son of Lancelot) married "Keziah Dennis" and they were the parents of nineteen children. Child number thirteen was "Keziah" who married Stephen Jones. The family moved to Western Pennsylvania, and John Strawn's will is dated 19 August 1801 and was filed for probate in Greene County, Pennsylvania, on 29 August 1808. The will mentions his wife Keziah (Dennis) (fig. 25) and his daughter Milly (who is lame and who is later cared for by Moses Jones) and appoints his son Jacob and his "son-in-law Stephen Jones" executors to his will (GREENE COUNTY, PENNSYLVANIA WILL BOOK I, #114, pp. 72-73).

As a matter of interest, Stephen did proxy work in Nauvoo for George Washington, Thomas Jefferson, and Andrew Jackson, as well as for General Marquee de Lafayette. He did the work as "friend", undoubtedly on the basis of his Revolutionary War service. Stephen was an early stalwart in the LDS Church, though modern historians have neglected to mention him. The contents of a letter he wrote indicate he must have been one of the earliest non-official missionaries for the Church. On 2 December 1831, Stephen Jones wrote from Delaware County in the state of Indiana ("20 miles from Winchester and eleven from Muncytown") to his son Moses, and others. In his letter he exhorted his children to hear the message of the Book of Mormon. The text of the letter, with slight variation from the original in punctuation and spelling, follows:

Dear Children I once more take up my pen to inform you that I enjoy a tolerable state of health, hoping these may find you all enjoying the same blessing, which ought to be a cause of thanksgiving to God. I feel it so and wish you all may also. Perhaps you may be anxious to know how I make a living--I can with rejoicing say that I have a plenty--having been blessed and prospered much in every thing I have undertaken, but horses, of them I have lost three since I have been here--but not any discouraged at that. Now a matter of more consequence lays on my mind which I hope may occupy yours also. For by means of a new revelation (to wit) the Book of Mormon which is now in the family said Book contains a record of a fallen people that once inhabited this land they being of the house of Israel, and tribe of Joseph and for their transgressions they were swept off all, except a

74

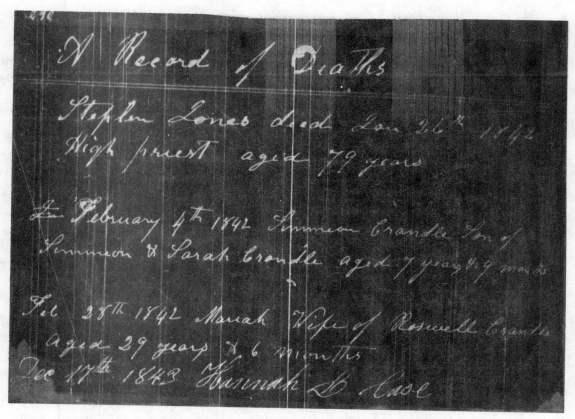

Fig. 24. LDS branch record showing Stephen Jones

Fig. 25. Tombstone found near Winchester, Indiana
--"Wife of Stephen Jones"

remnant of the Lamanites by us called Indians said people in the first year of the reign of Zedekiah King of Judah were led by the hand of God from Jerusalem to this land. They kept a record from the time they left it down to the time of their destruction--which was more than four hundred and twenty years from the coming of Our Lord and Saviour Jesus Christ of which they had a sign in this land at which time it was hiden by a prophet of the Lord whose name was Moroni and after being in secret from the world until the year 1829, said record was handed by an angel to Joseph Smith on plates of Gold, Witnessed by Oliver Cowdery, David Whitmer and Martin Harris. This will seem marvelous in your eyes but it is no more so than true therefor I your affec-tionate parent counsel you as you regard your Eternal welfare not to mock at it for I have a witness of the truth of it within me by the power and spirit of God who is merciful to all who call upon him with sincerity of heart. Now I wish you, if you can obtain one of the books, to read carefully and ask the Eternal Father in the name of Jesus Christ to manifest the truth of it to you and if you do so with pure intent it surely will be granted--read the prophecy of Isaih, Jeremiah, Daniel and Malechi for they all towards the last of the books speak of times and judgments that will take place in this very generation--I drop the subject and wish you Benjamin to see to Mary Ann I sent you word by Job Strawn to have her chose you her Guardian by that means you could have the control of her as she has no parents in the state--She now is a heavy burden on my mind. I have had several appointments to come and see you but often have been hinderd, now if I am spared & prospered I will come to you this winter--I live on the Mississinawa river 20 miles from Winchester and eleven from Munceytown--I request you to write as soon as you receive this and direct your letter to Winchester Post Office--I send my tender respects to you all, together with your step Mother--Adieu for the present. I subscribe myself your affec-tionate parent. Stephen Jones & Mary December 2--1831 Moses, Hiram, Benjamin & Stephen Jones Junr--George Carr and all my Daughters--May the Blessing of God be with you Amen.

The original letter is still in possession of Frank W. Jones of Lehi, Utah, a direct descendant of Stephen and Moses Jones (fig. 26).

After investigating the Nauvoo Baptisms for the Dead Index, selected searches should be made in post-Nauvoo Endowment House records. ENDOWMENT HOUSE BAPTISMS FOR THE DEAD and ENDOWMENT HOUSE ENDOWMENT AND SEALING RECORDS have been microfilmed and list considerable information about early Church members. Call numbers for many of them are listed on pages 366 and 367 of Jaussi's REGISTER.

Ordinance records for the Nauvoo and Utah periods (1840-1857) were filmed by the Genealogical Society in 1958 and were listed in

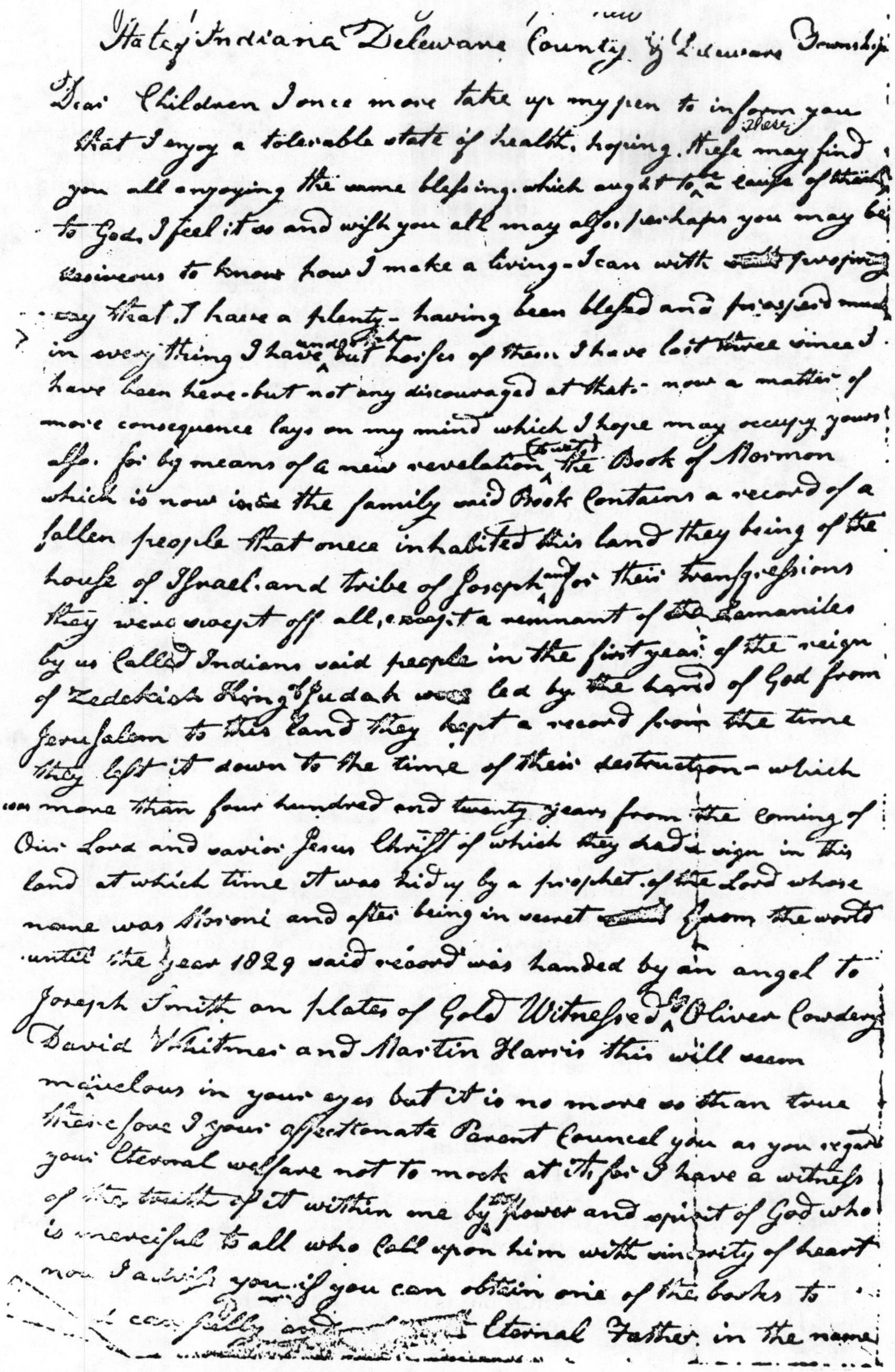

State of Indiana Delaware County of Delaware Township

Dear Children I once more take up my pen to inform you that I enjoy a tolerable state of health, hoping these may find you all enjoying the same blessing which ought to be a cause of thanks to God, I feel it so and wish you all may also, perhaps you may be desireous to know how I make a living — I can with ... saying that I have a plenty — having been blessed and prospered much in everything I have but horses of them I have lost three since I have been here — but not any discouraged at that — now a matter of more consequence lays on my mind which I hope may occupy yours also, for by means of a new revelation called the Book of Mormon which is now in the family said Book contains a record of a fallen people that once inhabited this land they being of the house of Israel and tribe of Joseph and for their transgressions they were swept off all, except a remnant of the Lamanites by us called Indians said people in the first year of the reign of Zedekiah King of Judah was led by the hand of God from Jerusalem to this land they kept a record from the time they left it down to the time of their destruction — which was more than four hundred and twenty years from the coming of Our Lord and savior Jesus Christ of which they had a sign in this land at which time it was hid up by a prophet of the Lord whose name was Moroni and after being in secret from the world until the year 1829 said record was handed by an angel to Joseph Smith on plates of Gold Witnessed by Oliver Cowdery David Whitmer and Martin Harris this will seem marvelous in your eyes but it is no more so than true therefore I your affectionate Parent Council you as you regard your Eternal welfare not to mock at it, for I have a witness of the truth of it within me by power and spirit of God who is merciful to all who call upon him with sincerity of heart now I wish you if you can obtain one of the books to ... I can fully ... Eternal Father in the name

Fig. 26. Extract from letter of Stephen Jones, 2 December 1831

the Genealogical Society's card catalog for several years; however, several microfilm rolls are not identified in Jaussi's REGISTER, and some have been withdrawn from public use because of their confidential nature. Film numbers for several early collections follow:

#25163 Pt 1 - Endowments 1845-46; Baptisms for the Dead performed by the Lima Branch in Illinois, Nov. 1840; & List of Nauvoo Temple Ordinance Workers, 1845-46.

#25163 Pt 2 - Washing & Annointings in the Nauvoo Temple, 1845-46. (This roll is known to have been withdrawn from public use because of its confidential nature.)

#25163 Pt 3 - Index to Sealings & Adoptions, 1846-1857.

#25163 Pt 4 - Sealings & Adoptions in the Nauvoo Temple & Utah, 1846-1857.

#25163 Pt 5 - Index to Baptisms for Dead, 1840-1845.

#25163 Pt 6 - Bapts. for the Dead, Bk. A, 1840-1841.

#25163 Pt 7 - Bapts. for the Dead, Bk. B, 1841-1842.

#25163 Pt 8 - Bapts. for the Dead, Bk. C, 1842-1843.

#25163 Pt 9 - Bapts. for the Dead, Bk. D, 1843-1845.

#25164 - Marriages & Sealings, 1853-1860, performed in Utah before the Endowment House was in use.

After investigating the Nauvoo and early Utah records, the worker may need to consult the later ENDOWMENT HOUSE RECORDS (1855-1889), the ST. GEORGE TEMPLE RECORDS (after 6 April 1877), the LOGAN TEMPLE RECORDS (after 17 May 1884), the MANTI TEMPLE RECORDS (after 21 May 1888), and the SALT LAKE TEMPLE RECORDS (after 6 April 1893). The baptism for the dead records among these seem to be the most important for genealogical purposes. They are indexed and may be searched by members of the Church in good standing. Film numbers for the early collections are listed on pages 365-93 of Jaussi's REGISTER. In addition, the following early ordinance collections not listed in Jaussi's REGISTER may prove helpful on certain early LDS problems:

(Ordinances performed in the Endowment House)

#25165 Pt 9 - Record Books of Proxies sealed for the dead, Books A-B, 1854-1857

#25165 Pt 10 - Index to Sealings, 1851-1854

#25165 Pt 11 - Index to Sealings, 1853-1873

#25165 Pt 12 - Index to Sealings, 1873-1889

#25165 Pt 13 - Sealings and Endowments, Books A-A1, 20 Feb. 1851 - 24 Apr. 1854

#25165 Pt 14 - Sealings, 1855-1856

#25165 Pt 15 - Sealings Books C-D, 1856-1866

#25165 Pt 16 - Sealings Books E-F, 1867-1870

#25165 Pt 17 - Sealings Book G, 1870-1871

#25165 Pt 18 - Sealings Book H, 1871-1873

#25165 Pt 19 - Sealings Book I, 1873-1874

```
#25165 Pt 20  -  Sealings Book J, 1874-1875
#25165 Pt 21  -  Sealings Book K, 1875-1878
#25165 Pt 22  -  Sealings, Books L-M, 1878-1889
#25165 Pt 23  -  Index to Endowments, Books A-J, 1851-1884
#25165 Pt 24  -  Endowments Books B-D, 1855-1864
#25165 Pt 25  -  Endowments Books E-F, 1864-1868
#25165 Pt 26  -  Endowments Book G, 1868-1872
#25165 Pt 27  -  Endowments Book H, 1872-1878
#25165 Pt 28  -  Endowments Book I, 1878-1884
#25165 Pt 29  -  Endowments Book J, 1884
```

After the Endowment House was erected in 1854, many Saints gathered genealogical facts and performed ordinances for deceased relatives and friends there. Families living in outlying settlements also performed work in the Endowment House, often spending a week or two with friends or relatives in Salt Lake City while doing the work. As temples were erected, similar work was done in them, sometimes repeating work which had been done previously in Nauvoo or the Endowment House. Husbands and wives often stood proxy for their counterparts among deceased relatives and friends. The patterns followed in this ordinance work sometimes make it possible to determine valuable relationship details from the records.

A typical entry for proxy work includes the name of the person for whom the work was performed, the name of the proxy and his or her relationship to the person, the date the work was performed, and sometimes birth and death information. Following is a copy of an actual entry from the St. George Temple:

```
Book A page 82-85 Jan. 1877 - James Pace proxy (GS F#23089 pts)
1481  -  James Pace b. 28 Jan 1778 d. 23 Dec 1814    Rel: Son
1482  -  John Pace d. 23 Dec 1814                     Rel: Nephew
1483  -  William Pace                                 Rel: Nephew
1484  -  Wilson Pace                                  Rel: Nephew
1485  -  Kenchon Pace                                 Rel: Nephew
1486  -  Jeremiah Pace                                Rel: Nephew
1487  -  Drewry Pace                                  Rel: Nephew
1488  -  Isaac Pace                                   Rel: Nephew
1489  -  William Pace                                 Rel: Gd Son
1490  -  Thomas Loveing                               Rel: Gd Son
1491  -  John Loveing                                 Rel: Nephew
1492  -  William Loveing                              Rel: Cousin
1493  -  Britton Pace                                 Rel: Cousin
1494  -  Barney Strickland                            Rel: 2nd Cou.
1495  -  John Christian d. 23 Dec 1814                Rel: Nephew
1496  -  George Williamson                            Rel: Nephew
1497  -  James Merida                                 Rel: Nephew
1498  -  James Gibson                                 Rel: Nephew
1499  -  Jacob Fortenberry                            Rel: Friend
1500  -  Fredrick G. Becklon                          Rel: Friend
1501  -  John M. Connelly                             Rel: Friend
```

```
1502  -  Joseph Fatherly                                    Rel:  Friend
1503  -  John Stroop                                        Rel:  Friend
1504  -  Horalis G. Galee                                   Rel:  Friend
1505  -  Jame King                                          Rel:  Cousin
1506  -  Samuel King                                        Rel:  Cousin
```

The genealogical value of such a record can readily be seen, and when used with other sources, valuable genealogical conclusions can sometimes be reached. In the above record some of the persons listed as "friends" were later identified to be blood relatives. Two of them were parents of relatives-in-law. The unusual names "Kenchon," "Drewry," and "Britton" could be extremely helpful in making family connections from local records. Also, the fact that Britton was listed as "cousin" could be of special genealogical significance if his ancestry could be determined.

In my own genealogy, St. George ordinance records helped clarify a rather difficult problem relating to early LDS membership. Professional genealogists had determined the father of an immigrant ancestor (Joseph Wright) to be John Wright born about 1780 (determined from his age at death in 1865). Searches in local parish registers revealed a christening entry for a John Wright who was the son of John Wright and Mary. The line was accepted as ancestral and further research was conducted, extending it three generations. However, another researcher was assigned the problem and located a third marriage for John Wright (the father of Joseph the immigrant) which took place in 1854. This marriage was confirmed through a marriage certificate from Somerset House in London, and the record stated the father of John Wright was William Wright. Which record was correct? St. George Baptisms for the Dead contained helpful information concerning proxy work done by my granduncle in 1877. He did proxy work for "John Wright as grandson" and for "William Wright as great grandson." A recheck of local parish registers revealed a christening entry for "John, son of William Wright and Ann" dated 10 August 1780 which fit the circumstances exactly.

Sealing records for couples are especially valuable because they may include birth information which may not be known by present family members. In one instance, an individual had a deceased sister of his living spouse sealed to him. The record entry gave her English parish of birth to be something quite different than that which the family knew to be ancestral. However, research disclosed that the place was an earlier family residence in England and the ancestral line was extended because of the new information.

Sealing records are especially convenient to use at the present time as well, because they are the only ordinance information which has been computerized. There is presently no master file listing all LDS ordinance information. Searching ordinance records is still largely a matter of investigating several collections in order to determine correct dates. The NAME TABULATION PROGRAM is a step toward a master ordinance file, but it contains information filed only since October of 1969 and sealing ordinances of couples. It is quite possible that additional ordinance information will be computerized in the near future and added to the new master file, but it will probably be several years before all ordinance information is available in a single file.

The following information is given as a guide to the researcher in locating original LDS ordinance facts pertaining to his ancestors and relatives:

BLESSING OF CHILDREN

1. To locate records of blessings, the worker should first search the ward or branch records where the child is or was resident, including individual membership certificates which were kept after 1948.

2. Duplicate copies of the individual membership certificates are also on file at the Church Membership Office in Salt Lake City and may provide the needed information.

3. If the member died after 1948, the DECEASED MEMBER'S FILE in the Church Historian's Office should be searched.

4. If the event took place after 1906, the FORM E or ANNUAL REPORTS for the ward or branch of residence may include the information.

BAPTISM, REBAPTISM, AND CONFIRMATION

1. The same procedure as outlined in 1, 2, 3, and 4 above can be followed.

2. In addition, some living persons were baptized in the Salt Lake Tabernacle, and special records have been kept for them. But the same information should also be of record in the person's ward or branch of residence.

3. Some living persons were baptized in the temples, and records for such ordinance work remain in those temples, as well as in ward or branch.

4. The EARLY CHURCH INFORMATION INDEX, mentioned earlier, contains some facts about "rebaptism" as do early ward and branch records. [1]

5. Proxy baptism and confirmation information (work for the dead) is recorded in books pertaining to Nauvoo, the Endowment House, the St. George Temple, and later temples.

6. Proxy baptisms are indexed by the name of the person at whose instance the work was done (the heir or proxy) and not by the name of the deceased, except for Nauvoo records which have been indexed by the name of both the deceased and the proxy.

7. The researcher must (1) have an idea of who would have done the work (usually some relative), (2) have an idea of which temple would have been used (usually the one nearest the family residence)[2] and (3) have an idea of the time period in which the work would have been performed.

8. When the person has been endowed, the baptism date may appear on a TEMPLE RECORDS INDEX BUREAU CARD or on an ARCHIVE RECORD at the Genealogical Society. [3]

SEALING OF COUPLES (MARRIAGES)[4]

1. Sealings of living couples, deceased couples, and combinations of the two, have been performed by persons holding the proper authority and may be found in records of the President of the Church, the Church Historian, the Endowment House, various Temples of the Church, the Temple Records Index Bureau, or the Church Records Archives.

2. Temple records of sealings of living couples are indexed by the names of each party.

3. Temple records of sealings of deceased couples are indexed by the name of the heir, except those for the St. George Temple covering the period 1877-1913.

4. In temple records of sealings where one member is deceased, there may be two indexes, one for the name of the living person and one for the name of the heir.

5. Some early sealing records of couples which were performed in the President's Office have been combined with Endowment House Sealings.

SEALING OF CHILDREN TO PARENTS

1. Children born to a couple after that couple has been properly sealed need not be sealed to their parents but are born in the covenant.

2. Records of children being sealed to their parents for time and eternity are included in records of the various temples of the Church.

3. No sealing of children is found in the Endowment House records.

4. Some sealing information of children to parents is included on TEMPLE RECORDS INDEX BUREAU CARDS and on ARCHIVE RECORDS at the Genealogical Society.

---

1. Some early members repeated ordinance work in their own behalf, often without apparent need. Perhaps there was some question in their minds about the work or perhaps accurate records had not been kept of the first ordinance. There is also the possibility that some reasoned that "if one baptism is good then two should be twice as good."

2. Church members usually attended to proxy work in the temples closest to their homes, but searches in records of other temples can sometimes reveal pertinent information. Another point to be considered in searching temple ordinance records is that relatives in one area, say Manti, may have performed work in "their" temple for their deceased relatives, while living relatives in Logan may have performed proxy work in the Logan temple for the same people. And it may be that the relatives in Manti had more information about the deceased persons than those in Logan, so that the Manti records might be more detailed. There was, after all, no system to prevent duplication of ordinance work until the Temple Records Index Bureau was established in the 1920s.

3. Sometimes discrepant dates for temple ordinances will be found in various records. In this case, the earliest recorded date is usually considered the correct one, if the individual was properly identified, and if the ordinance was properly performed by one holding the authority. In cases where complete dates cannot be ascertained or in cases where ordinance work itself is in question, the work may be done again to make sure it is valid.

4. Since sealings of couples from early temple records have recently been computerized, they can be verified through submission of the authorized "Marriage Entry Form."

CHAPTER 6

SEARCHING FOR THE FAMILY HISTORY IN PRINT

Steps should be taken early in research to investigate printed
family histories and genealogies because they can provide a variety
of genealogical facts, including information which might extend an
ancestral line several generations, details on the immigrant ancestral home, facts about other family members and relatives, and additional information which can give direction to later research.

When searching for family history in print, the researcher will
need to consider genealogies and family histories, genealogical and
historical periodicals, genealogical dictionaries, indexes, and compendia, regional and local histories, and biographical works. These
records might be located in a variety of places, including local and
regional libraries and historical societies, national and state archives,
and university libraries, as well as in special repositories such as the
Library of Congress, the DAR Library, and the Genealogical Society
Library in Salt Lake City. And the worker must be prepared to investigate many of the records himself, or through an agent, because
many organizations are unable to provide genealogical research
assistance.

While serving as Reference Librarian at the LDS Genealogical
Society, I frequently heard patrons say: "I have searched all the
records and still haven't solved this problem. Can you help me?"
or "I have done everything there is to do on this line. Can you give
me some suggestions?" Usually, as he was questioned further, it
was evident the worker had not done everything there was to do and
certainly had not searched "all the records." It is hard to believe
any one person has exhausted every research possibility on a particular line, especially with the amount of published and manuscript
material available. There is just too much in print and too many

places it might be located to say "everything has been done!"

The Surname and Locality Target Approach

Before making actual searches in the records, it is necessary to evaluate the pedigree problem carefully and note each name, place, and time period. Research should be based on these elements, and certain procedures should be followed in each library visited. It may also be necessary to repeat certain procedures each time a new ancestral name or locality is discovered.

The first step in actually beginning to solve a pedigree problem is to check each name through the card catalog at the library or genealogical society. In the problem in fig. 27, for instance, the names of Kindness Ann, Azariah, and Abraham Haines, Polly Ann and Aaron Newman, Nancy Ann Doty, and Kindness Drane should all be checked. References might be on file for any one of them and might be in the form of a biographical sketch, a genealogical article, a historical reference, or even an author reference.

After considering the individual names, the general surnames should be checked through the files, in this case Haines, Newman, Doty, and Drane. At this point the researcher should be looking for family histories and genealogies which concern themselves with any of the noted surnames. When the name is common, the localities, time periods, and given names should be considered, or time may be wasted.

When the record is located, it may be unindexed; it might be necessary, then, to check each family of the same approximate time period to make the proper connection. And many family histories and genealogies include information other than that identified on the title page or listed in the index, so general searches should be made in them so as not to miss something significant.

After the surnames have been researched, each locality should be noted, and printed references pertaining to them should be investigated. On the above problem this would include Salt Lake City and County in Utah, Greene County in Tennessee, Grant County in Indiana, Clinton County in Ohio, and the states of Virginia and Maryland. Perhaps genealogical periodicals should be investigated first, followed by town and county histories. The locality approach should also be used when investigating original source materials, such as census or land records, as well. This is outlined in this work.

Genealogies and Family Histories

Family histories and genealogies can provide facts which might extend a line several generations or may even include information about the immigrant ancestral home. The facts listed in these publications are not always correct or complete, but the information can be a helpful guide to searching other records. After all, it is much better to have a general idea of the family makeup--including some

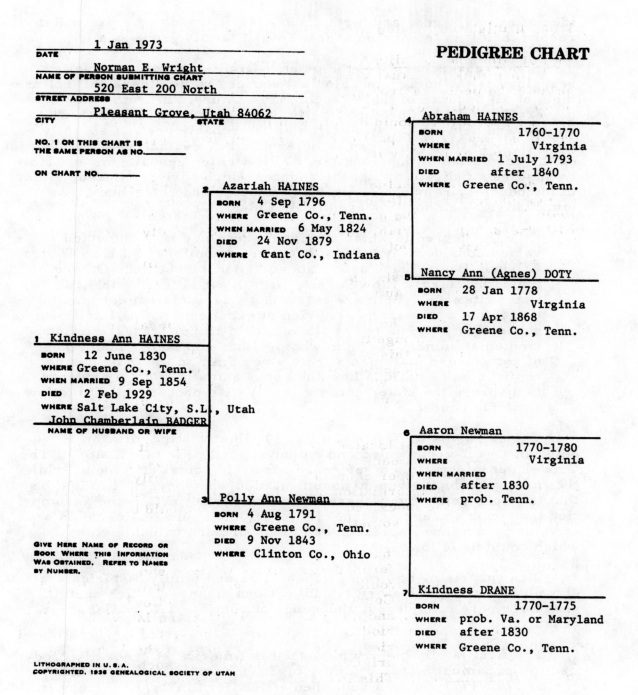

DATE   1 Jan 1973

NAME OF PERSON SUBMITTING CHART   Norman E. Wright

STREET ADDRESS   520 East 200 North

CITY   Pleasant Grove, Utah 84062   STATE

NO. 1 ON THIS CHART IS
THE SAME PERSON AS NO._____

ON CHART NO._____

2 Azariah HAINES
- BORN   4 Sep 1796
- WHERE   Greene Co., Tenn.
- WHEN MARRIED   6 May 1824
- DIED   24 Nov 1879
- WHERE   Grant Co., Indiana

4 Abraham HAINES
- BORN   1760-1770
- WHERE   Virginia
- WHEN MARRIED   1 July 1793
- DIED   after 1840
- WHERE   Greene Co., Tenn.

5 Nancy Ann (Agnes) DOTY
- BORN   28 Jan 1778
- WHERE   Virginia
- DIED   17 Apr 1868
- WHERE   Greene Co., Tenn.

1 Kindness Ann HAINES
- BORN   12 June 1830
- WHERE   Greene Co., Tenn.
- WHEN MARRIED   9 Sep 1854
- DIED   2 Feb 1929
- WHERE   Salt Lake City, S.L., Utah
- John Chamberlain BADGER
- NAME OF HUSBAND OR WIFE

6 Aaron Newman
- BORN   1770-1780
- WHERE   Virginia
- WHEN MARRIED
- DIED   after 1830
- WHERE   prob. Tenn.

GIVE HERE NAME OF RECORD OR
BOOK WHERE THIS INFORMATION
WAS OBTAINED. REFER TO NAMES
BY NUMBER.

3 Polly Ann Newman
- BORN   4 Aug 1791
- WHERE   Greene Co., Tenn.
- DIED   9 Nov 1843
- WHERE   Clinton Co., Ohio

7 Kindness DRANE
- BORN   1770-1775
- WHERE   prob. Va. or Maryland
- DIED   after 1830
- WHERE   Greene Co., Tenn.

LITHOGRAPHED IN U.S.A.
COPYRIGHTED, 1935 GENEALOGICAL SOCIETY OF UTAH

Fig. 27. Example pedigree problem

idea of names, ages, and birthplaces--when searching a particular record than it is to have no concept of the family group at all.

Some researchers feel the printed family history or compiled genealogy is the "only" genealogical source, while others will not use them at all because of their "secondary" nature. In truth, they can be very helpful when used correctly, and an attitude toward them somewhere between the two extremes is probably best. Generally the quality of the record can be determined by evaluating documentation or the reputation of the compiler. Well-written genealogies and family histories indicate or list the sources which have been used, either in introductory remarks or through footnotes and references. As family history authority Meredith B. Colket, Jr., says:

> The degree to which a printed genealogy is documented varies considerably. Some excellent compilers, such as Walter Goodwin Davis, have used almost no documentation. Others, including Mary Walton Ferris, literally load their work with exact citations. Both are extremes. . . . Detailed documentation is not a necessary criterion of excellence. One intelligent genealogist, and he is not alone, would rather trust the undocumented statement of one in whom he has confidence than a host of documented statements from a compiler in whom he has no confidence. Citations in some books actually contain evidence to disprove the statements made. A wise procedure is to follow a middle course. [1]

The examples in fig. 28 and fig. 29 illustrate the difference between a well-documented and an undocumented family history. The Grover genealogy cites a reference for each factual statement, while the Hoke genealogy gives no documentation whatsoever. It might be that the Hoke genealogy is based more upon imagination and assumption than upon sound evidence. However, both genealogies could be of value in continued research and might provide valuable clues which could be followed.

It is surprising how many genealogies and family histories are already in print. If historical publications, many of which contain genealogy, are considered, thousands of volumes are available for research.

The first family history published in America is generally credited to the Samuel Stebbins family of Connecticut. It covered the period 1707-1771 and was published at Hartford in 1771. A copy is on file at the Genealogical Society in Salt Lake City. Since the Stebbins publication, several thousand volumes have been printed and hundreds remain in manuscript covering other American families. "As Americans have become more conscious of their cultural heritage, they have written more genealogies," says Colket. "By the time of the Revolutionary War, hardly a genealogy had been printed. By the end of the Civil War, nearly three hundred genealogies had

GROVER*

THOMAS[1] GROVER** was resident in or near Charlestown before April, 1642, when his son LAZARUS[2] was born.[1,2] THOMAS[1] either settled on Mystic Side† or removed thereto for such mention as is found recorded of him, consistently calls him of Charlestown or Malden. He appeared not at all in public life, the only items found being the birth[4] at Malden of his daughter Elizabeth[2] in 1652, the death[4] of his daughter Grace[2] in 1658 and his own death there[4] in 1661. The period of his residence there presupposes that he was witness to, if not affected by, the church trouble relative to Rev. Marmaduke Matthews (see Call, pp. 135–6) for though we have no proof that he held church membership, it seems evident that his wife ELIZABETH did so, for she had joined the Charlestown Church[3] on September 10, 1644, and she was one of the thirty-six intrepid wives and mothers who dared on October 28, 1651, to address a petition to the General Court (see Call, p. 136) in behalf of their pastor, announcing the acceptability of his service to them and their strong desire that his "personall & perticul^r ffaylings" should be overlooked and that permission should be granted for him to continue as their minister.[5] Among the thirty-six women (who were the only signers of this petition) were ELIZABETH (——) GROVER, JOANNA (——) SHEPARDSON CALL, and Ann (——) Bibble whose husband John[1] appears to have been related[8] to the family of THOMAS[1] CARTER (see Carter, p. 142). Other women who signed were Mary (Hills) Waite, first wife of Capt. John[1] Waite who married secondly our SARAH (——) PARKER, widow of JACOB[1]; and Rachell (Batchelder) Atwood, first wife of Philip[1] Atwood who married secondly our ELIZABETH (——) GROVER.

On October 8, 1661, THOMAS[1] GROVER died, intestate, at Malden, and December 17, 1661, the inventory of his estate was filed by the widow ELIZABETH and the eldest son LAZARUS[2], who were appointed as administrators.[2] It showed a valuation of over £157 after debts of £34 were paid.[16]

After fifteen years as a widow, ELIZABETH married secondly on April 7, 1675, as his second wife, Philip[1] Atwood whose family, with those of her own son, Thomas[2] Grover, and of our PHINEAS[2] UPHAM were three of the five or six from Malden which ventured west that very month to form a new settlement in what is now Worcester County. As has been told (see Upham, p. 619) within three months after their arrival on the frontier, and when they would scarcely have completed their new homes, the Indian attacks on nearby towns forced the hurried return of

---

*This name was sometimes spelled[14] "Grovier" and a French origin has been claimed for it but with no evidence offered.

**It seems highly probably that the mother[1,2,3] and perhaps one or more brothers of THOMAS[1] emigrated also, for in Charlestown on November 30, 1643, "Ould Goodwife Grover" was admitted to the church and a John Grover lived there as early as 1640.

†Mystic Side was the outlying portion of Charlestown lying north of the Mystic River (see map, p. 255) the major part of which in 1649 was set off as Malden (see Call, p. 133 and Upham, p. 613).

337

Fig. 28. Extract from Grover genealogy

v. Andrew[5], b.[7,14] October, 1673; "he probably d. about 1751";[14] m. [7,14] about 1697 Mary (———); perhaps m. second by[14] 1734 Elizabeth. Removed about 1702 to Norton.[14]

The next two are the children of LAZARUS[2], *perhaps* by his second wife.

vi. Ephraim[3], b. (———); d.[14] at Norton February 25, 1766; m. at Malden[4,14] 1700 Mary Pratt. Removed to Norton[14] about 1702.

vii. Rebecca[3], b. (———); d. about[18] November, 1728; m.[4] at Malden October 18, 1709, Elias or Eliah Tottingham, often called[17] Totman.

The two children of LAZARUS[2] and MERCY (*Mudge?*) GROVER both born in Malden were[4]

viii. *MARY[3], b. prob. about 1692; d. about 1735–6 when her tenth child was born; m. at Malden[4,11] February 17, 1714–15 SAMUEL[4] UPHAM (see Upham, p. 634).

ix. **Ebenezer[3], b. at Malden[1,4] September 22, 1694; d.s.p. before July 19, 1725, when his estate was administered[18] by SAMUEL[4] UPHAM who "had married the sister and sole heir" of the deceased, except for his mother who was still living.

*An analysis of the origin and significance of the names given to the children of SAMUEL[4] and MARY (GROVER) UPHAM follows:

1. MARY[5] UPHAM, named for her mother.
2. Abigail[5] Upham, named for her father's mother.
3. Mercy[5] Upham, named for her mother's mother.
4. Samuel[5] Upham named for his father.
5. Jonathan[5] Upham, named doubtless for Jonathan[3] Mudge, uncle of the mother of these children whose legatee she was.
6. Ebenezer[5] Upham, named for his mother's brother who died unmarried.
7. Jacob[5] Upham, named for his father's brother.
8. Phebe[5] Upham.
9. William[5] Upham.

**Ebenezer[3], is said[1] to have married at Lyman in 1720 Anne (Wilson) Putt and to have had four children which is disproved as above.

REFERENCES

1. Genealogies and Estates of Charlestown, T. B. Wyman, 1879, pp. 26, 49–50, 196, 448–449, 721.
2. Savage, I, 14–15, 78; II, 320–1; Pope's Pioneers, pp. 23, 203.
3. History of the First Church, Charlestown, W. I. Budington, 1845, p. 248; New England Register, XXIII, 280–1.
4. Vital Records of Malden, pp. 35–6, 241, 348, 366; New England Register, X, 234–5, 237, 241–2; XII, 85; Malden Historical Society Register, III, 56, 58.
5. History of Malden, D. P. Corey, 1899, pp. 145–6.
6. Burnap Genealogy, H. W. Belknap, 1925, p. 49; History of Reading, L. Eaton, 1874, p. 85.
7. W. R. Cutter's New England Families, 1913, p. 389; Hills Genealogy, W. S. Hills and T. Hills, 1906, p. 261; Swan-Farwell Ancestry, J. C. Frost, 1923, p. 115.
8. Pope's Pioneers, p. 48; New England Register IX, 306–7; LXVI, 270–3; Weymouth, History and Genealogy, III, 4.
9. Wyman's Charlestown, p. 448.
10. History of Malden, D. P. Corey, 1899, pp. 259–60, 300–5, 318, 352, 370–1, 376, 606–7; History of Worcester County, D. H. Hurd, 1889, I, 780; Bicentennial Book of Malden, 1850, pp. 194, 197–9, 215–6; History of Worcester County, W. Lincoln, 1837, pp. 7–8, 11–15, 20.
11. Upham Genealogy, F. K. Upham, 1892, pp. 54, 71, 73, 78, 84.
12. New England Register, III, 347; IV, 267; VII, 28.
13. Wellman Genealogy, J. W. Wellman, 1918, pp. 84–5.
14. History of Norton, G. F. Clark, 1859, pp. 17, 23, 63, 69, 82, 165–6, 221, 287, 298–300, 377, 440–1, especially 82, 165, 440–1; Vital Records of Norton, pp. 65–7, 243–4, 373; Vital Records of Wrentham, p. 103; History of Taunton, S. H. Emery, 1893, pp. 136–7, 140–1.
15. Baldwin Genealogy, C. C. Baldwin, 1881, p. 617.
16. Research by Miss Eva L. Moffatt, Allston, Mass., Middlesex Probates, Administration No. 9989 (II, 51); No. 9990 (XII, 396).
17. Ibid., No. 9932 or No. 9982.
18. Ibid., No. 9974; Middlesex Deeds Vol. 29, p. 68.
19. Mudge Family, A. Mudge, 1868, pp. 177–81, 193–4; Descendants of JOHN UPHAM, F. K. Upham, 1892, pp. 78, 84.

DAWES-GATES ANCESTRAL LINES Vol. I. (GS #929.273 D321F)

Fig. 28a.

JOHN HOKE SETTLES IN ARKANSAS

In the beginning God created Heaven and Earth: When my grandfather first came to the United States of America, in the year of about 1756, he was 18 years old.

His name was John Hoke (in Dutch). Hoke in Dutch, is High in English, so hereafter we are called High.

When John Hoke came to the United States he brought with him a dog he thought lots of. One day he went out hunting, and found a porcupine. The beast hit the dog with his tail which was filled with sticky quills. They stuck so deep in the dog that the beast could not pull them out, so the man was obliged to kill them both. Then he was badly discouraged and out of heart, not knowing what to do. But he would not give up. He later married in the State of Ohio.

In 1832 he moved to Indiana, Warren County, Mound T. W. In 1838 he moved to Arkansas in Benton County, a few miles east of where Rogers now stands. He located on Prairie Creek, one-half mile from White River, and built a mill that run by water, to grind corn.

He was six weeks on the road to Arkansas.

They had three wagons pulled by oxen, and they drove a bunch of milk cows, which they would milk as they went along. After they had milked they would put the milk in a churn and by noon there would be a ball of butter instead of cream. It was in the summer and the stock would graze on the grass as they moved along. They came by way of St. Louis, Mo., and the city at that time was one mile wide and five miles up along the river. Now it is much larger.

This John High, as it is called in English, was a full-blooded Dutch, and he lived until 1845.

He and his wife came to Carroll County on Indian Creek, with four girls and eight boys. He bought out a claim, as in those days just a claim on land was all you got.

Later on Uncle Sam passed a law where one man or woman could homestead land, one hundred and sixty acres for their own use, if they would stay on it and improve it.

The government would give the man a deed to the said land if he would pay the small fee.

This John High's children, I will give you all of their names but will try to make it as short and interesting as I can. **(by Fred High GS #929.273 D321f)**

Fig. 29. Extract from Hoke genealogy

been printed. By the end of World War I an estimated eight thousand genealogies had been printed. Today (1968) over twenty thousand genealogies have been printed."[2]

Mr. Colket is currently working on a herculean project of identifying and classifying every American genealogy by its title and actual location. He is directing the work from the Western Reserve Historical Society Library in Cleveland, Ohio, and has already classified over five thousand genealogies and family histories. He is giving priority to well-written histories which include information on the immigrant ancestor, but he will include all others as time progresses.

The Genealogical Society in Salt Lake City holds over 110,000 volumes relating to genealogy and family history, many of which are rare volumes not found in other locations, and it is adding upwards of five hundred volumes per month to its collection. A few of the Society's genealogies and family histories have been microfilmed and may be borrowed through the branch library program.

Brigham Young University's Harold B. Lee Library is one of the largest university libraries in the Intermountain region. It has a respectable genealogical collection and has a generous acquisition program for additional genealogical materials. It is also a branch library to the Genealogical Society in Salt Lake City which gives it access to more than 775,000 rolls of microfilm which are equivalent to about three million volumes of 350 pages each.

The Library of Congress also contains thousands of volumes relating to genealogy and family history. In 1958 the collection included "14,000 volumes of compiled American genealogy, 3,300 volumes of compiled British genealogy, 5,400 volumes of Continental European genealogy, 2,400 volumes of heraldry, and 77,500 volumes of United States local history, or a total of 102,600 volumes."[3] Several hundred volumes have been added since 1958, making it one of the more important repositories in the country for compiled genealogy. Marion J. Kaminkow edited GENEALOGIES IN THE LIBRARY OF CONGRESS: A BIBLIOGRAPHY (Baltimore: Magna Carta Book Company, 1972) in two volumes which includes more than 25,000 references. (The work supersedes the 1954 microcard edition of AMERICAN AND ENGLISH GENEALOGIES IN THE LIBRARY OF CONGRESS and the second edition with the same title published in 1919.)

The LIBRARY OF CONGRESS CATALOG OF PRINTED CARDS, with its "Supplement," is available at many reference counters, and the Library of Congress sells copies of its printed cards to many participating libraries, including the BYU library and the GS Library in Salt Lake City (fig. 30).

Photocopy and microfilming services are available at the Library of Congress for those who desire copies of material in their files and the cost is quite reasonable.

McCleskey, Charles S   1897–
    Descendants of Thomas Trammell, Revolutionary soldier.
Compiled by Charles S. McCleskey. Baton Rouge, La.,
1972.

        vi, 399 p. illus. 29 cm.

        1. Trammell family.   I. Title.

    CS71.T77 1972   929'.2'0973   72–192748
                                                             MARC
    Library of Congress   72 [4]

Shurtleff, Benjamin, 1866–1952.
    John Atwood of Plymouth, Massachusetts; the descend-
ants of John Atwood of Plymouth, Massachusetts, 1614–
1676 and his wife Sarah Masterson, 1620–1701/2. Typing
from the original unpublished manuscript by Loraine Fair
Sanford. Edited and indexed by the Genealogical Records
Committee, Fort Dearborn Chapter, National Society
Daughters of the American Revolution. [Evanston? Ill.,
1972]

        vi, 100 l. 28 cm.

        1. Atwood family.   I. Title.

    CS71.A91 1972   929'.2'0973   72–86089
                                                             MARC
    Library of Congress   72 [4]

Warren, John Trexler, 1923–
    History and genealogy of the Trexler family. [Trexler-
town, Pa.] 1972.

        xxxii, 339 p. illus. 24 cm.

        On cover: Trexler family and related kin.

        1. Trexler family.   I. Title.

    CS71.T817 1972   929'.2'0973   72–75594
                                                             MARC
    Library of Congress   72 [4]

Fig. 30.   Library of Congress printed cards

The Newberry Library at 60 West Walton Street, Chicago 60610 should also be considered an important genealogical repository, with its 250,000 volumes on local history and genealogy. It has created a unique tool for the searcher in its GENEALOGICAL INDEX (Boston: G. K. Hall, 1960) in four volumes, copies of which are at BYU. The four-volume index is a photographic reproduction of the "Analytic Index" at the Newberry Library and lists family names found in selected volumes. It contains over one million entries which have been arranged by surnames in variant spellings and also grouped under states, counties, and towns, or surnames allied by intermarriage.[4] The Library is open to the public but makes a strong point of the fact that it is unable to give any type of genealogical assistance through correspondence. A researcher must visit the library himself, or send his agent, if he desires to take advantage of the Newberry collection.

Many other excellent genealogical repositories exist, including the New England Historical Genealogical Society in Boston, the Long Island Historical Society and the New York Public Library in New York, the Pennsylvania Historical Society in Philadelphia, the New Jersey Department of Archives and History in Trenton, the Maryland Historical Society in Baltimore, the Virginia State Library in Richmond, the North Carolina Department of Archives and History in Raleigh, and others too numerous to mention. Sometimes local libraries have collections which pertain to local residents, and sometimes private genealogical collections have been filed with them. Many of the latter have also found their way into the larger libraries and societies. When the compiler did original research, including interviews with local people, the collections are even more valuable. Many of the persons interviewed and some of the records have long since disappeared.

A great deal of caution must be used when investigating private genealogical collections. Many include facts which are based on hearsay, and sometimes the compiler's ability to evaluate the evidence leaves something to be desired. However, when they include family Bible information and other facts which have been documented from original sources, they are quite valuable. The arrangement varies with each collection and while some are well organized and well indexed, others are nothing more than a conglomeration of papers, clippings, and cards in no apparent sequence.[5]

Locating printed family histories, whether published or in manuscript form, is a real test for the genealogist. Some catalogs and guides have been published, but much material must be located through original research.

P. William Filby recently compiled an excellent list of printed materials which relate to American genealogy in his AMERICAN & BRITISH GENEALOGY & HERALDRY (Chicago: American Library Association, 1970). It is a selected list of books which is by no means exhaustive but does include listings of popular reference works and printed materials. Mr. Filby has been the Librarian and Assistant Director of the Maryland Historical Society in Baltimore and created the book primarily out of his own need for such a reference tool.

Thomas Allen Glenn compiled a LIST OF SOME AMERICAN GENEALOGIES WHICH HAVE BEEN PRINTED IN BOOK FORM IN 1896, which has recently been reprinted by the Genealogical Publishing Company in Baltimore. Joel Munsell's Sons, et al., have published other lists which are useful. Editions of THE AMERICAN GENEALO-GIST (not to be confused with the Connecticut Quarterly of the same name) were published in 1862, 1868, 1875 and 1900. William H. Whitmore edited the 1862-1875 editions and Munsell's Sons were responsible for the 1900 edition. In 1899, Munsell's Sons also published A LIST OF TITLES OF GENEALOGICAL ARTICLES IN AMERICAN PERIODICALS AND KINDRED WORKS which was designed to be a companion volume to their AMERICAN GENEALOGIST. The two provide a bibliography of American genealogy, or a list of title pages of books and pamphlets on family history which have been published in America between 1771 and 1900. Filby says the collection contains only about 750 entries and is inferior to Glenn's work which includes some 2,000 entries. [6]

Munsell's Sons also published the INDEX TO AMERICAN GENE-ALOGIES in 1895 and 1900 (4th and 5th editions) and the SUPPLEMENT TO THE INDEX TO GENEALOGIES 1900-1908, which are also helpful in determining family history in print. The title page to the fifth edition indicates nearly fifty thousand references have been included, but this refers to names and not titles. The same work indicates Daniel S. Durrie edited the first and second editions. Filby says Durrie also edited the third edition under the title BIBLIOGRAPHICA AMERICANA. He says it is a "standard reference work for locating unknown family histories, i.e., those not cataloged in any library because they are mentioned in books and periodicals."[7] The significance of Munsell's Sons work is also noted by Donald Jacobus in his INDEX TO GENEA-LOGICAL PERIODICALS, vol. 1 (1932): "Some of the older periodicals which are no longer published have been indexed only with respect to the records of places, since it was found that Munsell's Index of 1900-1908 adequately covered the surnames of families of which some genealogy was published."

The Long Island Historical Society in Brooklyn has a very rich collection of American genealogy and published A CATALOG OF AMERICAN GENEALOGIES IN THE LONG ISLAND HISTORICAL SOCIETY in 1935. It was compiled under the direction of Emma Toedteberg and contains titles of over eight thousand printed books and pamphlets and 850 titles of manuscripts. The Society is also currently working on a project to gather and classify additional source material for the genealogist and historian.

The microfilm copy of THE LDS GENEALOGICAL SOCIETY'S

CARD CATALOG, with SUPPLEMENTS, as found in over 130 branch libraries of that organization is also useful. The Society has established branch libraries in many parts of the United States, Canada, and Mexico and provides each branch with a microfilm copy of its card catalog and updates the listings with supplements from time to time.

Other lists of printed genealogies and family history have been published on a local or regional basis. Robert Armistead Stewart's INDEX TO PRINTED VIRGINIA GENEALOGIES (reprinted by the Genealogical Publishing Company at Baltimore, 1965) and A KEY TO SOUTHERN PEDIGREES by William Armstrong Crozier (second edition published by the Southern Book Company at Baltimore, 1953) are examples. Crozier's work is a comprehensive guide to Colonial families in the states of Virginia, Maryland, Georgia, North Carolina, South Carolina, Kentucky, Tennessee, West Virginia, and Alabama.

From strictly a bibliographic standpoint, Charles Evan's and Shaw-Shoemaker's AMERICAN BIBLIOGRAPHY is an exhaustive list for items published between 1639 and 1819. They have listed all titles published in America up to and including 1819. The collection is on microcard at Brigham Young University under the title EARLY AMERICAN IMPRINTS.

GUIDES TO MANUSCRIPT COLLECTIONS and INVENTORIES created under Historical Records Survey Projects of the Works Progress Administration can also help to locate genealogy and family history. The Genealogical Society in Salt Lake City has a good collection of them.

With the renewed interest in genealogical research, more guides and registers will undoubtedly come forth, and the researcher should keep in touch with reference personnel and professional genealogists for the latest information. He might also correspond with libraries and historical societies from time to time in order that he might keep current on genealogy in print. The following references will be found useful in such efforts:

Brown, Karl, comp. AMERICAN LIBRARY DIRECTORY. New York: R. R. Bowker Co., 1965.

HISTORICAL SOCIETIES AND AGENCIES IN THE UNITED STATES AND CANADA 1965-1966; A DIRECTORY. Nashville, Tenn., 1965.

INTERNATIONAL LIBRARY DIRECTORY. London: A. P. Wales, 1963.

Genealogical Periodicals and Indexes
    A considerable amount of genealogy and family history, as well

as much valuable genealogical source material, has been included in genealogical periodicals which have been published over the years. America has published some excellent registers, magazines, digests, bulletins, and newsletters to assist the genealogist and historian. Lester J. Cappon compiled AMERICAN GENEALOGICAL PERIODICALS, A Bibliography with a Chronological Finding-List (New York: The New York Public Library, 1964) which lists most American periodicals. It does not list newsletters and some bulletins, but it does have rather wide coverage. To give an idea of the number of periodicals published in America and to show their regional importance, Cappon's Geographical Finding List[9] is reproduced here:

Alabama
ALABAMA GENEALOGICAL REGISTER
BIRMINGHAM GENEALOGICAL SOCIETY
    QUARTERLY
PIONEERS

Arizona
GENEALOGICAL AND HISTORICAL MAGAZINE
    OF THE ARIZONA TEMPLE DISTRICT

California
ANCESTOR
CALIFORNIA REGISTER
GENEALOGICAL DIGEST
GENEALOGY EXCHANGE
. MISSING LINK
NATIONAL GENEALOGIST

Colorado
COLORADO GENEALOGIST
EARLY AMERICAN FAMILIES

Connecticut
AMERICAN GENEALOGIST, ed Jacobus
JOURNAL OF AMERICAN HISTORY v. 1-5
NEW HAVEN GENEALOGICAL MAGAZINE
STAMFORD GENEALOGICAL BULLETIN

Delaware
DELAWARE HISTORICAL AND GENEALOGICAL
    RECALL

Florida
SOUTHERN GENEALOGICAL EXCHANGE

Georgia
GEORGIA GENEALOGICAL MAGAZINE
GEORGIA MAGAZINE
SOUTHERN GENEALOGICAL REVIEW

Idaho
IDAHO GENEALOGICAL QUARTERLY

Illinois
GENEALOGICAL REVIEW
MAGAZINE OF AMERICAN GENEALOGY

Indiana
HOOSIER GENEALOGIST
JOURNAL OF AMERICAN HISTORY v. 6-9

Iowa
GENEALOGIST'S WEEKLY QUERY INDEX

Kansas
SOUTHWEST KANSAS GENEALOGICAL
    SOCIETY NEWSLETTER
TREESEARCHER

Kentucky
KENTUCKY STATE HISTORICAL
    SOCIETY . . . REGISTER

Louisiana
GENEALOGICAL REGISTER (Baton Rouge)
LOUISIANA GENEALOGICAL AND
    HISTORICAL SOCIETY, BULLETIN
LOUISIANA GENEALOGICAL REGISTER
    (New Orleans)

Maine
BANGOR HISTORICAL MAGAZINE
GENEALOGY CLUB BULLETIN
KNOX COUNTY HISTORICAL AND GENEALOG-
  ICAL MAGAZINE
MAINE GENEALOGIST AND BIOGRAPHER
MAINE HISTORICAL AND GENEALOGICAL
  RECORDER
MAINE HISTORICAL MAGAZINE
OLD ELIOT
OLD TIMES
SPRAGUE'S JOURNAL OF MAINE HISTORY
WESTCUSTOGO CHRONICLE

Maryland
COUNTY COURT NOTE-BOOK
MARYLAND GENEALOGICAL BULLETIN
MARYLAND GENEALOGICAL SOCIETY
  BULLETIN
MARYLAND HISTORICAL AND GENEALOGICAL
  BULLETIN

Massachusetts
COLONIAL
DEDHAM HISTORICAL REGISTER
ESSEX ANTIQUARIAN
ESSEX COUNTY HISTORICAL AND GENEALOG-
  ICAL REGISTER
ESSEX INSTITUTE HISTORICAL COLLECTION
GENEALOGICAL ADVERTISER
GENEALOGICAL BULLETIN (Boston)
GENEALOGICAL MAGAZINE
GENEALOGICAL QUARTERLY (Salem)
GENEALOGIST'S NOTE BOOK
HERALDIC JOURNAL

Massachusetts (cont'd)
HISTORICAL MAGAZINE
MASSACHUSETTS MAGAZINE
MAYFLOWER DESCENDANT
MEDFORD HISTORICAL REGISTER
NEW ENGLAND HISTORICAL AND
  GENEALOGICAL REGISTER
OLD IPSWICH
PILGRIM NOTES AND QUERIES
PUTNAM'S (MONTHLY) HISTORICAL
  MAGAZINE
SALEM PRESS HISTORICAL AND GENEA-
  LOGICAL RECORD
WINCHESTER RECORD

Michigan
DETROIT SOCIETY FOR GENEALOGICAL
  RESEARCH MAGAZINE
FLINT GENEALOGICAL QUARTERLY
MICHIGAN HERITAGE
MICHIGANA
PEDIGREE   SEARCHLIGHT

Missouri
KANSAS CITY GENEALOGIST

Montana
GOLDEN GRAINS OF RESEARCH

Nebraska
NEBRASKA AND MIDWEST GENEALOG-
  ICAL RECORD

New Hampshire
NEW HAMPSHIRE GENEALOGICAL RECORD

New Jersey
CAPE MAY COUNTY NEW JERSEY MAGAZINE
    OF HISTORY AND GENEALOGY
GENEALOGICAL MAGAZINE OF NEW JERSEY
GENEALOGY
GENEALOGY MAGAZINE
JERSEYMAN
NEW JERSEY GENESIS
NEW JERSEY HISTORICAL SOCIETY
    PROCEEDINGS
SOMERSET COUNTY HISTORICAL QUARTERLY
VINELAND HISTORICAL MAGAZINE

New Mexico
FAMILY HISTORY MAGAZINE

New York
CHRONOTYPE
EARLY SETTLERS OF NEW YORK STATE
GENEALOGICAL EXCHANGE
GENEALOGICAL SOCIETY OF CENTRAL
    NEW YORK
GRAFTON MAGAZINE OF HISTORY AND
    GENEALOGY
JOURNAL OF AMERICAN GENEALOGY
    (Albany)
JOURNAL OF AMERICAN HISTORY v. 10-29
LONG ISLAND HISTORICAL SOCIETY QUARTERLY
MOORSFIELD ANTIQUARIAN
NEW ENGLAND FAMILY HISTORY
NEW YORK GENEALOGICAL AND BIOGRAPHICAL
    RECORD
NEW YORK GENEALOGICAL AND BIOGRAPHICAL
    SOCIETY BULLETIN
NIAGARA FRONTIER GENEALOGICAL MAGAZINE

New York (cont'd)
TREE TALKS
WESTCHESTER GENEALOGIST
YOUR ANCESTOR

North Carolina
ANCESTRAL PROOFS AND PROBABILITIES
NORTH CAROLINA HISTORICAL AND
    GENEALOGICAL RECORD
NORTH CAROLINA HISTORICAL AND
    GENEALOGICAL REGISTER
NORTH CAROLINIAN

Ohio
AMERICAN REGISTER; A MAGAZINE OF
    GENEALOGY, HISTORY, BIOGRAPHY
OHIO GENEALOGICAL QUARTERLY
OHIO RECORDS AND PIONEER FAMILIES
"OLD NORTHWEST" GENEALOGICAL
    QUARTERLY

Oklahoma
MAYFLOWER NEWSLETTER
OKLAHOMA GENEALOGICAL SOCIETY
    QUARTERLY

Oregon
FORUM EXCHANGE
FORUM QUARTERLY (Mount Hood)
GENEALOGICAL FORUM OF PORTLAND
ORGANIZATION NEWS

Pennsylvania
AMERICAN GENEALOGIST; A MONTHLY
    MAGAZINE OF GENEALOGY AND
    LOCAL HISTORY, ed Glenn

Pennsylvania (cont'd)
AMERICAN REPOSITORY
BOOGHER'S REPOSITORY
GENEALOGICAL REGISTER (Philadelphia)
GENEALOGICAL SOCIETY OF PENNSYLVANIA,
  PUBLICATIONS
HISTORICAL JOURNAL
HISTORICAL RECORD OF WYOMING VALLEY
HISTORICAL REGISTER
LAUREL MESSENGER
MISCELLANEOUS AMERICANA
OUR ANCESTORS
PENNSYLVANIA GENEALOGICAL MAGAZINE
PENNSYLVANIA MAGAZINE OF HISTORY AND
  BIOGRAPHY
YOUR FAMILY TREE

Rhode Island
MAGAZINE OF NEW ENGLAND HISTORY
NARRAGANSETT HISTORICAL REGISTER
NEWPORT HISTORICAL MAGAZINE
RHODE ISLAND HISTORICAL MAGAZINE
RHODE ISLAND HISTORICAL SOCIETY
  PUBLICATIONS

South Carolina
SOUTH CAROLINA HISTORICAL MAGAZINE
SOUTH CAROLINA MAGAZINE

Tennessee
AMERICAN HISTORICAL MAGAZINE AND
  TENNESSEE HIST SOC QUARTERLY
ANSEARCHIN' NEWS
TENNESSEE HISTORICAL SOCIETY QUARTERLY
TYLER'S QUARTERLY

Texas
AMARILLO GENEALOGICAL SOCIETY
  BULLETIN
AUSTIN GENEALOGICAL SOCIETY
  QUARTERLY
CENTRAL TEXAS GENEALOGICAL
  SOCIETY, BULLETIN
CORONADO HERITAGE
(Dallas) QUARTERLY BULLETIN
FORTH WORTH GENEALOGICAL SOCIETY,
  BULLETIN
GENEALOGICAL BULLETIN
GENEALOGICAL BULLETIN OF THE
  WEST TEXAS GENEALOGICAL SOCIETY
GENEALOGICAL RECORD
NEW AUSTIN GENEALOGICAL QUARTERLY
OUR HERITAGE
SOUTHERN HISTORICAL RESEARCH
  MAGAZINE
STRIPES
TEXAS GENEALOGIST
TWIGS AND TREES
WEST TEXAS GENEALOGICAL SOCIETY.
  BULLETIN OF LOCAL HISTORY AND
  GENEALOGY

Utah
GENEALOGICAL HELPER
UTAH GENEALOGICAL AND HISTORICAL
  MAGAZINE

Vermont
ANCESTRAL NOTES
. . NEWS-LETTER FOR ALL AND
  SUNDRY ENGAGED IN THE PLEASANT
  WORK OF MAKING GENEALOGIES

Virginia
CRITIC
LOWER NORFOLK COUNTY VIRGINIA ANTIQUARY
RESEARCHER
RICHMOND STANDARD
TYLER'S QUARTERLY HISTORICAL AND GENEA-
    LOGICAL MAGAZINE
VIRGINIA GENEALOGIST
VIRGINIA HISTORICAL MAGAZINE
VIRGINIA MAGAZINE OF HISTORY AND
    BIOGRAPHY
WILLIAM AND MARY COLLEGE QUARTERLY
    HISTORICAL MAGAZINE

Washington, D. C.
AMERICAN SOCIETY OF GENEALOGISTS,
    NEWSLETTER
COUNTY COURT NOTE-BOOK
GENEALOGICAL NEWSLETTER
GENEALOGIST
GENEALOGY AND HISTORY

Washington, D. C. (cont'd)
HISTORICAL BULLETIN
KENTUCKY GENEALOGIST
MARYLAND AND DELAWARE
    GENEALOGIST
MILLS' LETTERGRAM
MISSISSIPPI GENEALOGICAL EXCHANGE
NATIONAL GENEALOGICAL SOCIETY
    QUARTERLY

Washington (State)
PACIFIC NORTHWEST FOUNDATION
    FOR GENEALOGICAL RESEARCH,
    BULLETIN
SEATTLE GENEALOGICAL SOCIETY,
    BULLETIN

West Virginia
SOUTHERN HISTORICAL MAGAZINE
WEST VIRGINIA HISTORICAL MAGAZINE
    QUARTERLY

Wisconsin
WISCONSIN FAMILIES
WISCONSIN STATE GENEALOGICAL
    SOCIETY

From Lester J. Cappon's AMERICAN GENEALOGICAL PERIODICALS, A Bibliography with a
Chronological Finding-List, pp. 30-32.

102

It would be helpful if a cumulative index existed for all genealogical periodicals, family histories, and genealogies, but this is not
yet the case. With modern electronic computers, it is certainly possible to create such a tool, but financial backing seems to be the problem. Perhaps some philanthropist will come forth and make this a
reality in the near future, but until such time, the genealogist must
be satisfied with a few indexes, dictionaries, and compendia.

Several thousand names have been indexed in Fremont Rider's
AMERICAN GENEALOGICAL INDEX (Middletown, Connecticut: The
Godfrey Memorial Library, 1952-53) in forty-eight volumes. Individual names have been indexed from genealogies and histories, and a
key to bibliographic information is provided in selected volumes.

The AMERICAN GENEALOGICAL-BIOGRAPHICAL INDEX, also
by Rider (Middletown, Connecticut: The Godfrey Memorial Library,
1952+), is a second series currently under compilation. At this writing there are seventy-four volumes in the second series and the alphabet has been covered "A-H" only (fig. 31).

Both series have indexed names from genealogies and local histories selected at random by the library or suggested by its subscribers, and no particular cut-off point has been reached, although plans
are already underway for a third series.[10] It will probably be several
years before the second series is completed.

A key to bibliographic information on titles indexed is provided in
various volumes, and hints for using the index are given periodically
in selected volumes. The last consolidated key was the "fourteenth"
and is included in the front of volume 54.

It is estimated that over twelve million references will have been
included in the second series when it is completed. Over two million
references have been included from the genealogical column of the
BOSTON TRANSCRIPT alone, according to Mrs. Francis Bielfield
of the Godfrey Memorial Library, and all names from the 1790 federal
U.S. census have been indexed in it.[11]

Munsell's Sons' INDEX TO AMERICAN GENEALOGIES and their
SUPPLEMENT, mentioned previously, should also be considered a
general index to genealogy. They contain over fifty thousand references
and should be used with their companion works, THE AMERICAN
GENEALOGIST, and A LIST OF TITLES OF GENEALOGICAL ARTICLES
IN AMERICAN PERIODICALS AND KINDRED WORKS, also mentioned
previously.

The late Donald Lines Jacobus is responsible for an excellent
three-volume series which indexes family names and localities in
American genealogical periodicals. His first volume was published
in 1932 and covered the chief genealogical periodicals through 1931,
except those which provided their own complete general indexes, such

Fourteenth
Consolidated
KEY TITLE INDEX (1966)

Key title designations with a prefixed asterisk (*) were indexed in the early days of the *Index* (i.e. only by surname or first name). These asterisk titles are being re-indexed as rapidly as possible.

This cumulation includes all
key index entries to date

Abbe Fam: Abbe-Abbey gen., John Abbe des. By Cleveland Abbey, et al. New Haven, 1916. *(511p.)*

Abbe Gen: Abbe gen. By F. J. A. Wallace. Frankford, Pa. n.d. *(7p.)*

Abbey Mem: Memorial of Thom. Abbey anc. and des. of Ct. East Orange, NJ., 1917. *(175p.)*

Abbot Reg: Genealogical reg. of Geo. Abbot des. of Andover [et al.] By Abiel Abbot, Boston, 1947. *(20, 197p.)*

*Abbot, Geo: Descendants of Geo. Abbott of Rowley, Ms. [et al.] By Lemuel Abijah Abbott. 1906. *(2v.)*

Abeel Fam: Abeel and allied fams. By Henry Whittemore. New York, 1899. *(24p.)*

*Achenbach Mem: Family mem. of John Phillip Achenbach and des. By Sarah Jane (Kline) Houtz. Topeka, 189- *(39p.)*

*AdamsCoPa, 1886: History of Cumberland and Adams cos, Pa. Chicago, 1886. *(132, 588, 516p.)*

*Adams-Evarts: History of the Adams and Evarts fams. By J. M. Adams. Chatham, NY., 1894. *(81p.)*

Adams Fam: History of the Adams fam, des. of Henry Adams of Braintree, Ms. By Henry Wittemore. New York, 1893. *(84p.)*

*Adams Gen: Genealogical hist. of Henry Adams of Braintree, Ms. and des; also John Adams of Cambridge, Ms. By And. Napoleon Adams. Rutland, Vt. 1898. *(1238p.)* (Has no first name index except to key family and that does not index wives under their married surnames. One surname index is selective only. The "Supplement" is not indexed at all, and thousands of family names are omitted entirely. Numerous serious mistakes in alphabeting cause even included matter to be overlooked. Our complete re-indexing added over 26,000 new entries to those already in the book's indexes—a good example of the work necessary to make completely available the contents of even the most important and apparently well indexed genealogies.)

Fig. 31. Key page of AMERICAN GENEALOGICAL-BIOGRAPHICAL INDEX

as the first fifty volumes of the NEW ENGLAND HISTORICAL AND GENEALOGICAL REGISTER and early volumes of COLLECTIONS OF THE ESSEX INSTITUTE. The second volume was published in 1948 and covered the fifteen years 1932-1946 inclusive; it contained a few titles which were overlooked in the first volume. His third volume was published in 1952 and covered the period 1946-1952 inclusive.[12]

The foundation for Jacobus's index was a card file which he made for his own use from complete sets of the NEW YORK GENEALOGICAL AND BIOGRAPHICAL RECORD through 1931 and volumes 51-85 of the NEW ENGLAND HISTORICAL AND GENEALOGICAL REGISTER. They were two of the oldest publications of their type and contained a mass of important genealogical material. From there, Mr. Jacobus expanded his work to include many other publications. Following are publications covered in Jacobus's indexes, with key references:

A1. THE NEW ENGLAND HISTORICAL AND GENEALOGICAL REGISTER, vols. 51-106 (1897-1952).
A2. THE NEW YORK GENEALOGICAL AND BIOGRAPHICAL RECORD, vols. 1-83 (1870-1952).
B1. THE GENEALOGICAL MAGAZINE OF NEW JERSEY, vols. 1-25 (1925-1950).
B2. THE NEBRASKA AND MIDWEST GENEALOGICAL RECORD, vols. 1-18 (1923-1943).
B3. THE CONNECTICUT QUARTERLY, vols. 1-4 and THE CONNECTICUT MAGAZINE, vols. 1-8 (1895-1908).
B4. NEW HAVEN GENEALOGICAL MAGAZINE, vols. 1-9 (1923-1931) and THE AMERICAN GENEALOGIST, vols. 9-48 (1932-1952).
B5. THE VINELAND HISTORICAL MAGAZINE (N.J.), vols. 1-36 (1916-1951).
B6. SOMERSET COUNTY HISTORICAL QUARTERLY (N.J.), vols. 1-8 (1912-1919).
B7. CAPE MAY COUNTY NEW JERSEY MAGAZINE OF HISTORY AND GENEALOGY, vols. 1-2 (1931-1943).
C1. THE SALEM PRESS HISTORICAL AND GENEALOGICAL RECORD, vols. 1-2 (1890-1891).
C2. PUTNAM'S MONTHLY HISTORICAL MAGAZINE, vols. 1-7 (1892-1899).
C3. THE GENEALOGICAL QUARTERLY MAGAZINE, vols. 1-5 (1900-1905).
C4. THE GENEALOGICAL MAGAZINE, vols. 1-4 (1905-1907, 1915-1917).
C5. THE GRAFTON MAGAZINE OF HISTORY AND GENEALOGY, vols. 1-2 (1908-1910).
Col. THE COLORADO GENEALOGIST, vols. 1-13 (1939-1952).
D. THE MAYFLOWER DESCENDANT, vols. 1-34 (1899-1937).
Dt. THE DETROIT SOCIETY FOR GENEALOGICAL RESEARCH MAGAZINE, vols. 2-10 (1938-1952).
Dx. PILGRIM NOTES AND QUERIES, vols. 1-5 (1913-1917).).
E. THE OLD NORTHWEST GENEALOGICAL QUARTERLY, vols. 1-15 (1898-1909).

E1. THE COUNTY COURT NOTE-BOOK, vol. 10 (1931).
E2. THE DELAWARE HISTORICAL AND GENEALOGICAL RECALL, vol. 1 (1933).
E3. EARLY SETTLERS OF NEW YORK STATE, vols. 1-8 (1934-1952).
F1. BANGOR HISTORICAL MAGAZINE, vols. 1-9 (1885-1895).
F2. MAINE HISTORICAL RECORDER, vols. 1-9 (1884-1898).
F3. NEW HAMPSHIRE GENEALOGICAL RECORD, vols. 1-7 (1903-1910).
F4. NARRAGANSETT HISTORICAL REGISTER, vols. 1-8 (1882-1890).
F5. DEDHAM HISTORICAL REGISTER, vols. 1-14 (1890-1903).
G1. RECORDS OF THE AMERICAN CATHOLIC HISTORICAL SOCIETY OF PHILADELPHIA, vols. 1-44 (1887-1933).
G2. THE JOURNAL OF THE AMERICAN-IRISH HISTORICAL SOCIETY, vols. 1-29 (1898-1931).
H. NORTH CAROLINA HISTORICAL AND GENEALOGICAL REGISTER, vols. 1-3 (1900-1903).
H1. NORTH CAROLINA HISTORICAL AND GENEALOGICAL RECORD, vols. 1-2 (1932-1933).
H2. THE NORTH CAROLINA HISTORICAL REVIEW, vols. 9-13 (1932-1936).
J. SOUTH CAROLINA HISTORICAL AND GENEALOGICAL MAGAZINE, vols. 1-53 (1900-1952).
JM. THE JERSEYMAN, vols. 1-10 (no dates given).
K. THE GENEALOGICAL ADVERTISER, vols. 1-4 (1898-1901).
K2. THE FILSON CLUB HISTORY QUARTERLY, vols. 15-20 (1941-1946).
L1. YEAR BOOK, CHURCH OF THE ADVENT, Cape May, N.J., nos. 1-6 (1927-1932).
LI. THE LONG ISLAND HISTORICAL SOCIETY QUARTERLY, vols. 1-4 (1939-1942).
M. THE NATIONAL GENEALOGICAL SOCIETY QUARTERLY, vols. 1-40 (1912-1952).
N1. THE TRANSALLAGHANY HISTORICAL MAGAZINE (West Va.), vols. 1-2 (1901-1902).
N2. THE WEST VIRGINIA HISTORICAL MAGAZINE, vols. 1-5 (1901-1905).
N3. REGISTER OF THE KENTUCKY STATE HISTORICAL SOCIETY, vols. 1-21 (to 1923) and vols. 30-50 (1932-1952).
N4. EAST TENNESSEE HISTORICAL SOCIETY PUBLICATIONS, vols. 1-14 (1929-1942).
NAH. PUBLICATIONS OF THE NORWEGIAN-AMERICAN HISTORICAL ASSOCIATION. STUDIES AND RECORDS, vols. 1-17 (1926-1952).
NE. MAGAZINE OF NEW ENGLAND HISTORY, vols. 1-3 (1891-1893).
Ng. THE NIAGARA FRONTIER GENEALOGICAL MAGAZINE, vol. 7 (1948).
NH. HISTORICAL NEW HAMPSHIRE (no dates - occasional publ.).
O. THE OHIO GENEALOGICAL QUARTERLY, vols. 1-8 (1937-1944).

O1. BULLETIN OF THE HISTORICAL AND PHILOSOPHICAL SOCIETY OF OHIO, vols. 1-10 (1942-1953).

OU. OLDE ULSTER, vols. 1-10 (1905-1914).

P. PUBLICATIONS OF THE GENEALOGICAL SOCIETY OF PENNSYLVANIA, vols. 1-19 (1895-1952). (Name changed to PENNA. GENEA. MAG. 1948).

Pw. PROCEEDINGS AND COLLECTIONS OF THE WYOMING HISTORICAL AND GEOLOGICAL SOCIETY, vols. 1-22 (1858-1926, 1930, 1938).

Q1. THE PENNSYLVANIA MAGAZINE, vols. 1-63 (1877-1939).

Q2. PENNSYLVANIA-GERMAN SOCIETY PROCEEDINGS, vols. 1-39 (1891-1928).

Q3. HISTORICAL REGISTER: NOTES AND QUERIES, HISTORICAL AND GENEALOGICAL, RELATING TO INTERIOR PENNSYLVANIA, vols. 1-2 (1883-1884).

Q4. WESTERN PENNSYLVANIA HISTORICAL MAGAZINE, vols. 1-12 (1918-1929) (listed but not indexed).

Q5. LANCASTER COUNTY HISTORICAL SOCIETY PAPERS, vols. 1-34 (1896-1930) (listed but not indexed).

R1. PUBLICATIONS OF THE SOUTHERN HISTORY ASSOCIATION, vols. 1-11 (1897-1907).

R2. GULF STATES HISTORICAL MAGAZINE (Ala.), vols. 1-2 (1902-1904).

S1. AMERICAN, ILLUSTRATED (also called AMERICAN HISTORICAL MAGAZINE), vols. 1-37 (1906-1943).

S2. THE GRANITE MONTHLY (N.H.), vols. 1-30 (1877-1901).

S3. THE BULLETIN OF THE CALIFORNIA STATE SOCIETY SONS OF THE REVOLUTION, vols. 1-6 (1928-1932) and vols. 9-17 (1932-1938).

S4. THE JOURNAL OF AMERICAN GENEALOGY, vols. 1-5 (1921-1925).

T1. REPORTS AND PAPERS, FAIRFIELD COUNTY HISTORICAL SOCIETY (Conn.), irregular publ. (1882-1899).

T2. NEW HAVEN HISTORICAL SOCIETY PAPERS, vols. 1-9 (1865-1918).

T3. CONNECTICUT HISTORICAL SOCIETY COLLECTIONS, vols. 1-22 (1860-1928).

T4. BULLETIN OF THE NEWPORT HISTORICAL SOCIETY, 81 issues (1912-1931).

T5. RHODE ISLAND HISTORICAL TRACTS (listed but not indexed).

T6. PUBLICATIONS OF THE RHODE ISLAND HISTORICAL SOCIETY, vols. 1-8 (1893-1900).

T7. COLLECTIONS OF THE NEW YORK HISTORICAL SOCIETY, vols. 1-64 (1868-1931).

T8. BULLETIN OF THE CONNECTICUT HISTORICAL SOCIETY, vols. 1-11 (1934-1944).

T9. NEW YORK HISTORICAL SOCIETY QUARTERLY BULLETINS, vols. 21-30 (1937-1946) and vols. 31-36 (1947-1952).

U. THE UTAH GENEALOGICAL AND HISTORICAL MAGAZINE, vols. 1-30 (1910-1939).

V1.   TYLER'S QUARTERLY HISTORICAL AND GENEALOGICAL
      MAGAZINE, vols. 1-32 (1919-1951).
V2.   THE RESEARCHER, A MAGAZINE OF HISTORY AND
      GENEALOGICAL EXCHANGE (Va.), vols. 1-2 (1926-1928).
V3.   THE VIRGINIA MAGAZINE OF HISTORY AND BIOGRAPHY,
      vols. 40-60 (1932-1952). (Vols. 1-38 indexed in Swem.)
V4.   VIRGINIA COUNTY RECORDS, vols. 1-10 (1905-1912).
W1.   WILLIAM AND MARY COLLEGE QUARTERLY MAGAZINE,
      vols. 1-27 (1892-1919) (listed but indexed in Swem).
W2.   WILLIAM AND MARY COLLEGE QUARTERLY MAGAZINE
      (New Series), vols. 1-10 (1921-1930) (listed but indexed in
      Swem), also vols. 12-24 (1932-1944) (Subsequent vols. con-
      tain no genea.).
WF.   WISCONSIN FAMILIES, vol. 1 (1940-1941).
X1.   MARYLAND HISTORICAL MAGAZINE, vols. 1-47 (1906-
      1952).
X2.   MARYLAND GENEALOGICAL BULLETIN, vols. 1-21
      (1930-1952).
Y1.   THE ESSEX INSTITUTE HISTORICAL COLLECTIONS, vols.
      1-88 (1859-1952) (Vols. 68-85 have their own index.)
Y2.   THE ESSEX ANTIQUARIAN, vols. 1-13 (1897-1909).
YA.   YOUR ANCESTORS, vols. 1-6 (1947-1952).
 Z.   THE AMERICAN MONTHLY (42 vols.) and THE DAUGHTERS
      OF THE AMERICAN REVOLUTION MAGAZINE, vols. 1-84
      (1892-1950).
Z1.   THE HYDE PARK HISTORICAL RECORDS, vols. 1-9
      (1891-1913).
Z2.   THE REGISTER OF THE LYNN HISTORICAL SOCIETY,
      vols. 1-24 (1897-1929).
Z3.   PROCEEDINGS OF THE NEW JERSEY HISTORICAL SOCIETY,
      vol. 1 (1st series) and vol. 16 (4th series).
Z4.   THE ATLANTIC COUNTY HISTORICAL SOCIETY YEARBOOKS,
      vols. 1-2 (1948-1952).

Volume 3 of Jacobus includes his "own index" consisting of names
indexed for his own personal use, chiefly concerning families of New
England and New York. In his last volume, Jacobus writes that he
"now lays down the task, feeling that his efforts have been of great
aid to many seekers and that he now deserves a rest from his labors,
but with the hope that some altruist may assume the thankless task
and continue an index of this type."[13]

Since 1962, the GENEALOGICAL PERIODICAL ANNUAL INDEX
(GPAI) has attempted to fulfill Mr. Jacobus's wishes with its annuals.
Ellen Stanley Rogers edited volumes 1-4 (Bladensburg, Maryland:
The Genealogical Recorders, 1963-1967) and George Ely Russell has
edited those since (volumes 5-8, Bowie, Maryland: The Genealogical
Recorders, 1968-1970).

The GPAI is the standard and authoritative topical and author
index to genealogical literature appearing in American, Canadian,

and British periodicals each year. It seeks out hidden subjects not indicated by titles of articles as well as family data buried in more general articles.[14] A "key" to genealogical periodicals indexed is included with each edition and the following periodicals were listed in the 1966 edition:

AFH	ARKANSAS FAMILY HISTORIAN
AGR	ALABAMA GENEALOGICAL REGISTER
AH	AMERICAN HERITAGE
AN	ANCESTRAL NOTES
AUG	THE AUGUSTAN
AUS	AUSTIN GEN. SOC. QUARTERLY
BEE	BALKAN & E. EUROPEAN . . . QUARTERLY
BMGS	BULLETIN, MD. GEN. SOC.
CEN	CENOTAPH, HUTCHINSON CO. GEN. SOC.
CHSB	CONN. HIST. SOC. BULLETIN
CinB	CINCINNATI HIST. SOC. BULLETIN
COG	COLORADO GENEALOGIST
CSM	CHRONICLES OF ST. MARY'S
CT	CENTRAL TEXAS GEN. SOC. QRTRLY.
DAR	DAR MAGAZINE
DSGQ	DEEP SOUTH GENEALOGICAL QRTRLY.
DSGR	DETROIT SOC. FOR GEN. RESEARCH
ECH	ECHOES, E. TENN. HIST. SOCIETY
EK	THE EAST KENTUCKIAN
FFF	FAULKNER FACTS & FIDDLINGS
FGQ	FLINT GENEALOGICAL QUARTERLY
FW	FT. WORTH GEN. SOC. BULLETIN
GGM	GEORGIA GENEALOGICAL MAGAZINE
GM	GEORGIA MAGAZINE
GMNJ	GENEALOGICAL MAGAZINE OF N. J.
GP	THE GENEALOGIST'S POST
GPGM	GEORGIA PIONEERS GEN. MAGAZINE
GRN	GENEALOGICAL RESEARCH NEWS
HG	THE HOOSIER GENEALOGIST
HH	HAWKEYE HERITAGE, IOWA GEN. SOC.
HOU	HOUSTON GENEALOGICAL RECORD
HW	HISTORICAL WYOMING
IF	INTERNATIONAL FINDERS
IG	THE ILLIANA GENEALOGIST
IGSQ	IDAHO GEN. SOC. QUARTERLY
JLIH	JOURNAL OF LONG ISLAND HISTORY
KCG	KANSAS CITY GENEALOGIST
KG	KERN GEN, KERN CO. GEN. SOC.
KK	KANSAS KIN, RILEY CO. GEN. SOC.
LGR	LOUISIANA GENEALOGICAL REGISTER
LHGS	LOCAL HIST. & GEN. SOC. QRTRLY.
LM	LAUREL MESSENGER, SOMERSET CO. HIST.
MDG	MARYLAND & DELAWARE GENEALOGIST
MGE	MISS. GENEALOGICAL EXCHANGE
MHM	MARYLAND HISTORICAL MAGAZINE

```
MHT     MT. HOOD TRACKERS
MI      MICHIGANA, W. MICH. GEN. SOC.
ML      MISSING LINKS
NCG     JOURNAL OF N. C. GENEALOGY
NCHR    NORTH CAROLINA HIST. REVIEW
NER     NEW ENGLAND HIST. & GEN. REGISTER
NGSQ    NATIONAL GEN. SOC. QUARTERLY
NJG     NEW JERSEY GENESIS
NMG     NEW MEXICO GENEALOGIST
NOG     NEW ORLEANS GENESIS
NYR     NEW YORK GEN. & BIOG. RECORD
OCQ     ORANGE CO. GEN. SOC. QUARTERLY
OGS     OREGON GENEALOGICAL BULLETIN
OGSB    ONTARIO GEN. SOC. BULLETIN
OGSQ    OKLAHOMA GEN. SOC. QUARTERLY
OH      OUR HERITAGE, SAN ANTONIO G & H S.
ORPF    OHIO RECORDS & PIONEER FAMILIES
PGF     GEN. FORUM OF PORTLAND
PGM     PENNSYLVANIA GENEALOGICAL MAGAZINE
PH      PIONEER HERITAGE
REF     REFLECTOR, AMARILLO GEN. SOC.
REP     REPORT, OHIO GENEALOGICAL SOC.
RIH     RHODE ISLAND HISTORY
RV      ROGUE VALLEY GEN. SOC. QRTRLY.
SAB     S. ARIZONA GEN. SOC. BULLETIN
SCC     SANTA CLARA CO. H. & G. SOC.
SCGR    SOUTH CAROLINA GENEAL. REGISTER
SGB     STAMFORD GEN. SOC. BULLETIN
SGE     SOUTHERN GEN. EXCHANGE QUARTERLY
SGSB    SEATTLE GEN. SOC. BULLETIN
STI     STIRPES, TEXAS STATE G. S. QRTRLY.
STQ     S. TEXAS G. & H. SOC. QUARTERLY
SWG     THE SOUTHWESTERN GENEALOGIST
TAG     THE AMERICAN GENEALOGIST
TAN     ANSEARCHIN' NEWS, TENN. GEN. SOC.
TGH     THE GENEALOGICAL HELPER
TGM     THE GENEALOGISTS' MAGAZINE
THH     THE HAPPY HUNTER, CUMBERLAND CO. G.
TIPS    GENEALOGICAL TIPS, TIP-O'-TEXAS G. S.
TKG     THE KENTUCKY GENEALOGIST
TPT     THE PENNSYLVANIA TRAVELER
TR      TAP ROOTS, E. ALABAMA GEN. SOC.
TRI     TRI-CITY GEN. SOC. BULLETIN
TS      THE TREESEARCHER, KANSAS GEN. SOC.
TSG     THE SCOTTISH GENEALOGIST
TT      TREE TALKS, CENTRAL N. Y. G. S.
TVG     THE VIRGINIA GENEALOGIST
VC      VIRGINIA CAVALCADE
VGSQ    VIRGINIA GEN. SOC. QUARTERLY
VMHB    VIRGINIA MAGAZINE OF HIST. & BIOG.
WIS     WISCONSIN STATE G. S. NEWSLETTER
YY      YESTERYEARS
```

The gap between Jacobus (1952) and the GPAI (1962) has been partially filled by Robert W. Carder's INDEX TO GENEALOGICAL PERIODICALS, 1953-1967 (Madison, Connecticut) and by Inez Waldermaier in various issues of her GENEALOGICAL NEWSLETTER. Both publications are on file at the Genealogical Society in Salt Lake City.

Another excellent genealogical index, which does for the South what Jacobus did for the North, is Earl G. Swem's VIRGINIA HISTORICAL INDEX (Gloucester, Massachusetts: Peter Smith, 1965). It indexes names and subjects from the following periodicals:

CALENDAR OF VIRGINIA STATE PAPERS
HENING'S STATUTES OF VIRGINIA
LOWER NORFOLK COUNTY VIRGINIA ANTIQUARY
VIRGINIA HISTORICAL REGISTER
TYLER'S HISTORICAL AND GENEALOGICAL QUARTERLY
VIRGINIA MAGAZINE OF HISTORY AND BIOGRAPHY
WILLIAM AND MARY COLLEGE QUARTERLY HISTORICAL
    MAGAZINE

Copies of this index are at BYU and Salt Lake City, and each of the periodicals indexed is available at the Genealogical Society in Salt Lake City.

Perhaps the most popular genealogical compendium is Frederick A. Virkus's THE ABRIDGED COMPENDIUM OF AMERICAN GENEALOGY in seven volumes (Chicago: A. N. Marquis & Company, 1952). It includes descent information on many of the first families of America and, to a degree, is a continuation of Savage's GENEALOGICAL DICTIONARY AND FARMER'S REGISTER. It is known to be rather brief and in some cases inaccurate, but some family listings are quite complete and correct. The arrangement is a little unusual, listing the modern descendant's name and birth date at the bottom of each entry and then showing direct-line descent from names listed above. The ascent order is shown in numerical sequence from the bottom of each entry to the top (fig. 32).

John Farmer's A GENEALOGICAL REGISTER OF THE FIRST SETTLERS OF NEW ENGLAND (Lancaster, Massachusetts: Carter-Andrews, 1829) was the first real attempt to publish a genealogical dictionary in America and has served the genealogist well. James Savage, former president of the Massachusetts Historical Society, followed with his GENEALOGICAL DICTIONARY OF THE FIRST SETTLERS OF NEW ENGLAND (reprinted in four volumes by the Genealogical Publishing Company at Baltimore in 1965). The original work appeared in one volume and some libraries have copies of the original edition. The Dictionary includes facts on three generations of those who came to New England before May 1692 and is based on Farmer's Register of 1829. Savage did not conduct original research on the families listed in his work, and some listings contain error. One can often do better in more recent family histories which have

BOWEN, Henry, *b* Providence, R.I., Aug. 5, 1852.

9–Richard **Bowen** (qv);

8–Thomas, *m* Elizabeth –;

7–Dr. Richard, *m* Mercy Titus;

6–Dr. Thomas, *m* Sarah Hunt;

5–Dr. Ephraim, *m* Mary Fenner;

4–Jabez, LL.D. (1739-1815), dep. gov. and chief justice of R.I., chancellor Brown U., 1785-1815, *m* 1st, Sarah Brown;

3–Henry (1785-1867), atty. gen. of R.I., 1817-19, and sec. of state, 1819-49.

2–Son of William Horatio **Bowen** (1824-1897), flour merchant, Providence, *m* Ednah Baker Goodhue (1828-55); issue: 1–Ednah Goodhue (1848-1913); 2–Henry (above); 3–Joseph Tilton (1854-1911; *m* Louise de Koven, qv); 4–Frank.

2–*M* Sept. 4, 1882, Clara Belle, dau. George D. Flagg, Providence, R.I.; issue (all *b* at Providence): 1–Joseph, *b* Dec. 15, 1887; served with 314th Supply Train in U.S. and France, World War; 2–Henry (twin; *d* May 18, 1910); 3–Dorothy Flagg, *b* Jan. 19, 1892; *m* Feb. 1, 1913, Francis Henshaw Dewey, Jr. (qv); 4–Donald Flagg (twin), *b* Jan. 19, 1892; Williams, '13; sergt. 78th Div. Inf., A.E.F. in France.

Mem. S.A.R.   Summer place: Kenyon Cottage, Narragansett Pier, R.I.   Residence: 84 Benefit St., Providence, R.I.

BOWEN, Louise de Koven (Mrs. Joseph T.), *b* Chicago, Ill., Feb. 26, 1859.

4–Capt. John Louis **de Koven,** of the Hanoverian army, came to America ca. 1778, and settled at Fort Washington, N.Y., *m* Elizabeth Sebor, of Middletown, Conn.;

3–Henry Louis, banker, Chicago, *m* 1813, Margaret Yates Sebor.

Fig. 32.   Example page from ABRIDGED COMPENDIUM

been published for those early New England families. An excellent collection is at the Genealogical Society in Salt Lake City.

Another dictionary of special importance to New England research is the GENEALOGICAL DICTIONARY OF MAINE AND NEW HAMPSHIRE, compiled in two volumes by Charles T. Libby and published in 1928-39. It attempts to cover every family in Maine and New Hampshire which was established by 1699 and carries information on some well into the eighteenth century. In 1959, the Research Department of the LDS Genealogical Society was conducting research on Henry Pendexter of Biddeford, York, Maine, but they had been unable to extend the line in America earlier than 1727. Henry first appeared in Biddeford records when he purchased a "Pew at the head of the stairs" in the First Church of Christ (Congregational). Searches in original records failed to provide the needed information, but an entry in the GENEA-LOGICAL DICTIONARY OF MAINE AND NEW HAMPSHIRE provided an entirely new outlook on the problem. An entry was noted for an "Isaac Pendexter" of Portsmouth (Strawberry Bank), New Hampshire, who was contemporary with the Henry in question. The Dictionary indicated Isaac was a seaman from St. Hilliary in the Channel Isles. An agent searched early registers there and located information about Isaac, but more importantly, located a christening entry for a "Henry Pendexter" who could well be the same person as the one in Biddeford, Maine. These early genealogical dictionaries should not be overlooked.

John Osborn Austin compiled the GENEALOGICAL DICTIONARY OF RHODE ISLAND in 1887. It lists three generations of Rhode Island settlers who came to America before 1690. Frank T. Calef added to the work (GS FILM #5303 pt 2) and corrections and additions were published in volumes 19, 21, 26, and 30 of the AMERICAN GENEALOGIST (Jacobus's work and not Munsell's). The correction work was done by G. Andrews Moriarty, and the listed volumes are found at the Genealogical Society in Salt Lake City.

A variety of biographical material is available to help the American genealogist accomplish his work, and most libraries and archives are important repositories. Many collections pertain to prominent citizens, but some include information about the ordinary "silent majority." Where an ancestor was prominent in the military, or in education, medicine, engineering, religion, or some other special field, there is a good possibility he might be located in specialized biographical collections. It is also a good procedure to check for biographical information pertaining to brothers, uncles, granduncles, etc., for their genealogy is the same as the ancestor's.

The LDS Genealogical Society in Salt Lake City has a wonderful collection of biographical material covering America and welcomes investigation by the genealogist and historian.

Regional and Local Histories
    A considerable amount of genealogical information can be found

in regional and local histories. They often contain special genealogical or biographical sections and include a variety of genealogical fact, including names and kinship, previous places of residence, birth and marriage information, details on death and burial, as well as other interesting facts. Early settlers are often identified, with migration details included.

County and town histories are excellent reference tools for the genealogist. Some include early township and county boundary maps, while others include plat-book information which gives the names of residents and their land ownership in pictoral view. Details about early church organizations and fraternal orders are provided, with political and military history included.

There are over three thousand counties in the United States, and each has had at least one work published for it; some have as many as five or six. There are also regional and national publications which are similar in format to local histories but which have broader coverage. They tend to include the more prominent individuals and do not meet the specific needs of the genealogist as often as the local publications do.

A major problem in using historical publications is their indexes. Often they are not indexed, or if they are, the genealogical information is not included. Some states have programs to index these materials, but usually the researcher must approach the records by locality and investigate them page by page. A state with an excellent indexing program is Indiana. Local and regional histories at the State Library at Indianapolis have been indexed by subject and by surname. Indexes are typescript and are shelved beside the historical publications they cover. The author was able to discover the Maryland birthplace of an ancestor who lived and died in Indiana by using these special indexes. The ancestor was listed in a biographical sketch of his father-in-law with pertinent birth information included.

The general indexes mentioned previously should be considered when investigating historical publications. This would include those of Durrie, Glenn, Jacobus, Munsell, Rider, Whitmore, and Swem. The NEWBERRY LIBRARY INDEX and the AMERICAN GENEALOGICAL-BIOGRAPHICAL INDEX can be considered both for genealogy and history.

Clarence Stewart Peterson's CONSOLIDATED BIBLIOGRAPHY OF COUNTY HISTORIES IN FIFTY STATES IN 1961 (Baltimore: The Genealogical Publishing Company, 1963) is also a popular and valuable bibliographic guide to historical material. It lists many publications such as biographical publications, maps, atlases, which are not county histories in their true form, but which are useful to the genealogist. The work is by no means exhaustive but can give useful information for a start.

The LDS Genealogical Society in Salt Lake City has an excellent collection of local and regional histories for America as does the library at Brigham Young University. Local libraries and societies should also be checked because they often have published and manuscript collections which are not found in larger repositories. The search never really ends for genealogical facts in historical records. The researcher should be alert to locate them wherever his travels take him.

---

1. Meredith B. Colket, Jr., "Creating a Worthwhile Family Genealogy," NATIONAL GENEALOGICAL SOCIETY QUARTERLY 50 (December 1968):257.

2. Ibid., p. 243.

3. Noel C. Stevenson, THE GENEALOGICAL READER (Salt Lake City: Deseret Book Company, 1958), p. 131.

4. From Joseph C. Wolf, Custodian of Local History and Genealogy at The Newberry Library, Chicago, letter dated 19 November 1968.

5. For excellent information on "Tracing U.S. Ancestry in Family Collections," see World Conference on Records Papers 14a, 14b, and 14c in Area I (The LDS Genealogical Society: World Conference on Records and Genealogical Seminar, Salt Lake City, 5-8 August 1969).

6. P. William Filby, AMERICAN & BRITISH GENEALOGY & HERALDRY (Chicago: American Library Association, 1970), p. 5.

7. Ibid., pp. 5-6.

8. Donald Lines Jacobus, INDEX TO GENEALOGICAL PERIODICALS, 1 (1932): "Introduction."

9. Lester J. Cappon, AMERICAN GENEALOGICAL PERIODICALS: A BIBLIOGRAPHY WITH A CHRONOLOGICAL FINDING-LIST (New York: The New York Public Library, 1964), pp. 30-32.

10. From Mrs. Frances S. Bielfield, Office Manager at Godfrey Memorial Library, Middletown, Connecticut, in a letter dated 10 December 1968.

11. Ibid.

12. Jacobus, 3:ii.

13. Ibid.

14. George Ely Russell, GENEALOGICAL PERIODICAL ANNUAL INDEX, 6:iii.

SECTION THREE - SEARCHING ORIGINAL RECORDS

CHAPTER 7

BEGINNING THE SEARCH IN ORIGINAL RECORDS

After determining the extent of previous research, it is time to define specific research objectives and get into original records in order to confirm survey data and extend the pedigree.

The late Donald Lines Jacobus felt that many modern texts dealing with genealogy spend too much time talking about the classification of evidence and not enough about searching original records. On one occasion he said: "I still think the best course of training is to go to the original record sources, and dig, dig, dig, until one gets the 'feel' of the time and place."[1] The author would agree with him but at the same time would suggest that survey work in secondary or compiled sources is also very important in genealogy.

Defining Research Objectives

In most cases, the researcher will gather conflicting information from his survey work or will be unable to determine the validity of all the facts he has located. It soon becomes evident that investigation of original source materials is necessary if he is to be convinced of the correctness of these facts. If the facts located are correct, the researcher must still proceed to the original sources to gain new facts and extend the pedigree.

The worker should first evaluate all his survey data and tabulate it in appropriate form. The pedigree charts, family group records, and summary forms shown previously are sufficient to accomplish this. He should then note all conflicts or note where information is lacking and define objectives to reconcile the differences or add to the missing information.

Consideration should be given to the name, the time period, the event, and the sources which might best fill the need. If it is a matter of determining the correct date of death or burial in a modern time period, it might only be necessary to obtain a copy of a death record from the state office of vital statistics registration.[2] However, if the time period was such that death records were not kept in state or county, it might be necessary to investigate probate, cemetery, church, or some other record to gain the desired information.

The researcher should carefully evaluate the problem and list the objectives he has in mind, i.e., "(1) Obtain the death record of "Kindness Ann Haines Badger who died in Salt Lake City in 1929" or (2) Obtain an obituary notice for Kindness Ann Haines Badger who died in Salt Lake City in 1929" to confirm the correct day and month of death and burial. Research objectives should be listed in some organized form so they can be easily identified and completed. As research is undertaken, the objectives can be checked off as they are accomplished. The research notes and summary charts will show the final conclusions reached.

Death and Burial Records

In genealogical research, one should work from the known to the unknown and from the more modern events to the earlier happenings because the more modern records usually contain more information and often provide facts which lead to records and sources for earlier periods.

When the individual of concern died in a modern period, say between 1850 and 1900 or later, an official death or burial record should be obtained from the state office of vital statistics. When a state record is not available, a death or burial record from the county or town should be obtained. The modern record calls for important genealogical facts about birthplace and parentage and often provides clues for continued research.

The typical record includes the name and age of the deceased, his birth date and birthplace, his parents and their birthplaces, his death date and death place, his place of burial and burial date, and the names and addresses of the informant and the undertaker (fig. 33).

Many state offices did not begin vital statistics registration until the latter part of the nineteenth century, though some towns and counties were recording much earlier. New England towns were recording birth, marriage, and death information from the very beginning of the town's settlement, and New England churches have recorded similar information since the 1640s. The middle and southern states did not record vital statistics on a town, county, or a state basis until after the 1880s, except for marriages, but churches in those states recorded vital statistics from the 1680s. Many midwestern states recorded births and deaths on a county basis after the 1850s and 1860s, but most of them recorded marriages on a county basis

STATE OF NEW MEXICO, DEPARTMENT OF HEALTH
CERTIFICATE OF DEATH

1 PLACE OF DEATH
County of _San Juan_　　　　Registered No. _19_

School District of _____ or Village of _____
or City of _New Aztec_ No. _____ St., _____ Ward

(If death occurred in hospital or institution, give its NAME instead of street and number)

2 FULL NAME _William Adelbert Pound_

(a) Residence. No. _____ St., _____ Ward.
(Usual place of abode)　　　(IF NONRESIDENT give city or town and State)
LENGTH OF RESIDENCE in city or town where death occurred _9_ yrs _1_ mos _20_ days. How long in U. S., if of foreign birth? _____ yrs. mos. ds

PERSONAL AND STATISTICAL PARTICULARS	MEDICAL CERTIFICATE OF DEATH

PERSONAL AND STATISTICAL PARTICULARS

3 SEX _male_　4 COLOR OR RACE _white_　5 Single, Married, Widowed, or Divorced (write the word.) _married_

5a If married, widowed, or divorced
HUSBAND OF
(or) WIFE of _Mary A. Pound_

6 DATE OF BIRTH _Sept._ month _3_ day _1852_ year

7 AGE _69_ Years _8_ Months _16_ Days | If LESS than 1 day _____ hrs. or _____ min.

8 OCCUPATION OF DECEASED
(a) Trade, profession, or particular kind of work _Farmer_
(b) General nature of industry, business, or establishment in which employed (or employer) _____
(c) Name of employer _Self_

9 BIRTHPLACE (city or town) (State or county) _Near Buffalo New York_

10 NAME OF FATHER _Geo. Pound_
11 BIRTHPLACE OF FATHER (City or town) (State or county) ✓
12 MAIDEN NAME OF MOTHER ✓
13 BIRTHPLACE OF MOTHER (City or town) (State or county) ✓

14 Informant _Kate Pound_
(Address) _Denver, Colo._

15 Filed _June 15_ 19 22, _Mrs. E. B. Dixon_ Sub. REGISTRAR

MEDICAL CERTIFICATE OF DEATH

16 DATE OF DEATH _May_ _19_, 19 _22_
MONTH　DAY　YEAR

17 I HEREBY CERTIFY, That I attended deceased from _May 12_ 19 _22_ to _May 19_ 19 _22_
that I last saw him alive on _May 19_, 19 _22_
and that death occurred, on the date stated above, at _3 a._ m.
The CAUSE OF DEATH* was as follows:

Angina Pectoris

(duration) _8.9_ yrs. _3_ mos. _____ ds.

CONTRIBUTORY (SECONDARY) _____
(duration) _____ yrs. _____ mos. _____ ds.

18 Where was disease contracted if not at place of death? _____
Did an operation precede death? _no_ Date of _____
Was there an autopsy? _no_
What test confirmed diagnosis? _clinical_
(Signed) _M. D. Taylor_ M. D
Date _____, 19 _____ (Address) _Aztec, N. Mex._

*State the Primary Disease causing death. See reverse for instructions as to statement of cause of death.

19 PLACE OF BURIAL, CREMATION OR REMOVAL _Aztec, N. Mex._ DATE OF BURIAL _May 20, 1922_

20 UNDERTAKER _J. W. Dial_ ADDRESS _Aztec, N. M._

STATE OF NEW MEXICO
COUNTY OF SANTA FE

I HEREBY CERTIFY THIS TO BE A TRUE AND CORRECT COPY OF AN ORIGINAL CERTIFICATE REGISTERED WITH THE VITAL RECORDS UNIT, NEW MEXICO HEALTH AND SOCIAL SERVICES DEPARTMENT--THE LEGAL DEPOSITORY FOR SUCH RECORDS, SIGNED AND SEALED December 8, 1969

BY: _Betty Alva_
DEPUTY STATE REGISTRAR

Joseph A. Maracchini
STATE REGISTRAR

Fig. 33. Modern death record from state office

119

from the organization of the county. Churches in the midwest were recording vital statistics as early as the 1820s.

Local records are not usually as inclusive as those issued by the state offices but they do provide helpful information. The local records are usually copies of register entries while those from the state offices are generally photostats or certified copies of certificates (fig. 34).

When a death record cannot be obtained from the state or county office, searches should be conducted in records of local churches, cemeteries, and funeral homes. It is surprising how many morticians have kept good records of death and burial, many dating from the 1830s, and most offices will make their information available for genealogical purposes. In many instances, the mortician was responsible for initiating the official state or county death record, and his record is often similar to theirs (fig. 35).

A few years ago, an attempt was made to obtain a death record from Illinois for a death which was thought to have taken place in Chicago in 1932. No record could be located for the deceased in the state, county, or city offices, but a local mortician was able to produce a record of the person's burial. The mortician's record indicated the person died in New Orleans but was buried in Chicago. A copy of the death record was obtained from Louisiana and it indicated our man had been "hung" in the parish prison. Of course mortician's records do not always include that kind of information, but they can be useful in genealogy.

Church or parish records relating to death are usually burial or funeral entries, though some include both the date and place of death and the date and place of burial. Some records include parentage, but most only give the name of the deceased and burial information.

American church records are not generally as useful as those of most foreign countries because the United States has not had a state church but has been a melting pot of national and ethnic groups.

After obtaining the death record, an attempt should be made to locate an obituary or death notice from a local newspaper, especially when the death occurred in a modern time period. These notices can supply facts about kinship, surviving relatives, places of residence, and even the foreign place of birth, as well as other important facts which will help future research.

Research on a St. Lawrence County, New York, problem indicated Margaret Fitzgerald was buried in Rossie, New York, in 1911 but other known facts were meager. Information suggested she was the wife of John Fitzgerald and mother of Jack and Lottie, but little else was known about her family. A death record was obtained from the State of New York which gave her death date as 19 December 1911 and her death place as Yonkers, New York. Her obituary

GRANT COUNTY
DEPARTMENT OF HEALTH
MARION, INDIANA

Certificate of Death

THIS IS TO CERTIFY, That our records show:

Name ....

died ....August..........22.........1903.........at.................at..Upland, Indiana
........(Month)........(Day)........(Year)........(Hour)........(Street, Hospital or Rural)

Age at death..83........Sex..Female..Color..White......Widow
........(Years)..(Married, Single or Other)

Primary cause of death given was ..Senility and Dysentery.....

Certified by ...O. L. Stout.................Upland, Indiana
........(Physician)........................(Address)

Place of burial or removal..Wabash........Wabash, Indiana
........(Cemetery)........................(Address)

Date of burial.8-24-1903.....Holden....Upland, Indiana
........(Funeral Director)........................(Address)

Record was filed....August 22, 1903.....Book No..Upland-1..Page No....45.

........(SEAL)........Lester S. Railsaur M.D.
....Grant County Health Officer

Issued on ...August 9, 1967

Fig. 34. Local death record

THE BLUNT MORTUARY

No.

Name

Place of Death

Usual Residence

Length of Time in Community _____ Social Security No.

Date of Birth—Month _____ Day _____ Year _____ Age: _____ Years

_____ Months

Date of Death _____ Hour _____ Days

Sex _____ Color _____ Veteran of _____ War

Name of Husband or Wife _____ Age if Alive

Birthplace _____ Occupation

Mother's Maiden Name _____ Birthplace

Father's Name _____ Birthplace

Cause of Death _____ Physician

Place of Burial _____ Lot _____ Block

Service _____ Date _____ Hour

Fig. 35. Mortician's record

notice was then located from a local newspaper (the GOUVERNOUR FREE PRESS) and gave the following interesting information about her:

On Saturday morning at three o'clock at the home of her daughter in Yonkers, New York occurred the death of Mrs John Fitzgerald a beloved and highly esteemed resident of this village. Death came suddenly after a four days illness from pleurisy, age 78 years. Mrs Fitzgerald went to Yonkers on the New York excursion and had planned on coming home last week in company with her daughter Mrs W. A. Smith but was taken suddenly ill last Tuesday.

Mrs Fitzgerald was born December 19, 1833 in Dublin Ireland and came to this country 60 years ago, settling with her parents in Rossie where several years of her life was spent and where she was married to John Fitzgerald who died several years ago. Her maiden name was Margaret Gillon. She has resided in this village for the past 28 years.

She is survived by four daughters, Mrs W. A. Smith of Yonkers, Mrs Homer Clapp of Watertown, Mrs William Pound of Silver City, New Mexico and Miss Tinnie Fitzgerald of this village and two sons, Michael and James, both of Gouvernour. The funeral was held yesterday at 9 a.m. from the St. James Roman Catholic Church, Rev. M. F. Gillivan officiating. Interment was made at Rossie.

Research was at a standstill until this notice was received, but after it was studied, new leads could be followed to gain more information about Margaret and her family.

It is also a good practice to locate similar records for other persons associated with the pedigree problem, because their records may add facts which might not be listed in the ancestor's. The researcher should try to obtain death or burial records for the spouse and for each of the children, and even for brothers, sisters, and parents of the deceased. They may all provide new leads for continued research, and when all facts are correlated, a much more complete picture of the family will be available. Gregory and Brigham's newspaper guides, explained in chapter 3, are excellent tools for determining the location of existing newspapers.

Cemetery-sextons' records are not as easy to locate and must often be investigated by a personal visit to the place of burial; however, some inscriptions and interments have been published and are located in libraries and historical societies. Cemeteries come in a variety of types and sizes, including national, state, county, township, town/city, church, and private. Some have records of burial, plot layout, and ownership, while others consist solely of inscriptions and epitaphs (fig. 36).

Sometimes the inscriptions and epitaphs are sorrowful while some

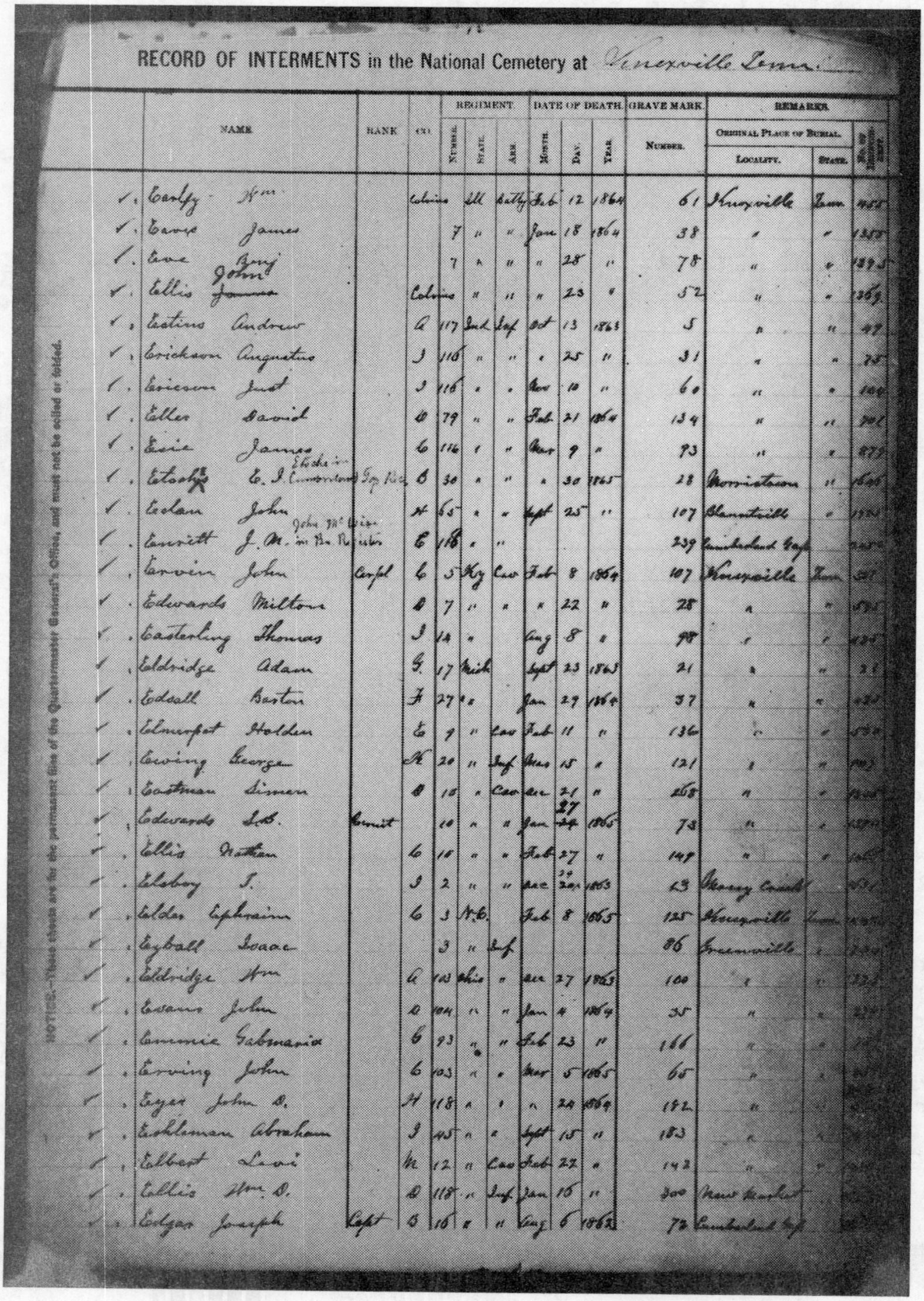

RECORD OF INTERMENTS in the National Cemetery at Knoxville Tenn.

NOTICE.—These sheets are for the permanent files of the Quartermaster General's Office, and must not be soiled or folded.

	Name	Rank	Co.	Regiment: Number	State	Arm	Date of Death: Month	Day	Year	Grave Mark: Number	Remarks: Original Place of Burial: Locality	State	No.
✓	Earlfy Wm		Colored		Ill	Batty	Feb	12	1864	61	Knoxville	Tenn	455
✓	Eaves James			7	"	"	Jan	18	1864	38	"	"	1355
✓	Eave Benj			7	"	"	"	28	"	78	"	"	1395
✓	Ellis John (James struck through)		Colored	"	"	"	"	23	"	52	"	"	1369
✓	Eastins Andrew		A	117	Ind	Inf	Oct	13	1863	5	"	"	47
✓	Erickson Augustus		I	116	"	"	"	25	"	31	"	"	75
✓	Ericsson Just		I	116	"	"	Nov	10	"	60	"	"	100
✓	Eller David		D	79	"	"	Feb	21	1864	134	"	"	701
✓	Essie James		G	116	"	"	Mar	9	"	93	"	"	877
✓	Etsolfs E. I. (Etsche in Enrollment)	Top Rec	B	30	"	"	"	30	1865	28	Morristown	"	1646
✓	Eolan John		H	65	"	"	Sept	25	"	107	Blountville	"	[illegible]
✓	Emmitt J. M. (John McWire in the Register)		G	118	"	"				239	Cumberland Gap		[illegible]
✓	Ervin John	Corpl	G	5	Ky	Cav	Feb	8	1864	107	Knoxville	Tenn	[illegible]
✓	Edwards Milton		D	7	"	"	"	22	"	28	"	"	[illegible]
✓	Easterling Thomas		I	14	"		Aug	8	"	98	"	"	[illegible]
✓	Eldridge Adam		G	17	Mich		Sept	23	1863	21	"	"	[illegible]
✓	Edsall Barton		F	27	"		Jan	29	1864	37	"	"	[illegible]
✓	Elmerfort Holden		E	9	"	Cav	Feb	11	"	136	"	"	[illegible]
✓	Ewing George		K	20	"	Inf	Mar	15	"	121	"	"	[illegible]
✓	Eastman Simeon		B	10	"	Cav	Dec	21	"	268	"	"	[illegible]
✓	Edwards S. B.	Recruit		10	"	"	Jan	27 (24 struck through)	1865	73	"	"	[illegible]
✓	Ellis Nathan		G	10	"	"	Feb	27	"	149	"	"	[illegible]
✓	Elsboy T.		I	2	"	"	Dec	24 (20)	1863	23	Mossy Creek		[illegible]
✓	Elder Ephraim		G	3	N.C.		Feb	8	1865	125	Knoxville	Tenn	[illegible]
✓	Eyball Isaac			3	"	Inf				86	Greenville	"	[illegible]
✓	Eldridge Wm		A	103	Ohio	"	Dec	27	1863	100	"	"	[illegible]
✓	Evans John		D	104	"	"	Jan	4	1864	35	"	"	[illegible]
✓	Emmie Gabmarix		G	93	"	"	Feb	23	"	166	"	"	[illegible]
✓	Erving John		G	103	"	"	Mar	5	1865	65	"	"	[illegible]
✓	Eyer John D.		H	118	"	"	"	24	1864	182	"	"	[illegible]
✓	Eshleman Abraham		I	45	"	"	Sept	15	"	183	"	"	[illegible]
✓	Elbert Levi		M	12	"	Cav	Feb	27	"	142	"	"	[illegible]
✓	Ellis Wm. D.		D	118	"	Inf	Jan	16	"	300	New Market		[illegible]
✓	Edgar Joseph	Capt	B	16	"	"	Aug	6	1862	72	Cumberland Gap		[illegible]

Fig. 36. Record of burial in a national cemetery

are quite humorous. An inscription on a child's headstone in a Tennessee cemetery evidently was intended to read "Blossomed on Earth to Bloom in Heaven," but it actually read "Blossomed on Earth to Boom in Heaven," undoubtedly a slip of the stonemason's chisel.

Personal investigation of the cemetery or burial plot can sometimes uncover valuable information which might not otherwise be located. Adjoining plots might be those of close relatives, and copied records might not allow this discovery when the surnames are different. Also, many cemeteries have not been visited by copiers, and sextons' records do not always exist. On an Ohio genealogical trip, the writer had to pass an owner's home, open a gate to his corral, drive past the barn into a cattle driveway, and go several rods along a field fence to locate the burial place of an ancestor.

On another occasion, the writer was nearly frightened to death by a three-foot-long snake while he was attempting to uncover a half-buried headstone (fig. 37).

Sometimes the headstones are so badly weathered that a clear interpretation of the inscription is almost impossible, and it is necessary to make a "rubbing" or scrape the headstone with pumicestone or some other substance. Dusting the inscription with chalk or using a crayon to mark the inscription will sometimes bring out the details. After chalking a very badly weathered stone, my wife was able to calculate a 1732 birth date for her fifth great-grandmother, which aided in identifying that person in a Connecticut church record.

Sometimes a central family monument with surrounding headstones for each member of the family is located, and sometimes all persons buried in a particular area are related. Better than 95 percent of the people buried in the Traylor Union Church Cemetery at Otwell, Pike County, Indiana, are descendants or relatives of Joel Traylor and Catherine (Bomar) Traylor who were from Spartanburg, South Carolina, and earlier from Chesterfield County, Virginia.

The researcher should be very careful when using copied cemetery and sextons' records because many contain errors. It is better to see the original when possible, and it is good to talk with old-timers and family associates to correlate information obtained from the copied records. Willard Hardin, age 84 in 1962, was able to identify burial plots of his grandparents and could give actual dates of burial for some persons buried in the family cemetery, even though headstones did not exist.

Various chapters of the Daughters of the American Revolution have carried out restoration projects in cemeteries and have placed headstones on the graves of veterans. They have also copied and published tombstone inscriptions from many cemeteries and made them available to local libraries and historical societies. The Genealogical Society Library in Salt Lake City recently obtained

125

Fig. 37. Half-buried and badly weathered headstones

Fig. 37a.

Fig. 38. Revolutionary veteran's tombstone

microfilm copies of cemetery and tombstone record collections from the National DAR Library in Washington, D. C., and has had several miscellaneous published collections for years (fig. 38).

Other groups have also been involved in copying cemetery sextons' records, especially local historians and genealogists. The LDS Church initiated a cemetery copying project several years ago through its wards and branches, and the Genealogical Society Library in Salt Lake City has several hundred volumes of these copied inscriptions.

Parents, grandparents, and even great-grandparents lived into the life of their descendants, and this should be remembered when searching the records. The searcher should not limit himself to a single time period or to a single surname but should consider earlier time periods and all surnames. Genealogical research is actually a series of repeated procedures with only the time period, record source, and locality changing.

After investigating death and burial records, the researcher should move to marriage and then to birth or baptism records for additional information. In practice it may not always be possible to separate these searches because birth, marriage, and death entries may be scattered throughout the record being investigated, but the sequence should be followed when possible.

Marriage Records
With exception of New England towns, the county has been the most important jurisdiction recording marriages in the United States. Many counties and towns initiated marriage registers at the date of their organization and have maintained records since then. Some counties failed to record them at all, and many recorded have been destroyed through neglect or catastrophe. This has caused considerable sorrow among genealogists.

There has been some duplication of marriage registration between state and local offices, but this has helped, not hindered, the genealogist. When a record cannot be obtained from the state office, the searcher should try to obtain one from the county, the town/city, or from the church.

New York and Pennsylvania left marriage registration entirely to the churches prior to 1880 and did not keep civil marriage records in the early days. South Carolina recorded some marriages in the office of the Secretary of State as early as 1778, but the counties were not recording until after the Civil War. Most of the southern and midwestern states were recording marriages on a county basis from the organization of their respective counties.

A variety of marriage documents have been created over the years in America, including applications, banns, bonds, certificates, consent notices, intentions, licenses, proclamations, register entries, and returns. Some ministers also kept diaries and journals where marriage information was recorded. These often remain the personal property of the minister or his family.

Fig. 39 shows a marriage license and return combined. The license is generally issued by county or town officials upon application and payment of a fee. It authorizes the Justice of Peace or a Minister to join the couple in matrimony. After the marriage ceremony has been performed, the official is to return the facts of marriage to the county or town hall where they are recorded. Information contained in the license or return has varied with each county or town but usually includes the names of the parties to be married, the date the license was issued, the place it was issued, and signatures and titles of officials. In some cases, the license includes the ages and places of residence of the bride and groom and sometimes their parentage. The return generally includes the names of the parties, the date and place of marriage, and the signature and title of the officiator. It may not include the ages and places of residence of the consenting parties (fig. 40).

The marriage certificate was usually given to the bride after the ceremony and became her personal property, though some have been filed in county or town offices. The original from which fig. 41 was made measured 24 by 36 inches and was purchased for fifty cents at a farmhouse auction north of Kokomo, Indiana, in 1968.

Some offices did not keep marriage licenses or returns, destroying them after essential facts were recorded in registers. Some recorded the information in special marriage entry books and also retained all related documents (fig. 42).

Many churches kept marriage registers, and some ministers kept diaries and journals where such information was recorded. A few private books have found their way into local libraries and historical societies, but many remain in possession of the ministers or their families. Churches were also permitted to publish "banns" or "proclamations" (usually for two or three consecutive sabbath days) of marriage, and if no protest was registered, the minister could perform the ceremony without license or marriage bond. The minister was still responsible to return a notice for such marriages to the county or town office within a reasonable length of time, generally thirty days. Many Maryland returns are annual.

In New England, the marriage "intention" was similar to the proclamation or banns but was a civil rather than an ecclesiastical record. The intention was usually recorded in the town meeting books and published for a two- or three-week period before the marriage took place. If no protest was registered, the couple could be married by a civil or ecclesiastical officer, evidently without a license. Cynthia B. Putnam and George Eastman filed their intention to be married in York County, Maine, in 1850, but shortly after their

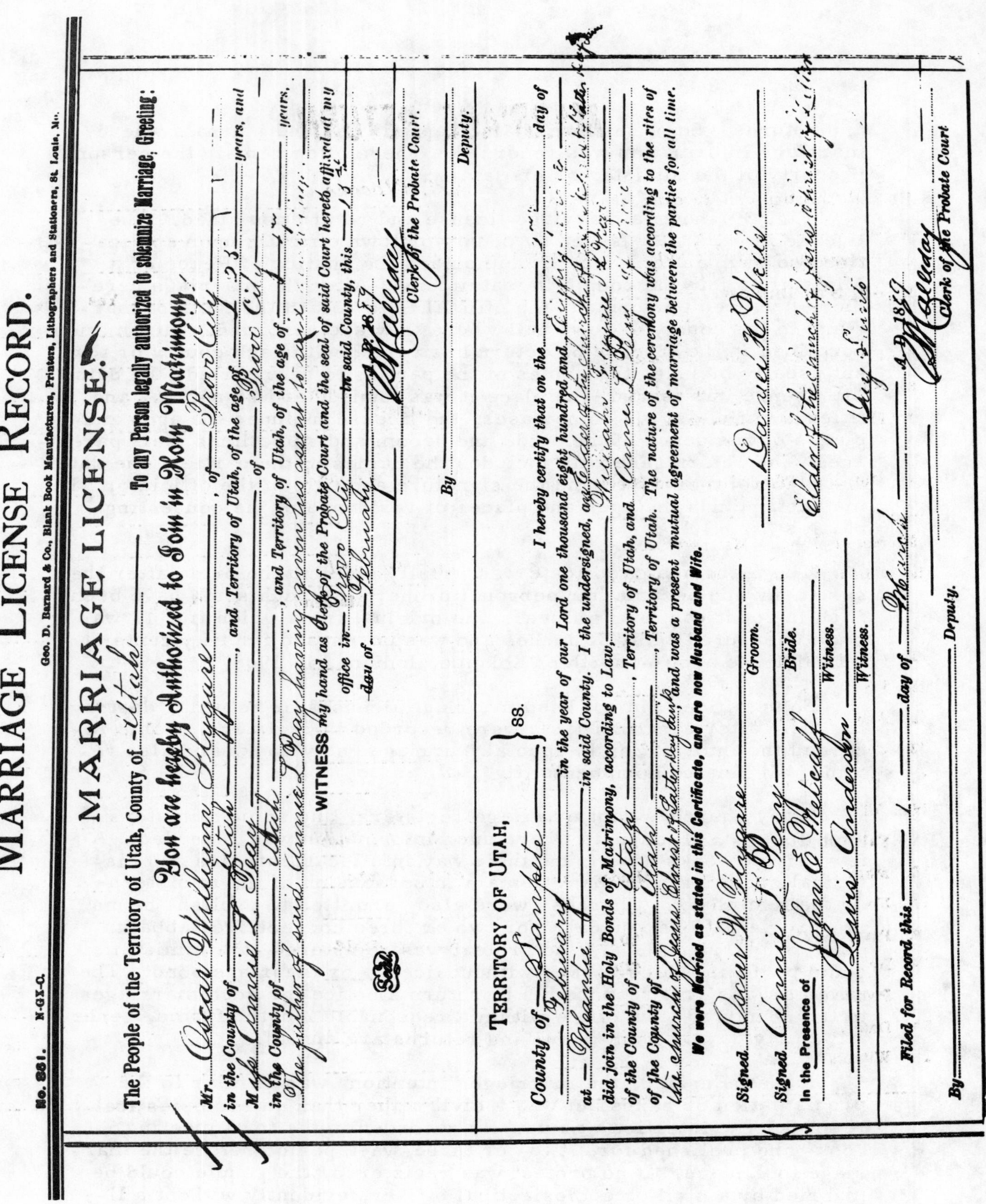

MARRIAGE LICENSE RECORD.

No. 251. N-GX-C.

Geo. D. Barnard & Co., Blank Book Manufacturers, Printers, Lithographers and Stationers, St. Louis, Mo.

MARRIAGE LICENSE.

The People of the Territory of Utah, County of _Utah_ ___ To any Person legally authorized to solemnize Marriage, Greeting:

You are hereby Authorized to Join in Holy Matrimony:

Mr. _Oscar William Hague_ ___ , of _Provo City_

in the County of _Utah_ ___ , and Territory of Utah, of the age of _25_ ___ years, and

Miss _Annie L Peay_ ___ of _Provo City_

in the County of _Utah_ ___ , and Territory of Utah, of the age of _17_ ___ years,

the further of said Annie L Peay having given his consent to such marriage.

WITNESS my hand as Clerk of the Probate Court and the seal of said Court hereto affixed at my

office in _Provo City_ ___ in said County, this _13_

day of _February_ ___ , 18 87.

L M Coliney ___
Clerk of the Probate Court.

By _____ Deputy.

TERRITORY OF UTAH, }
County of _Sanpete_ } 88.

I hereby certify that on the _1st_ ___ day of

February ___ in the year of our Lord one thousand eight hundred and _eighty seven_

at _Pleasant_ ___ in said County. I the undersigned, an Elder of the Church of Jesus Christ of Latter day Saints,

did join in the Holy Bonds of Matrimony, according to Law, _William Hague_ ___

of the County of _Utah_ ___ , Territory of Utah, and _Anna L Peay_ ___

of the County of _Utah_ ___ , Territory of Utah. The nature of the ceremony was according to the rites of

the Church of Jesus Christ of Latter day Saints, and was a present mutual agreement of marriage between the parties for all time.

We were Married as stated in this Certificate, and are now Husband and Wife.

Signed _Oscar W Hague_ ___ Groom.

Signed _Annie L Peay_ ___ Bride.

In the Presence of _John E Metcalf_ ___ Witness.

Lewis Anderson ___ Witness.

David H Wells ___

Elder of the Church of Jesus Christ of Latter day Saints

By _Linzlo_

A. D. 1887

Filed for Record this _1_ ___ day of _March_ ___ ,

L M Coliney ___
Clerk of the Probate Court

By _____ Deputy.

Fig. 39. Combined marriage license and return

130

MARRIAGE RETURN

1. **Full Christian and Surname of Groom** _John W. Bloomer_

2. **Present Residence** _Lafountain Wabash Co._ **No.** _____ **St.**

3. **Age Next Birthday** _22_ _____ **Years** _____

4. **Color** _white_

5. **Present Occupation** _farmer_

6. **Where Born** _Wabash Co., Ind._ **6a. When Born** _____

7. **Full Christian Surname of Father** _Ellis Bloomer_

8. **Mother's Full Christian and Maiden Name** _Julia Stewart_

9. **No. of Groom's Marriage** _1st_

10. **Full Christian and Surname of Bride** _Floy Edith Hubbard_
    Maiden Name, if a Widow

11. **Present Residence** _Washington County, Ind._

11a. **Present Occupation** _____

12. **Age Next Birthday** _22_ _____ **Years** _____

13. **Color** _white_

14. **Where Born** _Lafountain Wabash Co., Ind._

14.a. **When Born** _____

15. **Full Christian and Surname of Father** _Douglas M. Hubbard_

16. **Mother's Full Christian and Maiden Name** _Leona Myers_

17. **No. of Bride's Marriage** _1st_

18. **Place of Marriage** _Paoli, Ind._ **No.** _Orange Co., Ind._ **St.**

19. **By** _Edwin J. Cranford_

Post Office Address _____

20. **Date of Marriage** _June 29, 1911_

21. **Witness** _____

Fig. 40. Marriage return

131

Fig. 41. Marriage certificate

132

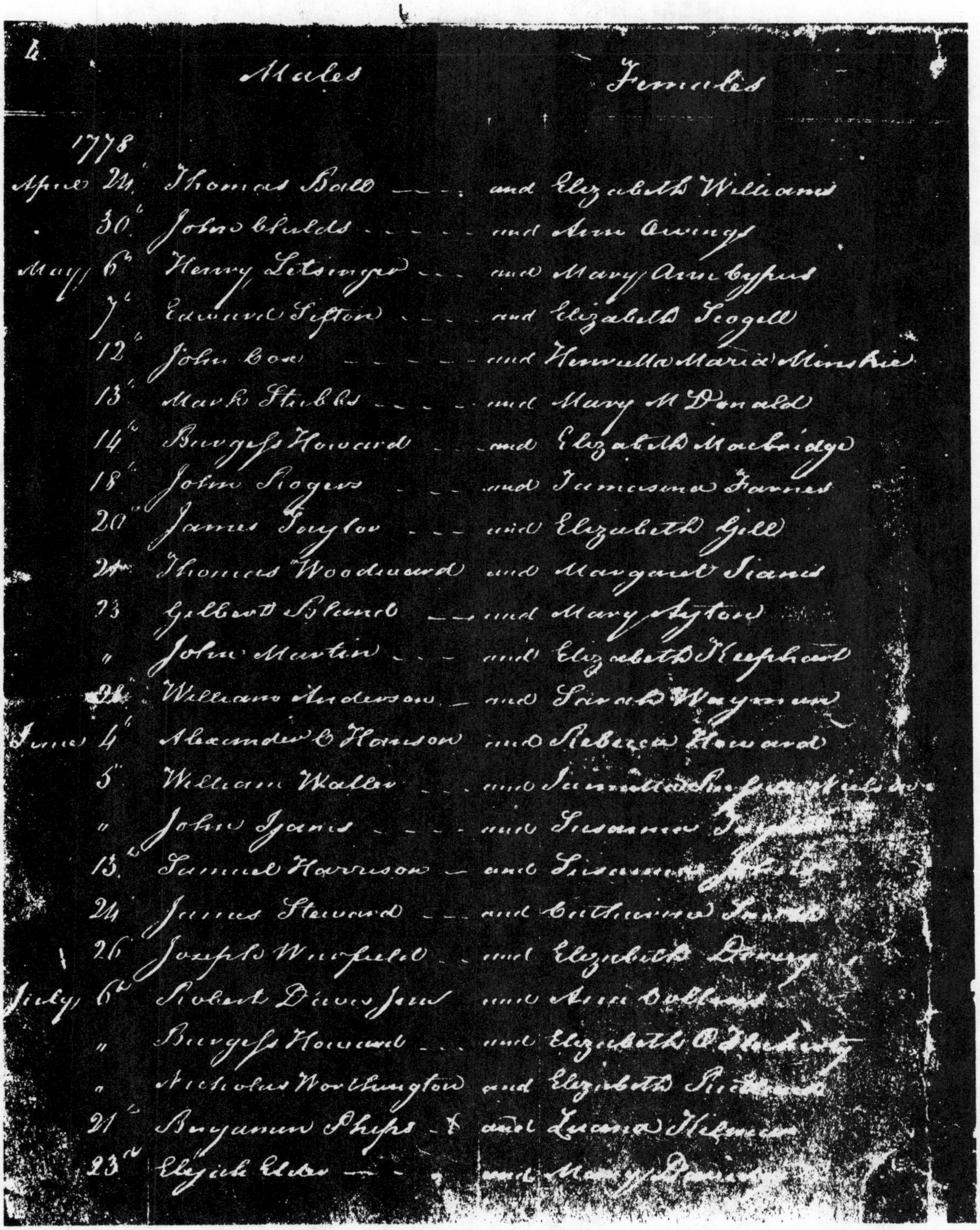

Males   Females

1778

April 24 Thomas Ball   and Elizabeth Williams
    30 John Shields   and Ann Owings
May 6 Henry Litsinger   and Mary Ann Cyrus
    7 Edward Tifton   and Elizabeth Scogell
    12 John Cox   and Henrietta Maria Minskie
    13 Mark Stubbs   and Mary McDonald
    14 Burgess Howard   and Elizabeth Macbridge
    18 John Rogers   and Tamasine Farnes
    20 James Taylor   and Elizabeth Gill
    22 Thomas Woodward   and Margaret Sians
    23 Gilbert Island   and Mary Ayton
    " John Martin   and Elizabeth Keephart
    24 William Anderson   and Sarah Wayman
June 4 Alexander C Hanson   and Rebecca Howard
    5 William Waller   and Jannett Shefield
    " John Sians   and Susanna ___
    13 Samuel Harrison   and Susanna ___
    24 James Steward   and Catharine ___
    26 Joseph Warfield   and Elizabeth ___
July 6 Robert Davis Jun   and Ann ___
    " Burgess Howard   and Elizabeth ___
    " Nicholas Worthington   and Elizabeth ___
    21 Benjamin Phips   and Lucana ___
    23 Elijah Elder   and Mary ___

Fig. 42. Marriage register entries

intention was published a notice appeared in the town records stating that Israel Putnam "forbad the marriage of Cynthia Putnam" because she was his minor. However, Cynthia did marry George, and many Utah and Wyoming people owe their existence to this couple.

In some of the southern states, a marriage bond showing the groom's eligibility to marry was completed after the license has been issued, usually in favor of the Governor. Sometimes this was done at the time the license was issued. In North and South Carolina, Virginia, Kentucky, and some other states, bonds are often the only marriage documents which have been preserved (fig. 43).

In addition to the names of the bride and groom, the bond included the date and place issued, the name of the bondsman (or surety), and the condition of the obligation. The bondsman or surety may have been the parent, a brother or sister, or some other relative to the bride or groom, so this information should be given special attention..

Some persons rightly hesitate to use marriage bonds as proof of marriage, because they do not guarantee the marriage actually took place. However, a majority of the bonds issued were undoubtedly followed by marriage. Of course the certificate, return, or register entry should be located whenever possible because they indicate the date the ceremony was performed.

Sometimes a note or document showing consent of a parent for his minor child to marry is filed among the other courthouse records (fig. 44). They are valuable but were not usually kept in any organized manner until after the nineteenth century. Some are nothing more than penciled notes found between pages of the register. Annulment or cancellation information might also be found in the marriage records, but they are usually a court action, and detail concerning them must be located in the civil-criminal court records (fig. 45).

It is also interesting to note that some counties did not require parent's consent for minors to marry when the bride-to-be was in a "family way" before marriage. A statement from a physician stating "such was the case" was sufficient information to authorize the issuance of a license.

Marriage applications are fairly modern documents, though some exist in Indiana counties as early as 1854. Some contain excellent genealogical information, including the names and ages of the couple, their birth dates and birthplaces, or their residence, their parentage, and their previous marital status (figs. 46 and 47).

Other documents relating to marriage might be located in court, military, land, and other records. Anti-Nuptial Agreements, Marriage Contracts, and Dower-Rights are examples. A widow and a widower might make special arrangements concerning their properties before they marry, or some special agreement for the disposition of their

PHOTOCOPY OF NORTH CAROLINA'S OLDEST EXTANT MARRIAGE BOND, ISSUED 2 JUNE 1741, CHOWAN COUNTY, NORTH CAROLINA, TO JOHN NORCOMB AND ANN BENTLEY.

Fig. 43. Marriage bond

CONSENT OF PARENT OR GUARDIAN TO THE MARRIAGE OF A MINOR

STATE OF UTAH, } ss.
County of _____

I, _____ do solemnly swear that I am the _____

of _____

the person named in the foregoing application for a Marriage License, and do hereby give my consent
to _____ marriage.

Subscribed and sworn to before me this _____ day of _____ 19 _____

Signed in the presence of _____

_____ County Clerk

By _____ Deputy Clerk

_____
_____ Witnesses

CONSENT OF PARENT OR GUARDIAN TO THE MARRIAGE OF A MINOR

STATE OF UTAH, } ss.
County of _____

I, _____ do solemnly swear that I am the _____

of _____

the person named in the foregoing application for a Marriage License, and do hereby give my consent
to _____ marriage.

Subscribed and sworn to before me this _____ day of _____ 19 _____

Signed in the presence of _____

_____ County Clerk

By _____ Deputy Clerk

_____
_____ Witnesses

Fig. 44. Marriage consent notice

136

1
2
3   Plaintiff,   :   C O M P L A I N T
4   vs.   FOR A N N U L M E N T
5
6   Civil No. _____
7   Defendant.   :
8

9   Comes now plaintiff by and through her guardian ad litem and

10 alleges as follows:

11   1. That plaintiff is a resident of Utah County, State of

12 Utah, and has been for more than one year last past.

13   2. That on December 21, 1965, plaintiff and defendant enter-

14 ed into a purported marriage in Clayton, New Mexico.

15   3. That at the time of the purported marriage, plaintiff

16 was mentally ill, and did not have sufficient mental capacity to

17 realize the nature of the contract or the significance thereof,

18 and because of plaintiff's lack of mental capacity, said marriage

19 contract was void in law.

20   4. That there have been no children born as issue of the

21 purported marriage and plaintiff is not pregnant at the present

22 time.

23   5. That it is reasonable and proper that the marriage con-

24 tract should be declared nul and void by this Court.

25   WHEREFORE, plaintiff prays judgment against defendant as

26 follows:

27   1. That the purported marriage be annulled and held for

28 naught from the beginning.

29   Dated and signed at Provo, Utah, this 21st day of September, 1966.

30

31

32   RAY H. IVIE
                             Attorney for Plaintiff
                             48 North University Avenue
                             Provo, Utah

Fig. 45. Annulment record

APPLICATION FOR LICENSE TO MARRY

STATE OF UTAH, } ss.
County of Utah

We, _____ of _____

and _____ of _____

desiring to procure a license to marry, each do solemnly swear that we are single and unmarried and may lawfully contract and be joined in marriage; that we are not related to each other within the fourth degree of consanguinity and that the following detail data is true, according to our best knowledge and belief:

1. County in which issued _____ UTAH _____ . Date issued _____

2. Place of marriage: County _____ City or Town _____ Date of Marriage _____
Title _____

3. Name and address of person officiating _____

Full name **GROOM**	Maiden name **BRIDE**
4.	18.
5. Residence: State _____ County _____	19. Residence: State _____ County _____
City or town _____	City or town _____
6. Color or race _____	20. Color or race _____
7. Age last birthday _____ (Years) 8. Birth date _____	21. Age last birthday _____ (Years) 22. Birth date _____
9. Previous marital status _____ (Single, widowed, or divorced)	23. Previous marital status _____ (Single, widowed, or divorced)
10. Number of this marriage _____ (1st, 2d, 3d, etc.)	24. Number of this marriage _____ (1st, 2d, 3d, etc.)
11. Birthplace _____ (State or country)	25. Birthplace _____ (State or country)
12. Usual occupation _____	26. Usual occupation _____
13. Industry or business _____	27. Industry or business _____
Father { 14. Birthplace _____ (State or country)	Father { 28. Birthplace _____ (State or country)
A. Name _____	A. Name _____
15. Usual occupation _____	29. Usual occupation _____
Mother { 16. Birthplace _____ (State or country)	Mother { 30. Birthplace _____ (State or country)
A. Name - Maiden _____	A. Name - Maiden _____
17. Usual occupation _____	31. Usual occupation _____

(Signed) _____
Male

(Signed) _____
Female

Subscribed and sworn to before me this _____ day of _____ 19 _____

By _____ Deputy Clerk _____

County Clerk.

Fig. 46. Application for marriage license

138

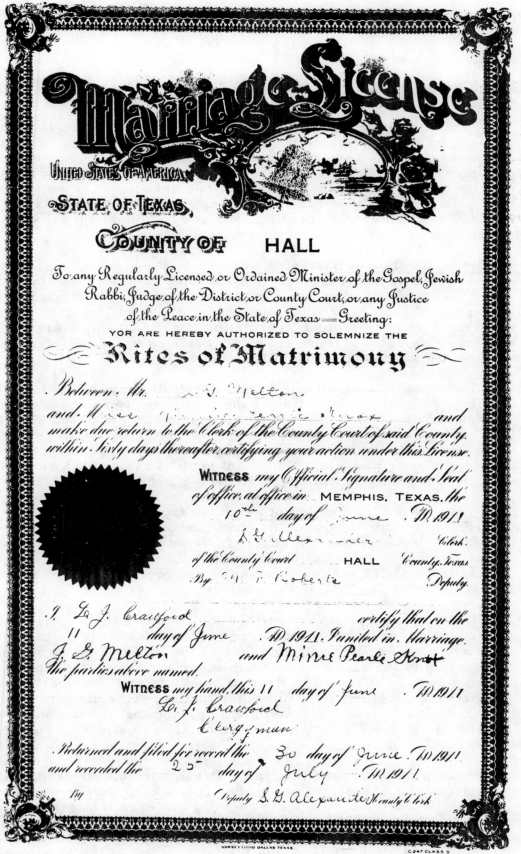

Fig. 47. Marriage license

139

property might be documented before marriage.

It should also be noted that some persons were married by their consent only and not by civil or ecclesiastical authority. Such marriages are usually referred to as common-law marriages and are not documented at first but may be recorded at a later date. Family tradition or the testimony of old-timers and associates is generally the only evidence available for such unions. It is interesting, however, that such marriages are binding, and are considered legal when the couple moves from one state to another.

Birth and Baptism-Christening Records

After death and marriage records have been located and investigated, birth and baptism (or christening) records should be searched. Modern birth records from state offices are very inclusive and contain excellent genealogical information (fig. 48). However, those of an earlier period and those from local offices are usually somewhat lacking in content and availability.

The typical birth record includes the full name of the individual, his place of birth; usually listing the town, county, and state; his birth date and whether the birth was legitimate; his parentage and their ages, residence, color, and occupation; facts concerning previous births for the mother; and the name and address of the attending physician or midwife. Document content varies with each state and also according to time period, even after 1900 (fig. 49).

When a birth record is not available from the state office, the county, town, city, hospital, or church should be considered and their records should be investigated. It might be wise to obtain copies from each jurisdiction because a document from one might include information not found in another; however, the cost of the documents might be a factor to consider.

Birth information is sometimes included in church christening or baptism records and can be used just as effectively as information from civil records. It may be that the christening or baptism information is the only evidence available to confirm a birth, and though they may differ a few days or weeks from the actual birth, they provide excellent substitute information. Of course many churches did not practice infant baptism, and the baptism dates found in their records may pertain to adults or children who are several years old.

Catholic, Episcopal (Anglican), Presbyterian, Congregational, and most of the "Reformed" churches (Lutheran, Dutch, German, etc.) baptized infants, and their records are excellent genealogical sources. However, many of the "pietist" or so-called "Christian" churches did not keep such records, among these American Baptist, Unitarian, and Methodist. Some pietist groups of the eighteenth and nineteenth centuries, the Quakers (Friends) and the Moravians

TEXAS DEPARTMENT OF HEALTH
BUREAU OF VITAL STATISTICS
STANDARD CERTIFICATE OF BIRTH

1. PLACE OF BIRTH

STATE OF TEXAS

COUNTY OF **Hall**

CITY OR PRECINCT NO. **Memphis,**

GIVE STREET AND NUMBER OR NAME OF INSTITUTION

2. FULL NAME OF CHILD **Ronald J. Melton**

RESIDENCE OF THE MOTHER — STREET AND NO. _____ CITY **Memphis** COUNTY **Hall** STATE **Texas**

3. SEX	FOR PLURAL BIRTHS ONLY:		6. LEGITIMATE?	7. DATE OF BIRTH
male	4. TWIN, TRIPLET, OTHER	5. NUMBER. IN ORDER OF BIRTH	**yes**	**March 24th** 19**12**

FATHER	MOTHER
8. FULL NAME John G. Melton	**14. FULL MAIDEN NAME** Minnie Pearl Knox
SOCIAL SECURITY NUMBER	SOCIAL SECURITY NUMBER
9. POSTOFFICE ADDRESS Memphis, Texas	**15. POSTOFFICE ADDRESS** Memphis, Texas.
10. COLOR OR RACE white **11. AGE AT LAST BIRTHDAY** 22 (YEARS)	**16. COLOR OR RACE** white **17. AGE AT LAST BIRTHDAY** 20 (YEARS)
12. BIRTHPLACE (STATE OR COUNTRY) Rockwall, Texas	**18. BIRTHPLACE (STATE OR COUNTRY)** Tennessee
13A. TRADE, PROFESSION OR KIND OF WORK DONE Farmer	**19A. TRADE, PROFESSION OR KIND OF WORK DONE** Housewife
13B. INDUSTRY OR BUSINESS IN WHICH ENGAGED Farm	**19B. INDUSTRY OR BUSINESS IN WHICH ENGAGED** Home
20. NUMBER OF CHILDREN BORN TO THIS MOTHER INCLUDING THIS BIRTH 1	**21. NUMBER OF CHILDREN BORN TO THIS MOTHER AND NOW LIVING** 1
SIGNATURE OF INFORMANT John Gordon Melton	**ADDRESS OF INFORMANT** Wilmington, Calif. XXX

22. MEDICAL ATTENDANCE

I HEREBY CERTIFY THAT I ATTENDED THE BIRTH OF THIS CHILD BORN ALIVE XXXXX AT _____ M. ON THE ABOVE DATE, AND THE PROPHYLACTIC

USED TO PREVENT OPHTHALMIA NEONATORUM WAS _____

3-24-, 19**12** **Chas. F. Wilson** M.D. XXXX **Memphis,** TEXAS
DATE — SIGNATURE — POSTOFFICE ADDRESS

23. FILE NUMBER	FILE DATE	SIGNATURE OF LOCAL REGISTRAR	POSTOFFICE ADDRESS
1212	3-24 .19 12	S. G. Alexander	Memphis, . TEXAS

MILITARY EX-SERVICE RECORD OF FATHER

(A) IS THE FATHER REPORTED TO HAVE BEEN IN SUCH SERVICE?

(B) NAME OF ORGANIZATION IN WHICH SERVICE WAS RENDERED

(C) SERIAL NUMBER OF DISCHARGE PAPERS OR ADJUSTED SERVICE CERTIFICATE

THE STATE OF TEXAS

County of **Hall** }

I hereby certify that the above certificate is a true and accurate copy of the record of birth of _____

Ronald J. Melton _____, filed in my office, and is of record on

Page **24** Vol **2** of the Record of Births of **Hall** County, Texas.

Witness my hand and seal of office this **16th** day of **November** 19 **42.**

G. M. Dial

By *Gladys Johnson* **County Clerk, Hall** County, Texas.
Deputy

Fig. 48. Modern birth record from state office

141

GRANT COUNTY HEALTH DEPARTMENT

MARION, INDIANA

Certificate of Birth

THIS IS TO CERTIFY, That our records show:

Name   James Robert Bloomer

Was born in   Marion, Ind.   GRANT COUNTY, on   September 4   , 19 13

Child of   John Bloomer and Floy Edith Hubbard

Birthplace of father   Indiana   Birthplace of mother   Indiana

Record was filed   9-10-1913   Book No.   9   Page No.   174
                    (Date)

Lester E. Rauharver, M.D.

DEPARTMENT OF HEALTH

(SEAL)

Issued on   August 9, 1967

Fig. 49.   Local birth records

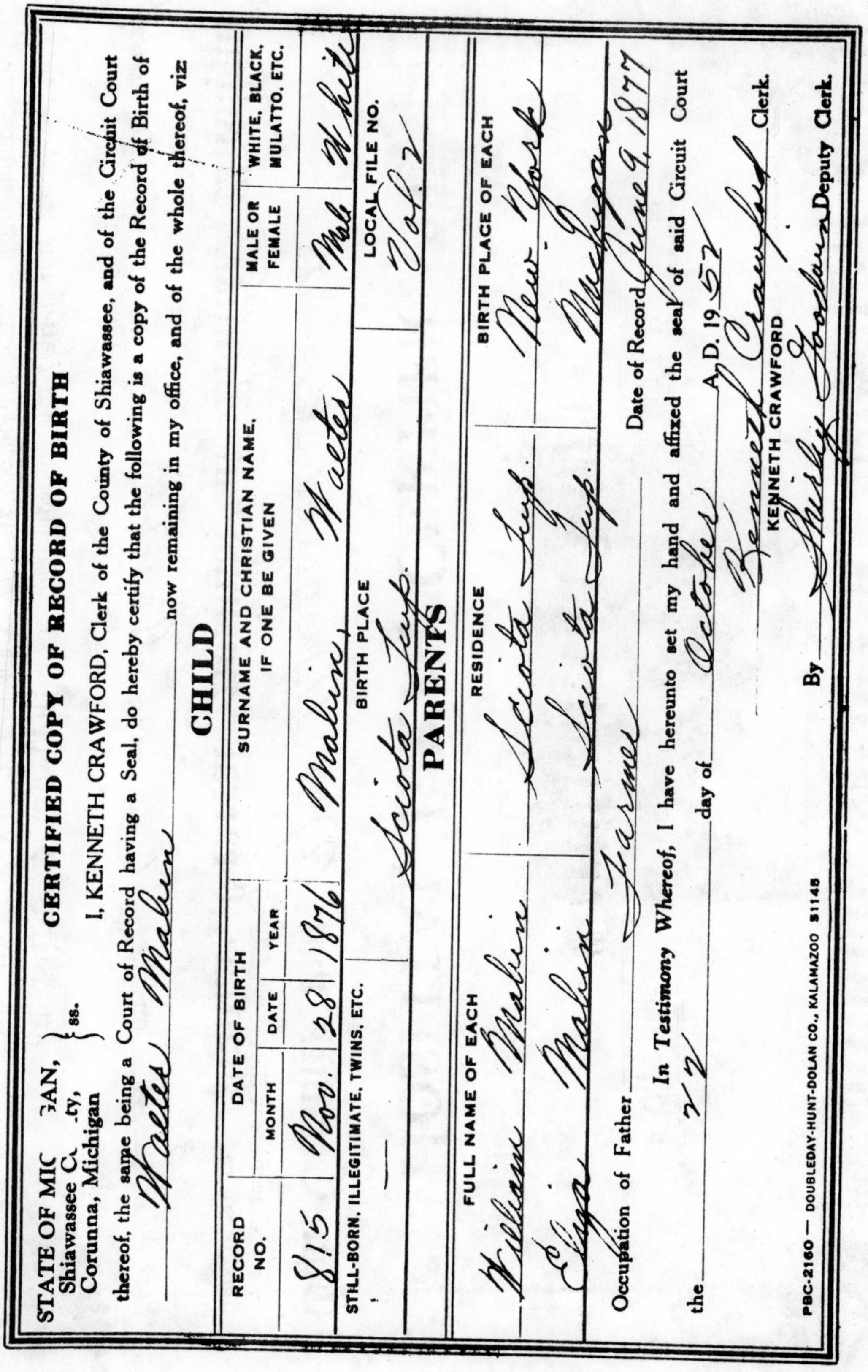

STATE OF MIC GAN, }
Shiawassee C ty, } ss.
Corunna, Michigan }

CERTIFIED COPY OF RECORD OF BIRTH

I, KENNETH CRAWFORD, Clerk of the County of Shiawassee, and of the Circuit Court thereof, the same being a Court of Record having a Seal, do hereby certify that the following is a copy of the Record of Birth of Walter Malin now remaining in my office, and of the whole thereof, viz

CHILD

RECORD NO.	DATE OF BIRTH MONTH	DATE	YEAR	SURNAME AND CHRISTIAN NAME, IF ONE BE GIVEN	MALE OR FEMALE	WHITE, BLACK, MULATTO, ETC.
815	Nov.	28	1876	Malin, Walter	Male	White

STILL-BORN, ILLEGITIMATE, TWINS, ETC.	BIRTH PLACE	LOCAL FILE NO.
—	Sciota Twp.	Vol. 2

PARENTS

FULL NAME OF EACH	RESIDENCE	BIRTH PLACE OF EACH
William Malin	Sciota Twp.	New York
Eliza Malin	Sciota Twp.	Michigan

Occupation of Father Farmer Date of Record June 9, 1877

In Testimony Whereof, I have hereunto set my hand and affixed the seal of said Circuit Court the 22 day of October A.D. 1957

Kenneth Crawford Clerk.
KENNETH CRAWFORD

By Shirley [illegible] Deputy Clerk.

PBC-2160 — DOUBLEDAY-HUNT-DOLAN CO., KALAMAZOO 51145

Fig. 49a.

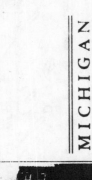
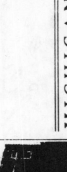

Pontiac General Hospital

PONTIAC   MICHIGAN

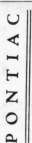

HOSPITAL BIRTH CERTIFICATE

This Certifies that _Mae Margaret Evans_

was born in Pontiac General Hospital of Pontiac, Michigan

at _12 ³¹ p m_ on the _1_ day of _October_ _____ A. D. 19 _44_

In Witness Whereof the said Hospital has caused this Certificate to be signed by its duly authorized officer and its Corporate Seal to be hereunto affixed.

Chas Astley M D Physician

Herbert J H Superintendent

Hospital
Number _G 3203._

Fig. 49b.   144

Thursday December 25th 1845

The weather is still cold and Boreas is still whistling over the plains causing his power to be felt by all living Creatures. It is clear overhead and light under foot; that is there is just snow enough to cover up the dust and make the roads good as well as the bridge over the great Mississippi, which is certainly famous to the poor Saints, in getting their wood.

Pres. J. M. Grant left the Temple at 5: a m. to attend to some matters at home, inasmuch as there was time to do them, the High Priests having permission to work till evening.

Pres. J. Young and Sherman came about 7: am.

Male Department

6:pm

Name		Born		
Lyman A Shurtliff	Born	Mar	12th	1807
Francis Smith	"	Oct	15"	1816
Hiram Moss	"	May	5"	1811
John H Farnham	"	Dec	15"	1799
Samuel Smith	"	June	11"	1807
Augusta A Farnham	"	May	20"	1815
Jesse K. Nichols	"	Sept	15"	1812
Uriah C Brewer	Passover	June	18"	1817
John E. Troxell		Nov	7"	1816
Thomas A Houston (Hessler)	"	Feb	12"	1805
Waldo Littlefield	"	May	24"	1797
Lester Clinton	"	Feby	17"	1813
James Hoyt	"	No date		
Wm S Moore	"	July	19"	1822
John Haron	"	Dec		1816
George Cannon	"	Jan.	11"	1827
Trueman Leonard, Jr.	"	Sept	17"	1820
Jackson Redden (Redding)	"	"	26	1817
Hezekiah Peck	"	Mar	18	1820

Washed by B. L. Clapp, J. D. Lee and A Lytle
Anointed by Jos Clapp & Pres J. M. Grant

Female Department

Name		Born		
S Shurtliff (wife)	Born	Augt	7th	1816
Laura Owens	"	Jany	11"	1806
Mary Ann Hunt (Troxell)	"	Sept	2"	1827
M A Troxell	"	Oct.	28"	1812
Maretta Smith	"	April	20"	1807
Mary A Farnham				

Fig. 49c.

145

for instance, did keep good records. But they were in the minority.

American church records have not been centralized to any great extent and must be found in their respective towns, cities, or villages. The Genealogical Society Library in Salt Lake City has an excellent collection of American church records from the eastern states but has relatively few from the Midwest and Southwest. However, they have an excellent acquisition program and are microfilming in those areas, so their church record collection is constantly growing.

In colonial New England, the Congregational church was predominant with Baptist, Unitarian, Universalist, and Protestant Episcopal (Church of England or Anglican) following, in that order. The Methodist church was popular after 1800 and Quakers (Friends) were there in good numbers, especially in Rhode Island, from the mid 1600s.

The mid-Atlantic states of New York, New Jersey, Pennsylvania, Maryland, and Delaware were a melting pot of ethnic groups, and the church of predominance was that of the national or ethnic group which settled a particular locality. Dutch Reformed congregations were strong in New York, but so were Lutheran and German groups. Congregationalists and Baptists from New England made their way into New York and New Jersey, and their influence was strong after 1700. English Welsh Quakers were strong in southeastern Pennsylvania after 1682, and many pietist groups moved into the southern part of the state after 1700, including Mennonites, Dunkards, and other "anabaptist" groups. The Scotch-Irish moved into Pennsylvania and Maryland in large numbers after 1710 and the Presbyterian church made its mark. The Scotch-Irish also settled in parts of New England, especially New Hampshire, at this same period, and their numbers were significant. West Jersey was primarily Quaker after 1680, but East Jersey and Delaware had a mixture of the other denominations.

The Church of England was the predominant church in the South during the colonial period but many other denominations settled there also. French Huguenots (Protestants) were numerous in Virginia and South Carolina from the early settlement, and Scottish Highlanders (Presbyterians) were strong in North and South Carolina after 1710. Scotch-Irish from Pennsylvania and Maryland moved into the western valleys of Virginia after 1750, and many found their way into Tennessee, Kentucky, and North Carolina by the end of the Revolution. Baptists were numerous in all of the South as were Methodists and other Christian denominations after 1800. Quakers, Moravians, and other pietist or anabaptist groups were also strong in the South after 1700.

E. Kay Kirkham's A SURVEY OF AMERICAN CHURCH RECORDS, vol. 1, 3rd ed. enl. (Logan, Utah: Everton Publishers, 1971) is an excellent listing of church records in America and covers major denominations before 1880. The book includes a majority of the church record listings at the Genealogical Society Library in Salt Lake City, but of course it is not complete.

146

<u>Other Records</u>
Searching vital records is only a beginning in the quest for new facts pertaining to the pedigree. The researcher must next move to other original records, including census, probate, land, military, and a variety of other original records. Their time period, content, and availability must be carefully considered if they are to be used efficiently. Later chapters of this work are designed to present such information for the researcher who is interested in proceeding further in genealogical research.

---

1. Donald Lines Jacobus "The Value of Searching Original Records." THE AMERICAN GENEALOGIST 40 (July 1964):171.

2. Detailed instructions for obtaining vital statistics information can be found in appendix 4.

CHAPTER 8

USING THE CENSUS TO CONFIRM AND TO FIND

Next to vital and church records, census enumerations provide the genealogist with some of his best information. They are great finding tools and often contain kinship and family information which cannot be found in any other source. They are popular with most professionals and few persons need to be convinced of their genealogical value once they have used them. Names, ages, places of birth and death, residence information, marital and military status, citizenship, and a variety of other facts may be gained from them. Some censuses are indexed, but many are not. And though some census records contain error, they can still provide information to confirm facts already known and provide facts which will assist in directing future research.

Federal population enumerations have been taken decennially on a county and state basis since 1790. Existing schedules have been microfilmed and are public for the years 1790-1900. (The 1890 population schedules, however, have been destroyed, except for a few fragments and for veteran's enumerations which were taken concurrently.) The modern schedules, 1910-1970, are confidential, and special requirements must be met to gain information from them. The 1900 schedules have recently been made public, with some restrictions.

Enumerations for the period 1790-1840 are statistical in format and only list the names of heads of households, including women, but enumerations after 1840 list each person by name and give other personal facts.

The official census year was June 1 through May 31, and enumerations were made during the entire twelve-month period; however, in 1880 and later schedules, the enumerators were instructed not to include the names of persons born after June 1 of the census year. Records prior to 1880 may include children born before the date of enumeration, regardless of the time of year.

Mortality schedules (death listings) were also compiled concurrently with the 1850-1880 enumerations, and a few were taken after that date. They are similar in format and content to their corresponding census counterparts and include the names of persons who died during the twelve-month period prior to the census year, that is, during 1849, 1859, 1869, 1879. Unfortunately, the 1890 mortality schedules were consumed by fire in March 1896.

State and local census records vary considerably in time and content. Some were taken much earlier than federal enumerations and some were taken at intervals between the federal censuses. Examples of early enumerations are those for Long Island in 1664 and 1701 and those for Maryland in 1777 and 1778. Some states enumerated their populations prior to statehood--Illinois in 1810, 1818, and 1820 for example. Wisconsin also took a preparatory census in 1836. Most state census records taken after 1840 closely resemble the federal enumerations, but some include special information and statistics, such as the number of years a person resided in that particular county or facts about citizenship and previous places of residence. State enumerations for New York and Kansas were taken decennially between federal enumerations (1855, 1865, 1875) down to a modern period, and the Genealogical Society Library has microfilm copies to about 1915.

Good research sequence would suggest searching the 1850 or 1860 census first and proceeding with later, then earlier enumerations. Special emphasis should be given the 1850-1880 schedules because they include name and age listings of the entire household. Earlier enumerations can also be useful, however, as they are excellent for locating people and giving the researcher an idea of possible ancestral connections.

After investigating the 1850-1880 records, it might be well for the worker to search the 1900 or later enumerations before searching the earlier records. The month and year of birth were included in the 1900 census, and that information may not be available in any other source. Sometimes it is necessary to search the records of several different counties when the place of residence is not known, but usually it is better to learn that information from land or probate records before searching the census.

A good axiom for original research in census records is "pick them up and run them out," that is, locate the family in one census, say the 1850, then follow that family through the 1860, 1870, and 1880 schedules. Then locate the same family or counterparts in the 1840, 1830, 1820, and so on. If this procedure is followed, a much more complete picture of the family can be made, and other relatives may be located who might not be found by other methods. Family group records can be constructed using the census information, and other sources can then be used to supplement the entries.

Federal Census Schedules 1850-1880

The 1850 schedules were the first to list each member of the household by name and are excellent genealogical tools (fig. 50). The 1850 schedules called for the following information:

Heading: Name of the district, precinct, ward, city, or town; the county and state; the day, month, and year of enumeration; and the name of the Assistant Marshal.
Column 1:   Dwelling-house numbered in the order of visitation.
Column 2:   Families numbered in the order of visitation.
Column 3:   Name of every person whose usual place of abode on the first day of June, 1850, was in this family.
Column 4:   Age.
Column 5:   Sex.
Column 6:   Color (White, Black, or Mulatto).
Column 7:   Profession, Occupation, or Trade of each male over 15 years of age.
Column 8:   Value of Real Estate owned.
Column 9:   Place of birth, naming the State, Territory, or Country.
Column 10:   Married within the year.
Column 11:   Attended School within the year.
Column 12:   Persons over 20 years of age who cannot read and write.
Column 13:   Whether deaf and dumb, blind, insane, idiotic, pauper, or convict.

The following is an extract showing Jesse James, the outlaw. in his father's family in the 1850 census:

CLAY COUNTY, MISSOURI

700	Platt Township		28 Sep 1850			351/52	
	732/732	James, Robert	31	Preacher	Ky.	$2100	
		Sarelda	28		Ky.		
		Franklin	10		Mo.		
		Jesse W.	4		Mo.		
		Susan	9/12		Mo.		

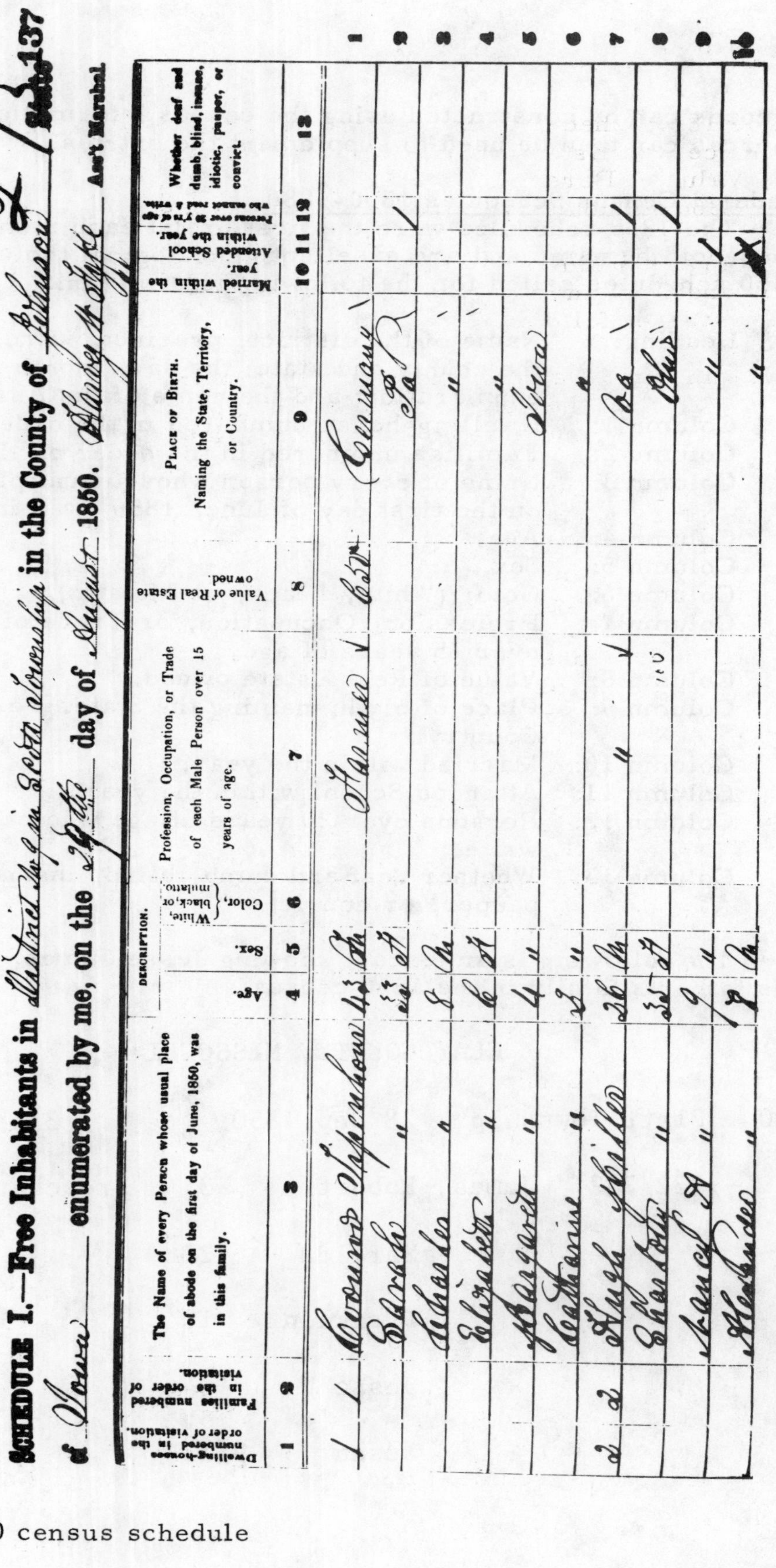

Fig. 50. 1850 census schedule

The 1860 schedules were identical to the 1850, except that the Post Office was listed in the heading and column 8 was divided to include "Value of Personal Estate." This resulted in fourteen columns for the 1860 schedules (fig. 51).

Federal schedules for 1870 and 1880 differed somewhat from those of 1850 and 1860 and included more personal information. Format of the 1870 was as follows:

Heading: Name of the district, precinct, ward, city, or town; the county and state; the day, month, and year of enumeration; the post office; and the name of the Assistant Marshal.

Column 1: Dwelling-houses numbered in the order of visitation.

Column 2: Families, numbered in the order of visitation.

Column 3: The name of every person whose place of abode on the first day of June, 1870, was in this family.

Column 4: Age at last birthday. If under 1 year, give months in fractions, thus 3/12.

Column 5: Sex (Males-M), (Females-F).

Column 6: Color (White-W), (Black-B), (Mulatto-M), (Chinese-C), (Indian-I).

Column 7: Profession, Occupation, or Trade of each person, male or female.

Column 8: Value of Real Estate owned.

Column 9: Value of Personal Estate.

Column 10: Place of birth, naming State or Territory of U.S.; or the Country, if of foreign birth.

Column 11: Father of foreign birth.

Column 12: Mother of foreign birth.

Column 13: If born within the year, state month (Jan., Feb., etc.).

Column 14: If married within the year, state month (Jan., Feb., etc.).

Column 15: Attended school within the year.

Column 16: Cannot read.

Column 17: Cannot write.

Column 18: Whether deaf and dumb, blind, insane, or idiotic.

Column 19: Male Citizens of U.S. of 21 years of age and upwards.

Column 20: Male Citizens of U.S. of 21 years of age and upwards, whose right to vote is denied or abridged on other grounds than rebellion or other crime.

Columns 7, 16, and 17 were not to be asked with regard to infants and numbers 11, 12, 15, 16, 17, 19, and 20 were to be answered, if applicable, merely by making a mark in the proper column. Perhaps columns 11 and 12 were the single most important addition to the 1870 over the 1860 census. Most enumerators in the 1870 and 1880 schedules listed surname first followed by given names, but those working the 1850 and 1860 schedules listed the names in the order spoken.

The 1880 schedules included the relationship of each person to the

SCHEDULE 1.—Free Inhabitants in *Manchester District* in the County of *Carroll* State of *Maryland* enumerated by me, on the 26th day of *July* 1860. *J. H. Busby* Ass't Marshal.

Post Office *Manchester.*

Dwelling	Family	Name	Age	Sex	Color	Profession, Occupation, or Trade	Value of Real Estate	Value of Personal Estate	Place of Birth				Remarks
757	758	Joseph Shanor	31	m		Farmer	1200		Md				
		Matilda	29	f					"				
		Davis	5	m					"				
		Mary	7	f					"				
		Alexander	6	m					"				
		Manual	5	f					"				
		Joseph	4	m					"				
		Marina	1	f					"				
758	759	Frederick Vaders	27	m		Cooper	600	50	Saxony Germany				
		Christena	24	f					"				
		Frederick	3	m					Md				
		Davis	1	m					"				
759	760	Grahal Hammond	35	m		Farmer	1500	500	Bavaria Germany				
		Margaret	35	f					"				
		Elizabeth	15	f					Pa		1		
		Davis	6	m					Md				
		Leonora	3	f					"				
760	761	Jacob Shanor	32	m		Farmer	2500	800	"				
		Christian	30	f					"				
		Henry	3	m					"				
		William	1	m					"				
761	762	Elizabeth Shanor	65	f		Farmer	900	200	Pa				
		Maryann	39	f					Md				
		Andrew Stone	35	m					"				
762	763	Joseph Shanor	30	m		Farmer	1400	400	"				
		Matilda	29	f					"				
		Davis	8	m					"		1		
		Amanda	4	f					"				
763	764	Daniel Smith	26	m		Farmer	800	150	"				
		Catharine	19	f					"				
		William	1	m					"				
764	765	Paul Ticket	45	m		Laborer		100	Hanover Germany				
		Susan	30	f					Baden Germany				
		Mary	9	f					Md		1		
		John	7	m					"		1		
		Simon	5	m					"				
		George	4	m					"				
		Adam	2	m					"				
765	766	Joseph Shambach	65	m		Laborer	800	50	Pa				
		Lydia	50	f					Md				

No. white males 23   No. colored males ____   No. foreign born ____   No. blind ____

No. white females 17   No. colored females ____   No. deaf and dumb ____   No. insane ____

Fig. 51. 1860 census schedule

154

head of the household and also called for the place of birth of parents for each person listed. This has been a great help to the genealogist.

The page number, the Supervisor's District number, and the Enumeration District number were to be listed in the upper left-hand corner of each schedule (fig. 52). Three special notes were included before the schedules themselves:

NOTE A: The census year begins 1 June 1879 and ends 31 May 1880.

NOTE B: All persons will be included in the enumeration who were living on the 1st day of June 1880. Children born since June 1, 1880 will be omitted. Members of families who have died since June 1, 1880 will be included.

NOTE C: Questions Nos. 13, 14, 22 and 23 are not to be asked in respect to persons under 10 years of age.

Heading: Name of the district, precinct, ward, city, township, town; county and state; the day, month, and year of the enumeration; and the name of the enumerator.

An unnumbered column on the left side of each schedule was to contain the name of the street and the house number of the resident when they lived in a city but few entries have any information recorded in that column.

Column 1: Dwelling-house numbered in the order of visitation.

Column 2: Families numbered in the order of visitation.

Column 3: The name of each person whose place of abode on the 1st day of June 1880 was in this family.

Column 4: Color; White W, Black B, Mulatto M, Chinese C, Indian I.

Column 5: Sex; Male M, Female F.

Column 6: Age at last birthday prior to June 1, 1880. If under 1 year of age, give month in fractions, thus 3/12.

Column 7: If born within the year give the month.

Column 8: Relationship of each person to the head of the family, whether wife, son, daughter, servant, boarder or other.

Column 9: Single.

Column 10: Married.

Column 11: Widowed - Divorced.

Column 12: Married during census year.

Column 13: Profession, Occupation, or Trade of each person, male or female.

Column 14: Number of months this person has been unemployed during the census year.

Column 15: Is the person (on the day of the Enumerator's visit) sick or temporarily disabled so as to be unable to

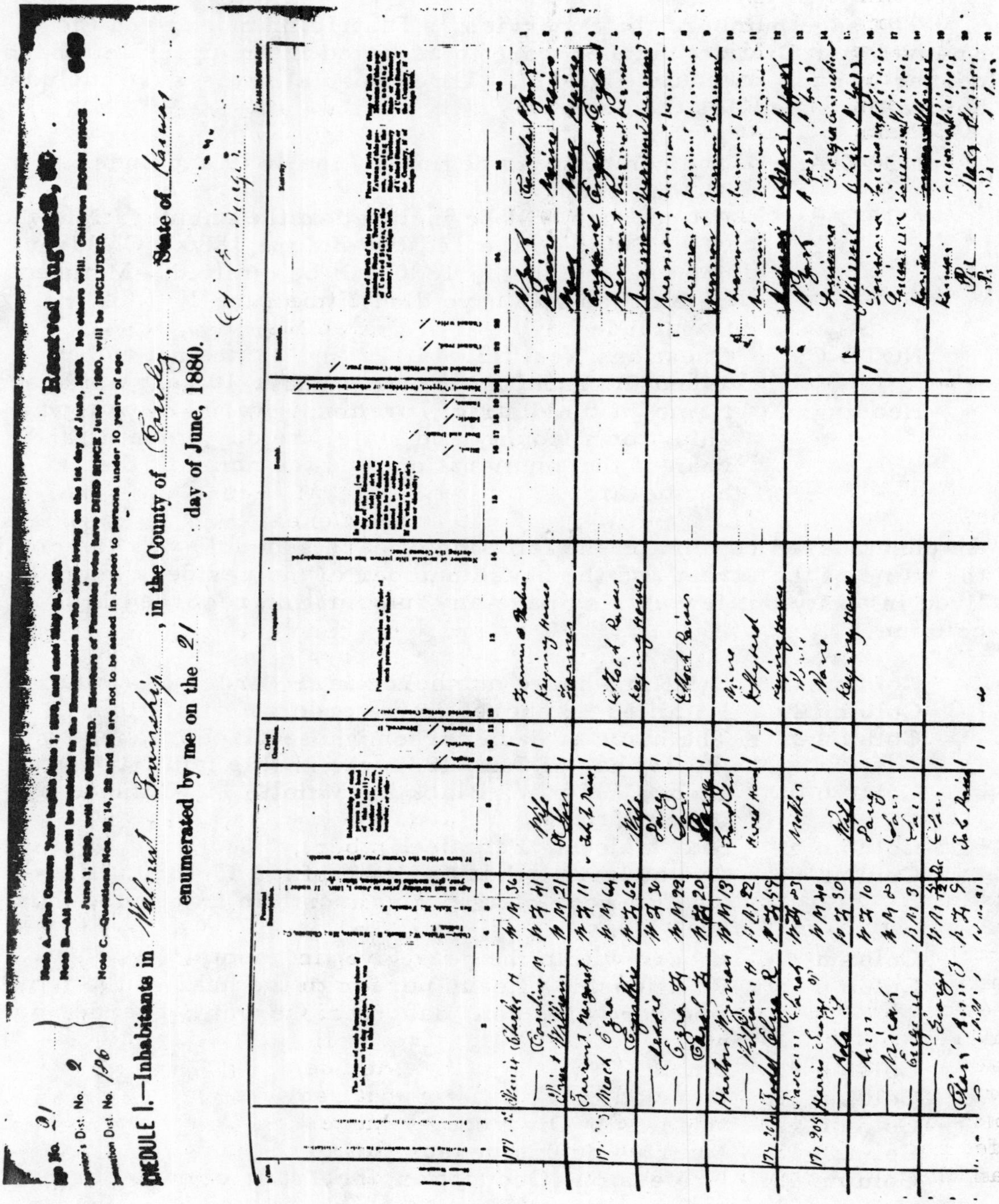

Fig. 52. 1880 census schedule

156

attend to ordinary business or duties. If so what is the nature of the disability.

Column 16: Blind.

Column 17: Deaf and dumb.

Column 18: Idiotic.

Column 19: Insane.

Column 20: Maimed, crippled, bedridden or otherwise disabled.

Column 21: Attended school within the census year.

Column 22: Cannot read.

Column 23: Cannot write.

Column 24: Place of birth of this person, naming State or Territory of United States, or the Country if of foreign birth.

Column 25: Place of birth of the father of this person, naming the State or Territory of United States, or the Country if of foreign birth.

Column 26: Place of birth of the mother of this person, naming the State or Territory of United States, or the Country if of foreign birth.

A SOUNDEX (partial index) to the 1880 federal census has been constructed, and film copies are on file at the Genealogical Society Library and at BYU. The index is by state or territory and is arranged phonetically by the name of the heads of households. It includes all persons living in households where there were children ten years of age or younger. When an elderly couple was living alone or when a family did not have a member ten years of age or under, they were not indexed and must be located in the original schedules.

The soundex cards do not show all facts which were contained in the originals, so they must be used together with the original schedules for maximum benefit. Reference to the original record is listed in the upper right-hand corner of each card, giving volume number, enumeration district, sheet number (page number), and the line number of the original entry. The name of the head of the family is listed at the top of each card and shows color, sex, age, and birthplace. The county of residence is listed along with the "M.C.D." (Municipal Civil District) which is usually the township. Space for the house number, street number, and the city is also provided. The lower half of each card is used to identify other members of the family, by name and relationship to the head of the family, as well as age and birthplace. The place of birth of parents is not included on the soundex cards and must be determined from the original schedules. Continuation cards are used when additional space is necessary, and cross-reference cards are filed for children when the surname is different than that of the head of the family with whom they are living (fig. 53).

The soundex filing system is alphabetical for the first letter of the surname and then numerical as indicated by special divider cards in the original file. This keeps names of the same and similar sound, but which have variant spellings, together. A guide to the soundex system follows.

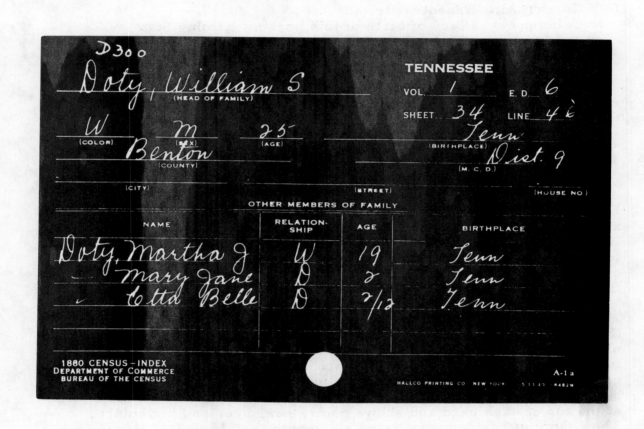

Fig. 53.   Example card from 1880 Soundex

158

Code	Key Letters and Equivalents
1	b, p, f, v
2	c, s, k, g, j, q, x, z
3	d, t
4	l
5	m, n
6	r

The letters a, e, i, o, u, y, w, and h are <u>not</u> coded.
The first letter of a surname is <u>not</u> coded.

Every Soundex number must be a 3-digit number. A name yielding no code numbers, as Lee, would thus be L 000; one yielding only one code number would have two zeros added, as Kuhne, coded as K 500; and one yielding two code numbers would have one zero added, as Ebell, coded as E 140. Not more than three digits are used, so Ebelson would be coded as E 142, <u>not</u> E 1425.

When two key letters or equivalents appear together, or one key letter immediately follows or precedes an equivalent, the two are coded as one letter, by a single number, as follows: Kelly, coded as 400; Buer<u>ck</u>, coded as 620; <u>Ll</u>oyd, coded as 300; and <u>Sch</u>aefer, coded as 160.

If several surnames have the same code, the cards for them are arranged alphabetically by given name. There are divider cards showing most code numbers, but not all. For instance, one divider may be numbered 350 and the next one 400. Between the two divider cards there may be names coded 353, 350, 360, 364, 365, and 355, but instead of being in numerical order they are interfiled alphabetically by given name.

Such prefixes to surnames as "van," "Von," "Di," "de," "Di," "D'," "dela," or "du" are sometimes disregarded in alphabetizing and in coding.

The following names are examples of Soundex coding and are given only as illustrations.

Name	Letters Coded	Code No.
Allricht	l, r, c	A 462
Eberhard	b, r, r	E 166
Engebrethson	n, g, b	E 521
Heimbach	m, b, c	H 512
Hanselmann	n, s, l	H 524
Henzelmann	n, z, l	H 524
Hildebrand	l, d, b	H 431
Kavanagh	v, n, g	K 152
Lind, Van	n, d	L 530
Lukaschowsky	k, s, s	L 222
McDonnell	c, d, n	M 235
McGee	c	M 200
O'Brien	b, r, n	O 165
Opnian	p, n, n	O 155
Oppenheimer	p, n, m	O 155

Name	Letters Coded	Code No.
Riedemanas	d, m, n	R 355
Zita	t	Z 300
Zitzmeinn	t, z, m	Z 325

The soundex to the 1880 census is an excellent finding tool, and each person born in the 1870s should be included. When the town or county of birth is unknown but the state is known, the soundex can be used to locate the family; it might also be possible to locate the family even when the state is not known, if one is willing to search the alphabetical listings for two or more states.

Unfortunately, the 1890 federal census schedules were destroyed, and only fragments and veteran's enumerations for that year remain. Fragments of the 1890 schedules are contained on three rolls of microfilm at BYU and include part of Perry County, Alabama; part of the District of Columbia; part of Muscogree County, Georgia; part of McDonough County, Illinois; part of Wright County, Minnesota; part of Hudson County, New Jersey; parts of Westchester and Suffolk counties, New York; parts of Gaston and Cleveland counties, North Carolina; parts of Hamilton and Clinton counties, Ohio; part of Union County, South Dakota; and parts of Ellis, Hood, Rush, Trinity, and Kaufman counties in Texas.

Veteran's enumerations for 1890 have been preserved and have been microfilmed by state. No ages or places of birth are listed in the schedules, but they can be used to provide places of residence and give information about military units and organizations of assignment.

Even when census records are available, problems arise in securing correct information from them. For instance, the legibility of each census enumeration varies considerably, according to the education and writing skills of the enumerator, the type of ink, the kind of paper used. Even microfilming techniques used on them affect the legibility of the records, and it may be necessary to consult the originals in the National Archives in order to decipher them correctly. The original filming of the 1860 and 1870 schedules was done by the National Archives and was not of the best quality. Both sets have recently been refilmed, and copies are at the Genealogical Society Library in Salt Lake City. The first filming of the 1860 was a double frame arrangement where two pages of the original were included on one microfilm frame. The refilming includes only one page per frame, so the picture is much larger and easier to read. Film copies of the 1870 schedules at Salt Lake were originally reverse exposures, that is, white writing on a black background, and are very hard to read, but the new copies are black on white and are of a much higher quality.

Some census entries defy interpretation, even by experts searching the originals. Some clues to deciphering are useful to know. For instance, the method of entering names has varied with each enumerator.

Sometimes he listed the head of the household by his given name and surname but listed other members by initials or by first name only. Sometimes the surname was "dittoed" after the first entry or even left blank; other times it was written for each entry. The "Color" column in the 1850 and 1860 schedules was often left blank if the person was white, but if he was Black or Mulatto, a "B" or "M" was entered. Negro slaves were enumerated and often took names very similar to those of their owners; however, schedules prior to 1850 listed no slave names but merely statistics by sex and age groupings.

The place of birth should always be carefully noted in the later records as it may lead to other sources. The enumerator was instructed to list only the state, territory, or country of birth but some listed the county or even the town of birth. Enumerations for Kane County, Utah, in 1880 included the English parish of birth for many persons residing in Duncan's Retreat (actually in Washington County but enumerated by the Kane County Marshal), but of course this is the exception rather than the rule.

Sometimes unusual abbreviations are used and duplicate listings are dittoed or left blank. It may be necessary to evaluate the writing on several pages in order to determine the system a particular enumerator was using. Pennsylvania might be abbreviated "Pa.", "Penn.", or "Penna.", or it might be spelled out. Likewise, Connecticut can be found entered as "Ct.", "Cn.", "Conn." and "Cnct." The reader must evaluate several entries and determine how the enumerator formed various letters and how he made particular entries. This procedure should also be followed when deciphering names and other facts.

Before searching the records, it is a good idea to take careful notice of how each surname sounds as well as how it is spelled. Many unusual spellings will be noticed in the records, and if the names are sounded out loud, they are sometimes easier to recognize when searching the records.

A researcher should not be too concerned when the ages and places of birth do not correspond with known family information. Census records are notoriously inaccurate. Male members of a family seem to gain more than ten years between each enumeration, while females only gain seven or eight years during the same period. This is not unusual even in modern times. Amos Harris and his wife Emily Jane were located in federal schedules of Carroll County, Maryland; Schyler County, Illinois; and Smith County, Kansas, each time with differences in names, ages, and places of birth.

1850 - Carroll County, Maryland

Amos Harris	age 28	born Maryland
Emiley	age 21	born Maryland

1860 - Schuler County, Illinois

Amis Harras	age 32	born Illinois
Emily Jane	age 28	born Maryland

1870 - Schuyler County, Illinois

Amos Harris	age 47	born Canada
Emily J.	age 37	born Illinois

1880 - Smith County, Kansas

Amis Harris	age 59	born Maryland
Emily	age 51	born Maryland

The names and ages of their children also varied considerably. Perhaps the informant did not really know the correct ages and places of birth; maybe a neighbor was called upon to provide the information.

Individuals and families have also been known to be listed more than once in the same enumeration. The family may have been enumerated in one county and then moved to another before its census had been taken. Or a person may have been visiting friends or relatives and appear in their family listing as well as in his own. Harrison Long appears in the 1850 census of Athens County, Ohio, in two different households, in two different townships, with two different ages and places of birth, though it is known he is the same person in both cases. He is listed as age "83," born in "Va.," in Rome Township and is living with his son-in-law Arastus Buckley. Harrison Long also is listed in Canaan Township, age "84," born in "Md." But this time he is living with "Wheeler Warren," another son-in-law. Which is the correct listing? Another family was listed in both Davis and Salt Lake Counties in Utah in the 1850 federal census. When the facts found in both records were compared with family information, details came to light concerning a "second wife and her children" who were not previously known.

Census records can be helpful in supplying primary information or in verifying data, though care must be taken to correctly analyze and evaluate this often highly circumstantial evidence. A few years ago, a young black student at Brigham Young University was able to trace her ancestry four generations using the census as her primary source. She was able to locate good information on collateral relatives as well, and she compiled a good record using the census and family information as her source. On another occasion, an individual was able to verify certain facts which indicated he descended from a slave. Using family information, he located his people in the 1880, 1870, and 1860 censuses of a Tennessee county. In these records his apparent ancestor was shown to be "Mulatto" in a white family. The 1850 schedule listed a "Negro Winch," age "32," as living with the family. This individual was also listed in the 1860 census, and a young male child--age "5," color "M"--was listed immediately under her entry. It was this child who was apparently the ancestor of the researcher. The child--age "16," color "M"--also appeared with the family in the 1870 census, but by 1880 he had married and had a family of his own. The entry located for him in the 1880 census also listed "color M." Was the evidence too circumstantial to lead to a correct conclusion? Sometimes census records can bring "ticklish" detail that is for some reason or other unknown in a family. One researcher located the record of an ancestor in the 1850 census of Kentucky. This ancestor was living with her son-in-law at the time, and column 13 of the schedule listed her "Insane." (Upon discovering this entry, the modern descendant said, "Huh! Anyone living in Kentucky in 1850 was insane.")

An American Fork, Utah, family had been unable to extend a particular line because of missing information. The census helped to make the connection. Their ancestor (William B.) was shown in the 1880 census of Utah County as age "22" and born in "Illinois." A death entry for him in an LDS ward record gave his birth date as "1858" and his birthplace as "Alton, Madison, Ill." The 1850 census of Madison County, Illinois, was searched, and a likely family was found. But of course the ancestor was not listed, because he had not been born by 1850. The 1860 schedules were investigated and the same family was located, this time listing a "William B." who fit the description of the Utah man, but not including "Joseph" who was listed at the head of the household in 1850. Perhaps he had died or was visiting relatives in another county, the researchers thought. A thorough search of the entire county was undertaken, and a person of the right name, age, and birthplace was located. Where was he? At Alton, in the "State Prison." Column 13 of the entry indicated "Joseph" was a "Horse Thief."

Before finishing with census records, it is usually a good procedure to search the entire county in order to make certain a proper investigation has been made (though this may not be wise for larger metropolitan cities). One should also consider other families in the same localities who have the same surnames, because they may be related. The man down the street two houses may be a brother or even the father.

It might also be necessary to repeat census searches from time to time when new information has been determined. One may not have known the maiden surname of the wife at the time a particular search was made and may want to look at the census again when the new name is known. Perhaps her family is listed in the same area but were overlooked because the surname was not known when the first search was made. Her parents, brothers and sisters, cousins, aunts and uncles, and even her grandparents may have been listed in the same census.

A single search, or even a county-wide search, which fails to yield results does not necessarily indicate that there is no record of the family in question. People do not always appear in the county enumeration which is supposed to include them. Sometimes they were enumerated by a marshal from an adjoining county or were living with other relatives in a county more distant. Persons may also own real estate in two or three different counties and might be living away from their usual residence when the census was taken. It is also possible the researcher's basic information is incorrect, and that is why the family cannot be located in the county being searched. One must use imagination along with known information to find some families. When the birthplaces of children are known, or when other events have been identified by time and place, these can be helpful in determining places of residence for census purposes.

Other sources can also be used to locate families in a particular census year--land, probate, court, and military records, for instance. Deeds showing land title transfer are excellent to list previous and present places of residence. Probate records also often include information about localities where relatives live. A son may have moved from the Kentucky ancestral home to an Illinois county many years prior to his father's death, and when the father's estate is probated, reference may be found in court records of the Illinois county as well as the Kentucky county where the father died. Relatives in the East may be mentioned in records of the family in the West, and movement patterns can sometimes be plotted from such records. In a Virginia county court order book, there was reference to an "8 shilling account" which an administrator had used to purchase whiskey "for the long ride into Lincoln County, Kentucky" to inventory property of the deceased.

Federal Mortality Schedules
     Mortality schedules taken concurrently with the 1850-1880 federal census enumerations may also be helpful in locating families in the census year or may provide additional facts to make the family record more complete. As mentioned previously, they contain the names of persons who died during the twelve-month period prior to the census year, or during 1849, 1859, 1869, and 1879.

The 1850 and 1860 schedules were identical in content, listing the names of persons who died during the year ending June 1. They included the following information:

Heading:	Name of the district, precinct, ward, city, or town; the county and state; and the name of the Assistant Marshal.
Column 1:	Name of every person who died during the year ending 1st of June (1850 or 1860) whose usual place of abode at the time of death was in this family.
Column 2:	Age.
Column 3:	Sex.
Column 4:	Color (White, Black, or Mulatto).

164

Column 5:	Free or Slave.
Column 6:	Married or widowed.
Column 7:	Place of Birth, Naming the State, Territory or County.
Column 8:	The Month in which the person died.
Column 9:	Profession, Occupation, or Trade.
Column 10:	Disease or cause of death.
Column 11:	Number of days ill.

The 1870 schedules included the following information (fig. 54):

Heading:	Name of the district, precinct, ward, city, or town; county or territory; and the name of the Assistant Marshal.
Column 1:	Number of the family as given in the same area of schedule 1 (the 1870 census enumeration).
Column 2:	Name of every person who died during the year ending June 1st, 1870 whose place of abode at the time of death was in this family.
Column 3:	Age last birth day. If under one year, give months in fractions, thus 3/12.
Column 4:	Sex (Male-M), (Female-F).
Column 5:	Color (White-W), (Black-B), (Mulatto-M), (Chinese-C), (Indian-I).
Column 6:	Married (M), Widowed (W).
Column 7:	Place of Birth, Naming State or Territory of U.S.; or the Country, if of foreign birth.
Column 8:	Father of foreign birth.
Column 9:	Mother of foreign birth.
Column 10:	The month in which the person died.
Column 11:	Profession, Occupation or Trade.
Column 12:	Disease or cause of death.

There was also a "Remarks" column at the bottom of the schedules where the Marshal could note special situations and circumstances. The Marshal who completed the above Arizona schedule said: "In making the enumeration, I find a very few deaths when they are of any family so I am not able to fill Column No. 1 as required by the regulations. I report a great many violent deaths, this being a frontier country where all disputes are settled by the use of weapons and occure between transients and single men who have no families."

The 1880 federal schedules contain all the information included in the 1870 schedules plus a listing for the birthplaces of parents of the deceased.

An interesting article concerning federal mortality schedules was included in the NATIONAL GENEALOGICAL SOCIETY QUARTERLY 31 (June 1943):45-46. Dr. Jean Stephenson, who edited the article, commented on the fortunate preservation of the schedules:

165

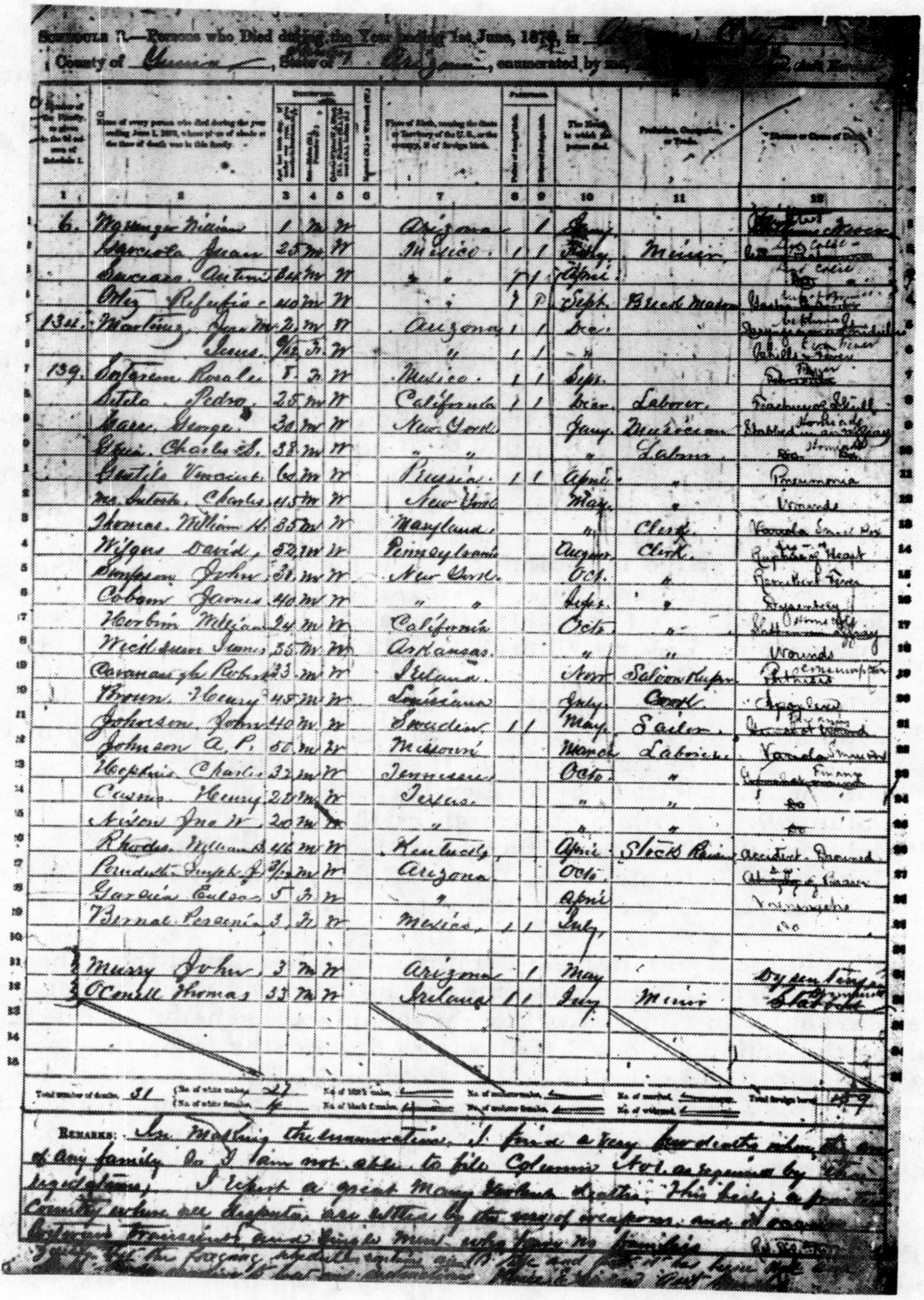

Fig. 54. 1870 mortality schedule

A number of years ago, when the mortality schedules had served their purpose and the matter of their destruction as useless papers arose, the Daughters of the American Revolution requested them. After consideration by the appropriate committees of Congress, the Director of the Census was authorized to return each schedule to the state concerned by presentation to the State Library, Archives or similar department, or to a recognized historical society of the state, at the request of such state agency or historical society, or in the absence of such request, to give them to the Daughters of the American Revolution in Washington.

Dr. Stephenson then listed the existing schedules along with their locations. The same information and list were reproduced on pages 251-55 of Derek Harland's GENEALOGICAL RESEARCH STANDARDS (Salt Lake City: Bookcraft, 1963), and similar lists have been placed in circulation among genealogists.

The list, however, is apparently incomplete and incorrect in some respects. Mr. W. Neil Franklin recently included a more current list in an article entitled "Availability of Federal Mortality Census Schedules, 1850-85," in volume 52, pp. 205-209 of the NATIONAL GENEALOGICAL SOCIETY QUARTERLY (GS #973 BZng). Among other things, Mr. Franklin said:

> The coverage of the Stephenson list was restricted to the mortaliy census schedules that were distributed by the Bureau of the Census in 1918 and 1919. In that list, therefore, no reference was made to the 1885 mortality schedules for 3 States and 2 Territories. These schedules, however, are available and this fact adds to the desirability of an updated version of the Stephenson list.
> Nearly all of the 1890 mortality census schedules were consumed in a fire of March 1896. The remnant schedules, moreover, had been so damaged that they were destroyed by order of the Department of the Interior. It is doubtful, therefore, that a single completed 1890 mortality schedule is available.
> The 1900 mortality census schedules were destroyed before World War I. Those for 1900 were the last of the mortality schedules created in connection with Federal decennial censuses. As directed by the Act approved March 6, 1902, which established the Bureau of the Census as a permanent agency, the Bureau has since obtained mortality data directly from records maintained by States and municipalities. These twentieth century data, unlike those included in the nineteenth century schedules, do not include the names of the persons to whom they relate.

His list follows:

Alabama
    State Department of Archives and History, Montgomery, Alabama, 1850-80.

Arizona
    National Archives, Washington, D. C., 1870-80.
    Library, National Society, Daughters of the American
    Revolution, Washington, D. C., 1870-80.
Arkansas
    Department of Archives and History, Little Rock, Arkansas,
    1850-80.
California
    California State Library, Sacramento, California, 1850-80.
Colorado
    National Archives, Washington, D. C., 1870-85.
    Library, National Society, Daughters of the American
    Revolution, Washington, D. C., 1870-80.
Connecticut
    Connecticut State Library, Hartford, Connecticut, 1850-80.
Delaware
    Public Archives Commission, Hall of Records, Dover,
    Delaware, 1850-80.
District of Columbia
    National Archives, Washington, D. C., 1850-80.
    Library, National Society, Daughters of the American
    Revolution, Washington, D. C., 1850-80.
Florida
    National Archives, Washington, D. C., 1885.
Georgia
    National Archives, Washington, D. C., 1850-80.
    Library, National Society, Daughters of the American
    Revolution, Washington, D. C., 1850-80.
Idaho
    Idaho Historical Society, Boise, Idaho, 1870-80.
Illinois
    Illinois State Archives, Springfield, Illinois, 1850-80.
Indiana
    Indiana State Library, Indianapolis, Indiana, 1850-80.
Iowa
    State Historical Society of Iowa, Iowa City, Iowa, 1850-80.
Kansas
    Library, National Society, Daughters of the American
    Revolution, Washington, D. C., 1870-80.
    Kansas State Historical Society, Topeka, Kansas, 1860-80.
Kentucky
    National Archives, Washington, D. C., 1850-80.
    Library, National Society, Daughters of the American
    Revolution, Washington, D. C., 1850-80.
Louisiana
    National Archives, Washington, D. C., 1850-80.
    Library, National Society, Daughters of the American
    Revolution, Washington, D. C., 1850-80.
Maine
    Office of Vital Statistics, Department of Health and Welfare,
    Augusta, Maine, 1850-80.

Genealogical Society of The Church of Jesus Christ of Latter-
day Saints, Salt Lake City, Utah, 1850-70.

Maryland

State Library, Annapolis, Maryland, 1850-80.

Massachusetts

National Archives, Washington, D. C., 1850-70.
Library, National Society, Daughters of the American
Revolution, Washington, D. C., 1850.
Massachusetts State Library, State House, Boston,
Massachusetts, 1850-80.

Michigan

National Society, Daughters of the American Revolution,
Washington, D. C., 1860-80.
Michigan Historical Commission, Lansing, Michigan,
1860-80.

Minnesota

National Archives, Washington, D. C., 1870.
Library, National Society, Daughters of the American
Revolution, Washington, D. C., 1850-70.
Minnesota Historical Society, Saint Paul, Minnesota, 1850-70.
Genealogical Society of The Church of Jesus Christ of Latter-
day Saints, Salt Lake City, Utah, 1850-70.

Mississippi

State Department of Archives and History, Jackson,
Mississippi, 1850-80.

Missouri

Missouri Historical Society, Saint Louis, Missouri, 1850-80.

Montana

National Archives, Washington, D. C., 1870-80.
Historical Society of Montana, Helena, Montana, 1870-80.

Nebraska

National Archives, Washington, D. C., 1885.
Nebraska State Historical Society, Lincoln, Nebraska, 1860-80.

Nevada

Library, National Society, Daughters of the American
Revolution, Washington, D. C., 1870.
Nevada Historical Society, Reno, Nevada, 1860-80.

New Hampshire

New Hampshire State Library, Concord, New Hampshire,
1850-80.
Genealogical Society of The Church of Jesus Christ of Latter-
day Saints, Salt Lake City, Utah, 1850-70.

New Jersey

Library, National Society, Daughters of the American
Revolution, Washington, D. C., 1850-80.
New Jersey State Library, Trenton, New Jersey, 1850-80.

New Mexico

National Archives, Washington, D. C., 1885.

New York

New York State Library, Albany, New York, 1850-80.

North Carolina
    National Archives, Washington, D. C., 1850-80.
    Department of Archives and History, Education Building,
    Raleigh, North Carolina, 1850-80.
North Dakota
    Library, State Historical Society, Bismarck, North Dakota,
    1885.
    Genealogical Society of The Church of Jesus Christ of Latter-
    day Saints, Salt Lake City, Utah, 1880.
Ohio
    Ohio Historical Society, Columbus, Ohio, 1850-60, 1880.
Oregon
    Oregon State Archives, Salem, Oregon, 1850-80.
Pennsylvania
    Pennsylvania State Library, Harrisburg, Pennsylvania,
    1850-80.
Rhode Island
    Library, National Society, Daughters of the American
    Revolution, Washington, D. C., 1860-80.
    Rhode Island State Library, Providence, Rhode Island,
    1850-80.
South Carolina
    Library, National Society, Daughters of the American
    Revolution, Washington, D. C., 1850-80.
    South Carolina Archives Department, Columbia, South
    Carolina, 1850-80.
South Dakota
    South Dakota Historical Society, Memorial Building, Pierre,
    South Dakota, 1885.
    Genealogical Society of The Church of Jesus Christ of Latter-
    day Saints, Salt Lake City, Utah, 1880.
Tennessee
    National Archives, Washington, D. C., 1850-60, 1880.
    Library, National Society, Daughters of the American
    Revolution, Washington, D. C., 1850-60, 1880.
Texas
    National Archives, Washington, D. C., 1850-80.
    Archives Division, Texas State Library, Austin, Texas,
    1850-80.
Utah
    National Archives, Washington, D. C., 1870.
    Archives Division, Texas State Library, Austin, Texas, 1870.
Vermont
    National Archives, Washington, D. C., 1870.
    Library, National Society, Daughters of the American
    Revolution, Washington, D. C., 1850-60.
    Archives Division, Texas State Library, Austin, Texas, 1870.
    Vermont State Library, Montpelier, Vermont, 1850-80.
Virginia
    National Archives, Washington, D. C., 1860.
    Library, Duke University, Durham, North Carolina, 1860.

170

Genealogical Society of The Church of Jesus Christ of Latter-
day Saints, Salt Lake City, Utah, 1870.
Washington
Library, National Society, Daughters of the American
Revolution, Washington, D. C., 1860-80.
State Library, Olympia, Washington, 1860-80.
West Virginia
State Department of Archives and History, Charleston, West
Virginia, 1860-80.
Wisconsin
Library, National Society, Daughters of the American
Revolution, Washington, D. C., 1850-70.
State Historical Society, Madison, Wisconsin, 1850-80.
Milwaukee Public Library, Milwaukee, Wisconsin, 1860-70.
Wyoming
Library, National Society, Daughters of the American
Revolution, Washington, D. C., 1870-80.

Recent correspondence with the NSDAR Library in Washington,
D. C., indicates that many researchers do not understand the services
and facilities of that organization, particularly with regard to federal
mortality schedules. The Society sent a list of their current mortality
schedule holdings and also instructions pertaining to the use of their
facilities by researchers and historians. The list varies somewhat
from information contained in Mr. Franklin's article, and the NSDAR
list indicates whether or not the record is indexed. Federal Mortality
Schedules on microfilm and in typescript form at the NSDAR Library,
1776 D Street, N.W., Washington, D. C., are as follows:

On Microfilm

(Asterisk indicates original volume also in Library)

*ARIZONA - 1870, Mohave Co. thru Yuma Co. only, & 1880,
complete. (Indexed)
*COLORADO - 1870 & 1880. (Not indexed)
*DISTRICT OF COLUMBIA - 1850, 1860, 1870 & 1880. (Indexed)
*GEORGIA - 1850, 1860 & 1870. (Indexed) 1880 available on
microfilm only. (Not indexed)
 KANSAS - 1870 & 1880. (Not indexed)
*KENTUCKY - 1850, Pendleton Co. thru Woodford Co. only,
1860, 1870 & 1880. (Indexed) (1880 indexed
giving pertinent information, typescript in
Library.)
*LOUISIANA - 1850, 1860, 1870 & 1880. (Indexed)
 MICHIGAN - 1860, 1870 & 1880. (Not indexed)
 NEW JERSEY - 1850, 1860, 1870 and 1880. (Not indexed)
 SOUTH CAROLINA - 1850, 1860, 1870 & 1880. (Not indexed)
*TENNESSEE - 1850 & 1860. (Indexed) 1880 available on micro-
film only. (Not indexed)

Typescripts

CALIFORNIA - <u>1870</u>; by Calif. Gen. Rec. Com., DAR, 1961.
   (Indexed)
INDIANA - <u>1850</u>, <u>1860</u>, <u>1870</u> & <u>1880</u>, Jefferson Co. only; by Mary
   Hill, 1944. (Indexed)
KANSAS - <u>1860</u>; by Ruby G. Kistler, 1945-47. (Not indexed)
MASSACHUSETTS - <u>1850</u>; by Mass. Gen. Rec. Com., DAR, 1947,
   2 vols. (Indexed)
MICHIGAN - <u>1850</u>; by Ethel W. & E. Gray Williams, 1961.
   (Indexed)
MINNESOTA - <u>1850</u>, <u>1860</u> & <u>1870</u>; by Edith H. Janssen, 1947.
   (Not indexed)
MISSOURI - <u>1850</u> & <u>1860</u>; by Elizabeth P. Ellsberry, 1964.
   (Indexed)
NEVADA - <u>1870</u>; compiled 1944-45. (Indexed)
NEW YORK - <u>1850</u>, City of Buffalo only (in N. Y. Cemetery,
   Church & Town Records, Volume 144).
   (Indexed)
PENNSYLVANIA - <u>1850</u>, <u>1860</u>, <u>1870</u> & <u>1880</u>, Mifflin Co. only; by
   Emma O. Ickes, 1957. (Indexed)
RHODE ISLAND - <u>1860</u>, <u>1870</u> & <u>1880</u>; by Rhode Island Gen. Rec.
   Com., DAR, 1946-47. (Indexed)
VERMONT - <u>1850</u> (in Vermont Gen. Rec. Com., DAR, Report,
   1948, Vol. 17). (Indexed)
   <u>1860</u> (in Vermont Gen. Rec. Com., DAR, Report,
   1950, Vol. 18). (Indexed)
WASHINGTON - <u>1860</u>, <u>1870</u> & <u>1880</u>; by Washington Gen. Rec.
   Com., DAR, 1956. (Indexed)
WISCONSIN - <u>1850</u>; by John Bell Chapter, DAR-Wisc., 1945.
   (Not indexed)
   <u>1860</u>; by Wisc. Gen. Rec. Com., DAR, 1947.
   (Not indexed)
   <u>1870</u>; by Wisc. Gen. Rec. Com., DAR, 1948.
   (Not indexed)
WYOMING - <u>1870</u>; compiled 1944. (Not indexed)
   <u>1880</u>; by Winifred C. Delzell, 1947. (Not indexed)

Following are instructions from the Librarian General of the
NSDAR Library pertaining to use of the library and its services:

We are sorry to advise you the Library does not maintain a
genealogical, heraldic or historical research service. It is our
practice to refer the inquirer to professional workers in this
area who do research for a stipulated fee.
We consider the workers whose names we furnish to be competent and reliable. However, the National Society assumes no
responsibility for their work, nor is it in a position to quote
prices. If you wish the name of a local researcher, we shall
be glad to furnish one upon request.
If you wish to visit the Library and do research here

personally, we shall be glad to have you. The Library is open to the public, except during the month of April, at which time it is open to members of DAR only. There is a fee of one dollar a day, or fifty cents a half-day to non-members for the use of the Library; there is no fee charged to members. The Library is open from 9:00 a.m. to 4:00 p.m. Monday through Friday. It is closed on Saturday, Sunday and all legal holidays.

The Library is entirely a reference library, and no material of any kind may be borrowed or rented from it. In addition, we do not have copies of books for sale. If you wish to purchase books of a genealogical nature, we shall be pleased to send you a list of dealers in old and rare books.

In some cases we can provide photostats of published material. To request photostating, you must furnish us the title, author and year of publication of the volume, and the page numbers you wish photostated. The fee for photostating is fifty cents per page, plus postage. We prefer to bill you at the time photostats are mailed out, as we must add in the postage which is determined by the weight of the completed photostats.

For information concerning application papers of DAR members and the Revolutionary War ancestors of such members, address your inquiry to the office of the Registrar General, NSDAR, at this same address.

The Genealogical Society Library in Salt Lake City has a fair collection of federal mortality schedules, but they are not identified in a single register or in a single file; rather, they are scattered among the cards pertaining to the respective states. The 1850-1880 schedules for Kentucky have been published, and the 1880 includes abstracts of the actual genealogical facts, but most other collections are on microfilm.

State and Local Census Records

State and local enumerations were made either contemporary to federal enumerations or between them, and they can sometimes be used to supplement the federal schedules. Additional information about family members--including names, ages, birthplaces, and residences--may be included in them. The modern state enumerations are not usually considered confidential like the federal records, and they might provide needed information where the federal records cannot be used (fig. 55).

New York took a state census decennially between the federal enumerations, and the records contain more information than the federal records. Kansas also took a similar census, and the Genealogical Society Library has copies to a very modern period.

State census schedules have not been centralized like the federal records, and many remain in state historical societies and libraries. The 1810, 1818, and 1820 state census enumerations for Illinois have been published in volumes 24 and 26 of the ILLINOIS STATE

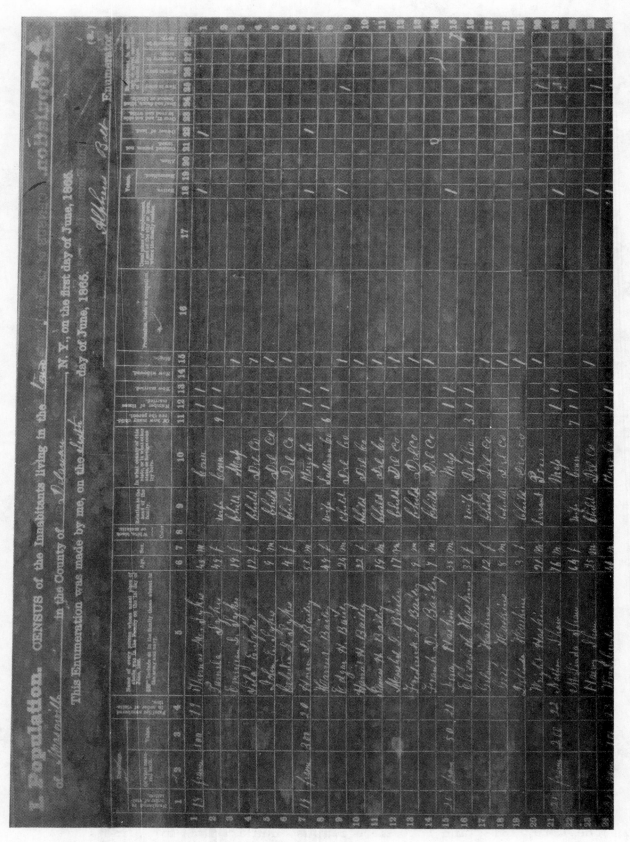

Fig. 55. 1865 New York State census

174

HISTORICAL SOCIETY PROCEEDINGS, and copies are at BYU and Salt Lake. Early census enumerations for Maryland have been listed in James M. Magruder's MARYLAND COLONIAL RECORDS, and early listings for Long Island are included in Earl B. O'Callahan's DOCUMENTARY HISTORY OF THE STATE OF NEW YORK. An annotated bibliography of censuses of population taken after the year 1790 by states and territories was published by the Department of Commerce, Bureau of the Census in 1948 under the title STATE CENSUSES (BYU Ref. 1 & 4 317.3 Un 342s).

Territorial censuses have been published for Arizona and New Mexico as SENATE DOCUMENT NO. 13, 89th Congress, 1st Session (2 February 1965) and can be obtained from the Government Printing Office in Washington. It included "Arizona Country in the Territory of New Mexico" in 1860 and the "Territory of Arizona" in 1865 and 1870 (fig. 56).

Wisconsin also took territorial censuses in 1836, 1838, 1842, 1846, and 1847. The enumeration for 1836 has been published and includes the Iowa counties of Dubuque and Des Moines. Montana and Wyoming Territories were included in the 1860 Federal census of Nebraska (GS F#3624), which also contains information on "Paunee Indian Reservation" inhabitants.

Federal Census Records 1900
Census schedules since 1900 are particularly valuable as they have requested considerable helpful genealogical information. The 1900 schedules, for instance, requested the month and year of birth, number of years married, and the year of immigration to the U.S. (fig. 57).

The 1900 federal census has recently been made available for search by genealogists, historians, and biographers. The original records remain in the National Archives and must be searched by the interested person himself or by his qualified agent. Indications are that copies of the schedule will soon be available in various regions of the United States. At the present time, however, searchers of the 1900 census must present, in person, proper identification as blood relatives of persons of interest, as qualified historians or biographers, or as their agents. Also required is a signed statement to the effect that the search is for good reason (genealogy, history, social studies) and that the information obtained will not be used to do harm.

Confidential Census Records
Federal enumerations since 1910 and some modern state census records are confidential, and information can be gained from them only by those meeting certain requirements set by the Bureau of Census.

Information recorded in the 1910 and later censuses will be furnished by the Bureau of the Census only upon the written request of the person about whom it relates or his legal representative such as

Excerpts from the special Territorial census of 1864 taken in Arizona—Continued

CERRO COLORADO MINE[1]

Gilbert W. Hopkins, deputy marshal

[Census 1864]

Name	Age (years)	Sex	Marital status	Length of residence	Occupation	Value of property	Place of birth
Adams, George	26	Male	Single	3 months	Laborer		New York.
Altorán, Besento	30	...do	Married		...do		Arizona.
Baker, Elihu	32	...do	Single	3 months	Manager of mine.		New York.
Bean, Henry	30	...do	...do	...do	Laborer		Connecticut.
Belcher, James	30	...do	...do	...do	Miner		Mississippi.
Casey, Michael	32	...do	...do	...do	...do		Ireland.
Castro Felicián	30	...do	Married		Laborer		Arizona.
Clark, James	27	...do	Single	7 months	Miner		Ireland.
Cooper-Cold, Charles	46	...do	Married	6 years	Cook		Delaware.
Davidson, Mathias Oliver.	44	...do	...do	3 months	Civil engineer		New York.
Day, James S	26	...do	Single	...do	Master miner.		Ohio.
Donly, Joseph	47	...do	Married	10 months	Miner		Do.
Farrar, William	23	...do	Single	2 months	Gunsmith		New York.
Felix, Andrés	24	...do	...do		Laborer		Arizona.
Fitzgerald, John	30	...do	Married	2 months	...do		North Carolina.
Gonzales, Lesardo	28	...do	Single		...do		Arizona.
Gonzales, Prudencia	48	...do	Married	2 months	...do		Do.
Gray, James	45	...do	Single	1 year	...do		Missouri.
Guyado, Juan	30	...do	...do		...do		Arizona.
Guydecán, Lorenzo	32	...do	...do		...do		Do.
Herrick, William H	23	...do	...do	3 months	Miner		Maine.
Higgins, Norman S	28	...do	...do	...do	Mineralogist		South Carolina.
Jac, Guillermo	30	...do	Married		Laborer		Arizona.
Lambert, Charles	32	...do	do	3 months	Miner		Maine.
Long, J. W	35	...do	Single	...do	...do		North Carolina
Mendoza, Foleno	26	...do	...do		Laborer		Arizona.
Miguel, José	25	...do	...do		...do		Do.
Mitchell, Alexander	24	...do	...do	2 months	Clerk		New York.
Murphy, Sylvester	28	...do	...do	3 months	Miner		Indiana.
Nebot, Joseph	30	...do	...do	...do	...do		France.
Pennypacker, Lewis	28	...do	...do	...do	Carpenter		Pennsylvania.
Ponsonby, Francis	43	...do	...do	...do	Miner		France.
Rualo, Crescencio	23	...do	...do		Laborer		Arizona.
Scobel, N	32	...do	...do	10 months	Miner		England.
Soto, Francisco	24	...do	do		Laborer		Arizona.
Sim, William	49	...do	Married	3 months	Mechanical engineer.		Scotland.
Swaine, Joseph D	27	...do	Single	...do	Watchman		New Hampshire.
Sweeten, Clark	25	...do	...do	...do	Carpenter		Pennsylvania.
Tanory, Miguel	23	...do	...do		Laborer		Arizona.
Weeger, J. A	45	...do	...do	3 months	Harnessmaker.		Canada.

[1] Forty-two Papago Indians with their families are laboring at this mine. Ditto 8 tame Apaches.

Fig. 56. 1864 Arizona territorial census

TWELFTH CENSUS OF THE UNITED STATES

7—224

SCHEDULE No. 1—POPULATION

{Supervisor's District No._____
{Enumeration District No._____ } Sheet No._____

State_____

County_____

Township or other division of county_____ Name of Institution,_____

Name of incorporated city, town, or village, within the above-named division,_____ Ward of city,_____

Enumerated by me on the_____ day of June, 1900,_____ Enumerator

LOCATION			NAME	RELATION	PERSONAL DESCRIPTION								NATIVITY			CITIZENSHIP			OCCUPATION, TRADE OR PROFESSION		EDUCATION				OWNERSHIP OF HOME			
IN CITIES			of each person whose place of abode on June 1, 1900, was in this family. Enter surname first, then the given name and middle initial, if any. Include every person living on June 1, 1900. Omit children born since June 1, 1900.	Relationship of each person to the head of the family	Color or race	Sex	DATE OF BIRTH		Age at last birthday	Whether single, married, widowed, or divorced	Number of years married	Mother of how many children	Number of these children living	Place of birth of each person and parents of each person enumerated. If born in the United States, give the State or Territory; if of foreign birth, give the Country only						of each person TEN years of age and over		Attended school (in months)				Owned or rented	Owned free or mortgaged	Farm or house	Number of farm schedule
Street	House Number	Number of dwelling house, in the order of visitation	Number of family, in the order of visitation					Month	Year						Place of birth of this Person	Place of birth of Father of this person	Place of birth of Mother of this person	Year of immigration to the United States	Number of years in the United States	Naturalization	Occupation	Months not employed		Can read	Can write	Can speak English				
		1	2	3	4	5	6	7		8	9	10	11	12	13	14	15	16	17	18	19	20	21	22	23	24	25	26	27	28
		1																												
		2																												
		3																												
		4																												

Fig. 57.   1900 census heading

177

guardian or administrator of estate. In the latter cases, a certified copy of the court order naming the legal representative is required. [1] If the record requested relates to a deceased person, the application must be signed by (1) a blood relative in the immediate family (parent, brother, sister, or child), (2) the surviving wife or husband, (3) the administrator or executor of an estate, or (4) a beneficiary who can present legal evidence of such beneficiary relationship. In all cases involving deceased persons, a certified copy of the death certificate is required (fig. 58).

After noting the many requirements to obtain copies of the confidential records, one might decide that it isn't worth it. However, there are times when facts from a confidential record might be the only evidence available. For many persons born prior to state registration there are no birth records, and other sources must be used for proof of dates. The official extract from a modern census is often accepted in lieu of an official birth record (fig. 59).

An extract from the confidential census usually includes the names of all persons enumerated in the household with their relationship to the head of the house shown. Age and birthplace information is provided for only one individual per fee. An additional fee is required for each person whose statistics are requested. It should be noted that genealogical information on parents and even grandparents could be available from the modern schedules, depending on who was living when the enumeration was taken (fig. 60).

A system for filing names by sound was used with the 1900 and 1920 records and information can usually be located when only the name and state of residence are known. More information is required to locate persons in the 1910, 1930, and later schedules. If a person was residing in a city at the time these enumerations were made, it is necessary to furnish the Census Bureau with the house number, the name of the street, the locality, and the name of the parent or other head of household with whom the person was living. For a resident of a small town or a rural area, such information as cross-streets, road names, township, district, precinct or beat is necessary. If the district or township is unknown, the distance and the direction from the nearest town should be included on the request.

Not more than two censuses will be searched, and only one transcript will be furnished for one fee. Should it be necessary to search more than two censuses to find the family, the Bureau will notify the sender to remit another fee before further searches will be made. The Personal Service Branch of the Census Bureau is not supported by tax monies and if a record cannot be found after a search has been made, the fee is not refunded.

Federal Census Records 1790-1840

After modern schedules have been investigated, the earlier records should be searched--both federal and state or local. The federal records for 1790-1840 include heads of households by name only but give statistical

FORM BC-600
(4-5-68)

U.S. DEPARTMENT OF COMMERCE
BUREAU OF THE CENSUS

APPLICATION FOR SEARCH OF CENSUS RECORDS

BUDGET BUREAU NO. 41-R2181.1
APPROVAL EXPIRES FEBRUARY 28, 1973

DO NOT USE THIS SPACE

CASE NO.

$_____ (Fee)

☐ Money Order
☐ Check ☐ Cash

PURPOSE FOR WHICH RECORD IS TO BE USED
(MUST BE STATED HERE) (See Instruction 1)

RETURN TO: U.S. Department of Commerce, Bureau of the Census, PITTSBURG, KANSAS 66762

FULL NAME OF PERSON WHOSE CENSUS RECORD IS REQUESTED: (Print or type)

FIRST NAME | MIDDLE NAME | MAIDEN NAME (If any) | PRESENT LAST NAME | NICKNAMES

DATE OF BIRTH (If unknown — estimate) | PLACE OF BIRTH (City, county, State) | RACE | SEX

FULL NAME OF FATHER (Stepfather, guardian, etc.)

FULL MAIDEN NAME OF MOTHER (Stepmother, etc.)

Please give FULL name of husband or wife of person whose record is requested.

FIRST MARRIAGE (Name of husband or wife) | YEAR MARRIED (Approximate)
SECOND MARRIAGE (Name of husband or wife) | YEAR MARRIED (Approximate)
THIRD MARRIAGE (Name of husband or wife) | YEAR MARRIED (Approximate)

GIVE PLACE OF RESIDENCE AT EACH DATE LISTED BELOW

CENSUS DATE	NUMBER AND STREET (Very important)	CITY, TOWN, TOWNSHIP (Precinct, beat, etc.)	COUNTY AND STATE	NAME OF PERSON WITH WHOM LIVING (Head of household)	RELATIONSHIP
JUNE 1, 1880 (See Instruction 3)					
★ JUNE 1, 1900 (See Instruction 2)					
APRIL 15, 1910 (See Instruction 3)					
JAN. 1, 1920 (See Instruction 2)					
APRIL 1, 1930 (See Instruction 3)					
APRIL 1, 1940 (See Instruction 3)					
APRIL 1, 1950 (See Instruction 3)					
APRIL 1, 1960 (See Instructions 3 and 8)					

If the census information is to be sent to someone other than the person whose record is requested, give the name and address, including Zip code, of the other person or agency.

This authorizes the Bureau of the Census to send the record to: (See Instruction 4)

See INSTRUCTIONS 5 AND 6 on the reverse side and indicate below the service desired.

FEE REQUIRED: A money order or check payable to "Census, Department of Commerce," must be sent with this application.

DO NOT SEND CASH

☐ $__.00 regular service
☐ $__.00 expedited search

____ extra copies (at $1.00 each)

TOTAL AMOUNT SENT WITH APPLICATION
$

I certify that information furnished about anyone other than the applicant will not be used to the detriment of such person or persons by me or by anyone else with my permission.

SIGNATURE OF APPLICANT (Do not print) (See Instruction 7)

PRESENT ADDRESS OF APPLICANT

NUMBER AND STREET

CITY | STATE | ZIP CODE

IF SIGNED ABOVE BY MARK (X), TWO WITNESSES MUST SIGN HERE

SIGNATURE | SIGNATURE

NOTICE — Intentionally falsifying this application may result in a fine of $10,000 or five years imprisonment, or both (Title 18, U.S. Code, Section 1001).

★ The 1890 Census records were destroyed by fire.

Fig. 58. Census application form

179

FORM BC-600
(4-5-68)

U.S. DEPARTMENT OF COMMERCE
Bureau of the Census
PERSONAL CENSUS SERVICE BRANCH
PITTSBURG, KANSAS 66762

INSTRUCTIONS FOR COMPLETING THIS FORM

1. Purpose

The purpose for which the information is desired must be shown so that a determination may be made under 13 U.S.C. 8(a) that the record is required for a proper use. The statement of purpose also provides a basis for determining which census records would best serve such purpose and, thereby, save the expense of additional searches.

2. Censuses 1900-1920

A system for filing names by sound is available for these census years. Information can be furnished in many instances when only the following information is given:

The name of the person about whom the information is desired.

The name of the city or county and State where the person resided.

The name of the head of the household with whom this person was living on the various dates of these censuses.

Additional information is desirable if it can be furnished.

3. Censuses--years 1880-1910-1930-1940-1950-1960

If residing in a city at the time these censuses were taken, it is necessary to furnish the house number, the name of the street, city, county, and State and the name of the parent or other head of household with whom residing at the time of the census. If residing in a small town or a rural area, give all available information as to cross-streets, road names, township, district, precinct or beat, etc. If the district or township is unknown, give the distance from the nearest town and the direction, also the rural route number.

4. Confidential information given to other than person to whom it relates

(a) Census information for the years 1900 and on is confidential and ordinarily will not be furnished to another person unless the person to whom it relates authorizes this in the space provided or there is other proper authorization as indicated in 4(b), 4(c), and 4(d) hereof.

(b) Minor children

Information regarding a child who has not reached legal age may be obtained upon the written request of either parent or the legal guardian.

(c) Mentally incompetent persons

Information regarding persons who are mentally incompetent may be obtained upon the written request of the legal representative supported by a certified copy of the court order naming such legal representative.

(d) Deceased persons

If the record requested relates to a deceased person, the application must be signed by (1) a blood relative in the immediate family (parent, brother, sister, or child), (2) the surviving wife or husband, (3) the administrator or executor of the estate, or (4) a beneficiary by will, intestacy, or insurance. In all cases involving deceased persons, a certified copy of the death certificate must be furnished. Legal representatives must also furnish a certified copy of the court order naming such legal representatives; and beneficiaries must furnish legal evidence of such beneficiary relationship.

5. Fee required

The $4.00 fee is for a search in regular turn, based on the date the request is received, of two suggested censuses about one (1) person only. The time required to complete $4.00 searches depends upon the number of cases on hand at the particular time and the difficulty encountered in searching a particular case. Normally from four to six weeks is required to process $4.00 cases.

The $5.00 fee is for a search ahead of $4.00 searches. When extensive searches are not required, the information can be furnished in about two weeks.

Not more than two censuses will be searched and one transcript furnished for one fee. Should it be necessary to search more than two censuses to find the record, you will be notified to send another fee before further searches are made. Tax monies are not available for the furnishing of this information. Accordingly, even though the information is not found, if a search has been made, the fee cannot be returned.

6. Additional copies of Census information

Additional copies of the information furnished will be prepared at a cost of $1.00 for each additional copy. Fill in the amount of money enclosed and the number of extra copies desired in the spaces provided.

7. Applicant

In general, the signed name of the applicant should be the same as that shown on the line captioned "full name of person whose census record is requested." When the application is for the census record concerning another person or persons the authority of the applicant must be furnished as set forth in Instruction 4 above.

8. 1960 Census

Since the place of birth and citizenship were obtained only on a sample basis during the 1960 Census, this information will not be shown on transcripts.

GENERAL INFORMATION

The application on the reverse side of this sheet is for use in requesting a search of the census records and a copy of the personal information found which includes age, place of birth and citizenship. This application should be filled in and mailed to the Bureau of the Census, Pittsburg, Kansas 66762, together with a money order or check payable to Census, Department of Commerce, in an amount based upon the fees stated on the face of this form.

Birth certificates, including delayed birth certificates, are not issued by the Bureau of the Census but by the Health Department or similar agency of the State in which the birth occurred. In Federal Censuses, the census takers obtained the age and place of birth of individuals. Copies of these census records are often accepted as evidence of age

and place of birth for employment, social security benefits, insurance and other purposes.

Census records for 1880 and prior years are not confidential for genealogical, historical or other proper purposes not detrimental to the persons recorded therein and have been transferred to the National Archives and Records Service, Washington, D.C. 20408. Requests for information from these Censuses should be addressed to that Agency.

If you authorize the Bureau of the Census to send your record to someone other than yourself, attention is called to the possibility that the information shown in the census record may not agree with that given in your application. The record must be copied exactly as it appears and will be sent as you direct regardless of what it shows.

U.S. GOVERNMENT PRINTING OFFICE : 1968 O—290—898

Fig. 58 continued.

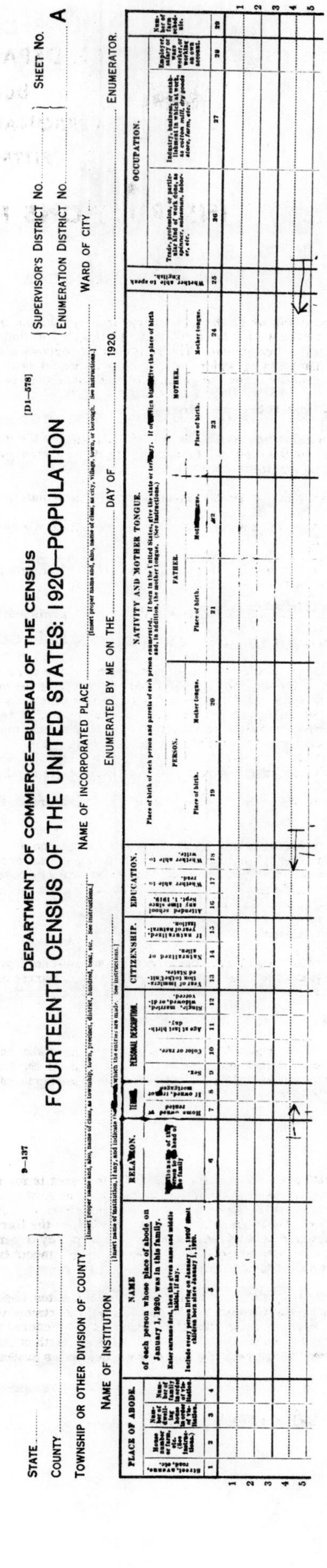

Fig. 59. 1920 census heading

DEPARTMENT OF COMMERCE—BUREAU OF THE CENSUS

[D1—678]

FOURTEENTH CENSUS OF THE UNITED STATES: 1920—POPULATION

SUPERVISOR'S DISTRICT NO. _____ SHEET NO. **A**

ENUMERATION DISTRICT NO. _____

STATE _____

COUNTY _____

TOWNSHIP OR OTHER DIVISION OF COUNTY _____

NAME OF INCORPORATED PLACE _____ WARD OF CITY _____

NAME OF INSTITUTION _____

ENUMERATED BY ME ON THE _____ DAY OF _____ 1920. _____ ENUMERATOR.

PLACE OF ABODE. | NAME | RELATION. | HOME. | PERSONAL DESCRIPTION. | CITIZENSHIP. | EDUCATION. | NATIVITY AND MOTHER TONGUE. | | | OCCUPATION.

U. S. DEPARTMENT OF COMMERCE
BUREAU OF THE CENSUS
WASHINGTON 25, D. C.

742-867

DEC 11 1962

Re: Israel G. Crawford

Sarah Crawford Patterson
315 Briar Street
Mound City, Missouri

Genealogical Society - New
P. O. Box 749
Salt Lake City 10, Utah

The following information, including spelling of name, relationship, age, etc., is an **EXACT COPY** of the census record as reported by the census taker on the original schedule.

Census of 1900, taken as of June 1

Hughes township

County _____ Nodaway _____ State _____ Missouri _____

Name	Relation-ship	Age	Month and year of birth	Place of birth	Citizenship
Crawford, William E.	Head				
- Ida M.	Wife				
- Fred E.	Son				
- Lela	Daughter				
- Lloyd	Son				
- Emmett B.	Son				
- Ermel B.	Daughter				
* - Israel G	Father	84	July 1815	Pennsylvania	
Carver, Adonice C.	Cousin				

*Place of birth of father - Pennsylvania; place of birth of mother - Scotland

Bureau of the Census

The above information is furnished upon application with the understanding that in no case shall the information furnished be used to the detriment of the person or persons to whom the information relates, in accordance with Title 13, United States Code, Section 8.

The Bureau of the Census does not issue birth certificates, but this record is often accepted in place of one.

U.S. GOVERNMENT PRINTING OFFICE: 1960 O - 551886

Fig. 60. Extract from a confidential census

information on other persons included in the household. The statistical information is helpful in research, especially when correlated with information from modern schedules so that a much more complete family record can be made.

Assuming the family of interest had been located in the 1850, 1860, 1870, and 1880 census, it would be a good policy to search schedules for the earlier years, including the 1840, 1830, 1820, 1810, 1800, and 1790. The individual of interest may not appear by name, but his father or grandfather might.

The 1840 and 1830 federal schedules are identical in format, except for statistical information on opposite pages from heads of household. Heads of household are shown by name with males and females classified according to sex and age group. Males are shown first, then females. The first four classifications represent five-year periods and the rest are for ten years. A special column shows persons one hundred years of age and upwards.

Original federal census schedules are bound volumes with statistics included on pages opposite to the name listings. When the pages were microfilmed, the left-hand page (containing the names) was copied first, then the right-hand counterpart was filmed. As the microfilm copy is viewed, the pages are shown in vertical sequence with every other page showing statistics only. The statistical page includes listings of slaves (in identical age groupings as free whites), occupation, and military service (fig. 61).

In 1841, the Government published a one-volume listing of military pensioners shown in the 1840 federal census. It was titled A CENSUS OF PENSIONERS FOR REVOLUTIONARY OR MILITARY SERVICE, WITH THEIR NAMES, AGES, AND PLACES OF RESIDENCE, UNDER THE ACT FOR TAKING THE SIXTH CENSUS. It was arranged by state, county, and town but was not indexed. The LDS Genealogical Society compiled a typescript index to it, and the Genealogical Publishing Company published it in hardback in 1965. Most genealogical libraries have copies, and the publication should be investigated along with the 1840 census schedules.

The researcher should be cautious when using the 1830 and 1840 records. The person shown as "head of the household" may not be the oldest according to the statistics given. Perhaps elderly parents or grandparents were living with a younger man and his wife, or perhaps the household is merely a listing of brothers and sisters. On the other hand, a young man and his recent wife and even a child or two may have been enumerated with parents or grandparents. Boarders and servants might also be among those listed, so correct family numbers cannot always be ascertained from the statistics given. However, when the records are used in conjunction with other schedules and sources, fairly complete family information can be compiled.

The 1820, 1810, and 1800 federal schedules are similar to those for 1840 and 1830, except they have broader age groupings. The 1820

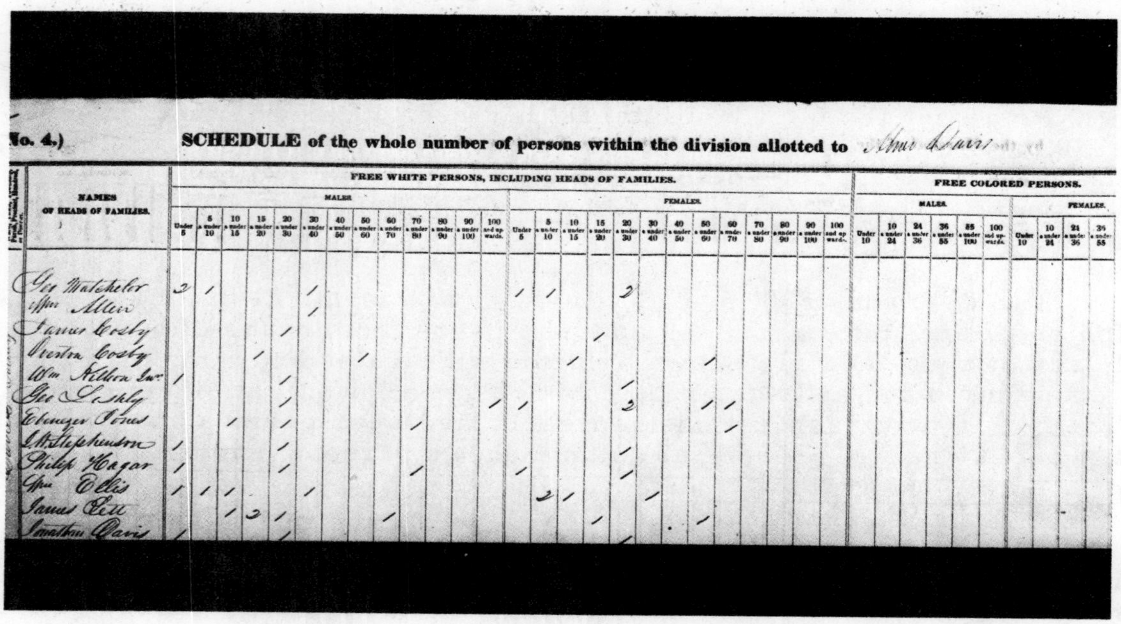

No. 4.) **SCHEDULE** of the whole number of persons within the division allotted to Abner Davis

FREE WHITE PERSONS, INCLUDING HEADS OF FAMILIES. — FREE COLORED PERSONS.

NAMES OF HEADS OF FAMILIES.
Geo Watcheler
Wm Allen
James Cosby
Overton Cosby
Wm Killion Jun.
Geo Lashly
Ebenezer Jones
J. M. Stephenson
Philip Hagar
Wm Ellis
James Pett
Jonathan Davis

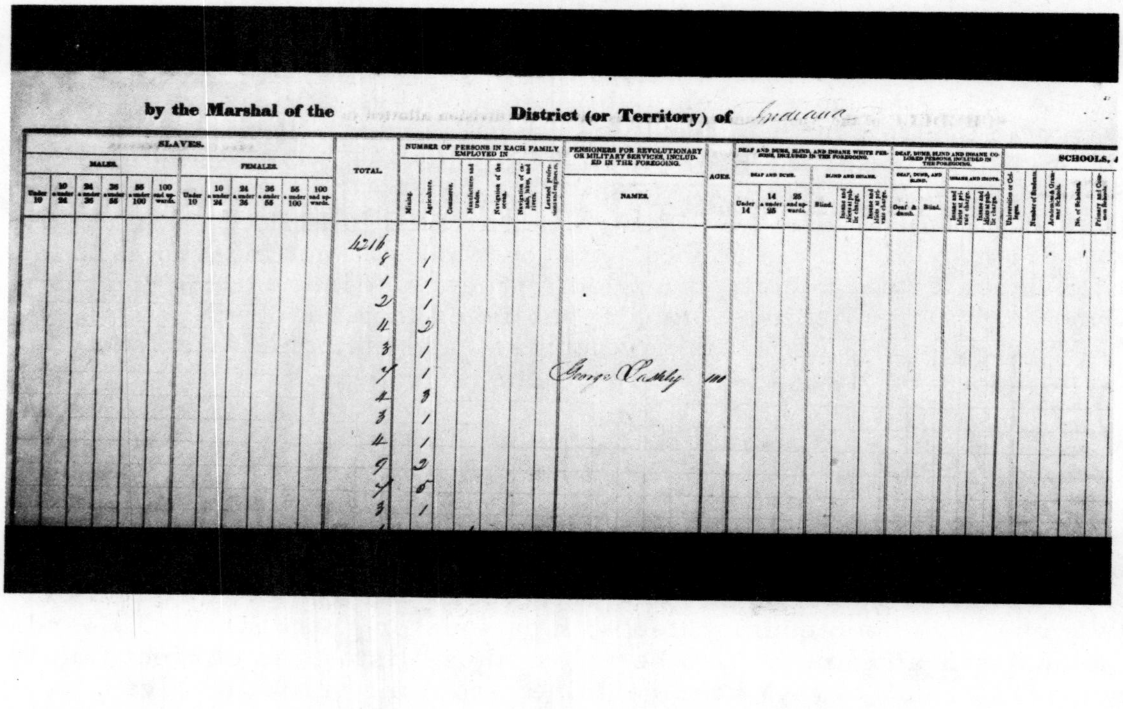

by the Marshal of the District (or Territory) of Indiana

SLAVES. — TOTAL. — NUMBER OF PERSONS IN EACH FAMILY EMPLOYED IN — PENSIONERS FOR REVOLUTIONARY OR MILITARY SERVICES, INCLUDED IN THE FOREGOING. — AGES. — SCHOOLS, &c.

TOTAL.	Agriculture.	Pensioners: NAMES.	AGES.
4216			
8	1		
1	1		
2	1		
4	2		
3	1		
7	1	George Lashly	100
4	3		
3	1		
4	1		
9	2		
7	5		
3	1		

Fig. 61. 1840 census schedule showing military service

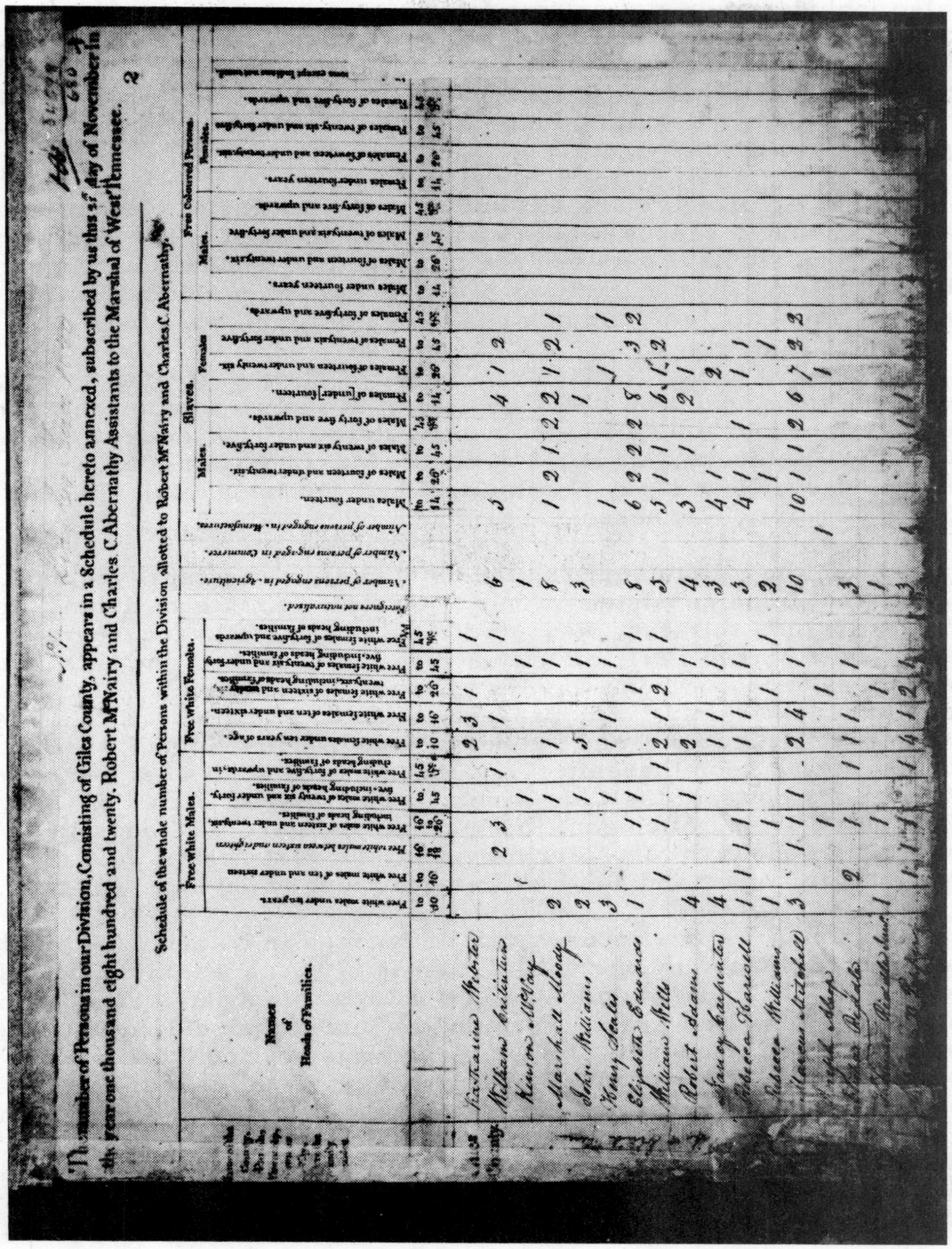

Fig. 62. 1820 census schedule

also includes a special column for males age 16-18 but are otherwise identical to the 1810 and 1800 (fig. 62). Some state enumerations were taken concurrently with these early federal records and include additional information, as is true of an 1800 census for Hancock County, Maine, which includes a special column showing the town "from whence a person came."

Indexing projects are and have been operating in various states, and many early census records have been indexed. The Genealogical Society in Salt Lake City and the library at Brigham Young University both have excellent collections of these and are participating in acquisition programs to obtain others as they become available.

The 1790 federal census was the first attempt to enumerate the entire white population in the colonies. It included enumeration of free, white inhabitants in the present states of Connecticut, Delaware, Georgia, Kentucky, Maine, Maryland, Massachusetts, New Hampshire, New Jersey, New York, North Carolina, Pennsylvania, Rhode Island, South Carolina, Tennessee, Vermont, and Virginia.

When the bill authorizing the 1790 census was approved on 1 March 1790, the Union consisted of only twelve states. Rhode Island, the last of the original thirteen, was admitted 29 May 1790, and Vermont was added on 4 March 1791, shortly before the results of the first census were announced. Maine was then part of Massachusetts, and Kentucky was part of Virginia. The present states of Alabama and Mississippi were part of Georgia, and Tennessee was part of North Carolina, though it was soon thereafter organized as the Southwest Territory or "Territory South of the Ohio River." The present states of Ohio, Indiana, Illinois, Michigan, Wisconsin, and part of Minnesota, were known as the Northwest Territory, and the vast region west of the Mississippi River and south of Georgia country belonged to Spain.[2]

Although the first census was authorized in March 1790, it was not ordered to commence until 2 August 1790 and was to be completed within nine calendar months. Some returns bear dates several months after that time, however. Vermont's enumeration did not commence until the first Monday in April 1791 and was not required to be completed for an additional five months. South Carolina marshals "experienced difficulty in getting assistants at the lawful rate of pay," and "the enumeration met with some opposition from the people," so it was not returned until 5 February 1792.[3] The enumeration of the Southwest Territory was taken by captains of the militia, probably without remuneration, and its schedules were returned on 19 September 1791.[4]

The returns of the enumerators were made to the marshals, who made summaries which were sent to the President, the originals being filed with clerks of the district courts. The returns were arranged for each state by counties, but those for North and South Carolina, Georgia, and the Southwest Territory had the counties grouped under districts. Some also included minor civil divisions.[5]

According to summary reports prepared by the marshals and sent to the President, the total population of the United States (including the Southwest Territory) in 1790 was just under four million persons.[6] The totals for states and territories are summarized on the population chart (fig. 63).

There seems to be some question among authorities as to the disposition of the original 1790 schedules. Summary returns were prepared from the originals shortly after they were taken, but these were statistical only and did not include the names of heads of households. The "enumerators' returns," which did include the names of heads of households, were evidently filed with the clerks of the various district courts for safe-keeping. By an act of Congress approved 28 May 1830, the clerks of the several district courts were directed to "transmit to the Secretary of State such schedules of the first four censuses as were in their respective offices."[7] This was completed in 1849, and in 1904 the schedules were evidently placed in custody of the Census Office.[8] Schedules of the 1790 census filed with that office included the following:

Maine	1 volume
New Hampshire	2 volumes
Vermont	2 volumes
Massachusetts	1 volume
Rhode Island	1 volume
Connecticut	3 volumes
New York	4 volumes
Pennsylvania	8 volumes
Maryland	2 volumes
North Carolina	2 volumes
South Carolina	1 volume
Total	27 volumes

Obviously, 1790 schedules for Delaware, Georgia, Kentucky, New Jersey, Tennessee, and Virginia are missing. Writers have suggested that these schedules were destroyed when the British burned the Capitol at Washington during the War of 1812, but this is probably not true because the schedules remained in their respective districts until at least 1849. If census records were destroyed when the British burned the Capitol, they were probably summaries and not the original enumerations.

According to A CENTURY OF POPULATION GROWTH, census schedules prior to 1890 were carefully examined by the Census Bureau in 1897, and those missing for the period 1790-1820 were cataloged as follows:

POPULATION OF THE UNITED STATES
AS RETURNED AT THE FIRST CENSUS, BY STATES: 1790

DISTRICT	Free white males of 16 years and upward, including heads of families.	Free white males under 16 years.	Free white females, including heads of families.	All other free persons.	Slaves.	Total.
Vermont	22,435	22,328	40,505	255	16	85,539
New Hampshire	36,086	34,851	70,160	630	158	141,885
Maine	24,384	24,748	46,870	538	None	96,540
Massachusetts	95,453	87,289	190,582	5,463	None	378,787
Rhode Island	16,019	15,799	32,652	3,407	948	68,825
Connecticut	60,523	54,403	117,448	2,808	2,764	237,946
New York	83,700	78,122	152,320	4,654	21,324	340,120
New Jersey	45,251	41,416	83,287	2,762	11,423	184,139
Pennsylvania	110,788	106,948	206,363	6,537	3,737	434,373
Delaware	11,783	12,143	22,384	3,899	8,887	59,094
Maryland	55,915	51,339	101,395	8,043	103,036	319,728
Virginia	110,936	116,135	215,046	12,866	292,627	747,610
Kentucky	15,154	17,057	28,922	114	12,430	73,677
North Carolina	69,988	77,506	140,710	4,975	100,572	393,751
South Carolina	35,576	37,722	66,880	1,801	107,094	249,073
Georgia	13,103	14,044	25,739	398	29,264	82,548
Total number of inhabitants of the United States exclusive of Southwest and Northwest territories.	807,094	791,850	1,541,263	59,150	694,280	3,893,635

	Free white males of 21 years and upward.	Free males under 21 years of age.	Free white females.	All other persons.	Slaves.	Total.
Southwest Territory	6,271	10,277	15,365	361	3,417	35,691
Northwest Territory	...	...	...	...	...	...

Fig. 63. Totals by state from the 1790 census

State or Territory	1790	1800	1810	1820
Rhode Island				*
New Jersey	*	*	*	*
Delaware	*			
Virginia	*	*		
South Carolina				*
Georgia (including Alabama[1] and Mississippi)	*	*	*	
Kentucky	*	*		
Southwest Territory (Tennessee)	*	*	*	
Northwest Territory[2] (Ohio,[3] Indiana, Illinois, Michigan, Wisconsin)	*	*	*	*

1 The schedules for Alabama in 1820 are not in existence.
2 There is no evidence of any enumeration of Northwest Territory in 1790.
3 The schedules for Ohio in 1820 are in existence.

Of the schedules for all the remaining states and organized territories, those for Arkansas in 1820 alone are missing. It is probable that the missing 1790 schedules were destroyed or lost in their respective district offices, because they were not received by the Secretary of State in 1849 or the Census Office in 1904. It is estimated that about 30 percent of the inhabitants were not accounted for because of missing 1790 schedules.[10]

Reconstructed schedules for the missing 1790 census of Delaware, Kentucky, and Virginia have been published. Those for Delaware and Kentucky are reasonably complete, but those for Virginia are estimated to be only about two-thirds complete. Tax lists for New Jersey, referred to as "ratables," have been preserved for the period 1773-1822 but are incomplete. "Lottery" lists which include the names of persons who drew land in seven lotteries between 1803 and 1832 have been published for Georgia and serve as an incomplete substitute for the 1790 of that state. Some lottery lists for Georgia have been published, and the complete set has been microfilmed by the LDS Genealogical Society.

In 1908, the Census Bureau compiled a tax-list substitute for Virginia's 1790 census using state tax records which covered the period 1782-1785. It was published under the title HEADS OF FAMILIES AT THE FIRST CENSUS. In 1940, Augusta B. Fothergill and John Mark Naugle published a sequel entitled VIRGINIA TAX PAYERS 1782-1787. They maintained they had located many names not reported in the Census Bureau's publication. Their work included records of a two-year period not covered by the 1908 publication. Neither of these volumes is complete however, and both should be used with caution.

Charles Heinemann copied tax lists for about nine Kentucky counties while doing research on some of his own Kentucky ancestors. In 1940, his compilation was enlarged by Gaius Marcus Brumbaugh, and this serves as a substitute for Kentucky's missing 1790 schedules. [11] A similar volume was published for the 1800 census of Kentucky, and copies are on file at BYU and Salt Lake City.

New Jersey "Ratables" (lists of taxpayers) covering the period 1773-1822 are in custody of the Archives and History Bureau in the New Jersey State Library at Trenton, New Jersey. Though they are incomplete, they do serve as a substitute for New Jersey's missing 1790 schedules. Ken Stryker-Rodda, Fellow of the American Society of Genealogists, has been responsible for published lists of ratables in the NEW JERSEY MAGAZINE OF HISTORY. The Gendex Corporation of Salt Lake City recently published NEW JERSEY IN 1793, using "Ratables" as its source.

North Carolina's 1790 census is published and indexed, but names from the counties of Granville, Caswell, and Orange are missing. Individuals resident in a particular locality are sometimes listed in schedules for another locality, and this should be considered when using the lists.

One difficulty encountered by the enumerators in certain sections of the country was the unwillingness of the people to give the information requested. Many persons had never been enumerated before and were reluctant to participate. Some were very superstitious regarding the census. As an example, an early colonial enumeration in New York had been followed by much sickness, and the people recalling that a similar experience had befallen the children of Israel as the result of an enumeration made by King David, ascribed this sickness directly to the census. But a very much more potent factor arousing opposition to the enumeration was the belief that the census was in some way connected with taxation. [12]

Genealogical information in the 1790 census is somewhat meager, compared with later records, but the schedules are excellent "finding tools" and are very popular with genealogists. The 1790 schedules include the names of the heads of households and then show statistically (1) free white males of 16 years and upward, including heads of families, (2) free white males under 16 years, (3) free white females, including heads of families, (4) all other free persons, and (5) slaves (fig. 64).

In some of the returns the names of heads of families are arranged alphabetically, indicating they were copied from preliminary notes

Berks County State of Pennsylvania

The Number of Persons within my division consisting of Twentysix thousand nine hundred & thirty as appears in a Schedule hereto annexed, subscribed by me, this fifth ——— day of May Anno Domini One thousand seven hundred and Ninety one

Nich Lotz

Schedule of the whole number of Persons within the division allotted to

Names of Heads of Families	Free White Males of 16 years & upwards, including Heads of Families	Free White Males under sixteen Years	Free White Females including Heads of Families	All other Free Persons	Slaves
Borough of Reading					
Nicholas Lotz	2	1	2		
Marg.t Bingeman		1	3		
Michael Lotz	1	1	6		
Samuel Wollison	2	1	2		
Daniel Ely	2	1	2		
Hartman Leitheiser	1	2	1		
John Goodman	2	3	6		

Fig. 64. 1790 census schedule

191

gathered while making the enumeration. In many cases the name of the minister, as the chief personage in the town, heads the list, regardless of alphabetical or other arrangement. Many of the entries are picturesque. Few men had more than one Christian name; hence, in order to make it clear what person was meant, additional information was often given, such as "Leonard Clements (of Walter)," "Sarah Chapman, (Wid. of Jno.)," "Walter Clements (Cornwallis Neck)." In the South there were many plantations whose owners were absent at the time of the enumeration; frequently the name of the owner was given along with his large number of slaves, while not one other white person was enumerated. Some slaves who were living apart from their owners, either alone or as heads of households, were entered separately, as "Peter, negro (Chas. Wells property)." Heads of free colored families were often stated to be "free," as "Ruth, Free negro," "Brown, John (free mulatto)." Some enumerators obtained the number of free colored males, as well as free whites, above and below sixteen years of age.[13]

As a "finding tool," the 1790 schedules are hard to beat. Sally Long was located in the 1850 federal census of Athens County, Ohio, as "age 57" and born in "Massachusetts." She was married in Athens County to one Isaac Long and the marriage record indicated her maiden surname to be "Paulk." If this information was correct, she should have been born somewhere in Massachusetts in about 1793. Because the 1790 schedules are indexed, it was quite easy to check those for Massachusetts, and it was noted that only three persons by that surname were shown. Xerxes Paulk was shown resident in Springfield, Hampden County, Massachusetts, and a check of published vital records for the town of Springfield includes a "Sally (Sarah) Paulk, daughter of Xerxes Paulk, born December 1793." Could this be our Sarah (Paulk) Long of Athens County, Ohio?

An 1860 census of Brazos County, Texas, included a researcher's "Chitwood" ancestor, and the entry suggested he was born in North Carolina. The family had been traced as far east as Alabama and Georgia, but reference to the North Carolina residence could not be located in records thus far searched. A check of the 1790 census of North Carolina showed several "Chitwood" families, but no indication as to which family was the right one was apparent. Since all "Chitwood" names in the 1790 schedules were stratified according to county, records of each county were searched. Deeds and probates of one county included good evidence to tie that family to the one of Alabama and Georgia and later of Texas.

Of course a researcher cannot always find direct connecting evidence in this way--especially when the surname is common or when a large metropolitan city is involved, but the 1790 schedules often provide clues which help to determine the correct place of residence.

It may not be possible to investigate all census records in the sequence they have been presented in this chapter, and it may not be necessary to search all records covered in the chapter because each problem is somewhat different; however, all pertinent records should eventually be searched and the findings correlated with previously known facts. This information should then be posted to pedigree and family group records, or some other summary form, so that it might be used effectively in further research. And it is important to remember that one never really finishes searching census records, because new names and new facts are constantly coming to light which demand investigation and reinvestigation.

1. Form BC-600 "Application for Search of Census Records" can be obtained without charge from the United States Department of Commerce, Bureau of the Census, Pittsburg, Kansas 66762.

2. United States, Bureau of the Census, VIRGINIA HEADS OF FAMILIES AT THE FIRST CENSUS (Records of the State Enumerations 1782-1785), Introduction.

3. United States, Bureau of the Census, A CENTURY OF POPULATION GROWTH, From the First Census of the United States to the Twelfth, 1790-1900, (Washington, D. C.: U. S. Government Printing Office, 1909), p. 45.

4. Ibid., p. 46.

5. Ibid.

6. Ibid., p. 47.

7. Ibid., p. 48.

8. Ibid.

9. Ibid., p. 49.

10. Ibid.

11. Bayless E. Hardin, "Genealogical Research In Kentucky," THE NATIONAL GENEALOGICAL SOCIETY QUARTERLY 37 (September 1949):65.

12. CENTURY OF POPULATION GROWTH, p. 45.

13. Ibid., p. 50.

CHAPTER 9

INVESTIGATING AMERICAN COURT
RECORDS FOR GENEALOGY

Court records--civil, criminal, and probate--can provide excellent genealogical information to support known facts or to extend a pedigree. Perhaps an official death record is not available for a deceased ancestor. Still, his probate, or perhaps a court deposition, may be available, with marriage or birth information in it. Probate and guardianship documents are some of the best records available to prove kinship. Naturalization or citizenship records might also exist which could indicate the date and port of arrival in America or could even list the foreign place of origin. Any number of genealogical facts might be contained in the records, and when correlated with other sources, they help to build a solid pedigree.

The American court system is really a child of English law and custom, and though it has undergone considerable change, its fundamental objectives and concepts have remained the same; namely, to adjudicate disputes, to decide the guilt or innocence of persons accused of crime, to protect personal property rights, and to determine the constitutionality of laws.[1] The system has produced records at the federal, state, and local levels of the highest genealogical and historical quality.

This chapter will not attempt to deal with extensive background in matters of law or the judicial process but will concentrate on the genealogical value of selected court records, dealing only incidentally with court organization and the judicial process. For excellent background on the subject, the reader is invited to consult Henry J. Abraham's COURTS AND JUDGES; AN INTRODUCTION TO THE JUDICIAL PROCESS (New York: Oxford University Press, 1962) or a good college text on American state and local government.[2] Roscoe

Pound's ORGANIZATION OF COURTS (Boston: Little, Brown and Co., 1940) (BYU 347.99 P86o) covers the American colonial court system adequately and should also be consulted by those who are interested in records of that period.

Courts and court jurisdiction have changed considerably since colonial times, but, generally speaking, courts at the federal and state level have produced records of excellent genealogical content. Records at the town and county level seem to be more popular with genealogists than those of the federal system, perhaps because they are more readily available. However, federal and state records do include important genealogical facts.

A series of minor courts are found at the bottom of the state court system--including those of the justice of the peace and magistrate courts of one type or another. These may be called by different names, but where they have been preserved, important genealogical information can often be located. In colonial times, the minor courts handled matters pertaining to church attendance, swearing, trespass, petty larceny and minor civil disputes. In more modern times, different municipal courts have been established to care for such matters.

Major trial courts, which have original jurisdiction, are found in the state court system at the district and county levels. These courts are identified differently from state to state but include circuit, county, common pleas, ordinary, quarter sessions, and superior courts. They are the standard trial courts with judges and juries which hear and decide all cases of importance. They also have appellate jurisdiction in cases from the minor courts.

The business before the major trial courts may be divided into four types: civil cases at common law; equity cases; criminal prosecutions; and probate matters, that is, actions relating to the wills and estates of deceased persons.[3] Probate is probably the most important of these businesses to the genealogist, but adoption, adultery, bigamy, divorce, citizenship, change of name, murder, disputes regarding land and property, and other matters relating to law and equity are important.

George Puddington of Tiverton, Devon, England, died testate in York County, Maine (then a Province of Massachusetts), sometime before 5 June 1649. He left a wife Mary (Pooke) Puddington and children George, Mary, Joan, John, Frances, Rebecca, Elias, and Sarah The children George and Joan evidently died young, as they are not mentioned further in York records, but the remaining children are well accounted for in the records. George's will was dated 25 June 1647 but was not proved for nearly half a century--until 18 June 1696-- which seemed quite unusual under the circumstances. Research in Maine court records revealed some very interesting information.

Evidently George failed to mention the child "Sarah" in his will.

His wife Mary felt an injustice had been done, so she concealed the will during her lifetime. It was not produced for probate until after her death, when it became necessary to settle heirship matters for the grandchildren. [4]

Province and court records for Maine on file at the Genealogical Society in Salt Lake City contained interesting facts regarding the Puddingtons. In August 1640, Mr. George Burdett, then minister of the Plantation of Agamenticus (York, Maine), came into court and made a series of charges of "slander" against certain persons of the town. The following entries taken from York records seemed of special significance to the Puddington problem.

> The declaration of Mr. George Burdett plaint. against Elizabeth Brady defendant.
> Mr. George Burdett cometh into this Courte, and declareth that Elizabeth Brady defendant hath lewdly and maliciously published many reproachfull words against the said plaint. and amongst many other words hath reported that the said plaint. was taken upon a bed with Puddintons wife: the said defendant hath also slandered the plaint. with and concerning the mother of the said defendant maliciously and falsely affirming that she had seen passages of uncleannes twixt the said plaint. and her mother; whereby he saith he is greatly damaged, and thereupon brings his action or slander, and desireth a legall proceeding to the lawe. [5]

A jury, consisting of twelve local citizens, was called. They ruled in favor of Mr. Burdett, giving him five pounds for his damage and allowing the court "twelve shillings and six pence" for costs. Shortly after the above charge, Mr. Burdett made a similar declaration against one Danyell Knight.

> Mr. George Burdetts declaration against Danyell Knight defendant.
> Mr. George Burdett cometh into this Courte and declareth that the defendant Danyell Knight of Agamenticus hath uttered words of slander, affirming that the said plaint. hath had the use of the body of James Wall his wife many tymes, and that the said plaint. was with her in a private place all the night at Pascattaque, and that the said plaint. being then his master, used to send him out of dores at such time as Puddingtons wife resorted to his house, and that his bed was usually tumbled, with many other speeches, endeavoureing to raise and publish a suspicion of incontinency in the said plaint. Whereby he saith he is damnified a thousand pounds and thereunto commenceth his action of slander against the defendant and craveth a legall proceeding according to lawe. [6]

The same jury was called and again ruled in favor of Mr. Burdett, giving him "five pounds for his damage" and allowing the court its costs. The jury consisted of the following persons who were also found in other court actions:

Geo. Cleeve, gent.	Mr. William Cole
John Bonython, gent.	Mr. Richard Foxill
Mr. John Winter	Mr. Tho. Williams
Mr. Arthur Mackworth	Geo. Frost
Mr. Richard Tucker	Tho. Smith
Mr. Thomas Page	Richard Hitchcocke

The declaration of John Winter and Johane his wife plaintiffs against George Cleeve gent. defendant.

Mr. John Winter cometh into this Courte, and declareth that this defendant aboute some six yeares past, within this Province did unjustly and wrongfully slander the said plaintiffe his wife in reporting that the said plaint. his wife (who then lived in the Town of Plymouth in old England) was the veriest drunkenest whore in all that towne, with divers other such like scandalous reports not only of the said plaint. his wife, but also of the said town in generall in saying that there was not foure honest women in all that towne . . .[7]

Continuing in the same record, the following information was noted:

Mary the wife of Geo. Puddington of Agamenticus is here indicted by the whole bench, for often frequenting the house and company of Mr. George Burdett minister of Agamenticus afore-said privately in his bed chamber and else where in a verie sus-pitious manner, notwithstanding the said Mary was often fore-warned thereof by her said husband and the Constable of said Plantation with divers others, and for abuseing her said husband to the greate disturbance and scandall of the said plantation, contrary to the peace of our Soveraigne lord the King.

Whereupon the Court enjoyneth the said Mary to make this publike confession here in this Courte, and likewise at Agamenticus aforesaid when she shall be thereunto called by the Worshipfull Thomas Gorges and Edward Godfrey, two of the Councellors of this Province, her confession followeth:

I Mary Puddington doe here acknowledge that I have dishonoured God, the place where I live, and wrongd my husband by my disobe-dience and light carriage, for which I am heartily sorrie and desire foregiveness of this Courte and of my husband, and doe promise amendment of life and manners henceforth; and have made this confession to aske her husband forgiveness on her knees.[8]

By 8 September 1640, the "Courte" had done a complete reversal on its judgment regarding Parson Burdett, as the following information indicates:

Mr. George Burdett, minister of Agamenticus, is indicted by

198

the whole bench for a man of ill name and fame, infamous for incontinency, a publisher and broacher of divers dangerous speeches the better to seduce that weake sex of women to his incontinent practices, contrary to the peace of our Soveraigne lord the King, as by depositions and evidences etc.

Whereupon the said George Burdett is fyned by the Bench for this his offence ten pounds starling to our Soveraigne lord the King.

Mr. George Burdett is also indited by the whole bench for a turbulent breaker of the peace, contrary to the law and peace of our soveraigne lord the King as appeareth by depositions.

Whereupon the said George Burdett is fyned by the bench for this his offence the sume of five pounds starling to our sorveraigne lord the King.

Mr. George Burdett is also indited by the whole Bench for deflowring Ruth the wife of John Gouch of Agamenticus aforesaid, as by deposition and evidence appeareth, contrary to the peace of our soveraigne lord the King.

Whereupon the said George Burdett is fyned by the Bench for this offence twenty pounds starling to our soveraigne lord the King.

Mr. George Burdett being found guilty by the Grand Enquest for entertaining Mary the wife of George Puddington in his house, as by the first indictment against the said George Burdett appeareth, is therefore fined by the Bench ten pounds starling to the said George Puddington for those his wronges and damage sustained by the said Geo. Burdett.

Ruth the wife of John Gouch found guilty by the Grand Enquest of adulterie with Mr. George Burdett, is therefore censured by this Courte, that six weeks after she is delivered of Child she shall stand in a white sheete publiquely in the congregation at Agamenticus two severall Sabath dayes, and likewise one day at the Generall Courte when she shalbe thereunto called by the Counsellors of this Province, according to his Majesties lawes in that case provided. [9]

The following interesting court actions were found recorded in York deed books covering the date "4th of January 1697/8":

Presentments agreed upon . . . to ye Court of Sessions at York (Maine).
We present Sarah King for comitting fornication.
We present Samuel Bragdon Senr. for retailing strong strong drink without Lycence--answered in Court.
We present Alexander Maxwell for drinking to Excess.
We present John Bacie for cursing.
We present Thomas Feanor and Ruth Donnel his now wife for committing fornication.
We present Thomas Starboard for not frequenting the public worship of God upon ye Lords day.
We present ye Town of Kittery for not laying out highways

according to Law in said Town.
We present John Hoigh for swearing.
We present Francis Herloe for swearing he would cut his wifes throat.
We present ye Widdow Taylor, Walter Allen's wife, Nicholas Turbet and his wife, Samuel Brackett and his wife and John Fosts wife, for not frequenting the public worship of God upon the Lords day. [10]

Of course all court matters do not involve moral charges, but most of them include good genealogical information. For instance, on 25 June 1844, a sixteen-year-old orphan named William Jackson was bound until he was "21 years" to Catherine A. M. Maddox. According to the record, "the said apprentice [was] to serve his said Mistress during the time as a good and faithful apprentice should do and the said Mistress agree[d] to feed, clothe, wash, and lodge him during the time, to teach or cause him to be taught the antics of House Servant and when free to give him a new suit of clothes."[11]

On 20 January 1868, John Remakles, "Being an Alien, and free white person," made oath in the Circuit Court of Jay County, Indiana, that he was born in the town of "Illrich, County of Cookern, Prussia," and that he arrived in the United States at the "City of New York, State of New York on the 4th of July 1861, owing allegiance to William, King of Prussia."[12]

On 7 February 1883, "Jane E. Bennett, being first duly sworn on oath," deposed that she resided "in Nebraska City, Otoe County, Nebraska, that she [was] fifty five years of age," and that her mother "Hannah Baum" resided "at Provo City, Utah Territory." Mrs. Bennett further swore that she was "the daughter of the said Hannah Baum and John Baum," who had at that time "six children living," all of whose names and places of residence follow in the record. [13]

Court records of Arapahoe County, Colorado; Levenworth County, Kansas; and Gage County, Nebraska, show that "Royal Dunkle Salisbury" was born the son of Rosa Zimmerman and James Juvenal, who were not man and wife, and was first named "Oscar Juvenal." He was adopted at about two years of age by "Mary E. Dunkle" who changed his name to "Royal Dunkle." A few years later Mary E. Dunkle married a "Mr. Salisbury" and had her son's name changed to "Royal Dunkle Salisbury."

On 7 May 1917, "Martin Walter and Ester J. Walter, his wife," entered a petition in the "District Court of the Fourth Judicial District, Utah County, State of Utah" to adopt "Bertha Walter, a deserted minor child whose parents are unknown."[14]

On 10 March 1911, "Austin Sanderson, of the Village of Leland, in the County of LaSalle and State of Illinois" died testate leaving no wife or children, no descendants of any deceased children, no father and no mother, no brothers and no sisters. Yet, his estate papers included the following genealogy:

. . . Second, --I give and devise to my nephew Edward H. Farley, of Leland, Illinois, the following described real estate to wit . . .

Third, --I give and devise to my nephew Willis C. Farley of LaSalle, County, Illinois, and to Charles Kittleson of the State of Kansas, he being the surviving husband of my deceased niece, Adeline Kittleson, the following described real estate to wit . . . and, provided further, that said Willis C. Farely and Charles Kittleson shall and do jointly pay to Adolph Kittleson of Freedom, Illinois, my nephew, the sum of four hundred dollars . . .

Fourth, --I give and devise to my nephew, Knute Kittleson, of the County of LaSalle and State of Illinois, the following described real estate to wit . . .

Fifth, --I give and devise to my nephew, Alfred A. Farley of the Town of Earl in the County of LaSalle and State of Illinois, the following described real estate to wit . . .

Sixth, --I give and devise to my nephew, Henry Kittleson, of the Town of Earl, County of LaSalle and State of Illinois, the following described real estate to wit . . .

Seventh, --I give and devise to my nephew, Henry Sanderson of the Town of Paw Paw, Dekalb County, Illinois, and to my nephew Frank Farley of the Town of Adams, LaSalle County, Illinois, the following described real estate to wit . . .

Eighth, --I hereby instruct my executor hereinafter named . . .

Nineth, --I give and bequeath to the children of Samuel Sanderson, a deceased son of my brother, Sander H. Sanderson, deceased, the sum of twelve hundred fifty dollars . . .

Tenth, --I give and bequeath to the children of Charles Sanderson, the deceased son of my brother Sander H. Sanderson, deceased, the sum of twelve hundred fifty dollars . . .

Eleventh, --I give and bequeath to Austin Sanderson, Seward Sanderson, Martha Halverson, Mary Oakland, Isabelle Richolson and Josephine Richolson, they being the sons and daughters of my deceased brother, Sander H. Sanderson, the sume of twelve hundred fifty dollars to each of them.

Twelfth, --I give and bequeath to Henry Sanderson, Nettie Hill and Margary Rogers, my nephew and nieces, they being the children of my deceased brother, Knute Sanderson, the sum of two thousand five hundred dollars to each of them.

Thirteenth, --I give and bequeath to Amos Kittleson and Emmer Kittleson, the sons of my deceased niece, Adeline Kittleson, who was the daughter of my deceased brother, Knute Sanderson . . .

Fourteenth, --I give and bequeath to my nephew, Frank Farley, and to my niece, Hannah Anderson, they being the children of my deceased sister Ellen Farley . . .

Fifteenth, --I give and bequeath to Esther Johnson, the daughter of my deceased niece, Matilda Johnson, who was the daughter of my deceased sister, Ellen Farley, --and to Gertie Jacobs, the daughter of my deceased niece, Emma Jacobs, who was the daughter of my deceased sister Lavina Kittleson . . .[15]

At the end of his will, Austin Sanderson placed the following limitations on the distribution of his estate:

Should any of my heirs at law, devisees or legatees, or any person in this will mentioned, or any person having an interest in my estate, by proceedings in court, attempt to contest or set aside this will, or object to the probate of same; or shall by legal proceedings attempt or endeavor to have this will declared of no force or null and void, or shall endeavor to have set aside any conveyance of property made by me, it is my desire and I hereby direct that he or she, or they shall receive nothing from my estate, and any portion herein devised or bequeathed to him or her, or them, shall pass to and vest in my residuary legatee and devisee, Leonard Johnson.[16]

Can there be any question as to the value of court records in genealogical research? Not simply the facts included, but the historical information and implied personality traits as well are very important.

Probate Court Records

It is usually better to investigate probate court records before civil and criminal records because of their genealogical content and general arrangement. The probates often include personal information of the highest quality. And most probate courts have indexed their probate and estate records by individual name and time period, so the records are generally more accessible than civil and criminal records.

Actions relating to guardianship, heirship, insanity, and the distribution of deceased persons' estates are included in probate records. A few courts have placed some restrictions on probates, but most of them are accessible to the genealogist during reasonable hours. Some probates have been published. Others have been microfilmed, which makes them even more accessible for genealogical use.

Probate procedure has varied somewhat from jurisdiction to jurisdiction and from one time period to another, but in the main it has followed a similar pattern in most American counties or towns. At the death of a person possessed of an estate, which need not be large, some interested party usually petitions the court to probate (prove) the estate. This person may be the spouse of the deceased, some other relative, a friend, a creditor, or some public official (fig. 65).

The petition usually contains the name of the deceased, his date and place of death, the name and place of residence of his spouse, and the names and addresses of all heirs to the estate. Sometimes an heir may be living in another locality and the information included in the petition might help trace family movement patterns, though in some cases the residence was not known and the scribe may have listed "of parts unknown" or "in Ohio Territory." The author has seen petitions in New York Counties which had a copy of the deceased's obituary

PETITION OF _____Jane Cadwallader_____in the matter of the Estate

of_____John Cadwallader_____ deceased for Letters of Administration

To the Hon._____Thompson Chandler_____ Judge of the County Court

of___McDonough_____County

_____

    The Petition of the undersigned_____Jane Cadwallader_____respectfully

represents that_____John Cadwallader_____late of__McDonough County_____

deceased, died at_____Prairie City_____in_____said County_____

on or about the_____first_____ day of_____October_____A.D. 1859

leaving property and effects in this County____but_____leaving_____no_____

last Will and Testament as far as known to and believed by this petitioner.

That said deceased left him surviving ____your petitioner Jane Cadwallader____,

as his widow, and__the following named children, towit: Morris, George,_____

Eva May, and Luella Carrie Cadwallader

Your Petitioner being_____the widow_____of said deceased, therefore

prays that __Letters of Administration upon the Estate of_____the said

John Cadwallader_____ deceased may be granted to her

Macomb, October 31st___1859

                                 _____Jane Cadwallader_____

STATE OF ILLINOIS   )
) SS.
MCDONOUGH COUNTY   )

_____Jane Cadwallader_____being duly sworn, deposes and says that the

facts averred in the above petition are true according to the best of her knowledge,

information and belief.

Sworn to and subscribed before me_J. H. Baker_____)
)

pro teno_____Clerk of the County Court of_____)   Jane Cadwallader

McDonough County, this 31st day of_____)

___October_____A.D. 1859.   )

J. H. Baker Pro teno_____)
                  CLERK

S. H. Bradbury   )
Edwin Reed   )   Appraisers
Ezra D. Smith   )

Fig. 65. Probate petition

notice attached, evidently from a local newspaper.

The petition is usually filed among related probate papers which are stored in special file boxes in some offices. Such records are usually referred to as "the files" or "packets" and contain loose documents and papers relating to the estate. Some files have been lost or destroyed, but many remain in their respective courts. A few have been transferred to libraries and historical societies for deposit, as is the case with early Connecticut files which are deposited at the State Library at Hartford.

In most Pennsylvania counties, the "files" (loose documents) have been copied into docket books and civil court order books, and the original papers are not usually available. New York "surrogate" (probate) offices usually have special metal filing cabinets specially designed for probate packets, and most officials do not object to their use by genealogists. The loose documents are usually referenced or numbered in the probate indexes (fig. 66).

Probate packets (files) for Grant County, Indiana, on the other hand, are located in a dusty, unventilated, and poorly lighted room in the attic of the courthouse. They are in no apparent system of arrangement, and officials in that county are very reluctant to let a genealogist consult the records. Of course all Indiana courthouses are not like that, and many Indiana officials are very cordial to the genealogist. Pike County, Indiana, files are kept in manila folders in the County Clerk's Office and are numbered in the general probate index.

After the petition for probate has been received by the court, further probating procedures take place. Where a will exists, evidence to that effect is presented, and a record is made in special will books.

After it has been copied into a will book, the original will may be placed in the "files" or it may be returned to the family for keeping. Sometimes a "nuncupative" (oral) will may be given by the testator shortly before his death, and the researcher sometimes finds such information also recorded in the will books (fig. 67).

An estate is "testate" when there is a will and "intestate" when there is no will. A will has to receive the approval of the court before it is probated, and if it is not approved, the estate becomes intestate. It is customary for the will to name one or more executors to carry out its provisions, but when an executor is not named, or if he died before the testator did, the court appoints an administrator and the will is annexed. In intestate estates, the court appoints an administrator, whose duties are similar to those of the executor, and distribution is made according to laws of inheritance for that particular state.[17] When the executor refuses to assume the responsibility given to him in the will, a "renunciation" (refusal to act) is usually made, and an administrator is appointed to carry out the provisions

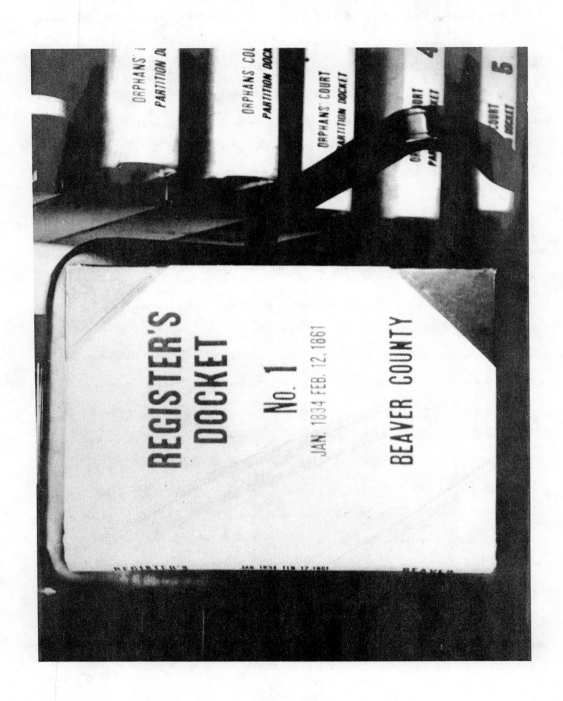

Fig. 66. Register's docket

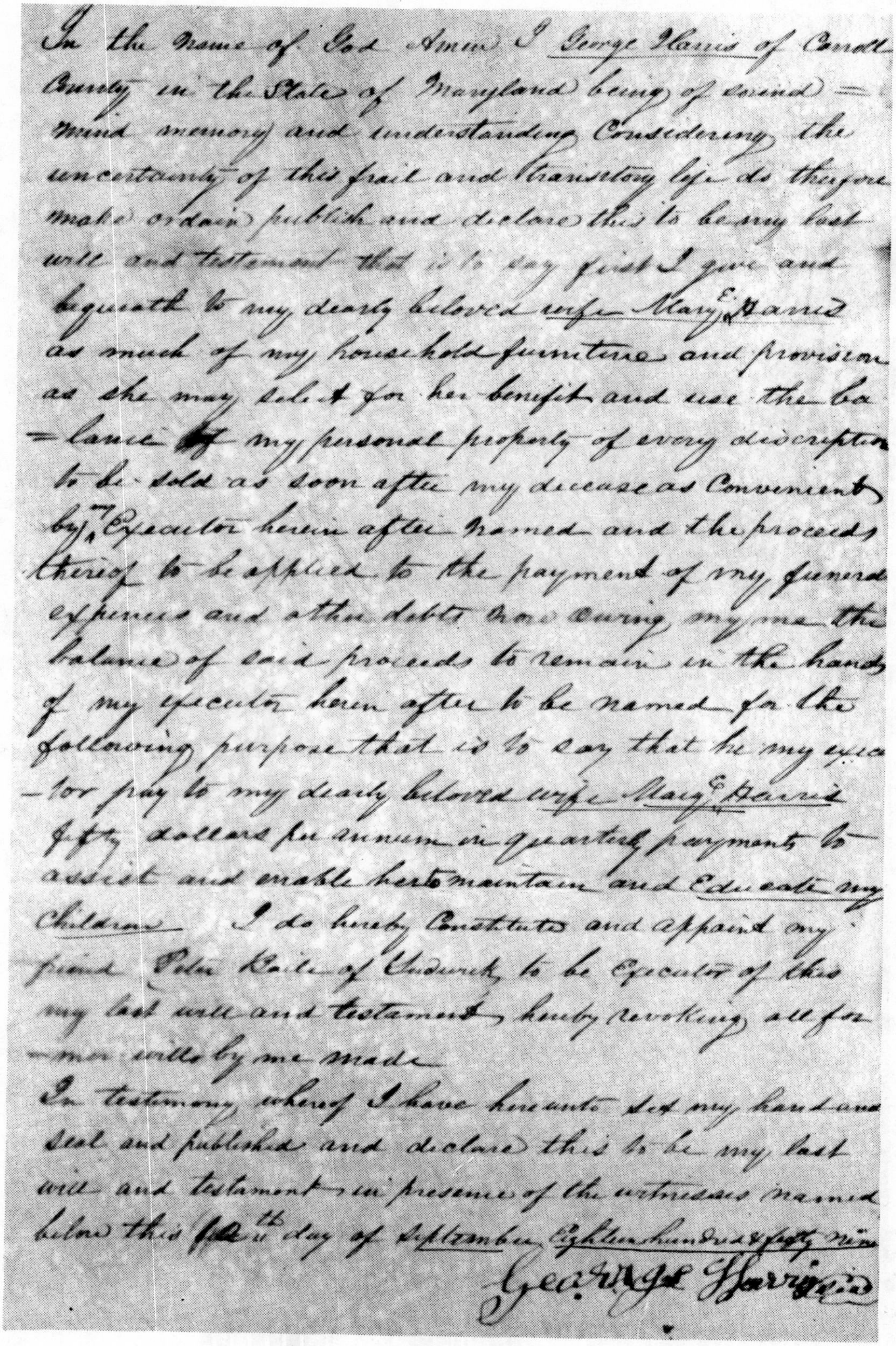

In the Name of God Amen I George Harris of Carroll
County in the State of Maryland being of sound —
mind memory and understanding Considering the
uncertainty of this frail and transitory life do therefore
make ordain publish and declare this to be my last
will and testament that is to say first I give and
bequeath to my dearly beloved wife Mary E Harris
as much of my household furniture and provision
as she may select for her benefit and use the ba
=lance of my personal property of every description
to be sold as soon after my decease as Convenient
by my Executor herein after named and the proceeds
thereof to be applied to the payment of my funeral
expenses and other debts now owing, my one the
balance of said proceeds to remain in the hands
of my executor herein after to be named for the
following purpose that is to say that he my execu
-tor pay to my dearly beloved wife Mary E Harris
fifty dollars per annum in quarterly payments to
assist and enable her to maintain and Educate my
Children   I do hereby Constitute and appoint my
friend Peter Keile of Uniontown to be Executor of this
my last will and testament hereby revoking all for
mer wills by me made
In testimony whereof I have hereunto set my hand and
seal and published and declared this to be my last
will and testament in presence of the witnesses named
below this 16th day of September Eighteen hundred & fifty nine
                              George Harris

Fig. 67. Handwritten will

206

of the will (fig. 68).

Two or three witnesses are usually signers of a will, whether written or oral, and they may be close relatives of the deceased. Witnesses are also required to acknowledge their signatures in court after the testator dies and are required to express their beliefs that he was of sound mind when he signed the will or expressed it orally in their presence. [18]

Frequently a testator wishes to change or modify some aspect of a will without rewriting it. (Perhaps a legatee originally named in the will had died or had fallen from the grace of the testator.) The addition he makes is called a "codicil" and may be attached to the will or be recorded along with it (fig. 69).

The genealogical content of wills varies considerably. Some are very informative, while others are brief and of little genealogical value. A will filed in a Georgia county included the statement, "I leave my entire estate to my loving wife and children," but it failed to name any of the parties. Wills such as that of Austin Sanderson, quoted previously, may meticulously name and identify all living (and some deceased) relatives.

All children of the deceased may not be listed in his will; some may have preceded him in death, and others may already have received their share of the estate. But usually those who are living and potential heirs to the estate are mentioned and given some portion to meet legal requisites. The amount of the bequest might actually be a clue to the status of the person. The record might indicate one daughter was to receive a larger cash amount "to make her equal with her sisters" or some other statement might be made to show a daughter is single while others are married. A son may have already been given his portion of his father's estate in the form of real estate and may only receive "one shilling" as his share from the will. Jacobus says that while the "eldest son by English law received the landed estate . . . in this country land was so plentiful at first that it was not considered good public policy. . . . In New England he received a double portion in consideration of his 'birthright.' Therefore, when the genealogist finds a deed that Samuel Smith conveyed a one-seventh interest in the estate of his father John Smith deceased, he may conclude that John Smith left six surviving children, each of whom received one-seventh except the eldest son who received two-sevenths." [19]

Other special arrangements might also have been made by a man before his marriage to a widow who had children and property from a previous marriage. An "antenuptial agreement" might have been made by the two before their marriage and before their deaths, and probate actions pertaining to either party might reveal some very unusual distribution practices.

Court procedure usually specifies that the administrator of an

IN THE PROBATE COURT OF UTAH COUNTY.
TERRITORY OF UTAH.

In the matter of the Estate | Notice of Application
of | *FOR*
John C. Baum | *Letters of Administration*
deceased |

Notice is hereby given that *Robert McKinley*

has filed with the Clerk of this Court a petition praying

for *Letters of Administration jointly with Hannah Baum*

of the Estate of *John C. Baum, deceased*

and that *Tuesday* the *20* day of *February*
A. D. 18*83*, at *10* o'clock A M. of said day, at the
Court House in Provo City, County and Territory of Utah,
has been set for hearing said petition, when and where any
person interested may appear and show cause why the said
petition should not be granted.

W. A. Dusenberry ......Clerk.

By *V. L. Halliday* Deputy Clerk

Provo City, U. T.,

Feb 10 A. D. 18*83.*

Fig. 68. Letter of administration

208

eceive one share to be divided equally among said children of said deeased daughter.   VIII.

Hereby commending my soul to God, I direct my said executors to follow strictly my wishes in the division of my property as hereinbefore set forth: hereby revoking any and all other wills, at any time by me heretofore made.

IN WITNESS WHEREOF, I, the said John D. Holladay, have signed, sealed published and declared this instrument to be my last will and testament, on this 20th. day of March, A.D. 1908.

<u>   John D. Holladay   (SEAL)</u>

SIGNED? SEALED, PUBLISHED AND DECLARED in the presence of us and each of us, by the said John D. Holladay to be his last will and testament, and we, at the request of the said John L. Holladay and in his presence and in the presence of each other, have hereunto subscribed our names as witnesses.

<u>   W.H. Boyle   </u>
Address: Santaguin, Utah.

<u>   Thomas B. Heelis   </u>
Address: Santaquin, Utah.

<u>CODICIL,   TO MY LAST WILL AND TESTAMENT.</u>

I Hereby direct that my executors Isaiah Holladay and John W. Holladay shall have the monument over my Father and Mothers, grave at Spring Creek put up properly, that is that the Marble Column be set up on its foundation and fastened in place with Portland (or other) Cement to hold it steady and also that a good, neat and substantial Iron Fence be placed around it to protect it from molestation.

I also further direct that when my body is laid in the family plot, in the Santaquin Cemetery, that a Monument be placed at my head, consisting of a Granite foundation with a four square Marble Column four or five feet high, about eight inches square on which suitable inscriptions may be placed regarding myself and my three wives previously mentioned in the accompanying will, and that a neat good and substantial Iron fence be built around said family plot of burying ground.

And I especially direct that the expences of Carrying out and executing his my Codicil be taken out of my property, of which I may die seized, before any division or distribution is made for any purpose whatever.

Fig. 69. Codicil to a will

estate must be bonded; however, in many testate estates the testator specifically indicates the executor may act without bond. Such a record as an administrator's bond may not be too valuable from a genealogical standpoint, but it might contain the date (or approximate date) and place of death of the deceased (fig. 70).

One of the first acts of the executor or administrator is to locate and inventory all property of the deceased and have it appraised prior to any settlements. Again, the inventory or appraisal document might not contain too much genealogical information but it may give some idea of the deceased person's occupation or economic status. The actual inventory usually lists all the property, whether real or personal, and the appraisal states their value. The persons chosen to inventory and appraise the estate may or may not be related to the deceased; however, when sales are made, the names of the buyers should be of special concern because they are often family members and close relatives. Some sales documents specify "widow" or "son" while others leave relationship to the reader's imagination (fig. 71).

One family doing research in Pike County, Indiana, was not able to determine whether the correct surname for the family of interest was "Taylor" or "Traylor." Research in other sources had failed to clarify the matter, but a search of probate files at Petersburg, Indiana, disclosed a "sale document" (closely approximating a quit-claim deed) in the probate files which had been signed by each heir to the estate as well as all spouses of heirs. The ancestor of interest was a party to the sale and signed his name "Jesse Taylor," not "Traylor." In addition, Jesse's wife (Mary Ellen Hardin) had signed her name as "Mary E. Taylor."

Other documents may also be filed with those relating to sales and accounts. In an Oneida County, New York, packet there was a letter from a son who was living in Springfield, Massachusetts. In the letter the son asked, "please send my share of the estate in money because I cannot use the hay." Further research revealed that this son was living in an earlier ancestral home, which information had not been known previously by the family.

In some cases, it is necessary to give the widow or the minor children an "allowance" while the estate is in probate, and documents relating to such actions can also be helpful for the genealogist. Allowance in the past may have been in cash or in kind, and the records vary considerably in their content.

When minor heirs exist or when an heir or legatee is named, special records may be initiated. Guardianship and apprentice records can also provide excellent vital statistics and relationship information. In a York County, Maine, probate Henry Pendexter named his two sons "Henry Jr. and Sibley" executors to his estate. Sibley was a minor, and he chose Henry Jr. as his guardian. The court usually appoints guardians for children under fourteen years

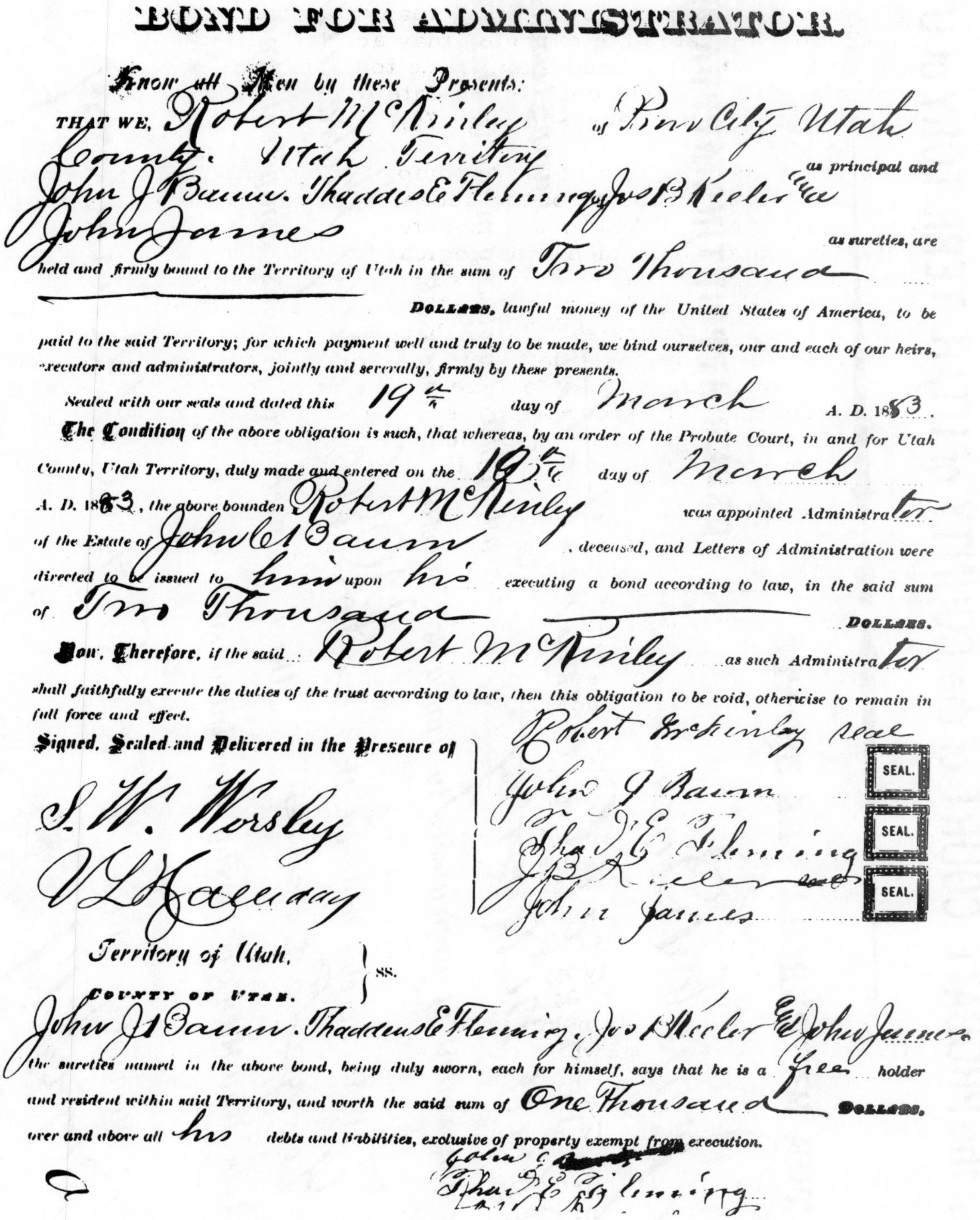

BOND FOR ADMINISTRATOR

Know all Men by these Presents:

THAT WE, *Robert McKinley* of *Provo City Utah County. Utah Territory* as principal and *John J Baum. Thaddeus E Fleming, Jos B Keeler &c John James* as sureties, are

held and firmly bound to the Territory of Utah in the sum of *Two Thousand*

DOLLARS, lawful money of the United States of America, to be paid to the said Territory; for which payment well and truly to be made, we bind ourselves, our and each of our heirs, executors and administrators, jointly and severally, firmly by these presents.

Sealed with our seals and dated this *19th* day of *March* A. D. 18*83*.

The Condition of the above obligation is such, that whereas, by an order of the Probate Court, in and for Utah County, Utah Territory, duly made and entered on the *19th* day of *March* A. D. 18*83*, the above bounden *Robert McKinley* was appointed Administrator of the Estate of *John Baum*, deceased, and Letters of Administration were directed to be issued to *him* upon *his* executing a bond according to law, in the said sum of *Two Thousand* DOLLARS.

Now, Therefore, if the said *Robert McKinley* as such Administrator shall faithfully execute the duties of the trust according to law, then this obligation to be void, otherwise to remain in full force and effect.

Signed, Sealed and Delivered in the Presence of

S. W. Worsley

V L Halliday

Robert McKinley seal

John J Baum SEAL

Thad E Fleming SEAL

J B Keeler &c SEAL

John James

Territory of Utah. } ss.
COUNTY OF UTAH.

John J Baum. Thaddeus E Fleming. Jos B Keeler & John James the sureties named in the above bond, being duly sworn, each for himself, says that he is a *free* holder and resident within said Territory, and worth the said sum of *One Thousand* DOLLARS, over and above all *his* debts and liabilities, exclusive of property exempt from execution.

John C Baum

Thad E Fleming

Fig. 70. Administrator's bond

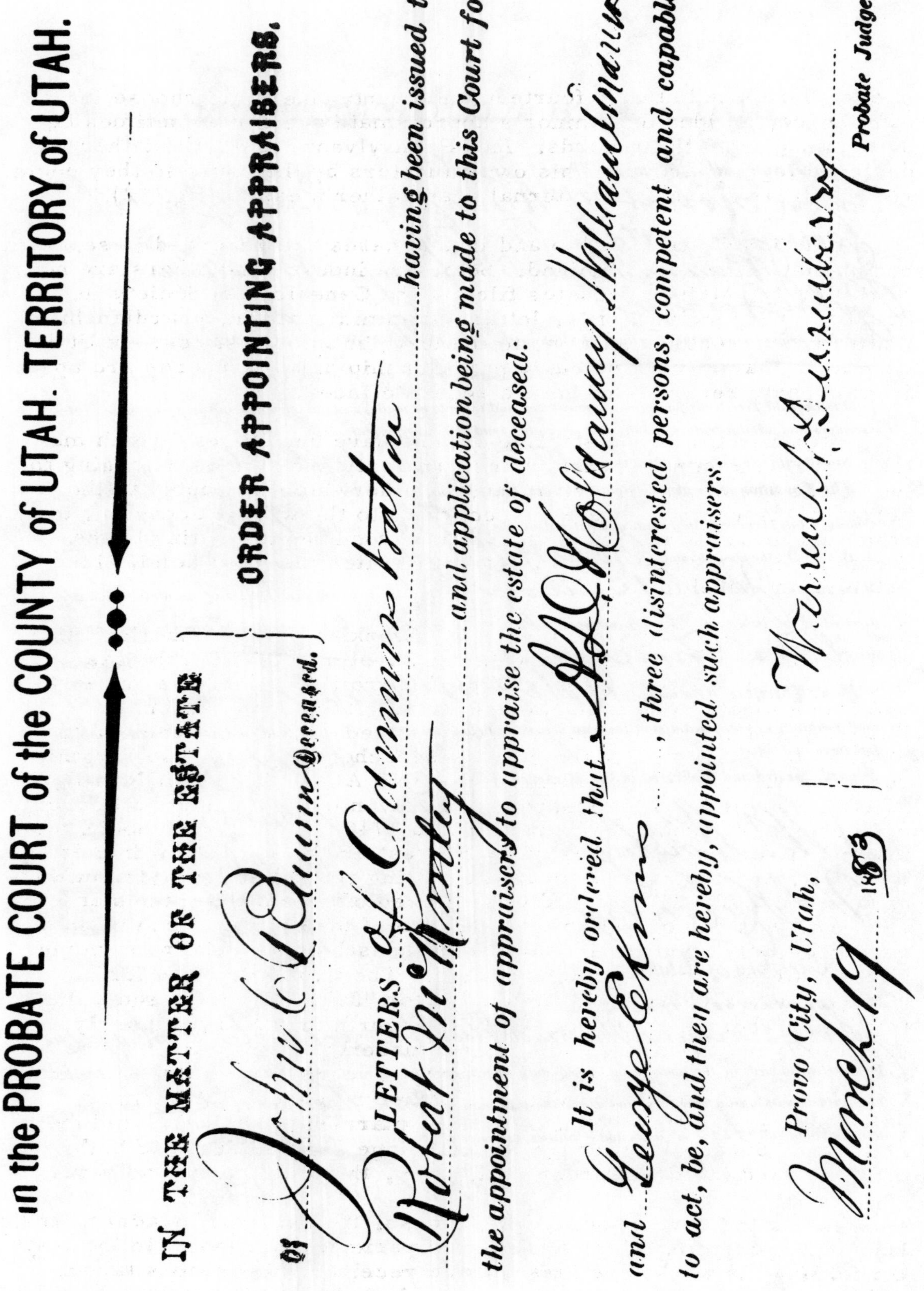

ın the PROBATE COURT of the COUNTY of UTAH. TERRITORY of UTAH.

ORDER APPOINTING APPRAISERS.

IN THE MATTER OF THE ESTATE

of John C. Dunn Deceased.

LETTERS of Administration

Letters of Administration _____ having been issued to

Peter McNulty _____ and application being made to this Court for

the appointment of appraisers to appraise the estate of deceased:

It is hereby ordered that _____ S. W. McCauley McLauthman

and _____ George Kno _____ , three disinterested persons, competent and capable

to act, be, and they are hereby, appointed such appraisers.

Provo City, Utah,

March 19 1883

Warren N. Dusenberry

Probate Judge.

Fig. 71. Order appointing appraisers

212

of age, but those between fourteen and twenty-one could choose their own; hence, an idea of a minor's approximate age can sometimes be determined from the records. In a Pennsylvania case, the father was declared legal guardian of his own daughters by the court so they could receive their share of a maternal grandfather's estate (fig. 72).

Sometimes guardianship and insane cases are recorded in separate books, but many are combined. Some are indexed and others are not. York County, Maine, probates filed at the Genealogical Society in Salt Lake City include wills, letters of administration, guardianship matters, and records relating to the distribution of estates. In Utah County, a majority of the early guardianship-insane records are apart from probate records and have a separate index.

After certain administrative actions have been taken, which may take several months or even years, property and monies belonging to the estate are divided, partitioned, or otherwise distributed to the heirs, devisees, and legatees, according to the will or according to state and local laws if there is no will. Documents relating to the division and distribution of an estate are often the most helpful in establishing kinship (fig. 73).

Several years ago, the author was working on a "Douberley" line of Florida, South Carolina, and North Carolina. The family was finally traced to Craven County, North Carolina, where the earliest reference located was a deed dated about 1756. John, Thomas, William, and Saccor Dubberly were involved. Research seemed to be at a standstill when some general searches were made in Virginia records. Torrence's EARLY WILLS AND ADMINISTRATIONS OF VIRGINIA included a reference to the "Inventory" of one John Dubberly of "Accomack" County, Virginia, dated 1740. Court order books for that county covering the period of interest are on microfilm in Salt Lake City and contained a most interesting record of the distribution of John's estate. The record was marked off in equal sections and each heir was named and given a portion of the estate. Each of them received 16-1/2 pounds of wool, some household items, and farming utensils which came to an equal value. The first entry was for "Grace Dubberly, widow"; the second for "John Dubberly, son"; the third for "Thomas Dubberly, son"; the fourth for "Mary Dubberly, daughter"; and the fifth for "William Dubberly, son." Could these children be the same persons who sixteen years later were living in Craven County, North Carolina? Further research in Accomack records revealed that "John Dubberly" married "Annabella" and their child was "Saccor." Through the marriage record, deeds of both counties, and the court order book entry, the problem was solved.

During the normal probating process, the executor or administrator keeps an accounting of his actions and periodically reports to the court concerning his work. Letters may be received, depositions taken, affidavits signed, and other documents initiated which might help solve a genealogical problem. Investigation of the files is the best way to

STATE OF KANSAS, } ss.
Leavenworth County.

In the Probate Court of Leavenworth County, State of Kansas.

Oscar Juvenal   a minor   male child aged *Two Years*   and *Rosa Zimmerman*   his *mother by her written statement*, now appearing before the Probate Court of Leavenworth County aforesaid, and the said *minor and said mother* thereto consenting.

1. *M. C. Dunkle*   the undersigned, do hereby offer to adopt *Oscar Juvenal*   the minor child above mentioned, as my own *child and heir to be known as Royal Dunkle*

M. E. Dunkle

DONE in the Probate Court of Leavenworth County this *9th* day of *May*   A. D. 18*91*.

Newton Mann

Probate Judge.

IN WITNESS WHEREOF, I the undersigned, Probate Judge of Leavenworth County, have hereto set my hand and affixed the seal of the said Probate Court this *7th* day of *May*   A. D. 18*91*

Newton Mann

Probate Judge.

Fig. 72. Guardianship record

214

In the Matter of the Last Will and)
) Proof of Heirship.
Testament of Austin Sanderson, Deceased.)

Now on this day comes Edward H. Farley, executor of the last will and testament of Austin Sanderson, deceased, in his own proper person and by Al. A. Clapsaddle his attorney, and makes proof of heirship in the estate of said Austin Sanderson, deceased; and the Court having heard the testimony of said Edward H. Farley, a competent witness of lawful age, produced, sworn and examined on oath in open court, finds therefrom that the said Austin Sanderson departed this life, testate, at his late home at Leland in this County, on or about March 10th, 1911, leaving him surviving no widow, and no child or children, and no descendant or descendants of any deceased child or children, and no father, and no mother, and no brother, and no sister, and Austin Sanderson, Seward Sanderson, Josephine Richolson, Isabelle Richolson, Martha Halverson and Mary Oakland children and only surviving children of Sander Sanderson a deceased brother of said Austin Sanderson, and Harvey Sanderson, Sander Sanderson, Eva Hill, Kinne Sanderson, Lester Sanderson and Vira Sanderson children and only children of Samuel Sanderson a deceased son of Sander Sanderson, and Mabel Knutson. Silas Sanderson, Otto Sanderson, Alma Sanderson, Edith Sanderson, Curtis Sanderson, Myrtle Sanderson, Herbert Sanderson, and Kenneth Sanderson children and only children of Charles Sanderson a deceased son of Sander Sanderson, and no descendant or descendants of any other deceased son or daughter of said Sander Sanderson;

Fig. 73. Proof of heirship

determine what actually exists. Some records are quite inclusive, while others are very disappointing.

In Virginia counties, particularly in the earlier days, probate matters were often recorded in "court order books" along with other civil and criminal court actions. Special probate documents may not exist in some instances. The will, a petition, a codicil to a will, or documents showing the distribution of property belonging to an estate might be recorded in the order books, in deed books, or in some other court record. This practice is not peculiar to Virginia, however, and may happen in other states.

When the executor or administrator appeared in court to give an accounting of his actions, such information may have been recorded in civil court docket books or court journals. In a Monroe County, Illinois, problem the researcher was unable to determine the exact date of death from the usual probate records but found a reference in a civil court journal: "Administrator of the estate of John Morgan, dec'd, who died in this County intestate on the 1st day of June 1841." That particular information was probably recorded in no other place.

Most probate offices have general indexes to their estate records which give reference to original will books and estate papers. Some do not, however, and one must search each volume's index separately. Moreover, records may not be indexed as expected. All probate documents relating to Austin Hammer of Henry County, Indiana, are indexed under the name of "Green P. Nelson," administrator of Hammer's estate.

It should also be noted that probate jurisdiction has varied from state to state over the years, both in court responsibility and the governmental level at which the probating process was handled. New England, Connecticut, and Vermont probated on a district level (one or more towns constituting a probate district), while Rhode Island operated at the town level. In Massachusetts and Maine the county has been responsible, while New Hampshire functioned on a "provincial" basis before 1772 but acted on a county basis thereafter. New Jersey, North Carolina, and South Carolina have each had periods when probates were handled on a state basis, but now the counties are responsible. Prior to the Revolution, New York probated all records through New York County, and it was after 1780 before upstate and western counties had probate responsibility.

In the colonial period, the General Court, Particular Court, or some other court handled probate action, but many states set up regular Probate Courts shortly thereafter. In early New York it was the Prerogative Court with Surrogates in the counties, but in Pennsylvania the Orphan's Court was responsible. In Georgia it was the Ordinary Court, while at an early period in New England the General Court held probate responsibility and the "Governor" was the "Ordinary." The Circuit Court, the County Court, and the Court of Common Pleas has been responsible in Indiana, Illinois, Ohio, and in several other states.

Civil and Criminal Court Records

After probate records have been investigated, it is a good practice to investigate certain civil-criminal court records, because many of our ancestors have been involved in court actions concerning law and equity. Cases dealing with adoption, adultery, divorce, citizenship, change of name, murder, and disputes involving personal property and real estate should be of special interest. Of course, not all adoptions were "legal" and of court record, and not all foreigners took out citizenship and left official records of the event. Neither have all persons who have changed their names made it a matter of court record, nor have all couples who separated gotten a legal divorce. Yet, a great number of our ancestors are of record in American courts, and most of the records are open for public inspection.

General indexes to civil and criminal court records do not exist as often as they do in probate matters but DOCKET BOOKS, JOURNALS, OR COURT ORDER BOOKS can usually be consulted to locate cases involving specific persons. Docket books and journals are usually chronological listings of cases which have come before the court with the names of the plaintiff and defendant or names of parties involved in a dispute listed. Actions and decisions of the court are generally recorded in order books, minute books, or books containing judgments and decrees. Sometimes the order books and minute books are indexed within each volume and arranged chronologically, but most of the time they are not indexed and one must consult the docket books or journals for reference to the persons of interest.

Not all adoptions are of record in the local courthouse but some are and give good genealogical information. Sometimes the parentage is not known by the court and hence is not recorded, but sometimes considerable detail is given in the records. Sometimes adoption records have been "sealed" by court order and can only be reviewed by authorized persons who gain a new court order to have the records opened. This is common with many modern adoptions (fig. 74).

Two or three examples at the first of this chapter indicated that adultery has been a matter of court action in America at least since 1641, and persons are still being charged for such acts. When persons are charged with adultery, the court records may give parentage, dates, and other facts of genealogical value. Frequently, the court record will give reference to docket and file numbers that can be used to locate the original files. In other situations, general docket books list the particular case, and reference is given to the files where additional information can be located.

Divorce records are separately indexed in some courts but might be listed among other civil court matters in others. In these instances, they are usually listed chronologically in docket books or journals.

In the District Court of the Fourth
Judicial District, Utah County
State of Utah

In the Matter of the adoption

Bertha Walter, a minor   {Agreement to Adopt

A petition having been filed in the
above entitled court by Martin Walter and
Esther J Walter, his wife, for leave to adopt
Bertha Walter, a deserted minor child,
whose parents are unknown.

Now, therefore, in consideration of
the entry of an order of said court, permitting said adoption to be made as prayed
for in said petition, the undersigned
the petitioners who are residents of Utah
County, Utah in which such order of adoption
is made hereby agree with said minor
that said minor, said Bertha Walter
shall be adopted, and is now adopted
as our own child, and that such minor
child shall be treated in all respects
as our own lawful child should be
treated including the right of support
protection and inheritance.

In witness whereof, we have here unto
set our hands and seals this 7th. day
of May, 1917.

Martin Walter
Esther J. Walter

Signed in open court in the presence
of A. B. Morgan, Judge

Fig. 74. Court record relating to adoption

218

The testimony given in court is usually recorded in the files, and documents relating to "Findings in Fact" are extremely important. The testimony can provide date and place of marriage, the names and number of children, their places of residence, death information, and other helpful facts. Affidavits, depositions, letters, and related documents may also be among the file papers.

Oaths of allegiance, declarations, intentions, and other documents relating to naturalization and citizenship are among local, state, and federal court records. Those dating prior to about 1900 are generally at the county level, but after that date they might be under federal custody. Records at the local courthouses or city halls are open for public inspection but cannot be duplicated or photocopied. Federal statute forbids it. However, genealogical information might be copied in longhand from the records without breaking the law (fig. 75).

It should be remembered that early colonists and settlers did not always follow legal procedures to become citizens as persons must do today. They were merely coming to another part of their own country and were citizens by decree. This was particularly true regarding British colonists. However, some German and other "foreign born" persons were required to take an oath of allegiance or make a declaration of their intention to become a citizen. These lists usually give the person's name, the date and place of debarkation, and the country to which he owes allegiance. They seldom give places of birth or other genealogical facts. Some records after 1860 are more inclusive.

The new immigrant may have settled in two or three different places before he initiated citizenship papers, or he may have done it immediately upon settling in his first county of residence. Existing papers are usually in the courthouse of the county where the person was residing, and a researcher must sometimes investigate the records of two or three counties before finding the needed material. The author has seen British subjects of record in Salt Lake County who made declarations during the "Mormon Era" of their intention to become citizens, but has seen none in the colonial period.

On one occasion the author wrote to Warren County, Minnesota, for a check of court records on an 1870 Scandinavian immigrant and was informed that a citizenship record was located but it could not be copied. It was necessary to send an agent to the courthouse and copy the information, but the effort was worthwhile because the record gave the village of birth as well as parentage and other helpful genealogical information.

After about 1902-1908, the laws for naturalization and citizenship were more effective, and officials kept better records at both the county or city and national levels. The following information was copied from a Montana court record and pertained to one David Thomas Evans from Wales:

Declaration of Intention

TO BECOME A CITIZEN OF THE UNITED STATES.

UNITED STATES OF AMERICA,
TERRITORY OF UTAH,
County of _Sanpete_

I, _Christian H Jacobsen_, do declare, on oath that it is bona fide my intention to become a citizen of the United States of America; and to renounce and abjure forever, all allegiance and fidelity, to all and any Foreign Prince, Potentate, State and Sovereignty whatever, and particularly to _the Kingdom of Denmark_ of whom I was a subject.

Christian H Jacobsen

Subscribed and sworn to before me, this _"16"_ day _October_ A. D. 189_5_.

George Hawncamp
Clerk of the U. S. First Judicial District Court, In and for the Territory of Utah.
By _Robert E. Knowlden_ D. C.

I, _George Hawncamp_, Clerk of the First Judicial District Court of the United States, in and for the Territory of Utah, do hereby certify that the above is a true and correct copy of the Original Declaration of Intention of _Christian H Jacobsen_ to become a

CITIZEN OF THE UNITED STATES OF AMERICA,

now of record in my office at Provo City, Utah.

In Testimony Whereof, the Seal of said Court is hereunto affixed this _"16"_ day of _October_ in the year One Thousand Eight Hundred and Ninety _five_.

George Hawncamp Clerk,

By _Robert E. Knowlden_ Deputy Clerk.

NOTE.—A copy of the above Declaration of Intention can be obtained at any time of the Clerk of the above Court for $1.00.

JOHN MORRIS COMPANY, PRINTERS, CHICAGO.

Fig. 75. Citizenship records

FACTS FOR PETITION FOR NATURALIZATION

Aaron Johnson

(Give here name used in Declaration of Intention, and do not abbreviate any part of name, by initial or otherwise.)

1. My place of residence is _Mapleton_ (Number and name of street.), _____ (City or town.)
Utah (County.), _Utah_ (State, Territory, or District.)

2. My present occupation is _Farmer_

3. I was born on the _22_ day of _May_, 18_50_, at _Council Bluffs_ (City or town.) _Iowa_ _____, and my last foreign residence was
Raber (City or town.) _Alberta Canada_ (Country.)

4. I emigrated to the United States from _Reber Canada_ (Port of embarkation.)
_____ (Country.), on or about the _23_ day of _Nov_, 19_07_,
and arrived at the port of _Coutts_ (Port of arrival.) _Montana_ (State.), ^or about^ on the _24_
day of _Nov._, 19_07_, ~~on the vessel~~ _by team_, of the _____ Line,
by first cabin _____, second cabin _____, steerage _____

(If the alien arrived otherwise than by vessel, the character of conveyance or name of transportation company should be given.)

at which time my height was _5_ feet _10_ inches; complexion, _White_; color of hair, _brown_;
color of eyes, _blue_; occupation, _Farmer_; destined to _Mapleton_ (City or town.)
Utah (State.), and accompanied by _My Son Leland_ _____;
destined to _Mapleton._ _Rest of my family came later._
(Person or persons to whom destined.)

(If the alien came under some other name than his own name, the name used on the steamship must be given here, or the record of arrival can not be found.)

(If the alien arrived as a stowaway or deserting seaman, or in any other manner than as a passenger, please so state.)

5. I declared my intention to become a citizen of the United States on the _____ day of _____,
19_____, at _Provo_ (Location of court.), in the _____ Court of _____

(OVER.)

14—267

Fig. 75a.

221

.6. I am _____ married. My husband's name was _Louisa M Johnson_
                         wife's   is
(Petitioner, if a widower, should give the name of his wife when living, and state place
of her birth; if not married, he should enter "not" in first sentence. In both cases
surplus words should be struck through.)

He
She was born in _Manti_____, _Sanpete_____, and is now deceased.
              (City or town.)   (Country.)   now resides at

_Mapleton_____, _Utah_____
       (City or town.)   (Country.)

I have _10_ children whose names, date and places of birth, and places of residence are
as follows:

A. _Wayne_____, born _14_ day of _July_, 1872, at _Springville_; resides at _Springville_

_Winnifred___, born _17_ day of _Nov._, 1874, at " ; resides at _died_

_Claudia_____, born _12_ day of _June_, 1877, at " ; resides at _Mapleton_

_Willis_____, born _16_ day of _Sep._, 1879, at " ; resides at "

_Frank_____, born _2_ day of _Oct._, 1881, at " ; resides at "

_Elmer_____, born _14_ day of _Nov._, 1884, at " ; resides at "
Hugh   " 27   _July_ 1887   _Mapleton_   "
_Louis_____, born _8_ day of _Dec._, 1889, at " ; resides at "
Leland   " 15   _Aug._ 1893   "   "
Bryan   " 20   _June_ 1897   "

7. I now owe allegiance to _King Geo. 5_____
                          (Name of sovereign and country.)

8. I am able to speak the English language.

9. I have resided continuously in the United States since the _____ day of _____, 19_07_,
              State
   and in the Territory of _____ since the _____ day of _____, 19_07_
              District

10. I have _not_ heretofore made petition for United States citizenship.

   (If petitioner has heretofore made application for citizenship, the facts required should be fully stated in the following
   blanks:)

   I previously petitioned for citizenship to the _____Court, at

   _____, _____
           (City or town.)   (State, Territory, or District.)

   on the _____ day of _____, 1_____, which was denied for the following reason:

   _____

   The cause of such denial has since been cured or removed.

                                    Aaron Johnson.
                                    (Sign name in full.)

Fig. 75a. continued.

222

#693795 Petitions Vol. 5, No. 723 Fugus County, Montana
DATE OF BIRTH: July 4, 1875
PLACE OF BIRTH: Swansea So. Wales, British Isles
DATE OF ARRIVAL IN U.S.: June 10, 1908
PLACE OF ARRIVAL IN U.S.: Lewistown, Montana
CITY IN WHICH NATURALIZED: Lewistown, Montana
NAME OF THE COURT: District Court of Fugus County, Montana
DATE OF NATURALIZATION: Feb. 6, 1917
ADDRESS AT TIME OF NATURALIZATION: Hanover, Montana
RESIDENCE TIME: July 1916 to 1918
WITNESSES: William Tierney and Wm. Duncan
FIRST PAPERS DATED: July 1910
CITY OF FIRST PAPERS: Lewistown, Montana
NAME OF OTHER CITIES: Kendall Mont. June 11, 1908 to
July 1916

Federal records relating to naturalization and citizenship may be located in district courts and in the National Archives in Washington, D. C. Some records pertaining to immigrants are also located at the federal centers of arrival, such as at "Ellis Island, New York," or at other Federal Record Centers. Genealogist Meredith Colket had the following to say about Federal records:

The first naturalization act passed by Congress on March 26, 1790 (1 Stat. 103), provided that an alien who desired to become a citizen should apply to "any common law court of record, in any one of the states wherein he shall have resided for the term of one year at least." Under this and later laws aliens were naturalized in Federal courts and also in State and local courts.

Records of naturalization proceedings in Federal courts are usually in records of the district court for the district in which the proceedings took place. These court records may still be in the custody of the court, they may have been transferred to a Federal Records Center operated by the General Services Administration, or they may have been transferred to the National Archives. Naturalization proceedings are often recorded in the minutes of both district and circuit courts; for example, see the minutes of both courts for the Southern District of New York, 1789-1913, now in the National Archives. Also in the National Archives, among the records of the U. S. District Court for the Eastern District of Virginia, are a few declarations, petitions, and certificates of naturalization for the years 1855 and 1867-96. And among the records of the U. S. District Court for the Western District of Virginia at Abingdon are a few petitions for naturalization, 1910-17, and a few petitions to set aside certificates of naturalization, 1909. Other naturalization records do not appear to have been transferred to the National Archives with court records.

Records of naturalization proceedings in State or local courts would normally be in the custody of the clerk of the court. Publications of the Historical Records Survey, described near the end

223

of this chapter, are sometimes useful in finding and using State and local court records.

Two Historical Records Survey publications that relate specifically to naturalization records are INDEX TO NATURALIZATION RECORDS, MISSISSIPPI COURTS, 1798-1906 (prepared by the Old Law Naturalization Records Project, Division of Community Service Programs, WPA, and issued in Jackson, Mar. 1942; classified in the National Archives Library as HRS 1857A), which lists individuals alphabetically under the county in which they were naturalized; and GUIDE TO NATURALIZATION RECORDS IN NEW JERSEY (prepared by the New Jersey Historical Records Program, Division of Community Service Programs, WPA, and issued in Newark, 1941; classified in the National Archives Library as HRS 1337), which describes series of naturalization records by county.

If a naturalized citizen or a person who had declared his intention to become a citizen applied for a homestead, or if a naturalized citizen applied for a passport before 1906, the application would normally be in the National Archives and give the name of the court where the naturalization took place. Duplicates of records relating to persons naturalized since September 27, 1906, are deposited with the Commissioner of Immigration and Naturalization, Washington, D. C., and are confidential.

Photocopies of Naturalization Records

To centralize the information in the naturalization records, which are among the records of more than 5,000 Federal, State, and other courts, the Work Projects Administration in the late 1930's began to make photographic copies of the records and to index them. Some of these copies and indexes are now in the National Archives.

The records. --The records consist of 5" x 8" photocopies of naturalization documents, 1787-1906, filed by courts in Maine, Massachusetts, New Hampshire, and Rhode Island. They are arranged by State, thereunder by court, and thereunder by date of naturalization.

Index to the records. --The index is on 3" x 5" cards arranged by name of petitioner for naturalization. A card contains the name and location of the court and identifies the papers by volume and page number and petition or entry number. The printed cards have spaces, often left blank, for other data that may be in the naturalization papers. The index cards are filed according to the Soundex system; that is, alphabetically by the first letter of the surname, thereunder by the sound of the surname, and thereunder alphabetically by the given name. There are some index cards for New York and Vermont, although neither the related naturalization records nor copies of them are in the National Archives.

Information in the records. --For each naturalization there are usually two pages of forms with spaces for some or all of the following: the petition for citizenship, the oath of allegiance to the United States, affidavits relating to U. S. residence, and a record of citizenship. Other information on the forms usually includes place and date of birth and of arrival in the United States, place of residence at the time of applying for citizenship, and sometimes the name of the ship on which the immigrant arrived and his occupation.

Use of the records. --A searcher may make an abstract of a naturalization record in the National Archives. According to section 346 of an act approved October 14, 1940 (54 Stat. 1163), however, it is a felony for any person "to print, photograph, make, or execute, or in any manner cause to be printed, photographed, made, or executed, without lawful authority, any print or impression in the likeness of any certificate of arrival, declaration of intention, or certificate of naturalization or of citizenship, or any part thereof."

Record group. --The records are in Record Group 85, Records of the Immigration and Naturalization Service.

Civil Service Commission List of Naturalization Certificates

The records. --A volume entitled "List of Naturalization Certificates Sent to the U. S. Attorney for Review, and Returned by Him to the Board of Civil Service Examiners, of Persons Taking Civil Service Examinations, 1905-06," was transferred to the National Archives from the New York district office of the Civil Service Commission. Naturalization certificates for persons taking Federal civil service examinations in New York State are entered under the initial letter of the surname and thereunder chronologically by date the certificate was sent to the U. S. attorney.

Information in the records. --For each naturalization certificate are given the name of the court that issued it, the name of the person who signed it, the kind of civil service examination taken and where, and the date the certificate was returned by the attorney.

Record group. --The volume is part of Record Group 146, Records of the United States Civil Service Commission.

RECORDS CONCERNING INHABITANTS OF THE DISTRICT OF COLUMBIA

The National Archives has certain court records relating to the part of the District of Columbia that was not retroceded to Virginia. They include naturalization records, transcripts of wills, administration papers relating to the estates of decedents, guardianship papers, and indentures of apprenticeship. They form part of the records of the courts created under terms of an act approved February 27, 1801 (2 Stat. 103), and later acts. Each kind of record is described separately below.

Naturalization Records

The records.--The naturalization records, 1802-1926, are based on an act approved April 14, 1802 (2 Stat. 153), and later acts. The ones described here, for the years 1802-1906, are less detailed than those filed in accordance with an act approved June 29, 1906 (34 Stat. 596).

The records include declarations of intention (or certified copies if the declarations had been filed elsewhere), petitions to become citizens (which succeeded "proofs of residence"), and orders of admission to citizenship. A declaration of intention normally preceded a proof of residence or a petition to become a citizen by two or more years, but the declaration was sometimes not required if the citizen had an honorable discharge from certain military service or had entered the country when a minor. The petition to become a citizen and the order of admission were handled at or about the same time and were often recorded on the same page. The early orders of admission to citizenship are normally available only in the minute books.

A list of the basic series of naturalization records to about 1906, with dates of each series, follows: unbound declarations of intention and such related records as proofs of residence, arranged chronologically, 1802-1903; a bound volume of abstracts (and, for 1818, transcripts) of declarations of intention, 1818-65; bound volumes of declarations of intention, 1866-1906; bound volumes labeled "naturalization records" consisting in part of orders of admission, 1824-1906; and a volume index to most series of naturalization records, 1802-1907.

Information in the records.--The declarations of intention normally show for each declarant his name, age, allegiance, the country or exact place of his birth, the date of his declaration, and, for those dated before 1866, the date and place of his arrival and the place of his embarkation. The proofs of residence contain the names of two citizens who testified.

The bound "naturalization records" show, for 1824-39, the date of admission of each person to citizenship and usually the same information as that contained in the declaration of intention and proof of age; for 1839-65, the name of each person and the term and year of admission, arranged by first letter of surname; for 1866-1906, the name, place of birth, and age of the person, the date of his declaration of intention, statement of honorable discharge, or statement of arrival as a minor (at first, before the age of 18, and later, 21); and from 1903, the date of arrival.[20]

A number of other events might be recorded in civil or criminal court records, including matters pertaining to real estate and personal property. Court action regarding these matters are probably more prevalent than any other type.

In 1680, John Shepard of York County, Maine, was charged with "Tresspass" by Nathaniel Keene for removing timber from certain property which Nathaniel claimed was his. John Shepard insisted he owned the right to such timber and brought his wife Mary, his daughter Margaret, and his son Mark into court to testify in his defense. Each witness stated his or her name and relationship to John and gave age and place of residence at the time. Previous searching in local records had failed to show the parentage of one "Mark Shepard" who fit the description of this person. But this court record seemed to solve the problem.

Unfortunately, the Genealogical Society in Salt Lake City has not acquired a great number of civil and criminal court records, and most work in them must be done in the respective courthouses. They should not be neglected, however, merely because they are not readily available.

The genealogical significance of law libraries also deserves some consideration here. True, these records are abridgments from original court cases, but they contain some excellent genealogy in readable form. In cases where courthouses have been burned, these abridgments might be especially useful. There is room for more study on this subject.

Another area where more study could be carried out is in the field of Session Laws and Statutes. They contain genealogy as well as other matters of interest but are not often used.

Noel C. Stevenson has written an excellent article relating to the significance of genealogical research in Session Laws and Statutes, and a portion of the article is reproduced below.

A number of years ago, a dealer in London sent me a shipment of books. Apparently due to a paper shortage there, the books were packed in a number of stray pages of a book containing acts of Parliament. While looking over one of these pages, an Act of 1672 was observed providing for the "Protection of William Dick, grandchild and appearand aire [sic] to Sir William Dick."
This brief title of the Act is illustrative of the wealth of genealogical facts contained in Session Laws and Statutes of the various legislative bodies of any state or nation. In this article it will be necessary to confine our analysis of these sources to the United States. It is obvious, however, that a study of the laws of other countries would produce results similar to those disclosed here.
Session laws are the laws passed at successive legislative sessions of the various states. Statutes at Large are statutes in full or at length as originally enacted as distinguished from abridgments, compilations, and revisions. If you could use the Session Laws exclusively, instead of the Statutes, you would be certain to have access to every law passed. One thing is certain, a person usually settles for what is available. Furthermore, don't use revised or compiled statutes if you can avoid it, as all

of the private acts and genealogical facts probably will be omitted. You should be safe using the statutes at large as they are supposed to contain all of the laws enacted whether private or public.

There are a few fine examples of compiled statutes available for the use of the genealogist and historian, such as Hening's STATUTES AT LARGE OF VIRGINIA, Smith's, Index to the Names mentioned in Litell's LAWS OF KENTUCKY, and similar material available for other colonies or states. What we haven't found, though, is a systematic explanation of how to use and where to find the session laws and statutes that haven't been reprinted and indexed like Litell and Hening, and which are buried in the local law libraries. Unfortunately, there are only a few Hening's and Litell's and their counterparts, whereas the number of volumes of session laws and statutes for the various colonies and states literally run into thousands. Furthermore, the large amount of authentic genealogical facts buried in them is indeed amazing. There can be no doubt that many genealogical mysteries that plague us now would be cleared up if enterprising genealogists methodically searched these sources.

A few practical examples from session laws will prove the value of this source. The same type of information will be found in statutes at large.

Chapter XIII, of Massachusetts Session Laws of 1787, is an act passed 16 Nov. 1787, and provides for the naturalization of some twenty persons. Their names, occupations, residences, and, in some instances, their wives and children's names are given. The best example is the family of Henry Smith, merchant, his wife, Elizabeth, and their children, Henry Lloyd Smith, Elizabeth, Catherina, Rebecca, and Anna Smith, all residents of Boston. Also mentioned is Kirk Boot, formerly of London, Great Britain, his wife, Mary Boot, and their daughter, Frances, all now residents of Boston.

An Act changing the name of Thomas Greaves Russell to Thomas Russell Greaves, of Boston, Gentleman, was passed as Chapter XII on 6 July 1787, by the General Court of Massachusetts. The reason for the change of name was that Thomas "being a lineal descendant of the Honourable Thomas Greaves, late of Charlestown, Esq., deceased, and being desirous from respect to his memory, to be called by his surname," petitioned that the court authorize the change.

Of course, a researcher expects to find records like the foregoing in Massachusetts, but what about some jurisdiction where records are generally lacking? To answer this question, Alabama was selected as a good case in point. The first Session Laws of Alabama Territory were examined with similar results. Quite a number of divorces were found and a similar number of marriages were made legitimate. On page 16, is the record of a divorce of William Henry from his wife, Ann Henry. Section 2 of the act provides "That the marriage of the said William Henry with Amelia Bradley previous to the granting of this divorce, be and the same is hereby declared to be good and valid in law, and that George Gaines, Caroline, Matilda, Cornelia, Julia Brunette, and William Jackson, the issue born of said marriage, be and the same are hereby declared to be legitimate." I believe I am safe in waiving further argument in behalf of Alabama. Several other similar acts were observed just as good as William Henry's.

A search was made of Pennsylvania Session Laws with the same gratifying results. Chapter 99 of the Session Laws of 1783 disclosed that Mary McKay of the town of Pittsburgh, widow of Colonel Aeneas McKay (late of this state, deceased), was granted a franchise to establish a ferry over the Monongahela River at the New-Store, on a tract of land late the property of her deceased husband, and now vested in his children, Samuel McKay and Elizabeth McKay.

Chapter 78 of the same year provided for the dissolution of the marriage of Charles Rubey of the town and county of Bedford, cordwainer, from Jane Rubey, his wife, late Jane Smith.

Abraham Comron of Philadelphia petitioned the General Assembly on 5 Nov. 1782, for what amounted to a statutory quiet title action. In his petition, he stated that his grandfather, Nicholas Cassell, deceased, did in his life-time, by deed of gift convey unto Mary Comron, the mother of the said Abraham, a certain lot on Race Street, between the Front and Second Streets, from the Delaware River in the City of Philadelphia. On this lot, John Comron, the father of Abraham, built a small brick house. John Comron and his wife, Mary, died intestate, leaving as heirs, the said Abraham and a daughter, Rebecca, their only issue. That when the enemy were in possession of Philadelphia, Abraham and his family moved to the county of Gloucester, New Jersey, to a place called Clonmwell, where the enemy came and broke and destroyed everything belonging to the family and burned all the papers, amongst which was the deed of gift from the said Nicholas Cassell to the said Mary Comron, the mother of said Abraham. Abraham's petition was granted, as the act providing for his relief was passed 6 Dec. 1783.

The foregoing actual examples are revelatory of the genealogical facts you will discover in these sources. During my search, I found many equally as good or better.

In order to make a thorough search of these sources, it is necessary to make a page by page search of the laws for the period in which you are interested, unless the archives department or library of the state in which you are searching has published a printed index or compiled a card index including all names mentioned in the laws. Therefore, before undertaking an extended search of these sources, be sure to ascertain if the state involved in your search has indexed the names appearing in its laws. If so, did they index all persons by Christian and surname? If not, you will still have to make a page-by-page search to be sure you are not missing your party. This problem will be with us until some public-spirited and genealogical minded person or organization realizes the value of financing the digesting and indexing of these excellent sources. Fortunately, progress has been made in indexing and in compiling bibliographies disclosing the available session laws and statutes which are of great value to genealogists.

Check Lists

Session Laws:

> CHECK-LIST OF SESSION LAWS, Compiled by Grace E. McDonald, N.Y., 1936, The H. W. Wilson Company, pp. 266.
> A SUPPLEMENT WITH BIBLIOGRAPHICAL NOTES, Emendations and Additions, compiled by Erwin H. Pollack, General Assistant, Columbia University Law Library. (This is a supplement to the Check-List compiled by Grace E. McDonald.) Preliminary Edition, Boston, National Association of State Libraries, 1941, pp. 48.

Statutes:

> CHECK-LIST OF STATUTES OF THE UNITED STATES OF AMERICA, etc. Compiled by Grace E. McDonald for the ------------ National Association of State Libraries. Providence, 1937, pp. 147.

To tap these sources on a local problem, the nearest county law library will probably have the session laws or statutes, or both, available to you. However, you can't very well ascertain what there is available as a whole without referring to the above mentioned check-lists. Even before working on a problem in the local law library, it is wise to check with the state law library or archives to see if there is a printed or card index to persons. If you find that no index of persons has been compiled and your search is extensive, it will be necessary to go to a large library, such as at the state library, or one of the larger county law libraries, or better yet, the law library of the Library of Congress. The larger law libraries have excellent collections of early statutes and session laws from all parts of the country. Of course, a searcher is bound to find incomplete collections as the early volumes are very costly, and in some instances, are not available at any price.

Assume you find the laws have not been indexed and you visit a law library and know the year or years most likely to contain the information you are seeking, you would first examine the check-lists mentioned above to see if the law library has the session laws or statutes for that period. You find that the library has the one you desire. After getting the volume or volumes, you examine the index, if any, or table of contents, in each volume for the name of the family for which you are searching. Then merely turn to the page containing the information about the family. If there is no index or table of contents, a page by page search will be necessary, which, of course, is the safest method.

For example, assume you are trying to find the wife and

children of John Gardiner, a lawyer residing in Boston, Massachusetts, in 1787. By referring to the above mentioned checklist of session laws, you find that the session laws are in the law library. Examination of the table of contents discloses a private act relating to Gardiner and his family on 25 October 1787. It is Chapter IV, and names "John Gardiner Esq., Barrister at Law, Margaret Gardiner, his wife, Ann Gardiner, John Silvester John Gardiner, and William Gardiner, their children." This act was passed to correct a previous act of 1784 which failed to include his wife's name.

A course in legal research is not necessary as there is really nothing complicated about the procedure.

As mentioned, a page by page search is the safest method. However, if you are lucky, you may spot what you are looking for in the index or table of contents, if any. If the index contains headings, such as, "Relief of - - -," "Persons," "Naturalization of - - -," "Divorces," "Private Acts," you are in luck.[21]

---

1. Henry J. Abraham, COURTS AND JUDGES: AN INTRODUCTION TO THE JUDICIAL PROCESS (New York: Oxford University Press, 1962), p. 2.

2. Two excellent paperbacks covering the subject adequately are Claudius O. Johnson's AMERICAN STATE AND LOCAL GOVERNMENT, 4th ed. (New York: Thomas Y. Crowell Co., 1965) and Joseph F. Zimmerman's STATE AND LOCAL GOVERNMENT (New York: Barnes and Noble, 1962).

3. Johnson, p. 155.

4. Charles Edward Banks, HISTORY OF YORK MAINE (Boston, 1931-1935; reprinted 1967 by The Regional Publishing Company, Baltimore), pp. 100-104.

5. PROVINCE AND COURT RECORDS OF MAINE (Maine Historical Society, Portland, Maine, 1928), 1:103.

6. Ibid., p. 71.

7. Ibid., p. 72.

8. Ibid., pp. 73, 74.

9. Ibid., pp. 74, 75.

10. YORK MAINE DEEDS, 5:103.

11. District of Columbia Court Records on file at the National Archives, Washington, D. C., copy in possession of the author.

12. Jay County, Indiana Citizenship Records, copy in possession of the author.

13. Utah County Probate Records, Estate of John C. Baum, copy in possession of the author.

14. Utah County Adoption Records, Adoption of Bertha Walter, a minor child, copy in possession of the author.

15. LaSalle County, Illinois Probate Records, Estate of Austin Sanderson, copy in possession of the author.

16. Ibid.

17. Donald Lines Jacobus, "Probate Law and Custom," THE AMERICAN GENEALOGIST 9 (July 1932):4.

18. Ibid.

19. Ibid.

20. Meredith B. Colket, Jr. and Frank E. Bridgers, GUIDE TO GENEALOGICAL RECORDS IN THE NATIONAL ARCHIVES (Washington: The National Archives, 1964), p. 142.

21. Noel C. Stevenson, ed., THE GENEALOGICAL READER (Salt Lake City: Deseret Book Co., 1958).

CHAPTER 10

SEARCHING LAND AND PROPERTY
RECORDS FOR GENEALOGY

Considering the entire spectrum of American genealogy, land and property records have probably helped solve more difficult problems than any other single source; yet, many researchers fail to make effective use of them. True, they do not provide such prime genealogical facts as exact birth and death dates, but they often contain excellent information about time and place and also valuable kinship information. An American pedigree should be built on land records.

Land and property records should be investigated in conjunction with probate and civil court records because the two are so closely related and complement each other. The sequence of search may vary with each problem, but generally it is advisable to investigate probate records first, then land records, and finally civil and criminal court records.

Facts Contained in Land and Property Records

Some of the more important genealogical facts contained in the records include the names of buyers and sellers (grantee-grantors), the given name of a spouse, the names of former spouses, clues to the maiden name of a wife, names of relatives and their kinship, and the names of friends and associates.

When it comes to time and place, property records often contain facts about previous places of residence, dates of settlement and removal from a particular area, places of residence of relatives and associates, dates and places of death (or clues to them), approximate birth and marriage dates and places, occupation, church affiliation, social status, clues to other sources, and sometimes the location of the immigrant ancestral home. They have even been known to include facts about illegitimacies and adoption as well as other unusual family circumstances and events. Almost anything might be listed in a land or property record.

Origin of Land Title

The story of America is really the story of land, and several factors have made land and property records valuable genealogical sources. Land has been plentiful and relatively cheap or easily obtained, and its ownership and use has been a matter of public record since colonial times. Personal property, as well as real estate, is involved, and the use of it during life and its disposition after death has resulted in the preservation of valuable genealogical information.

Original title to land in America rested with God and the Indians, but the English Crown assumed ownership through conquest and treaty and then chartered or granted the land to the thirteen colonies and her people. The thirteen original colonies included Connecticut, Delaware, Georgia, Maryland, Massachusetts, New Hampshire, New Jersey, New York, North Carolina, Pennsylvania, Rhode Island, South Carolina, and Virginia. Kentucky was part of Virginia, Maine was a province of Massachusetts, Tennessee was considered part of North Carolina, and Vermont was claimed by both New York and New Hampshire. The area south of Georgia--including what is now Alabama, Florida, and Mississippi--was held by France and Spain until 1819 (fig. 76).

The area north and west of the Ohio and Mississippi rivers, extending to the Pacific Ocean, was claimed by several of the colonies through their original charters and grants from the British Crown and was also claimed by France and Spain through their early exploration and settlement in that region. Through cession from the colonies after the Revolution and through various treaties and purchases, this vast region was finally acquired by the United States and became the "public domain" (fig. 77).

Land Jurisdiction and Ownership in the Colonial States

Three types of colonies administered land and property prior to the Revolution--ROYAL, PROPRIETARY, and CORPORATE colonies. Some were under more than one classification during certain periods.

Georgia, New Hampshire, New Jersey, New York, North Carolina, South Carolina, and Virginia were royal colonies at one time or another with the title to lands and the responsibility for its administration resting with the Crown and its governors. Delaware, Maryland, Pennsylvania, New Jersey (for a time), and the Carolinas (for a time), were proprietary colonies. Land and property matters in these colonies was the responsibility of selected proprietors in England and America and their agents. Connecticut, Massachusetts, Rhode Island, and Virginia (for a time), were corporate colonies with land ownership and its administration resting with various merchants and individuals

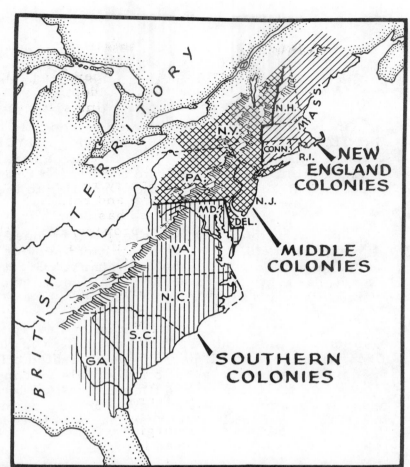

Fig. 76.
Colonial America

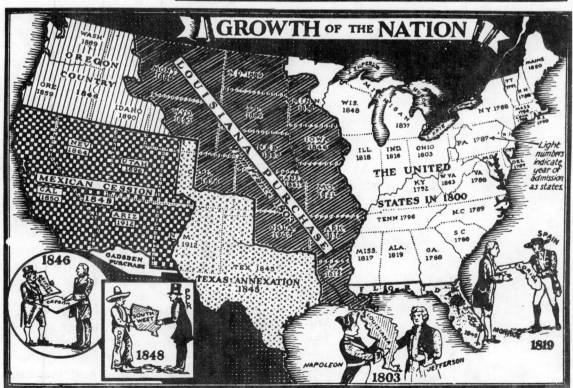

Fig. 77. N.S. land acquisitions

in England as well as with certain colonial leaders in America (fig. 78).

Individuals within the colonies gained title to their lands through SPECIAL PURPOSE GRANTS, through a HEADRIGHT SYSTEM, and through PRIVATE PURCHASE. Of course the records relating to the early charters and grants from the British Crown are not as valuable, genealogically speaking, as those relating to the individual, but they are of historical importance.

Special purpose grants were given in most colonies at one time or another for military and/or political service or merely for being a recognized member of the community. Grants were also given to extend the frontier, and some were given to protect the colonies from Indians and other outside forces.

The headright system was practiced early in Virginia but was also used in the middle colonies as well as in New England for a time. Under this system, all persons were treated alike, and land was granted in stated acreages to individuals settling or to persons bringing others into the colony for settlement. No orderly pattern was followed under the system, and it was abused by some; however, it did serve to attract many settlers to America as well as from one colony to another.

Individual or private purchase, important in all of the colonies from the beginning and even in the states to the present day, accounts for most land transfer. In certain periods, land or trading companies were organized. They acquired large tracts of land and then sold smaller parcels for a profit. However, in many instances, individuals purchased land directly from the town fathers or from other officials such as the proprietors.

Where land was surveyed in the colonies, a METES AND BOUNDS method was used which was based upon physical or topographical features of the land. The land description usually included the name of the water-course or the tributary it was situated on and listed measurement details showing boundaries and rights-of-way as well as restrictions or limitations for use, as follows:

> . . . a tract of land containing two hundred acres, running and bounded as followeth, Beginning at a post oak and hickory sapling a corner of Robert Crawfords survey, thence down the meanders of the river 532 poles to a chesnut oak on the bank of the river, then South 186 poles to a stake, then a Direct course to the Beginning, containing Two Hundred acres, with all and singular the woods, waters, mines, minerals, Hereditaments, and appurtenances unto the said Tract of Land belonging . . .

Records relating to land title acquisition, transfer, and taxation

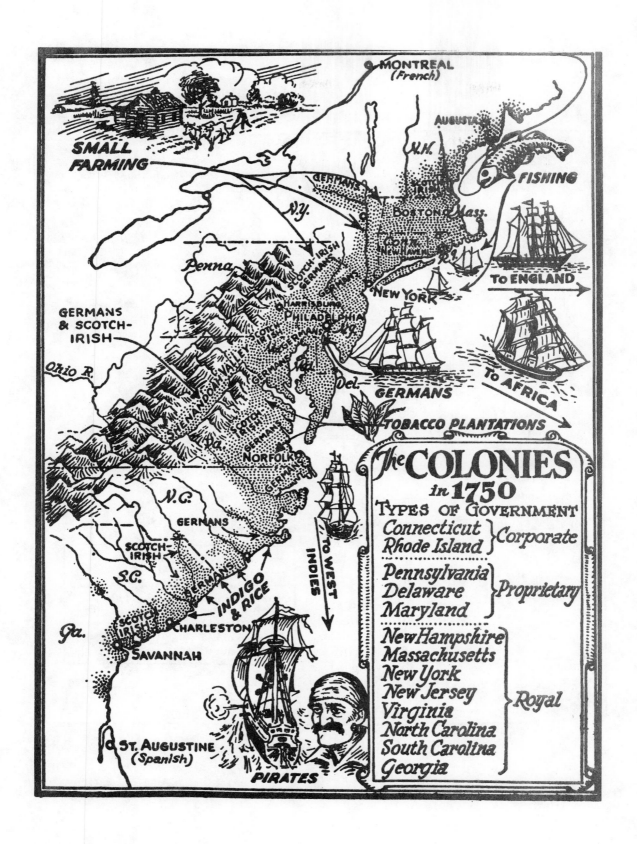

Fig. 78. Types of colonies

237

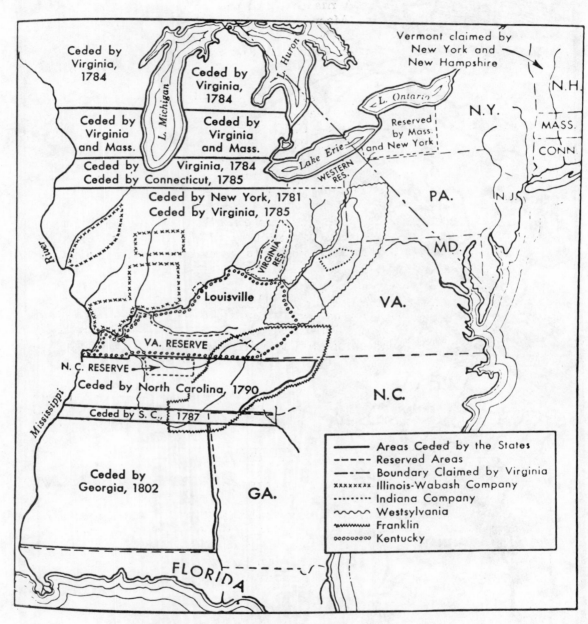

Ceded by Virginia, 1784

Ceded by Virginia, 1784

Ceded by Virginia and Mass.

Ceded by Virginia and Mass.

Ceded by Virginia, 1784
Ceded by Connecticut, 1785

L. Michigan

L. Huron

L. Ontario

Lake Erie

WESTERN RES.

Reserved by Mass. and New York

Vermont claimed by New York and New Hampshire

N.H.

N.Y.

MASS.

CONN.

PA.

N.J.

Ceded by New York, 1781
Ceded by Virginia, 1785

VIRGINIA RES.

MD.

River

Louisville

VA.

VA. RESERVE

N. C. RESERVE

Mississippi

Ceded by North Carolina, 1790

Ceded by S. C., 1787

N.C.

Ceded by Georgia, 1802

GA.

FLORIDA

——— Areas Ceded by the States
- - - Reserved Areas
—·—· Boundary Claimed by Virginia
xxxxxxx Illinois-Wabash Company
·········· Indiana Company
∿∿∿ Westsylvania
ⵡⵡⵡ Franklin
ooooooooo Kentucky

Western Land Cessions, 1780–1802

Fig. 79. Western land cessions

238

were kept in different jurisdictions in the colonial states with towns and counties being primary custodians but with some records kept on a provincial or state basis. A majority of the colonies, including Delaware, Kentucky, Maine, Maryland, Massachusetts, New Hampshire, New Jersey, New York, North Carolina, Pennsylvania, South Carolina, Tennessee, Virginia, and present-day West Virginia kept such records on a county basis.

Connecticut, Rhode Island, Vermont, and South Carolina recorded on a town basis. In South Carolina, the records for the entire colony were kept at Charlestown prior to 1785, but after that date they were filed in their respective counties. New Hampshire kept her land records on a provincial basis from 1635 until 1771 when the counties assumed jurisdiction. New Jersey recorded provincially, prior to 1701, but reverted to a county recording system after that date.

The LDS Genealogical Society has an excellent collection of town, district, and county land records for each of the colonial states and has copies of most provincial land records known to exist for that region.

Land Jurisdiction and Ownership in the Public Domain

Claim to land title in the public land states was based upon several factors, including cession of lands from the colonies, conquest, outright purchase, and treaty--principally with England and France, but also with the Indians (fig. 79).

The following two tables show the chronological sequence of cession of western lands[1] as well as historical and statistical data on all states and territories in 1880[2]:

CESSIONS OF WESTERN LANDS

1778, Sept. 19.	Congressional committee proposal that States cede lands.
1778, Dec. 15.	Maryland proposal that States cede their lands.
1779, May 12.	Maryland proposal presented to Congress.
1780, Feb. 19.	New York act, ceding her lands.
1780, Mar. 7.	New York cession laid before Congress.
1780, Sept. 6.	Congress recommends that all States cede their lands.
1780, Oct.	Connecticut resolution ceding lands.
1781, Jan. 2.	Virginia resolution ceding lands.
1781, Mar. 1.	New York cession presented to Congress.
1781, June 27.	Congressional committee reports New York, Virginia, and Connecticut cessions inexpediant in form.
1782, Apr. 18 to 1782, Sept. 26.	Congressional discussion of State cessions.
1782, Oct. 29.	New York cession accepted by Congress.

1783, Jan. 30. to	
1782, Sept. 13.	Congressional discussion of Virginia and other cessions.
1783, Oct. 20.	Beginning of Virginia session at which lands are ceded.
1784, Mar. 1.	Virginia cession accepted by Congress.
1784, June 2.	North Carolina act of cession.
1784, Nov. 13.	Massachusetts cession accepted by Congress.
1785, May 20.	Congress asked North Carolina to rescind her November act and be as liberal as in June.
1786, May 11.	Connecticut second act of cession.
1786, May 26.	Congressional expression of readiness to accept Connecticut when deed is drawn.
1786, Sept. 14.	Connecticut land cession completed in Congress.
1787, Mar. 8.	South Carolina act of cession.
1787, Aug. 9.	South Carolina cession accepted by Congress.
1788, Feb. 11.	Georgia act of cession.
1788, July 15.	Georgia offer rejected by Congress.
1789, Dec.	North Carolina act of cession.
1790, Feb. 25.	North Carolina deed presented to Congress.
1790, Apr. 2.	North Carolina cession accepted by Congress.
1800, Apr. 28.	Connecticut Reserve jurisdiction to be ceded to Congress.
1802, Apr. 24.	Georgia cession agreement entered into.
1802, May 3.	Georgia cession on new terms lost in Congress.
1802, June 16.	Georgia ratification of cession agreement.

HISTORICAL AND STATISTICAL TABLE OF THE U.S. AND TERRITORIES IN 1880

Colonial States	Counties-1878	Date of Orgn.	Date of Ratific.
New Hampshire	10		21 June 1788
Massachusetts	14		6 Feb 1788
Rhode Island	5		29 May 1789
Connecticut	8		9 Jan 1787
New York	60		26 Jul 1788
New Jersey	21		18 Dec 1788
Pennsylvania	67		12 Dec 1787
Delaware	3		7 Dec 1787
Maryland	23		28 Apr 1788
Virginia	105		26 June 1788
North Carolina	94		21 Nov 1789
South Carolina	33		23 May 1788
Georgia	137		2 Jan 1788
Legislative States			
Kentucky	117		4 Feb 1791
Vermont	14		18 Feb 1791
Tennessee	94		1 June 1796
Maine	16		3 Mar 1820

Legislative States	Counties-1878	Date of Orgn.	Date of Ratific.
Texas	151		29 Dec 1845
West Virginia	54		31 Dec 1862
Public Land States			
Ohio	88		30 Apr 1802
Louisiana	58	3 Mar 1805	
Indiana	92	7 May 1800	
Mississippi	75	7 Apr 1798	
Illinois	102	3 Feb 1809	
Alabama	67	3 Mar 1817	
Missouri	115	4 Jun 1812	
Arkansas	74	2 Mar 1819	
Michigan	76	11 Jan 1805	
Florida	39	30 Mar 1822	
Iowa	99	12 June 1838	
Wisconsin	60	20 Apr 1836	
California	52		9 Sept 1850
Minnesota	71	3 Mar 1849	
Oregon	23	14 Aug 1848	
Kansas	76	30 May 1854	
Nevada	14	2 Mar 1861	
Nebraska	62	30 May 1854	
Colorado	30	28 Feb 1861	
Territories			
Wyoming	5	25 July 1868	
New Mexico	12	9 Sept 1850	
Utah	20	9 Sept 1850	
Washington	24	2 Mar 1853	
Dakota	34	2 Mar 1861	
Arizona	6	24 Feb 1863	
Idaho	10	3 Mar 1863	
Montana	10	26 May 1864	
Alaska		27 July 1868	
Indian Territory			
District of Columbia		16 July 1790	

Survey of the public domain was authorized under an act of Congress dated 20 May 1785 and began in Ohio where the Ohio River crosses the west Pennsylvania border (fig. 80). Virginia claimed the region on the basis of her early grants and charters but ceded it to the United States after the Revolutionary War. She retained a portion of it as a military reserve, and many early settlers were actually Virginians (fig. 81).

The first survey was the "Old Seven Ranges," located in the eastern part of Ohio, but it was not long until lands had been entered and surveyed in other parts of the territory. Steubenville, in Jefferson County, Ohio, was the first local land office, but the number of offices steadily increased throughout the domain until well over three hundred offices were in existence by 1930.

A rectangular method of survey was employed in the public land

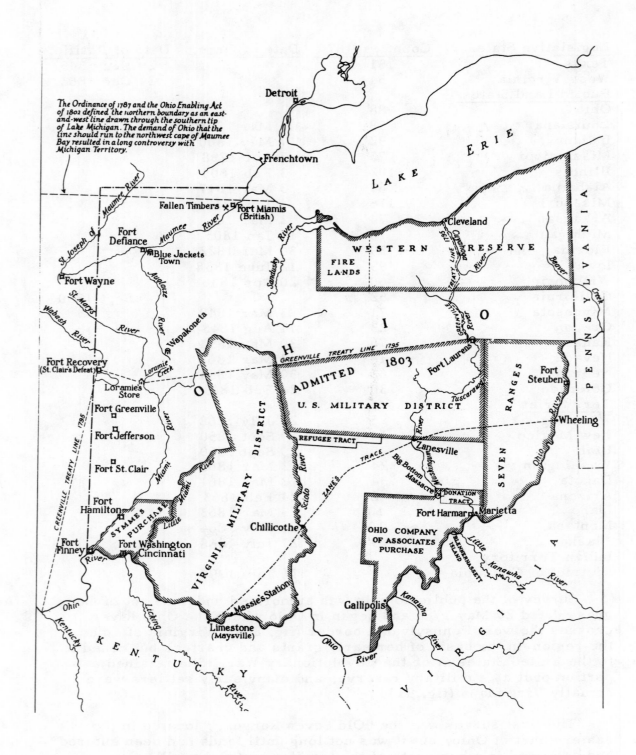

The Ordinance of 1787 and the Ohio Enabling Act
of 1802 defined the northern boundary as an east-
and-west line drawn through the southern tip
of Lake Michigan. The demand of Ohio that the
line should run to the northwest cape of Maumee
Bay resulted in a long controversy with
Michigan Territory.

Fig. 80. Ohio Country 1787-1803

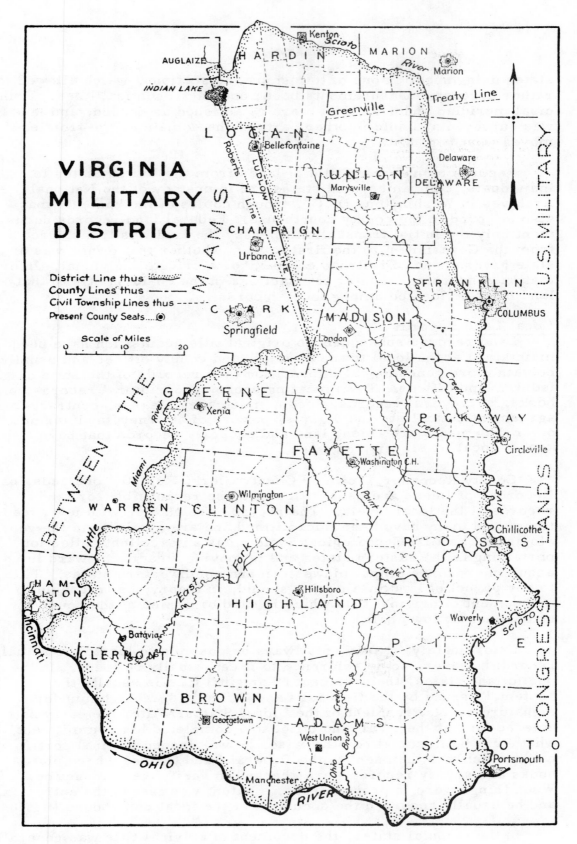

Fig. 81. Virginia Military District in Ohio

243

states using subdivisions of townships and sections, which allowed for rather accurate measurements based upon astronomical lines. Principal meridian and base lines were established as needed, and land was surveyed and sold in other parts of the domain as the frontier moved west (fig. 82).

Records transferring title of lands from the United States to individuals, companies, and states are in custody of the National Archives in Washington, D. C., though copies of the "patent" may also be found in the county courthouse. Federal land records document only the initial transaction whereby the land was transferred from the Government to the first owner, whether that owner was a state government, a railroad company or a private individual. Information concerning all later transactions in the chain of title to that land must be located among local records.

Local Land Records

Land records subsequent to original title acquisition have been maintained at the local town, district, and county offices and usually contain more genealogical information than records of the state or federal land offices. Town meeting books, proprietors' records, platbooks, surveyors' records, deeds, mortgages, leases, contracts and agreements, tax lists and digests, powers of attorney, and various other documents are among land and property records that have been kept at local levels (fig. 83).

County Recorder, Town or County Clerk, Register of Deeds, or Recorder of Deeds are usual titles of those responsible for land records at the local levels. The records are public, with few exceptions, and many have been microfilmed and are available to the genealogist. The LDS Genealogical Society has an excellent collection pertaining to the eastern states and is moving steadily forward in acquiring records of the midwestern and southwestern states. Title to any parcel of land in America should, in theory, be traceable to a document of original title which is filed or copied at the county courthouse or town hall.

Unfortunately, it may not always be possible to locate the actual record; however, some reference to it can usually be found. In the public land states, the document of original title is usually the "patent," issued by the General Land Office in Washington under signature of the President of the United States. After the entryman entered land at the local land office and completed his commitment, whether it be financial or otherwise, he was issued a "final certificate" which was then sent to the General Land Officer where platbooks and survey records were checked to verify the transaction. When things were in proper order, a patent was issued the entryman, and he usually recorded the document at the local courthouse (fig. 84).

In the colonial states, the document of original title was generally a charter or grant, though it might have been a special deed of

244

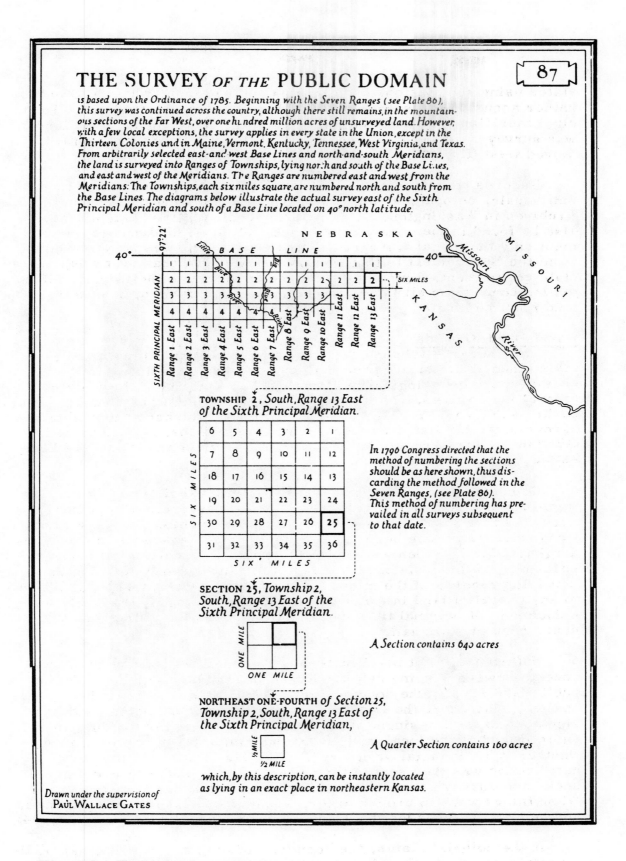

THE SURVEY OF THE PUBLIC DOMAIN

is based upon the Ordinance of 1785. Beginning with the Seven Ranges (see Plate 86), this survey was continued across the country, although there still remains, in the mountainous sections of the Far West, over one hundred million acres of unsurveyed land. However, with a few local exceptions, the survey applies in every state in the Union, except in the Thirteen Colonies and in Maine, Vermont, Kentucky, Tennessee, West Virginia, and Texas. From arbitrarily selected east-and west Base Lines and north-and-south Meridians, the land is surveyed into Ranges of Townships, lying north and south of the Base Lines, and east and west of the Meridians. The Ranges are numbered east and west from the Meridians: The Townships, each six miles square, are numbered north and south from the Base Lines. The diagrams below illustrate the actual survey east of the Sixth Principal Meridian and south of a Base Line located on 40° north latitude.

TOWNSHIP 2, South, Range 13 East
of the Sixth Principal Meridian.

In 1796 Congress directed that the method of numbering the sections should be as here shown, thus discarding the method followed in the Seven Ranges, (see Plate 86). This method of numbering has prevailed in all surveys subsequent to that date.

SECTION 25, Township 2, South, Range 13 East of the Sixth Principal Meridian.

A Section contains 640 acres

NORTHEAST ONE-FOURTH of Section 25, Township 2, South, Range 13 East of the Sixth Principal Meridian,

A Quarter Section contains 160 acres

which, by this description, can be instantly located as lying in an exact place in northeastern Kansas.

Drawn under the supervision of
PAUL WALLACE GATES

Fig. 82. Rectangular survey

Fig. 83. Iowa county courthouse and Massachusetts town hall

246

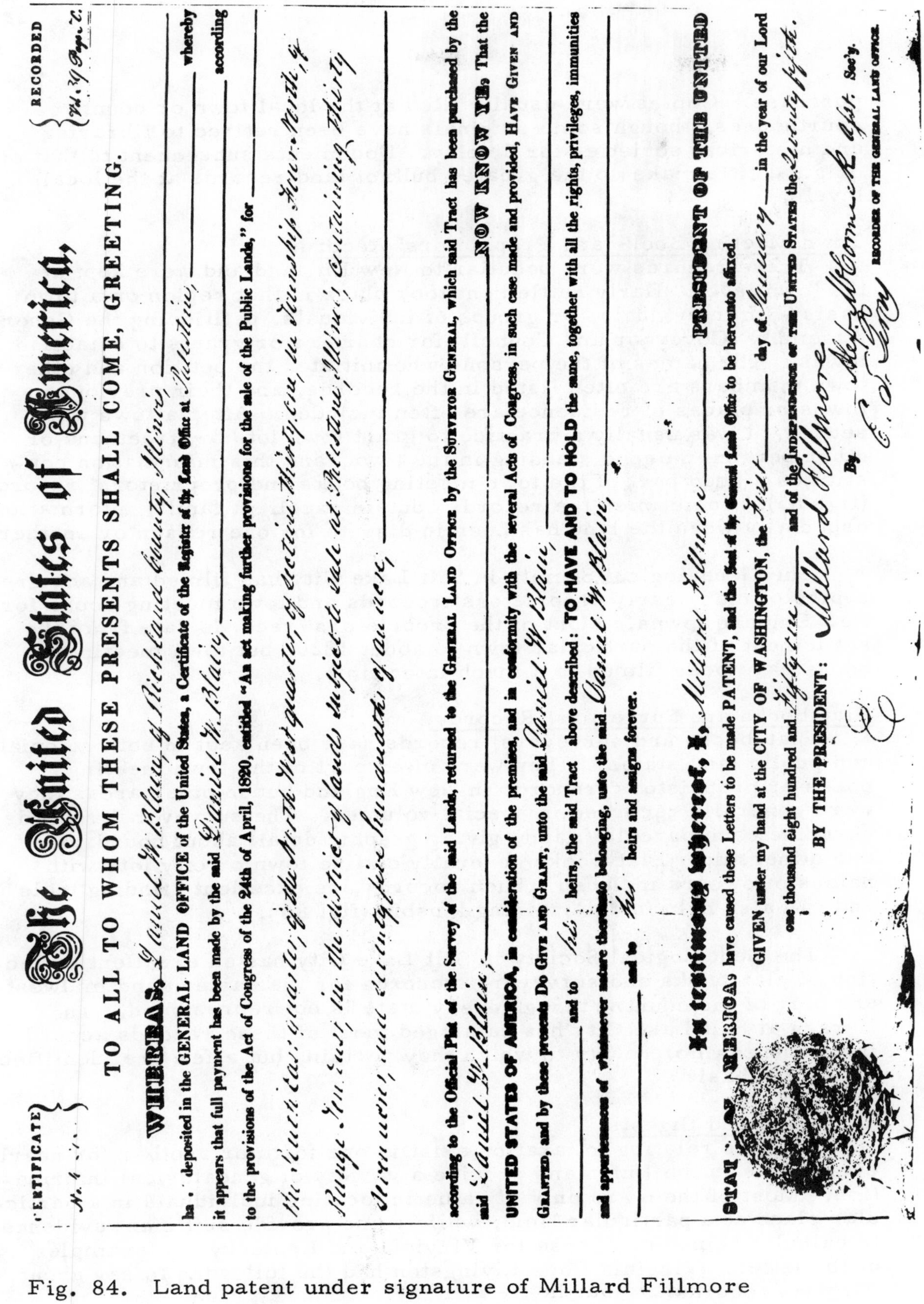

RECORDED
Vol. 24 Page 2.

The United States of America,

TO ALL TO WHOM THESE PRESENTS SHALL COME, GREETING.

WHEREAS, *Daniel W. Blair, of Richland County, Illinois,*

ha.. deposited in the GENERAL LAND OFFICE of the United States, a Certificate of the Register of the Land Office at *Palestine,* whereby

it appears that full payment has been made by the said *Daniel W. Blair* according

to the provisions of the Act of Congress of the 24th of April, 1820, entitled "An act making further provisions for the sale of the Public Lands," for

the South-east-quarter of the North-West-quarter of section thirty-six, in township four-North of
Range Ten East, in the district of lands subject to sale at Palestine, Illinois; Containing thirty
seven acres, and seventy-five hundredths of an acre;

according to the Official Plat of the Survey of the said Lands, returned to the GENERAL LAND OFFICE by the SURVEYOR GENERAL, which said Tract has been purchased by the said *Daniel W. Blair;*

NOW KNOW YE, That the

UNITED STATES OF AMERICA, in consideration of the premises, and in conformity with the several Acts of Congress, in such case made and provided, HAVE GIVEN AND GRANTED, and by these presents DO GIVE AND GRANT, unto the said *Daniel W. Blair,*

and to *his* heirs, the said Tract above described: TO HAVE AND TO HOLD the same, together with all the rights, privileges, immunities and appurtenances of whatsoever nature thereunto belonging, unto the said *Daniel W. Blair,*

and to *his* heirs and assigns forever.

In testimony whereof, I, *Millard Fillmore* PRESIDENT OF THE UNITED STATES OF AMERICA, have caused these Letters to be made PATENT, and the Seal of the General Land Office to be hereunto affixed.

GIVEN under my hand at the CITY OF WASHINGTON, the *First* day of *January* in the year of our Lord one thousand eight hundred and *fifty two* and of the INDEPENDENCE OF THE UNITED STATES the *seventy fifth.*

BY THE PRESIDENT: *Millard Fillmore*

By. *Jno. M. Connell* Apt. Secy.

E. A. Cozy RECORDER OF THE GENERAL LAND OFFICE.

Fig. 84.   Land patent under signature of Millard Fillmore

247

purchase. Copies were usually filed at the local town or county courthouses, though some originals have been retired to libraries and historical societies for display. Documents subsequent to that of original title make up the greater bulk of land records at the local levels.

Town Meeting Books and Proprietors' Records

These records were peculiar to New England and were kept at the town level. Early settlement took place in that region on a town basis with individuals, or groups of individuals, petitioning the General Assembly (Governor and Council) for charters or grants to establish towns. The names of the persons who initiated the petition and other town members are often listed in the records, and their previous towns or places of residence are often included. After a town was settled, it was usually a practice to grant town lots to "freemen" or other persons in good standing in the town, and this information constitutes a good part of the town meeting books and proprietors' records (fig. 85). Sometimes the records contain excellent family information, especially when the land has been in dispute for one reason or another.

The Genealogical Society in Salt Lake City has filmed and acquired copies of many early proprietors' records and town meeting books for New England towns. Most of the proprietors' records date from the settlement of the particular town to about 1820, but town meeting books have been filmed to a much later time.

Plat-books and Surveyors' Records

Plat-books and surveyors' records have been kept in both colonial and public land states. They were often part of the town meeting books or proprietors' records in New England but in other areas they were generally recorded in special volumes. The surveyors' records describe each parcel of land, giving graphic detail about boundaries and ownership. Plat-books generally outline town or city lots with names of owners included. Such records are excellent "finding tools" and can also help in determining kinship (fig. 86).

The Genealogical Society in Salt Lake City has an excellent collection of plat-books and surveyors' records for the eastern and midwestern part of the country though every state is not represented. The library at Salt Lake City has cataloged most of these records according to the town or county to which they pertain, but a few are identified on a state basis.

Tax Lists and Digests

Records relating to taxation exist in one form or another for nearly every state in the Union and provide a variety of genealogical information. Most of them are only of value in locating individuals in a particular place at a particular time, while some provide sufficient evidence to calculate kinship. Those for Virginia and Kentucky are examples of the latter. Virginia Pope Livingston had the following to say about Virginia records:

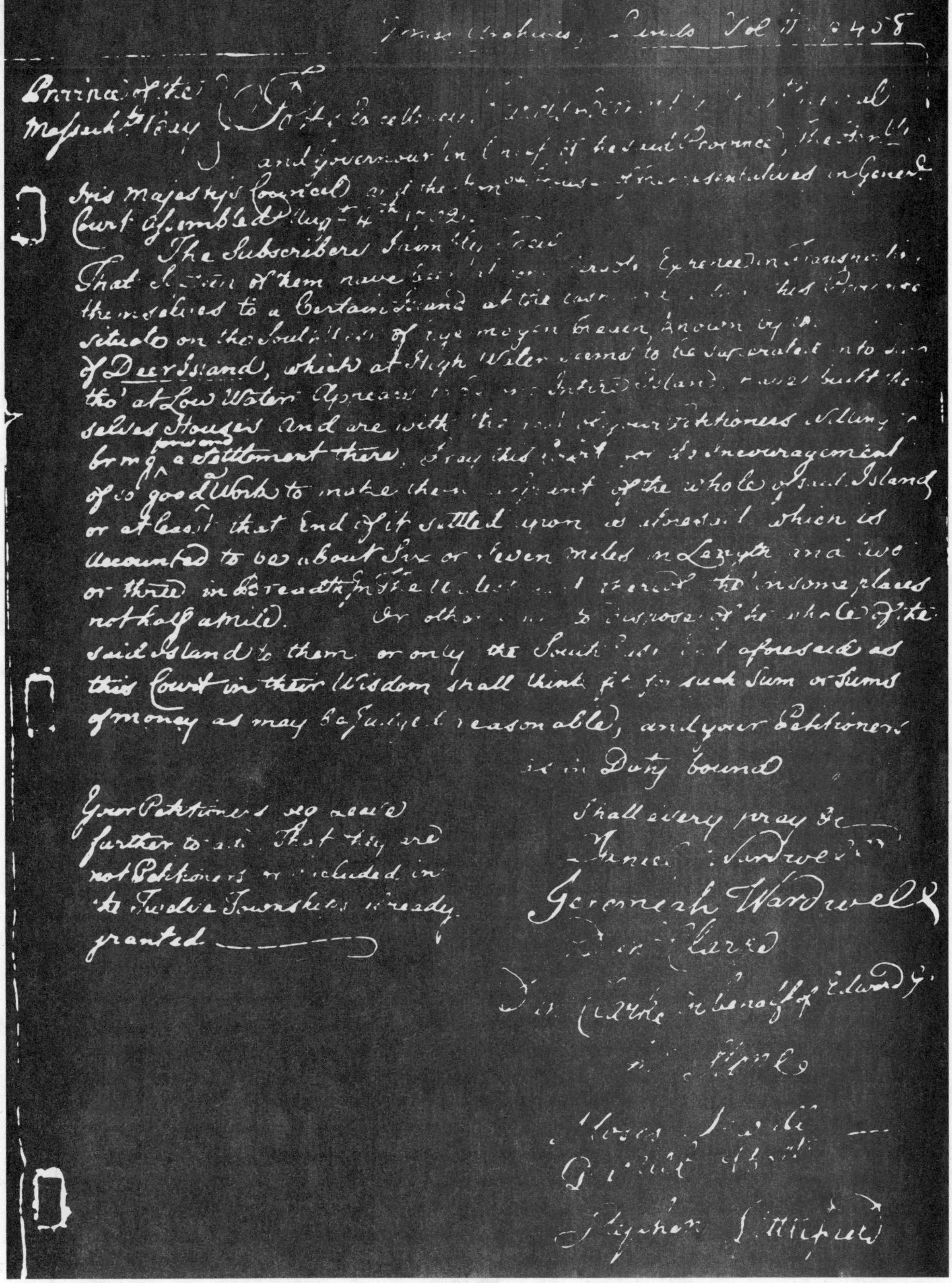

Province of the
Massachusetts } To His Excellency [illegible] and Governour in Chief of the said Province, the Honourable His Majesty's Council and the Honourable [illegible] Representatives in General Court Assembled Aug 4th 17[illegible].

The Subscribers Humbly Sheweth [illegible]

That [illegible] of them have [illegible] Expressed in Transporting themselves to a Certain Island at the East [illegible] situate on the South side of [illegible] now [illegible] known by [illegible] of Deer Island, which at High Water seems to be separated into two tho' at Low Water Appears to be one Intire Island, & have built themselves Houses and are with the rest of your Petitioners willing to bring [illegible] a Settlement there, [illegible] for its Encouragement of so good a Work to make them [illegible] of the whole of said Island or at least that End of it settled upon as aforesaid which is accounted to be about Six or Seven Miles in Length and in two or three in Breadth, in the widest [illegible] and [illegible] to in some places not half a mile. Or otherwise to dispose of the whole of the said Island to them or only the South side as aforesaid as this Court in their Wisdom shall think fit for such Sum or Sums of money as may be [Judged] [reasonable], and your Petitioners is in Duty bound

Your Petitioners do [illegible]
further to [illegible] That they are
not Petitioners or included in
the Twelve Townships already
granted ——————

Shall ever pray &c——
James [illegible]
Jeremiah Wardwell
[illegible]
[illegible]
Moses [illegible] ——
[illegible]
Stephen [illegible]

Fig. 85. Massachusetts proprietor's record

Signers. Narr. &t

William grenlla
Jonathan Grenlaw
Ebenezer Grenlaw
Charles Greenlaw
Alexander Greenlaw
William Wilson
William grenlaw
Nathan Closson
David Torey
Joseph Thoms
Michael Barney
John Tinker
George Lilly
John Urin
William Eaton
John Staple
Ebenezer Low
Samuel Low
Eliakim eaton
John Cane
Enoch hutchings
Nathaniel Webber

Pickard Daniel
Ward well & Mas
Feby 24 Refers to a
may Refers for consideration

1762

Fig. 85 continued.

JACKSON
1964

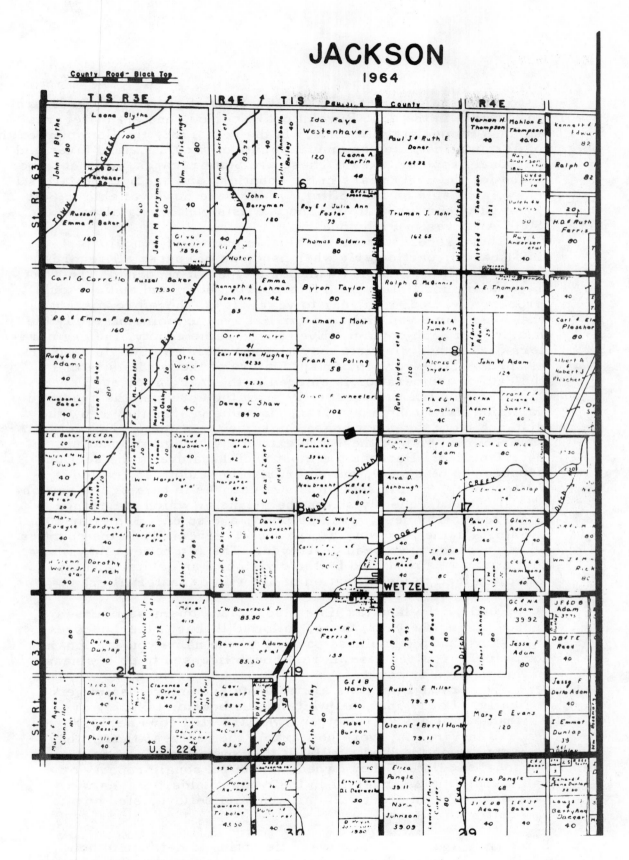

Fig. 86. Plat book

251

When one considers the peculiarities of genealogical research in Virginia in the post-Revolutionary period, one set of records springs immediately to mind. In the year 1782, the Commonwealth of Virginia instituted an annual series of tax lists, land taxes and personal property taxes. These are State records, are not to be found for the early years in the counties, and are not, so far as I know, available on microfilm. /Many are now available in Salt Lake City on microfilm. / The tax lists can be examined in the State Archives in Richmond.

These records are an invaluable source of genealogical information, particularly when used, as of course all records should be, in conjunction with other types of records. The regulations for listing taxable property, both land and personal property, varied from year to year. It is, therefore, essential that every time you pick up a tax list, you examine carefully the headings of each column. Even in the same county, the enumerators of different districts may arrange their columns in a different order. One very important feature of the tax lists is that the date of enumeration is entered in the margin for each entry.

The land tax lists generally show the acreage, the assessed valuation and the amount of tax. In some years, they show the distance from the court house, in some the name of the nearest watercourse; both of these are extremely helpful in locating your families. Perhaps the most useful feature is the section, supposed to be annual, but unfortunately seldom so, called "Alterations." This section shows changes in title or tax responsibility, and frequently shows the means by which the change occurred, as by deed, will, division, and so on. Sometimes the grantor's name is given--a great boon, especially in the counties whose records have been destroyed. The Alterations may show that a man received land by the division of an estate, and this can often lead to identification of his wife or maternal grandparent . . .

Finally, the land tax lists also include business licenses issued during the year; these, followed through other records, may show that the business partner by the name you are looking for actually resided elsewhere, though licensed to do business in this particular county.

The personal tax lists are perhaps even more useful genealogically. In Virginia, all white males became taxable, or "Tithable," at age 16. Women, who are still considerably ignored in Virginia, were not taxable themselves, though they may appear on the land tax list if they owned land, or on the personal tax lists if they owned taxable personal property or had taxable males under 21 in their households. Slaves were taxable at 12. In practically all years, I believe, stud horses and cattle were taxed."[3]

Some time ago, the author was attempting to determine how early William Pace and his family came to Georgia; tax digests were very helpful in solving the problem. William and his sons William, Jr., James, Jeremiah, Wilson, Kenchin, Drury, and Isaac were known to be resident in three counties of Tennessee after 1806 and two counties of Georgia prior to that date. A study of tax digests for Clarke County, Georgia, showed them to be resident there between 1802 and 1806, and Oglethorpe County records (parent county of Clarke) listed each of them from 1798 until 1802. The family could not be located in other Georgia tax digests earlier than 1798, but it was interesting to note individuals by the same names were indexed in the 1790 census for North Carolina. Could North Carolina be the family's residence prior to 1798? Records of Halifax, Edgecombe, and Northampton counties in North Carolina show family information too similar to that of Georgia for it to be otherwise.

When searching early tax records, it is a good practice to extract entries for all persons by the same surname and also to cover a wide time period. Individuals may not be located every year, even though they were known to be resident in that county, and some cannot be located because certain records are missing. People were no different in the early days than they are now, and anyone who could avoid the tax lists undoubtedly tried to do so. Sometimes by noting when a person first appears in the tax records and by noting that he was merely a "poll" or "tithable," and then by following him through each list for a number of years and identifying his taxable real estate, one can determine parentage and other important kinship information. In Kentucky tax records it is often possible to determine a young man's age and his father's name from the lists. Kentucky lists included free white male persons twenty-one years of age and upward, and when the person first turned twenty-one he was usually listed immediately under his father's entry. By following the records in succeeding years it is also possible to show a father's ownership of land decreasing by an amount equal to a son's newly acquired land. The land may also be shown to be entered in the same name and be situated on the same watercourse. In some cases, the records can be used to identify a female spouse or a widow, while in other instances the records might lead to the maiden name of the wife.

The LDS Genealogical Society has completed the filming of early tax records for New England and has copied many records for Kentucky, Georgia, and North Carolina. It has not yet filmed all tax records for Virginia, Maryland, Tennessee or for other southern states, though it does have some collections for each of them. The Society also has early tax lists for Philadelphia County, Pennsylvania, and for some New Jersey counties. Some early tax lists for Pennsylvania have been published in various volumes of the PENNSYLVANIA ARCHIVES, and New Jersey "Ratables" (taxables) have been listed periodically in the NEW JERSEY MAGAZINE OF HISTORY. The Society in Salt Lake has several New Jersey lists on microfilm covering the period 1773-1822, and the Gendex Corporation of Salt Lake City recently published NEW JERSEY IN 1793, which includes many names from New Jersey tax lists. The Society's microfilming program in Ohio also included tax records covering the period 1818-1838, and copies for many counties are available at Salt Lake City. Microfilming is currently under way in New York, Pennsylvania, and New Jersey, and exchange programs are also in effect in midwestern and southwestern states.

Deeds, Mortgages, and Leases

This record group is one of the most important to the American genealogist and accounts for the bulk of land record information on file at the Genealogical Society in Salt Lake City. Several thousand rolls of microfilm constitute the Society's deed and mortgage collection alone. As an example, over 1767 rolls of film are on file for Middlesex County, Massachusetts.

Deeds, mortgages, and leases were recorded on a county basis in each of the public land states, but registration practices varied in the colonial states. Connecticut, Rhode Island, and Vermont each registered land on a town basis while Delaware, Kentucky, Maine, Maryland, Massachusetts, New Hampshire, New Jersey, New York, North Carolina, Pennsylvania, South Carolina, Tennessee, Virginia, and West Virginia each recorded at the county level. New Hampshire recorded provincially before 1772 and New Jersey did the same prior to 1702. South Carolina recorded all land matters at Charleston until 1785 when the counties assumed the responsibility.

A majority of the deed and mortgage records are indexed alphabetically by the names of buyers and sellers (grantee-grantors) but a few counties and metropolitan cities file their records by description. Most counties in Illinois and Kansas are now filing by description, and many western counties are doing the same. In these jurisdictions it is necessary to know the "quarter-section" or address of the land before the officials can locate records concerning it. Family records can often help in locating such information, and sometimes the earlier county histories state section numbers where farmers resided. Sometimes the earlier indexes have been retired to the attic or basement storeroom and descriptions can be gained from them. If a general idea of the land's location is known, the County Auditor's Office can sometimes supply an interested person with description information.

Some deed and mortgage indexes are phonetic in arrangement and quite confusing. Names in the index are listed by sound rather than in alphabetical sequence, and similar sounding names are grouped on special pages accordingly. There is generally a "key" on the inside cover of the first index book which explains the system. By noting the first letter of the surname and by considering consonant sounds, one can follow the grid lines to a meeting point where page numbers are listed. By turning to the page indicated, one can locate his surname and find deed-book and page numbers where the actual information is recorded. New York and Pennsylvania both use this system to index their deed and mortgage records.

Deeds, both quit-claim and warrantee, were used to transfer title to lands from one individual to another. A warrantee deed indicates the seller holds the land in "fee simple" or that he has clear title to it and will defend the same against all persons whatsoever, whereas a "quit-claim" deed merely releases whatever right the person or persons have in the land. When a man dies intestate (without a will), his real estate usually becomes the property of his heirs, and one often finds quit-claim deeds used by such heirs to release their right to a particular parcel of land. Deeds of "gift" or "trust" might also be found in the records, but most of the deeds found by the genealogist are quit-claim or warrantee by definition. The quit-claim deed can be just as important, genealogically speaking, as the warrantee deed, so the researcher should not be too concerned with the type of deed but rather with the content of the record.

The opening of the typical deed usually gives reference to the date the deed was constructed and recorded, the names and places of residence of the parties involved, and the consideration or payment which changed hands. For example, the opening to the deed of Robert Wagganer et al. to Elizabeth W. Wagganer, entered 19 November 1867 follows:

> This Indenture made the twenty second day of March in the year of our Lord one thousand eight hundred and sixty six Between Robert Waggoner and Sarah his wife of Allegheny County, John Lowry and Sarah his wife, John McKee and Eliza Jane his wife, Martin Fisher and Therisa his wife, William McKee and Martha Ann his wife and William Waggoner of the County of Beaver and State of Pennsylvania of the first part and Elizabeth W. Waggoner of the borough of Freedom in the County of Beaver and State aforesaid of the second part Witnesseth that the said parties of the first part, for and in consideration of the sum of Sixty Dollars lawful money of the United States of America, unto them well and truly paid by the said party of the second part, at or before the sealing and delivery of these presents the receipt whereof is hereby acknowledged, have granted, bargained, sold, aliened, enfeoffed, released conveyed and confirmed and by these presents do grant, bargain, sell, alien, enfeoff, release, convey and confirm unto the said party of the second part, her heirs and assigns, All the right, title, interest and claim of the parties of the first part of, in, and to all that certain lot of ground situate in the borough of Freedom in the County of Beaver and State of Pennsylvania . . .

The body of the deed usually gives reference to the legal description of the property and outlines any limitations or restrictions which might be placed on it. In some deeds, the past history of that particular parcel of land is outlined, which can be very helpful to the genealogist:

> . . . being lot numbered twenty-eight in the general plan of

lots in said borough and bounded and described as follows Viz.
Beginning on Main Street at a post at the corner of lot No. 27
thence back by said lot one hundred feet to the corner of lot 76
thence sixty feet to the back corner of lot No. 29. Thence by
said lot one hundred feet to Main Street to a post, the place of
beginning, being the same premises which Stephen Phillips and
Rhoda his wife and Jonathan Betz and Mary his wife by Indenture
bearing date the 27th day of March, A.D. 1837 and recorded in
the office for recording deeds in and for the County of Beaver, in
Deed Book "R" page 310, did grant and confirm unto Elizabeth
Waggoner her heirs and assigns and the said Elizabeth Wagner in
and by her last will and testament--in writing bearing date May
19th 1846, since her decease duly proved and remaining in the
Registers Office at Beaver did divise the said lot of ground to
her two daughters Anne Waggoner and Elizabeth W. Waggoner
and the said Anne Waggoner being by virture of said last will and
testament--seized of the undivided half of said lot of ground in
fee, died intestate with out issue but leaving to survive her, two
brothers the said Robert Waggoner and William Waggoner, two
sisters the said Sarah Lowry and Elizabeth W. Waggoner, and
one Nephew and two Nieces Viz: the said Martin Fisher, Eliza
Jane McKee and Martha Ann McKee, who are children of Susan
Fisher a deceased sister of said intestate to whom the said undivided half of said lot of ground by the laws of Pennsylvania relating to intestates did decend and come together with all and singular the buildings, improvements, ways, waters, watercourses,
rights, liberties, privileges, hereditaments, and appurtenances,
whatsoever thereunto belonging, or in anywise appertaining, and
the reversions and remainders, rents, issues and profits thereof;
and all the estate, right, title, interest, property, claim and
deman whatsovever of the said parties of the first part in law
Equity or otherwise howsoever of, in, and to the same and
every part therof, to have and to hold the said right, title,
interest and claim of the said parties of the first part, of, in,
and to the lot of ground above described, hereditaments and
premises hereby granted or mentioned, and intended so to be
with the appurtenances unto the said party of the second part,
her heirs and assigns, to and for the only proper use and behoof
of the said party of the second part her heirs and assigns forever . . .

The closing of the deed usually contains information relating to
the claims of the owners and includes the names of the witnesses and
signers of the deed. The date of the deed and the date of recording
may also be found in the closing and other statements may be made,
such as information relating to the release of dower:

And, the said parties of the first part, for themselves, their
heris, executors and administrators, do by these presents grant
and agree to and with the said party of the second part, her heirs
and assigns that they the said parties of the first part and their

256

heirs, all and singular the hereditaments and premisis herein above described and granted, or mentioned, and intended so to be with the appurtenances, unto the said party of the second part, her heirs and assigns, against them the said parties of the first part, and their heirs and against all and every other person or persons whomsoever lawfully claiming or to claim the same or any part thereof shall and will warrant and forever defend. In witness whereof the said parties of the first part have to these presents, set their hands and seals. Dated the day and year first above written.

Sealed and delivered in the
presence of us
   H. Bryan

Robert Waggoner
Sarah X Wagoner
   (her mark)
John X Lowry
   (his mark)
Sarah X Lowry
   (her mark)
John McKee
Eliza Jane McKee
Wm McKee
Martha A. McKee
William Waggoner
Martin W. Fisher
Therisa Fisher

Beaver County--
. . . On the twenty second day of March, Anno Domini 1866 before me a Justice of the Peace in and for said County came the above named Robert Waggoner and Sarah his wife, John Lowry and Sarah his wife, John McKee and Eliza Jane his wife, Martin Fisher and Therisa his wife, Wm McKee and Martha Ann his wife and William Waggoner and acknowledged the above indenture to be their act and deed and desired that the same might be recorded as such they the said Sarah Waggoner, Sarah Lowry, Eliza Jane McKee, Theresa Fisher and Martha Ann Fisher being of full age and by me examined separate and apart from their said husbands and the contents of the said indenture being first made fully known to them declared that they did of their own free will and accord sign and seal, and as their act and deed, deliver the same without any coercion or compulsion of their said husbands.
   Witness my hand and seal the day and year aforesaid
                    H. Bryan J.P.

Not all deeds are as involved as the above document, but they can still provide a variety of helpful genealogical information. Sometimes the consideration is listed as "the love and affection I show my son" or some other similar statement which is most helpful in determining relationship. Other information listed in a deed might include information about adoption, illegitimacies, family disputes, and the like.

In 1960, genealogists visited the Oneida County, New York, courthouse at Utica, seeking information on "Lydia Guiteau" who migrated west with the Mormon pioneers in the 1840s. They knew little about her family or parentage but were able to locate a reference to her name in the deed indexes at Utica. She and her sister Hannah had joined in the sale of certain land in Oneida County, and by tracing the land to its earlier owners, we found the sisters had received the land from their father, Francis Guiteau. They proved to be close relatives of "Charles Julius Guiteau," the man who assassinated President Garfield in 1884, and other helpful facts were located in the deeds and mortgage records using his name.

Ezra S. E. Davis and his wife Catherine Ann (Stattler) were known to be resident in Dubuque County, Iowa, in 1845 when their son Isaac was born. Family records indicated Ezra's mother (Mary Davis) was living in Philadelphia when Ezra went west to the "Gold Fields" in 1853. A search of the 1850 federal census for Dubuque County, Iowa, listed the following:

NAME	AGE			BIRTHPLACE
#1582 Benjamin F. Davis	45	M	Painter	Pa.
Rachel	45	F		N.J.
William M. G.	17	M		Pa.
Lafeyette	13	M		Pa.
John W. F.	11	M		Iowa
Martha M.	9	F		Iowa
Julia B.	7	F		Iowa
#1583 Ezra S. E. Davis	35	M	Carpenter	Pa.
Catherine	33	F		Pa.
Marion	11	M		Iowa
Harrison	7	M		Iowa
Isaac	5	M		Iowa
Mary	1	F		Iowa

A search of Philadelphia deed indexes at the Genealogical Society in Salt Lake City disclosed two interesting entries in the 1844 period. The first was between "Benjamin F. Davis et al. and Mary Davis" and the second was between "Samuel M. Davis et al. and Mary Davis," both recorded in the same deed book (R. L. L. #35) and on succeeding pages. At the time of this search the Genealogical Society only had film copies of deed books to 1832, though their copy of the index covered the period 1682-1932. It was therefore necessary to write to the Recorder of Deeds at Philadelphia for photocopies, but the result was well worth the effort. The two deeds were extremely helpful and provided the following genealogical information:

1. That Benjamin Franklin Davis of Dubuque, Iowa, was a brother of Ezra S. E. Davis.

2. That Ezra's middle initials stood for "Stiles and Ely."

3. That Ezra and Benjamin were the sons of Mary Davis, a

"widow" of Philadelphia in 1844 and were brothers to "Samuel Meeker Davis of Natchez, Mississippi," and "Caroline H. M. Shubert of Philadelphia."

4. That Ezra Stiles Ely Davis was the son of Isaac Davis and grandson of Samuel Davis, both of whom died in Philadelphia.

5. That Ezra's father Isaac Davis had a brother John and a sister Hannah (fig. 87).

Special attention should be given transactions where the consideration (payment) is unusually small or excessively large, because this may indicate a special family relationship. The father may sell his son or son-in-law a sizeable piece of property for "one dollar and other good and valuable consideration," or he may sell property for a very large amount in relation to its relative value, but the body of the record might indicate some other consideration is involved, such as care in old age.

Some deeds were not recorded until several years after their construction, so one should also investigate the indexes for a rather wide time period. Some of the author's people were "Mennonites" from Lancaster County, Pennsylvania, and though they failed to leave probate records, they certainly were listed in land records. The immigrant Christian Musser purchased over two hundred acres in Lancaster County shortly after 1729 but left no will when he died in 1755. No deeds were on file for the property between 1729 and 1800 but in 1811, nearly one hundred years after the land had been purchased, a series of deeds were recorded showing heirs of Christian and descent of his property to them. It seems his son and grandsons remained on the land but did not transfer title when Christian died. However, in 1811 there arose a need to clarify title, and excellent family information resulted because of it.

A close relationship exists between deed and probate records, and they should be used in conjunction with one another. Sometimes it is not possible to locate a particular deed showing descent or distribution of property from an estate because the will or some other instrument was considered legal transfer. It may be that the will was considered sufficient legal evidence for the transfer and deeds were not constructed to show it. In cases where deeds fail to indicate the origin of title to a particular parcel of real estate, probate and other court records should certainly be investigated. Deeds might also be recorded in will books and vice versa, particularly in the southern states, which is another reason the two record groups should be used to complement each other.

It may be wise to start in the earliest indexes and copy all references which seem significant to a particular problem and then proceed to read and copy the records. In other cases it might be better to locate references only in the time period of interest and investigate

Fig. 87. Fragment of photocopy of very early Philadelphia deed

them selectively. It is usually better, however, to evaluate the indexes carefully before proceeding to the actual deed and mortgage records.

By paying special attention to names and places in the deeds, and by noting the description of the property, it is sometimes possible to gain kinship information which cannot be obtained from any other source. Also, by noting the names listed in the body of the deed and the names of witnesses, other genealogical conclusions can be reached. That a person signed his name by using his "mark" might help to distinguish him from another person of the same name in the same records.

It is usually a good practice to copy reference information from the indexes over a wide time period before checking the actual records. Careful evaluation of the index entries will allow the researcher to be selective in his reading and may save him valuable time. Evaluation of both grantor and grantee indexes should be made so that records will not be missed, and sufficient reference detail should be copied to allow effective searching of the records. For example, a researcher looking for an ancestor surnamed Kelsey would copy the following entries from Ontario County, New York, deed indexes, 1789-1945:

1809 Elijah Kelsey to Amasa Kneeland	13:619
1809 Elijah Kelsey & Ux (wife) to Lewis Miller	13:737
1815 Elijah Kelsey & Ux to Lewis Miller	23:511
1815 Eli Kelsey & Ux to Michael Pipher	24:186
1815 James Kelsey to Walter Adams et al.	24:240
1818 Elijah Kelsey to Eli Kelsey	29:477
1818 Eli Kelsey to Abel Peck	29:480
1819 Henry Kelsey to Truman Spencer	33:160
1819 Elijah Kelsey to Henry Kelsey	33:162
1821 Simeon Kelsey & Ux to Philip Cool	38:149
1836 Camp Kelsey & Ux to Loring Tesdale	61:102
1841 Camp Kelsey & Ux to Jesse H. Cowen	70:386
1845 Solomon Kelsey & Ux to Shotwell Powell	79:315

(Grantees)	
1798 Elijah Kelsey from James Wadsworth	5:345
1807 James Kelsey from David Warner	12:59
1807 Elijah Kelsey from John V. Henry et al.	13:38
1808 Elijah Kelsey from Sebastian Visscher	13:39
1809 Elijah Kelsey from Caleb Benton & Ux	13:618
1812 Jehiel Kelsey from James Wadsworth	16:539
1818 Eli Kelsey from Elijah Kelsey	29:477
1819 Henry Kelsey from Elijah Kelsey	33:162
1821 Alexander Kelsey from John Shaver & Ux	37:215
1821 Simeon Kelsey from Timothy Barnes & Ux	38:148
1836 Eli Kelsey from Isaac Kimmy & Ux	59:562
1838 Camp Kelsey from Henry B. Gibson & Ux	64:388
1840 Solomon Kelsey from Wm. P. Underhill	68:308
1842 Camp Kelsey from Nathaniel W. Howell	72:321

After references have been copied from the indexes, the actual records should be read and copied or extracted. When the surname and/or given names of interest are common, it may be necessary to do selective reading and copying, but at other times it might be well to read each deed. Where a deed is known to be relevant, it should be copied verbatum or photocopied, but where the researcher is not sure, it might be best to extract only essential facts which might help at a later date. For example:

13:39   15 Apr 1796 . . between Sebastian Visscher of the City of Albany, New York to Elijah Kelsey of Renssalaer, New York, for 240 pounds, 200 acres in Ontario Co; lot #38 twp 8.

13:619   16 Mar 1807 Elijah Kelsey of Vernon, Ontario Co, to Amasa Kneeland of Marcellis, Onondaga, for $50, part of lot #10 in Vernon, Elisha Woodworth Jr., witness, signed "Elijah Kelsey."

13:737   2 May 1809 Elijah Kelsey and "Cattiline Kelsey" of the town of Snell, Ontario Co, New York to Lewis Miller of New York City, for $400, land in Phelps-Gorham Purchase, 100 acres, signed "Elijah Kelsey" and "Cateline" (her mark)

Sometimes after extracting all deeds which seem relevant, relationships can be determined which would not otherwise be possible.

The Genealogical Society in Salt Lake City has an excellent collection of deed, mortgage, and lease records for the eastern states, and the program to acquire those of the midwestern and southwestern states is moving forward rapidly. These records have long been considered good genealogical sources, and microfilmers have done a respectable job of copywork in most cases.

Earlier filming programs of the 1940s and '50s included indexes and record volumes dating from the town or county formation to about the Civil War period, but later programs have included records to a relatively modern time (1935-1972). In some cases the Society has sent its filmers back to the towns and counties to bring the records up-to-date, while in other instances they have purchased records on an exchange basis. Their collection is undoubtedly one of the best in the world.

Other Land Records

Other records and documents--including rent rolls, powers of attorney, ante-nuptial agreements, and contracts of various types-- may also be kept in local courthouses. Some are closely allied to probate and guardianship matters, while others are associated with civil-criminal court records.

Powers of attorney are often associated with land use, though they may pertain to other matters. They authorize parties of the first part to act in behalf of parties of a second part and are often found among records relating to the distribution of an estate. Perhaps an older son moved from his Kentucky place of birth to an Illinois county and after several years received word of his father's death and settlement of his estate. Rather than make the journey back to the Kentucky home, the older son might initiate a "power of attorney" in favor of his younger brother who resides in Kentucky and have him act in his behalf in matters pertaining to the estate. Of course other types of business could also be handled under such power.

Ante-nuptial agreements are also useful and are sometimes found among land records. They concern persons who are about to marry but who desire to make special arrangements regarding their properties before the marriage is contracted. A widower may plan to marry a widow and both may have children from previous unions. They may desire to make special arrangements regarding land or property acquired previously or may desire to make special arrangements regarding their estates. Such records sometimes give the maiden name of a female spouse, previous married names, childrens' names, and serve to clarify problems regarding marital unions which might not otherwise be understood.

Contracts and agreements of other types may also be among local land records. Each must be located and evaluated to determine its relative worth. Conveyances in one county may be the same as evidences in another and both may pertain to deeds or transfer of title. In some counties the mortgages and leases may be included with the deed records, but in another county they might be recorded in separate volumes. However, all the counties of a particular state usually have similar recording systems and use similar nomenclature regarding their records. Land records as a general group have some consistencies, but the records and documents making up the group are divergent.

Federal or National Land Records

Records of the former General Land Office, now in the National Archives, include the land-entry papers for the thirty public land states, including Alaska. They include all of the United States except the thirteen original states and Kentucky, Maine, Vermont, West Virginia, Tennessee, Texas, and Hawaii.

The land-entry papers in the National Archives are in two main arrangement patterns. Before 1908 they are arranged alphabetically by state and according to the district land office where the entry was made. For each land office there is a separate series for each class of entry. Within each series the individual entry files are arranged in numerical order according to the number assigned to each entry at the time the final certificate was issued by the register of the local land office. With minor exceptions, warrants, scrip, mineral lieu selection entries, and all patented cases after 1908 are arranged in an unbroken numerical series, regardless of state or land office, according to the number assigned at the time of patenting.

There is no general overall index to entrymen or patentees for land-entry papers prior to 1908. There is such an index in the Bureau of Land Management, Department of the Interior, for the patented cases after 1908. There are partial indexes, however, either in the Bureau of Land Management or in the National Archives for the following series prior to 1908: (1) Warrants under the Military Bounty Land Act of 1788 (incomplete), (2) Virginia Military Bounty Land Warrants, (3) Private Land Claims, (4) Coal Cash Entries, and (5) Mineral Entries. There is also a consolidated name index (by name of entryman or patentee) for those land entries that are arranged by district land office in Alabama, Arizona, Florida, Louisiana, Nevada, Utah, and Alaska. This does not include names of persons who located land under military bounty land warrants. As the index is consolidated and the names are in one alphabetical sequence, it is not possible to select all entries for any particular state. Each index card shows the name of the entryman, description of the land, name of land office, date, type, and number of entry. No personal information of any kind regarding the entryman appears on these cards.

Among the records of the Veterans Administration in the National Archives, there is an alphabetical index to applications for military bounty land warrants issued under the acts of 1847, 1850, 1852, and 1855. For all land entry files other than those covered by name indexes, it is necessary, in order to find a file relating to a particular entry, to know either the legal description of the land in terms of township, range, section, and fraction of section or the date (or approximate date) of the entry and the name of the land office through which the entry was made.

Land-entry papers in the National Archives include (1) records relating to entries based on purchase or special conditions of settlement, 1800-1951, (2) bounty-land-warrant records, ca. 1789-1908, (3) homestead entries, and (4) private land-claims records, 1789-1908. The first class, records relating to entries based on purchases or special conditions, may be divided into several groups. The credit entry files and the cash entry files contain relatively little information of genealogical value; the donation entry files contain genealogical data in varying amounts.

The Bureau of Land Management has retained all of the record copies of the patents issued for all types of land entries, 1800 to date. No personal information about the entryman, however, appears on these record copies. To obtain information from these record copies it is necessary to have the date of the patent and the volume and page number of the record copy as shown on each individual land-entry paper now filed in the National Archives (fig. 88).

Credit Prior Entries

Most of the land sold by the federal government between 1800 and 1820 was sold on credit at no less than $2.00 an acre in accordance

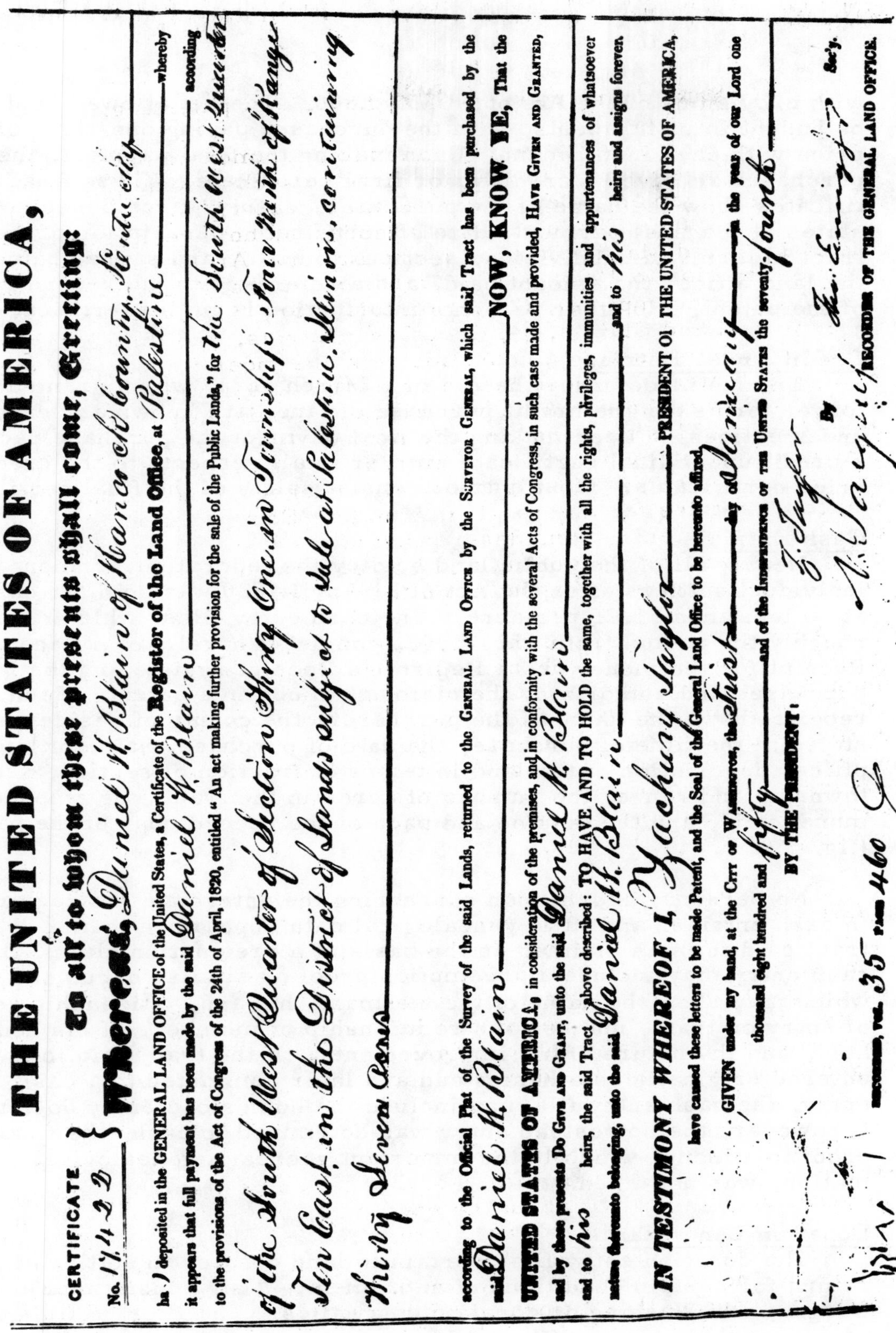

THE UNITED STATES OF AMERICA,

To all to whom these presents shall come, Greeting:

CERTIFICATE
No. 14,733

Whereas, Daniel M. Blair, of Marion County, Kentucky ———— whereby

ha_ deposited in the GENERAL LAND OFFICE of the United States, a Certificate of the **Register of the Land Office,** at Palestine ———

it appears that full payment has been made by the said _Daniel M. Blair_ ———— according

to the provisions of the Act of Congress of the 24th of April, 1820, entitled "An act making further provision for the sale of the Public Lands," for the _South West Quarter_

of the South West Quarter of Section Thirty One, in Township Fourteenth, of Range

Ten East, in the District of Lands subject to sale at Palestine, Illinois, containing

thirty seven acres ———

according to the Official Plat of the Survey of the said Lands, returned to the GENERAL LAND OFFICE by the SURVEYOR GENERAL, which said Tract has been purchased by the

said _Daniel M. Blair_ ———— **NOW, KNOW YE,** That the

UNITED STATES OF AMERICA, in consideration of the premises, and in conformity with the several Acts of Congress, in such case made and provided, HAVE GIVEN AND GRANTED,

and by these presents Do GIVE AND GRANT, unto the said _Daniel M. Blair_

and to _his_ heirs, the said Tract above described: TO HAVE AND TO HOLD the same, together with all the rights, privileges, immunities and appurtenances of whatsoever

nature thereunto belonging, unto the said _Daniel M. Blair_ ———— and to _his_ heirs and assigns forever.

IN TESTIMONY WHEREOF, I, _Zachary Taylor_ ———— **PRESIDENT OF THE UNITED STATES OF AMERICA,**

have caused these letters to be made Patent, and the Seal of the General Land Office to be hereunto affixed.

"" GIVEN under my hand, at the CITY OF WASHINGTON, the _first_ ———— day of _January_ ———— in the year of our Lord one

thousand eight hundred and _fifty_ ———— and of the INDEPENDENCE OF THE UNITED STATES the seventy _fourth_ ————

BY THE PRESIDENT:

Z. Taylor

By _R. Waugh_

Tho. Ewing Secy.

RECORDER OF THE GENERAL LAND OFFICE.

RECORDED VOL. 35 PAGE 460 E.

Fig. 88. Land patent under signature of Zachary Taylor

265

with provisions of the Act of 10 May 1800. The act allowed land to
be bought in installments, with the purchaser paying one-third of the
price with each installment. Upon making the final payment, the
purchaser received a credit prior final certificate. These final certificates show the name of the purchaser, county of residence he
stated at the final payment, date of certificate, description of the
tract in terms of subdivision, section, township and range, name of
the land office, the amount paid, and a reference to the record copy
of the patent. No other personal information is in the certificates.

Credit Under Entries

Entries made under the Act of 3 March 1821, which granted
longer terms for the credit purchase of land, are known as "credit
under entries." Upon making the final payment the purchase received
a credit under final certificate similar in all respects to the credit
prior certificates. Most entries consist solely of the final certificate.

Cash Entries

Nearly all of the public land sold by the federal government to
individual settlers after the Act of 21 April 1820 was sold for cash
at no less than $1.25 per acre. The cash entry files, which cover
roughly the period from 1820-1908, consist generally of a Receiver's
Receipt for the money and a Register's Receipt registering the land
purchases and authorizing the claimant to obtain a patent. Each
receipt shows the name of the purchaser, the county of residence
stated at the time of purchase, the date of purchase, name of land
office, description of the land in terms of fraction of section, section,
township and range, the number of acres in the tract, the amount of
money paid, and the volume and page of the record copy of the patent
(fig. 89).

No personal information concerning the entryman was required
in cash entries, and little genealogical data appears in them. If the
tract paid for was claimed on the basis of a preemption claim, the
cash entry may include a preemption proof or similar document
which may show the name of the claimant, his age, citizenship, date
of entry on tract, number and relationship of members of his household, and the nature of his improvements. If the tract paid for was
entered originally as a homestead and later commuted to a cash
entry, the cash entry file may include the homestead entry documents.
If however, the homestead entry was commuted to cash, the final-
proof testimony, which is the important source of genealogical information, was not taken.

Donation Land Claims

The donation entry files pertain to land donated to settlers in
return for certain conditions of settlement. They consist of Florida,
Oregon, and Washington donation entry files. The Florida files
usually include a permit to settle, an application for a patent, a
report of the land agent, and a final certificate authorizing the
issuance of patent. A permit to settle shows the name of the applicant,

266

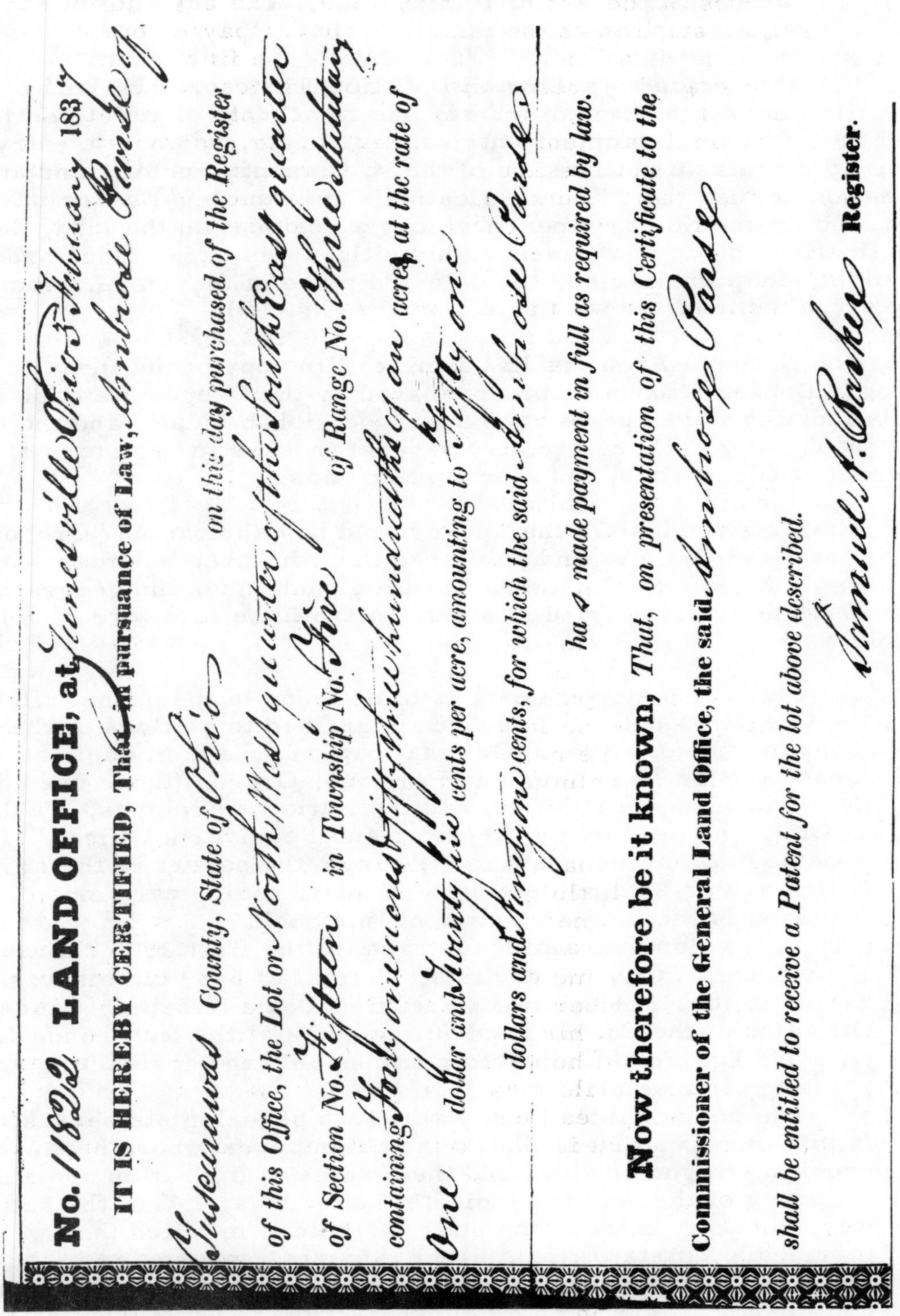

No. 1182. **LAND OFFICE, at** *Zanesville Ohio 3 February* 183*7*

IT IS HEREBY CERTIFIED, That, in pursuance of Law, *Ambrose Pardee of*

Muskingum County, State of *Ohio* on this day purchased of the Register of this Office, the Lot or *North West* quarter of the *South East* quarter of Section No. *Fifteen* in Township No. *Five* of Range No. *Three Military*; containing *forty one acre fifty three hundredths* of an acre, at the rate of *Fifty one* dollar and *twenty five* cents per acre, amounting to *Fifty one* *dollars* and *twenty* *cents, for which the said* *Ambrose Pardee*

ha *s* made payment in full as required by law.

Now therefore be it known, That, on presentation of this Certificate to the **Commissioner of the General Land Office, the said** *Ambrose Pardee*

shall be entitled to receive a Patent for the lot above described.

Samuel F. Parker **Register.**

Fig. 89. Receiver's receipt, Ohio 1837

267

his marital status, the month and year he began residing in Florida, and a legal description of the land.

The Oregon and Washington Donation Files for each land office are files in two numerical series, one relating to complete entries, and the other to incomplete entries. A file for a complete entry usually contains a notification of the settlement of public land and the donation certificate. The notification shows the legal description of the land, name of entryman, how long a resident on the land, date of application, place of residence, his citizenship, age, place and date of birth, and, if married, the date and place of marriage. Sometimes, the given name of the wife also appears (fig. 90).

The National Archives has a microfilm copy of the Index to Oregon Donation Land Claims prepared by the Oregon State Library. This index is in two parts, one arranged alphabetically and the other geographically. There are also several indexes to registers of these donation claims, but they contain gaps.

The Genealogical Forum of Portland has abstracted "Oregon Donation Land Claims" and published them in three volumes--vol. 1, 1957; vol. 2, 1959; vol. 3, 1962--with alphabetical and geographical indexes available (fig. 91). An extract from the foreword of volume 1 follows:

Much genealogical data is to be found in the papers filed for the Oregon Donation Land Claims granted to settlers of the Oregon Territory before 1853. Original papers, made in duplicate, are located at the Land Office in Portland, Oregon (those used by the Surveyor General's Office) and the National Archives, Washington, D. C. (those used by the Register and Receiver's Office). The genealogical material abstracted from the papers in the Land Office at Portland by members of the Genealogical Forum of Portland is the subject matter of this book.

This volume contains abstracts of the first 2500 claims filed at the Oregon City Land Office. A total of 5289 claims were filed at this office, 2141 claims were filed at the Roseburg Land Office, 5 at the Dalles Land Office and 2 at the La Grande Land Office. The Forum plans to continue with the abstracting and printing of these claims.

The books should be of interest to genealogists because of the family data contained, and to historians everywhere because proof of Oregon settlers and their paths of migration are shown. A survey of the records indicate that at least 45% of the settlers were not born in the same state as the one in which they were married. All states existing in 1853 are represented in the list from which Oregon settlers emigrated with the greatest number coming from Missouri, Kentucky, Virginia, Ohio, Indiana, Tennessee, Illinois, New York, Pennsylvania, North Carolina, South Carolina, Connecticut, Iowa, Maryland, Massachusetts, and Vermont.

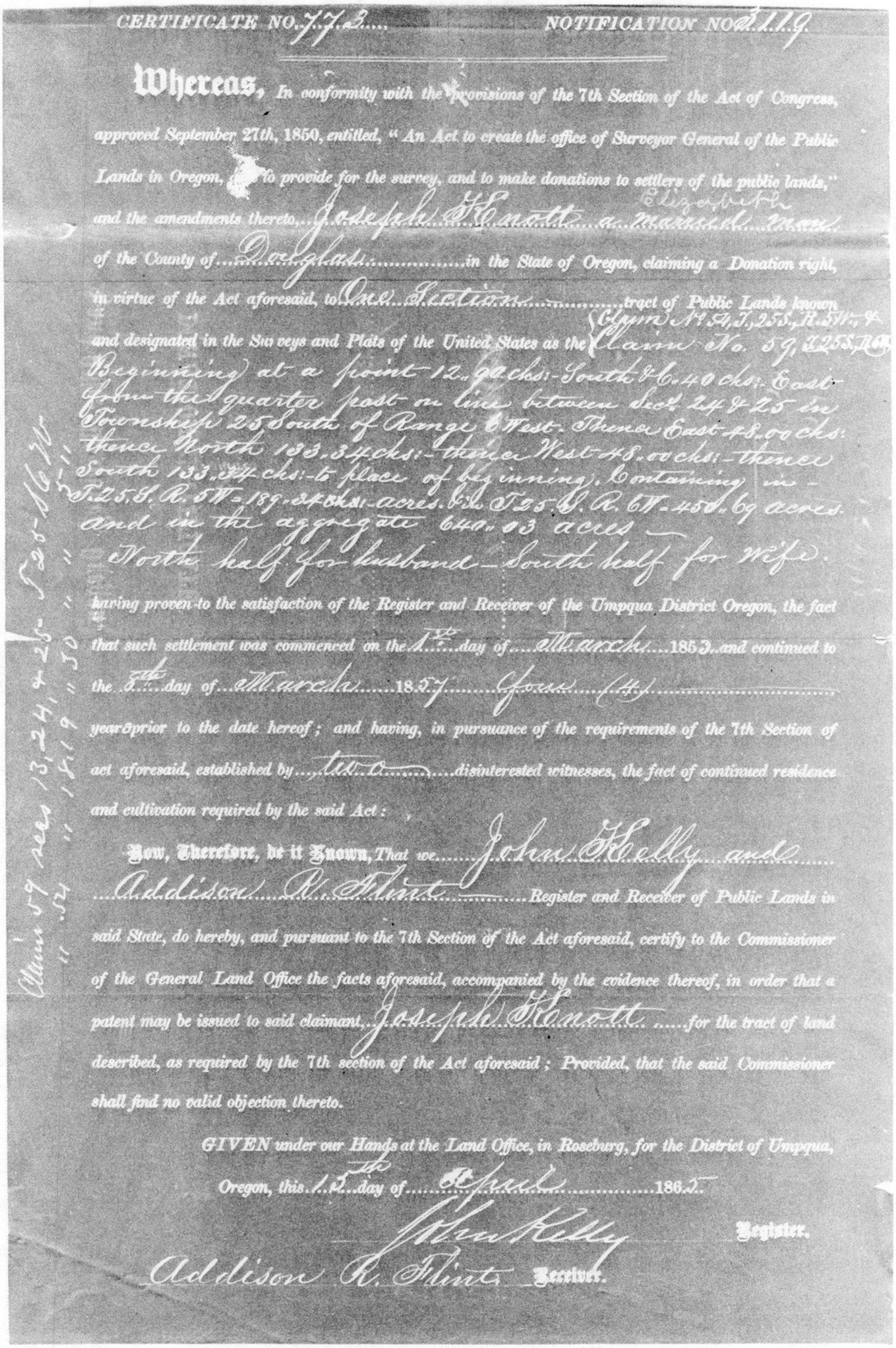

CERTIFICATE NO. 773 NOTIFICATION NO. 3119.

Whereas, In conformity with the provisions of the 7th Section of the Act of Congress, approved September 27th, 1850, entitled, "An Act to create the office of Surveyor General of the Public Lands in Oregon, and to provide for the survey, and to make donations to settlers of the public lands," and the amendments thereto, Joseph Knott & Elizabeth a married man of the County of Douglas in the State of Oregon, claiming a Donation right, in virtue of the Act aforesaid, to One Section tract of Public Lands known and designated in the Surveys and Plats of the United States as the Claim No. 54, T. 25 S., R. 5 W., & Claim No. 59, T. 25 S., R. 6 W.

Beginning at a point 12.90 chs:- South & 6.40 chs:- East from the quarter post on line between Secs. 24 & 25 in Township 25 South of Range 6 West. Thence East 48.00 chs: thence North 133.34 chs:- thence West 48.00 chs:- thence South 133.34 chs:- to place of beginning. Containing in - T. 25 S. R. 5 W. = 189.34 acres. & in T. 25 S. R. 6 W. = 450.69 acres. and in the aggregate 640.03 acres

North half for husband - South half for wife.

having proven to the satisfaction of the Register and Receiver of the Umpqua District Oregon, the fact that such settlement was commenced on the 1st day of March 1853 and continued to the 3rd day of March 1857 four (4) years prior to the date hereof; and having, in pursuance of the requirements of the 7th Section of act aforesaid, established by two disinterested witnesses, the fact of continued residence and cultivation required by the said Act:

Now, Therefore, be it Known, That we John Kelly and Addison R. Flint Register and Receiver of Public Lands in said State, do hereby, and pursuant to the 7th Section of the Act aforesaid, certify to the Commissioner of the General Land Office the facts aforesaid, accompanied by the evidence thereof, in order that a patent may be issued to said claimant, Joseph Knott for the tract of land described, as required by the 7th section of the Act aforesaid; Provided, that the said Commissioner shall find no valid objection thereto.

GIVEN under our Hands at the Land Office, in Roseburg, for the District of Umpqua, Oregon, this 15th day of April 1865.

John Kelly **Register.**

Addison R. Flint **Receiver.**

Claim 59 secs 13, 24, & 25 - T 25 - R 6 W
" 54 " 18, 19, " 30 " " 5 "

Fig. 90. Donation land claim

No. 763 WILKERSON, Elijah, Marion Co; b 1817, Ky; SC 20 Jan 1848; m Elizabeth J. 10 Jan 1839, Mo. Aff: Peter Polly, Joseph C. Polly.

No. 764 DELANY, David, Marion Co; b 1828, East Tenn; Arr. Ore. Nov 1845; SC 18 Apr 1852; m Jane 12 July 1855, Ore. T. Aff: Daniel Delany, Geo. Delany.

No. 765 PERHAM, Eugene L., Benton Co; b 1825, N.H.; Arr. Ore. Oct 1850; SC 19 July 1853. Aff: Theodore Wygant, Geo. A. Pease, Abraham B. Springer, John J. McFarland.

No. 766 BARLOW, John L., Clackamas Co; b 1828, Ind; Arr. Ore. prior 1 Dec 1850; SC 20 Sept/Dec 1852; m Mary E. 9 Oct 1850, Ore. T. Aff: Samuel K. Barlow, A. F. Hedges, Wm. D. Demont, John E. Millon.

No. 767 PARRISH, Edward E., Marion Co; b 1791, Va; SC 15 July 1845; m Rebecca, Mar 1827, Pa. Boundary conflict with Samuel Whittey (Whitley). Statements included from: John H. Whittey, Hiram A. Johnson, Isaac McCully, J. R. Robb, Thomas M. Romsdel (Ramsdell), Hamilton Campbell, Samuel Miller, Charles Miller. Aff: Jesse Loony, Joseph Cox.

No. 768 WHITLEY, Samuel, Marion Co; b 1789, Va; SC 15 Mar 1848; m Catharine L. 30 Mar 1817, Ind. Aff: Thomas Cox, Jesse Looney.

No. 769 JOHNSON, Hiram A., Marion Co; b 1819, N.Y.; SC 5 Feb 1849; m Elizabeth J. 25 July 1841, Ill. Aff: Samuel Whitney, Jesse Looney, Joseph Z. Himsaker, Jacob Conser.

No. 770 MILLER, William T., Marion Co; b 1829, Cole Co, Mo; Arr. Ore. Sept 1847; SC 15 Mar 1851; m Elizabeth 7 Sept 1851, Marion Co, Ore. T. Aff: Wm. H. Hillams, Joseph C. Polley, Reason Roby.

No. 771 MILLER, Charles, Marion Co; b 1830, Ind; Arr. Ore. 10 Sept 1848; SC 1 May 1852. Aff: Isaac Miller, Sr., Samuel Miller, Ralph Waltr.

Fig. 91. Abstracts from donation land claims

Each abstract will show for the settler in the following order his certificate number; his name; his place of residence; date and place of birth; date and place of marriage; first name of wife and last name when it appears in the record; date he settled his claim; names of those who signed affidavits (here will be found names of friends and relatives of the family). Pertinent family material entered in the file or any data on naturalization will also be included in the abstracts.

Bounty-Land Warrants and Scrip

The entry papers for the Virginia Revolutionary Warrants are dated chiefly 1795-1830 and include such documents as a surrendered warrant, a certificate of location, a survey, power of attorney, an assignment, and possibly an affidavit concerning the veteran's heirs. Most Virginia warrants were used in the Virginia Military District of Ohio prior to 1830 and were exchanged for scrip after that date. By the five acts beginning in 1830, Congress provided that holders of unused Virginia and United States Revolutionary War Warrants could surrender them for scrip certificates. These certificates could be used for land location anywhere on the public domain that land was offered for selection. A scrip application file includes such documents as the surrendered bounty-land warrant, power of attorney, assignment, an affidavit of relationship, and related correspondence (fig. 92).

The records relating to United States Revolutionary War Warrants surrendered for land in the United States Military District of Ohio are dated chiefly 1789-1833. In most instances the surrendered warrant and the certificate of location are the only documents on file, but occasionally an affidavit, power of attorney, or similar document is filed with the warrant. Warrants based upon the Act of 1803 as extended in 1806 show the location of the tract in terms of lot, sub-division, township, and range.

The records relating to United States War of 1812 Warrants include the notification of the filing of the warrant with the General Land Office, a power of attorney, and a letter of transmittal. A typical file contains such information as the name of the veteran, the location of the land, date of patent, and volume and page number of the record copy of the patent.

The last important group of warrant files consists of records relating to United States Warrants issued for unspecified land based on a series of acts passed between 1847 and 1855. Many of these warrants involve veterans of the Mexican War. The Mexican War is the last war for which veterans were granted bounty lands; no warrants have been issued for any service after 3 March 1855, the date of the last set. The Homestead Act, enacted in 1862, served to take the place of bounty-land acts.

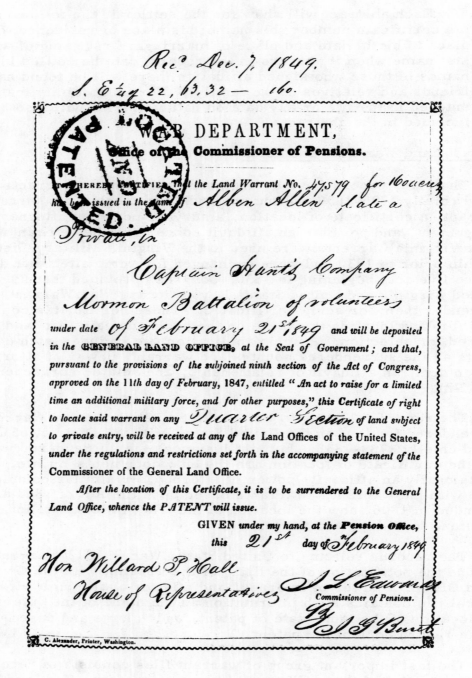

Rec.ᵈ Dec. 7, 1849.

S. E ¼ ᵠ 22, 63.32 — 160.

WAR DEPARTMENT,

Office of the Commissioner of Pensions.

IT HEREBY CERTIFIES, That the Land Warrant No. *47579* for *160 acres* has been issued in the name of *Alben Allen*, late a *Private, in*

Captain Hunt's Company

Mormon Battalion of volunteers

under date *of February 21ˢᵗ, 1849* and will be deposited in the **GENERAL LAND OFFICE**, at the Seat of Government; and that, pursuant to the provisions of the subjoined ninth section of the Act of Congress, approved on the 11th day of February, 1847, entitled "An act to raise for a limited time an additional military force, and for other purposes," this Certificate of right to locate said warrant on any *Quarter Section* of land subject to private entry, will be received at any of the Land Offices of the United States, under the regulations and restrictions set forth in the accompanying statement of the Commissioner of the General Land Office.

After the location of this Certificate, it is to be surrendered to the General Land Office, whence the *PATENT* will issue.

GIVEN under my hand, at the **Pension Office**, this *21ˢᵗ* day of *February 1849*

Hon Willard P. Hall.
House of Representatives

J. L. Edwards
Commissioner of Pensions.

By J. G. Burt

C. Alexander, Printer, Washington.

Fig. 92.   Bounty land warrant for member of the Mormon Battalion

Homestead Entries

Under the Homestead Act of 20 May 1862, citizens and persons who had filed their intentions to become citizens were given 160 acres of land on the public domain provided they fulfilled certain conditions, such as building a house on the land, cultivating the land, and residing on the homestead for five years.

The homestead entry papers, filed by names of land office, are dated 1863-1908. There are usually two separately numbered series for each land office, one relating to complete homestead entries, the other to unperfected entries. A complete file includes the homestead application, the certificate of publication of intention to make a claim, the homestead final proof and a final certificate authorizing the claimant to obtain a patent. The Homestead Final Proof Testimony, the only document in the file that includes personal information about the claimant, shows the name, age, and post office of the claimant, a description of the tract, a description of the house and the date when residence was established, the number and relationship of members of the family (but seldom their names), evidence of citizenship, the nature of the crops and number of acres under cultivation, and testimony of witnesses as to the truth of the claimant's statements (fig. 93).

Private Land Claims

These claims were made on the basis of grants or settlements that occurred before the United States acquired sovereignty. They relate chiefly to persons who claimed to have received grants from foreign sovereigns to their descendants, and to pioneer citizens of the United States who settled in these lands with the permission of the foreign governments (fig. 94).

Private land claims in the National Archives related to land in portions of fourteen states: Alabama, Arizona, Arkansas, California, Colorado, Florida, Illinois, Indiana, Iowa, Louisiana, Michigan, Mississippi, Missouri, New Mexico, and Wisconsin.

The private land claims of the General Land Office are filed in separate dockets containing such documents as correspondence, affidavits, and copies of court decisions. Since all of these dockets are poorly indexed with regard to the personal names of the applicants or grantees, it is essential to have a legal description of the land in order to locate an individual docket. Records relating to individual claims presented between 1790 and 1837 were reported to Congress and transcribed and indexed in the American State Papers, Class VIII, Public Land, Gales and Seaton, 8 vols.[4]

The Gendata Corporation of Salt Lake City recently published GRASSROOTS OF AMERICA (1972) which is a computerized index to the American State Papers, Class VIII, 1789-1837. The work was

HOMESTEAD PROOF—TESTIMONY OF CLAIMANT

James L. Wells_____, being called as a witness in his own behalf in support of homestead entry, No. 4235_____, for SW¼ Sec. 12 , T. 28N., R. 9 W. testifies as follows:

Ques. 1.—What is your name, age, and post-office address?

Ans. James L. Wells, age 41 years, Manchester, Okla

Ques. 2.—Are you a *native-born* citizen of the United States, and if so, in what State or Territory were you born?*

Ans. I am. Kansas.

Ques. 3.—Are you the identical person who made homestead entry, No. 4235_____, at the Alva Okla Ty_____ land office on the 17_____ day of Jany, 1894_____, 18 , and what is the true description of the land now claimed by you?

Ans. I am. I claim the SW¼ Sec. 24, T. 28N., R. 9 W.

Ques. 4.—When was your house built on the land and when did you establish actual residence therein? (Describe said house and other improvements which you have placed on the land, giving total value thereof.)

Ans. Dug out, 12 x 16, built Sept. 27, 1893, and actual residence established therein same date. Stone house, 16 x 33, addition, 14 x 16, stone hen house, stables, well, 65 acres cultivated, 15 acres fenced, 2300 fruit and forest trees. Value $800.

Ques. 5.—Of whom does your family consist; and have you and your family resided continuously on the land since first establishing residence thereon? (If unmarried, state the fact.)

Ans. Wife and six children. We have.

Ques. 6.—For what period or periods have you been absent from the homestead since making settlement, and for what purpose; and if temporarily absent, did your family reside upon and cultivate the land during such absence?

Ans. None

Ques. 7.—How much of the land have you cultivated each season, and for how many seasons have you raised crops thereon?

Ans. 65 acres cultivated to crops each season.

Ques. 8.—Is your present claim within the limits of an incorporated town or selected site of a city or town, or used in any way for trade and business?

Ans. No sir

Ques. 9.—What is the character of the land? Is it timber, mountainous, prairie, grazing, or ordinary agricultural land? State its kind and quality, and for what purpose it is most valuable.

Ans. Prairie land, most valuable for farming.

Ques. 10.—Are there any indications of coal, salines, or minerals of any kind on the land? (If so, describe what they are, and state whether the land is more valuable for agricultural than for mineral purposes.)

Ans. None

Ques. 11.—Have you ever made any other homestead entry? (If so, describe the same.)

Ans. No sir

Ques. 12.—Have you sold, conveyed, or mortgaged any portion of the land; and if so, to whom and for what purpose?

Ans. No sir

Ques. 13.—Have you any personal property of any kind elsewhere than on this claim? (If so, describe the same, and state where the same is kept.)

Ans. No sir

Ques. 14.—Describe by legal subdivisions, or by number, kind of entry, and office where made, any other entry or filing (not mineral), made by you since August 30, 1890.

Ans. No sir

(Sign plainly with full christian name.) James L. Wells

*(In case the party is of foreign birth a certified transcript from the court records of his declaration of intention to become a citizen, or of his naturalization, or a copy thereof, certified by the officer taking this proof, must be filed with the case. Evidence of *naturalization* is only required in final (*five-year*) homestead cases.)

6—577

Fig. 93. Homestead proof

FS-2
(August 1962)

6.05b-1L

PRIVATE LAND CLAIM INFORMATION

Misc. No. or Serial No. _____ State _Louisiana_

Is case docketed? _yes_ What is docket number? _858_

Grantee or Confirmee _Pierre Chasson_

Claiming Under _____

Cert. No. _598_ Date Issued 11/20/1816 Date Entered _filed 12/20/1803_

Location of claim _Both sides of Bayou Lafourche_

Area of claim _____ Nature of claim _settlement & cultivation_

American State Papers _Gales & Seaton_ Volume _3_ Page _264_

Confirmed by ____ or under section _____ of Act of _May 11, 1820 (3 Stat 573)_

Description of Land	Sec.	Twshp.	Range	Meridian	Area	Date of Plat
	4	18 S	18 E	La	90.80	4/5/1832
	3	18 S	19 E	"	136.29	. . . . .
					227.09 total	

Conflicts on Plat _none_

Conflicts on Tract Book _none_

Any record of R & R decision on conflict _/_

Information from Archives and Remarks _Report 247 - Reg. & Receiver_
for land claims Eastern District of La

Application for Patent _____ Applicant _____

Is possession claimed _____ Any adverse claimants _____

Has applicant served notice on adverse claimants _____

G.H. Wallace
(Signature of Adjudicator)

_5/8/64_
(Date)

Fig. 94. Private land claim

275

edited by Phillip W. McMullin and printed by Universal Printing.

The Genealogical Society in Salt Lake City has not yet obtained copies of the federal land records in the National Archives, though it does have several rolls of microfilm pertaining to Ohio State Land Records which concern federal lands. It also has miscellaneous state collections for other states, but the general group of federal land records outlined above are not yet among its collections.

Sequence for Search in Land Records

The sequence of search may vary with each genealogical problem, but usually it is effective to locate the individual of interest through the use of tax lists or deed indexes. In New England it may be best to search town meeting books and proprietors' records when they are indexed. But since the majority are not, tax lists or deed indexes will serve the purpose. Plat-books and surveyors' records might also be useful as locating tools, but they are not always indexed or convenient to use.

Once the county or town of residence has been established, the deeds and mortgages should be investigated. If there are only one or two entries for the surname, they should be evaluated and copied verbatim, but if many entries are located, time should be taken to copy the index references, and extracts should be made of the actual records. Tape recorders and cameras make excellent copy tools for land records, though one must be careful of spelling and arrangement when using the tape recorder.

After the deeds, mortgages, and leases have been examined, plat-books, surveyors' records, special agreements and contracts, and related records should be searched. Documents relating to ante-nuptial agreements and powers of attorneys should be noted when they are filed among the other land records; otherwise they should be located in their respective record volumes.

Following the local land records, existing state records should be investigated followed by federal or national land records. However, it should be remembered that land records pertaining to the public land states are in the National Archives, while those for the colonial states remain in their respective town, county, and state land offices.

Documents and records other than those explained in this chapter may also be found among local, state, and federal land records, and methods regarding their use may also be determined which will supersede or supplement those listed here. However, it is hoped the information presented will serve as a guide and provide new motivation for genealogical research.

1. C. E. Sherman, ORIGINAL OHIO LAND SUBDIVISIONS (Ohio State Reformatory Press, 1925), 2:19.

2. Public Land Commission, THE PUBLIC DOMAIN: ITS HISTORY, WITH STATISTICS, 1880 (Washington, D. C.: Government Printing Office), pp. 28, 29.

3. Virginia Pope Livingston, SOME PECULIARITIES OF GENEALOGICAL RESEARCH IN VIRGINIA, A paper delivered at the World Conference on Records and Genealogical Seminar, Salt Lake City, August 1969, pp. 1, 2.

4. Meredith B. Colket, Jr. and Frank E. Bridgers, GUIDE TO GENEALOGICAL RECORDS IN THE NATIONAL ARCHIVES (Washington, D. C.: Government Printing Office, 1964), pp. 104-128.

CHAPTER 11

USING MILITARY RECORDS AS A PEDIGREE SUPPLEMENT

On the 31st of October 1787, a training of the militia soldiers was held at this place. About four o'clock in the afternoon of that day, David Downs left his house, now occupied by Treat Davidson, and went to the tavern for the purpose of getting his son excused from going to the General Training, to be held the next day at Southbury. Thomas Hurlbut was present with a gun, in the house of Ransom, and one Hitchcock asked him if his gun was a good one. He replied "Try it and see." On being asked by Hitchcock if it was loaded, he replied in the negative, on which he pulled the trigger, and the gun being loaded, the ball which it contained passed through the head of David Downs, above the eyes, and dashed his brains on the wall, or ceiling, near which he stood, the stain from which remained indelible for many years after. (From THE HISTORY OF WOODBURY CONNECTICUT, 1:174.)

Military records may not provide solution to every American pedigree problem, but they can certainly be used as a pedigree supplement. It is surprising the number of persons who have been involved with the military and the amount of genealogical information which has been recorded since the earliest settlement of this land because of it.

Records relating to the earliest conflicts are primarily historical accounts and contain little genealogical information, but many created since the Revolution contain facts relating to birth, marriage, death, parentage, as well as other family data.

An article that appeared in the DESERET NEWS of 12 November 1968 indicated that over 26 million Americans, more than 10 percent of the population, are veterans of military service, and most of them have served in wartime. This has probably been the case in earlier periods also. At the time of the article, there were over 14 million veterans of World War II, over 5 million veterans of the Korean conflict, and more than 200,000 veterans of Vietnam. About 1.8 million veterans of World War I were still on the government pension rolls at that time, and about 10,000 veterans of the Spanish-American War were still alive. Only 2 veterans from Indian wars were listed as living, and it was indicated that the last veteran of the Civil War died in 1959, though the Veteran's Administration was still serving more than one thousand widows of Civil War veterans.

Service and pension files were first created as a result of the Revolutionary War (1775-1784), and they sometimes contain valuable genealogical information. Records relating to the earlier conflicts consist primarily of historical accounts with rather incomplete and meager genealogical data included. When it comes to the conflicts prior to 1775, one must approach the problem on a locality basis, looking for local and regional histories or special publications which covered the conflicts. SOLDIERS IN KING PHILIP'S WAR by George Madison Bodge (Baltimore: The Genealogical Publishing Company, 1967) is an example. It contains a concise history of the Indian wars of New England from 1620 through 1677 with lists of soldiers and sketches of principal officers (GS #973 M26 or BYU #973.24 B632s).

Records created during and after the Revolutionary War are much more complete than those of the earlier periods and contain varying amounts of genealogical information, but pension files are by far the most important to genealogy. They include claims, depositions, affidavits, information briefs and summaries, letters and correspondence, agency reports, personal papers, and miscellaneous documents relating to the soldier and his family.

Service files do not contain as much genealogical information as pension files because they relate more to events which concerned the serviceman while in service. Typical documents include enlistment and induction registers, rosters, and papers; muster rolls, payrolls, and vouchers; orders and citations; applications and recommendations for promotion; requests and orders for leave; oaths of fidelity for some officers; disciplinary proceedings; medical reports; death and interment reports; and miscellaneous correspondence.

With exception of a few record groups destroyed in 1800 and 1814 when public buildings were burned in Washington, most pension and service records have been preserved, though service files for the early wars are rather incomplete. Records concerning personnel who served prior to World War I have been centralized in the National Archives in Washington, D.C., and many have been microfilmed. Records relating to personnel who served after that period are housed in various other federal repositories.

The service and pension records in the National Archives apply to personnel who served in various branches of the service--in the Revolutionary War, the War of 1812, Indian Wars, the Mexican War, the Spanish-American War, and in peacetime during the same periods. They relate to service in the Continental Army, U.S. Volunteers, U.S. Regular Army, U.S. Navy, U.S. Marine Corps, and the Confederate States Army, Navy, and Marines. Many of the records have been compiled (combined) by the name of the serviceman and arranged according to organization and service. Each record group has one or more indexes, most of which have also been microfilmed.

The following information relates primarily to military pension records in the National Archives and only incidentally covers the service files. For an excellent treatise on the service records which date prior to World War I, a researcher should see pp. 44-102 of GUIDE TO GENEALOGICAL RECORDS IN THE NATIONAL ARCHIVES by Meredith B. Colket, Jr., and Frank E. Bridgers (Washington: The Government Printing Office, 1964). The information presented in this chapter is based on the above publication and on U.S. MILITARY SERVICE AND PENSION RECORDS HOUSED AT THE NATIONAL ARCHIVES by James D. Walker (a paper read at the World Conference on Records and Genealogical Seminar, 5-8 August 1969); however, some information has been omitted or rearranged, and document examples have been included to show the genealogical value of the records.

Revolutionary War Pension Records
        Pension records relating to service in the Revolutionary War were created under various Congressional acts beginning 26 August 1776 and continuing into the twentieth century. (The last Revolutionary War widow died 11 November 1906.) The burden to provide the actual benefits rested first with the states and applied mainly to officers, but by 1818 pensions were provided others who served and were based upon need and length of service. The rate of pay was twenty dollars per month for officers but only amounted to eight dollars for others. No provisions were made in the first laws to establish need; as funds became limited, some pensioners were dropped from the rolls. An 1821 act restored many persons who had previously been dropped, and pension requirements were gradually liberalized, especially by acts in 1828 and 1832. These allowed for widows' and orphans' benefits; though various later acts altered the requirements for proving a claim (fig. 95).

An act dated 4 March 1789 transferred the responsibility for providing pension benefits from the states to the federal government, and the Secretary of War became responsible for examining and approving cases submitted. On 3 March 1849, the Pension Office was transferred to the Department of Interior where it remained until the Veteran's Administration was established.

The general procedure for initiating an early pension claim

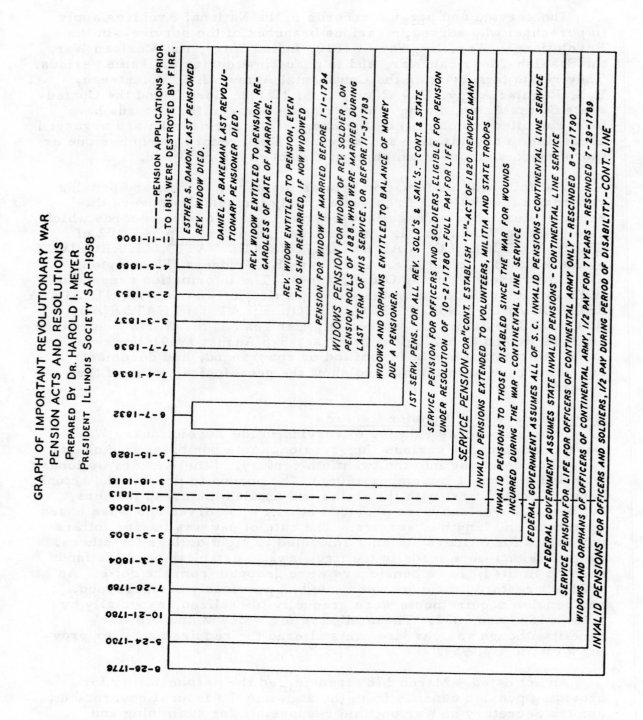

Fig. 95. Graph of pension acts and resolutions

was for the soldier, or his widow or heir, to go before a court of record in the county of residence and state his service by oath or present evidence to prove that service was rendered.

Nathaniel Morrill of Sanbornton, Strafford, New Hampshire, appeared before a Judge of the County Court and requested a pension under the Act of 7 June 1832. He completed a "brief" showing his age, service, and place of enlistment and also provided supporting documents, such as a discharge and depositions from others. His pension was approved, and he was placed on the pension rolls at the rate of $26.66 per annum under the law of 7 June 1832 (fig. 96).

Sometimes the facts given in the declarations can lead to other helpful sources. Paul Gammit applied for a pension in Otsego County, New York, in 1833, giving his age and place of birth in the declaration. He stated he was born in West Greenwich, Rhode Island, in 1747 but did not know of any record of his birth being available. Searches by a private researcher in the Arnold collection of Rhode Island vital records at Salt Lake City failed to show his birth entry in the town records for West Greenwich, but there was a marriage entry in 1745 for Abraham Gammit and Sarah Gardiner, who turned out to be his parents. The age and place of birth were the most helpful facts in that deposition, but other information might be just as important in other depositions.

The widow's pension claim and deposition usually contains more genealogical information than the soldier's, including her name and age, place of birth or residence, the death date and place of her husband, their marriage date and place, and other family information (fig. 97). The law provided that such evidence be presented by discharge certificate, statements of persons having knowledge of such service, by testimony of the soldier's officers and comrades, or by custodians of records reflecting such service. The Acts of 1820 and 1832 necessitated the inclusion of a schedule of the personal property owned by the claimant and various acts required that widows provide evidence of their marriage and proof of death by certificate, court record, minister's statement, statement of witnesses to the actual marriage service, and statements of witnesses to the veteran's death (fig. 98).

The Act of 1832, and many subsequent acts, required record of proof of the claimant's age. Dependency of children as well as evidence of legal guardianship was also necessary. In addition, evidence of fidelity in the form of proof that no remarriage had occurred was required. The requirement to prove need also served to provide information about other family members, depending upon the applicant and his situation.

Files for Francis Montey, a private who served in the Revolution from Clinton County, New York, helped to extend a pedigree three generations for an Idaho family. Their ancestor, Abraham Montey,

BRIEF in the case of *Nath'l Morrill* of *Sanbornton* *of Strafford* in the State of *New Hampshire*
(Act 7th June, 1832.)

1. Was the declaration made before a Court or a Judge? *Court*

2. If before a Judge, does it appear that the applicant is disabled by bodily infirmity?

3. How old is he? *70*

4. State his service, as directed in the form annexed.

Period.	Duration of Service.			Rank.	Names of General and Field Officers under whom he served.
	Years.	Months.	Days.	As a	Gen.
*In 177_*		*2*		*Pri*	*Capt'n Brown*
July 4 1780		*6*			*Runniman, Lt. Col. Drayton*
				3	*Col Scammel, Gen'l Lafayette*

5. In what battles was he engaged?

6. Where did he reside when he entered the service? *Rockingham County New Hampshire*

7. Is his statement supported by living witnesses, by documentary proof, by traditionary evidence, by incidental evidence, or by the rolls?
Documentary

8. Are the papers defective as to form or authentication? and if so, in what respect? *Defective papers not attached as required*

I Certify that the foregoing statement and the answers agree with the evidence in the case above mentioned.

J. Wilson, Examining Clerk.
_y 15 1833

Nathaniel Morrill of Hawk in the in the State of N. Hampshire a Soldier in the N. Hampshire Regiment inlisted for Six Months from the fourth of July last has faithfully served as a Soldier and agreeable to gen'l orders is discharged the service and has liberty to return to said State N. Hampshire Village Decm'r

H. Dearborn Lt. Col'o

Fig. 96. Documents from pension file of Nathaniel Morrill

284

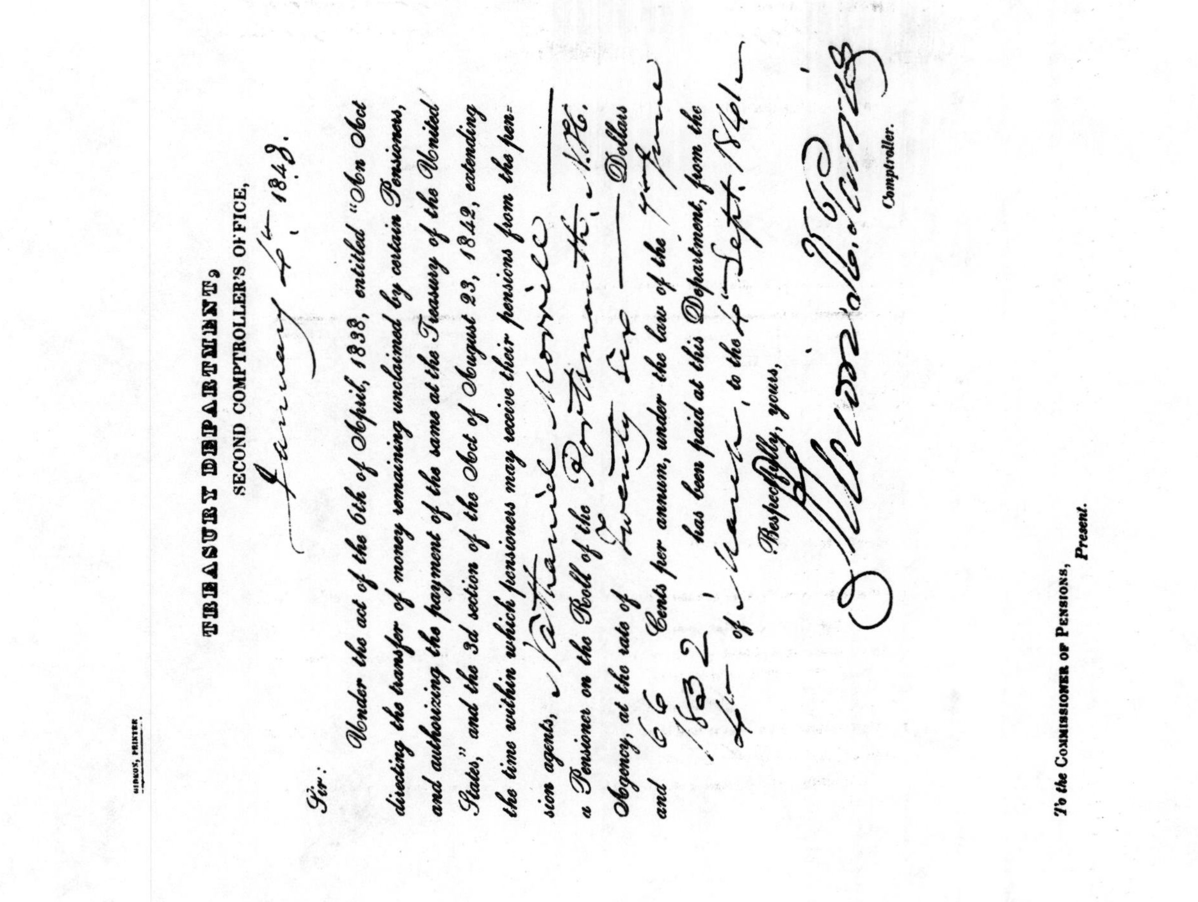

GIBSON, PRINTER.

TREASURY DEPARTMENT,

SECOND COMPTROLLER'S OFFICE,

January 4, 1848.

Sir:

Under the act of the 6th of April, 1838, entitled "An Act directing the transfer of money remaining unclaimed by certain Pensioners, and authorizing the payment of the same at the Treasury of the United States," and the 3d section of the Act of August 23, 1842, extending the time within which pensioners may receive their pensions from the pension agents, Nathaniel Norris

a Pensioner on the Roll of the Portsmouth, N.H. Agency, at the rate of Twenty Six ———— Dollars and 66 Cents per annum, under the law of the 7 June 1832, has been paid at this Department, from the 4th of March, to the 4th of Sept. 1846,

Respectfully, yours,

Comptroller.

To the COMMISSIONER OF PENSIONS, *Present.*

New Hampshire 4746.

Nathaniel Norris

of Stafford in the State of N.H. who was a Private in the company commanded by Captain ———— of the Reg't commanded by Col. Dearborn in the N.H. line for 8 Mos

Inscribed on the Roll of N.H. at the rate of 26 Dollars 66 Cents per annum. to commence on the 4th day of March, 1831.

Certificate of Pension issued the 30th day of Jany 1833 and Sent to Col. Harper Hs'd Rep's

Arrears to 4th of Sep 1832 $39.99
Semi-annual allowance ending 4 Mar 33   13,33

$53,32

Revolutionary Claim,
Act June 7, 1832.

Recorded by J. H. McBlair Clerk
Book D.   Vol. 12   Page 170.

Fig. 96a.

285

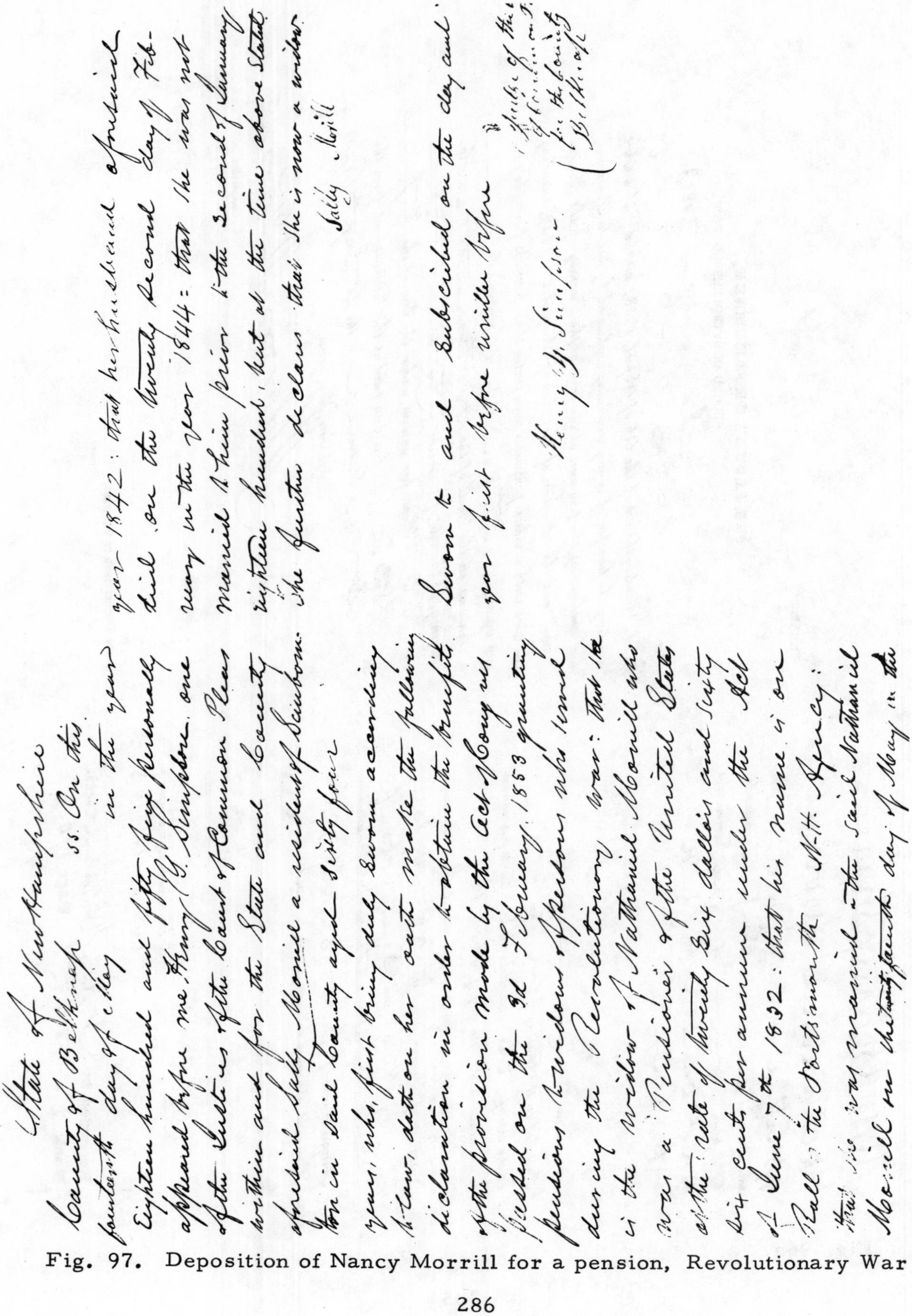
State of New Hampshire
County of Belknap ss. On this fourteenth day of May in the year Eighteen hundred and fifty five personally appeared before me Henry G. Simpson one of the Justices of the Court of Common Pleas within and for the State and County aforesaid Sally Morrill a resident of Sanbornton in said County aged sixty four years, who, first being duly sworn according to law, doth on her oath make the following declaration in order to obtain the benefit of the provision made by the Act of Congress passed on the 3d February 1853 granting pensions to widows of persons who served during the Revolutionary war: that she is the widow of Nathaniel Morrill who was a Pensioner of the United States at the rate of twenty six dollars and sixty six cents per annum under the Act of June 7th 1832: that his name is on Roll of the Portsmouth N.H. Agency: that she was married to the said Nathaniel Morrill on the twenty fourth day of May in the year 1842: that her husband aforesaid died on the twenty second day of February in the year 1844: that she was not married to him prior to the second of January eighteen hundred, but at the time above stated. She further declares that she is now a widow.

Sally Morill

Sworn to and subscribed on the day and year first before written before

Henry G. Simpson (Judge of the C of Common P for the County Belknap

Fig. 97. Deposition of Nancy Morrill for a pension, Revolutionary War

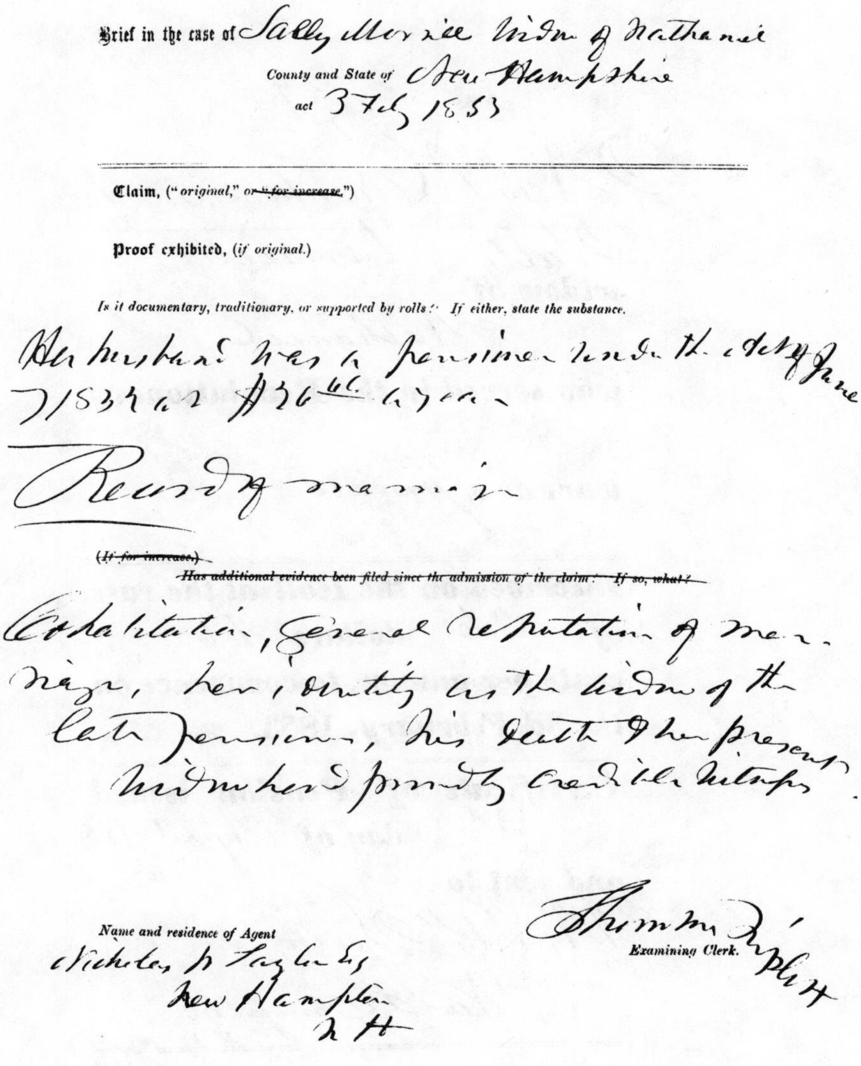

Brief in the case of *Sally Merrill Widow of Nathaniel*

County and State of *New Hampshire*

act *3 Feby 1853*

Claim, ("*original,*" or "*for increase.*")

Proof exhibited, (*if original.*)

Is it documentary, traditionary, or supported by rolls? If either, state the substance.

Her husband was a pensioner under the Act of June 7 1832 at $36.66 a year —

Record of marriage

(If for increase.)

Has additional evidence been filed since the admission of the claim? If so, what?

Cohabitation, general reputation of marriage, her identity as the widow of the late pensioner, his death & her present widowhood proved by credible witnesses.

Thomas
Examining Clerk.

Name and residence of Agent

Nicholas W Taylor Esq
New Hampton
N H

Fig. 98. Documents supporting a Revolutionary War pension claim

287

5729.

New Hampshire. In

Sally Morrill,

widow of *Nathaniel,*

who served in the Revolutionary

war, as a *private*

Inscribed on the Roll at the rate
of *26* **dollars** *66*
cents per annum, to commence on
the 3d February, 1853.

Certificate of Pension issued
3d **day of** *April 185*
and sent to

W, M, Taylor,

New Hampton,

N. H.

Recorded on Roll of Pensioners under act
February 3, 1853, Page 161. Vol. 36.

Fig. 98a.

who was born in Plattsburg, New York, in 1800 and lived in McDonough County, Illinois, in the 1870s and in Sandusky County, Ohio, in the 1850s proved to be a brother of Christopher Montey who applied for benefits from Francis Montey's pension. Christopher, after being "duly sworn" said he was of Plattsburg, Clinton County, New York, and was "one of the children of Francis Montey, late of Plattsburg, deceased," and was also "administrator of his father, the said Francis Montey." Christopher further stated that his father, Francis Montey, "was the oldest son of Francis Montey, a Lieutenant in Captain Olivers Company in said Regiment and who was an invalid pensioner of the United States at the rate of Eighty dollars per year and died at Chazy in 1809." He went on to say that "the father of deponent, the said Francis (Private) died at Plattsburgh on the 10th day of August 1818 and was on the pension rolls at the time of his death" (fig. 99).

A pension application file relating to an approved claim for a veteran usually contains evidence of service, evidence of age, an application, a jacket which holds the documents, the rate of pension, the certificate number, and the name of the pension agency. Miscellaneous papers in the files usually provide the best genealogical information. The property schedules not only list the veteran's land holdings, household effects, and sources of income, but also frequently list his wife and dependent children by name and age. Sometimes the declaration contains unusual genealogical information, such as that shown in fig. 100, which explains how Robert Givens, Sr., was really Robert Givens, Jr.

The Act of 1832 set forth guidelines by which applications for pensions were to be made. They required (1) a declaration of service rendered and proof of discharge or commission, (2) certification of an evaluation of the evidence given by the court, (3) relinquishment of prior claims, (4) evidence of a minister or other witnesses acknowledging acquaintanceship with the claimant, (5) certification by the court of the veracity of the witnesses, and (6) statements as to birthplace, age, residence at the time of application, form of enlistment, names of officers under whom each period of service was rendered, and certification of the court clerk by signature and seal.

An application by a widow or by another in behalf of orphaned children required additional evidence. An application for a minor necessitated all information required to be furnished by a widow, and also evidence of her death or remarriage. The applicant would, under court appointment, be the legal guardian of the children and would be required to provide strict accounting of the pension monies paid to minors. All minors' pensions terminated at age sixteen.

Approved widow's pension claim files contain a record of the soldier's service, a record of affidavits relating to her marriage, evidence of continued widowhood, some evidence of need, a jacket similar to that found in the soldier's file, and if she claimed pension in behalf of a minor child, proof of his age and date of birth. A file

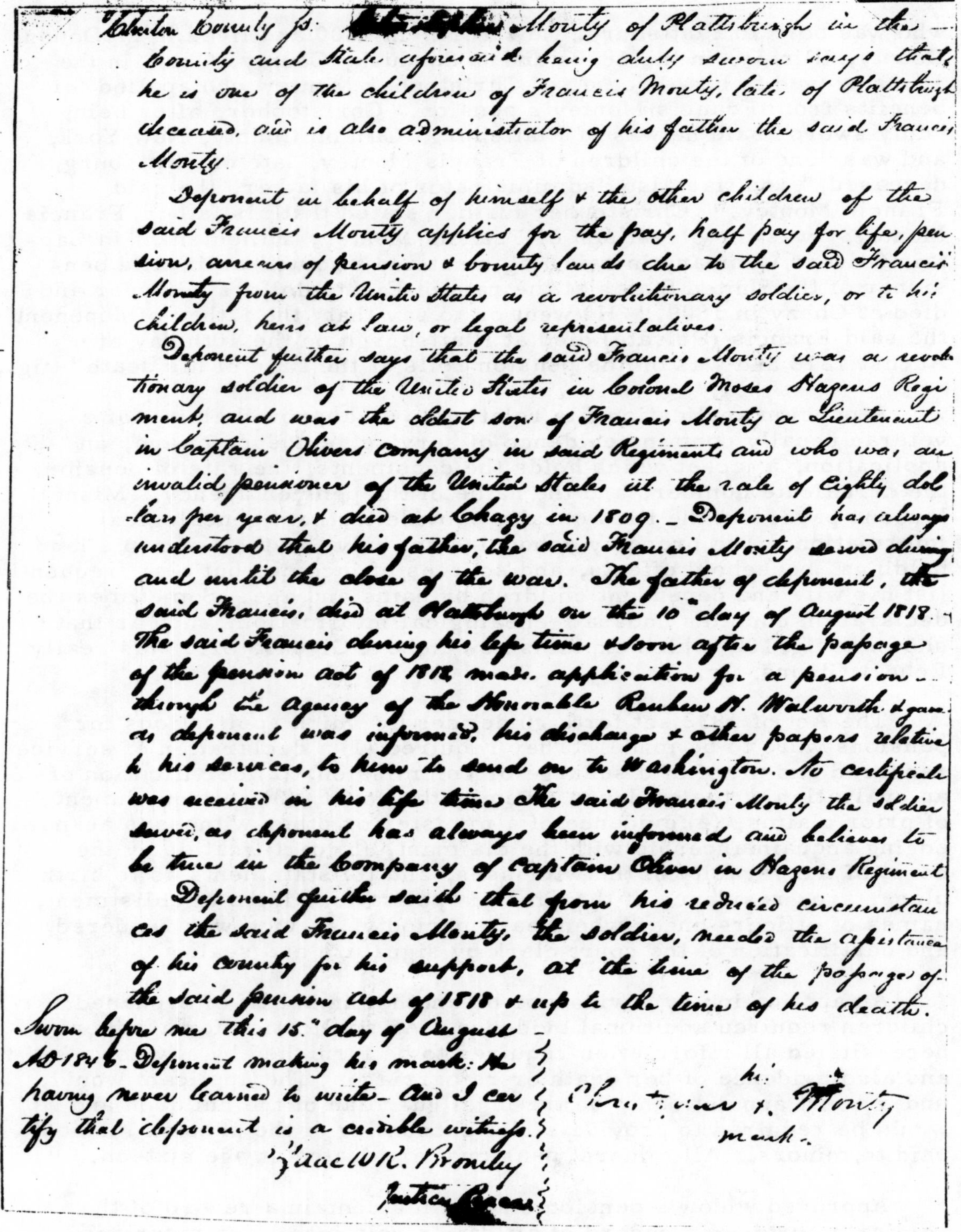

Clinton County ss. ~~Christopher~~ Monty of Plattsburgh in the County and State aforesaid having duly sworn says that he is one of the children of Francis Monty, late of Plattsburgh deceased, and is also administrator of his father the said Francis Monty.

Deponent in behalf of himself & the other children of the said Francis Monty applies for the pay, half pay for life, pension, arrears of pension & bounty lands due to the said Francis Monty from the United States as a revolutionary soldier, or to his children, heirs at law, or legal representatives.

Deponent further says that the said Francis Monty was a revolutionary soldier of the United States in Colonel Moses Hazens Regiment, and was the eldest son of Francis Monty a Lieutenant in Captain Olivers company in said Regiment and who was an invalid pensioner of the United States at the rate of Eighty dollars per year, & died at Chazy in 1809.— Deponent has always understood that his father, the said Francis Monty served during and until the close of the war. The father of deponent, the said Francis, died at Plattsburgh on the 10th day of August 1818. The said Francis during his life time & soon after the passage of the pension act of 1818 made application for a pension through the Agency of the Honorable Reuben H. Walworth & gave, as deponent was informed, his discharge & other papers relative to his services, to him to send on to Washington. No certificate was received in his life time. The said Francis Monty the soldier served, as deponent has always been informed and believes to be true in the Company of Captain Oliver in Hazens Regiment.

Deponent further said that from his reduced circumstances the said Francis Monty, the soldier, needed the assistance of his country for his support, at the time of the passage of the said pension act of 1818 & up to the time of his death.

Sworn before me this 15th day of August AD 1848. Deponent making his mark: He having never learned to write— And I certify that deponent is a credible witness.

Isaac W R. Bromley
Justice of Peace

Christian + Monty
his
mark

Fig. 99. Deposition of Christopher Montey, Revolutionary War

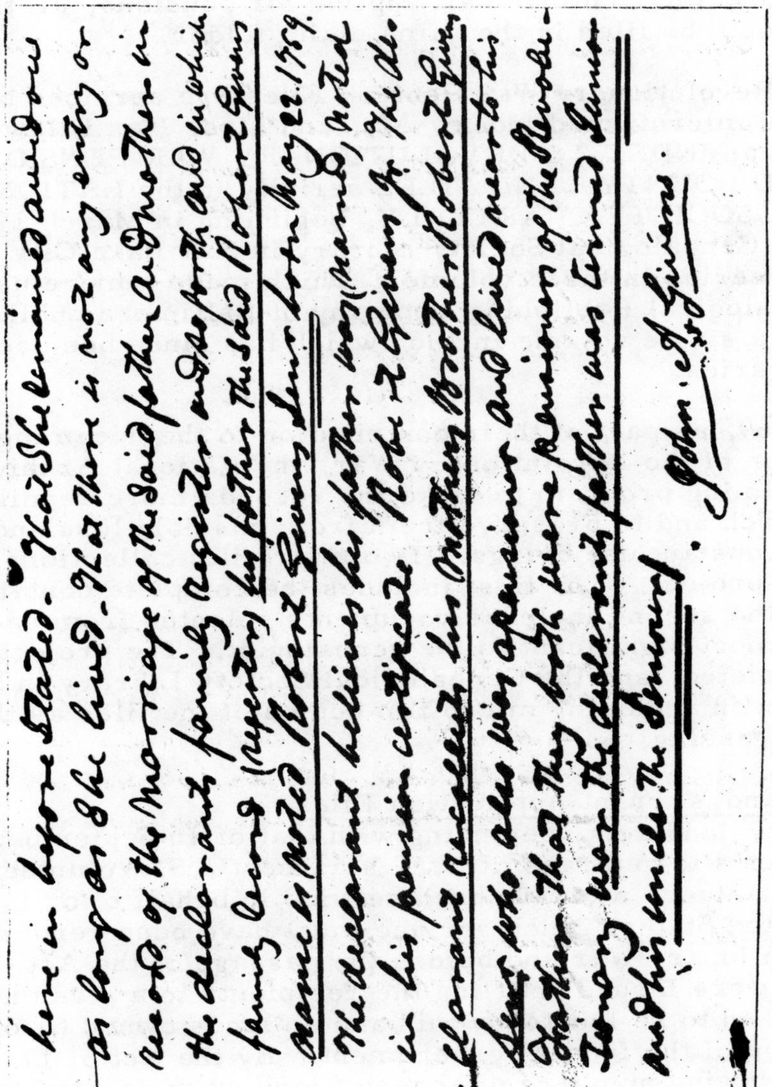

here in before stated. That She remained a widow
as long as She lived. That there is not any entry or
record of the marriage of the said father and mother in
the declarants family register and so forth and in which
family record (regester) his father the said Robert Givens
name is noted Robert Givens Senr born May 22. 1759.
The declarant believes his father was named, noted
in his pension certificate Robert Givens Jr. The declarant recollects his mothers Brother Robert Givens
Senr who also was a pensioner and lived near to his
father that they both were pensioners of the Revolutionary war the declarants father was termed Junior
and his uncle the Seniors.
John A. Givens

Fig. 100. Declaration clarifying kinship

relating to claims in behalf of minors would normally contain all of the items found in the widow's file plus letters of guardianship.

It was the policy of the pension agencies to combine all related papers into a single file. Therefore, if the soldier, his widow and guardian of minor children all applied for pensions, all three sets of papers would be filed in the same claim folder.

The Revolutionary War Pension Files are serviced by both a published and microfilmed index. Mr. and Mrs. Max Ellsworth Hoyt published an INDEX TO REVOLUTIONARY WAR PENSION APPLICATION AND BOUNTY LAND FILES serially in the NATIONAL GENEALOGICAL SOCIETY QUARTERLY, beginning in March 1943. In 1960, the Genealogical Society Library in Salt Lake City bound the complete series in three volumes, which made a more usable index. The Genealogical Publishing Company of Baltimore published the same series in a single volume in 1967 which has since been acquired by many libraries.

In 1969, as part of their contribution to the upcoming bicentennial celebration of the Revolutionary War, the National Archives initiated a microfilming program to make the records more readily available for research and to preserve them from possible loss and the deterioration that constant use brings. Two microfilm collections resulted from this project. The first includes the complete contents of each file, and the second includes documents selected from each file which would be most significant to the genealogist. The project has just been completed, and the Genealogical Society Library in Salt Lake City has been acquiring microfilm copies of the files as the work has been progressing.

Bounty-Land Warrant Application Files

Bounty-land acts, beginning with that of 16 September 1776, granted lands to veterans of U.S. service, U.S. Volunteers of State Militia, or others who rendered service in behalf of or in the interest of the United States. Such service must have been rendered between the Revolutionary War and before the passage of the Act of 1855. Warrants were issued entitling the recipients to a given number of acres of land to be located within and on lands owned by or under the jurisdiction of the federal government. By the Act of 1776, warrants for the following numbers of acres of land were granted to each qualified veteran upon the presentation of satisfactory evidence of service which was terminated by honorable discharge or death:

Major General	1,100 acres
Brigadier General	850 acres
Colonel	500 acres
Lieutenant Colonel	450 acres
Major	400 acres
Captain	300 acres
Lieutenant	200 acres

Ensign	150 acres
Noncom'd Officer or Private	100 acres

(All papers relating to land warrants received in Washington prior to the fire of 8 November 1800 were destroyed.)

Bounty-land laws served as inducement to foster enlistments and deter desertions or resignations. They were also given at subsequent dates as a reward for service rendered. Relatively few veterans applied for regular pensions, but very few refused or failed to apply for and receive a bounty-land warrant. As in the case of a pension certificate, the warrant was a negotiable instrument, and many warrants were sold for their ready cash value to land speculators (fig. 1 01).

After the Revolutionary War, grants of land based upon military service were limited to 160 acres. During the Mexican War (1846-48) noncommissioned officers and other enlisted men serving in either the U.S. or Volunteer Regiments were entitled to receive 160 acres of land or one hundred dollars in script for twelve months' service. Those serving less than twelve months were entitled to twenty-five dollars in script or 40 acres of land.

The Act of 28 September 1850 extended land benefits to some enlisted men who failed to qualify under previous acts passed since the Revolutionary War and to officers for the first time. That law also allowed those who received less than 160 acres for nine months' service during the War of 1812, Mexican War, or in the Indian Wars (1812-1850) to receive the amount of land, which when added to the amount previously granted, totaled 160 acres. Those who served for six months were entitled to 80 acres and those who served one month were entitled to 40 acres. The Act of 22 March 1852 amended the Act of 1850 to include those state or territorial troops who had served since 1812.

The Act of 3 March 1855 provided 160 acres to all who had served fourteen days or more in any battle in any war in which the U.S. had been engaged from 1790 to the passage of the act. Revolutionary War veterans who had received less than 160 acres could also apply under the act.

A claim file for bounty land can include several approved claims and some disapproved claim papers. As in the case of a pension claim, satisfactory evidence of service was required. The files contain little more genealogical information than is normally found in a military service file, except in the case of a claim by a widow or a legal guardian, where additional genealogical data might be included. A soldier's claim will, if based upon volunteer service, contain an application on which is stated his age, residence, alleged service, reference to previous warrants issued, and certification by a court clerk (fig. 102).

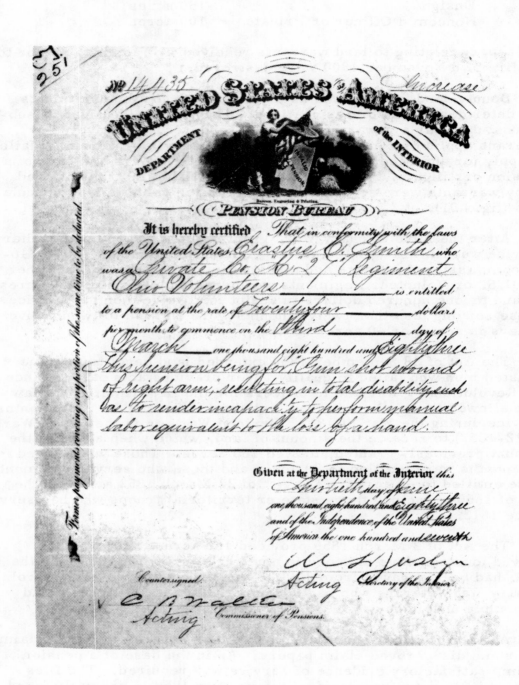

Fig. 101. Pension certificate

STATE OF NEW-YORK,
County of Madison, }

On this *19th* day of *March* A. D., one thousand eight hundred and fifty-five, personally appeared before me, *M Spear* a justice of the peace, within and for the county and State aforesaid, *James Anderson* aged *52* years, a resident of *Nilson* in the state of New-York, who, being duly sworn according to law, declares that he is the identical *James Anderson* who was a *Corporal* in the company commanded by Captain *B Bicknell* in the regiment of *New York Militia* commanded by *Col E Farnham* in the war with Great Britain, declared by the United States, on the 18th day of June, 1812, for the term of *nearly two Month* and continued in actual service in said war for fourteen days: that he has heretofore made application for bounty land under the act of September 28, 1850, and received a land warrant, No. *forgotten* for *forty* acres, which he has since legally disposed of, and cannot now return. *his discharge from service is on file in the War Off*

He makes this declaration for the purpose of obtaining the additional bounty land to which he may be entitled under the act approved the 3d day of March, 1855. He also declares, that he has never applied for nor received, under this or any other act of Congress, any bounty-land warrant except the one above mentioned.

James Anderson

We, *B. T. Clarke* and *John Hobbie* residents of *Cazenovia* in the state of New York, upon our oaths, declare that the foregoing delaration was signed and acknowledged by *James Anderson* in our presence, and that we believe, from the appearance and statements of the applicant, that he is the identical person he represents himself to be.

B. T. Clarke

John Hobbie

The foregoing declaration and affidavit were sworn to and subscribed before me on the day and year above written; and I certify that I know the affiants to be credible persons; that the claimant is the person he represents himself to be, and that I have no interest in this claim.

M Spear Justice of the peace

Fig. 102. James Anderson's application for bounty land, War of 1812

State of New Hampshire
County of Belknap ss. On this fourteenth
day of May   in the year Eighteen
hundred and fifty five personally appeared
before me, a Justice of the Peace in and
for the State and County aforesaid
Sally Morrill aged sixty four
years a resident of Sanbornton in said
County, who being duly sworn according
to law declares that she is the widow of
Nathaniel Morrill who was a Pensioner
of the United States at the rate of Twenty Six
Dollars and Sixty Six cents per annum
under the Act of June 7th 1832 and that
his name was on the Roll of the
N.H. Pension Agency: Portsmouth
She further declares that she was married
to the said Nathaniel Morrill on the twentyfourth
day of May A.D. 1842 = that her said husband
died on the twenty Second day of February
A.D. 1844 = that her name before her said
marriage was Sally Flanders and that
she is now a widow = that for proof of
the facts Stated in this declaration She refers

Fig. 103. Deposition of a widow for bounty land

to the evidence filed in the Pension Office
in support of her claim for Pension under
the 2d Section of the Act of Feb. 3d 1853.

She makes this declaration for the
purpose of obtaining the bounty land to
which she may be entitled under the
Act approved March 3d 1855—.
Attest
—Samuel Tilton—   Sally Morrill
Lowel Long

We Samuel Tilton   and Lowel Long
            residents of Sanbornton in the
State of New Hampshire upon our oaths
testify and say that the foregoing declaration was signed and acknowledged
by the said Sally Morrill in our presence
and that from the appearance & statements of the
applicant we believe her to be the person she
represents herself to be.—

                        Samuel Tilton
                        Lowel Long

Fig. 103 continued.

A regular army soldier generally proved his service by the presentation of his original discharge certificate. A widow or legal guardian had to follow very nearly the same process of assembling and submitting evidence to prove relationship as that normally followed in a pension claim (fig. 103).

There are 450,000 separately filed bounty-land claim folders in the National Archives, and all papers relating to a particular claim have been filed together. Each file includes the warrant number, the act, the acreage granted, the name of the veteran, his rank, and his organization.

The Montey family, mentioned previously, was represented in the Revolution by several family members, each of whom applied for bounty lands. Microfilm copies of each file were obtained from the National Archives, and a surprising amount of genealogical information was contained in them. One had over eighty-five separate documents in it, and most of them contained more than twenty-five. Among the documents were depositions, affidavits, letters, vital certificates, and other official papers. Documents in the files helped establish direct relationship between each of the families and gave evidence of the family ancestral home in Canada.

"Claude Montey" stated in one deposition that "he was unable to speak English" but said "his brother John could verify that he (Claude) served in the Revolution." A deposition of John's, in Claude's file, did verify that Claude served in Moses Hazen's Regiment in the Revolutionary War, that he (Claude) could not speak English, and that he was previously from Quebec, Canada. Each of the files gave reference of one kind or another to persons named in other files, and before many were investigated, it was evident that at least seven of the applicants were brothers, each of whom had received bounty land.

Perhaps it should be noted here that many individuals remained loyal to the British government during and after the Revolutionary War. Many of these people removed to Canada and Great Britain or to the Louisiana Territory which was under jurisdiction of the French and Spanish. Of course many remained in the colonies and were particularly numerous in New York, Massachusetts, Virginia, Georgia, South Carolina, and in the Cape Fear region of North Carolina.

After the 1783 peace treaty, both the United States and Great Britain provided means whereby those who suffered losses because of their loyalty to the British Crown could claim compensation from the British government. Records created as a result of the claims have been filed in the Public Record Office, London, as part of records in custody of the Exchequer and Audit Department. They are titled CLAIMS, AMERICAN LOYALISTS, SERIES I (A.O. 12) and SERIES II (A.O. 13) and consist of 146 volumes and over 140 bundles of records. The collection was microfilmed in London on behalf of the Public Archives of Canada, and the Genealogical Society Library in Salt Lake City has a complete set (GS F#366,693-366,869). A typescript name index to both series has also been microfilmed and is available at Salt Lake City (GS F#162,010). The collection was microfilmed according to bundle numbers as follows:

#1-10	Supplied Donations
#11-16	New York Claims
#17-20	New Jersey Claims
#18-22	New Brunswick Claims
#23	New Hampshire Claims
#24-26	Nova Scotia Claims
#27-33	Virginia Claims
#34-38	Georgia Claims
#39-40	Maryland Claims
#41-42	Connecticut Claims
#43-51	Massachusetts Claims
#51-52	New Hampshire Claims
#54-57	New York - Temporary Assistance
#58	Virginia Claims
#59	Va., R.I., Vt., N.H., and Bahamas Claims
#59-62	Maryland Support Claims
#63-67	New York Support Claims
#68-69	Rhode Island Support Claims
#70-72	Pennsylvania Claims
#73-75	Massachusetts Assistance
#76	Connecticut Claims
#79	Miscellaneous Letters
#80	Late Claims, S.C. and Pa.
#81-85	Canada Claims
#86-107	Miscellaneous Letters
#108-116	New York Assistance
#117-124	North Carolina Assistance
#125-135	South Carolina Assistance
#136	S.C. and Georgia Assistance
#137-140	Miscellaneous Papers

The following published references to Loyalists are also on file at the Genealogical Society in Salt Lake City:

975.6   Demond, Robert O.
H2d   The loyalists in N. Carolina during the revolution.
              Durham N. C., Duke University Press, 1940.
                  vii, 286 p. index.

N. Y.   Loyalist Estates, Disposition of
55   The disposition of Loyalist Estates in the Southern
              District of the State of New York. By Harry B.
              Yoshpe. Columbia University Press, 1939, 226 pages.

971.7434   Eaton, Arthur Wentworth Hamilton
         The history of Kings County, Nova Scotia, heart
of the Acadian land, giving a sketch of the French
and their expulsion: and a history of the New England
planters who came in their stead, with many genealogies, 1604-1910. Salem, Mass., The Salem Press
Company, 1910. xii, 898 p. index.

970   Gandy, Wallace, ed.
F2L   The Association oath rolls of the British plantations (New York, Virginia, etc.) A.D. 1696, being a
contribution to political history; edited with an introduction by Wallace Gandy . . . London. Printed for
private distribution by the editor, 1922.
         9-86p. index. facsim.
         The oath of association was drawn up after the
discovery of a plot to assassinate William III, and
was signed by Englishmen at home and abroad. The
present volume contains the lists of signers in
Barbados, Virginia, New York, Bermudas, Antigua,
Nevis, Montserratt, Antego, St. Chrostophers, Dort,
Rotterdam, The Hague, Malaga, and Geneva.

P.B.A.   Gibbon, John Murray.
#1092   The new Canadian Loyalists. Toronto, The
Macmillan Company of Canada Limited, 1941. 39p.

971.74   Gilroy, Marion, comp.
R2g   Loyalists and land settlement in Nova Scotia.
A list compiled by Marion Gilroy. Under the direc-
tion of D. C. Harvey, archivist. Published by author-
ity of the Board of Trustees of the Public Archives of
Nova Scotia. Halifax, 1937. 154 p. (Nova Scotia.
Public archives. Publication no. 4)

975.1   Hancock, Harold Bell.
F2L   The Delaware Loyalists. Wilmington, Del.,
Historical Society of Delaware, 1940. xi. 76 p.

974.4   Jones, Edward Alfred.
F2Lj   The loyalists of Massachusetts, their memorials,
petitions and claims, with 63 portraits in photogravure.
London, The Saint Catherine Press, 1930.
         xxiv, 341 (1) p. index. ports.
         "The genesis of this work is to be found in the
bundles of original and unpublished loyalist manuscripts in the Public record office in London."-
introd.

974.9   Jones, Edward Alfred.
C4n   The loyalists of New Jersey, their memorials,
V.10   petitions, claims, etc., from English records.
           Newark, N.J., New Jersey Historical Society, 1927.
               346p. port. (New Jersey Historical Society.
           Collections, vol. X)
               "Republished from the New Jersey Historical
           Society Proceedings in 1926-7."

971.577   Macdonell, John Alexander.
               Sketches illustrating the early settlement and
           history of Glengarry in Canada, relating principally
           to the revolutionary war of 1775-83, the war of 1812-
           14 and the rebellion of 1837-8, and the services of the
           King's royal regiment of New York, the 84th or Royal
           Highland emigrant regiment, the Royal Canadian
           volunteer regiment of foot, the Glengarry fencible or
           British Highland regiment, the Glengarry light infantry
           regiment, and the Glengarry militia. Montreal, W.
           Foster, Brown & Co., 1893. 337 p.

974.7   Orderly book of the three battalions of loyalists, com-
M25c   manded by Brigadier-General Oliver De Lancey, 1776-
           1778, to which is appended a list of New York loyalists
           in the City of New York during the war of the Revolu-
           tion--compiled by William Kelby. New York, N.Y.,
           printed for the New York Historical Society, 1917.
           147p. index. (The New York Historical Society.
           The John Divine Jones Fund series of histories and
           memoirs, III)

974.6   Peck, Epaphroditus.
               . . . The Loyalists of Connecticut. (New Haven,
           Published for the Tercentenary Commission by the
           Yale University Press, 1934.) 31p. (Connecticut.
           Tercentenary Commission. Committee on Historical
           Publications. (Tercentenary pamphlet series, XXXI)

974.62   Phelps, Richard Harvey.
J4p   A history of Newgate of Connecticut, at Simsbury,
1860   now East Granby; its insurrections and massacres,
           the imprisonment of the Tories in the revolution, and
           the working of its mines. Also, some account of the
           state prison, at Wethersfield. Albany, N.Y., J.
           Munsell, 1860. 151p. index. illus. port.

974.62
J4p
1876

Phelps, Richard Harvey.
  Newgate of Connecticut; its origin and early history. Being a full description of the famous and wonderful Simsbury mines and caverns, and the prison built over them. To which is added a relation of all the incidents, insurrections, and massacres, connected with their use as a prison for the Tories during the revolution . . . Also. An illustrated description of the state prison at Wethersfield. By Richard H. Phelps. Hartford, Conn., American Publishing Company, 1876. 117p. illus., plates.
  "The first edition . . . and the larger work published in 1860 have been revised, and additional matter of interest herein incorporated." pref.

971.5
H2p

Pringle, Jacob Farrand.
Lunenburgh, or The old Eastern district, its settlement and early progress: with personal recollections of the town of Cornwall, from 1824; to which are added a history of the King's royal regiment of New York and other corps; the names of all those who drew lands in the counties of Stormont, Cundas and Glengarry, up to November, 1786; and several other lists of interest to the descendants of the old settlers. By J. F. Pringle . . . Cornwall (Ont.) Standard Printing House, 1890.
  xix, 421. (2) p. fold. table.

971.5
F2u

Reid, W. D., comp.
  Data on United Empire Loyalists. n.p., Typed by Mrs. Mahala M. Waywell, 1947-49. 2v.
  Reproduced from typewritten copy.

971.5
F2u
index

---Index to persons who married into or were connected with the United Empire Loyalists. n.p., Typed by Mrs. Mahala M. Waywell, 1950. 52 leaves. index.
  Reproduced from typewritten copy.

973
F2-Lr

Ryerson, Adolphus Egerton, 1803-1882.
  The loyalists of America and their times: from 1720 to 1816. By Egerton Ryerson . . . 2d ed., Toronto, W. Briggs, 1880, 2v. port.

973
F2-Ls

Sabine, Lorenzo, 1803-1877.
  Biographical sketches of loyalists of the American Revolution, with an historical essay. Boston, Little, Brown and Company, 1864, 2v.

974.4
F2Ls   Stark, James Henry.
              The loyalists of Massachusetts and the other side
          of the American Revolution. Boston, J. H. Stark, 1810.
              vii, 5-509p. index. illus., plates, ports., maps
          (1 fold.)

Am   Loyalists during the American Revolution
Pub.
AR   Story of the men who remained loyal to England during
Vol.   the American Revolution.
2   Journal of Amer. History. Vol. 2, p. 339.

929.271   Tucker, W. Bowman.
M612t   The romance of the Palatine Millers, a tale of
          Palantine Irish-Americans and United Empire Loyalists.
          2d ed. of "The Camden colony," rev. and enlarged.
          Montreal, the author, 1929. xxxiv, 369p. index. illus.,
          plates, ports.

971   Wallace, William Stewart.
H2cc   The United empire loyalists; a chronicle of the
V.13   great migration. Toronto, Glasgow, Brook & Company,
          1920.
              xi, 148p. index. plates, ports., fold. map.
          (Chronicles of Canada, vol. 13.)

971.72   Wright, Esther (Clark).
F2a   The loyalists of New Brunswick. (1st ed.)
          Fredericton (1955)
              365p. index. map.
              "List of New Brunswick loyalists": p.253-345.

974.72   Yoshpe, Harry Beller.
              The disposition of loyalist estates in the southern
          district of the state of New York. New York, 1939.
              226p. index. plates, maps, diagra. facsim.

Regular Army Records
     The United States Army (Regular Army) was created as a perma-
nent establishment in 1789, and records relating to it also contain
some genealogical information. The size and composition of the army
has varied from time to time, being very small at first and in times
of peace, but expanding during wartime and periods of unrest.

     The records relate to officers and enlisted men and consist
primarily of enlistment papers, registers, and rosters, though some
published material is also available for officers. The original
records for the period 1789-1821 were subjected, in part, to the fires
of 1800 and 1814 in Washington, but most of those after that date
remain intact. Records of both officers and enlisted men are reflected

in registers of enlistment, which were prepared from various original documents created during the actual period of service (fig. 104).

Entries within the registers are in strict alphabetical sequence showing the name of the soldier; his organization; the date and place of enlistment; by whom enlisted; period of enlistment; town, county, and state of birth; age; occupation; physical description including color of eyes and hair, complexion, and height; and a special remarks section showing discharge, death information, and other details.

The registers for the period 1789-1821 are arranged in two groups. The first group relates to service from 1789 to the establishment of peace at the end of the War of 1812 (15 May 1815). The second group relates to service from 17 May 1815 to 30 June 1821. There are one or more registers relating to soldiers whose surname begins with a particular letter of the alphabet.

Registers of enlistment for the period 1 July 1821 through 31 October 1912 are arranged by the initial letter of the soldier's surname only and chronologically by the month of enlistment. A single register may relate to a part of a year, a whole year, or more than one year. As the soldier's enlistment was received, an entry was made in the register and the number corresponding to the entry in the register was added to it. The basic entries of name, enlistment date, place and period, nativity, age, and physical description were made from the enlistment papers. Other details were added later. The registers for the period 1821-1912 reflect, as do subsequent entries, the various organizations in which the soldier served and the date, place, reasons, and character of his discharge. Most enlistment papers have two or more numbers, and it is presumed they were separately arranged at one time and then renumbered to correspond with their enlistment register entry number.

A few years ago, a request was sent to the Early Wars Branch at the National Archives for a check of Regular Army records for William B. Stilson, who supposedly married Susannah Young, a sister of Brigham Young. William was known to have been in the military in the St. Louis, Missouri, area in about 1845, but no other facts were known about him. Archives personnel graciously searched Regular Army enlistment records and located two entries pertaining to the man. The first gave his age as thirty-two, his eyes hazel, his hair black, his complexion dark, his height five feet eight-and-one-half inches, and his birthplace Fairfield, Connecticut. His occupation was given as "painter," and he enlisted on 8 May 1839. The second entry noted him to be "absent without leave" (fig. 105).

Enlistment papers were prepared for all enlisted men serving in the Regular Army except for principal musicians and drum majors. The enlistment papers reflect the agreement to serve a specified number of years and contain the soldier's name, the date and place of enlistment, the soldier's age and birthplace, a brief physical

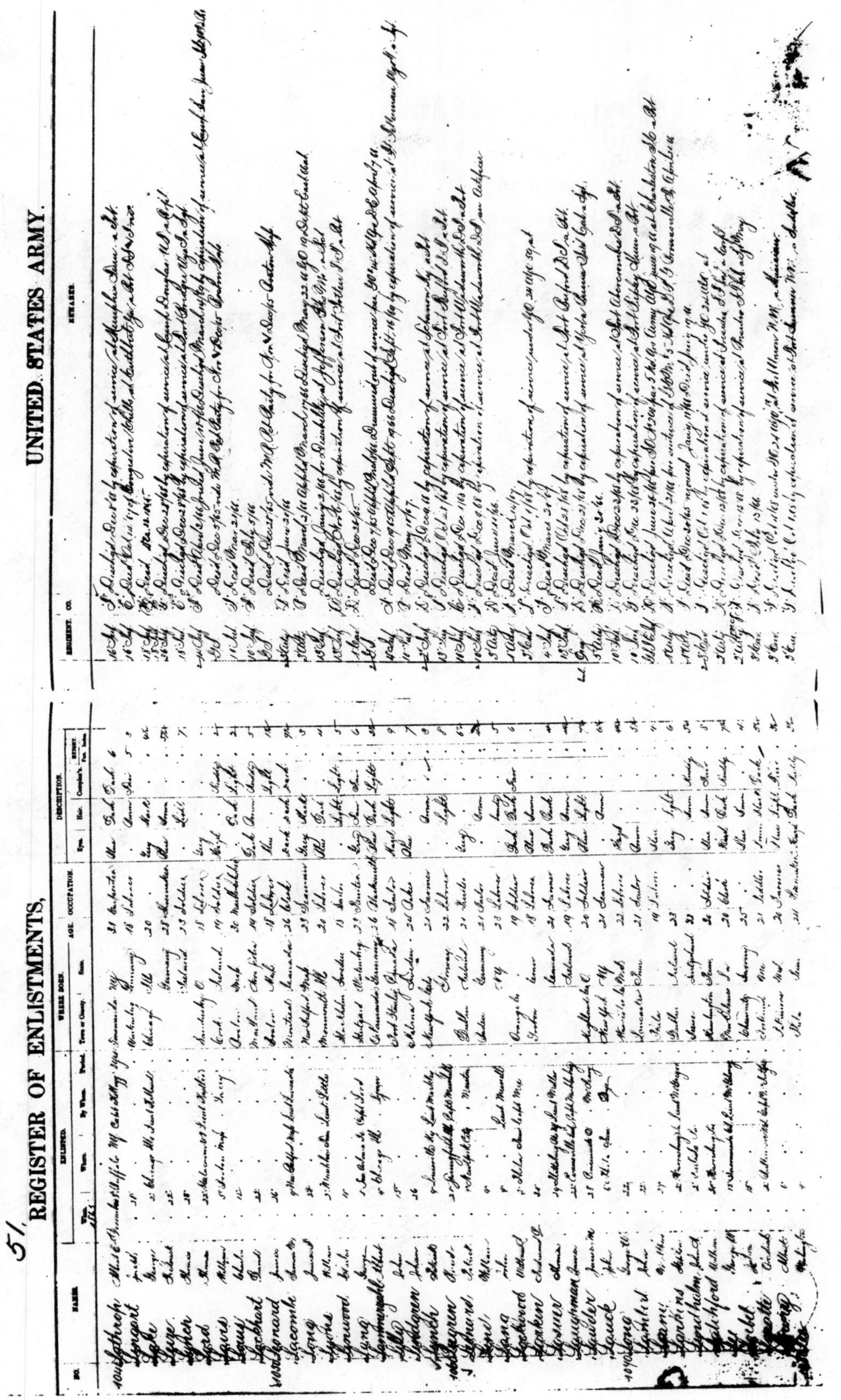

Fig. 104. Regular Army enlistment register

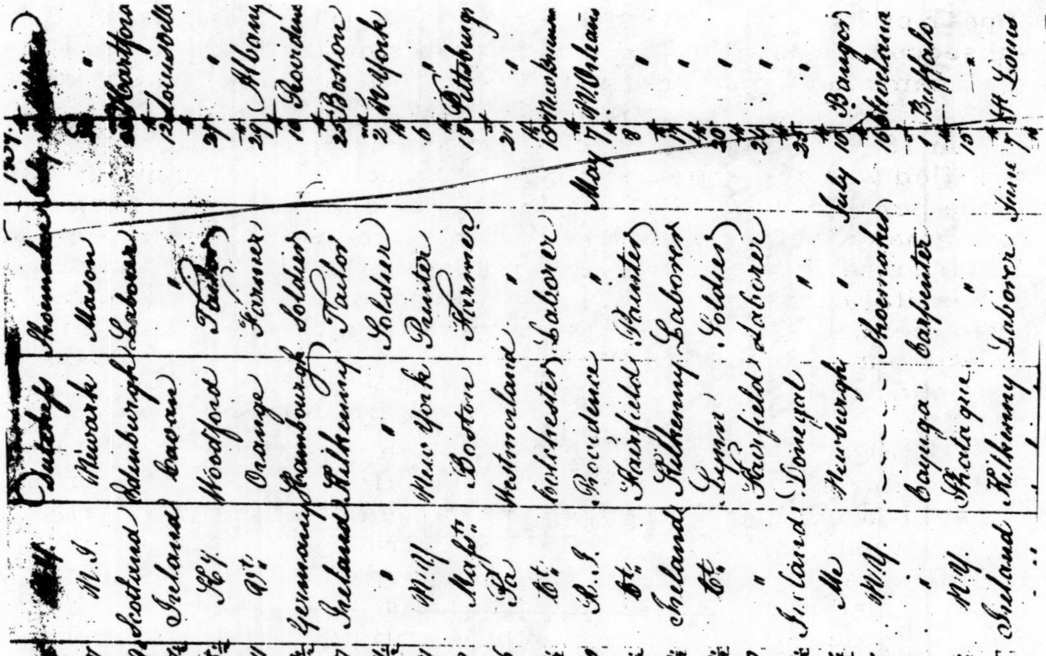

207	Shaw	Alexander	21	hazel	black	fair	[illegible]	[illegible]	Dutchess	Shoemaker	1857 July	[illegible]
8	Sheeran	John	30	blue	brown	dark	5.7	N.S.	Newark	Mason	23	Hartford
9	Sinclair	Alexander	24	hazel	"	ruddy	5.9	Scotland	Edinburgh	Laborer	12	Louisville
210	Smith	Edward	25	blue	brown	fair	5.7½	Ireland	Cavan	"		
1	Stevenson	John T.	24	grey	black	"	[illegible]	Ky.	Woodford	Tailor	24	"
2	Smith	Thomas	27	hazel	brown	ruddy	5.11	Vt.	Orange	Farmer	29	Albany
3	Smythe	Charles	30	blue	brown	dark	5.6	Germany	Hamburgh	Soldier	16	Providence
4	Shotwell	Richard	24	"	"	fair	5.7	Ireland	Kilkenny	Tailor	25	Boston
5	Shields	Martin	38	"	"	fair	5.5½	"	"	Soldier	2	N. York
6	Shippey	Charles	28	grey	"	ruddy	5.7	N.Y.	New York	Printer	6	"
7	Sprague	John S.	24	blue	"	fair	5.8	Mass.	Boston	Farmer	19	Pittsburg
8	[illegible]	James	20	hazel	"	"	5.6	Pa.	Westmoreland	"	27	"
9	Sullivan	James	21	blue	"	light	5.7½	Ct.	Colchester	Laborer	18	Ft. Leavenworth
220	[illegible]	Robert	32	grey	"	dark	5.10	R.I.	Providence	"	May 7	N. Orleans
1	Stilson	William B.	32	hazel	black	"	5.8½	Ct.	Fairfield	Printer	8	"
2	[illegible]	Thomas	20	"	brown	"	5.8¼	Ireland	Kilkenny	Laborer	[illegible]	"
3	Sanders	Charles	21	"	"	"	5.8¾	Ct.	Lynn	Soldier	20	"
4	Smith	William	20	grey	light	dark	5.8	"	Fairfield	Laborer	24	"
5	Sweeney	Patrick	29	hazel	black	"	5.9½	Ireland	Donegal	"	23	"
6	Smith	John	25	blue	sandy	ruddy	5.5½	Me.	Newburgh	"	July 10	Bangor
7	Shepherd	Alexander	27	grey	brown	light	5.7	N.Y.	[illegible]	Shoemaker	16	Cleveland
8	Stevens	George H.	21	blue	dark	ruddy	5.6	"	Cayuga	Carpenter	1	Buffalo
9	Stafford	Orlando	22	"	"	ruddy	5.6¼	N.Y.	[illegible]	"	[illegible]	"
230	[illegible]	Thomas	29	grey	brown	ruddy	5.5	Ireland	Kilkenny	Laborer	June 7	St. Louis

Fig. 105. Enlistment register showing William B. Stilson

description, and in the case of a minor, the consent of his parent. In 1885, the name of an emergency addressee was added. The enlistment officer's signature and the signature or mark of the enlistee also appear on each enlistment paper. A new paper was prepared for each subsequent enlistment and the reverse side included the name of the serviceman and his organization (fig. 106).

In 1894, a physical description and assignment card was prepared and filed with the enlistment papers. Such cards do not add materially to the personal data found on the enlistment paper, but they do show the name of the organization to which a soldier was initially assigned. A station card is also found beginning in 1894 in the enlistment papers of hospital corps personnel. When a soldier served more than one enlistment, his enlistment papers are filed together in a single jacket. Enlistment papers are arranged in two series--1818 through 14 July 1894 and 15 July 1894 through 31 October 1912.

Records of U. S. Army officers are found in the registers of enlistment, consolidated files, and in official military communications. The Adjutant General was charged with matters pertaining to the command, discipline, and administration of the military establishment and has had the duties of recording, authenticating, and communicating to troops and individuals in the military service. His records relating to officers included enlistment papers, muster rolls, returns, reports of battles, official reports of all officers, reports of the status of the militia, reports of absences, records of court-martials, inventories of the effects of deceased soldiers and officers, communications relating to appointments, requests for warrants for soldiers, and requests for promotion.

Each communication received and retained was filed by the serial assigned chronologically each year. In 1863, efforts were made to create consolidated files of papers relating to individual officers, but this was usually done only when such papers were needed in the course of regular business. Otherwise, the records of officers can be located only by a detailed search of the annual registers of letters sent and received by the Adjutant General. In some instances, military histories of officers were prepared, usually by the bureau or special office to which they were assigned.

In 1890, a new record-keeping system was employed by the War Department--the record card system, which allowed for the continuous indexing and referencing of communications received. The records were not always filed together, but the system allowed for continuous referencing of communications about an individual and resulted in most officers' files being consolidated.

By a special act in 1815, annual registers of officers serving in the U. S. Army were published under the title THE OFFICIAL ARMY REGISTER. Other published sources containing biographies

I, *John Purcell* do acknowledge that I have voluntarily enlisted myself to serve four years in the Marine Corps of the UNITED STATES, unless sooner discharged, upon the terms mentioned in the act passed the 11th day of July, 1798, entitled "An act for establishing and organizing a Marine Corps;" also the act passed the 2d day of March, 1833, entitled "An act to improve the condition of the non-commissioned Officers and Privates of the Army and Marine Corps of the United States, and to prevent desertion;" and also the acts passed the 2d day of March, 1837, entitled "An act to provide for the enlistment of boys for the Naval service, and to extend the term of the enlistment of seamen;" and February 20, 1845, entitled "An act to amend an act entitled 'An act to provide for the enlistment of boys for the Naval service, and to extend the term of the enlistment of seamen;'" and also the 9th section of an act passed March 3d, 1845, "making appropriations for the Naval service for the year ending the 30th of June, 1846;" and that I have had read to me the Rules and Articles of the Army and Navy against Mutiny and Desertion.

Witness my hand, this *1st* day of *January* 185*3*.

John Purcell

I, *John Purcell* do solemnly swear or affirm, (as the case may be,) that I will bear true allegiance to the United States of America, and that I will serve them honestly and faithfully against all their enemies or opposers whatsoever, and observe and obey the orders of the President of the United States, and the orders of the officers appointed over me, according to the Rules and Articles for the government of the Army and Navy of the United States. And, further, that I am of the full age of twenty-one years.

Sworn before me, at *New York*
this *1st* day of *January* 185*3*.   *John Purcell*

Michl. Connolly

SIZE ROLL.

John Purcell ——— a private, born in the *United States*
State of *New York* ——— County of *New York* ——— Town of ———
New York City ——— enlisted *1st January 1853* ——— at
——— for four years, by *Capt. Reynolds*,
aged *21* years, *5* feet *11¼* inches high, *blue* eyes,
Sandy hair, *Ruddy* complexion, by trade or occupation a *Clerk*.

REMARKS.

Jno. Geo. Reynolds
Capt. & Bt. Maj. Comdg.

I CERTIFY, That the above recruit is free from bodily defects, and is qualified to perform the duty of a soldier. *George Peck Asst Surgeon U.S.M.*
Marine Rendezvous
N. York City

Fig. 106. Enlistment document

and histories of officers are as follows:

HISTORICAL REGISTER AND DICTIONARY OF THE U.S. ARMY
1789-1903 by Francis B. Heitman (Washington: Government Printing
Office, 1903)

BIOGRAPHICAL REGISTER OF THE OFFICERS AND GRADUATES
OF THE U.S. MILITARY ACADEMY by George W. Cullum (Boston:
1891)

ARMY LIST AND DIRECTORY by the War Department (Washington:
GPO, 1891-1942)

OFFICIAL ARMY REGISTER OF THE VOLUNTEER FORCE OF
THE UNITED STATES ARMY FOR THE YEARS 1861-65 (8 vols.) by
the War Department Washington: GPO, 1865)

OFFICIAL REGISTER OF OFFICERS OF VOLUNTEERS 1899-
1900 IN THE SERVICE OF THE U.S. (Washington: GPO, 1900)

Records of all officers whose service terminated during the
period 1789 through 31 October 1916 are on file in the National Archives,
but if service terminated after 1916, papers have been transferred to
the National Personnel Records Center at St. Louis, Missouri.

The Old Wars Series Pension Records

The "Old Wars" series of pension application files relates to claims
based on death or disability incurred in service, both peacetime and
wartime, rendered between the end of the Revolutionary War (11 April
1783) and 4 March 1861. The series does not include files relating
to claims based on death or disability incurred in service in the War
of 1812. It does, however, include a few files for those whose death
or disability claims are based on service in the Civil War before 14
July 1862. The series consists of several sub-series--Mexican War
death or disability files, Civil War death or disability files, and
miscellaneous service death or disability files. The miscellaneous
sub-series contains claims relating to service in the various Indian
wars and in the Regular Establishment. All of the War of 1812 death
or disability claims are interfiled with the War of 1812 series of pension application files whose claims are based on service alone. Some
death or disability claims based on service in the War of 1812, the
Mexican War, the Civil War, and the Indian wars have been consolidated
with other series of pension application files relating to claims based
solely on service rendered.

The files within each of the sub-series of the "Old Wars" pension
application files are arranged alphabetically by name of veteran.
Within the "miscellaneous" sub-series, the files are arranged not
only alphabetically by the name of the veteran but also chronologically
by the period of service. An alphabetical name index has been reproduced on seven rolls of microfilm and covers the period 1815-1926
(microcopy T-316).

The War of 1812 Pension Records

The War of 1812 pension application files relate to claims based on service between 1812 and 1815. The claims include those based on death or disability incurred in service as well as those based on service alone. Some War of 1812 bounty-land warrant application files are interfiled with the pension files. The application files are arranged alphabetically by the name of the veteran. The face side of each jacket or envelope has been reproduced on 102 rolls of microfilm and arranged alphabetically by the name of the veteran (microcopy M-313).

The records are similar to those of the Revolutionary War period, though the pension acts relating to the War of 1812 were passed several years after termination of the war. The first service pension act exclusively for veterans of the War of 1812 was passed on 14 February 1871, some fifty-six years after the war ended. It granted pensions to those who served sixty days, or to widows who married prior to the treaty of peace which took place on 17 February 1815. An act on 9 March 1878 reduced the service provision to fourteen days and removed the marriage date restriction (fig. 107).

The Indian Wars Pension Records

The pension application files in the Indian Wars series relate to claims based on service performed in various Indian wars and disturbances between 1817 and 1898. The claims are primarily those based on service alone and were filed from 1892 to 1926.

The files are arranged in four sub-series numerically by either the application number or the certificate number, depending on the class of the claim. The four sub-series are designated as (1) Indian Survivors' Originals, (2) Indian Survivors' Certificates, (3) Indian Widows' Originals, and (4) Indian Widows' Certificates. An alphabetical name index has been reproduced on twelve rolls of microfilm and covers the period 1892-1926 (microcopy T-318).

The Mexican War Pension Records

The Mexican War series of pension application files relates to claims based on service between 1846 and 1848. The claims are chiefly those based on service alone and filed between 1887 and 1926. Pension legislation for Mexican War veterans and their widows was passed on 29 January 1887, some thirty-nine years after the war. They provided pensions to soldiers and sailors who had served at least sixty days--if they had reached age sixty-two or were disabled or dependent--and to their widows or orphans.

The Mexican War pension application files consist of four subseries: (1) Mexican Survivors' Originals, (2) Mexican Survivors' Certificates, (3) Mexican Widows' Originals, and (4) Mexican Widows' Certificates. The files in the series of originals are arranged numerically by the original numbers assigned the claims when they were submitted, and the files in the certificate series are arranged numerically by the certificate numbers assigned the claims when they were approved.

[3—405.]
(Pensioner Dropped.)

U. S. Pension Agency,

Buffalo N.Y.
June 15, 1896

Hon. D. I. Murphy
Commissioner of Pensions.

Sir:

I hereby report that the name of Catharine Anderson widow of James, Corp Lt Abner Camp's Co. N.Y. Mil. War of 1812, the Widow of pensioner on the rolls of this Agency, under Certificate No. 13332, and who was last paid at $ 12, to 4 October, 1892, has been dropped because of Statute limitation

Very respectfully,
Samuel E. Nichols
Pension Agent.

(8550—50 M.) 6—163 Every name dropped to be thus reported at once.

Head Quarters, Sackets Harbor, Nov. 8th 1814.

James Anderson a Corp'l in Capt. J. Birkmelbrefs Company, in the Regiment of New-York Militia commanded by Lieut Col Elisha Farnham and 3d Brigade commanded by Brigadier General J. N. M. Hurd, having entered the service of the United States, the 8th day of October last, and faithfully performed his duty, is hereby HONORABLY DISCHARGED.

By order of Major General
NATHANIEL KING.
Commanding Militia at that post and vicinity.
JARVIS K. PIKE, Aid de Camp.

Fig. 107. Documents from War of 1812 pension files

SUMMARY OF PROOF.

Marriage Date *April 28, 1859* of *James Anderson* to *Catharine VanBuren. Alleged by Claimant and Corroborated by affidavit of George D. & Eveline Richardson who were present at the wedding.*

Proof as to capacity to marry. *Claimant alleges that soldiers first wife Hannah Stebbins died in 1857 in Madison Co. N.J. Claimant And soldier were married in same Co. And continued to live there up to soldiers death, And she in same place since*

Death of soldier. Date *June 17, 1875 Alleged by Claimant And Corroborated by affidavit of Augustin P. Clode And Chas R. Corell.*

Widowhood. *Shown by affidavit of George D and Eveline Richardson in declaration*

INCIDENTAL MATTER.

Soldier received Land Warrant. His Application for pension under Act of 1871 was rejected by reason of insufficient service. He Alleged that the Captain of his Co. was Bricknell who was away in the N.J. Legislature at the time And that Lieut. Camp had charge of the Company. Rejd Claim # 5,079. Report of Auditor in B.L. claim gives rank as Corporal. Soldier alleged marriage to Hannah Stebbins in 1815.

Owen

SERVICE PENSION,
War of 1812.

WIDOW'S BRIEF.

Claim No. *17,068*

Certificate No.

Act of *March 19, 1876*

Claimant *Catharine Anderson*

Soldier *James Anderson*

Action, *Admitted*

Examiner, *D. J. Waters*

Admitted Dec 4th 1878 Claim

Fig. 107a.

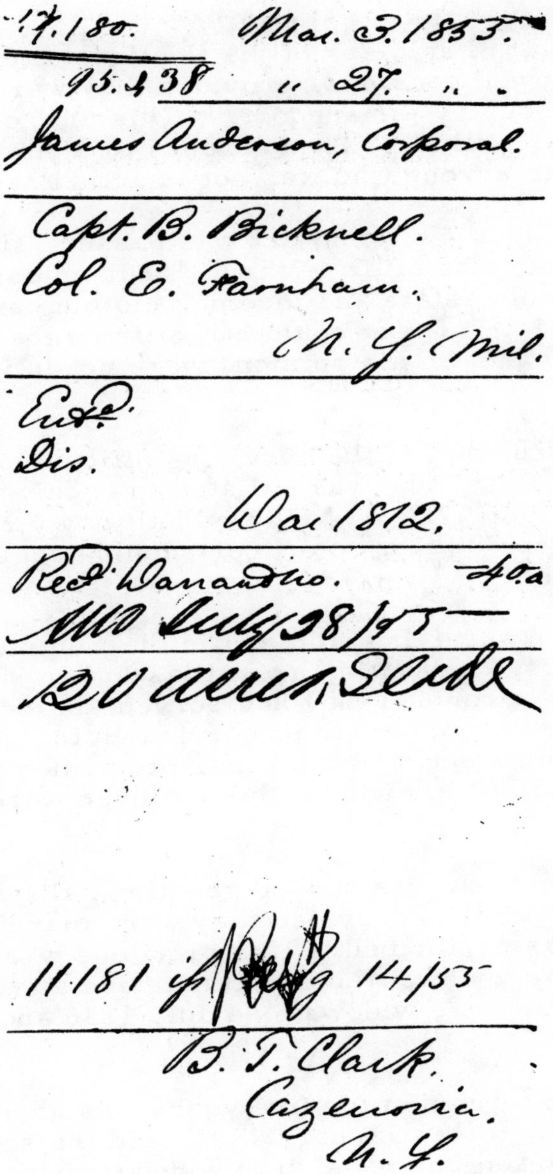

17.180.   Mar. 3. 1855.
95.438   " 27.   " .

James Anderson, Corporal.

Capt. B. Bicknell.
Col. E. Farnham.
                M. Y. Mil.

Entd.
Dis.
                War 1812.
Recd Wanantno.   40.a
MWD July 28/95 —
120 acres Slide

11.181 if WVH g 14/55

B. T. Clark.
Cazenovia.
            N. Y.

Fig. 107b.

313

An alphabetical name index has been reproduced on fourteen rolls of microfilm and covers the period 1887-1926 (microcopy T-317).

A summary of the more important pension acts passed prior to the Civil War follows:

On 18 March 1818 soldiers of the Continental establishment and Marines were allowed pensions, provided they were "in need of assistance from their country for support." This did not entitle any of the men serving in the Militia or State Troops to a pension, nor could the pension be given to anyone who was not in actual need.

On 1 May 1820 an additional act was passed, stating that no person should receive a pension after 4 March 1820 "unless he exhibits a schedule of his whole estate and income, clothing and bedding excepted," and that the Secretary of War could strike from the pension list the names of persons who, in his opinion, were not in indigent circumstances.

On 15 May 1826 each of the surviving officers of the Revolution in the Continental Line, who was enlisted to receive half pay by the Resolve of 21 October 1780 was allowed half pay for life, beginning 3 March 1826--provided that no officer should receive more than full pay of a captain.

On 7 June 1832 surviving soldiers in the Continental Line, State Troops, Volunteers, or Militia, as well as Indian spies, were placed on the pension list, provided they had served six months; the amount of pay was to increase for length of service up to two years. In case of death of the soldier between the times of payment of pension, his widow, or if he had left his widow, his children were entitled to the amount due.

On 4 July 1836 a law was passed granting half pay for life to widows of Revolutionary soldiers, provided they were married before the last term of service was performed. This privilege was extended on 3 March 1837 to those widows who had remarried after their husband's death, provided they were widows on 4 July 1836 and continued to remain widows.

On 7 July 1838 a pension for five years was granted to those widows who were married before 1 January 1794, and the same day another act was passed granting the pension to widows whose husbands had died after 4 July 1836.

On 23 August 1842 the remarriage of the widows claiming under the Act of 7 July 1838 was not considered a bar to a pension, provided the applicant was a widow at the time of making application; and in any event, marriage after receiving a pension caused it to stop automatically.

On 3 March 1843 the time of widows' pensions granted under the

Act of 7 July 1838 was continued for one more year, and on 17 June 1844, for four more years. On 2 February 1848 the pensions were continued for life, and on 29 July 1848 the date of marriage was extended to 1 January 1800. Not until 1853 was all restriction as to date of marriage removed.

On 3 March 1855 Congress voted bounty land to all soldiers and sailors, or their legal representatives, who had served six weeks or more in any of the wars of the United States. Thus, some who could not obtain a pension because of not having served six months could and did obtain bounty lands.

The basic congressional act designed to benefit Civil War veterans, their widows, and certain other dependents was the Act of 14 July 1862. This act granted pensions to all veterans disabled in service since 4 March 1861 and to the widows and children under sixteen years of age and other dependents of veterans who died in or as a result of such service. In an act of 27 June 1890, Congress extended pension benefits to veterans of the Civil War who had served ninety days and were honorably discharged and could not earn a living because of disabilities not service connected. Widows and minor children were also eligible for pension under certain conditions.

Disabled veterans of the Spanish-American War, the Philippine Insurrection, and the Boxer Rebellion and widows, minor children, and other dependents of veterans who were killed in or died as a result of service rendered in these wars were eligible for pensions under the act of 14 July 1862 which applied not only to the Civil War but also to all future wars in which the United States might be engaged. It was not until an act of 16 July 1918 that the widows and minor children of these veterans could apply for pensions on the basis of service alone. Surviving veterans of these wars did not receive pensions on the basis of service alone until the passage of a congressional act dated 5 June 1920.

Civil War Records--Union Forces
Service and pension records of volunteers serving in the Civil War with the Union Army contain more personal information than those of the earlier wars. Many early enlistments (1861-62) were for very short periods and reflect little more than enlistment and discharge information, but records relating to service for three or more years are more comprehensive.

The pension application files in the "Civil War and Later Series" relate to claims based chiefly on service, 1861-1934, excluding service rendered for the Confederacy and in World War I. The files in this series may, however, include some relating to claims based on service rendered as early as 1817.

The pension files are divided into nine sub-series, each of which is arranged numerically. The sub-series are (1) Navy Survivors'

Originals, (2) Navy Survivors' Certificates, (3) Navy Widows' Originals, (4) Navy Widows' Certificates, (5) Survivors' Originals, (6) Survivors' Certificates, (7) Widows' Originals, (8) Widows' Certificates, and (9) "C" and "XC" files. The first four sub-series relate to claims submitted between 1861 and 1910 and are based on service in the Navy, 1861-1910. The next four sub-series relate to claims submitted between 1861 and 1934 for service in the United States Army and to claims submitted between 1910 and 1934 for service in the United States Navy. These claims were based on both death or disability incurred in service and on service alone from 1861-1917. The "C and XC" sub-series include all types of claims filed between 1861 and 1934 and are based on service, 1817-1934, excluding World War I service.

Pensions based on Civil War service in the Union forces are serviced by an alphabetical index on 544 rolls of microfilm and cover the period 1861-1934 (microcopy T-288). There is also an "Organization Index" on 764 rolls of microfilm (microcopy T-289) arranged alphabetically by name of state, thereunder numerically by regiment, thereunder alphabetically by company, and thereunder alphabetically by veteran's name.

There is also a card index known as the REMARRIED WIDOWS INDEX as well as a "C and XC" index which relates to the Civil War. The "Remarried Widows Index" is an incomplete listing of pension claims by widows based on their first husbands' service. The index lists a widow's remarried name and the name of her former husband. The "C and XC Index" shows the new numbers assigned to some claims previously approved and originally numbered under an elaborate system employed by the Pension Bureau prior to the introduction of the "flat file" or "C and XC" system which is now in use. A pension payment card index also exists for files after 1907 which list the pensioner's name, the pension agency, amount of payment and increases, notations of payments made, and the individual's date of death. Occasionally there is listed the name of the heir who received his death benefits.

Documents contained in the pension claim files can be as few as six pages and as many as several hundred, but significant genealogical data can usually be found on fewer than ten pages. The documents are similar in format and content to those contained in pension files of the earlier wars but are generally a little more inclusive.

Daniel J. Dill of Pierce County, Wisconsin, made application for an invalid pension. He said he was "injured by a vicious horse which he was riding" and "received injury to his back from which he has never recovered." He stated that he was never admitted to a hospital but was placed in a private house where certain doctors visited him. Supporting documents were also filed pertaining to his claim which provided considerable family information (fig. 108).

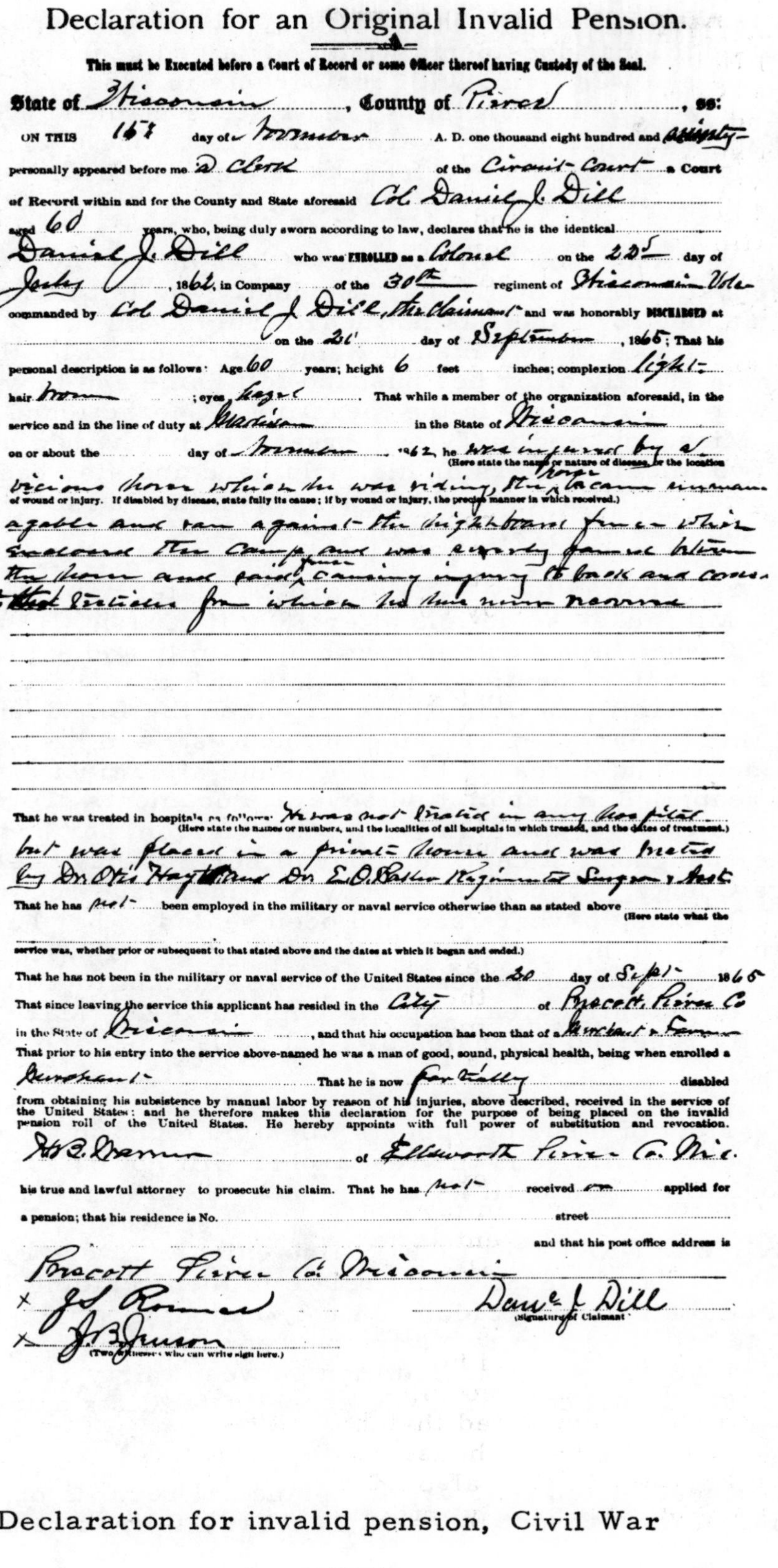

Declaration for an Original Invalid Pension.

This must be Executed before a Court of Record or some Officer thereof having Custody of the Seal.

State of _Wisconsin_, County of _Pierce_, ss:

ON THIS _15th_ day of _November_ A. D. one thousand eight hundred and _eighty-_

personally appeared before me _a Clerk_ of the _Circuit Court_ a Court

of Record within and for the County and State aforesaid _Col Daniel J. Dill_

aged _60_ years, who, being duly sworn according to law, declares that he is the identical

Daniel J Dill who was ENROLLED as a _Colonel_ on the _25_ day of

July, 186_4_, in Company _of the_ 30th regiment of _Wisconsin Vols._

commanded by _Col Daniel J Dill, the claimant_ and was honorably DISCHARGED at

_____ on the _21_ day of _September_, 1865; That his

personal description is as follows: Age _60_ years; height _6_ feet ___ inches; complexion _light_

hair _brown_; eyes _hazel_. That while a member of the organization aforesaid, in the

service and in the line of duty at _Madison_ in the State of _Wisconsin_

on or about the ___ day of _November_ 1862 he _was injured by a_

vicious horse which he was riding, the horse became unmanageable and ran against the lightboard fence which enclosed the camp and was severely forced between the horse and said causing injury to back and causes to the sections for which he has now recover

_____

_____

That he was treated in hospitals as follows: _He was not treated in any hospital but was placed in a private room and was treated by Dr Otis Hoyt and Dr E. O. Butler Regiment Surgeon & Asst_

That he has _not_ been employed in the military or naval service otherwise than as stated above

That he has not been in the military or naval service of the United States since the _20_ day of _Sept_ 1865

That since leaving the service this applicant has resided in the _City_ of _Prescott Pierce Co_

in the State of _Wisconsin_, and that his occupation has been that of a _Merchant & Farmer_

That prior to his entry into the service above-named he was a man of good, sound, physical health, being when enrolled a

Merchant That he is now _partially_ disabled

from obtaining his subsistence by manual labor by reason of his injuries, above described, received in the service of the United States; and he therefore makes this declaration for the purpose of being placed on the invalid pension roll of the United States. He hereby appoints with full power of substitution and revocation.

H.B. Warner of _Ellsworth Pierce Co. Wis._

his true and lawful attorney to prosecute his claim. That he has _not_ received ___ applied for

a pension; that his residence is No. ___ street

and that his post office address is

Prescott Pierce Co Wisconsin

x _J.S. Rowe_   _Danl J Dill_
x _J.B. Jurson_   (Signature of Claimant)

(Two witnesses who can write sign here.)

Fig. 108. Declaration for invalid pension, Civil War

317

After Daniel's death, his widow applied for a pension and produced several additional documents which contained genealogical information. She stated she was living with her parents in 1850 and 1860, giving their names as well as her brothers' and sisters' names, along with their places of residence if they were still living. She even went so far as to submit an extract from a federal census which showed her father's household as proof of her identity (fig. 109).

George Anderson Story was a veteran of the Civil War who resided in Wisconsin during the 1870s. Evidently, he left home looking for work in about 1871 and was not heard from again for nearly thirty years. His wife Mary Amanda Kump Story joined the LDS Church in Wisconsin shortly after her husband left home and moved to Moroni, Utah, with her family. In the meantime, George found work in St. Louis, Missouri, and in Tyler, Arkansas, but he had been injured, losing two middle fingers on his right hand and also badly crippling his forefinger. His left eye had also been injured in 1887, "which caused the loss of eyesight in that eye."

George applied for a pension and was later admitted to a soldier's home in Milwaukee sometime after 1890 (fig. 110). He remained there until 1900 when he got in touch with his family and expressed a desire to see them before he died. His wife sent him money, and George came to his family in Utah where he joined the LDS Church. George died within a year after arriving in the West, and his widow applied for "benefits and arrears" of his pension. Her first claim was rejected, so she reapplied and submitted several documents proving her relationship to George--including a deposition from her brother, a letter from her daughter, a certified copy of her marriage record from Portage County, Wisconsin, a copy of a marriage record from the Manti LDS Temple where she had been sealed to her husband upon his return to Utah, and other documents of genealogical interest. Evidently the Pension Bureau had been reluctant to allow the pension because of the thirty-year separation of the two. Mary persisted and finally received a pension of eight dollars per month until her death.

A variety of other documents might be found in a Civil War service or pension file, and the researcher will not be sure of their genealogical content until he investigates them (fig. 111).

Civil War DRAFT RECORDS also exist and were created under the Act of 3 March 1863. They relate to men residing in the part of the United States under Union control, including single male persons subject to military duty who were between the ages of twenty and thirty-five years, and married men between thirty-five and forty-five years. The records include consolidated lists and descriptive rolls.

The consolidated lists are the principal records of the Washington office of the Provost Marshal General's Bureau relating to

MARGIN RESERVED FOR BINDING

Write Plainly With Unfading Ink--This is a Permanent Record

This form of certificate is to be used only by LOCAL REGISTRARS for reporting to the REGISTER OF DEEDS. Send this certificate to the REGISTER OF DEEDS when the monthly report is mailed to the state office. DO NOT distribute these blanks to undertakers or other persons required to report deaths to you. All original certificates must be sent to the state office with the monthly reports.

STATE OF WISCONSIN

Department of Health—Bureau of Vital Statistics

COPY OF DEATH RECORD

1 PLACE OF DEATH

County Pierce

Township —

or Village —

or City Prescott (No. ..... St. ..... Ward)

Page No. ..... (To be filled out by the Register of Deeds)

2 FULL NAME Daniel J. Dill

PERSONAL AND STATISTICAL PARTICULARS

3 Sex Male

4 Color or Race White

5 Single, Married, Widowed or Divorced (Write the word) Married

6 Date of Birth Feb. (Month) 24th (Day) 1830 (Year)

7 Age 86 yrs. 11 mos. 14 ds. If LESS than 1 day, ... hours or ..... min.?

8 Occupation (a) Trade, profession, or particular kind of work Retired Merchant

(b) General nature of industry, business or establishment in which employed (or employer)

9 Birthplace (State or country) Dillsburg, Pa.

Parents

10 Name of Father Matthew Dill

11 Birthplace of Father (State or country) Pennsylvania

12 Maiden Name of Mother Hannah Brawley

13 Birthplace of Mother (State or country) Penna.

14 The above is true to the best of my knowledge

(Informant) Geo. M. Dill.

(Address) Prescott, Wis.

15 Filed Feb. 8th 1917 Geo. M. Dill. Registrar

Filed ..... 191... ..... Sub-Registrar

MEDICAL CERTIFICATE OF DEATH

16 Date of Death Feb. (Month) 7th (Day) 1917 (Year)

17 I HEREBY CERTIFY, That I attended deceased from Jan. 1st 1917, to Feb. 7th 1917, that I last saw him alive on Feb. 7th 1917, and that death occurred on the date stated above, at 7:30 P. m.

The CAUSE OF DEATH* was as follows:

Senile Debility

(Duration) 2 yrs. ..... mos. ..... ds.

Contributory (Secondary) ..... (Duration) ..... yrs. ..... mos. ..... ds.

(Signed) Geo. M. Dill M.D.

Feb. 8th 1917 (Address) Prescott, Wis.

*State the disease causing death, or in deaths from violent causes state (1) means of injury; (2) whether accidental, suicidal or homicidal.

18 Length of Residence (For hospitals, institutions, transients, or recent residents)

At place of death ..... yrs. ..... mos. ..... ds. In the State ..... yrs. ..... mos. ..... ds.

Where was disease contracted, if not at place of death?

Former or usual residence

19 Place of burial or removal Prescott Wis. Date of burial Feb. 10th 1917

20 Undertaker Dot. Engelbert Address Hastings, Minn.

(over)

MARRIAGE LICENSE

State of Minnesota } ss
District Court for the County of Goodhue

To Any Person Lawfully Authorized to Solemnize Marriage Within Said State:

KNOW YE, That license is hereby granted, to join together as Husband and Wife

Daniel J. Dill, *of the County of* Pierce *and State of* Wisconsin *and* Mary P. Johnson *of the County of* Pike *and State of* Illinois *being satisfied by the oath of said* Daniel J. Dill,

that there is no legal impediment thereto.

THEREFORE, This shall be your sufficient authority for solemnizing the marriage of said parties and making return thereof as provided by law.

IN TESTIMONY WHEREOF, I have hereunto set my hand and affixed the seal of said District Court, at Red Wing, this 16th, *day of* March *A. D.* 1867

Seal,

Robert Deakin

Clerk.

Deputy.

This license may be detached at the dotted line next below, and retained by the person solemnizing the marriage, as a proof of authority for the same

MARRIAGE CERTIFICATE

State of Minnesota } ss
COUNTY OF GOODHUE

I hereby certify that on the 17th, *day of* March *in the year of our Lord one thousand* eight *hundred and* sixty-seven *at* Red Wing Minn, *in said County, I, the undersigned, a* Minister of the Gospel *did join in the holy bonds of matrimony, according to the laws of this state* Daniel J. Dill *of the County of* Pierce *and State of* Wisconsin *and* Mary P. Johnson *of the County of* Pike *and State of* Illinois

IN PRESENCE OF

L. F. Hubbard

E. R. Otis

Jabez Brooks

This Certificate must be filled up and returned to the Clerk of Court who issued it, within one month after marriage, under penalty of not more than one hundred dollars. And if marriage is solemnized in any other than Goodhue County, a similar certificate must be filed with the Clerk of that County.

Fig. 109. Documents relating to Mary Johnson Dill's pension

"Thrive By Thrift, Buy War Saving Stamps."

DEPARTMENT OF COMMERCE

BUREAU OF THE CENSUS

WASHINGTON

February 7, 191[illegible].

Sir:

Referring to your letter of February 1, 1918, "[illegible] Civil War Division Wid. Orig. 1095057, Mary [illegible]. Dill, Daniel J. Dill, Col. 30 Wisconsin Inf.," I give below data secured from the Census records of 1860:

Pittsfield, Perry County, Ill.,
enumerated July 23, 1860.

Name.		Age.
Stephen	Johnson	42
[illegible]	"	41
Geo	"	19
Mary [illegible]	"	17
J. [illegible].		14
A. [illegible].		12
Oliver		9
[illegible]. [illegible].		7
Eliza		4

You are advised that the schedules for Griggsville and surrounding Townships, Pike County, Illinois, as returned at the Census of 1850, have been carefully examined but we fail to find the pensioner's name enumerated therein.

Very respectfully,

[illegible]

Director.

Commissioner of Pensions,
Washington, D. C.

FEB 11 [illegible]

U. S. PENSION OFFICE
M FEB 11 1918

Fig. 109a.

Adjutant General's Office, Wisconsin—Pension Division

GENERAL AFFIDAVIT FOR ANY PURPOSE

In the matter of the _____Widow's_____Pension Claim_____Mary P. Dill_____

No.___1,095,057_____account of____Daniel J. Dill_____

(Here give soldier's name.)

late a__Colonel_____, of Co " _____," ____20th. Regiment __Wisconsin Vol. Inf._____

(Grade)

State of_____Wisconsin_____, County of_____Pierce_____}ss.

On this____15th__day of_____June_____, A. D. 1917, personally appeared before me

_____Mary P. Dill, the claimant_____, a respectable citizen, entitled to credit, who

being duly sworn, says that __she is a resident of_____Prescott_____, in the County of

_____Pierce_____, State of_____Wisconsin_____, her postoffice

address is_____Prescott, Wisconsin_____, and is__72____years old; ~~and~~

decl~~~~~~~~~~~~~~~~~~~~~~~~~~~~~~~~.

That the said affiant is the claimant in this case;

That she was born October 22, 1844;

That there is no family or church record of her birth;

That she was born in the Village of Griggsville, Pike County, Illinois;

That prior to the year 1878 birth records were not kept in the State of
    Illinois;

That during the summers of the years of 1850 and 1860 the claimant lived
    with her parents, Stephen Johnson and Abigail Johnson;

That her brothers names are;
        William Johnson, now dead,
        John Johnson, now dead,
        Elliot Johnson, now living at Kendall, Kansas,
        Oliver Johnson, address unknown,

That her sister's name was Annie Johnson, now Annie Morris, of
    Ogden, Utah.

Mary P. Dill

Fig. 109b.

CLAIMANT'S AFFIDAVIT.

Note.—This may be sworn to before any officer authorized to administer oaths, having a seal of office.

State of Wisconsin, County of Milwaukee.—ss.

In the Matter of Invalid Pensions Claim No. 820839 of Geo. A. Story late a _Private_ in Co. _I_ Regiment of _20" Wis. Inf._ Volunteers.

On this _2_ day of _July_ A. D. 189_2_, personally appeared before me, a Notary Public in and for the aforesaid County, duly authorized to administer oaths, _Geo. A. Story_ aged _65_ years, a resident of NATIONAL HOME, in the COUNTY OF MILWAUKEE and STATE OF WISCONSIN, well known to me to be reputable and entitled to credit, and who, being duly sworn, declared in relation to the aforesaid case as follows:

I am claimant in the above cited case. I have not been in the military or naval service of the United States since the _14_ day of _July_ 186_5_.

As to call 2. He states that he lost 2 middle fingers on his right hand while to work in a shingle Mill at _Tiller Ark._ in the year 1888 — his fore finger is also badly crippled. his left eye was injured in 1887. at St Louis Mo. while working at Carpenter work, a sliver struck his left eye which caused the loss of eyesight in said eye.

My Post Office address is National Home, Wisconsin.

Geo. A. Story
Signature of Applicant

3

If affiant signs by mark, two witnesses who write will sign here

Fig. 110. George A. Story's affadavit for an invalid pension

322

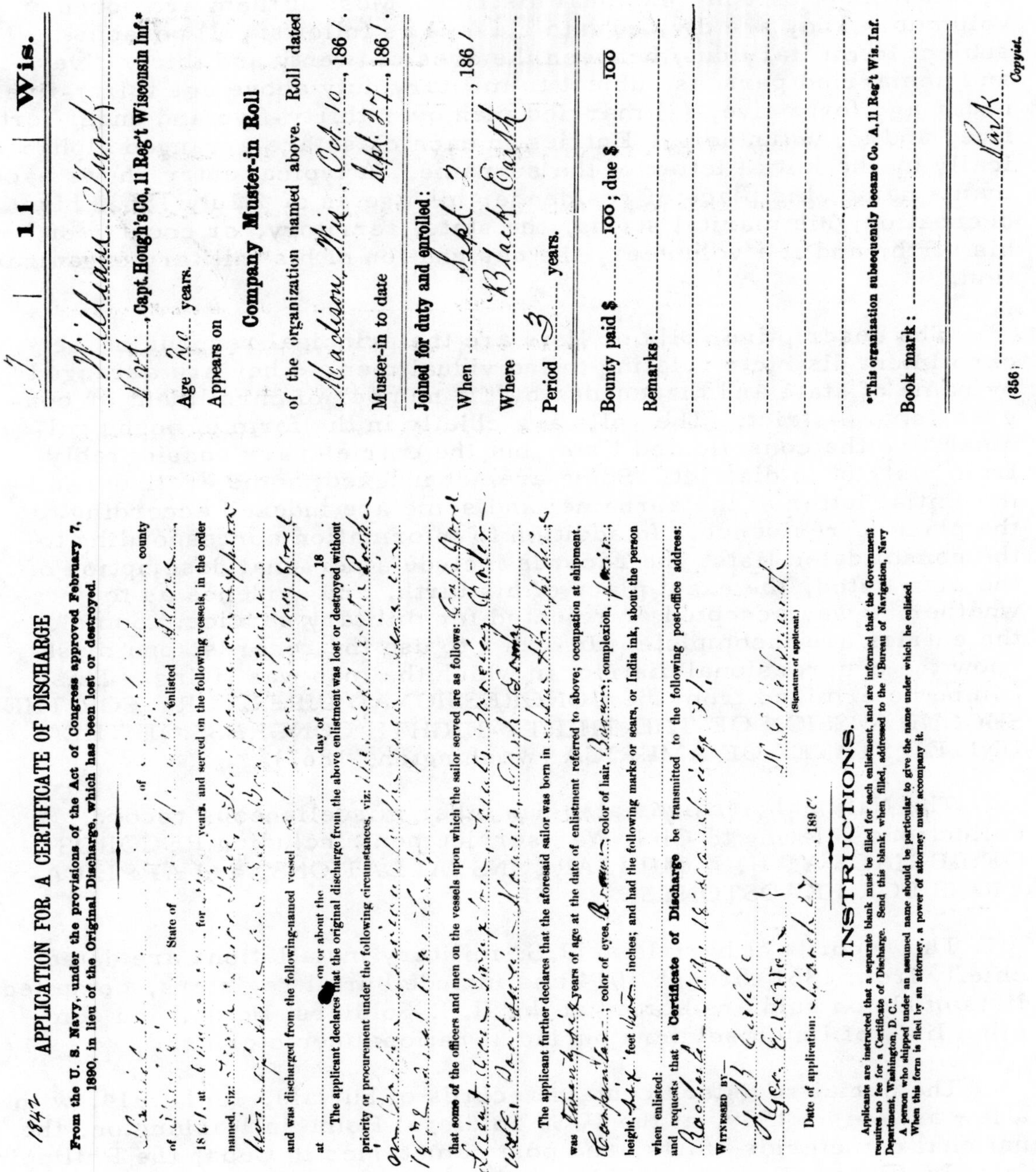

William Clark

Pat...., Capt. Hough's Co., 11 Reg't Wisconsin Inf.*

Age ... years.

Appears on

Company Muster-in Roll

of the organization named above. Roll dated

Madison Wis... Oct. 10, 1861.

Muster-in to date Sept. 27, 1861.

Joined for duty and enrolled:

When Sept 2 , 1861

Where Black Earth

Period 3 years.

Bounty paid $ ...100; due $ ...100

Remarks:

*This organisation subsequently became Co. A, 11 Reg't Wis. Inf.

Book mark:

Park

(856.)   Copyist.

1842   APPLICATION FOR A CERTIFICATE OF DISCHARGE

From the U. S. Navy, under the provisions of the Act of Congress approved February 7, 1890, in lieu of the Original Discharge, which has been lost or destroyed.

... of .... State of .... enlisted ....

1861 at .... for ...... years, and served on the following vessels, in the order named, viz: ...

and was discharged from the following-named vessel ...

at .... on or about the .... day of .... 18....

The applicant declares that the original discharge from the above enlistment was lost or destroyed without priority or procurement under the following circumstances, viz: ...

that some of the officers and men on the vessels upon which the sailor served are as follows: ...

The applicant further declares that the aforesaid sailor was born in ...

was .... years of age at the date of enlistment referred to above; occupation at shipment ...

Complexion ...; color of eyes, Brown; color of hair, Black; complexion, fair ...;

height, five feet .... inches; and had the following marks or scars, or India ink, about the person when enlisted: ...

and requests that a Certificate of Discharge be transmitted to the following post-office address:

Rockdale, No. 18 Cambridge St ...

Witnessed by:

Date of application: ...., 189 .

INSTRUCTIONS.

Applicants are instructed that a separate blank must be filled for each enlistment, and are informed that the Government requires no fee for a Certificate of Discharge. Send this blank, when filled, addressed to the "Bureau of Navigation, Navy Department, Washington, D. C."

A person who shipped under an assumed name should be particular to give the name under which he enlisted. When this form is filed by an attorney, a power of attorney must accompany it.

Fig. 111.   Documents from pension file

individual men. They are arranged by name of state and thereunder by enrollment or congressional district. Most of them are bound volumes. They are divided into classes as follows: (1) persons subject to military duty between the ages of twenty and thirty-five and unmarried persons subject to military duty above age thirty-five and under age forty-five, (2) married men over thirty-five and under forty-five, and (3) volunteers. Entries in each class are arranged alphabetically by the initial letter of the surname. A typical entry shows each man's name, his place of residence, his age as of 1 July 1863, his occupation, his marital status, the state, territory, or country of his birth, and if a volunteer, the designation of his military organization.

The descriptive rolls or lists are the principal records of the enrollment districts relating to individual men. They are arranged by name of state and thereunder by the number of enrollment or congressional district. The rolls are chiefly in the form of bound volumes like the consolidated lists, but the entries vary considerably from district to district. Some are not indexed; some are indexed by the initial letter of the surname; and some are indexed according to the place of residence. In addition to information corresponding to the consolidated lists, the records include a personal description of the man listed, the exact place of his birth, and evidence as to whether he was accepted or rejected for military service. Some of the entries are incomplete. In order to use the records, one must know the congressional district in which the man was living. This can be determined from the CONGRESSIONAL DIRECTORY FOR THE SECOND SESSION OF THE THIRTY-EIGHTH CONGRESS OF THE UNITED STATES OF AMERICA (Washington, 1865).

The National Archives also has other miscellaneous record collections relating to Civil War servicemen, including RECORDS OF BURIALS AT U.S. MILITARY INSTALLATIONS, and APPLICATIONS FOR HEADSTONES.

The records of burials at U.S. military installations are dated chiefly from 1861 through 1914 and include burial registers, compiled lists of Union soldiers buried at the U.S. Soldiers' Home, and compiled lists of Union soldiers buried at national cemeteries.

The burial registers contain records of burials, 1861-1914, with a few as late as 1939, at the U.S. Soldiers' Home in Washington, the national cemeteries, forts, and post cemeteries in Cuba, the Philippine Islands, Puerto Rico, and China. Filed with registers are a very few registers for burials at private cemeteries. Most of the registers are arranged alphabetically by the name of the installation, and as a minimum they show each soldier's name, his military organization, and the date and place of his burial. The registers for the U.S. Soldiers' Home also show the soldier's rank; the town, county, and state of residence before enlistment; the name and residence of his widow, relative, or friend; his age; his nativity; the cause, date, and place of his death; the date of his burial; and, sometimes, the place of his burial.

The compiled lists of Union soldiers buried at the U.S. Soldiers' Home relate to burials between 1861 and 1918. The entries are arranged alphabetically by initial letter of the surname, and there are separate lists arranged by the name of the state. A typical entry usually shows the name of the soldier, his military organization, the date of his death, and the place of his burial.

The compiled lists of Union soldiers buried in national cemeteries relate chiefly to burials during the years 1861-1865, but some are as late as 1886. They are arranged alphabetically by the name of the state of burial. The lists for each state are divided into three parts; on one the names are arranged by the name of the cemetery, on another by the name of the military organization, and on another alphabetically by the initial letter of the surname of the soldier. There are lists arranged by surname, however, only for Connecticut, Delaware, District of Columbia, Iowa, Maine, Maryland, Massachusetts, Michigan, New Hampshire, New Jersey, Pennsylvania, Rhode Island, Vermont, and Wisconsin. A typical entry usually shows the name of the soldier, his military organization, the date of his death, and the place of his burial.

Lists of Union soldiers who were buried in public and private cemeteries during the Civil War are published in Quartermaster General's Office, ROLL OF HONOR (Washington, 1865-1871). Entries are arranged by the name of the cemetery and thereunder alphabetically by the name of the soldier, showing his date of death. Accompanying the volumes is a place index to volumes 1-13 entitled ALPHABETICAL INDEX TO PLACES OF INTERMENT OF DECEASED UNION SOLDIERS (1868). The National Archives has an unpublished place index to all volumes. The Memorial Division, Quartermaster General's Office, Washington, D.C., has an alphabetical card file identifying nearly all soldiers who were buried in national cemeteries and other cemeteries under its jurisdiction from 1861 to the present time.

The APPLICATION FOR HEADSTONES are dated 1879-1925 and relate to servicemen who were buried in private village or city cemeteries. Under terms of an act approved 3 February 1879, headstones were erected by the Government at the graves of Union servicemen. Headstones were erected later at the graves of servicemen of the Revolutionary War and other wars in which the United States had been engaged. Most of the applications are arranged by the name of the state of burial and thereunder by the name of the county, giving the date of application. A few of the applications that relate to servicemen who were buried at the branches of the National Home for Disabled Volunteer Soldiers are arranged by the name of the branch and thereunder by the date of application. Each application shows the name of the serviceman, his rank and military organization, the date of his death, the name and location of the cemetery in which he was buried, and the name and address of the applicant for the headstone (fig.112).

Many other records in the National Archives relate to the Civil War, but those listed above are of special interest to genealogy. For an exhaustive work on additional records pertaining to the Union forces, see GUIDE TO FEDERAL ARCHIVES RELATING TO THE CIVIL WAR, by Kenneth W. Munden and Henry Putney Beers (Washington: Government Printing Office, 1962 $4.50).

Civil War Records--Confederate States

Civil War records relating to Confederate servicemen are not nearly as complete as those pertaining to the Union forces. But still, a fair amount of information is available concerning the Confederate veteran, his widow, and his heirs. Many Confederate service records were destroyed in the war, but some have been preserved and are filed in the National Archives as well as in state repositories. A majority of the pension records were created by the states themselves, and the records remain in their custody and jurisdiction, though several collections have been microfilmed and are available at the Genealogical Society Library in Salt Lake City.

Before the Confederate Government evacuated Richmond, some of its records were moved south under directions from President Jefferson Davis. According to Henry P. Beers "the Union Army penetrated the defenses of Petersburg," on 2 April 1865, "forcing a Confederate retreat from the southern approach to Richmond. On that day President Davis directed all department heads to complete arrangements for leaving the Capital. Some records were then boxed for rail transportation; clerks piled up other records in the streets and set them afire and other records were simply abandoned in the Government offices. Some records were saved by Union Army officers who entered the city and some were carried off by soldiers and individuals. Government offices were set aflame and most of the buildings that had been occupied by Confederate Government departments and agencies were destroyed along with quantities of records."[1]

Fig.113 is a letter which was written at the very time the above events were taking place and graphically illustrates the conditions which existed at the time.

After occupying Richmond, the Union Army seized considerable quantities of Confederate records and sent them to the War Department in Washington for deposit and evaluation. Other records were also acquired from time to time, and on 1 July 1878 the War Department appointed Marcus J. Wright, a former Confederate brigadier general, its agent for the collection of Confederate records.[2] He did a great work in purchasing, borrowing and copying, and otherwise obtaining important Confederate records for a more complete archives on the Confederacy.

Form 1

SAW 14 JUL 1967 ORIGINAL

1. NAME OF DECEASED - LAST - FIRST - MIDDLE (Print or Type)
Frank, Nelson T.

14. NAME AND LOCATION OF CEMETERY (City and State)
Oakland Cemetery, Taunton, Mass.

IMPORTANT - Item 18 on reverse side must be completed. See attached instructions and complete and submit both copies.

2. SERVICE NUMBER | **3. PENSION OR VA CLAIM NUMBER**

15. This application is submitted for a stone or marker for the unmarked grave of a deceased member or former member of the Armed Forces of the U. S., soldier of the Union or Confederate Armies of the Civil War or for an unmarked memorial plot for a non-recoverable deceased member.
I hereby agree to accept responsibility for proper placement at the grave or memorial plot at no expense to the Government.

4. ENLISTMENT DATE (Month, day, year) Enl. 4/24/1898
5. DISCHARGE DATE (Month, day, year) 3/31/1899

6. STATE July 1, 1878 **7. DECORATIONS**

NAME OF APPLICANT (Print or Type) Mrs. Emma F. Rudine **RELATIONSHIP** Daughter

8. GRADE OR RANK Pvt. **9. BRANCH OF SERVICE, COMPANY, REGIMENT, DIVISION**
Co. D. 5th Mass Inf.
Fifth Reg. Mass Infantry U. S. Vols.

ADDRESS OF APPLICANT (Street address, City and State)
83 Park Ave., Meridan, Conn.

10. DATE OF BIRTH (Month, day, year) NOT SHOWN Jan. 20, 1876
11. DATE OF DEATH (Month, day, year) July 6, 1967

SIGNATURE OF APPLICANT Emma F Rudine **DATE** July 7, 1967

12. RELIGIOUS EMBLEM (Check one)
X LATIN CROSS (Christian)
STAR OF DAVID (Hebrew)
NO EMBLEM

13. CHECK TYPE REQUIRED
UPRIGHT MARBLE HEADSTONE
FLAT MARBLE MARKER
XX FLAT GRANITE MARKER
FLAT BRONZE MARKER

16. FREIGHT STATION Brockton, Mass.

17. NAME OF CONSIGNEE WHO WILL TRANSPORT STONE OR MARKER
Dahlborg Funeral Home, Inc.

DO NOT WRITE HERE

FOR VERIFICATION 13 JUL 1967 **ORDERED**

ADDRESS OF CONSIGNEE (Street address, City and State)
647 Main St., Brockton, Mass. 02401

I HAVE AGREED TO TAKE THE STONE OR MARKER TO THE CEMETERY.

B/L | **CONTRACTOR**

SIGNATURE OF CONSIGNEE

DD FORM 1330, 1 NOV 62 NNO EDITION OF 1 DEC 61 MAY BE USED. APPLICATION FOR HEADSTONE OR MARKER JBR 8/14/67

Form 2

WW I   WW II   KOREA   20 JUL 1967 ORIGINAL

1. NAME OF DECEASED - LAST - FIRST - MIDDLE (Print or Type)
HENDRIX, William Wesley

14. NAME AND LOCATION OF CEMETERY (City and State)
New Home Cemetery
RFD, Monroeville, Alabama 36460

IMPORTANT - Item 18 on reverse side must be completed. See attached instructions and complete and submit both copies.

2. SERVICE NUMBER Unknown **3. PENSION OR VA CLAIM NUMBER** Unknown

15. This application is submitted for a stone or marker for the unmarked grave of a deceased member or former member of the Armed Forces of the U. S., soldier of the Union or Confederate Armies of the Civil War or for an unmarked memorial plot for a non-recoverable deceased member.
I hereby agree to accept responsibility for proper placement at the grave or memorial plot at no expense to the Government.

4. ENLISTMENT DATE (Month, day, year) Sept. 1, 1861
5. DISCHARGE DATE (Month, day, year) After war ended 5-26-1865. Was P.O.W. when war ended

6. STATE Alabama **7. DECORATIONS** Unknown

NAME OF APPLICANT (Print or Type) W. H. Hendrix **RELATIONSHIP** Son

8. GRADE OR RANK Pvt. **9. BRANCH OF SERVICE, COMPANY, REGIMENT, DIVISION**
Georgia
Co. H, 1st Confederate Volinteers

ADDRESS OF APPLICANT (Street address, City and State)
Route "E"
Repton, Alabama 36475

10. DATE OF BIRTH (Month, day, year) Unknown
11. DATE OF DEATH (Month, day, year) May, 1921

SIGNATURE OF APPLICANT **DATE** 7-11-67

12. RELIGIOUS EMBLEM CONFEDERATE VETERAN
X LATIN CROSS (Christian)
STAR OF DAVID (Hebrew)
NO EMBLEM

13. CHECK TYPE REQUIRED
X UPRIGHT MARBLE HEADSTONE
FLAT MARBLE MARKER
FLAT GRANITE MARKER
FLAT BRONZE MARKER

16. FREIGHT STATION Monroeville, Alabama (Monroe County)

17. NAME OF CONSIGNEE WHO WILL TRANSPORT STONE OR MARKER
W. H. Hendrix

DO NOT WRITE HERE

FOR VERIFICATION 18 JUL 1967 **ORDERED**

ADDRESS OF CONSIGNEE (Street address, City and State)
Route "E", Repton, Alabama 36475

I HAVE AGREED TO TAKE THE STONE OR MARKER TO THE CEMETERY.

B/L | **CONTRACTOR**

SIGNATURE OF CONSIGNEE

DD FORM 1330, 1 NOV 62 EDITION OF 1 DEC 61 MAY BE USED. APPLICATION FOR HEADSTONE OR MARKER Form Approved Budget Bureau No. 22-R205

Fig. 112. Application for headstone

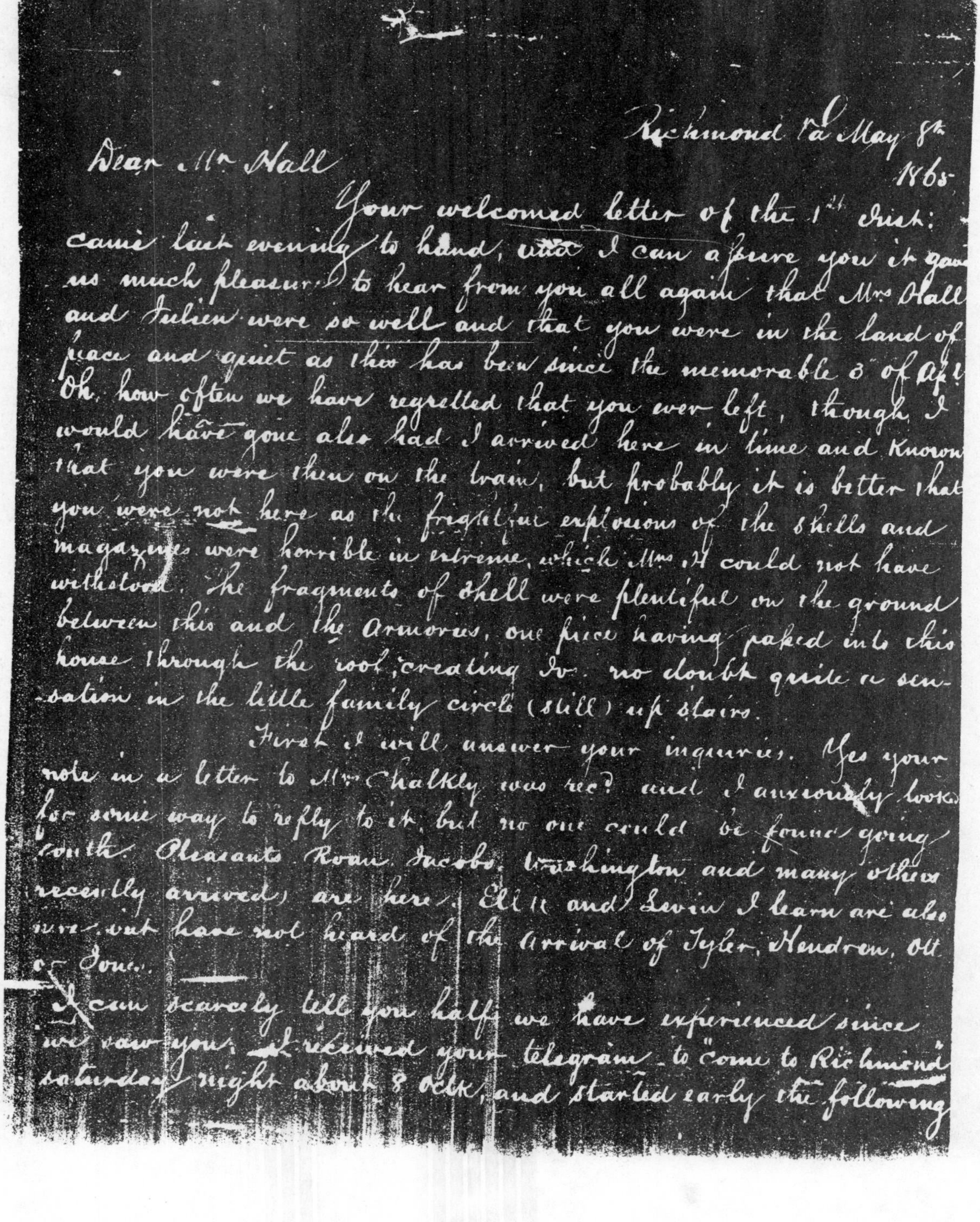

Richmond Va May 8th 1865

Dear Mr Hall

Your welcomed letter of the 1st Inst: came last evening to hand, and I can assure you it gave us much pleasure to hear from you all again that Mrs Hall and Julien were so well and that you were in the land of peace and quiet as this has been since the memorable 3 of Apl. Oh, how often we have regretted that you ever left, though I would have gone also had I arrived here in time and known that you were then on the train, but probably it is better that you were not here as the frightful explosions of the shells and magazines were horrible in extreme, which Mrs H could not have withstood. The fragments of shell were plentiful on the ground between this and the Armories, one piece having passed into this house through the roof, creating &c. no doubt quite a sensation in the little family circle (still) up stairs.

First I will answer your inquiries. Yes your note in a letter to Mr Chalkly was recd and I anxiously looked for some way to reply to it, but no one could be found going south. Pleasants Roan Jacobs, Washington and many others recently arrived) are here. Ellis and Levin I learn are also here, but have not heard of the arrival of Tyler, Hendren, Ott & Jones.

I can scarcely tell you half we have experienced since we saw you, I received your telegram to "come to Richmond" Saturday night about 8 oclk, and started early the following

Fig. 113. Letter from Richmond, Virginia, 8 May 1865

328

morning (sunday) to the depot with Mrs N. Tommie and Ida
we left the city under a furious shelling each as it came sc
reaming along would increase Mrs N speed, we remained
at the station till about 5 oclk PM before we succeeded in
getting on the train and arrived at Manchester about dark
from there we walked over to the city where we found all excite
-ment I met Philbrook and Wingfield (and hundreds of others
running) to the depots but they said nothing of your or Mr I
or of any one else being on the train or that you thought of
going or anything of the kind. We got home, had supper and
I immediately went up to your house to see you as to what
should be done, no one answered the bell so I returned home
and sent up to Mrs Chalkly then about 9½ oclk to inquire if
you were there, and was informed to my great surprise that
you had all gone. Next morning (monday) we were awakened
before day by the terrific explosions and as soon as it was light
witnessed from our windows a scene that cannot here be described
jaded horses and men flying through the streets the troops smash-
-ing the windows and rushing along with the spoils, the fire roaring
was crashing amid the explosions of the magazines and thousands
of shells and other ammunition the whole city enveloped in a cloud
of black smoke following the troops rushed the pillagers from store
to store white and black filling the streets running in every direction
with valuable clothing provisions, hats, shoes, beautiful dress goods dr-
aging around their feet, fine furniture, mirrors, in short everything
that cand be imagined, but hundreds of piles piles of their newly
gotten wealth burned in the streets while they were flying lest they

Fig. 113 continued.

329

should share the same fate, many (like the true owners) after a day
of breathless struggling found their goods only in a better place to
burn. Soon the shout was raised that the "yankees" were coming"
and surely there they were the flames roaring and cracking over
them as they dashed up the streets; they immediately placed gu-
-ards on the streets who immediately restored order. captured
every negroe and set them at work extinguishing the fire, which
was finally done but not untill our little all had been des-
-troyed; yes of all of our little plunder, furniture pictures carpets
&c &c we saved nothing except a few armfulls of clothing and
a few chairs. and can assure you that the kindness of you and
Mrs Hall will ever be remembered as also Mrs C. we immediately
came up to your house after finding it had not been burned) and
took posession and are very comfortably fixed and anxiously
waiting for you to come. Mr Nowlan has been with us about three
weeks. our farm flat was also destroyed by fire during the
night of Sunday &c. we have concluded to make this city
our future home Mr Nowlan having ruled out the store in
Petersburg, but the trouble now is where we will get a house
to do business in as all of the fine store of Main St. have
been destroyed. There is little money and no business except
with the sutlle stores, these can fruits meats and confectionaries,
nearly in fact all I meet on the St. are like myself doing not-
-hing except Tiller & Blankenship who are employed at the U S
com up: Depot. but for the loss of my tools and watch material
I would have long ago been at work, but can do nothing now
without (one of us) first going north I want you to come to Richmd

for I am sure if anyone can find employment here you can. and if there is nothing now there will be soon I hope as the debris of the ruins are fast being cleared away. and nearly every one preparing to rebuild. this city is destined to be within a few years the second New York.

Of the extent of the fire you can form no idea without walking over the ruins. on the South side of Main St. nothing is standing between 9th St. and the Traders bank. on the North side nothing b 'ween 8th & Franklin to Mitchell & Tylers except the Treasy: building and those Iron front buildings on 13th bet: Main & Franklin — on Carey froming 9th to 15th St. on Canal from 8th St. R & P. R. R Shops up to 4th St. and all of the buildings below the canal up to the Tredegar works. then down about Main & 21 & 22nd two Sqrs: all of the bridges to Reid Church, & the Court house on the square. The city is perfectly quiet and the new rule working splendidly we have been politely even kindly treated by the soldiery and I have yet to meet a single person who has been treated otherwise, thousands have been furnished with provisions from their commy: depots and no passes are required to walk about the streets

Excuse the errors &c of this letter for I am so anxious to get it to the office that you may get it early, that I cannot look it over to correct — Remember me to Mrs. Hall. and Julien.

Truly Your Friend Ro: E Macomber

Mrs. Nowlan sends much love to M Hall and often wishes her here - she has seen Mrs. Chalkly and · tif Mattie once or twice a day since you left and would have gone to Petersburg but thought best to remain here and keep anyone else from taking possession of her house and save further expense in moving her furniture believing that you would return as soon as the road was in order, and now will expect you every day. We have not decided yet whether we will live here or go further north, having very little desire to go south at present. if we can get a store and residence

Fig. 113 continued.

331

I think we will remain here as this is my preference. Our farm place was burned. It seemed hard that I should have been burnt out entirely here and there both, but yet I feel very thankful that we yet have a comfortable house left if we are compelled to live in Petersburg. I hope you will come soon I will remain here till you do. I have many many things to tell you and if we remain here I do hope you will do the same. For I have sadly missed you. The two old ladies, daughter and son still occupy the upper floor, and from thier conversation I think expect to do so the remainder of thier lives as they say thier grandmother is too old to be again removed. Not one of my servants either here or in Petersburg have left me. and I have not experienced the inconvenience on account of the changes which I must say are very agreeable to me after the suffering, losses, and trials of the last four years. the pleasure thing of having my husband again with me is a happiness unsurpasable. Love to Mr Hall & Julien. And remain

   Truly Your friend
 Signed Mrs Nowlan.

Write to us early

   Your

   R. E. W.

Fig. 113 continued.

Over the years the records were arranged in various groupings with several thousand index cards created to identify facts which pertained to a particular individual. In 1903, legislation authorized the creation of COMPILED MILITARY SERVICE RECORDS for Confederate veterans. They are in three parts, and each has been microfilmed. Part 1 consists of jacket envelopes for men who served in organizations connected with one of the Confederate states during 1861-1865, arranged alphabetically by state, thereunder by branch of service, thereunder by designation of organization, and thereunder alphabetically by the name of the individual. Part 2 consists of jacket envelopes for men who served in organizations raised directly by the Confederate Government and not identified with any particular state. Part 3 consists of jackets known as the "General and Staff Officers' Papers," containing carded records of general officers, officers and enlisted men of the staff departments, and officers attached to other units.

A CONSOLIDATED INDEX TO CONFEDERATE VETERANS' COMPILED MILITARY SERVICE RECORDS has been created, and the microcopy numbers for it as well as for the three record groups follow:

GROUP 1:
Alabama	M 311 (508 rolls);	Index M 374 (49 rolls)
Arizona Terr.	M 318 (1 roll);	Index M 374 (1 roll)
Arkansas	M 317 (256 rolls);	Index M 376 (26 rolls)
Florida	M 251 (104 rolls);	Index M 225 (9 rolls)
Georgia	M 266 (607 rolls);	Index M 226 (67 rolls)
Kentucky	M 319 (136 rolls);	Index M 377 (14 rolls)
Louisiana	M 320 (414 rolls);	Index M 378 (31 rolls)
Mississippi	M 269 (427 rolls);	Index M 232 (45 rolls)
Missouri	M 322 (193 rolls);	Index M 380 (16 rolls)
No. Carolina	M 270 (580 rolls);	Index M 230 (43 rolls)
So. Carolina	M 267 (392 rolls);	Index M 381 (35 rolls)
Tennessee	M 268 (359 rolls);	Index M 231 (48 rolls)
Texas	M 323 (445 rolls);	Index M 227 (41 rolls)
Virginia	M 324 (1,075 rolls);	Index M 382 (62 rolls)

GROUP 2: M 258
GROUP 3: M 331 (275 rolls)
CONSOLIDATED
  INDEX: M 253 (535 rolls)

The CONSOLIDATED INDEX contains the names of all military personnel in the compiled military service records. The cards give the name of the soldier, his rating or rank, the designation of the unit with which he served, and often information concerning the origin of the unit (fig. 114).

Since some records of the Confederate Army were lost during the war and at its close, the compiled military service records are not complete; however, the pension records in custody of each state are just as inclusive if not more so than Civil War pension records

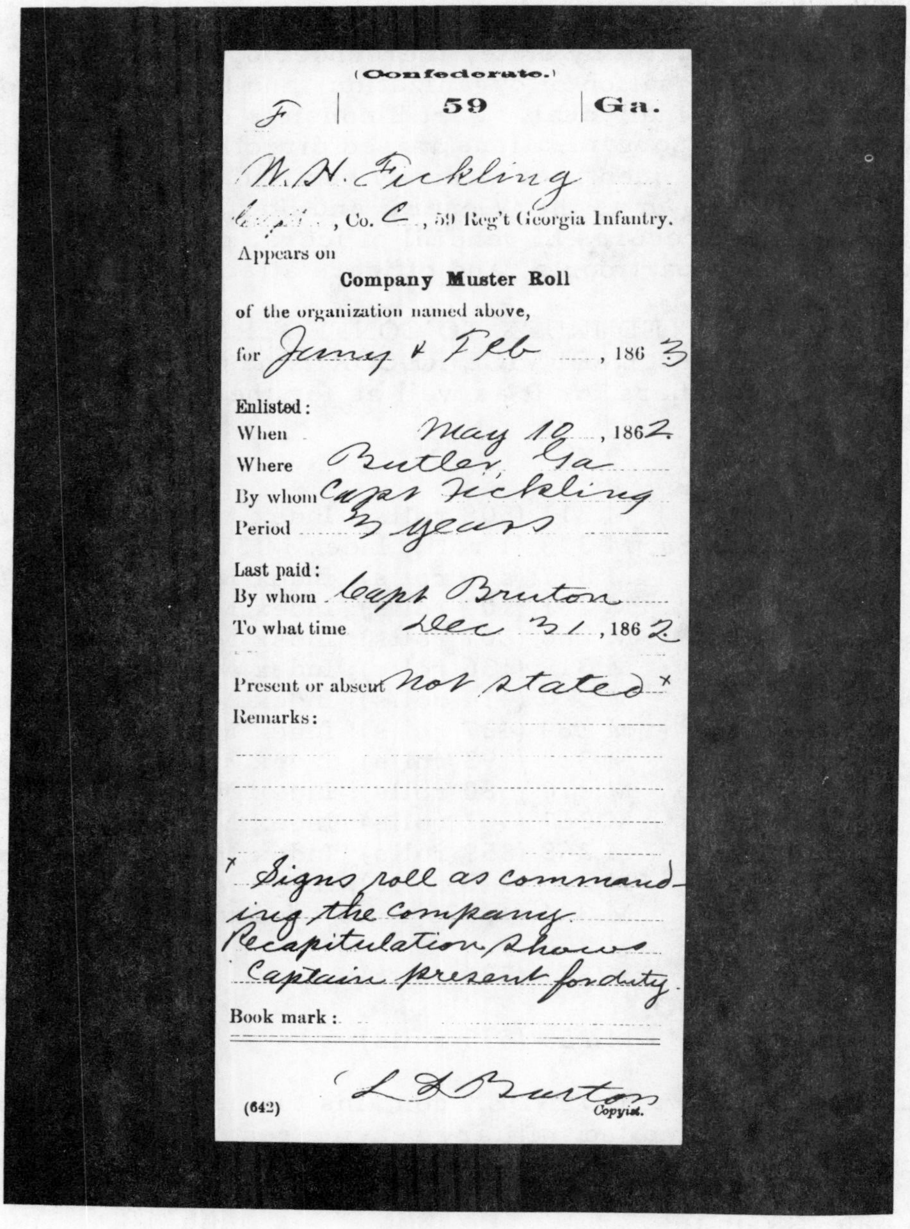

(Confederate.)

F. | 59 | Ga.

W. H. Fickling

Capt. , Co. C , 59 Reg't Georgia Infantry.

Appears on

Company Muster Roll

of the organization named above,

for Jany & Feb , 186 3

Enlisted:
When May 12 , 1862
Where Butler, Ga
By whom Capt Fickling
Period 3 Years

Last paid:
By whom Capt Bruton
To what time Dec 31 , 1862

Present or absent Not stated ×

Remarks:

_____

_____

_____

× Signs roll as command-
ing the company.
Recapitulation shows
Captain present for duty.

Book mark : _____

L. D. Bruton
(642)   Copyist.

Fig. 114. Document from Confederate service file

334

of the Union forces.

Other compiled records relating to the Confederacy are also available in the National Archives, and under certain conditions, they might help solve a particular pedigree problem. They include special files about individuals and businesses compiled by the U.S. War Department, Union Provost Marshals' records concerning certain individuals from the South, and special records relating to military and civilian personnel in prisons and in other situations.

A file compiled by the U.S. War Department on individual Confederate citizens or business firms, 1861-1865, is available on 1,240 rolls of microfilm (M 346). It contains original documents with cross-references to other compiled files and to book records. Vouchers, receipts, affidavits, and correspondence relate to payments for materials purchased by or services performed for the Army and Navy. Other documents include abstracts of expenditures, contracts for armament, contractors' bonds, certificates of deposit, passes, powers of attorney and other documents.

The Union Provost Marshals' papers relating to civilians, 1861-1867, are available in two microfilm collections (M 345 and M 416) and might also be useful for genealogy. They contain papers relating to the arrest and trial of persons suspected of aiding or spying for the enemy, of disloyalty, and of other war crimes.

A file has also been compiled relating to military and civilian personnel, 1861-1865 (M 347). It contains correspondence, card abstracts, and cross-reference slips relating to officers, soldiers, civilian employers, citizens, Confederates in Union prisons, Federals in Confederate prisons, and British subjects in Confederate service. The files are arranged alphabetically by surname (fig. 115).

Other records of various quantity and quality relating to the Confederacy have been centralized in the National Archives, and the genealogist should consult GUIDE TO THE ARCHIVES OF THE GOVERNMENT OF THE CONFEDERATE STATES OF AMERICA, by Henry Putney Beers (Washington: Government Printing Office, 1968 $3.75) for more detail concerning them.

As mentioned previously, pension records pertaining to Confederate veterans and their families are in custody of the respective southern states, and several collections are available at the Genealogical Society Library in Salt Lake City. The genealogical information included in them is similar to that shown in files of the Union forces.

Spanish-American War Records
Compiled records in the National Archives pertaining to the Spanish-American War and the Philippine Insurrection are not open to public examination at the present time, but Archives personnel will provide selected information from the files concerning a

ROLL OF PRISONERS OF WAR PAROLED AT

WE, the undersigned, Prisoners of War, do give our parole of honor, that we will not take up arms again, nor serve as military police or constabulary force in any fort, garrison, or constabulary force, nor as guards of prisons, depots, or stores, nor to discharge any duty usually performed by soldiers, until exchanged under the provisions of the Cartel entered into July 22, 1862.

NO.	NAMES—IN ALPHABETICAL ORDER. (BY REGIMENTS AND COMPANIES.)	RANK OR TOWN.	REGIMENT OR COUNTY AND STATE.	CO.	WHERE CAPTURED.	WHEN CAPTURED.	SIGNATURES.	REMARKS. (CHARGES, &c., &c.)

Fig. 115. Prisoner of war record

particular soldier upon written request. Usually information in the written response from the Archives will include a summary of the soldier's service, as well as genealogical data--including his age, place of birth, next of kin, and place of residence at enlistment. Restrictions on the use of records relating to military service within the last seventy-five years preclude public examination or the reproduction of the records.

The records themselves vary in form and content from other volunteer compiled military service records. An enlistment paper usually contains the soldier's birthplace, his age and physical description, the name of a person to be notified in case of emergency, a statement of the soldier's physical condition with particular details to past illnesses, a physical examination paper, and other miscellaneous records and documents.

Records of the Modern Wars

Records relating to servicemen and women who have served in World War I and later conflicts are housed in various federal repositories throughout the country. They are confidential, but information can be obtained from most of them by writing to the appropriate office.

World War I draft records have been deposited at a Federal Records Center (Region 4), 221 St. Joseph Avenue, East Point, Georgia. Personnel at the Center will investigate their records and provide genealogical data from the files of a particular individual when basic identifying information is provided. World War I Selective Service System Draft Boards were established according to population, and records at the Federal Records Center are filed according to the Local Draft Board. The larger cities had a great number of Boards, each covering a particular district of the city, and the Federal Records Center personnel must have the home address of the individual at the time of his registration to locate his records.

A few years ago, the Genealogical Society in Salt Lake City was attempting to verify certain genealogical information about Abraham Randall and was able to get helpful facts from World War I records. The Federal Records Center was not able to assist until Abraham's residence was determined, but after it was learned he lived at "Eagle Rock, California" (near Los Angeles), they were able to locate his records and provided facts concerning his parentage, birth date, and birthplace.

Modern records concerning personnel who have been separated from the service are deposited in the National Personnel Records Center at St. Louis, Missouri. The records are not open to public inspection, but genealogical data will be provided close relatives upon application. Sufficient identifying information must be submitted with a request in order for the personnel to locate the proper records; usually required are the name, service number, branch of service, and approximate time period.

SYMBOLS RD Replacement Depot
         MS Months Service (computed as of 2 Sept 45)
         RA Regular Army
         ** Quartered at 4th RD Annex
         *   Quartered at Special Training Det #1
      BFAGMT By 1st available govt mtr T
      BFAGRT By 1st available govt rail T

HEADQUARTERS
FOURTH REPLACEMENT DEPOT

SPECIAL ORDER)   APO 703
              :   15 February 1947
NUMBER.....43)   E X T R A C T

     48. Following named (14) EM, BR SV & MOS indicated,
RA, reld atchd unasgd Repl Co indicated, this RD, trfd
in grade from indicated BR SV to AAF, asgd 1539th AAF Base
Unit WPW PACD ATC, APO 226, EM are project "ZAMA", & WP
BFAGMT or RT. TDN. TCNT. EDCMR 17 Feb 1947. EM WP with
least practicable delay. (Auth: Cite AG 200.3 (1 Feb 47),
AG-OP, dtd 1 Feb 1947 from CINFE, APO 500).

RANK	NAME	ASN	BR SV	MOS	REPL
Cpl	ONSTED, RICHARD E	RA15212870	QMC	262	259
Tec 5	OSHIRO, EIKA	RA30126905	BI	405	260
Pfc	KOHATSU, JAMES J	RA30126879	BI	521	260
Pfc	STROHL, DONZEL B	RA17199116	MD	264	259
Pfc	VALENTINE, HARRY E JR	RA12256341	INF	821	259
Pfc	BUCK, ELMER E	RA16219645	CAC	433	260
Pvt	HIGASHI, HARUO	RA10101732	BI	521	260
Pvt	HOLMAN, WILSON T JR	RA18291036	MD	858	259
Pvt	MELSON, LEROY M	RA19247495	INF	522	259
Pvt	NACHSTEIN, JAMES J	RA12261767	MD	521	259
Pvt	PERRY, CLIFFORD G	RA10735267	BI	521	260
Pvt	SPOUSTA, LESLIE A	RA11155221	INF	820	259
* Pvt	* WRIGHT, NORMAN E	RA39773444	INF	745	259
Pvt	YAMADA, WALTER K	RA10102319	BI	521	260

BY ORDER OF COLONEL DISSINGER:

                                      THEO. F. PRESLEY
                                      Major   AGD
                                      Asst Adm Officer

OFFICIAL:

[signature: Theo F Presley]

THEO. F. PRESLEY
Major   AGD
Asst Adm Officer

END OF ORDERS

DISTRIBUTION:
   "B"
                              - 11 -

Fig. 116. Documents relating to personnel in modern wars

REPORT OF SEPARATION FROM THE ARMED FORCES OF THE UNITED STATES

HONORABLE

DEPARTMENT: **ARMY**

1. LAST NAME—FIRST NAME—MIDDLE NAME WRIGHT NORMAN EDGAR	**2. SERVICE NUMBER** US 39 773 444 **3. GRADE–RATE–RANK AND DATE OF APPOINTMENT** SFC(T) 22Feb52 **4. COMPONENT AND BRANCH OR CLASS** AUS Unasgd

5. QUALIFICATIONS

SPECIALTY NUMBER OR SYMBOL: 1502 · RELATED CIVILIAN OCCUPATION AND D.O.T. NUMBER: Administrative Clerk

6. EFFECTIVE DATE OF SEPARATION DAY 13 MONTH Nov YEAR 52

7. TYPE OF SEPARATION Trf to ERC

8. REASON AND AUTHORITY FOR SEPARATION (See Item 38)
Released to ERC, SR 615-363-5 ETS

9. PLACE OF SEPARATION Fort Leonard Wood, Missouri

10. DATE OF BIRTH DAY 9 MONTH Jan YEAR 27 · **11. PLACE OF BIRTH** (City and State) Murray, Utah

12. DESCRIPTION SEX Male · RACE Cau · COLOR HAIR Brown · COLOR EYES Brown · HEIGHT 68 1/2 · WEIGHT 205

13. REGISTERED YES X NO · **SELECTIVE SERVICE NUMBER** 42 24 27 15

14. SELECTIVE SERVICE LOCAL BOARD NUMBER (City, County, State) #24, Ft Douglas, St Lake Co., Utah

15. INDUCTED DAY 14 MONTH Nov YEAR 50

16. ENLISTED IN OR TRANSFERRED TO A RESERVE COMPONENT YES X NO · **COMPONENT AND BRANCH OR CLASS** ERC · **COGNIZANT DISTRICT OR AREA COMMAND** Utah Military District, Sixth Army Area

17. MEANS OF ENTRY OTHER THAN BY INDUCTION ☐ ENLISTED ☐ REENLISTED ☐ COMMISSIONED ☐ CALLED FROM INACTIVE DUTY

18. GRADE–RATE OR RANK AT TIME OF ENTRY INTO ACTIVE SERVICE Rct (now Pvt-1)

19. DATE AND PLACE OF ENTRY INTO ACTIVE SERVICE DAY 14 MONTH Nov YEAR 50 PLACE (City and State) Ft Douglas, Utah

20. HOME ADDRESS AT TIME OF ENTRY INTO ACTIVE SERVICE (St., R.F.D., County, City and State) 4288 S 5th East, St Lake Co, Murray, Utah

STATEMENT OF SERVICE FOR PAY PURPOSES

	A. YEARS	B. MONTHS	C. DAYS
21. NET ( ) SERVICE COMPLETED FOR PAY PURPOSES EXCLUDING THIS PERIOD	Not Applicable		
22. NET SERVICE COMPLETED FOR PAY PURPOSES THIS PERIOD	2	0	0
23. OTHER SERVICE (Act of 16 June 1942 as amended) COMPLETED FOR PAY PURPOSES	0	7	13
24. TOTAL NET SERVICE COMPLETED FOR PAY PURPOSES	2	7	13

25. ENLISTMENT ALLOWANCE PAID ON EXTENSION OF ENLISTMENT, IF ANY DAY — MONTH — YEAR NotApplicable AMOUNT None

26. FOREIGN AND/OR SEA SERVICE YEARS None MONTHS None DAYS None

27. DECORATIONS, MEDALS, BADGES, COMMENDATIONS, CITATIONS AND CAMPAIGN RIBBONS AWARDED OR AUTHORIZED
None

28. MOST SIGNIFICANT DUTY ASSIGNMENT
Co A, 25th Armd Engr Bn
6th Armd Div Ft Leonard Wood Mo

29. WOUNDS RECEIVED AS A RESULT OF ACTION WITH ENEMY FORCES (Place and date, if known)
None

30. SERVICE SCHOOLS OR COLLEGES, COLLEGE TRAINING COURSES AND/OR POST-GRAD. COURSES SUCCESSFULLY COMPLETED	DATES (From-To)	MAJOR COURSE	31. SERVICE TRAINING COURSES SUCCESSFULLY COMPLETED
None MOP included in total payment V.C. CURTIS LT COL FC	Not Applicable	Not Applicable	Military Justice Leadership Clerk Typist

GOVERNMENT INSURANCE INFORMATION: If premium is not paid when due, or within thirty-one days thereafter, insurance will lapse. Make checks or money orders payable to the Treasurer of the United States. Forward payments for National Service Life Insurance to the Collections Unit, Veterans Administration District Office having jurisdiction of area in which you maintain your mailing address for insurance purposes. Forward payments for United States Government Life Insurance to Collections Division, Veterans Administration, Washington 25, D.C. When making insurance payments be sure to give full name and mailing address for insurance purposes, service number and policy number(s), if known.

32. KIND OF INSURANCE (amount and premium due each month) N.S.L.I. Free Indemnity · U.S.G.L.I. None

33. MONTH ALLOTMENT DISCONTINUED Not Applicable

34. MONTH NEXT PREMIUM DUE

35. TOTAL PAYMENT UPON SEPARATION 237.41

36. TRAVEL OR MILEAGE ALLOWANCE INCLUDED IN TOTAL PAYMENT 94.38

37. DISBURSING OFFICER'S NAME AND SYMBOL NUMBER V. C. CURTIS, LT COL., FC 215-334

38. REMARKS (Continue on reverse)
No time lost UP Sec 6(a), App 2b, MCM 1951.
Ref Item 8: Released fr active mil svc & transferred to ERC for 5 yrs.
Blood Group "O". 5 das excess lv.

39. SIGNATURE OF OFFICER AUTHORIZED TO SIGN *James A Gifford*
NAME, GRADE AND TITLE (Typed) JAMES A GIFFORD 1st Lt Inf Actg Asst Adjutant General

40. V.A. BENEFITS PREVIOUSLY APPLIED FOR (Specify type) COMPENSATION, PENSION, INSURANCE BENEFITS, ETC. None · **CLAIM NUMBER** Not Applicable

41. DATES OF LAST CIVILIAN EMPLOYMENT: FROM 1950 TO 1950 · **42. MAIN CIVILIAN OCCUPATION** Farmer 3-06.100 · **43. NAME AND ADDRESS OF LAST CIVILIAN EMPLOYER** E O Wallin, Salt Lake City, Utah

44. UNITED STATES CITIZEN ☒ YES ☐ NO

45. MARITAL STATUS Single

46. NON-SERVICE EDUCATION (Years successfully completed) GRAMMAR 8 · HIGH SCHOOL 4 · COLLEGE 0 · DEGREE(S) None · MAJOR COURSE OR FIELD Academic

47. PERMANENT ADDRESS FOR MAILING PURPOSES AFTER SEPARATION (St., R.F.D., County, City and State) See Item #20

48. SIGNATURE OF PERSON BEING SEPARATED *Norman E Wright*

DD FORM 214 JAN 50

INDIVIDUAL'S COPY (TO BE DELIVERED TO THE INDIVIDUAL BEING SEPARATED) 1

Fig. 116a.

SEPARATION QUALIFICATION RECORD

SAVE THIS FORM. IT WILL NOT BE REPLACED IF LOST

This record of job assignments and special training received in the Army is furnished to the soldier when he leaves the service. In its preparation, information is taken from available Army records and supplemented by personal interview. The information about civilian education and work experience is based on the individual's own statements. The veteran may present this document to former employers, prospective employers, representatives of schools or colleges, or use it in any other way that may prove beneficial to him.

1. LAST NAME—FIRST NAME—MIDDLE INITIAL			MILITARY OCCUPATIONAL ASSIGNMENTS		
WRIGHT NORMAN E			10. MONTHS	11. GRADE	12. MILITARY OCCUPATIONAL SPECIALTY

2. ARMY SERIAL No.	3. GRADE	4. SOCIAL SECURITY No.
39 773 444	Pvt	529 24 2664

10. MONTHS	11. GRADE	12. MILITARY OCCUPATIONAL SPECIALTY
1	Pvt	Basic (521)
6	Pvt	Clerk Typist (405)

5. PERMANENT MAILING ADDRESS (Street, City, County, State)
4288 S 5TH E
MURRAY UTAH

6. DATE OF ENTRY INTO ACTIVE SERVICE	7. DATE OF SEPARATION	8. DATE OF BIRTH
12 Oct 1946	24 May 1947	9 Jan 1927

9. PLACE OF SEPARATION
CAMP STONEMAN
CALIFORNIA

SUMMARY OF MILITARY OCCUPATIONS

13. TITLE—DESCRIPTION—RELATED CIVILIAN OCCUPATION

CLERK TYPIST (405): Worked in subsistance warehouse typing requisitions and other military correspondence. Was assistant manager of warehouse. Issued out food supplies to different units.

WD AGO FORM 100
1 JUL 1945

This form supersedes WD AGO Form 100, 15 July 1944, which will not be used.

16—43815-1

Fig. 116b.

THE

PRESIDENT

OF

THE UNITED STATES OF AMERICA

To all who shall see these presents, greeting:

Know Ye, that reposing special trust and confidence in the patriotism, valor, fidelity and abilities of IVAN CLEEO WRIGHT, I do appoint HIM, SECOND LIEUTENANT in the RESERVE, USAF

United States Air Force

to DATE as such from the NINTH day of JUNE, nineteen hundred and FIFTY-EIGHT. This Officer will therefore carefully and diligently discharge the duties of the office to which appointed by doing and performing all manner of things thereunto belonging.

And I do strictly charge and require those Officers and other personnel of lesser rank to render such obedience as is due an officer of this grade and position. And this Officer is to observe and follow such orders and directions, from time to time, as may be given by me, or the future President of the United States of America, or other Superior Officers acting in accordance with the laws of the United States of America.

This commission is to continue in force during the pleasure of the President of the United States of America, for the time being, under the provisions of those Public Laws relating to Officers of the **Armed Forces of the United States of America** and the component thereof in which this appointment is made.

Done at the City of Washington, this NINTH day of JUNE in the year of our Lord one thousand nine hundred and FIFTY-EIGHT, and of the Independence of the United States of America the one hundred and EIGHTY-SECOND.

By the President:

E O'Donnell
Lieutenant General, USAF
Deputy Chief of Staff, Personnel

DEPARTMENT OF THE AIR FORCE
UNITED STATES OF AMERICA
MCMXLVII

James H. Douglas
Secretary of the Air Force

DD 1AF

Fig. 116c.

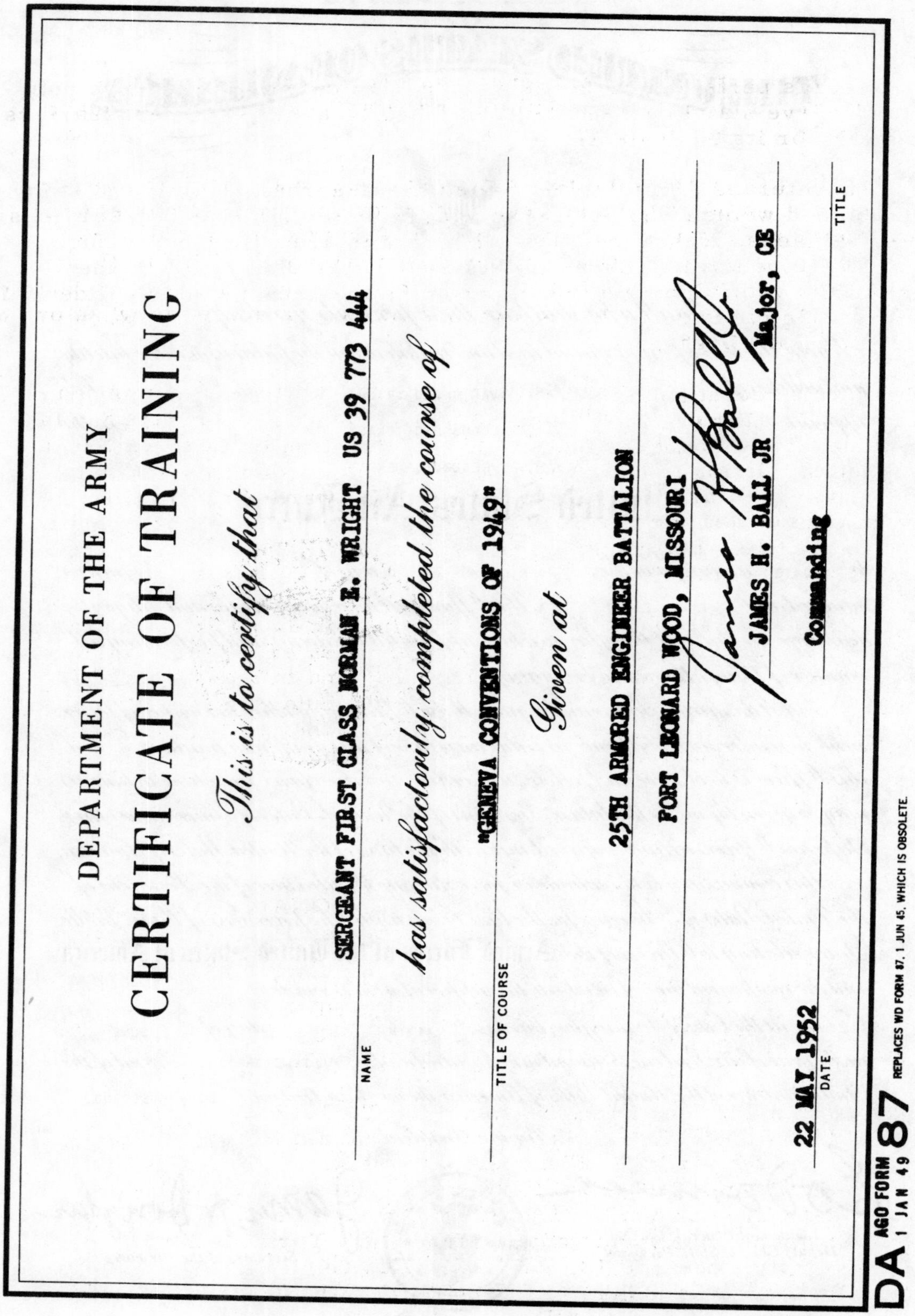

DEPARTMENT OF THE ARMY

CERTIFICATE OF TRAINING

This is to certify that

SERGEANT FIRST CLASS NORMAN E. WRIGHT   US 39 773 444

NAME

has satisfactorily completed the course of

"GENEVA CONVENTIONS OF 1949"

TITLE OF COURSE

Given at

25TH ARMORED ENGINEER BATTALION

FORT LEONARD WOOD, MISSOURI

James H. Ball

JAMES H. BALL, JR   Major, CE

Commanding

22 MAY 1952

DATE   TITLE

DA AGO FORM 87   REPLACES WD FORM 87, 1 JUN 45, WHICH IS OBSOLETE.
1 JAN 49

Fig. 116d.

Records pertaining to personnel who are currently on active duty or on reserve status remain with their units--generally "Headquarters Company" or its equivalent.

The Veterans Administration also has records pertaining to servicemen and women who have been separated from the armed services where pensions, insurance, or other benefits are concerned. Such records are generally housed in the nearest regional office to the home of the veteran or his family. Again, the records are confidential and genealogical facts from the files might only be available when proper credentials are presented.

In most recent times the rather inclusive "201 file" or personnel record is kept for each individual in government service. It contains a considerable amount of genealogical information in most instances. Documents relating to enlistment or induction, promotion, travel, allotments, special duty, special schooling, awards and citations, medical and dental work, and even disciplinary proceedings may be found in the file. Letters and affidavits relating to family life are found in many of the files.

It should be recognized that the information and document examples presented here which pertain to the military are selected. Any number of other examples and documents might be found in other files. The researcher should carefully evaluate his particular pedigree problem and begin to investigate the records as though they were going to provide him with the information he is seeking; and well they might (fig. 116).

A Selected Bibliography Relating to American Military Records

GENERAL

Colket, Meredith B., Jr., and Frank E. Bridgers. GUIDE TO GENEALOGICAL RECORDS IN THE NATIONAL ARCHIVES. Washington, D.C.: The National Archives, 1964. (BYU 929. 373 C682g)

Cullum, George, Bvt. Maj.-Gen. BIOGRAPHICAL REGISTER OF THE OFFICERS AND GRADUATES OF THE U.S. MILITARY ACADEMY AT WEST POINT, N.Y. 3rd ed. 9 vols. Boston: Houghton, Mifflin & Co., 1891. (GS 973 M2cu and BYU 920.073 C898b V.2)

Gardner, Charles K. A DICTIONARY OF THE ARMY OF THE UNITED STATES. New York: G.P. Putnam & Co., 1853. (GS Ref. 973 M2g and GS Film 496,461 1st item)

Glasson, William H., Ph.D. FEDERAL MILITARY PENSIONS IN THE UNITED STATES. Edited by David Kinley. Carnegie Endowment for International Peace. New York: Oxford University Press, 1918. (BYU 330 C21 G46)

Hamersly, Lewis Randolph. RECORDS OF LIVING OFFICERS OF THE U.S. ARMY, 1884. (BYU 923.5 H17r)

Hamersly, Thomas H.S. COMPLETE REGULAR ARMY REGISTER OF THE UNITED STATES: FOR ONE HUNDRED YEARS (1779-1879). Washington, D.C.: T.H.S. Hamersly, 1880. (BYU Ref. 4 929.173 H17c)

Heitman, Francis. HISTORICAL REGISTER AND DICTIONARY OF THE UNITED STATES ARMY FROM ITS ORGANIZATION SEPTEMBER 29, 1783 TO MARCH 2, 1903. Washington, D.C., 1903. (BYU Ref. 4 929.059 H36)

_____. HISTORICAL REGISTER OF OFFICERS OF THE CONTINENTAL ARMY. 2nd ed. Baltimore: The Genealogical Publishing Co., 1967. (GS 973 M23h and BYU 929.173 H36h V.1-2)

Kirkham, E. Kay. SOME OF THE MILITARY RECORDS OF AMERICA (BEFORE 1900). Salt Lake City, Utah: Deseret Book Co, 1964. (GS Ref. 973 M2k and BYU Ref. 4 929.373 K63m)

de Kraft, E. A LIST OF ALL THE PENSIONERS OF THE UNITED STATES, THE SUM PAID TO EACH. Baltimore: Southern Book Co., 1959. (GS Ref. 973 M24upa)

Powell, William Henry. LIST OF OFFICERS OF THE ARMY OF THE UNITED STATES FROM 1779-1900. Detroit: Gale Research Co., 1967. (GS 973 M23pw and BYU Ref. 4 929.373 P871)

Robinson, Fayette. AN ACCOUNT OF THE ORGANIZATION OF THE U.S. ARMY. 2 vols. Philadelphia: E.H. Butler & Co., 1848. (BYU 973 R554a)

Smith, Paul Tincher. "Militia of the United States from 1846-1860," INDIANA MAGAZINE OF HISTORY 15 (1919): 20-47.

U.S. Adjutant-General's Office. OFFICIAL ARMY REGISTER 1896 TO PRESENT. (BYU Documents Collection D102.9)

U.S. Army. BRIEF HISTORIES OF ARMY COMMANDS (ARMY POSTS) AND DESCRIPTIONS OF THEIR RECORDS. (BYU Film RG393 T912)

U.S. Bureau of Census. ELEVENTH CENSUS OF THE UNITED STATES, 1890. Washington, D.C.: The National Archives, 1945. (BYU Film RG15 M123 pts.1-118; BYU Ref. 4 929.373 B76 (Guide); BYU Film RG29 M496 (Index); and GS Film 561,375-561, 377)

U.S. Bureau of Pensions. ANNUAL REPORT OF THE COMMISSIONER OF PENSIONS FOR THE YEAR ENDING JUNE 30, 1881. Washington, D.C.: Government Printing Office, 1881.

_____. LIST OF PENSIONERS ON THE ROLL JANUARY 1, 1883. 5 vols. Baltimore: The Genealogical Publishing Co., 1970. (BYU Ref. 4 939.373 Un3p V.1-5; BYU Documents Collection Serial Set #2078, #2080, #2082; and GS 973 M3L)

_____. REPORT OF THE COMMISSIONER OF PENSIONS FOR THE YEAR ENDING JUNE 30, 1892. Washington, D.C.: Government Printing Office, 1892.

U.S. Congress. AMERICAN STATE PAPERS, DOCUMENTS, LEGISLATIVE AND EXECUTIVE OF THE CONGRESS OF THE UNITED STATES, FROM THE FIRST SESSION OF THE FIRST TO THE SECOND SESSION OF THE SEVENTEENTH CONGRESS, INCLUSIVE. COMMENCING MARCH 4, 1789 AND ENDING MARCH 3, 1823. Washington, D.C., 1834.

U.S. Congress, House. MUSTERING-OUT PAY. House Committee on Military Affairs. Washington, D.C.: Government Printing Office, 1943. (BYU 328 Un3d #10764)

_____. OFFICIAL ARMY REGISTER FOR 1907 OF THE COMMISSIONED AND WARRANT OFFICERS OF THE NAVY OF THE UNITED STATES AND OF THE MARINE CORPS TO JANUARY 1, 1907. Washington, D.C.: Government Printing Office, 1907. (GS 973 M23hr and GS Film 618,272p (Index))

U.S. Congress, Senate. LIST OF PRIVATE CLAIMS BROUGHT BEFORE SENATE OF THE U.S., 1880-1881. (BYU Ref.4 929.373 Un3rk)

_____. LIST OF PRIVATE CLAIMS BROUGHT BEFORE SENATE OF THE U.S., 1893-1894. (BYU Ref.4 929.373 Un3rl)

_____. LIST OF PRIVATE CLAIMS BROUGHT BEFORE SENATE OF THE U.S., 1905-1909. (BYU Ref.4 929.373 Un3rp)

U.S. Department of the Interior. REPORT OF THE SECRETARY OF THE INTERIOR, WITH A STATEMENT OF REJECTED AND SUSPENDED APPLICATIONS FOR PENSION. Washington, D.C., 1852. (BYU Documents Collection Serial Set #618 and GS 973 M24ur)

U.S. National Archives. REGISTERS OF ENLISTMENTS IN THE UNITED STATES ARMY, 1798-1877. Washington, D.C.: National Archives Microfilm Publications, 1963. (GS Film 350, 307-350,350)

U.S. Navy Department. REGISTER OF COMMISSIONED AND WARRANT OFFICERS OF THE U.S. NAVY AND MARINE CORPS. (BYU Documents Collection D208.12)

U.S. Veterans Administration. PENSION FILE, SERVICE RECORDS, LAND WARRANTS, 1775-1913. Washington, D.C.: The National Archives, 1970. (GS Film 833,170-833,175; 833,308-833,313)

U.S. War Department. LETTER FROM THE SECRETARY OF WAR TRANSMITTING A REPORT OF THE NAMES, RANK, AND LINE OF EVERY PERSON PLACED ON THE PENSION LIST, IN PUR-SUANCE OF THE ACT OF JANUARY 20, 1820. Baltimore: Southern Book Co., 1959.

_____. LETTER FROM THE SECRETARY OF WAR TRANS-MITTING A REPORT OF THE NAMES, RANK, AND LINE OF EVERY PERSON PLACED ON THE PENSION LIST, IN PURSU-ANCE OF THE ACT OF THE 18TH OF MARCH, 1818. Baltimore: Southern Book Co., 1955. (BYU Ref.4 929.373 Un3L)

_____. THE PENSION OF 1835 IN FOUR VOLUMES. 4 vols. Baltimore: The Genealogical Publishing Co., 1968. (GS Ref. 973 M24ua)

_____. A TRANSCRIPT OF THE PENSION LIST OF THE UNITED STATES . . . NUMBER OF PENSIONERS IN THE SEVERAL DISTRICTS AND AMOUNTS ALLOWED. Washington, D.C.: A. and G. Way, Printers, 1813. (GS 973 M24us)

_____. A TRANSCRIPT OF THE PENSION LIST OF THE UNITED STATES FOR 1813. Baltimore: Southern Book Co., 1959. (GS 973 A1 #6; GS Film 845,477 2nd item; GS 973 M24uw; and BYU Ref.4 929.373 Un3pr)

Walker, James D. U.S. MILITARY SERVICE AND PENSION RECORDS HOUSED AT THE NATIONAL ARCHIVES. Salt Lake City, Utah: The Genealogical Society, 1969. (BYU 929.1 W893 V.9 #1-11 and GS 929.1 W893 J11)

PRE-REVOLUTION

Baker-Crothers, Hayes. VIRGINIA AND THE FRENCH AND INDIAN WAR. Chicago: The University of Chicago Press, 1928. (BYU 975.502 B178u)

"(A Bibliography of) Journals and Orderly Books Kept by Massachusetts Soldiers During the French and Indian War (1755-1760)," THE NEW ENGLAND HISTORICAL AND GENEALOGICAL REGISTER 95: 118-121. (BYU 929.06 N44 V.95)

Bodge, George Madison, A.B. SOLDIERS IN KING PHILIP'S WAR. 3rd ed. Baltimore: The Genealogical Publishing Co., 1967. (GS 973 M26 and BYU 973.24 B632s)

Burd, J. FRENCH AND INDIAN WAR. (BYU 974.802 P38u)

Busch, Clarence M. FRONTIER FORTS OF PENNSYLVANIA. (BYU 974.8 P38r V.1-2)

Clark, D.S. "Journals and Orderly Books Kept by Connecticut Soldiers During the French and Indian War, 1755-1762," NEW ENGLAND HISTORICAL AND GENEALOGICAL REGISTER 94 (July 1940): 225-330. (BYU 929.06 N44 V.94)

Connecticut Historical Society. ROLLS OF CONNECTICUT MEN IN THE FRENCH AND INDIAN WAR, 1755-1762. (GS 974.6 B4C V.9-10)

Crozier, William Armstrong. VIRGINIA COLONIAL MILITIA, 1651-1776. Baltimore: Southern Book Co., 1954. (BYU 975.520 C887u)

Darlington, Mary Carsot (O'Hara). HISTORY OF COL. HENRY BOUQUET AND THE WESTERN FRONTIERS OF PENNSYLVANIA, 1747-1764. New York: Arno Press, 1971. (BYU 973.802 D249h)

GENERAL ORDERS OF 1757; ISSUED BY THE EARL OF LOUDOUN AND PHINEAS LYMAN IN THE CAMPAIGN AGAINST THE FRENCH. (BYU 973.26 C762g)

Hunter, William Albert. FORTS OF PENNSYLVANIA FRONTER. Harrisburg: Pennsylvania Historical Society, 1755-1763. (BYU 974.802 H919f)

Jacobus, Donald Lines. LIST OF OFFICIALS, CIVIL, MILITARY AND ECCLESIASTICAL OF CONNECTICUT COLONY FROM MARCH 1636 THROUGH 11 OF OCTOBER 1677, AND OF NEW HAVEN COLONY THROUGHOUT ITS SEPARATE EXISTENCE: ALSO SOLDIERS IN THE PEQUOT WAR WHO THEN OR SOON AFTER RESIDED WITHIN THE PRESENT CONNECTICUT BOUNDRY. (GS 974 D3j)

Johnson, W. FRENCH AND INDIAN WAR. (BYU 923.9 J63pa)

Kentucky Land Office. A CALENDAR OF THE WARRANTS FOR LAND IN KENTUCKY, GRANTED FOR SERVICE IN THE FRENCH AND INDIAN WAR. Baltimore: The Genealogical Publishing Co., 1967. (BYU 929.3769 K419c)

KING GEORGE'S WAR. (BYU 974.802 P28u)

Lee, Enoch Lawrence. INDIAN WARS IN NORTH CAROLINA, 1663-1763. Carolina Charter Tercentenary Commission, 1963. (BYU 975.602 L511i)

Lewis, Virgil Anson. THE SOLDIERY OF WEST VIRGINIA IN THE FRENCH AND INDIAN WAR; LORD DUNMORE'S WAR; THE REVOLUTION; THE LATER INDIAN WARS; THE WHISKEY INSURRECTION; THE SECOND WAR WITH ENGLAND; THE WAR WITH MEXICO, AND ADDENDA RELATING TO WEST VIRGINIANS IN THE CIVIL WAR. Baltimore: The Genealogical Publishing Co., 1967. (BYU 975.4 L589s)

MacLean, John P. AN HISTORICAL ACCOUNT OF THE SETTLEMENTS OF SCOTCH HIGHLANDERS IN AMERICA PRIOR TO THE PEACE OF 1783. Baltimore: The Genealogical Publishing Co., 1968.

MISCELLANEOUS FRENCH AND INDIAN WAR RECORDS. (GS Film 1471)

New Hampshire Adjutant-General's Office. MILITARY HISTORY OF NEW HAMPSHIRE FROM ITS SETTLEMENT IN 1623 TO THE YEAR 1861.

Nolan, James Bennett. OFFICERS AND SOLDIERS IN THE SERVICE OF THE PROVINCE OF PENNSYLVANIA, 1744-1764. Philadelphia: The University of Pennsylvania Press, 1936. (BYU 929.2 P85ng)

OFFICERS AND SOLDIERS IN THE SERVICE OF THE PROVINCE OF PENNSYLVANIA, 1744-1764. (BYU 929.2748 P38n)

PAPERS RELATING TO THE PROVINCE OF PENNSYLVANIA PRIOR TO THE REVOLUTION. (BYU 929.3748 P38n)

Pennsylvania Provincial Secretary's Office. SOLDIERS IN THE SERVICE OF THE PROVINCE OF PENNSYLVANIA. (BYU 929.3748 P38n)

Potter, Chandler. THE MILITARY HISTORY OF THE STATE OF NEW-HAMPSHIRE. 2 vols. Baltimore: The Genealogical Publishing Co., 1972.

Putnam, Isreal. LT. COL. ISREAL PUTNAM, MUSTER AND ORDERLY BOOK OF COMM. REGIMENT, HAVANAH CAMPAIGN, 1762. Flushing, New York: Filmed by the Library of Congress, n.d. (GS Film 513,823 2nd item)

Shepard, James. CONNECTICUT SOLDIERS IN THE PEQUOT WAR OF 1637. (GS Film 428,342)

Sipe, Chester Hale. THE INDIAN WARS OF PENNSYLVANIA. Harrisburg, Pennsylvania: Telegraph Press, 1931. (BYU 970.4 Si74)

Society of Colonial Wars, Illinois. LIST OF OFFICERS AND MEMBERS TOGETHER WITH A RECORD OF THE SERVICE PERFORMED BY THEIR ANCESTORS IN THE WARS OF THE COLONIES. Chicago, 1900. (GS 977.3 C4s)

Stuart, John. MEMOIR OF INDIAN WARS AND OTHER OCCURRENCES. Edited by Charles A. Stuart. New York: The New York Times, 1971. (BYU 973.26 St92M)

REVOLUTIONARY WAR

Abbott, Wilbur C. NEW YORK IN THE AMERICAN REVOLUTION. New York: Charles Scribner's Sons, 1929. (BYU 974.7 Ab29)

347

Ainsworth, Mary Bouvier. "Recently Discovered Records Relating to Revolutionary War Veterans Who Applied for Pensions Under the Act of 1792." NATIONAL GENEALOGICAL SOCIETY QUARTERLY 46 (March & June 1958). (BYU 929.05 N21 V.46)

Allen, Penelope Johnson. TENNESSEE SOLDIERS IN THE REVOLUTIONARY WAR IN THE COUNTIES OF WASHINGTON AND SULLIVAN. 1935.

Armstrong, Zella. TWENTY-FOUR HUNDRED TENNESSEE PENSIONERS, REVOLUTION, WAR OF 1812. 1937.

Bailey, J.D. SOME NEGROES OF THE AMERICAN REVOLUTION.

Bell, Annie W.B. REVOLUTIONARY WAR SOLDIERS WHO SETTLED AND LIVED IN KENTUCKY COUNTIES. 1935.

Bill, Alfred Hoyt. NEW JERSEY AND THE REVOLUTIONARY WAR. Princeton: D. Van Nostrand Co., 1964. (BYU 974.9 N46h V.11)

Blair, Anna. "A List of Revolutionary Soldiers Buried in North Carolina," HISTORICAL COLLECTIONS OF THE GEORGIA CHAPTERS, DAUGHTERS OF THE AMERICAN REVOLUTION, I (1926): 353-364.

Blair, Ruth. REVOLUTIONARY SOLDIERS' RECEIPTS FOR GEORGIA BOUNTY GRANTS. Atlanta: Foote & Davies Co., 1928. (GS Film 22353 and GS Q975.8 reg.)

Bowman, J.E. OBITUARY NOTICES OF REVOLUTIONARY SOLDIERS FROM CONNECTICUT, MAINE, PENNSYLVANIA, RHODE ISLAND, AND SOME CENTRAL, WESTERN, AND SOUTHERN STATES.

Brumbaugh, Gaius M., and Margaret Hodges. REVOLUTIONARY WAR RECORDS OF VIRGINIA. Baltimore: The Genealogical Publishing Co., 1967.

_____. REVOLUTIONARY RECORDS OF MARYLAND. Baltimore: The Genealogical Publishing Co., 1967.

Burgess, Louis Alexander. VIRGINIA SOLDIERS OF 1776. 3 vols. Richmond: Richmond Press, 1927. (BYU 929.3755 B91v)

Chamberlain, George Walter. SOLDIERS OF THE AMERICAN REVOLUTION OF LEBANON, MAINE. Weymouth, Massachusetts: Weymouth & Braintree Publishing Co., 1897. (GS 974.195/L1 M2c)

Chandler, Ora. COPIES OF PENSION PAPERS OF REVOLUTIONARY, 1812, AND INDIAN WAR SOLDIERS WHO SETTLED IN HENDERSON COUNTY, KENTUCKY. Corydan, Kentucky, n.d. (GS PB #1558)

Clark, H.A. "A Connecticut Revolutionary Roll," NEW ENGLAND HISTORICAL AND GENEALOGICAL REGISTER 60 (October 1906): 331. (BYU 929.06 N44 V.60)

Coggins, Jack. SHIPS AND SEAMEN OF THE AMERICAN REVOLUTION; CREWS, WEAPONS, GEAR, NAVAL TACTICS, AND ACTIONS OF THE WAR FOR INDEPENDENCE. Harrisburg: Stackpole Books, 1969. (BYU 973.35 C786g)

Collections of the New York Historical Society. MUSTER AND PAY ROLLS OF THE WAR OF THE REVOLUTION, 1775-1783. 2 vols. New York: The New York Historical Society, 1914-1915. (GS 974.7 B4n V.47-48; GS Film 547,506; and BYU 974.7006 N48c 1891)

Connecticut Historical Society. LISTS AND RETURNS OF CONNECTICUT
MEN IN THE REVOLUTION, 1775-1783. Edited by Albert C.
Bates. (GS 974.6 B4C V.12)
_____. ORDERLY BOOK AND JOURNALS KEPT BY CONNECT-
ICUT MEN WHILE TAKING PART IN THE AMERICAN REVOLUTION,
1775-1778. (GS 974.6 B4C V.7)
_____. ROLLS AND LISTS OF CONNECTICUT MEN IN THE
REVOLUTION, 1775-1783. (BYU 974.6 C76c V.8)
Crockett, Walter Hill. "Revolutionary Soldiers Interred in Vermont,"
PROCEEDINGS OF THE VERMONT HISTORICAL SOCIETY (1903-
1904):114-165; (1905-1906):189-203.
Dandridge, Dankse. AMERICAN PRISONERS OF THE REVOLUTION.
Baltimore: The Genealogical Publishing Co., 1967.
Daughters of the American Revolution. "Graves of Revolutionary
Soldiers," NATIONAL HISTORICAL MAGAZINE (June 1940):
36-37.
_____. "Graves of Soldiers of the American Revolution,"
ANNUAL REPORT OF THE DAUGHTERS OF THE AMERICAN
REVOLUTION, 1898. (BYU 369.1 D26a and BYU 369.1 D26b
(Index))
_____. INDIANA. Baltimore: The Genealogical Publishing
Co., 1968. (BYU 929.3772 D265)
_____. REVOLUTIONARY PENSIONERS, 1827-1831.
Washington, D.C.: National Society of the D.A.R., n.d.
_____. REVOLUTIONARY RECORDS FROM CONGRESSIONAL
REPORTS. 5 vols. Washington, D.C.: National Society of the
D.A.R., n.d.
_____. SUPPLEMENT: REVOLUTION REGISTERS, LISTS.
Washington, D.C.: National Society of the D.A.R., 1966.
(BYU Ref.4 369.1 D26p)
_____. VETERANS GRAVE REGISTRATION, LOS ANGELES
COUNTY TO 1940. 2 vols. Genealogical Records Committee.
(GS Film 844,432 3rd item)
Daughters of the American Revolution of North Carolina. ROSTER
OF SOLDIERS FROM NORTH CAROLINA IN THE AMERICAN
REVOLUTION. Baltimore: The Genealogical Publishing Co.,
1967. (BYU 929.3756 D265)
David Humphrey's Branch, Connecticut Society. REVOLUTIONARY
CHARACTERS OF NEW HAVEN. 1911.
DOCUMENTS RELATING TO THE REVOLUTIONARY HISTORY OF
THE STATE OF NEW JERSEY. 5 vols. Trenton: J.L. Murphy
Publishing Co., 1901-1917.
Draper, Belle (Merrill). HONOR ROLL OF MASSACHUSETTS
PATRIOTS HERETOFORE UNKNOWN, BEING A LIST OF MEN
AND WOMEN WHO LOANED MONEY TO THE FEDERAL
GOVERNMENT DURING THE YEARS 1777-1779. Boston, 1899.
Duncan, Louis C. MEDICAL MEN IN THE AMERICAN REVOLUTION,
1775-1783. 1931.
Eckenrode, J.J. LIST OF REVOLUTIONARY SOLDIERS OF VIRGINIA.
2 vols. 1931.

Egle, William Henry. OLD RIGHTS, PROPRIETORY RIGHTS, VIRGINIA ENTRIES, AND SOLDIERS ENTITLED TO DONATION LANDS. (BYU 333.16 Eg530)

_____. PENNSYLVANIA WOMEN IN THE AMERICAN REVOLUTION. Cottonport, Louisiana: Polyanthose, 1972. (BYU 920.7 Eg53p)

Ervin, Sara Sullivan, ed. SOUTH CAROLINIANS IN THE REVOLUTION. Baltimore: The Genealogical Publishing Co., 1965. (BYU 929.3757 Er93s)

Flagg, Charles Alcott. AN ALPHABETICAL INDEX OF REVOLUTIONARY PENSIONERS LIVING IN MAINE. Baltimore: The Genealogical Publishing Co., 1967. (GS 974.1 M24f 1968)

The Genealogical Society of The Church of Jesus Christ of Latter-day Saints. A GENERAL INDEX TO A CENSUS OF PENSIONERS FOR REVOLUTIONARY OR MILITARY SERVICE, 1840. Baltimore: The Genealogical Publishing Co., 1965. (GS 973 X2pc; GS Film 219,463; and BYU Ref.4 929.373 Un3c)

Georgia Department of Archives and History. GEORGIA ROSTER OF THE REVOLUTION. Atlanta: Index Printing Co., 1920. (GS Film 547,588)

Giller, Sadye. CORRECTIONS TO THE INDEX OF REVOLUTIONARY WAR PENSION APPLICATIONS. Washington, D.C., 1965. (BYU Ref.4 929.173 N213s #31)

Godfrey, Carlos E. THE COMMANDER-IN-CHIEF'S GUARD: REVOLUTIONARY WAR. Baltimore: The Genealogical Publishing Co., 1972.

Goodrich, John E. ROLLS OF THE SOLDIERS IN THE REVOLUTIONARY WAR, 1775-1783. Rutland, Vermont, 1904.

Goold, Nathan. HISTORY OF COLONEL EDMUND PHINNEY'S EIGHTEENTH CONTINENTAL REGIMENT: TWELVE MONTH'S SERVICE IN 1776 WITH COMPLETE MUSTER ROLLS OF THE COMPANIES. Portland, Maine: The Thurston Print, 1898. (GS PB #362)

Gould, Edward Kalloch. REVOLUTIONARY PENSIONERS OF KNOX COUNTY, MAINE. Rockland, Maine: The Courier-Gazette, 1935. (BYU q974.153 M24g)

"Green Mountain Boys," THE VERMONT ANTIQUARIAN, 3:138-143.

Gwathmey, John Hastings. HISTORICAL REGISTER OF VIRGINIANS IN THE REVOLUTION: SOLDIERS, SAILORS, MARINES, 1775-1783. Richmond: The Dietz Press, 1938. (BYU 929.3755 G995h)

Hammond, Isaac Weare. ROLLS OF THE SOLDIERS OF THE REVOLUTIONARY WAR. 4 vols. Concord, 1885-1889.

Headley, Joel Tyler. THE CHAPLAINS AND CLERGY OF THE REVOLUTION. New York, 1864.

_____. WASHINGTON AND THE GENERALS OF THE AMERICAN REVOLUTION. Philadelphia: J.B. Lippincott, 1859. (BYU 923.11 H34)

Hedden, J.S. CONNECTICUT SOLDIERS OF 1775-1783 BURIED IN NEW HAVEN, CONNECTICUT. 1934.

_____. NEW HAVEN COUNTY REVOLUTIONARY GRAVES. 1932.

Herbert, Charles. A RELIC OF THE REVOLUTION. Boston:
    C.H. Pierce, 1847. (BYU 973.371 H415r)
Hinman, Royal Ralph. A HISTORICAL COLLECTION FROM
    OFFICIAL RECORDS, FILES, OF THE PART SUSTAINED BY
    CONNECTICUT DURING THE REVOLUTION. 1842. (BYU 974.603
    H593h)
Historical Records Survey. INDEX OF OFFICIAL REGISTER OF THE
    MEN OF NEW JERSEY IN THE REVOLUTIONARY WAR. Newark,
    New Jersey: Works Progress Administration, 1941. (BYU
    929.3749 H627i and BYU 929.059 Un3n)
House, Charles J. NAMES OF SOLDIERS OF THE AMERICAN
    REVOLUTION WHO APPLIED FOR STATE BOUNTY UNDER
    RESOLVES OF MARCH 17, 1835, MARCH 24, 1836, AND
    MARCH 20, 1836, AS APPEARS OF RECORD IN THE LAND
    OFFICE. Baltimore: The Genealogical Publishing Co., 1967.
    (BYU 929.3741 H816n and GS 974.1 M2h)
Houston, Martha Lou. SIX HUNDRED REVOLUTIONARY SOLDIERS
    LIVING IN GEORGIA IN 1827-1828. Washington, D.C., 1932.
    (GS PB #601)
Houts, Alice. REVOLUTIONARY SOLDIERS BURIED IN MISSOURI.
    Kansas City, Missouri, 1966. (BYU 929.3778 H819)
Hoyt, Max Ellsworth, et al. INDEX OF REVOLUTIONARY WAR
    PENSION APPLICATIONS. Washington, D.C.: The National
    Genealogical Society, 1966. (BYU Ref.4 929.173 N213s #32)
Jones, Alexander. THE CYMRY OF '76; OR, WELSHMEN AND
    THEIR DESCENDANTS OF THE AMERICAN REVOLUTION.
    2nd ed. Baltimore: The Genealogical Publishing Co., 1968.
Jones, Chester. NEW JERSEY REVOLUTIONARY WAR VETERANS.
    New Brunswick, New Jersey: Filmed by The Genealogical
    Society, 1971. (GS Film 855,165-855,185)
Judd, Sylvester. CONNECTICUT ARCHIVES FOR THE REVOLUTIONARY
    WAR, 1763-1820. (GS Film 1462)
Kaminkow, Marion, and Jack Kaminkow. MARINERS OF THE
    AMERICAN REVOLUTION. Baltimore: Magna Carta Book Co.,
    1967. (GS 973 M25k and BYU 929.373 K128m)
Knight, Lucian L. GEORGIA'S ROSTER OF THE REVOLUTION.
    Baltimore: The Genealogical Publishing Co., 1967. (GS 975.8
    M23k)
LIST OF AMERICAN SEAMEN WITH NAME AND VITAL INFORMATION
    ABOUT EACH OF PROVIDENCE DISTRICT, PURSUANT TO THE
    ACT FOR AND PROTECTION OF AMERICAN SEAMEN, FOUND
    AT THE U.S. CUSTOMS HOUSE, PROVIDENCE, RHODE ISLAND -
    1829 THROUGH 1857. (GS Film 5313)
LIST OF HESSIAN PRISONERS, WAR OF THE REVOLUTION. (GS
    Film 5058)
Maryland Historical Society. MUSTER ROLLS AND OTHER RECORDS
    OF SERVICE OF TROOPS IN THE AMERICAN REVOLUTION,
    1775-1783. Baltimore: The Genealogical Publishing Co., 1972.
Massachusetts Secretary of the Commonwealth. MASSACHUSETTS
    SOLDIERS AND SAILORS OF THE REVOLUTIONARY WAR. 17
    vols. Boston: Wright & Potter Printing Co., State Printers,
    1896-1908. (BYU 929.374 M38g)

Mather, Frederic Gregory. THE REFUGEES OF 1776 FROM LONG ISLAND TO CONNECTICUT. Baltimore: The Genealogical Publishing Co., 1972. (BYU 974.703 M42r)

McAllister, Joseph Thompson. VIRGINIA MILITIA IN THE REVOLUTIONARY WAR. Hot Springs, Virginia: McAllister Publishing Co., 1913.

McCall, Ettie. ROSTER OF REVOLUTIONARY SOLDIERS IN GEORGIA. 3 vols. Baltimore: The Genealogical Publishing Co., 1968. (GS Film 2328; GS 975.8 M23m; and BYU 929.3758 M124r)

McGhee, Lucy. MARYLAND REVOLUTIONARY PENSIONERS, WAR OF 1812 AND THE INDIAN WARS. 1962.

Mell, Patrick Hues. REVOLUTIONARY SOLDIERS BURIED IN ALABAMA. Montgomery, 1904. (GS 976.1 M2m)

"The Men with Ethan Allen at Ticonderoga," THE VERMONT ANTIQUARIAN, 3:138-43.

Ministère des Affaires Etrangères, France. LES COMBATTANTS FRANCAIS DE LA GUERRE AMERICAINE, 1778-1783. (FRENCH SOLDIERS IN THE REVOLUTIONARY WAR.) Baltimore: The Genealogical Publishing Co., 1969.

New Jersey Adjutant-General's Office. RECORDS OF OFFICERS AND MEN OF NEW JERSEY IN WARS, 1791-1815. Baltimore: The Genealogical Publishing Co., 1970. (GS 974.9 M25no 1970)

New Jersey State Library. ALPHABETICAL LIST OF OFFICERS IN THE REVOLUTION IN NEW JERSEY. Trenton: Filmed by The Genealogical Society, 1969. (GS Film 573,334 2nd item)

New York Comptroller's Office. NEW YORK IN THE REVOLUTION AS A COLONY AND A STATE. 2 vols. Albany, New York: J.B. Lyon Co., 1901-1904. (BYU 929.3747 N489n)

New York Division of Archives. THE AMERICAN REVOLUTION IN NEW YORK: ITS POLITICAL, SOCIAL, AND ECONOMIC SIGNIFICANCE. Albany, New York: The University of the State of New York, 1926. (BYU 974.7 N42a)

NEW YORK PENSION ROLL (REVOLUTIONARY WAR), 1815-1840. (GS Film 832,846 1st item)

New York Secretary of State. THE BALLOTING BOOK, AND OTHER DOCUMENTS RELATING TO THE MILITARY BOUNTY LANDS IN THE STATE OF NEW YORK. Albany, New York: Packard & Benthuysen, 1825. (BYU Film 900 #255)

Newman, Harry Wright. MARYLAND REVOLUTIONARY RECORDS. Baltimore: The Genealogical Publishing Co., 1967. (BYU 929.3752 N464m and GS 975.2 M2n 1967)

North Carolina State Archives. REGISTER OF CONTINENTAL LINE FROM NORTH CAROLINA.

O'Byrne, Mrs. Roscoe C. ROSTER OF SOLDIERS AND PATRIOTS OF THE AMERICAN REVOLUTION BURIED IN INDIANA. Baltimore: The Genealogical Publishing Co., 1968.

Ohio Adjutant-General's Office. GRAVE REGISTRATIONS OF SOLDIERS BURIED IN OHIO. (GS Film 182,702-182,793)

_____. THE OFFICIAL ROSTER OF THE SOLDIERS OF THE
    AMERICAN REVOLUTION BURIED IN THE STATE OF OHIO.
    3 vols. Columbus, Ohio: The F.J. Heer Printing Co., 1929-1959.
    (BYU 929.3771 Oh3o)
Owen, Thomas M. REVOLUTIONARY SOLDIERS IN ALABAMA.
    Baltimore: The Genealogical Publishing Co., 1967.
PENSION RECORDS OF REVOLUTIONARY SOLDIERS OF SOUTH
    CAROLINA. Lane Historical Collection.
Perkins, E.P. WEST VIRGINIA REVOLUTIONARY PENSIONS, vol.
    1. 1935.
Peterson, Clarence Stewart. KNOWN MILITARY DEAD DURING THE
    AMERICAN REVOLUTIONARY WAR, 1775-1783. Baltimore:
    The Genealogical Publishing Co., 1967. (BYU 973.36 P44k)
Quisenberry, Anderson C. REVOLUTIONARY SOLDIERS IN KENTUCKY.
    Baltimore: The Genealogical Publishing Co., 1968. (BYU 973.345
    Q48r)
Reddy, Anne Walker. WEST VIRGINIA REVOLUTIONARY ANCESTORS
    WHOSE SERVICES WERE NON-MILITARY AND WHOSE NAMES,
    THEREFORE, DO NOT APPEAR IN REVOLUTIONARY INDEXES
    OF SOLDIERS AND SAILORS. Baltimore: The Genealogical
    Publishing Co., 1963. (BYU 929.3754 R246w)
Revill, Janie. COPY OF THE ORIGINAL INDEX BOOK SHOWING
    THE REVOLUTIONARY CLAIMS FILED IN SOUTH CAROLINA.
    Baltimore: The Genealogical Publishing Co., 1969.
REVOLUTIONARY WAR INDEX, A COMPILATION OF REVOLUTIONARY
    WAR SLIPS AND DOCUMENTED MATERIALS FROM OTHER
    SOURCES. (GS Film 568,699-568,724; 569,421-569,425)
REVOLUTIONARY WAR MANUSCRIPTS, NEW JERSEY NUMBERS
    1-10811. (GS Film 579,876-579,883; 580,786-580,807)
"Revolutionary War Pay Roll, 1777," NATIONAL GENEALOGICAL
    SOCIETY QUARTERLY 9 (October 1920): 45. (BYU 929.05 N21
    V.9)
REVOLUTIONARY WAR RECORDS OF NEW JERSEY. (GS Film
    573,001-573,080; 573,314-573,320)
REVOLUTIONARY WAR SLIPS, SINGLE CITATIONS OF THE NEW
    JERSEY DEPARTMENT OF DEFENSE MATERIALS. (GS Film
    568,988-568,996; 569,426-569,456; 569,680-569,697; 570,170-
    570,187; 571,307-571,324; 573,036-573,060)
Richards, J.E. HONOR ROLL OF LITCHFIELD COUNTY REVOLU-
    TIONARY SOLDIERS. 1912.
Rosengarten, Joseph George. AMERICAN HISTORY FROM GERMAN
    ARCHIVES WITH REFERENCE TO THE GERMAN SOLDIERS
    IN THE REVOLUTION AND FRANKLIN'S VISIT TO GERMANY.
    Lancaster, Pennsylvania: The Pennsylvania-German Society,
    1904.
Saffell, W.T.R. RECORDS OF THE REVOLUTIONARY WAR. 3rd
    ed. Baltimore: The Genealogical Publishing Co., 1969. (BYU
    973.3 Sal7r and GS 973 M26s)
South Carolina Treasury. STUB ENTRIES OF INDENTS ISSUED IN
    PAYMENT OF CLAIMS AGAINST SOUTH CAROLINA GROWING
    OUT OF THE REVOLUTION. Columbia, 1910.

Steiny, Bernard C. WESTERN MARYLAND IN THE REVOLUTION. New York: Johns Hopkins University Press, 1902.

Stewart, Robert Armistead. THE HISTORY OF VIRGINIA'S NAVY OF THE REVOLUTION. 1934.

Stryker, William S. OFFICIAL ROSTER OF THE OFFICERS AND MEN OF NEW JERSEY IN THE REVOLUTIONARY WAR. Baltimore: The Genealogical Publishing Co., 1967. (BYU 929. 3749 N489 and GS 974.9 M23n)

Tate, Mrs. Percy L. ROSTER AND ANCESTRAL ROLL; MAINE DAUGHTERS OF THE AMERICAN REVOLUTION AND THE LIST OF MAINE SOLDIERS AT VALLEY FORGE, 1777-1778. 1948. (GS 974.1 C4d)

Tower, J.M., M.D. THE MEDICAL MEN OF THE REVOLUTION. Philadelphia, 1876.

U.S. Bureau of Census. A CENSUS OF PENSIONERS FOR REVOLU- TIONARY OR MILITARY SERVICES. Baltimore: The Genealog- ical Publishing Co., 1967. (GS 973 X2pc; GS Film 002,321; GS Film 594,466; GS Film 816,370; and BYU Ref.4 929.373 Un3c 1841)

U.S. Bureau of Pensions. PENSION RECORDS OF THE REVOLU- TIONARY SOLDIERS FROM CONNECTICUT. Washington, 1919.

U.S. Congress, House. DIGESTED SUMMARY AND ALPHABETICAL LIST OF PRIVATE CLAIMS. Baltimore: The Genealogical Publishing Co., 1970. (BYU Ref.4 929.373 Un3d V.1-3)

U.S. Congress, Senate. LIST OF THE NAMES OF SUCH OFFICERS AND SOLDIERS OF THE REVOLUTIONARY ARMY AS HAVE ACQUIRED A RIGHT TO LANDS FROM THE UNITED STATES AND WHO HAVE NOT YET APPLIED THEREFOR. Washington, D.C., 1828.

U.S. General Land Office. REGISTERS OF REVOLUTIONARY WAR LAND WARRANTS, ACT OF 1788; MILITARY DISTRICT OF OHIO, 1789-1805. (GS Film 847,553)

U.S. Secretary of War. WAR OF THE REVOLUTION. (BYU Documents Collection Serial Set #249 and #514)

U.S. Veterans Administration. SELECTED RECORDS FROM REVOLUTIONARY WAR PENSION AND BOUNTY-LAND WARRANT APPLICATION FILES. Washington, D.C.: National Archives Microfilm Publications, 1969. (GS Film 840,256-840, 406)

U.S. War Department. CLAIMS AGAINST THE U.S. GOVERNMENT FOR SERVICES OF THE MILITIA OF GEORGIA, IN THE YEARS 1793 AND 1794. (BYU Documents Collection Serial Set #6 and #27)

_____. PENSIONERS OF REVOLUTIONARY WAR - STRUCK OFF THE ROLL. Baltimore: The Genealogical Publishing Co., 1969. (GS 973 M24usa)

_____. REVOLUTIONARY PENSIONERS; A TRANSCRIPT OF THE PENSION LIST OF THE UNITED STATES FOR 1873. Baltimore: Southern Book Co., 1959. (BYU Ref.4 929.373 Un3pr)

_____. REVOLUTIONARY WAR ROLLS, 1775-1783.
Washington, D.C.: National Archives Microfilm Publications,
1957. (GS Film 830,280-830,417)

Virginia Department of Archives and History. LIST OF THE REVOLU-
TIONARY SOLDIERS OF VIRGINIA. Richmond: Virginia State
Library, 1913.

von Eelking, Max. THE GERMAN ALLIED TROOPS IN THE NORTH
AMERICAN WAR OF INDEPENDENCE, 1776-1783. Baltimore:
The Genealogical Publishing Co., 1969.

Waters, Margaret R., REVOLUTIONARY SOLDIERS BURIED IN
INDIANA WITH SUPPLEMENT. 2 vols. Baltimore: The
Genealogical Publishing Co., 1970. (BYU 929.3772 W317r)

Welch, Alice T. FAMILY RECORDS: MISSISSIPPI REVOLUTIONARY
SOLDIERS. Baltimore: The Genealogical Publishing Co., 1956.

Whiteley, William Gustavus. THE REVOLUTIONARY SOLDIERS OF
DELAWARE. Wilmington, 1896.

Wilson, Samuel Mackay. CATALOGUE OF REVOLUTIONARY SOLDIERS
AND SAILORS OF THE COMMONWEALTH OF VIRGINIA TO
WHOM LAND BOUNTY WARRANTS WERE GRANTED BY VIRGINIA
FOR MILITARY SERVICES IN THE WAR FOR INDEPENDENCE.
Baltimore: Southern Book Co., 1953. (BYU 929.3755 W697c)

Winge, Elizabeth B. NORFOLK COUNTY, VIRGINIA (NOW CHESA-
PEAKE CITY, VIRGINIA) REVOLUTIONARY WAR AND WAR OF
1812 APPLICATIONS FOR PENSIONS, BOUNTY LAND WARRANTS,
AND HEIRS OF DECEASED PENSIONERS. Norfolk, Virginia,
1964. (BYU 929.37552 W757n)

WAR OF 1812

Barton, Henry W. TEXAS VOLUNTEERS IN THE MEXICAN WAR.
Wichita Falls, Texas: Texian Press, 1970. (BYU 973.62 B285t)

Bowen, Daniel. A HISTORY OF PHILADELPHIA. Philadelphia, 1820.
(BYU 974.811 B675h)

Carr, Deborah Edith (Walldridge). INDEX TO CERTIFIED COPY LIST
OF AMERICAN PRISONERS OF WAR, 1812-1815. n.p.: United
States Daughters of 1812, 1924. (GS PBA #116)

Clark, Byron N. A LIST OF PENSIONERS OF THE WAR OF 1812
(VERMONT CLAIMANTS). Baltimore: The Genealogical Publishing Co., 1969.

Connecticut General Assembly. RECORD OF SERVICE OF CONNECT-
ICUT MEN IN THE REVOLUTION, THE WAR OF 1812, AND THE
MEXICAN WAR. 1889.

Diefenbach, Mrs. H.B. INDEX TO THE GRAVE RECORDS OF SOL-
DIERS OF THE WAR OF 1812 BURIED IN OHIO. (GS 977.1 V22d)

Frost, John. THE MEXICAN WAR AND ITS WARRIORS. New Haven:
H. Mansfield, 1848. (BYU 973.62 F92m)

Hitsman, J. McKay. THE INCREDIBLE WAR OF 1812. (BYU 973.523
H638i)

Illinois Adjutant-General's Office. RECORD OF SERVICES OF
ILLINOIS SOLDIERS IN THE BLACK HAWK WAR, 1831-1832,
AND IN THE MEXICAN WAR, 1846-1848.

Indiana Adjutant-General's Office. INDIANA IN THE MEXICAN WAR.
Indianapolis: W.B. Burford, 1908. (BYU 973.62 In2i)

Isaac, George. HEROES AND INCIDENTS OF THE MEXICAN WAR.
n.p.: Review Publishing Co., 1903. (BYU Hafen 973.62 Islh)

Kentucky Adjutant-General's Office. REPORT OF THE ADJUTANT
GENERAL OF KENTUCKY - SOLDIERS OF THE WAR OF 1812.
Frankfort, 1891.

Kentucky Historical Society. COMMISSIONED OFFICERS IN THE
WAR OF 1812. ABRELL TO ZURNETTE. (GS Film 482,878)

Linn, John B., and William H. Egle. MUSTER ROLLS OF THE
PENNSYLVANIA VOLUNTEERS IN THE WAR OF 1812-1814.
Baltimore: The Genealogical Publishing Co., 1967. (BYU 929.
3748 M978)

Louisiana Adjutant-General's Office. THE COMPILED SERVICE
RECORDS OF LOUISIANIANS IN THE WAR OF 1812.

Marine, William N. BRITISH INVASION OF MARYLAND, 1812-1815.
Baltimore, 1913.

Marshall, A.F. SOLDIERS OF 1812, ETC. WHOSE BOUNTY LAND
GRANTS WERE LOCATED IN WOODFORD COUNTY, ILLINOIS.
(GS Film 823,572 and GS 977.3 AL #1)

Marshall, Donald William. THE MISSISSIPPI SAINTS AND SICK
DETACHMENTS OF THE MORMON BATTALION, WINTER,
1846-1847. (BYU 979.205 T344 V.2)

Massachusetts Adjutant-General's Office. RECORDS OF MASSACHU-
SETTS VOLUNTEER MILITIA CALLED OUT BY THE GOVERNOR
OF MASSACHUSETTS TO SUPPRESS A THREATENED INVASION
DURING THE WAR OF 1812-1814. Published by Brig. Genl.
Gardner W. Pearson, the Adjutant General of Massachusetts, 1913.

THE MEXICAN WAR AND ITS HEROES. Philadelphia: J.B. Lippincott
& Co., 1857. (BYU 973.62 M574)

Miller, Alice Turner. SOLDIERS OF THE WAR OF 1812 WHO DIED
IN MICHIGAN. Ithaca, Michigan, 1962. (GS 977.4 M23m; GS
Film 844,961; and GS Supp 977.4 M23m)

Mississippi Department of Archives and History. ROSTER OF
MISSISSIPPI MEN WHO SERVED IN THE WAR OF 1812, AND
IN THE MEXICAN WAR.

Nebraska Secretary of State. ROSTER OF SOLDIERS, SAILORS
AND MARINES OF THE WAR OF 1812, THE MEXICAN WAR,
AND THE WAR OF THE REBELLION RESIDING IN NEBRASKA,
JUNE 1, 1891. Lincoln: State Journal Co., 1892. (GS 978.2
M23n and GS Film 844,966 4th item)

New Jersey State Library. NEW JERSEY IN THE WAR OF 1812,
BOOKS 1-52. Trenton: Filmed by The Genealogical Society,
1969. (GS Film 573,377-573,351)

_____. NEW JERSEY PENSIONERS, WAR OF 1812.
Trenton: Filmed by The Genealogical Society, 1969. (GS Film
578,153-578,154)

New York Adjutant-General's Office. INDEX OF AWARDS ON
CLAIMS OF THE SOLDIERS OF THE WAR OF 1812. Baltimore:
The Genealogical Publishing Co., 1969.

North Carolina Adjutant-General's Office. MUSTER ROLLS OF THE
SOLDIERS OF THE WAR OF 1812 DETACHED FROM THE
MILITIA OF NORTH CAROLINA IN 1812 AND 1814. Winston-
Salem, North Carolina: Barber Printing Co., 1969.

Ohio Adjutant-General's Office. ROSTER OF OHIO SOLDIERS IN THE
WAR OF 1812. Baltimore: The Genealogical Publishing Co.,
1968. (BYU 973.52741 Oh3r)

_____. VETERAN'S AFFAIRS, STATE HOUSE, COLUMBUS.

Pennsylvania Archives. MUSTER ROLLS OF THE PENNSYLVANIA
VOLUNTEERS IN THE WAR OF 1812-1814. Baltimore: The
Genealogical Publishing Co., 1967. (BYU 929.3748 M978 Ser.2
V.12)

Pennsylvania Historical and Museum Commission. PENNSYLVANIA
RECORDS COVERING THE WAR OF 1812.

Rowland, Mrs. Dunbar. MISSISSIPPI TERRITORY IN THE WAR OF
1812. Baltimore: The Genealogical Publishing Co., 1968.

Sapio, Victor A. PENNSYLVANIA AND THE WAR OF 1812. Lexington:
The University of Kentucky Press, 1970. (BYU 973.52 Sa67p)

South Carolina Confederate Relic Room and Museum. ROSTER OF
THE SOUTH CAROLINA MEN WHO SERVED IN THE WAR OF
1812.

U.S. Adjutant-General's Office. MUSTER PAY AND RECEIPT ROLLS
OF INDIANA TERRITORY VOLUNTEERS OR MILITIA OF THE
PERIOD OF THE WAR OF 1812. 4 vols.

U.S. Daughters of 1812. HEROES OF 1812.

U.S. National Archives. THE COMPILED SERVICE RECORDS OF
LOUISIANIANS AND THE INDEX.

_____. COMPILED SERVICE RECORDS OF VOLUNTEER
SOLDIERS WHO SERVED DURING THE MEXICAN WAR IN
MORMON ORGANIZATIONS. Washington, D.C.: National
Archives Microfilm Publications, 1961. (GS Film 536,226-536,
227; 471,465; and BYU Film RG94 M351 pts.1-3)

_____. INDEX TO WAR OF 1812 PENSION APPLICATION
FILES. Washington, D.C.: National Archives Microfilm Publications, 1960. (GS Film 840,431-840,500; 847,501-847,532;
and BYU Film RG15 M313 pts.1-102)

_____. MEXICAN WAR SERVICE RECORDS, 1845-1877.
Washington, D.C.: National Archives Microfilm Publications,
1961. (GS Film 471,465-471,583; 536,241)

U.S. Veterans Administration. MEXICAN WAR INDEX TO PENSION
FILES, 1887-1926. Washington, D.C.: The National Archives,
1967. (GS Film 537,000-537,013 and BYU Film RG15 T317 pts.
1-14)

_____. OLD WAR INDEX TO PENSION FILES, 1815-1926.
Washington, D.C.: The National Archives, 1959. (GS Film
821,603-821,609 and BYU Film RG15 T316 pts.1-7)

Vermont Adjutant-General's Office. ROSTER OF SOLDIERS IN THE
WAR OF 1812-1814. Published by Herbert T. Johnson, the
Adjutant General, 1933.

Virginia State Library. MUSTER ROLLS OF THE VIRGINIA MILITIA
IN THE WAR OF 1812. 1852.

_____. PAY ROLLS OF MILITIA ENTITLED TO LAND
   BOUNTY UNDER THE ACT OF CONGRESS 28 SEPTEMBER 1850,
   1851.
WAR OF 1812. (BYU 973.52447 N489p)
Welch, Richard W. MICHIGAN IN THE MEXICAN WARS. 1967.
   (GS 977.4 M23w)
Wilder, Minnie S. KENTUCKY SOLDIERS OF THE WAR OF 1812.
   Baltimore: The Genealogical Publishing Co., 1969.

CIVIL WAR
Arkansas Adjutant-General's Office (Union). REPORT OF THE ADJU-
   TANT GENERAL (A.W. BISHOP) OF ARKANSAS FOR THE PERIOD
   OF THE LATE REBELLION, AND TO NOVEMBER 1, 1866.
   Washington, 1867.
Army Department of Northern Virginia. THE APPOMATTOX
   ROSTER. New York: The Antiquarian Press, 1962. (BYU 929.
   3755 C76a)
Barrett, John Gilchrist. THE CIVIL WAR IN NORTH CAROLINA.
   Chapel Hill: The University of North Carolina Press, 1963.
   (BYU 975.603 B275c)
Bates, F.A. GRAVES-MEMOIRS OF THE CIVIL WAR. Edinburgh:
   William Blackwood and Sons, 1927.
Beatty, John. MEMOIRS OF A VOLUNTEER, 1861-1863. New York:
   W.W. Norton & Co., 1946. (BYU 973.781 B38m)
Booth, Andrew B., Commissioner of Louisiana Military Records.
   RECORDS OF LOUISIANA CONFEDERATE SOLDIERS AND
   LOUISIANA CONFEDERATE COMMANDS. 3 vols. 1920.
California Adjutant-General's Office. RECORDS OF CALIFORNIA
   MEN IN THE WAR OF THE REBELLION, 1861 TO 1867. Sacra-
   mento: State Office, 1890. (BYU 979.404 C128r)
Candler, Allen D. THE CONFEDERATE RECORDS OF THE STATE
   OF GEORGIA. Atlanta: C.P. Byrd, State Printer, 1909-1911.
   (GS 975.8 M26c)
Chemung County Historical Society. LIST OF CONFEDERATE
   SOLDIERS BURIED IN WOODLAWN CEMETERY, ELMIRA,
   NEW YORK. Elmira, New York, n.d. (GS Film 896,803 3rd
   item)
CIVIL WAR INDEX. (BYU Ref. 4 973.7 C4oi)
CIVIL WAR MONOGRAPHS. (BYU 973.7 C49m)
CIVIL WAR ROSTER. (BYU 973.7 C49r)
CIVIL WAR VETERANS BURIED IN WICHITA, TEXAS. Filmed by
   The Genealogical Society. (GS 976.4745 V22 and GS Film 823,
   664 10th item)
COMPLETE RECORD OF THE NAMES OF ALL THE SOLDIERS AND
   OFFICERS IN THE MILITARY SERVICE. Filmed by The
   Genealogical Society. (GS Film 482,217)
CONFEDERATE NAVAL AND MARINE PERSONNEL RECORDS.
   Washington, D.C.: Microcopy no. 26, n.d. (GS Film 25940)
CONFEDERATE SOLDIERS, SAILORS AND CIVILIANS WHO DIED
   AS PRISONERS OF WAR AT CAMP DOUGLAS, CHICAGO,
   ILLINOIS. Kalamazoo, Michigan: Edgar Gray Publications,
   n.d. (GS 977.31/CL V23c)

Connecticut Adjutant-General's Office. CATALOGUE OF CONNECTICUT VOLUNTEER ORGANIZATIONS (INFANTRY, CAVALRY AND ARTILLARY) IN THE SERVICE OF U.S., 1861-1865. Published by order of C.M. Ingersoll. (GS 974.6 M25cc)

_____. CATALOGUE OF CONNECTICUT VOLUNTEER ORGANIZATIONS WITH ADDITIONAL ENLISTMENTS AND CASUALTIES TO JULY 1, 1864. (GS 974.6 M25cc 1864)

_____. PENSION RECORDS FOR CONNECTICUT MEN IN THE CIVIL WAR, 1861-1865.

Croffut, William Augustus. THE MILITARY AND CIVIL HISTORY OF CONNECTICUT DURING THE WAR OF 1861-1865. (GS 974.6 M25c and BYU 973.74 C874m)

Currie, George E. WARFARE ALONG THE MISSISSIPPI. Clarke Historical Collection. Mount Pleasant: Central Michigan University Press, 1961. (BYU 973.73 C93w)

Delaware County Clerk's Office. U.S. REGIMENT RECORDS, NEW YORK, 1862-1864. Delhi, New York: Filmed by Reproduction Systems, 1970. (GS Film 831,889 2nd item)

DISCHARGE PAPERS OF MAINE SOLDIERS, 1863-1865. Auburn, Maine: Filmed by The Genealogical Society, 1956. (GS Film 2765)

Dunlop, William S. LEE'S SHARPSHOOTERS. Little Rock, Arkansas: Tunnah E. Pittard, Printers, 1899. (BYU 973.742 (D921L)

Dyer, Frederick Henry. A COMPENDIUM OF THE WAR OF THE REBELLION, COMPILED FROM OFFICIAL RECORDS OF THE FEDERAL AND CONFEDERATE ARMY AND OTHER SOURCES. New York: Yesoloff, 1959.

Foster, John Y. NEW JERSEY AND THE REBELLION. Newark: Martin R. Dennis & Co., 1868. (BYU 973.74 F814n)

Gaines, George Towns. FIGHTING TENNESSEANS. (BYU 976.8 G127f)

Georgia Department of Archives and History. CONFEDERATE PENSION ROLLS. Atlanta: Filmed by the State of Georgia, 1963. (GS Film 315,678-323,742)

Georgia Historical Society. CONFEDERATE STATE OF AMERICA SERVICE RECORDS, MILITARY AND NAVAL. Savannah: Georgia Historical Society, 1938. (GS Film 30192)

Gilman, C. Malcomb. NEW JERSEY INFANTRY - STORY OF JERSEY BLUES. Trenton: Trenton Printing Co., 1962. (BYU 356 G42s)

Hall, Charles Bryan. MILITARY RECORDS OF GENERAL OFFICERS OF THE CONFEDERATE STATES OF AMERICA. New York: Lockwood Press, 1898. (BYU q923.5 H13m)

Hall, Granville Davisson. LEE'S INVASION OF NORTHWEST VIRGINIA IN 1861. Chicago: Mayer and Miller Co., 1911. (BYU 975.4 H142L)

Henderson, Lillian. ROSTER OF THE CONFEDERATE SOLDIERS OF GEORGIA, 1861-1865. Haperville, Georgia: Longings & Porter, 1960-1964. (GS 975.8 M22h)

Hicken, Victor. ILLINOIS IN THE CIVIL WAR. Urbana: The University of Illinois Press, 1966. (BYU 973.7473 H525i)

Hopkins, Owen Johnston. UNDER THE FLAG OF THE NATION:
DIARIES AND LETTERS OF A YANKEE VOLUNTEER IN THE
CIVIL WAR. Columbus: Ohio State University Press, 1961.
(BYU 973.7 Oh3p)

Illinois Adjutant-General's Office. REPORT OF THE ADJUTANT
GENERAL OF THE STATE OF ILLINOIS, 1861-1866. 9 vols.
Springfield, Illinois: Phillips Brothers, 1900-1902.

Indiana Adjutant-General's Office. INDIANA IN THE WAR. Indianapolis: A.H. Conner, 1865-1869. (BYU 353.9772 In2)

Iowa Adjutant-General's Office. ROSTER AND RECORD OF IOWA
SOLDIERS IN THE WAR OF THE REBELLION. 6 vols. Des
Moines: E.H. English, State Printer, 1908-1911. (BYU 929.
3777 Io9r)

Kansas Adjutant-General's Office. REPORT OF THE ADJUTANT
GENERAL (C.K. HOLLIDAY) DECEMBER 31, 1864. Leavenworth, 1865.

_____. REPORT OF THE ADJUTANT GENERAL (T.J.
ANDERSON) OF THE STATE OF KANSAS IN 1861-1865. 2 vols.
1867-1870.

Kansas State Historical Society. REGISTRATION LISTS OF ALL
VETERANS OF CIVIL WAR DUE TO ENROLLMENT.

Katz, Irving I. THE JEWISH SOLDIER FROM MICHIGAN IN THE
CIVIL WAR. Columbus: Ohio State University Press, 1961.
(GS 977.4 M25k)

Kenly, John Reese. MEMOIRS OF A MARYLAND VOLUNTEER.
Philadelphia: J.B. Lippincott & Co., 1873. (BYU 973.628
K356m)

Kentucky Adjutant-General's Office. REPORT ON THE STATE OF
KENTUCKY, CONFEDERATE KENTUCKY VOLUNTEERS WAR,
1861-1865. (GS Film 467,975 3rd item)

Kentucky Adjutant-General's Office (Union). REPORT OF THE
ADJUTANT GENERAL (D.W. LINDSEY), 1861-1866. 2 vols.
Frankfort, 1866-1867.

Laney, Clara. UNION COUNTY CEMETERIES, 1910-1914, AND A
ROSTER OF CONFEDERATE AND REVOLUTIONARY SOLDIERS.
1958. (BYU 929.3756 L248u)

Langley, Elizabeth B. TANEY COUNTY, MISSOURI SOLDIERS WHO
FOUGHT IN THE CIVIL WAR INCLUDING SOLDIERS OF SOUTH-
WEST MISSOURI AND NORTHWEST ARKANSAS; ALSO THE
CHEROKEES UNDER STAND WATIE. (GS 977.8797 M23L)

Libby Prison General Hospital. MORNING REPORT OF SICK AND
WOUNDED IN THE LIBBY PRISON GENERAL HOSPITAL AT
RICHMOND VIRGINIA, MONDAY, MAY 15, 1865. (GS Film
496,745 4th item)

Maine Adjutant-General's Office. SUPPLEMENT TO THE ANNUAL
REPORTS OF THE ADJUTANT GENERAL OF THE STATE OF
MAINE FOR THE YEARS 1861, 1862, 1863, 1864, 1865, and
1866. Augusta: Stevens & Sayward, 1867. (GS 974.1 M26m
Supp.)

Manarin, Louis H. NORTH CAROLINA TROOPS, 1861-1865, A
    ROSTER. Raleigh: North Carolina Department of Archives
    and History, 1966. (GS 975.6 M23m)
Maryland General Assembly. HISTORY AND ROSTER OF MARYLAND
    VOLUNTEERS, WAR OF 1861-1865. Baltimore, 1898-1899. 2
    vols.
Maryland Hall of Records Commission. INDEX TO THE MARYLAND
    LINE IN THE CONFEDERATE ARMY, 1861-1865. Annapolis:
    Publication No. 3, 1944.
Massachusetts Adjutant-General's Office. RECORD OF MASSACHU-
    SETTS VOLUNTEERS, 1861-1865. 2 vols. Boston, 1868-1870.
Massachusetts Bureau of Labor Statistics. A LIST OF SOLDIERS,
    SAILORS, AND MARINES OF THE WAR OF THE REBELLION
    IN THE COMMONWEALTH OF MASSACHUSETTS ON MAY 1,
    1905; ARRANGED ALPHABETICALLY BY CITIES AND TOWNS.
    Boston, 1907.
MASTER LIST OF MISSOURI CIVIL WAR VETERAN BURIALS.
    (GS Film 483,686-483,687)
Mebane, John. BOOKS RELATING TO THE CIVIL WAR. (BYU
    973.7016 M464b)
Michigan Adjutant-General's Office. MICHIGAN IN THE WAR.
    Edited by Jno. Robertson. Lansing, Michigan: W.S. George
    & Co., State Printers, 1882. (GS 977.4 M25a and BYU 973.7474
    M582m)
_____. RECORD OF SERVICE OF MICHIGAN VOLUNTEERS
    IN THE CIVIL WAR, 1861-1865. 46 vols. Kalamazoo, Michigan:
    Ihling Brothers & Everard Printers, n.d. (GS 977.4 M2m)
Minnesota Adjutant-General's Office. ANNUAL REPORT OF THE
    ADJUTANT (H.P. VAN CLEVE) FOR THE YEAR ENDING
    DECEMBER 1, 1866, AND OF THE MILITARY FORCES OF THE
    STATE FROM 1861-1866. St. Paul, 1866.
_____. ANNUAL REPORTS OF THE ADJUTANT GENERAL,
    1861-1865.
Missouri Adjutant-General's Office (Union). ALPHABETICAL REGISTER
    OF OFFICERS OF MISSOURI VOLUNTEERS AND MISSOURI STATE
    MILITIA ACCOMPANYING ADJUTANT GENERAL'S REPORT FOR
    1865. Jefferson City, Missouri, 1865.
Moore, Robert Augustus. A LIFE FOR THE CONFEDERACY. Jackson,
    Tennessee: McCowat-Mercer Press, 1959. (BYU 973.782 M78L)
Munden, Kenneth White. GUIDE TO FEDERAL ARCHIVES RELATING
    TO THE CIVIL WAR. (BYU 973.7016 M923g)
Murdock, Eugene Converse. OHIO'S BOUNTY SYSTEM OF THE CIVIL
    WAR. Columbus: Ohio State University Press, 1963. (BYU
    973.7 Oh3p V.13)
Nebraska Adjutant-General's Office. ROSTER OF NEBRASKA VOLUN-
    TEERS FROM 1861-1869. Hastings, 1888.
Nebraska State Historical Society. CIVIL WAR VETERANS INDEX.
_____. D.A.R. MEMBERS BURIED IN NEBRASKA CEMETERIES.
_____. MICROFILM OF VETERANS RECEIVING PENSIONS
    IN 1890.
_____. ROSTER OF ALL KNOWN VETERANS IN 1887.

_____. ROSTER OF VETERANS FOR OTHER STATES.

New Hampshire Adjutant-General's Office. REVISED REGISTER OF
THE SOLDIERS AND SAILORS OF NEW HAMPSHIRE IN THE
REBELLION, 1861-1866. Concord, 1895.

New Jersey Adjutant-General's Office. RECORDS OF OFFICERS
AND MEN OF NEW JERSEY IN THE CIVIL WAR, 1861-1865.
2 vols. Trenton, 1876.

New York Adjutant-General's Office. ANNUAL REPORTS OF THE
ADJUTANT GENERAL, REGISTERS OF NEW YORK REGIMENTS
IN THE WAR OF THE REBELLION. 46 vols. Albany, 1894-.

Nicholson, John Page. PENNSYLVANIA AT GETTYSBURG.
Harrisburg, 1893. (BYU 973.7349 P38p)

Nix, Bennie Edgar. COMPILED LIST OF CONFEDERATE SOLDIERS
OF SHELBY COUNTY, TEXAS. Center, Texas: J.B. Sanders,
c1965. (GS 976.4179 M23n)

North Carolina General Assembly. ROSTER OF NORTH CAROLINA
TROOPS IN THE WAR BETWEEN THE STATES. 4 vols.
Raleigh: J.W. Moore, 1882.

OFFICERS OF THE ARMY & NAVY (REGULAR AND VOLUNTEER
WHO SERVED IN THE CIVIL WAR). Philadelphia: L.R.
Hamersly & Co., 1894. (BYU q923.5 Of2)

Ohio Roster Commission. OFFICIAL ROSTER OF THE SOLDIERS
OF THE STATE OF OHIO IN THE WAR OF THE REBELLION,
1861-1866. 12 vols. Akron, 1886-1895.

Pemlico County, North Carolina. RECORDS OF EX-CONFEDERATE
VETERANS OF THE CIVIL WAR, 1889-1918. Raleigh, n.d.
(GS Film 593,285)

Pennsylvania Adjutant-General's Office. ANNUAL REPORT OF THE
ADJUTANT-GENERAL (A.L. RUSSELL) FOR 1863-1866.
Harrisburg, 1864-1867.

Phisterer, Frederick. NEW YORK IN THE WAR OF THE REBELLION,
1861-1865. 3rd ed. 5 vols. 1912. (BYU 973.7447 P559n)

Pleasants, Henry. INFERNO AT PETERSBURG. Philadelphia:
Chilton Co. Book Division, 1961. (BYU 973.737 PL71i)

Pompey, Sherman Lee. CIVIL WAR VETERAN BURIALS. 2 vols.
(GS Film 483,688-483,689)

_____. CIVIL WAR VETERANS' BURIALS FROM CALIFOR-
NIA, NEVADA, OREGON, AND WASHINGTON REGIMENTS
BURIED IN COLORADO. Independence, California: Historical
and Genealogical Publishing Co., c1965. (GS 978.8 M2ps)

_____. CONFEDERATE SOLDIERS BURIED IN COLORADO.
Independence, California: Historical and Genealogical
Publishing Co., 1965. (GS 978.8 M2p)

_____. INTERRMENT OF UNION SOLDIERS IN UNITED
STATES TERRITORIES DURING THE CIVIL WAR. Independence,
California: Historical and Genealogical Publishing Co., c1965.
(BYU 973.76 P772i)

_____. MILITARY RECORDS: ALABAMA, ARIZONA,
ARKANSAS, INDIANS OF NORTH AMERICA, MARYLAND,
MISSOURI, TEXAS, GEORGIA, MISSISSIPPI, TENNESSEE.
(GS 973 X2pg)

_____. MUSTER LISTS OF THE ALABAMA CONFEDERATE
TROOPS. 3 vols. Independence, California: Historical and
Genealogical Publishing Co., c1965. (GS 976.1 M23p)

_____. MUSTER LISTS OF THE AMERICAN RIFLES OF
MARYLAND, BALTIMORE ARTILLERY, DIAS MARYLAND
ARTILLERY, MARYLAND GUERILLA ZOUAVES AND CAPTAIN
WALTER'S COMPANY. Bakersfield, California, c1965. (GS
975.2 M23p)

_____. MUSTER LISTS OF THE ARKANSAS CONFEDERATE
TROOPS. 2 vols. Independence, California: Historical and
Genealogical Publishing Co., c1965. (GS 976.7 M23p)

_____. MUSTER LISTS OF THE CHEROKEE CONFEDERATE
INDIANS. Independence, California: Historical and Genealogical
Publishing Co., c1965.

_____. MUSTER LISTS OF THE CREEK AND OTHER CON-
FEDERATE INDIANS. Independence, California: Historical and
Genealogical Publishing Co., n.d. (GS 970.3 C861p)

_____. MUSTER LISTS OF THE MISSOURI CONFEDERATES.
9 vols. Independence, California: Historical and Genealogical
Publishing Co., c1965. (GS 977.8 M23p)

_____. MUSTER LISTS OF THE TEXAS CONFEDERATE
TROOPS. 8 vols. Independence, California: Historical and
Genealogical Publishing Co., c1966. (GS 976.4 M23p)

Reid, Whitelaw. OHIO IN THE WAR: HER STATESMEN, HER
GENERALS, AND SOLDIERS. Cincinnati: Moore, Wilstach and
Baldwin, 1868. (BYU 977.103 R272o)

Rhode Island General Assembly. OFFICIAL REGISTER OF RHODE
ISLAND OFFICERS AND SOLDIERS WHO SERVED IN THE
UNITED STATES ARMY AND NAVY FROM 1861 TO 1866.
Providence, 1866.

Rhode Island Soldiers and Sailors Historical Society. PERSONAL
NARRATIVES OF EVENTS IN THE WAR OF THE REBELLION.
Providence, 1889. (BYU 973.781 B619f)

Ripley, Edward Hastings. VERMONT GENERAL: THE UNUSUAL
WAR EXPERIENCES OF EDWARD HASTINGS RIPLEY, 1862-1865. Ed.
Otto Eisenschiml. New York: Devin-Adair, 1960. (BYU 973.
781 R48u)

Salley, A.S. SOUTH CAROLINA TROOPS IN CONFEDERATE SERVICE.
Columbia.

THE SOLDIER OF INDIANA IN THE WAR FOR THE UNION. Indianapolis: Merrill & Co., 1866-1869. (BYU 977.204 So42)

Stegeman, John F. THESE MEN SHE GAVE, THE CIVIL WAR DIARY
OF ATHENS, GEORGIA. Athens, Georgia: The University of
Georgia Press, 1964. (GS 975.808 M25st)

Stillwell, Leander. THE STORY OF A COMMON SOLDIER OF ARMY
LIFE IN THE CIVIL WAR, 1861-1865. Erie, Kansas: Franklin
Hudson Publishing Co., 1920. (BYU 973.781 St54s)

Strong, Robert Hale. A YANKEE PRIVATE'S CIVIL WAR. ed. Ashley
Halsey. Chicago: H. Regnery Co., 1961. (BYU 973.781 St89y)

Stutler, Boyd Flynn. WEST VIRGINIA IN THE CIVIL WAR. 2nd ed.
Charleston, West Virginia: Education Foundation, 1966.
(BYU 975.403 St98w)

U.S. Adjutant-General's Office. COMPILED SERVICE RECORDS OF
VOLUNTEER UNION SOLDIERS WHO SERVED IN ORGANIZA-
TIONS FROM THE TERRITORY OF UTAH, 1862. (CAPT. LOT
SMITH'S COMPANY, UTAH CAVALRY). (GS Film 821,588)

_____. OFFICIAL ARMY REGISTER OF THE VOLUNTEER
FORCE OF THE UNITED STATES ARMY FOR THE YEARS
1861, 1862, 1864, 1865. Washington, 1865-1867. 8 vols.
(GS 973 M23ua)

U.S. Congress, Senate. DAKOTA MILITIA IN THE WAR OF 1862.
Washington, D.C., 1904.

U.S. National Archives. CONSOLIDATED INDEX TO COMPILED
SERVICE RECORDS OF CONFEDERATE SOLDIERS. Washington,
D.C.: National Archives Microfilm Publications, 1957. (GS
Film 25939 pts.1-535; BYU Film RG94 M253 pts.1-535; and BYU
Ref.4 929.373 B76p (Guide to Consolidated Index))

_____. DOCUMENTS FROM THE PENSION APPLICATION
FILES RELATING TO THE CIVIL WAR SERVICE OF SOLDIERS
WHO HAVE THE SURNAME OF CHRYSLER. Salt Lake City:
Received from Mrs. Paul E. Haldreg, n.d. (GS Film 475,630)

_____. MILITARY OPERATIONS OF THE CIVIL WAR.
Washington, D.C.: U.S. Government Printing Office, 1970.
(GS 973 M2us V.2 pt.3)

U.S. Record and Pension Office. COMPILED SERVICE RECORDS
OF CONFEDERATE GENERAL AND STAFF OFFICERS AND
NONREGIMENTAL ENLISTED MEN. Washington, D.C.:
National Archives Microfilm Publications, 1961. (GS Film
881,105-881,379)

_____. COMPILED SERVICE RECORDS OF CONFEDERATE
SOLDIERS WHO SERVED IN ORGANIZATIONS FROM THE
STATE OF ARKANSAS. Washington, D.C.: National Archives
Microfilm Publications, 1962. (GS Film 821,811-821,836 and
880,849-881,102)

_____. INDEX TO COMPILED SERVICE RECORDS OF
CONFEDERATE SOLDIERS WHO SERVED IN ORGANIZATIONS
FROM THE STATE OF ALABAMA. Washington, D.C.: National
Archives Microfilm Publications, 1962. (GS Film 821,949-821,
997 and 880,330-880,837)

_____. INDEX TO COMPILED SERVICE RECORDS OF
CONFEDERATE SOLDIERS WHO SERVED IN ORGANIZATIONS
FROM THE STATE OF FLORIDA. Washington, D.C.: National
Archives Microfilm Publications, 1959. (GS Film 880,001-880,
206)

U.S. Veterans Administration. GENERAL PENSION INDEX FILE,
1861-1934. Washington, D.C.: Veterans Administration
Publications Service, 1953. (GS Film 540,757-541,300; BYU
Film RG15 T288 pts.1-544 and BYU Ref.4 929.373 B76p
(Guide to General Index))

U.S. War Department. BIBLIOGRAPHY OF STATE PARTICIPATION
IN THE CIVIL WAR, 1861-1866. 3rd ed. Washington, D.C.:
War Department Library, n.d.
_____. OFFICIAL ARMY REGISTER OF THE VOLUNTEER
FORCE OF THE UNITED STATES ARMY FOR THE YEARS
1861-1865. Washington, 1865.
_____. THE WAR OF THE REBELLION: A COMPILATION
OF THE OFFICIAL RECORDS OF THE UNION AND CONFEDER-
ATE ARMIES. 68 vols. Washington, D.C.: Government Print-
ing Office, 1880. (GS 973 M26u and BYU 973.7 Un3os)
Vermont Adjutant-General's Office. REVISED ROSTER OF VERMONT
VOLUNTEERS AND LISTS OF VOLUNTEERS WHO SERVED IN
THE ARMY OF THE UNITED STATES DURING THE WAR OF THE
REBELLION, 1861-1866. Montpelier, 1892.
Walker, Charles D. BIOGRAPHICAL SKETCHES OF THE GRADUATES
AND ELEVES WHO FELL DURING THE WAR BETWEEN THE
STATES. Philadelphia: J.B. Lippincott & Co., 1875. (GS 975.5
D3u)
Warner, Ezra J. GENERALS IN BLUE. New Orleans: Louisiana
State University Press, 1964. (GS 973 M2war and BYU Ref.
923.5 W24gb)
_____. GENERALS IN GRAY. New Orleans: Louisiana State
University Press, 1959. (GS 973 M2wa and BYU 923.5 W24g)
Watson, William. LETTER OF A CIVIL WAR SURGEON. West
Lafayette, Indiana, 1961. (BYU 973.775 W331)
West Virginia Adjutant-General's Office. ANNUAL REPORT OF THE
ADJUTANT GENERAL (F.P. PIERPOINT) OF THE STATE OF
WEST VIRGINIA FOR THE YEAR ENDING DECEMBER 31, 1865.
Wheeling, 1866.
Wheeler, Kenneth W. FOR THE UNION: OHIO LEADERS IN THE
CIVIL WAR. Columbus, Ohio: Ohio State University Press,
1968. (BYU 920.0771 W564f)
White, William W. THE CONFEDERATE VETERAN. Confederate
Centennial Studies. Tuscaloosa, Alabama: Commercial
Publishing Co., 1962. (BYU 973.7 C761 V.22)
Wills, Charles W. ARMY LIFE OF AN ILLINOIS SOLDIER. Washing-
ton, D.C.: Globe Printing Co., 1907. (BYU 973.78 W68)
Wisconsin Adjutant-General's Office. ROSTER OF WISCONSIN
VOLUNTEERS OF THE REBELLION, 1861-1865. 2 vols.
Madison, 1886.
WISCONSIN STATE CENSUS OF CIVIL WAR VETERANS OF 1895
AND 1905.
Wood, William Charles Henry. CAPTAINS OF THE CIVIL WAR:
A CHRONICLE OF THE BLUE AND THE GRAY. New Haven:
Yale University Press, 1921. (GS 973 H2ch V.31)
Workman, Beth B. CONFEDERATE SOLDIERS SERVICE RECORDS.
Salt Lake City: The Genealogical Society, 1964. (GS Film
30172-30173 and BYU Ref.4 929.376 W892c)
Wright, Edward Needles. CONSCIENTIOUS OBJECTORS IN THE
CIVIL WAR. New York: A.S. Barnes, 1961. (BYU 973.715
W931c)

SPANISH-AMERICAN WAR

A MILITARY ALBUM, CONTAINING OVER ONE THOUSAND PORTRAITS OF COMMISSIONED OFFICERS WHO SERVED IN THE SPANISH-AMERICAN WAR. New York: L.R. Hamersly Co., 1902. (BYU 929.373 M599h)

RECORD OF MEMBERS OF THE CHURCH OF JESUS CHRIST OF LATTER-DAY SAINTS WHO ENTERED MILITARY SERVICE OF THE UNITED STATES AND ITS ALLIES UP TO DECEMBER 31, 1919. Salt Lake City: Filmed by the LDS Church Historian's Office. 1961. (GS Film 241,188)

SOLDIERS OF THE GREAT WAR. (BYU 940.467 So42)

U.S. Navy Department. COMBAT CONNECTED CASUALTIES OF WORLD WAR II. 2 vols. 1946. (GS 973 M23un)

_____. OFFICERS AND ENLISTED MEN OF THE U.S. NAVY WHO LOST THEIR LIVES DURING THE WORLD WAR FROM APRIL 6, 1910, TO NOVEMBER 11, 1918. (BYU 920.467 Un30)

U.S. Veterans Administration. INDIAN WARS INDEX TO PENSION FILES, 1892-1926. Washington, D.C., 1971. (GS Film 821, 610-821,621 and BYU Film RG15 T318 pts.1-12)

_____

1. Henry Putney Beers, GUIDE TO THE ARCHIVES OF THE GOVERNMENT OF THE CONFEDERATE STATES OF AMERICA (Washington, D.C.: The National Archives and Records Service, 1968), p. 413.

2. Ibid., p. 415.

CHAPTER 12

MISCELLANEOUS SOURCES FOR GENEALOGY

There are several miscellaneous record groups which do not fit the general categories covered in previous chapters but which might provide facts to help extend a pedigree, depending on the time period and location of the problem and on certain other factors. They include a variety of social and commercial records created by the private sector of the economy and by certain governmental agencies. Commercial business establishments, schools, hospitals, clubs, lodges, and other social organizations are among the number responsible for these records.

It should be clearly understood that all of the records and sources covered in this chapter are not immediately open to public inspection; in fact, many are extremely confidential. However, they are known to contain good genealogical information, and the determined researcher may be able to investigate them if he takes the proper approach. With determination and a little money, he can meet just about any objective.

These kinds of records are more numerous after 1900, but some exist much earlier; however, little has been done to gather them because of their confidential nature. Personal research in the localities of interest is usually necessary to locate them, though correspondence and even the telephone may bring results in some cases.

Outlining the Problem

Each problem should be individually evaluated according to time and place, and all pertinent events and circumstances should be considered before investigating the records. It might be advisable to list historical highlights about a particular ancestor and then define specific objectives from those highlights. The following approach was recently taken by a genealogy student and shows how a problem might be analyzed and research objectives outlined:

Social-Commercial Records Which Might Exist For
One of My Ancestors, William Stennett
Poppleton, Who Lived from
1844 to 1923

William Stennett Poppleton was born 14 August, 1844 in Moulton, Lincs., England. He was the oldest of six children born to William Poppleton and Sarah Stennett. His father became a member of the Church of Jesus Christ of Latter-day Saints in 1852, and emigrated to America that same year leaving his family in England. He at first located near St. Louis, Missouri where he worked to earn money to bring his family to America.

His wife and family arrived in America in the fall of 1853, and joined young William's father near St. Louis. The family next lived near Genoa, Nebraska from 1856 to 1860. In the spring of 1860 a member of the Church hired young William to drive a four mule team across the plains to Utah. Young William separated from his family and arrived in Bountiful, Utah the fall of 1860, and soon after moved to Cache Valley.

On 9 December, 1865 he married Celia Knox Riggs of Wellesville, and they had eleven children. On 6 June, 1884 he married Emma Mitton as a plural wife, and they had nine children.

About 1886 the anti-polygamy crusade started. William went underground using the assumed name of Wm. Grey. With some other men of the Church he went to Mexico, but he did not stay long. He returned to Utah and worked as a carpenter for the Union Pacific Railroad. In 1888 he went to Rock Springs, Wyoming with some other Church men and worked in the mines.

During 1888 he returned and was arrested three times for polygamy and paid a fine of $80.00 each time. In 1890 he was arrested again for polygamy, and served 45 days in the State Penitentiary. After the manifesto he was permitted to live with his wives in Wellsville.

He worked in various stores and small businesses in Wellsville. For 16 years he was Cache County Road Superintendant, for 8 years a town councilman. He was a prominent member of the Home Dramatic Company, and for 30 years he was a member of the Brass and String Band. He held numerous church positions in the Wellsville ward.

He enjoyed remarkable health until he was seventy years old when his health became poor and he underwent several critical bladder operations.

He died 27 August, 1923 in Wellsville, Cache County, Utah.

From this sketch of the life of William Stennett Poppleton I would hope that information of a genealogical nature would be found concerning him in social and commercial records at the following general locations:

a. School administration offices (1) near St. Louis where the family lived from 1853 to 1856, (2) near Genoa, Nebraska where the family lived from 1856 to 1860, and (3) from 1860 on in the Bountiful and Wellsville, Utah areas.

b. The Union Pacific Railroad offices in Ogden, Utah, the Cache County Road Commission in Logan, offices of a mine in Rock Springs, Wyoming, Wellsville town offices where he served as a councilman, and possibly some of the small business firms where he worked in Wellsville. A note in his wife's file indicates that he worked at Baugh Bros. store in Wellsville at one time.

c. With his active participation in dramatic and musical organizations in Cache Valley there should be considerable information about him in newspapers and possibly local histories of the area to be found in libraries in Logan, Salt Lake City, and possibly elsewhere.

d. The State Penitentiary where he served for practicing polygamy, and other offices where he paid fines.

e. Doctors offices in Wellsville, Logan, and possibly other towns where he worked during his life.

f. The hospital in Logan where his bladder operations likely were performed as this is the only place closer than Ogden where there was a hospital at the time.

g. The mortuary offices in Logan, the nearest to Wellsville.

h. Coroner's office only if further search should indicate something unusual or extreme about his death.

i. Possibly insurance records in Logan or Salt Lake City.

j. Possibly suppliers of road building supplies in the Cache Valley, Ogden, and Salt Lake areas.

Business or Employment Records

Consideration should be given the individual's occupation, profession, and social status in order to determine the best possible approach. What did he do for a living? Was he one of the great silent majority in early American history who were farmers and laborers, or was he a professional man, perhaps a physician, merchant, lawyer, engineer, schoolmaster, or minister? Records may exist pertaining to his education, training, employment, or work.

The document in fig. 117 was completed by the employee himself and gave his age, marital status, birthplace, parentage, and other valuable genealogical information. It was located among personnel records of the Southern Pacific Railroad in Ogden, Utah. On a similar problem, a researcher at the Genealogical Society used the telephone to contact the personnel manager of the Union Pacific Railroad at Omaha, Nebraska, and obtained genealogical information on one of their early employees (1898).

C. P. R. R.
AND LEASED LINES.

PERSONAL RECORD.

☞ Division and Assistant Superintendents will require all train, and station hands, on entering the service of this Company, under their supervision, to write answers to the following interrogatories in their own handwriting. Master Mechanics will conform to the above, regarding Engine men. This blank, when filled out and signed, must be forwarded to the Assistant General Superintendent, at San Francisco, together with a Photograph of the person, and all letters of recommendation the applicant may have. Superintendents and Master Mechanics will require these records to be signed in duplicate, keeping one copy in their own offices for reference.

J. A. FILLMORE, General Superintendent.

_____ Salt Lake _____ Division,
Ogden Station, Jan 5 ____ 1883

1. Age next birthday? 40 years   Married or single? Married
2. Where born? Town   Burks gardens Virginia
   County,   Bowell
   State, or Country   State of Virginia
3. Description—Height 5 ⁶⁄₈   Weight 156 lbs., Color of Eyes blue Color of Hair brown
4. Name of parents? Phillip and Elizabeth Heninger
   Residence? Burks gardens Virginia
5. Name of Nearest relative or friend to whom communications can be addressed, in case of sickness or injury? Chastina Heninger
   Residence? Ogden City
6. Were you ever injured, if so, when? No
   What road?
   Extent of injury?
7. In what business before entering Railroad employ? Farming
8. Name ALL roads on which you have been employed :

RAILROAD.	AT WHAT STATION OR DIVISION.	OCCUPATION.	YEAR.
Central Pacific	Ogden Salt Lake	Stevedore	5 years

10. On what foreign road last employed?
    Cause of leaving?
11. Number of letters of recommendation enclosed?
12. When did you last commence service on this Division? in 1877
    and what is your present position? Stevedore
13. By whom recommended? G R Hill

Witness:

Jeddiah Grant Heninger
[SIGN YOUR NAME IN FULL ; NOT INITIALS.]

Fig. 117. Central Pacific Railroad employment document

Most employment records dating prior to the 1900s consist of only a single document or two, but many after that period include detailed application forms and supporting documents which contain good genealogical data. When employment was with a governmental agency, there may also be documents relating to naturalization, citizenship, residence abroad, or security.

Information concerning the employee's membership in a local union or labor organization may also be on file, and records pertaining to his retirement or company benefits may exist. The records may be filed with the employer, the employee, the union, or with the organization providing and servicing the benefits (figs. 118 and 119).

If the individual was a doctor or lawyer and belonged to a medical association or the State Bar, special application and biographical forms might have been kept concerning him. Notice that each form calls for basic vital statistics and also includes space for such things as citizenship status or foreign residence (figs. 120 and 121).

The individual may also have purchased life insurance or may have borrowed money from an insurance company, a bank, a credit union, or from a mortgage-loan association, and they may have kept detailed personal information about him. It is even possible that credit bureaus could provide genealogical data on certain persons. Credit bureaus exist for the benefit of commercial institutions but probably would cooperate with a genealogist, if a little money and the right approach were taken (fig. 122).

Millions of Americans have also been individually identified by local, state, and federal agencies, such as the Internal Revenue Service, the Federal Bureau of Investigation, Social Security, or local and state law enforcement agencies. It is noted that the State of California maintains a master fingerprint file, but of course such records are highly confidential, and it is doubtful that a genealogist could gain information from them without committing a crime himself.

Morticians' and Coroners' Records

The local mortician sometimes has records which antedate official vital records, and many will provide genealogical information from their files without restriction or charge. Students at Brigham Young University recently conducted a survey of selected morticians in over thirty-four states, and it was surprising the number who had records dating prior to 1900 and who would open their files to genealogists. The following typical response was received from the Gilmartin Funeral Home in Batavia, New York:

Dear Mr. Kohut:

I am sorry for the delay in answering your letter of April 16. However, I have just returned to my office after being away for the past two weeks.

OFFICE EMPLOYES INTERNATIONAL UNION

APPLICATION FOR MEMBERSHIP

Desiring to become a member of a Local Union chartered by the Office Employes International Union, AFL-CIO, I hereby make application for admission to membership and authorize such organization to be my exclusive collective bargaining representative.

Name_____

(PRINT)

Social
Security
No._____

Street Address_____   Telephone_____

City_____   (_____) _____

ZONE   STATE OR PROVINCE

Occupation_____

Name of company where now employed _____

Date_____, 19_____

FORM 9   PRINTED IN U.S.A.   SIGNATURE OF APPLICANT

Fig. 118. Application for union membership

372

FORM NO. AA-1
(11-54)
UNITED STATES OF AMERICA
RAILROAD RETIREMENT BOARD

DO NOT WRITE IN THESE SPACES

APPLICATION FOR EMPLOYEE ANNUITY UNDER
THE RAILROAD RETIREMENT ACT

ALL ITEMS ON THIS FORM THAT PERTAIN TO YOU MUST BE ANSWERED. THE COMPLETED FORM IS TO BE RETURNED
TO THE RAILROAD RETIREMENT BOARD.

I.
(PRINT: FIRST NAME - MIDDLE NAME - MAIDEN NAME IF FEMALE - LAST NAME)   (SOCIAL SECURITY ACCOUNT NUMBER)

hereby apply for an employee annuity under the provisions of the Railroad Retirement Act.

PART I - GENERAL
(To be completed by all applicants)

1. Place of birth _____ _____ _____
   (TOWN OR CITY)   (COUNTY)   (STATE OR FOREIGN COUNTRY)

2. Date of birth _____ _____ _____
   (MONTH)   (DAY)   (YEAR)

3. Father's name _____ _____ _____
   (FIRST)   (MIDDLE)   (LAST)

4. Mother's name _____ _____ _____
   (FIRST)   (MIDDLE)   (MAIDEN LAST NAME)

5. Sex (indicate by check (✓) mark) Male ☐   Female ☐

6. Marital status (indicate by check (✓) mark) Single ☐   Married ☐   Widowed ☐   Divorced ☐
   If married give:
   Date of your marriage _____ _____ _____
   (MONTH)   (DAY)   (YEAR)
   Husband's name or wife's maiden name _____ _____ _____
   (FIRST)   (MIDDLE)   (LAST)
   Husband's or wife's date of birth _____ _____ _____
   (MONTH)   (DAY) (YEAR)

7. Did you work for any employer under the Railroad Retirement Act before 1937? _____
   (YES OR NO)

   If "Yes," have you filed with the Board a statement of such service on Form AA-15? _____
   (YES OR NO)

8. Give the following information about your service for all employers under the Railroad Retirement Act
   for whom you worked during the last 5 years (include any compensated service you may have performed
   for a local lodge or division, or for a general committee, of a railway labor organization.)

   (USE A SEPARATE BLOCK FOR EACH DIFFERENT EMPLOYER OR EACH DIFFERENT PERIOD OF SERVICE)

NAME OF EMPLOYER	NAME OF EMPLOYER
YOUR NAME ON PAYROLL	YOUR NAME ON PAYROLL
LAST OCCUPATION	LAST OCCUPATION
LAST DEPARTMENT	LAST DEPARTMENT
LAST DIVISION OR LOCATION	LAST DIVISION OR LOCATION
WORKED FROM _____ (DATE) TO _____ (DATE)	WORKED FROM _____ (DATE) TO _____ (DATE)

   (IF YOU NEED MORE SPACE, CONTINUE YOUR ENTRIES UNDER "REMARKS" OR ATTACH SEPARATE SHEET.)

9. Do you claim compensated service as an employee representative under the Railroad Retirement Act?

   _____ If "Yes," have you filed with the Board a statement of such service? _____
   (YES OR NO)   (YES OR NO)

Fig. 119. Application for railroad annuity

373

UTAH STATE MEDICAL ASSOCIATION

LICENSED PHYSICIAN'S BIOGRAPHICAL DATA

DATE

ACTIVE PRACTICE OR RETIRED

FULL NAME (NO INITIALS)
(PLEASE PRINT)

PLACE OF BIRTH

DATE OF BIRTH   SEX
(MO-DAY-YEAR)

COMPLETE OFFICE ADDRESS
CITY

DATE LOCATED AT ADDRESS
(MO-DAY-YEAR)

MARRIED—WIFE'S NAME

PREMEDICAL EDUCATION—NAME AND LOCATION OF SCHOOL

DEGREE   DATE OF DEGREE
(MO-DAY-YEAR)

MEDICAL EDUCATION—NAME AND LOCATION OF SCHOOL

DEGREE   DATE OF DEGREE
(MO-DAY-YEAR)

INTERNSHIP—NAME OF INSTITUTION AND LOCATION

INCLUSIVE DATES

RESIDENCIES, FELLOWSHIPS, OR POST GRADUATE TRAINING

FROM (MO-DAY-YEAR) TO (MO-DAY-YEAR)
INCLUSIVE DATES

SERIAL NUMBER AND DATE OF YOUR UTAH LICENSE   ISSUED BY EXAMINATION   BY RECIPROCITY WITH
FROM (MO-DAY-YEAR) TO (MO-DAY-YEAR)
(NAME STATE)

LICENSES HELD FROM OTHER STATES AND DATES OF ISSUE

PREVIOUS PRACTICE LOCATIONS IN UTAH

INCLUSIVE DATES
FROM (MO-DAY-YEAR) TO (MO-DAY-YEAR)

TYPE OF PRACTICE—GP OR SPECIALTY (NAME)   LIMIT PRACTICE?

BOARD CERTIFICATION
(BOARD NAME)   (DATE)

SOCIETIES—AMA, STATE, COUNTY, SPECIALTY

OFFICES HELD IN EACH AND YEAR

THIS INFORMATION IS FOR OFFICIAL FILES AND DIRECTORY SERVICE OF THE UTAH STATE MEDICAL ASSOCIATION.
PLEASE COMPLETE ALL ENTRIES AND RETURN TO U.S.M.A., 42 SOUTH 5TH EAST, SALT LAKE CITY, UTAH.

Fig. 120.   Biographical data form for physician

374

UTAH STATE BAR

IN RE APPLICATION OF

}

....

APPLICATION
FOR
ADMISSION TO THE BAR

Fee for filing application for admission on certificate $100.00
Fee for filing application for admission by examination $5.00

To the Board of Commissioners of the Utah State Bar:

I, ...
hereby apply for recommendation to the Supreme Court for admission to practice law
in the State of Utah.

1. (a) State your full name..

   (b) Have you ever been known by any other name or surname........................
                                                (Yes or No)

       If so, state and give details...

       ....

2. Date of Birth..............................Age ....

3. (a) State your Birth Place...

   (b) If born in a foreign country state age at which you came to the United

       States ....

   (c) If naturalized, state when and where, and file proof.................................

       ....

   (d) If claiming citizenship other than by birth in the United States or natural-
       ization, state why and file proof ....

4. (a) Are you a bona fide Resident of Utah? ....

   (b) Upon what date did you become such a resident?..................................

5. State every residence you have had since you were sixteen years of age.

CITY AND STATE   **STREET AND NUMBER**   **FROM**   **TO**

Fig. 121. Application for admission to Utah State Bar

Application to the Beneficial Life Insurance Company (PartI)

Policy Number _____

1. (a) Full name of Applicant _____
   (b) Sex _____ Color of eyes _____ Color of hair _____

2. (a) Present Residence: State _____ County _____
   City of _____ , Street No. _____

3. (a) Place of Birth: City _____ , State _____
   (b) Date of Birth: Month _____ , Day _____ , Year _____
   (c) Age (Nearest Birthday) _____ Years.

4. (a) Present occupation (Explain in detail) _____
   (b) Name of Employer _____
   (c) Do you contemplate making any change in your occupation? _____
       If so explain fully _____
   (d) Former occupations last five years _____

   (e) Have you taken flying lessons, owned or piloted a plane? _____
       If answer is "yes": (a) When did you last fly? _____
       (b) How many hours did you fly in the past 12 months? _____
       (c) How many hours contemplated in next 12 months? _____

5. Kind of Policy applied for _____

6. Sum to be Insured _____
   Do you desire
   (a) Disability?
   (b) Double Indemnity?
   (c) Extra
   (d) Total annual premium
   (e) Policy If issued to be dated
   (f) In one policy or how?

	Insurance	Annual Premium
	$	$
	Yes	No	$
			$
			$
			$

7. (a) Full name of person (or persons) proposed as ORIGINAL Beneficiary
   NAME _____ Relationship _____ Age _____
   (b) Residence _____
   (c) Occupation _____

8. (a) Full name of person (or persons) proposed as ALTERNATE Beneficiary
   NAME _____ Relationship _____ Age _____
   (b) Residence _____
   (c) Occupation _____

9. (a) Have you your life insured in this or any other company? _____
       Name of Company _____ Amount _____ Date Taken _____
   (b) Do your policies include Double Indemnity? _____
   (c) How much of Insurance was issued without Medical Examination? _____ Amount $ _____

10. (a) Have you ever applied or been examined for Insurance in any Company without receiving a policy of the exact
        kind and rate applied for? _____
    (b) Name of Company _____ When _____

11. Are any negotiations for Insurance now pending? _____ If so, explain: _____

12. (a) Are you a citizen of the U.S.A.? _____
    (b) If not a citizen, how long have you lived in the U.S.A.? _____

13. (If applicant is a woman) (a) Do you own property in your own right? _____
    (b) Will premiums be paid out of your personal funds? _____
    (c) How much life insurance does your husband carry in your favor? _____

14. For Home Office Endorsements Only

Fig. 122. Applications for life insurance

376

Part A

Application to the METROPOLITAN LIFE INSURANCE COMPANY (Herein called the Company)

(Ordinary Department)

Use PERMANENT INK—preferably black—for answers and signatures

Medical

Form O36K-9
Sept. 1948
PRINTED IN U.S.A.
(1-59)

1. What is your FULL NAME? (Print)

    FIRST NAME   MIDDLE INITIAL   LAST NAME

2. Have you ever changed your name by marriage or otherwise? (If yes, give the previous name or names.)

3. Residence. (If R.F.D. route, give route and approximate location.)
    No.   (PRINT) ——(ST., AVE., PL., TER., RD., ETC.—BE EXPLICIT)   Apt. No.
    Floor
    City or Town (Print)   State.   Postal Zone No.
    County
    How long have you resided at this address?   Give other addresses in last 3 years.

4. Place of birth   (STATE OR FOREIGN COUNTRY)

    Shall communications be sent to residence? ☐ Place of business? ☐
    (TOWN OR CITY)

5. Date of Birth | Month | Day | Year | Age nearest birthday........years

6. Single ☐ Married ☐ Widowed ☐ Divorced ☐ Separated ☐ (Give relationships and ages.)

7. How many are dependent on you for support? (Give relationship and ages.)

8. Occupation (a) Job title
    (b) Duties

9. (a) Employer (Name of Firm)
    (b) Business address——NO.——STREET——CITY AND ZONE——STATE
    (c) How long have you worked for this employer?
    (d) Nature of employer's business
    (e) If beer, wine, or liquor is manufactured or sold, is it a major part of the business?

10. Do you also have a part-time or seasonal occupation? (If yes, state when and give details of occupation and employer.)

11. Do you contemplate any change in occupation? (If yes, state when and give details of occupation and employer.)

12. Have you, within the last 5 years, been engaged in any occupation other than your present one? (If yes, state each occupation and the periods so engaged.)

16. Plan of insurance desired (as designated in the Rate Book).

17. Is the Accidental Means Death Benefit desired?

18. Amount of Insurance Desired:
    ☐ Annual ☐ Semiannual ☐ Quarterly ☐ Monthly
    Premium Payable
    Classification Applied For
    ☐ Ordinary ☐ Intermediate ☐ Special Class ☐ Special Class B
    $
    If premium payable is monthly and amount of premium is $10.00 or less, this application is for a policy in the Monthly Accounting Branch.

19. (a) Beneficiary in case of your death. (Print first name, middle initial, last name.)
    Relationship..Age.........
    Address..............................
    The right to change the above-named Beneficiary without the consent of said Beneficiary is........reserved.
    Unless otherwise indicated, if two or more beneficiaries are named, any payment to them shall be made in equal shares or to the survivors in equal shares or all to the last survivor.
    (b) Contingent Beneficiary (Print first name, middle initial, last name.)
    Relationship..Age.........
    Address..............................
    The right to change the above-named Contingent Beneficiary without the consent of said Contingent Beneficiary is........reserved.
    Unless otherwise indicated, if two or more contingent beneficiaries are named, any payment to them shall be made in equal shares or to the survivors in equal shares or all to the last survivor.

20. The following are the details of all Life insurance now in force on my life in all companies (including National Service Insurance, fraternals, etc.). (If none, so state.)

Name of Company	Amount	Plan of Insurance	Year Issued	If in Metropolitan, Give Policy Numbers

377

I am enclosing several forms which are used in conducting our funeral business. First of all is a copy of the "Certificate of Death" issued by the New York State Department of Health. This form must be completed and filed with the local health office within 72 hours after a person expires. The information which is necessary for this certificate is obtained from a member of the immediate family of the deceased and the enclosed card entitled "Gilmartin Funeral Home" is used for obtaining this information. This card becomes a part of our permanent records. The book of "Certificate of Death" furnished by the State of New York also includes a stub which contains the same information as is listed on the Certificate of Death. This, too, becomes part of our records.

The last form used for our complete record is the folder entitled "Funeral of". As you can see, this folder contains a record of the deceased, plus funeral charges, cash disbursements and record of payments.

The information listed above answers your first two questions. In answer to Question 3 - our records cover the period of time since our business was established - January 13, 1955 to the present time. In answer to Question 4 - the information in our records is available to the public except, of course, for the financial part. This is a private matter between the family making the arrangements and ourselves.

We hope the above information is helpful to you in completing your research paper.

Sincerely yours,

DARWIN GILMARTIN

The mortician has records contemporary with those of City Boards of Health and State Bureaus of Vital Statistics and his records may contain information which is not included in the official files. It was noted in the survey that some morticians had records which had been retained from previous owners and some had transferred such records to the city hall or county courthouse for keeping. It is also possible that some records are still in possession of the previous owners, or their families (fig. 123).

In 1958, the author was attempting to gain genealogical information about Isaac Myron Davis for a Los Angeles attorney who was probating Isaac's estate. The attorney was seeking heirs to the estate because Isaac had died in Los Angeles with considerable liquid assets and was apparently a bachelor. Isaac was known to have been a resident of Bingham Canyon, Utah, and his father and mother were known to have been resident there. Mortician and hospital records concerning the father were helpful in determining heirs to Isaac's estate. The town of Bingham Canyon has since been demolished because it was built on one of the richer copper ore deposits in Utah, but at the time of search, several homes were standing and the local

Place of Death		Usual Residence	
City	State	City	State
Name			
Birth Place	City	State	
Sex	Color	Single, Married, Widowed, Divorced	
Husband or wife			Age
Date of Birth			
Age — Years	Months	Days	Social Security Number
Occupation			
Father's Name			
Birth Place			
Mother's Maiden Name			
Birth Place			
Informant		Address	Phone No.
Date of Death — Year	Month	Day	Place Burial
Date of Burial — Year	Month	Day	Cemetery
Duration of Illness			
Principal Cause of Death			
		Address	
Doctor's Signature			
		Address	
Funeral Director's Signature			
Funeral Director No.		Embalmer No.	

Fig. 123. Morticians' records

AULTOREST MEMORIAL CORPORATION

Ogden, Utah

Deceased _____

Father's Name _____

Mother's Maiden Name _____

Wife's Maiden Name _____

Husband's Name _____

Where Born _____

When _____

Where Died _____

When _____ Age _____

Cause of Death _____

Physician _____

Crypt No. _____ in Row _____ Corridor _____

Lot No. _____ Plot _____ Position _____ Tier ____

Box Style _____ Size _____ in. x _____ in.

Cash _____

Opening $ _____ Charge Grave ordered by _____

I hereby certify that the above is correct.

Undertaker...

Funeral No.......................... Burial Permit No.......................

INDEX OF INTERMENTS

Name _____

        Surname   Christian Name

Record of Interment _____

                Date of Death

Lot Owner _____

Address _____

Place of Burial—Lot No. _____ Position _____

Burial Number _____ Plot _____

_____

_____

Fig. 123a.

mortician was residing in town. This mortician had recently purchased his business and had sent all the records he had inherited to the city hall for deposit. In a visit to the city hall (which has also since been demolished), genealogical information concerning Isaac's father was located in a 1903 mortician's record, which dated three years prior to state registration of vital statistics in Utah. Among other things, the record indicated Isaac's father had died in the Salt Lake County Hospital in Salt Lake City.

The names and addresses of morticians and funeral directors can be determined from the National Directory of Morticians which is usually in possession of any local funeral director.

In certain situations it might also be advisable to consult records of the COUNTY CORONER, especially when there was some question concerning the cause of death. An inquest may have been held, and important genealogical information might have been recorded. With few exceptions, the records in custody of the county coroner are public and open to inspection by genealogists, though a charge might be levied for copies of documents requested. A typical file might include a NECROPSY report giving technical causes of death, supported by PATHOLOGY and TOXOLOGY reports, TESTIMONY from involved individuals, and a JURY report.

During World War II, a Utah family received information that their son had died in San Francisco while in the service, but there was some question as to the actual cause of death. The official death record indicated the young man had committed suicide by jumping from the Bay Bridge, but the family questioned this. However, records from the coroner's office helped to clarify the matter. Documents relating to the inquest included the testimony of a Coast Guard member who stated that he "was on a routine patrol in the Bay when he sighted the body of the deceased, fully dressed, except for coat, lying face downward in the rocks about 50 feet southeast of the shoreline" and that he found identifying papers on the body. The testimony of an army buddy of the deceased indicated "he was a very quiet man and no one got to know him very well," and that "during the last week of his life he seemed depressed over an impending divorce." Testimony also indicated the young man had been seen "walking on the Bay Bridge before his death" and likely jumped from it. In addition, an extensive necropsy report indicated that death was caused by fractures, contusions, and injuries to internal organs, all due to "trauma."

In the case of another violent death which occurred at a place removed from the home of the deceased, a presumptive death certificate was filed which listed names and birth dates of family members as well as a summary of the evidence for the cause of death (fig. 124).

In addition, a letter from the Assistant Chief of the Weather Bureau, for which the deceased was working when he was killed, provided official information about the case (fig. 125).

ALASKA DEPARTMENT OF HEALTH
BUREAU OF VITAL STATISTICS

DEATH NO. **1258**

PRESUMPTIVE DEATH CERTIFICATE
(ORIGINAL)

U.S. COMMIS-
SIONER'S NO. *62-94b* (FOR REGISTRAR)
(FOR NUMBERING WITHIN PRECINCT)

NAME OF DECEASED (TYPE OR PRINT)
(FIRST) **JAMES** (MIDDLE) **W.** (LAST) **GRANT**

RECORDING DISTRICT WHERE DEATH OCCURRED **Anchorage, ?**
TOWN OR OTHER PHYSICAL LOCATION (SPECIFY IN OR NEAR) **near Skwentna**

USUAL RESIDENCE (TOWN) **325 11th Avenue, Anchorage, Alaska** (STATE OR TERRITORY)

SEX **male** | COLOR OR RACE **white** | MARRIED, NEVER MARRIED, WIDOWED, DIVORCED (SPECIFY) **Married** | IF MARRIED, NAME OF SPOUSE **Helen**

PRESUMED DATE OF DEATH **July 25, 1960** | BIRTHPLACE **Weiser, Idaho**

DATE OF BIRTH **November 25, 1918** | AGE **43** | SOCIAL SECURITY NUMBER **540 05 4494**

USUAL OCCUPATION **Meteorologist - G. S. 13** | IN WHAT KIND OF BUSINESS OR INDUSTRY? **UNITED STATES WEATHER BUREAU**

FATHER'S NAME **James William Grant, Sr.** | MOTHER'S MAIDEN NAME **Clair Georgia Jensen**

CAUSE OF DEATH (GIVE SHORT STATEMENT OF CAUSE OF PRESUMED DEATH. GIVE DETAILS ON REVERSE SIDE OF FORM.)
Aircraft wreck, summary on reverse side

WAS DEATH DETERMINED TO BE: ☒ ACCIDENT ☐ SUICIDE ☐ HOMICIDE

WAS MORE THAN ONE DEATH INVOLVED? **Yes** | IF SO, HOW MANY OTHERS? **Seven** *1243 1344*

WERE THERE ACTUAL WITNESSES? **No**

WAS EVIDENCE OF WRECKAGE OR OTHER PHYSICAL EVIDENCE FOUND? **No**

NAME OF PERSON PRESENTING PETITION **Helen Gardner** | ADDRESS **52 East 2nd North, Salt Lake City, Utah**

☒ ACCIDENTAL OR OTHER VIOLENT DEATH PRESUMED UNDER CHAPTER 89, SLA 1953.

DATE OF JURY VERDICT **March 7, 1962** | DATE VERDICT APPROVED BY U.S. COMMISSIONER **March 7, 1962** | DATE COMM. ORDER OF PRESUMED DEATH **March 14, 1962**

☐ MISSING PERSON PRESUMED DEAD AFTER SIX YEARS UNDER SECTION 62-1-15, ACLA 1949.

BEGINNING DATE OF PERIOD OF CONTINUOUS DISAPPEARANCE | DATE COMM. ORDER OF PRESUMED DEATH

I HEREBY CERTIFY THAT THE FACTS AND OTHER DATA GIVEN ON THIS CERTIFICATE, AND ON ANY ATTACHMENTS HERETO, ARE TRUE AND COMPLETE INSOFAR AS CAN BE DETERMINED; AND THAT ANY PRESUMPTION OF DEATH UNDER CHAPTER 89, SLA 1953, WAS THE UNANIMOUS VERDICT OF THE JURY AND APPROVED BY MYSELF.

SIGNED *Richard B Collins*   District Magistrate | RESIDING AT **ANCHORAGE**

DATE RECORDED **APR 4 1962** | RECORDING DISTRICT **ANCHORAGE** | *Richard B Collins*

DATE FILED BY REGISTRAR **MAY 4 1962** | REGISTRAR'S SIGNATURE *Francis E. Kester* | BY *Eufrasia Arcilla*

LIVING CHILDREN: (PLEASE LIST)

James W. Grant, III - born September 3, 1944
Marilyn Grant - born November 19, 1947
Judith Grant - born October 17, 1950
Susan Elizabeth Grant, born June 21, 1954
Robert David - born April 13, 1958

SUMMARY OF EVIDENCE: (IF NECESSARY, ATTACH ADDITIONAL SHEETS)

The evidence presented to the jury established that on the 25th day of July, 1960, James William Grant was a passenger on a United States Weather Bureau plane on a flight from Anchorage, Alaska, to Nome, Alaska. James William Grant was an employee of the United States Government working for the Weather Bureau, at Anchorage, Alaska, and was travelling on official business. That on the 25th day of July, 1960, radio contact with the aircraft was last reported over Skwentna, Alaska, and that no trace of the aircraft or the persons abroad the same or their remains have been discovered; and it further appeared that an extensive aerial search was made by the Air Force and Civil Air Patrol and others, and that the aircraft apparently struck the ground in a place where it cannot be seen from aerial observation.

Fig. 124. Presumptive death certificate

382

UNITED STATES DEPARTMENT OF COMMERCE
WEATHER BUREAU
WASHINGTON

SEP 17 1963

IN REPLY, PLEASE ADDRESS
CHIEF, U. S. WEATHER BUREAU
WASHINGTON 25, D. C.
AND REFER TO

A-1

Mrs. Owen Gardner
92 West Apricot Avenue
Salt Lake City, Utah

Dear Mrs. Gardner:

This is to confirm recent telephone conversations with Mr. Spangler regarding the sighting and identification of the wreckage of the Weather Bureau plane lost in Alaska on July 25, 1960, along with Jim and six other Weather Bureau employees.

The facts in the case briefly follow: On August 25, 1963, a local pilot, Mr. Howard Fowler, while on a hunting trip in the area, sighted the wreckage in the Johnson River Valley, about 50 miles due west of Skwentna. On August 26, the Air Force dispatched three H-21 helicopters to the scene carrying, in addition to Air Force personnel, FAA and Civil Aeronautics Board investigators and two state troopers. Positive identification of the wreckage was made at that time. Two representatives of the Weather Bureau in Anchorage accompanied Civil Aeronautics Board and FAA investigators on August 28. It was found that the wreckage was strewn over a considerable area and there was evidence of high speed impact followed by an explosion and fire. All occupants perished instantaneously.

Since the investigation at the scene of the accident has been completed, there will be no further official trips to the area.

If you should have questions or if this office can be of any assistance whatsoever, I hope that you will feel free to write.

Sincerely yours,

R. C. Grubb
Assistant Chief of Bureau
(Administration)

Fig. 125. Letter regarding death of Weather Bureau employee

383

Of course, not all deaths result in a coroner's inquest, and seldom does one find such unusual circumstances surrounding the deaths of his ancestors, but these records are certainly possibilities to be considered, and they might lead to useful genealogical information in some cases. There is a close relationship between records of the coroner, mortician, hospital, and the state department of vital statistics, and each should be considered when it comes to death information. Sometimes very unusual information is located by investigating each area.

In some of the larger metropolitan cities, special medical examiners are being trained and given the responsibility of examining deceased persons and determining the cause of death. It is a fact that crimes of violence, including murder, rape, felonious assault, and robbery, are increasing and are affecting more and more of us. According to Dr. Howard A. Rusk, a physician and NEW YORK TIMES writer, "in the past, elected coroners and their inexpert juries commonly decided how murder victims died. Medical examiners now perform this function in most places, but in some states it remains in the hands of laymen who know little of pathology and how it can enable dead men to tell tales." In an article which appeared in the DESERET NEWS of 17 July 1968, Dr. Rusk suggests that the archaic coroner's office is on its way out, that the participation of medicine in the administration of justice "in the administration of justice in the United States" is steadily increasing (fig. 126).

Medical Records
Medical records of doctors and hospitals are closely akin to those of the coroner and mortician, and some contain excellent genealogical information. Certain documents and records are, of course, confidential and cannot be searched even by immediate family members. For instance, in the case of the late Jeff Chandler who died as a result of a "back operation," about the same time as President John F. Kennedy was having his back problems, the hospital refused to open their records for inspection, even after a long court battle.

Medical records relating to diagnosis and treatment are strictly confidential, but some of those relating to hospital admittance or social register may be investigated under certain conditions. Most admittance or social register records include facts about the individuals's birth, parentage, religious affiliation, and next of kin (figs. 127 and 128).

On the Isaac Myron Davis problem mentioned previously, the mortician's record indicated Isaac's father had died in the "county hospital," now part of the University Medical Center in Salt Lake City, and personnel at the former institution located pertinent information in their records. In addition to containing basic vital statistics, the records included the names and addresses of two of Isaac's sisters, who were living in Connecticut and Massachusetts and who were indeed heirs to his estate.

Professionals Taking Over

Archaic Coroner Office Nears Demise

By Howard A. Rusk, M.D.

New York Times Writer

NEW YORK — Reported crimes of violence — murder, rape, felonious assault and robbery — increased by 16 percent last year. The toll included 7,600 persons shot to death and 4,400 who died from beatings and stabbings.

There is no quarrel with the basic validity of these statistics. But in some parts of the United States there is still no scientific approach to determining cause of death.

In the past, elected coroners and their inexpert juries commonly decided how murder victims died. Medical examiners now perform this function in most places, but in some states it remains in the hands of laymen who know little of pathology and how it can enable dead men to tell tales.

New York City was one of the earliest to give up the coroner system. It continues to pioneer. Last week it celebrated the 50th anniversary of the office of chief medical examiner by announcing establishment of an Institute of Forensic Medicine — the first of its kind in the United States.

The main purpose of the new institute is to strengthen teaching and research in forensic medicine and forensic pathology, according to Dr. Milton Helpern, the chief medical examiner of New York City and chairman of the department of forensic medicine at New York University School of Medicine.

The new institute is similar to institutes of legal medicine found in most European countries. These are governmental agencies but also are connected with universities.

When deaths are unattended by physicians, the bodies may not be buried without a death certificate. Certification of the cause of death in such cases historically was the responsibility of the coroner.

As recently as 15 years ago, when the National Municipal League, with approval of the American Medical Assn., the American Bar Assn. and other authorities, began recording progress in this field, state constitutions commonly provided for the election of a coroner in each county. Often he was required to impanel a half dozen bystanders as a coroner's jury and let them help him determine the cause of death.

Louisiana and Ohio limited candidates for coroner to physicians. Elsewhere physicians were occasionally induced to run for coroner. In many communities the candidates were competing morticians.

A murder by poison, with no obvious trace, would probably be discovered by the toxicological tests of a skilled pathologist. If a victim were hauled out of the river, the pathologist would look past the natural verdict of drowning and, finding no water in the lungs, determine that death had come from some other cause. And if a victim simply dropped dead, the examiner would know better than to call it heart failure unless there was corroborative medical history.

Under the leadership of the National Municipal League, the backward states may soon be adopting its model system. Richard S. Childs, an officer of the league, initiated the study in 1950 and invoked the technical guidance of Dr. Richard Ford of Harvard Medical School to formulate the model.

For many years Ford was the medical examiner of Massachusetts and developed the system for his state, later adopted by Maryland and Virginia.

To protect and improve the new scientific standards of the service, a new organization known as the National Association of Medical Examiners held its first annual meeting earlier this year. Its major objective is to improve and make more effective the official investigation of sudden, suspicious and violent deaths under the medical examiner system.

In 1954 the American Medical Assn. published a report which concluded: "Medicine participates less effectively in the administration of justice in the United States than it does in any comparable country in the world."

This situation is rapidly changing for the better.

(Copyright)

Fig. 126. Newspaper article, DESERET NEWS, 17 July 1968

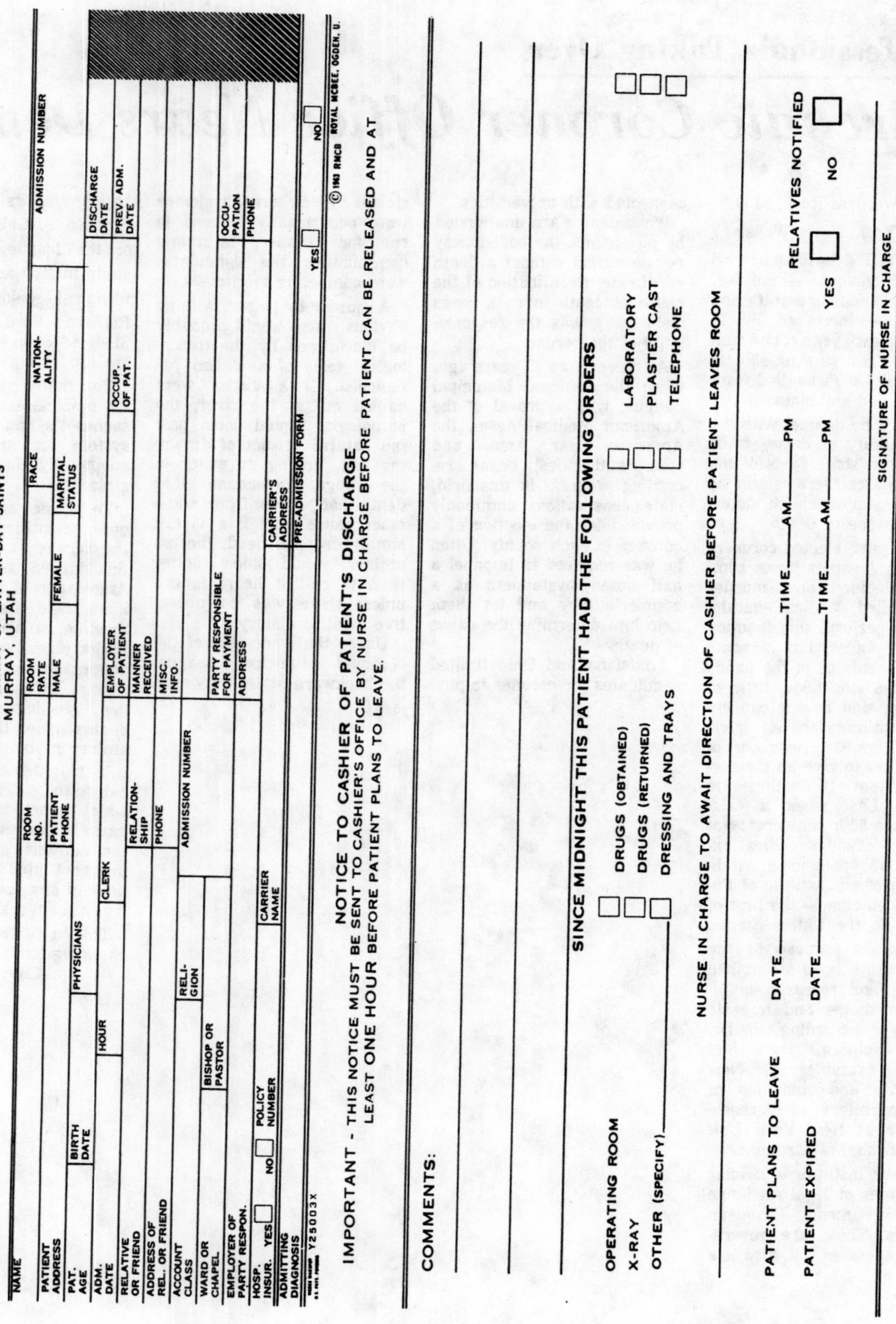

COTTONWOOD HOSPITAL
THE CHURCH OF JESUS CHRIST OF LATTER-DAY SAINTS
MURRAY, UTAH

NAME

| ROOM NO. | ROOM RATE | RACE | NATION-ALITY | ADMISSION NUMBER |

PATIENT ADDRESS

PATIENT PHONE | MALE | FEMALE | MARITAL STATUS

PAT. AGE | BIRTH DATE

PHYSICIANS | DISCHARGE DATE

ADM. DATE | HOUR | CLERK | EMPLOYER OF PATIENT | OCCUP. OF PAT. | PREV. ADM. DATE

RELATIVE OR FRIEND | RELATION-SHIP | MANNER RECEIVED

ADDRESS OF REL. OR FRIEND | PHONE | MISC. INFO.

ACCOUNT CLASS | ADMISSION NUMBER

WARD OR CHAPEL | RELI-GION

BISHOP OR PASTOR | PARTY RESPONSIBLE FOR PAYMENT | OCCU-PATION

EMPLOYER OF PARTY RESPON. | ADDRESS | PHONE

HOSP. INSUR. YES □ NO □ | POLICY NUMBER | CARRIER NAME | CARRIER'S ADDRESS

ADMITTING DIAGNOSIS | PRE-ADMISSION FORM YES □ NO □

Y25003X ROYAL McBEE, OGDEN, U. © 1963 RMCB

IMPORTANT - THIS NOTICE MUST BE SENT TO CASHIER'S OFFICE BY NURSE IN CHARGE BEFORE PATIENT CAN BE RELEASED AND AT LEAST ONE HOUR BEFORE PATIENT PLANS TO LEAVE.

NOTICE TO CASHIER OF PATIENT'S DISCHARGE

COMMENTS:

SINCE MIDNIGHT THIS PATIENT HAD THE FOLLOWING ORDERS

□ DRUGS (OBTAINED) □ LABORATORY
□ DRUGS (RETURNED) □ PLASTER CAST
□ DRESSING AND TRAYS □ TELEPHONE
□ OPERATING ROOM
□ X-RAY
□ OTHER (SPECIFY)

NURSE IN CHARGE TO AWAIT DIRECTION OF CASHIER BEFORE PATIENT LEAVES ROOM

PATIENT PLANS TO LEAVE   DATE _____ TIME _____ AM _____ PM

PATIENT EXPIRED   DATE _____ TIME _____ AM _____ PM

RELATIVES NOTIFIED   YES □   NO □

SIGNATURE OF NURSE IN CHARGE

Fig. 127.   Hospital admittance record

Cottonwood Hospital

Murray, Utah

Birth Certificate

This Certifies that Susanne Marie Wright

was born to Carolyn LaRene Bevan Wright in this Hospital

at 1:26 a. m. on Friday the Fifteenth day of November 1963.

In Witness Whereof the said Hospital has caused this Certificate to be signed by its duly authorized officer and its Official Seal to be hereunto affixed.

Jack T. Alp
Administrator

Val Swendwall
Attending Physician

HOLLISTER Registered BIRTH CERTIFICATE
H4

Fig. 128. Hospital birth record

387

Consultation with personnel at the Cottonwood Hospital in South Salt Lake County indicated they consider their records, including admittance records, "confidential" and "not open for public inspection," but it is likely that certain genealogical facts could be obtained if the right approach were taken with a practicing physician or with certain administrative personnel at the hospital.

Medical studies have also been made concerning individuals and families having unusual or rare diseases, and the results have been published in newspapers and medical journals. Sometimes the important genealogical facts are omitted, but often they are not. A recent newspaper article in a Salt Lake City paper provided detailed genealogical information about a family which had a disease of the central nervous system. The disease was hereditary, and testimony was printed indicating different family members' attitudes toward having children and passing the malady on to the next generation. In a similar case, a California family was able to determine their "southern states origin" by noting published medical information concerning a family with the same surname and same hereditary disease. Very few of the published medical reports contain exact names and vital statistics, but it is probable that official medical files pertaining to the cases do.

Records of Schools and Universities

A variety of records relating to schools, colleges, universities, academies, and social organizations connected with them exist and contain facts which can be useful to the genealogist. Perhaps the individual of interest attended a school or university or was an alumnus of some other institution. Perhaps he belonged to some social unit at that institution or to a fraternal or social order outside the school. Perhaps he was a member of the faculty or was on the board of trustees.

Records for early local schools are few in number and usually only exist where the schoolmaster preserved the records, but those of a more modern period are more readily available. One 1830 school record for the tuition of poor children included the names of children, their ages, guardians, and dates of entrance into school, as well as the names of their teachers and the local school commissioners (fig. 129).

Many of America's colleges and universities have outstanding records collections, including documents relating to admission, registration, credit, and graduation. Many have also published biographies, histories, and yearbooks which contain genealogy, and alumni association records as well as records of fraternal and social units also exist (figs. 130 and 131).

Detailed applications are required for admittance to some of the larger schools and supporting documents are also found in the files. Such records are usually in custody of the registrar or archivist at the school and are not generally considered confidential if a person

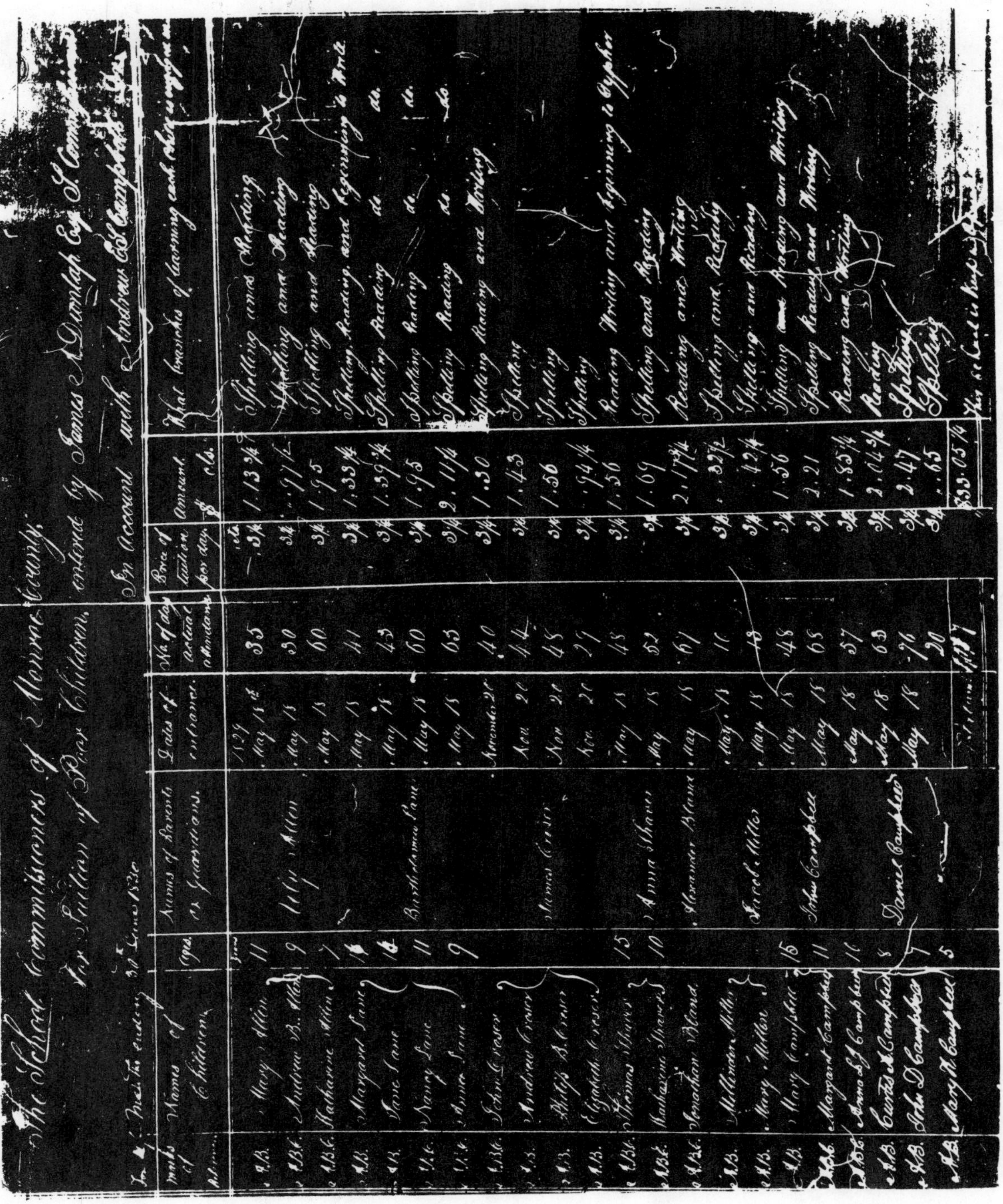

Fig. 129. List of children attending school

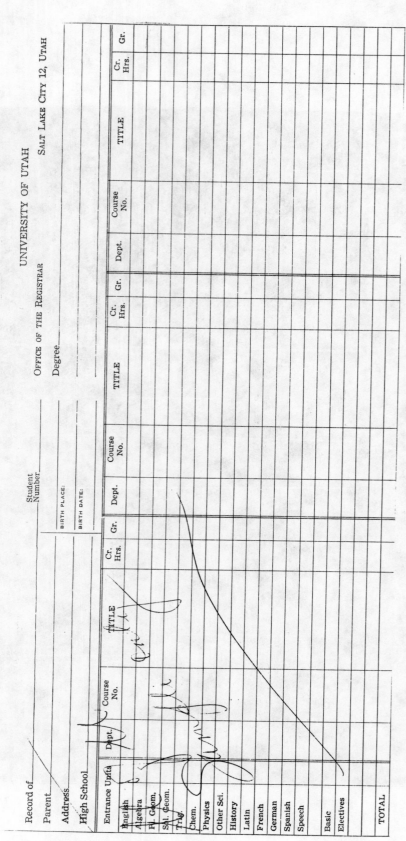

Fig. 130. Transcript of credits form

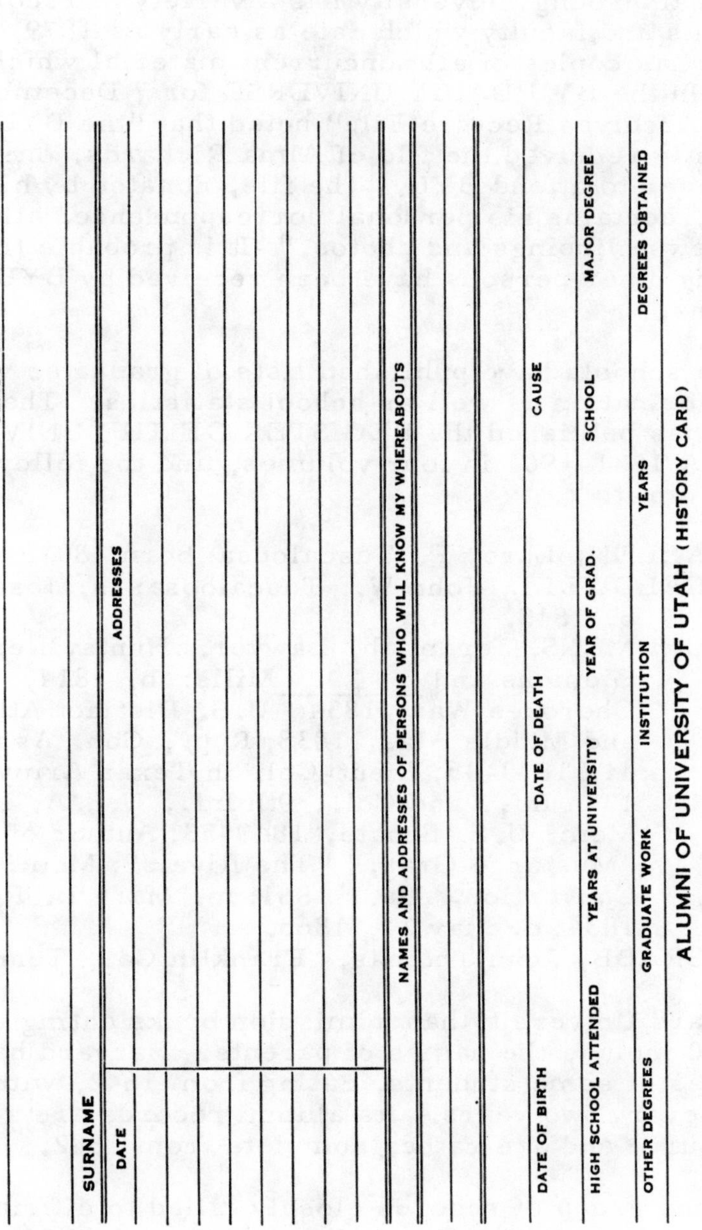

ALUMNI OF UNIVERSITY OF UTAH (HISTORY CARD)

SURNAME

CLASS OF

DATE | ADDRESSES

NAMES AND ADDRESSES OF PERSONS WHO WILL KNOW MY WHEREABOUTS

DATE OF BIRTH | DATE OF DEATH | CAUSE

HIGH SCHOOL ATTENDED | YEARS AT UNIVERSITY | YEAR OF GRAD. | SCHOOL | MAJOR DEGREE

GRADUATE WORK | INSTITUTION | YEARS | DEGREES OBTAINED

OTHER DEGREES

Fig. 131. Alumni history card

391

is courteous in his approach (fig. 132).

Brigham Young University has a variety of records concerning its students and faculty which date as early as 1879, and the University Archivist has copies of all noncurrent material which has been preserved. In the BYU DAILY UNIVERSE for 7 December 1972 an article entitled "Archives Receive File" noted that "the BYU Library Archives has recently received the file of Alma Richards, one of the greatest athletes ever to attend BYU. The file, donated by his widow Lenore Richards, contains his personal correspondence, athletic accomplishments, news clippings and photos." It is probable that similar files concerning other persons have been received by BYU and by other institutions.

Some schools have published lists of graduates which include family information as well as school statistics. The University of Alabama has published the REGISTER OF THE UNIVERSITY OF ALABAMA 1831-1901 in four volumes, and the following are typical entries from it:

> ALLEN, Leroy P. Tuscaloosa; born 1807.
> CALDWELL, John W. Tuscaloosa: s. Joseph Caldwell:
>   b. 1817.
> CLEMENS, Jeremiah, Lawyer. Huntsville: s. James
>   Clemens and _____ Mills: b. 1814, Private, U.S.A.,
>   Cherokee War, 1834: U.S. District Attorney, Northern
>   and Middle Ala., 1838; Rep., Gen. Assem. Ala., 1838-
>   41, 1843-45; Lieut-Col. in Texas Army, 1842, Major,
>   135h Inf., and Col., 9th Inf., U.S.A. Mexican War;
>   Mem. U.S. Senate, 1849-53; Author of "Barnard Lysle,"
>   "Mustange Gray," "The Rivals"; Mem. Constitu.
>   Convention, Ala., 1861; m. Mary L. Read, 4 Dec.
>   1834; d. May 21, 1865.
> CRABB, John Thomas. Franklin Co., Tenn; b. 1812.

Harvard University has admission books dating from 1725; records since 1820 include the names of parents. Harvard has also published biographies of some students, dating from 1642, with a volume appearing about every two years. Its alumni records are also a good genealogical source and are rather complete from 1882.

Another group of records closely allied to official school records are those of fraternities, sororities, and social units associated with the schools. Some have kept very complete records of their members and some units have national as well as local chapters (fig. 133).

Fraternal or social orders outside academic institutions--such as the Masonic Lodge, the Odd Fellows Lodge, the Elks, or the Mystic Shrine--also keep personal records. Some fraternal orders even have records pertaining to insurance and benefits for members and their families which might be used for genealogical purposes.

Date of Application: ....
                           Month   Day   Year

I hereby apply for admission to the two-year program leading to the degree of Master in Business Administration in the class entering in September, 1962.

1. Signature ....
                           First   Middle   Last

2. Age as of Sept. 12, 1962 ....3. Birth Date:...

4. Marital Status:.....................5. Number of Children:.........................6. Their Ages:.................

7. Are your parents living? Father...Mother.......................................

8. Father's Name:...

    Address ....

    Occupation ....

    (If father is deceased or his address is unknown, please give the above data for nearest relative and indicate relationship to you.)

9. Number of Brothers and Sisters:..........................10. Their Ages:...

11. Are you a citizen of the United States? Yes.............................No..

12. Supplemental questions for applicants who are not citizens of the United States:

    Citizen of ....

    Do you intend to return to your native land? ....

13. Please list all secondary schools, colleges, and universities attended. (If possible, it is preferred that you enclose with this application official transcripts of your record at *each* of the colleges and graduate schools listed. If for any reason you are unable to enclose an official transcript, please request of the appropriate official at your college that one be sent to the Admissions Board, Harvard Business School, Boston 63, Massachusetts. If the transcript must be sent separately, it would considerably expedite processing to have it sent *prior* to submission of this application.)

SECONDARY SCHOOLS, COLLEGES AND GRADUATE SCHOOLS	LOCATION	DATES ATTENDED FROM	TO	DEGREE, IF ANY, AND YEAR RECEIVED
....	....	....	....	....
....	....	....	....	....

Fig. 132. Application to Harvard School of Graduate Business

393

BIOGRAPHICAL DATA CARD
(MUST BE TYPEWRITTEN)

Historian Form 131
1958

Do Not Fold

_____ (Chapter) _____ (Yr. of Grad.) _____ (Leave Blank)

(Last, First and Middle Names)

PERMANENT HOME ADDRESS: _____ (Date of Pledging)

(Number, Street, City, Zone, State)

DATE OF BIRTH: _____ PLACE OF BIRTH: _____

(Month, Day, Year) (Town, County, State)

FATHER'S FULL NAME: _____ MOTHER'S MAIDEN NAME: _____

RACIAL ORIGIN: _____ RELIGIOUS PREFERENCE: _____

(Not Nationality)

ENTERED: _____ (Date) _____ (Course)

(University at which chapter is located;

ATTENDED: _____

(Any other colleges)

DATE OF INITIATION: _____ IF NOT INITIATED, WHY? _____

(To be inserted at General Headquarters)

RELATIVES IN GREEK-LETTER SOCIETIES:

Name   College   Class   Relationship

Signed, this _____ day of _____ 19____ _____

(Signature of Pledge in ink)

Fig. 133. Biographical data card for social unit

394

PETITION FOR INITIATION AND MEMBERSHIP
El Kalah Temple
Ancient Arabic Order Nobles of the Mystic Shrine

To the Illustrious Potentate, Officers and Members of El Kalah Temple,
Situated in Oasis of Salt Lake City, Desert of Utah:
I, the undersigned, hereby declare that I am a Master Mason in good standing in

....Lodge No..................F. & A. M., at...
A Royal Arch Mason in good standing in

....Chapter No..................R. A. M., at...
A Knight Templar in good standing in

....Commandery No..................K. T., at...
OR a 32° Ancient and Accepted Scottish Rite Mason in good standing in

....Consistory, A. & A. S. R., at...

Furthermore, I do not now, and never will, hold membership in or allegiance to any body claiming to be Masonic that has been declared clandestine by a Commandery or Preceptory of Knights Templar or Consistory of the Ancient and Accepted Scottish Rite of Free Masonry of the obedience of either the Supreme Councils of the Northern or Southern Masonic Jurisdiction of such Rite in the United States, or those Supreme Councils which are in amity with and recognized by them; that I have resided in the Jurisdiction of your Temple, or in unoccupied territory, not less than six months, as required by the Constitution of the Imperial Council, and that I am not under suspension or expulsion in either of the bodies prerequisite to this order, and respectfully pray that I may be made a Noble of the Mystic Shrine, and become a member of your Temple.

If I be found worthy, and my request granted, I promise to conform to all the Ceremonies, Engagements, Constitutions, Regulations and Edicts of the Imperial Council, together with those of your Temple.

Have you previously applied for admission to any Temple of the Order?...

If so, to what Temple... When?...

Birthplace... Date of Birth...

Profession or Occupation...

Business Address...Street, City...

Residence Address...Street, City...

Mail Address...Street, City...

Date... Size of Hat...

Signature (all names in full)...

Print name as you want same on **Addressograph**...

Recommended and vouched for on the honor of

Noble...No.........................

Noble...No.........................

(This space for Recorder)

Investigating Committee {
....
....
....
....
}

Fee Paid...

Elected......................... Created.........................

Shrine No...

Total Fee $125 Must Accompany Petition

Fig. 134. Membership documents for fraternal organizations

395

PETITION FOR DEGREES IN MASONRY

Salt Lake City, Utah, ...19.........

To the Worshipful Master, Wardens and Members of Mount Moriah Lodge No. 2, F. & A. M. of Utah:

I, the undersigned, freely and voluntarily offer myself as a candidate for the mysteries and privileges of Freemasonry and respectfully petition that I may become a member of your Lodge.

I make this request unbiased by the solication of friends and uninfluenced by mercenary or other unworthy motives, being prompted by a favorable opinion conceived of the institution, a desire for knowledge and a sincere wish to be serviceable to my fellow men. If found worthy and elected, I will conform to all the ancient usages and regulations of the fraternity.

Have you carefully read the Authorized Statement on the reverse side of this Petition? ....

What is your full name? (print or type) ....
(All Names in Full, Including Middle Name)

What is your age? ....years. Date of birth (month, day, year)..

Where were you born? ....

What is your residence address? .... Tel................... Postal Zone...........

What is your business address? .... Tel................... Postal Zone...........

Where do you want your mail sent? ....

Are you a proprietor of or a vendor in an establishment the principal business of which is the sale of malt or spiritous liquors as a beverage? ....

What is your occupation? ....

State explicitly your occupation for the past ten years an where conducted ....

....

Has the State of Utah been your place of legal residence for the last twelve months? ....

What towns have been your place of legal residence during the past six months? ....

Where have you resided the five years last past? If in more than one place, state the particular years in each place. ....

....

....

Have you ever presented a Petition to any Masonic Lodge? .... If so, when, to what Lodge and what action was taken?

....

Do you believe in the existence of a Supreme Being? .... Are you married? ....

Are you in sound bodily health? .... Have you any physical defect or deformity? .... If so, describe

....

List the Fraternal or Religious Organizations with which you are affiliated: ....

....

Will you see that your family understands that Masonry is NOT an Insurance or Benefit Society? ....

List two character references, other than your recommenders, and preferably Masons.

Name .... Address ....

Name .... Address ....

Do you upon your honor, declare all of the foregoing statements to be true? ....

(Signed) ....
(Usual Signature of Applicant)

Fig. 134a.

396

Form 1

ANCIENT AND ACCEPTED

Scottish Rite of Freemasonry

Southern Jurisdiction

Valley of Salt Lake, Orient of Utah

RECEIVED...........................

FEE PAID $...........................

DATE ENT. ....

....

TO THE OFFICERS AND MEMBERS OF
THE SCOTTISH RITE BODIES OF UTAH:

...., 19...........
(City or Town)   (Date)

I, the undersigned, certify that I am a Master Mason in good standing in...........................
         (Name of Lodge)

Lodge No. .... F. & A. M., located at ...., under the Jurisdiction of the

Grand Lodge of ....; and was raised to that degree in...........................
   (State)   (Name of Lodge)

Lodge No. ...., located at ...., on ....
                (Date Degree Received)

I have passed a satisfactory examination in the catechism of the Master Mason degree, and have resided in this State since

.... I have never *previously applied for any of the Scottish Rite Degrees, except as explained

on the reverse side hereof, and I now respectfully petition to receive the degrees from the .... inclusive,

promising always to bear true faith and allegiance to the Supreme Council of the Thirty-third Degree.

 I. The Supreme Council announces as fundamental principles the following:

   "The inculcation of patriotism, respect for law and order and undying loyalty to the Constitution of the United States of America.

   "The entire separation of church and state and opposition to every attempt to appropriate public monies — federal, state or local — directly or indirectly, for the support of sectarian or private institutions."

  Do you approve wholeheartedly of these principles? ....
           yes or no

 II. Have you ever held or expressed opinions contrary to the foregoing or been affiliated with any organization which has?

                     ....
                     yes or no

 If you answer this question in the affirmative, give particulars on the reverse side hereof.

List here the Fraternal and Religious organizations with which you are affiliated:

....

....

I am...........................(State whether single, married, divorced or widower.)

My occupation is ....
     (State fully and clearly your occupation, or particular kind of business engaged in)

In connection with or service of...........................
     (Give name of firm or corporation, kind of business, and its address)

My position is that of...........................
     (State fully and specifically the nature of your duties)

Residence .... Residence Phone...........................
     (Give city or town, street and number)

Business address .... Business Phone...........................

Please address my mail to... Zone Number ....

Date of birth...........................

Place of birth... , ... , ...
     (City or town)   (County)   (State)

Hight...........ft...........inches; color of eyes...........................; color of hair...........................; hat size...........................;

Recommended by:

....

....
          (Sign all names in full, not initials)

....
          (Then print or typewrite name in full)

Investigation Committee   Address

Fig. 134b.

YORK RITE OF FREEMASONRY   FEE $15.00

APPLICATION FOR MEMBERSHIP

To the officers and members of .... Council No........., R. & S. M.
of ....,Utah:

The subscriber respectfully represents that he was made a Master Mason in .... Lodge
No. .... in .... State of .... date ....

and now a member of .... Lodge No......... in .... State of ....

.... State of .... or has petitioned to receive the Capitular Chapter No......... at ....

Degrees of the York Rite in .... Chapter No......... at .... State of ....

.... and has never been proposed or rejected for the Degrees in any Council of Royal and
Select Masters and now prays to receive the Degrees in .... Council No........., R. & S. M.
of Utah, and if elected promises a cheerful compliance to all the laws, rules and regulations thereof.

Date of birth .... Place .... Residence ....

Occupation .... Employer ....

Business Address ....

Recommended by ....
.... (Name in full. No initials.)

Companion........................   *Refers to:*   Phone........................

Companion........................   Companion........................

Report of Committee   Companion........................

Companion........................   Elected........................

Companion........................

Companion........................   R. M. Degree........................

Ill. Master ....   S. M. Degree........................

Recorder ....   S. E. M. Degree........................

Fig. 134c.

Application for Membership in
Salt Lake City Lodge No. 85

Benevolent and Protective Order of Elks
of the United States of America

Brother_____under the obligation of the Order, proposes for membership in this Lodge,

Mr._____

_____
Signature of Proposer

QUESTIONS TO BE ANSWERED BY APPLICANT

IMPORTANT! Applicant's name, complete address including P.O. box, rural route, street address, Zone No. (if any), and correct post office should be given. Your home address will be used as mailing address unless otherwise specified.

1. Name_____ Occupation_____

   Home Address_____ Telephone_____

   Business Address_____ Telephone_____

2. State the place and date of your birth. Answer: Born in City of_____

   County of_____, State of_____, on the_____day of_____in year_____

3. Do you believe in the existence of God?   .   .   .   . Answer_____

4. Are you a Citizen of the United States of America?   .   .   .   .   .   . Answer_____

5. If foreign born, when and where were final naturalization papers issued? Answer_____

6. Are you willing to assume an obligation that
   (a) Will not conflict with your duties to yourself, or your family, or your religious or political opinions, and that
   (b) Will bind you to uphold the Constitution and laws of the United States of America? Answer_____

7. Are you now or have you ever been a member of the Communist party or directly or indirectly connected or affiliated with the Communist party, or with any organization or group advocating or believing in the overthrow of the government of the United States by force?   Answer_____

8. Have you ever pleaded guilty to, or been convicted of a felony? .   .   .   .   . Answer_____
   If your answer is in the affirmative, state nature of crime, date and place of conviction, and sentence imposed.

9. If you have ever been discharged from the Armed Services of the United States or any of its Allies, state the character of the discharge received   .   .   .   .   .   . Answer_____

10. Do you anticipate any pecuniary benefits by becoming a member of this Order?   Answer_____

11. Do you know of any physical ailment that might cause you to become a burden upon this Order?   Answer_____

12. Have you ever been proposed for membership in any lodge of this Order, and if so, where and when and with what result?   .   .   Answer_____

13. Have you been a bona fide resident within the jurisdiction of this Lodge for the period of six months immediately preceding the date of this application?   Answer_____

14. I understand and agree that the annual dues paid by me to your Lodge include the sum of $1.00, or any other sum that hereafter may be established by the Grand Lodge, to cover my subscription to The Elks Magazine.

15. Give references of at least two members of this Order, stating the name, home address, and business address of each.

NAME	HOME ADDRESS	BUSINESS ADDRESS

16. Give the name of each place of residence you have had during the five years last preceding the date of this application, specifying date of each change therein, also the occupation followed by you in each place.

PLACE OF RESIDENCE	WHEN ESTABLISHED	WHEN CHANGED	OCCUPATION

17. Give the name and address of at least two citizens of any city in which you have resided during the last five years, where a lodge of this Order is located.

NAME	HOME ADDRESS	BUSINESS ADDRESS

The above blank must be fully filled out by the Proposer and the Applicant, and to be accompanied by an Application Fee of _____Dollars, or it will not be considered. Balance of Initiation Fee_____Dollars, and proportionate Semi-Annual Dues up to next April 1st October 1st [strike out date not needed] must both be paid at time of initiation.

Date_____19____   _____
Signature of Applicant (in his own handwriting)

Fig.   134d.

WORK SHEET

OR

**PRELIMINARY APPLICATION
TO THE NATIONAL SOCIETY**

OF THE

DAUGHTERS OF THE AMERICAN COLONISTS

(Not to be used as a regular application)

I, ..., being of the age .... years,

hereby apply for membership in this Society by right of lineal descent in the following line from ....

who was born in .... on the .... day of ....

and died in .... on the .... day of ...., 1............

(1) I am the daughter of .... born .... died ....

married (date) .... place ....

to .... born .... died ....

(2) grand daughter of .... born .... died ....

married (date) .... place ....

to .... born .... died ....

(3) great grand daughter of .... born .... died ....

married (date) .... place ....

to .... born .... died ....

(4) great 2 grand daughter of .... born .... died ....

married (date) .... place ....

to .... born .... died ....

Fig. 135. Application for a patriotic society

Such records are often confidential and are generally in custody of the local lodge, temple, or shrine. Addresses of current organizations can be obtained from local telephone directories, but those for inactive or defunct units must be located through personal research in the localities of concern (fig. 134).

Records of Hereditary and Patriotic Societies

Membership records of hereditary societies and patriotic organizations have long been regarded as excellent genealogical sources. Most of these organizations require formal application for membership, usually including a family connection to some colonial group or citizen such as a Revolutionary War veteran or some other patriot. Membership is generally based on common objectives and purposes or, as with the hereditary and lineage societies, on a common background derived from having ancestors who lived during a certain period and were committed to a common cause (fig. 135).

The National Society Daughters of the American Revolution is perhaps the most widely known patriotic organization, and it has followed an active plan to recruit members for many years. The NSDAR has not only been responsible for the location and preservation of genealogical data concerning others, but has also been effective in preserving genealogical information about its own members. LINEAGE CHARTS have been published showing members and their ancestry, and a PATRIOT INDEX was published in 1966 which contains the names of 105,500 patriots, both men and women, who have served the nation in some capacity. Copies of these publications are on file at the Genealogical Society Library in Salt Lake City as well as other libraries and historical societies.

Some societies maintain a card index of ancestors claimed by their applicants for membership. The Sons of the American Revolution maintain a card for each Revolutionary ancestor, and on that card is shown the membership number of each member who has claimed that ancestor. They have also published lists showing members and their ancestors.

The following list gives the names and addresses of several hereditary and lineage societies in America and shows how early each was organized:

THE SOCIETY OF THE CINCINNATI, organized 1783; 2118 Massachusetts Ave. N.W., Washington, D.C. 20008
    DAUGHTERS OF THE CINCINNATI, organized 1894; 122 E. 58th Street, New York City, New York
    NATIONAL SOCIETY DAUGHTERS OF THE AMERICAN REVOLUTION, organized 1890; 1776 D Street, N.W., Washington, D.C. 20006
    NATIONAL SOCIETY DAUGHTERS OF THE REVOLUTION, organized 1891; 66 Hiehgts Road, Ridgewood, New Jersey 07450

NATIONAL SOCIETY SONS OF THE AMERICAN REVOLUTION, organized 1889; 2412 Massachusetts Avenue N.W., Washington, D.C. 20008

GENERAL SOCIETY SONS OF THE REVOLUTION, organized 1876; Fraunces Tavern, 54 Pearl Street, New York, New York 10004

DESCENDANTS OF THE SIGNERS OF THE DECLARATION OF INDEPENDENCE, organized 1907; 1300 Locust Street, Philadelphia, Pennsylvania 19107

GENERAL SOCIETY OF THE WAR OF 1812, organized 1814; Secretary General, 3311 Columbia Pike, Lancaster, Pennsylvania 17603

NATIONAL SOCIETY UNITED STATES DAUGHTERS OF 1812, organized 1892; 1461 Rhode Island Avenue N.W., Washington, D.C. 20005

AZTEC CLUB OF 1847, organized 1847; 5225 Westpath Way, Washington, D.C. 20036

MILITARY ORDER OF THE LOYAL LEGION OF THE UNITED STATES, organized 1865; 1805 Pine Street, Philadelphia, Pennsylvania 19103

DAMES OF THE LOYAL LEGION OF THE UNITED STATES, organized 1899; P.O. Box 24, Gettysburg, Pennsylvania 17225

AUXILIARY TO SONS OF THE UNION VETERANS OF THE CIVIL WAR, organized 1883; 2025 Cleveland Avenue, West Lawn, Pennsylvania 19609

LADIES OF THE GRAND ARMY OF THE REPUBLIC, organized 1886; 90 Conestoga Boulevard, Lancaster, Pennsylvania 17602

SONS OF CONFEDERATE VETERANS, organized 1896; Southern Station, Box 1, Hattiesburg, Mississippi 39401

ORDER OF STARS AND BARS, organized after 1889; Southern Station, Box 1, Hattiesburg, Mississippi 39401

UNITED DAUGHTERS OF THE CONFEDERACY, organized 1894; 328 North Boulevard, Richmond, Virginia 23220

SPANISH WAR VETERANS UNITED, organized 1898; 810 Vermont Avenue N.W., Box 1915, Washington, D.C. 20013

MILITARY ORDER OF THE WORLD WARS, organized 1920; 910 Seventeenth Street N.W., Washington, D.C. 10006

Sources for the American Indian

At a genealogical seminar in Tacoma, Washington, in 1964, the following pedigree information was produced by a fine-looking gentleman who said he was a Sioux Indian (fig. 136).

James (whose Indian name was Winter) indicated his wife Susan (whose Indian name was Snow) was a Blackfeet (not a Blackfoot) Indian and said they were the parents of two sons, namely, Sweet Pine (Gary) and Petrified Buffalo Medicine Boy (James, Jr.). Winter had married Snow and they had Sweet Pine and Petrified Buffalo Medicine Boy. (Of course this is not much different from "Comfort" marrying "Patience" and having two daughters named "Thankful Relief" and "Faith" or Mr. "Doolittle" marrying Miss "Longnecker" and naming a child Theodore, which means "Horselover." Unusual

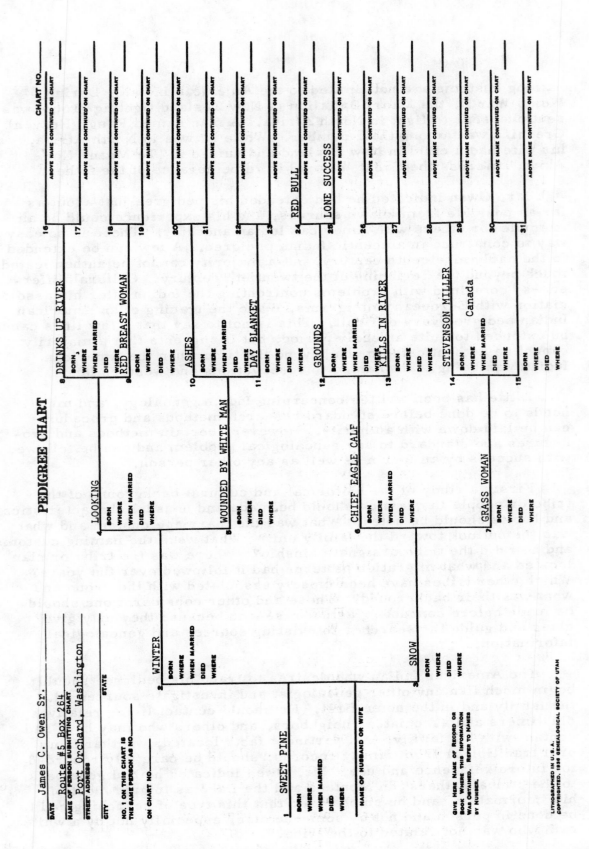

Fig. 136. Pedigree of James C. Owen (Winter) and Susan Ground (Snow)

naming customs are not limited to the American Indian. During World War II, the Maori Battalion (a New Zealand fighting group) was sent overseas to fight in North Africa. A man named Rangi (Heaven) Greening was among their number. While he was in North Africa, his wife had a child in New Zealand and named it "Te Moana Nui Akiwa" (Across the Great Waters) in remembrance of the father.

Mr. Owen indicated he had extended his pedigree just about as far as possible from known sources, and his experience could be an example for others with American Indian ancestry. There is no easy way to construct an authentic Indian pedigree. A few can be extended to the early nineteenth century, but a majority cannot be authenticated much beyond the beginning of the twentieth century. Cultural differences, combined with problems confronting the Indian after his association with European immigrants, make the tracing of an American Indian pedigree very difficult. This is not to say that a few lines cannot be extended to quite an early period, but it suggests that a majority cannot be authenticated much beyond the time when the American Indian was being transplanted to reservations and western lands.

Little has been written concerning Indian genealogy, and much needs to be done before standard research methods and procedures can be laid down with authority. However, certain methods and procedures are standard to any genealogical problem and can be followed with success by an Indian as well as any other person.

First, a study of the historical and cultural background of the tribe or people in question should be made and unusual characteristics and habits should be noted. What was the marriage custom and what was the outlook toward the family unit? What were the naming customs and how did the tribe designate kinship? Where was the tribe or clan located and what migration patterns had it followed over the years? Which other tribes have been closely associated with the group and what was their background? These and other considerations should be made before conducting actual research because they may give clues and guide the searcher to existing sources and genealogical information.

The American Indian who desires to trace his pedigree should begin much like any other genealogist and investigate sources with the family and in the home first. He should contact living relatives, old-timers and associates, neighbors, and others who may have had contact with his family. All pertinent facts located, whether from oral tradition or from family records, should be carefully recorded for future reference and use. Mr. Owen indicated he had gone back to the "tribal fathers" in Montana and the Dakotas to gain most of his information, and he emphasized that this type of searching had to be done in person and not by someone else, especially not by a white man who was not related to the tribe.

Some elderly tribal members have excellent memories and can

recall early family and tribal history. Many believe the Maori of New Zealand to be close kin of the American Indian. They were very effective in handing down genealogy ("whakapapa") through oral tradition, carvings, paintings, and through song and dance. Like the Indians, they did not have a written language when the white man first contacted them, but many Maoris could chant their genealogy back to the 1200s. According to Maori sages, the "tohunga" (priest) would choose a young intelligent man (usually between the ages of fourteen and sixteen) and train him to memorize the genealogies and sacred ("tapu") things. [2] It is possible that similar customs have been followed by some American Indian tribes, but it stands to reason that such information is sacred and probably not available to outsiders.

After gathering available oral and written testimony from the home jurisdiction, tribal records maintained by the council or clan should be investigated. Records may be found with individual members or in official council offices, dating primarily after the intervention of the U.S. Government in Indian affairs. A majority of these records only date to the 1920s, though some pertaining to the "five civilized tribes" (Cherokee, Chickasaw, Choctaw, Creek, and Seminole) date to about 1820. The records include such things as modern vital statistics, census and enrollment records, annuity and payment records, land records and other documents relating to the family and tribal connections.

Copies of a few tribal records have been filed with the Genealogical Society Library in Salt Lake City, and the following entry was taken from GENEALOGIES OF THE BLACKFOOT INDIAN TRIBE IN BROWNING, GLACIER, MONTANA (GS F#459,651). The record itself was copied in 1956 from "Books in the Tribal Office" of the Blackfoot Council at Browning by Anthony C. (Mose) Gilham and was microfilmed by the Genealogical Society in 1968.

RIDES AT THE DOOR   Full Peigan   44 yrs
    Father: LONE PITY, dead
        Grandfather: CHIEF BULL, dead
        Grandmother: SPRING WATER, dead
    Mother: YELLOW OWL WOMAN, dead
        Grandfather: SCREAMING OWL, dead
        Grandmother: DRY GOOD WOMAN WITH THE COAT,
                living
THE COAT, living, is a brother of YELLOW OWL WOMAN. GOOD MEDICINE PIPE WOMAN, living, is a sister of YELLOW OWL WOMAN. RED CALF, wife of SHOOTS FIRST, living, is sister of YELLOW OWL WOMAN. BIG ROBE was brother, no issue, dead. SCREAMING OWL, dead, brother, no issue. MANY TAIL FEATHERS is half brother of YELLOW OWL WOMAN. JAMES MANY TAIL FEATHERS is half brother of YELLOW OWL WOMAN. FINE VICTORY, wife of BIG WOLF MEDICINE, is half sister of YELLOW OWL WOMAN. HANDING BACK, wife of SPOTTED EAGLE, is half sister.

Wife: MARY GRANT RIDES AT THE DOOR   3/4 Peigan   37 yrs
married 1887 - Indian's Custom
Father: JAMES GRANT, dead, Blackfoot
Mother: MARY CADOTTE GRANT, living by herself.
Grandfather: CADOTTE
Grandmother: unknown

Paternal Aunts and Uncles unknown. CHARLES ROSE, living, is half brother of MARY GRANT. PETER CADOTTE is half brother of MARY. Brothers and sisters of MARY are JULIA MAGEE, living, wife of TOM MAGEE. MAGGIE LITTLE SKUNK and CECILE LITTLE SKUNK. JAMES GRANT, RICHARD GRANT, PETER GRANT, are half brothers.

Children:

RICHARD RIDES AT THE DOOR	18	md to AMY SLANNON
FRANK	13	
JAMES	10	
JOHNNY	7	
JOSEPH	5	
WILLIAM	2	
ANNIE		born 1908

Lives between Willow Creek and John Vielle. Wants boys to have land on Willow Creek and will take up land above FOX'S on upper Willow Creek.

There were several hundred entries in the above record, and the information had evidently been compiled from family knowledge and recorded in council books.

Part of another entry from the same record follows:

LITTLE DOG   Part Peigan   54 yrs
Paternal Uncles and Aunts all dead. LITTLE DOG stated that the mother of WALKING IN THE WATER was LONG TIME GOOD SUCCESS. SHORT RIB says that WALKING IN THE WATER was daughter of UNDER PETRIFIED ROCK, a sister of his. When UNDER PETRIFIED ROCK died, the child was taken and raised by LONG TIME GOOD SUCCESS, a cousin of UNDER PETRIFIED ROCK. SHORT RIB says that LITTLE DOG thinks his mother-in-law is LONG TIME GOOD SUCCESS but is in error. A cousin of LONG TIME GOOD SUCCESS was CALF BOSS RIBS, died 2 years ago, leaving BARNEY ROSS RIBS and MEDICINE RABBIT, a girl, and CAPTURING A GUN IN THE MORNING, a boy. Sister of LONG TIME GOOD SUCCESS is DOUBLE BLANKET WOMAN, living. The father of PETRIFIED ROCK is dead. The mother, VICTORY AT HOME is dead.

Family connections in the above record were cross-referenced when they appeared in more than one entry. It can readily be seen that such information is valuable to the searcher if he once finds a family connection, but very little "date" or "place" information is given.

It can also be seen that complex and unusual family relationships existed among the American Indians because of death, divorce, abandonment, and the like. Doctor James R. Clark in his THE CULTURAL AND HISTORICAL BACKGROUND OF THE INDIAN PEOPLE: A VITAL PART OF THE GENEALOGICAL RESEARCH PROBLEM (paper read at the World Conference on Records and Genealogical Seminar in Salt Lake City, August 1969) explains the complex nature of some Crow family units:

> In a small, light blue house on the east side of the highway leading out of Crow Agency, Montana our interviewer met MAY TAKES GUN CHILD IN MOUTH. Mrs. CHILD IN MOUTH was 73 years of age at the time of the interview. She was a widow. She was a 3/4 blood Crow or Absaraka. Living with her was IRA L. BAD BEAR, a grandson, age 19 who was single. Also living with her was DENNIS BIG HAIR, a grandnephew, age 27 who was divorced.
> ANDREW BIRD IN GROUND lived in Real Bird Land Southeast of the Crow Agency. Living with him in his home was a rather typical extended family. There was his wife, INEZ, his son-in-law, BURTON DARROW PRETTY ON TOP who had married ELEANOR, daughter of the BIRD IN GROUNDS'. Also living at home, with her daughter, CARLEN FAITH BIRD IN GROUND, was their 20 year old, single daughter, ANDREA. The BIRD IN GROUNDS had seven other children living at home with them ranging in age from 19 to 4 years of age (p. 9).

(This situation is not peculiar to Indian families; the white man sometimes creates problems which are just as complex or allow extended family association equal to that above. Several years ago, in a family in Corpus Christi, Texas, three generations were living in the same home with unusual and extended relationship. "Big Daddy" was the father and head of the house while "Daddy Boy" was a grandson, child of a daughter who was divorced and who was also living in the home. "Big Mama" was not the wife of "Big Daddy" as might be supposed but was his mother, having her own parlor and bedroom and also enjoying her own television set. The father-in-law of "Big Daddy" was also living with the family. The wife of "Big Daddy" and mother in the home was not known by any special nickname but was a loving mother, wife, daughter, daughter-in-law, grandmother, and a wonderful cook. The love and help given family members, and the hospitality shown visitors, was truly exemplary, as it is in many American Indian families of this kind.)

The tribal fathers may also have other records of genealogical value, including tribal enrollment records where individuals were identified as officially belonging to a particular tribe. The following is an example of a record which has been microfilmed and filed at the Genealogical Society Library:

HOMER ABERCROMBIE - Mineral Bluff, Georgia
Rejected: Applicant and ancestors never enrolled.
No affiliation or association with Eastern Band shown.
Applicant never recognized by Tribe as member.
Ancestors: Sallie Reid, Robert Wright and Riley Wright.
Decisions: Vol. V page 304.
(Cherokee Enrollment Records, vol. I, 1924 GS F#847, 750)

Entries for individuals whose applications were accepted by the Tribe are similar to those which were rejected; each includes the individual's name and residence and gives names of the ancestors he hoped to show were connected to the tribe. In some cases the entry also indicates the number of children in the family, though no entries were observed where their names were listed. Hundreds of "rejects" were noted in the above record, which suggests many persons applied who perhaps were never recognized as tribal members. This is good as far as genealogy is concerned.

After investigating records of the tribal councils and clans or bands, those of the Indian Agencies should be considered. Agencies under the Bureau of Indian Affairs administered government policy, and records were kept pertaining to land allotment, payment and receipt of monies, census, heirship and probate matters, and other events.

Census records were kept for some Cherokee Indians as early as 1835, and annual enumerations were required by an act of Congress dated 4 July 1884. Persons maintaining a formal affiliation with a particular tribe under federal supervision were enumerated. Some tribes, such as those in New York State, have never been under federal control and they are not included. Those with some degree of Indian blood who did not maintain a tribal connection are not included either, and the "white man's" census records should be consulted for them. No census rolls exist for some reservation Indians because of administrative problems, and some enumerations were probably incorrect and "padded"[3] (fig. 137).

The information given in the census varies with each annual enumeration, but each includes the name (usually the Indian name and the English name), age, sex, and sometimes relationship. The modern enumerations also include present and past residence information as well as other items (fig. 138).

It is advisable to search the modern rolls first and then proceed with earlier enumerations, because the families were listed in numerical order and reference is given to previous rolls. It should also be remembered that some individuals changed their names, some as many as four times, and careful evaluation of the appropriate rolls must be made.

Originals for the census rolls dated 1885-1940 and special rolls

Census of the Chehalis Indians of Chehalis Reservation
Puyallup Consolidated Agency W.T. for 1888

Indian Name	No	English Name	Age	Relation	Remarks
Sut-up	1	Jim Walker	48	Hush	
Se-ah-koht-ca	2	Susie Walker	50	wife	
Si-ya-hun	3	Charlie Walker	50	Hush	
Wah-bush	4	Mary Walker	48	wife	
Kutõ-hues	5	Geo Walker	53	Hush	
	6	Mary Walker	58	wife	
	7	Joe Walker	30	Hush	
	8	Clara Walker		wife	
Choke	9	William Choke	58	Hush	
Quad-chil-chu	10	Sally Choke	53	wife	
Kit-sun	11	Jack Choke	53	Hush	
Kla Klutsh	12	Nellie Choke	30	wife	
	13	Thomas Choke	14	Son	
	14	Joseph Choke	10	"	
	15	Millie Choke	6	Dau	
	16	William Choke	4	Son	
	17	Edwin Choke	2	"	
Que-hun-doh	18	Sally Hawanet	78		
Ho-wa-net	19	Harry Hawanet	43	Hush	
Kwe-pah	20	Josephine Hawanet	68	wife	
Hat-dut	21	Old Ben	78	Hush	
Ke-ka-ek	22	—	53	wife	
How-y-ah	23	Lucy Jack	32	Dau	
Qua-ok-sot	24	Dan Ben	25	Son	
Kla-u-til	25	Jack Ben	43	Hush	

Fig. 137. Census of the Chehalis Indians, 1888   409

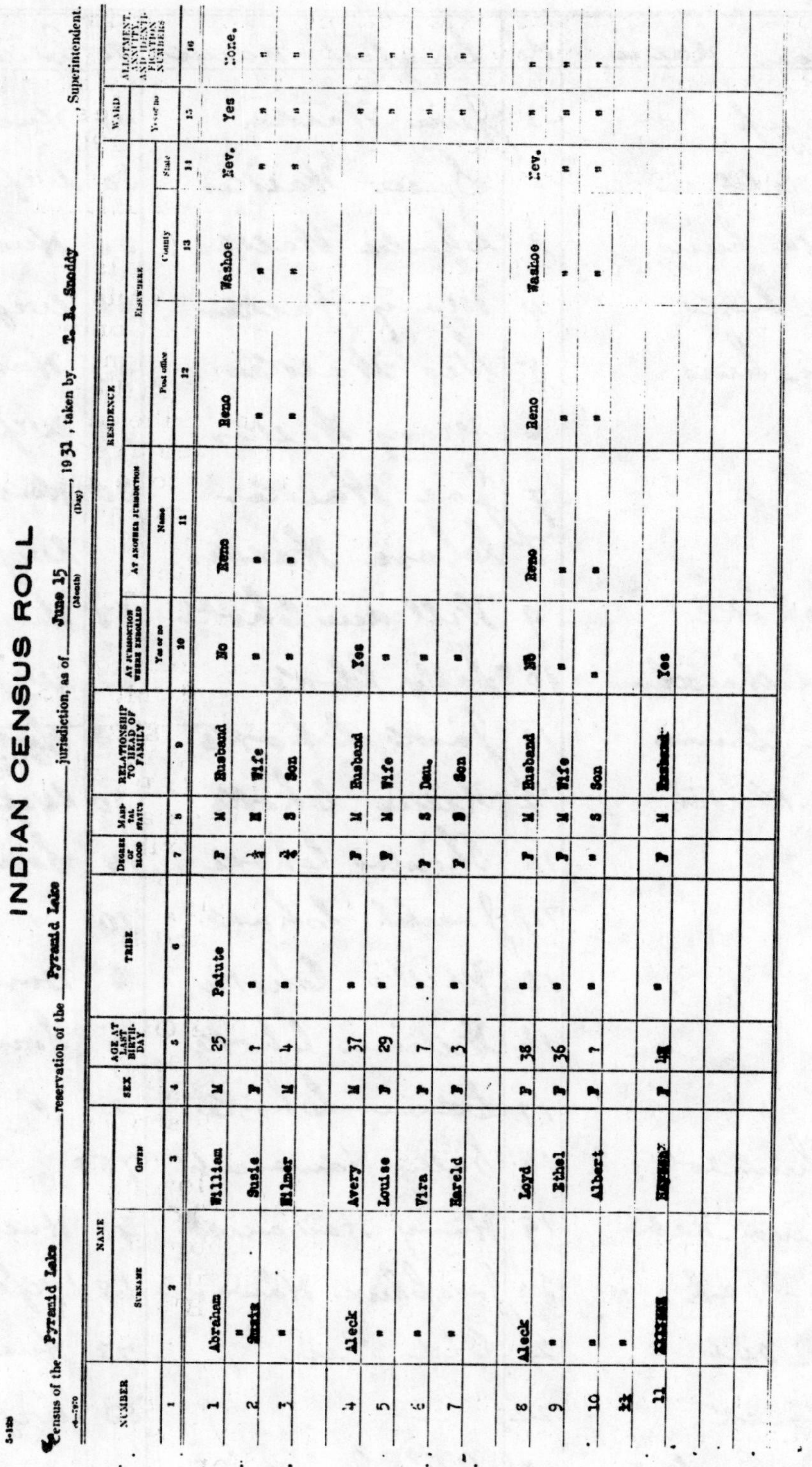

INDIAN CENSUS ROLL

Census of the Pyramid Lake reservation of the Pyramid Lake jurisdiction, as of June 15 (Month) 19 31 (Day), taken by T. B. Snoddy, Superintendent.

NUMBER	Surname	Given	SEX	AGE AT LAST BIRTH-DAY	TRIBE	Degree of blood	Marital match	RELATIONSHIP TO HEAD OF FAMILY	At jurisdiction where enrolled (Yes or No)	At another jurisdiction — Name	Post office	County	State	WARD (Yes or no)	ALLOTMENT, ANNUITY AND IDENTIFICATION NUMBERS
1	Abraham	William	M	25	Paiute	F	M	Husband	No	Reno	Reno	Washoe	Nev.	Yes	None.
2	Smith	Susie	F	4	"	F	M	Wife	"	"	"	"	"	Yes	"
3	"	Wilmer	M	4	"	M	S	Son	"	"	"	"	"	"	"
4	Aleck	Avery	M	37	"	F	M	Husband	Yes						
5	"	Louise	F	29	"	F	M	Wife	"						
6	"	Vira	F	7	"	F	S	Dau.	"						
7	"	Harold	F	3	"	F	S	Son	"						
8	Aleck	Loyd	F	35	"	F	M	Husband	No	Reno	Reno	Washoe	Nev.	"	"
9	"	Ethel	F	36	"	F	M	Wife	"	"	"	"	"	"	"
10	"	Albert	F	7	"	F	S	Son	"	"	"	"	"	"	"
11	Rodriguez	Rodriguez	F	48	"	F	M	Husband	Yes						

Fig. 138. Indian census role, 1931

410

for the Eastern Cherokees dating from 1835 are in the National Archives and have been microfilmed. Those for the period 1885-1940 have been microfilmed under "Microcopy 595" and consist of 692 rolls. The special rolls relating to the Eastern Cherokees cover the years 1835-36, 1848-49, 1851-52, 1868-69, 1884, 1907-8, 1909-10, and 1924 and have been microfilmed under number "T-496." Both collections are on file at the Genealogical Society Library in Salt Lake City.

Annuity payrolls and receipt rolls are also among the Agency records and are similar to the modern census rolls. The annuity payrolls resulted from treaties or acts of Congress providing that the Federal Government make annual payments to tribal members for a stated period of time. They are usually in bound volumes which are arranged by the name of the tribe and thereunder chronologically. Those in the National Archives are dated 1848-1940 and are especially valuable for the period before annual census rolls were taken in 1885.[4] The modern enrollment and annuity payment rolls sometimes include marriage information as well as the usual vital statistics. Notice the marriage date for Elizabeth Annamitta on the 1911 Annuity Pay Roll shown in fig. 139 (see also fig. 140).

C. George Younkin wrote an excellent paper concerning the tribal and agency records for the five civilized tribes which should be consulted by all persons interested in Indian genealogy. His paper is entitled HISTORICAL AND GENEALOGICAL RECORDS OF THE FIVE CIVILIZED TRIBES AND OTHER INDIAN RECORDS and was read at the 1969 World Conference on Records at Salt Lake City (Area I-42). He gives a brief history of each tribe and the government's association with them and includes details on record holdings at Federal Records Center 7 in Fort Worth, Texas. He also gives suggestions for searching the records and lists reference and finding aids.

The Indian Archives Division of the Oklahoma Historical Society, Historical Building, Oklahoma City has a volume entitled FINAL ROLLS OF THE CITIZENS AND FREEDMEN OF THE FIVE CIVILIZED TRIBES OF INDIAN TERRITORY which should also be consulted. It was completed and printed under authority of an act of Congress approved 21 June 1906 and lists the following: Choctaws by Blood, New Born Choctaws by Blood, Minor Choctaws by Blood, Choctaws by Marriage, Choctaw Freedmen, Minor Choctaw Freedmen, Mississippi Choctaws, New Born Mississippi Choctaws, Minor Mississippi Choctaws, Chickasaws by Blood, New Born Chickasaws by Blood, Minor Chickasaws by Blood, Cherokees by Blood, Delaware Cherokees, Cherokees by Intermarriage, Creeks by Blood, Minor Creeks by Blood, Creek Freedmen, New Born Creek Freedmen, Minor Creek Freedmen, Seminoles by Blood and Freedmen, New Born Seminoles by Blood, and New Born Seminole Freedmen. Using the Choctaw Rolls as an example, the ages of the Choctaws by Blood are calculated to 25 September 1902. The enrollment number is listed first, then the name, age, sex, degree of blood, and census

ANNUITY PAY ROLL.

Payment 4th. quarter 1910

We, the subscribers, severally acknowledge to have received of L. M. Nichols, Superintendent and Special Disbursing Agent, IN CASH,
the sums set opposite our respective names, in full payment of our shares in the payment to Indians made by said official in the **third** quarter, 19**11**,
on account of Menominee per-capita payment.

Amount per capita $25.00

No. Last	No. Present	NAME.	RELATION ship.	AGE.	SEX.	AMOUNT OF EACH CHECK OR CASH PAYMENT.	DATE OF CASH PAYMENT OR DATE AND NUMBER OF CHECK.	SIGNATURE FOR CASH OR NAME OF PERSON TO WHOSE ORDER CHECK IS DRAWN.	MARK.	WITNESS TO SIGNATURE BY MARK.	REMARKS.
1	1	Annis, Kate P.	mother	43	F						
2	2	---Isabell Pecore	Adop. Dau	11	F	2000 464		Kate P Annis			Cert. 1
3	3	Amour, Adolph	husband	36	M						
4	4	", Theressa M.	wife	31	F						
5	5	", Mitchell	SonHusb.	13	M						
6	6	", Christine	DauHusb	9	F						
7	7	--Joseph Menore	SonWife	14	M	75 20 470					
8	8	--Andrew "	" "	11	M	6 00 471					
9	9	--Videl "	" "	3	M	00 472					
10	10	--Fredz "	DauWife	1	F	00 473		Adolph Amour Sety 23 1911.			
14	11	Annamitta, Kasick	Orphan	15	M	2000		Reginald Oshkosh			Act'g Guardian
15	12	Annamitta, Frank, Jr.	Husband	28	M						
45	13	", Keshekokey	Wife	17	F						
498	14	", Elisabeth	Daughter	1	F	60 00		Frank Annamitta Jr			Married May 19, 1
16	15	Assisouit, Martin	Husband	67	M						
17	16	", Louise	Wife	57	F	0000		Martin Assisouit			
18	17	Awonohopay, John	Husband	57	M						
19	18	", Kinyeokey	Wife	34	F	13 00 476					
20	19	", Warsaw	Son	3	M	00 477		John Awonohopay			
21	20	Ahkenokoay, Mitchell	Father	87	M	20 00 478					
22	21	", Yawayaakah	Son	16	M	20 00 479		Mitchell Ahkenokoay			
23	22	Askenett, Peter	Husband	37	M						
24	23	", Catherine	Wife	24	F						
25	24	", Theresa	Daughter	4	F						
26	25	", Martha	"	2	F	80 00		Peter Askenett			
27	26	Ahnamah	Single	73	F	20 00 482		Ahnamah			
40	27	Ahyahsha, Gust	Husband	49	M	54 00					
41	28	", Mary	Wife	59	F	34 00		Gust Ahyahsha			

Amount carried forward 560 00

Fig. 139. Annuity payroll for the Menominee Tribe, 1911

[handwritten cursive paragraph, largely illegible]

Receipt role ... for the 1st semi annual pay ment of annuity to the Menomonee tribe of Indians, within the Green Bay Agency, for the ... hundred and sixty five. (1865.)

We the Chiefs, Warriors, Heads of Families and Individuals without families, of the Menomonee tribe of Indians, acknowledge the receipt of Two Thousand dollars (#2000) of Morgan L. Martin, U.S. Indian Agent, in the sums appended to our names, being our proportion of the 1st semi annual payment of annuity to said Tribe, for the year ... hundred and sixty five (1865) the same being paid to us at ... this ... day of August 1865.

Corrow's Band	Hd	Families				Distribution means		Amt paid	
Names		Men	Women	Children	Total	Goods	Cash	Dollars	Cents
Corrow	X	1	2	5	8	5	5	51	75
Me-shaw-Komick	X	1	1	1	3	"	"	17	25
Pah po-co-wah Kokiew	X		1		1	"	"	5	75
Ah pah ta ke sha	X	1	2		3	"	"	17	25
Wah po chick	X		1	2	3	"	"	17	25
Wah nak ka aha	X	1	1	3	5	"	"	28	75
Tah quah kah nah	X	1	2	1	4	"	"	23	00
Na ke ah kiew	X		1	1	2	"	"	11	50
Wah pa nas com	X	1	1	2	4	"	"	23	00
Py ah wa aha	X	1			1	"	"	5	75
Shaw ah no me tah	X	1	1	4	6	"	"	34	50
Shaw wa no ka sick	X	1	1	1	3	"	"	17	25
Ke she we ah tah	X	1	1		2	"	"	11	50
Wah hun naw nah	X	1	1	2	4	"	"	23	00
Mah nah	X		1		1	"	"	5	75
O she pe o kiew	X	1	2	1	4	"	"	23	00
Mah ka ta wa quett	X	2		1	3	"	"	17	25
Mah ke net	X		1	1	2	"	"	11	50
Sha che ah kiew	X	1	2		3	"	"	17	25
Moah she noah	X	1	1	3	5	"	"	28	75
Sha note	X		1	1	2	"	"	11	50
Pah mo ne kote	X	1	1	3	5	"	"	28	75
She she quon	X	1	1	1	3	"	"	17	25
Wah tah to	X		2		2	"	"	11	50
Mach o pa tow	X	1	1	8	10	"	"	57	50
Ka chis kah no	X		1		1	"	"	5	75
Ah nah quah	X				1	"	"	5	75
carried forward		20	31	41	92	"	"	529	00

Fig. 140. Receipt role from the Green Bay Agency, 1865

413

card number. The census card, which is on file in the Muskogee Area Office, Muskogee, Oklahoma, gives more information, including the names of parents, where in the nation they lived, and whether living or dead. The ages of the New Borns are calculated to 4 March 1905 and are the children born between 25 September 1902 and that date. The ages of the Minors are calculated to 4 March 1906, when the rolls of the five civilized tribes were closed forever. The Freedmen are the slaves or descendants of slaves of the enrollees.[5]

Some agency records remain in their respective agency offices, but many have been transferred to the National Archives in Washington, D.C., or to one of the twelve Federal Records Centers. The Genealogical Society Library in Salt Lake City has a good collection from the National Archives but not from any of the Federal Records Centers. However, it does have an excellent collection of miscellaneous records relating to the Indians, including private journals of missionaries and schoolteachers who worked with the Indians, church records (especially Catholic) which included Indians, journals of commissioners of Indian trade, some tribal records, and many military records.

The church records are especially important, for many early priests, ministers, elders, pastors, and missionaries worked closely with the Indians and in many instances converted them to Christianity and entered their names in the records.

Many Indians living in the Midwest and the East attended the CARLISLE INDIAN SCHOOL in Carlisle, Pennsylvania, during the period 1879-1918; records for them have been preserved and filed in the National Archives. The records include record cards which are filed in alphabetical order and individual student folders. Each record card relates to an individual student and shows his English name, Indian name, agency, nation, band, home address, degree of Indian blood, age, and the dates of his arrival and discharge. Each folder relates to an individual student and includes the name of one of his parents and his school record.[6]

Consideration should also be given other records of the white man as outlined in previous chapters, especially when the person in question was not under jurisdiction of the reservation or an agency. Birth, marriage, and death certificates are available from local and state offices, and census records as outlined in chapter 4 include some individuals with Indian blood. Indians have also been involved in land transactions and many appear in records of the courts. They have also been involved in the military, both on a voluntary and involuntary basis, and records of social and commercial organizations include them.

Following are selected titles on file at the Genealogical Society in Salt Lake which relate to American Indians:

AMERICAN STATE PAPERS - TREATIES WITH INDIANS OF THE
    SOUTHERN STATES

REPORT OF THE COMMISSIONER OF INDIAN AFFAIRS FOR
    THE YEAR 1859
INDIAN AGENCY NAMES, POST OFFICE, STATE AND TRIBE
    AS OF 1949
FAMOUS INDIAN CHIEFS
LIVES OF FAMOUS INDIAN CHIEFS
INDIAN GEOGRAPHICAL NAMES
INDIAN HISTORY, BIOGRAPHY AND GENEALOGY OF THE
    WAMPANOAG TRIBE
INDIAN JOURNALS OF LEWIS HENRY MORGAN, 1859-62
HANDBOOK OF AMERICAN INDIAN LANGUAGES
INDIAN TRIBES OF THE LOWER MISSISSIPPI VALLEY
SENECA INDIAN MYTHS AND FOLK TALES
INDIAN NOTES AND MONOGRAPHS - POWHATAN TRIBES OF
    VIRGINIA
HISTORY AND CHARACTERISTIC SKETCHES OF THE OJIBWAY
    NATION
INDIAN TRIBES AND THEIR LOCATIONS, 1782-1890
INDIAN TRIBES OF THE HUDSON RIVER
NOTES ON INDIAN WARS IN NEW ENGLAND FROM 1675
ADAIR'S HISTORY OF THE AMERICAN INDIAN
EARLY HISTORY AND NAMES OF THE ARAPAHO
INDIANS OF THE SOUTHERN COLONIAL FRONTIER
REGISTRATION OF VITAL EVENTS AMONG INDIANS
REPORT ON INDIANS TAXED AND NOT TAXED - 1890
PROVINCIAL NEGOTIATIONS WITH THE WESTERN INDIANS
    1754-58
ABENAKIS INDIANS OF VERMONT
ASSINIBOIN INDIANS OF THE UPPER MISSOURI
CODDO INDIANS
CHEROKEE INDIAN CHIEFS
CENSUS OF CHEROKEE INDIANS - 1835
CHEROKEE INDIANS 1755-63
INDEX TO AND THE FINAL ROLLS OF CITIZENS AND FREEDMEN
    OF THE FIVE CIVILIZED TRIBES IN INDIAN TERRITORY
HISTORY OF CHICKESAW INDIAN SCHOOLS
CHOCTAW INDIAN CENSUS - 1860
CREEK INDIAN CENSUS CARDS
IROQUOIS ANTHROPOLOGY AT THE MID CENTURY
THE MEMOMINI INDIANS
NAVAJO INDIANS
OJIBWAY INDIAN NATION
QUAPAW INDIANS
QUINNIPIOCK INDIANS
SEMINOLE INDIAN CENSUS CARDS
THE UNCONQUERED SEMINOLE INDIANS
SENECA INDIANS
SIOUX PERSONAL PROPERTY CLAIMS
TAOVAYAS INDIANS
UTE INDIAN TRIBE CENSUS
UTE INDIAN TRIBE MEMBERSHIP ROLLS

UTE INDIAN VITAL RECORDS
UTES OF ROYAL BLOOD
YUTA INDIANS
PIMA AND MARICOPA INDIANS
GENEALOGY OF A FEW INDIAN FAMILIES OF THE PIMA,
    MARACOPA AND PAPAGOS
CANALINO INDIANS
INDIAN DEEDS OF RHODE ISLAND - 1638
HISTORY OF THE INDIANS OF CONNECTICUT
TEKESTA INDIANS - SOUTHERN FLORIDA
TIMUCUA INDIANS - FLORIDA
REMOVAL OF CHEROKEE INDIANS FROM GEORGIA
INDIAN DEPREDATIONS 1787-1825
INDIAN LETTERS, TALKS, AND TREATIES
INHABITANTS IN THE CHEROKEE COUNTRY
INDIANS OF IDAHO
SHOSHONI INDIANS
INDIAN TREATIES AND CONVENTIONS EFFECTING KANSAS
SHAWNEE INDIANS IN KANSAS
KANSA OR KAW INDIANS
POTTAWATOMIE INDIANS
INDIAN TREATIES BY THE COLONY OF MASSACHUSETTS
    1717-53
INDIAN WARS IN MAINE - 1675
SIOUX INDIANS OF NEBRASKA
SIOUX INDIAN WARS
SENECA INDIANS
CHEROKEE INDIANS IN NORTH CAROLINA - 1835
CONFEDERATE INDIAN SOLDIERS
MISSIONS AND MISSIONARIES AMONG OKLAHOMA INDIANS
INDIAN STUDENTS 1826-1835
INDIAN TRIBES OF OKLAHOMA 1889-1891
MISSIONARIES AMONG CHEROKEE INDIANS
INDIAN WARS OF THE NORTHWEST
INDIAN PATHS OF PENNSYLVANIA
ACCOUNTS AND BELIEFS OF DELAWARE AND IROQUOIS
    INDIANS - 1746-49
CREEK INDIAN TRIBES
RED CAROLINIANS
TRADERS AMONG CHEROKEE INDIANS 1690-1760
INDIAN DEPREDATIONS IN UTAH
INDIAN WARS IN DESERET
CENSUS OF UTE INDIAN TRIBE - 1944
UTE INDIAN VITAL RECORDS
ABENAKIS INDIANS
INDIANS OF VERMONT
INDIANS OF VIRGINIA
YAKIMA INDIANS

The maps shown as fig. 141 may also be helpful to the researcher.

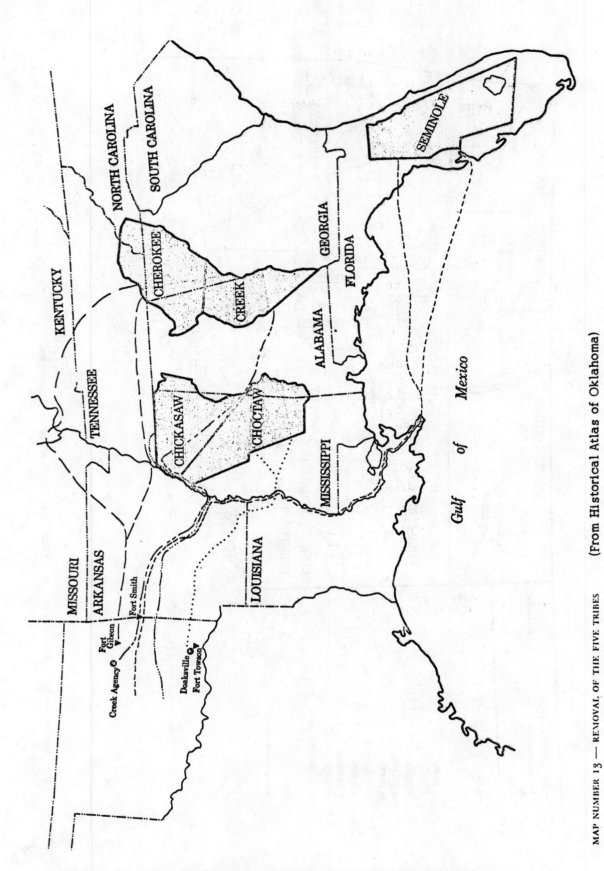

MAP NUMBER 13 — REMOVAL OF THE FIVE TRIBES

Fig. 141. Maps showing removal of five civilized tribes

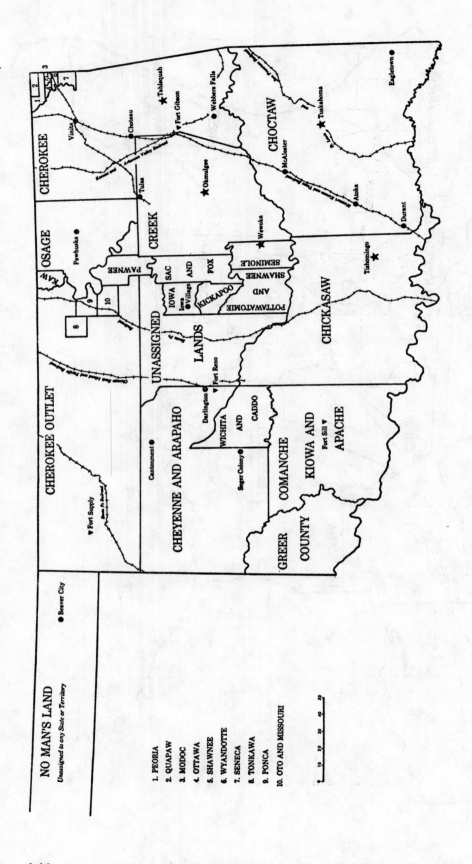

Fig. 141a.

418

Fig. 141b.

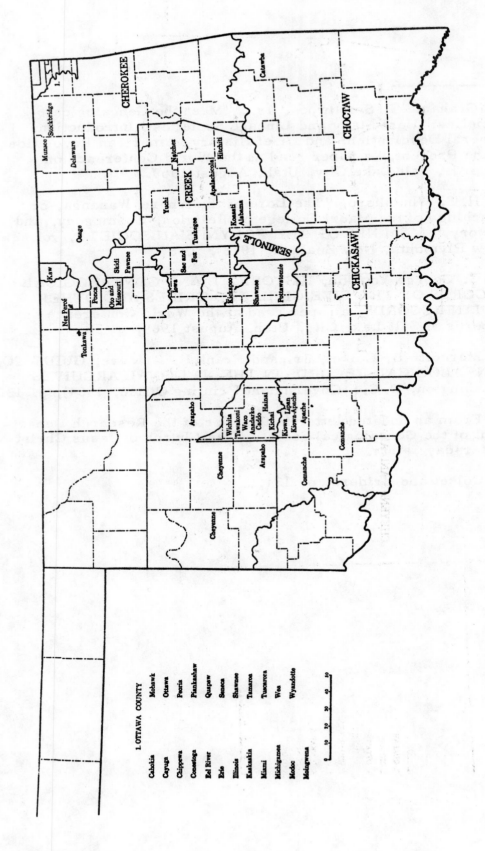

MAP NUMBER 14 — TRIBAL LOCATIONS IN OKLAHOMA   (From Historical Atlas of Oklahoma)

1. OTTAWA COUNTY

Cahokia	Mohawk
Cayuga	Ottawa
Chippewa	Peoria
Conestoga	Piankashaw
Eel River	Quapaw
Erie	Seneca
Illinois	Shawnee
Kaskaskia	Tamaroa
Miami	Tuscarora
Michigamea	Wea
Modoc	Wyandotte
Moingwena	

419

1. Grahame T. Smallwood, Jr., "Meet the Genealogical Societies: Hereditary and Lineage Societies: Introduction, General Description, and Brief History, American Revolution to the Present," a paper read at the World Conference on Records, Salt Lake City, Utah, August 1969.

2. H. T. Whatahoro, "The Lore of the Whare-Wananga, or Teachings of the Maori College on Religion, Cosmogony, and History," MEMOIRS OF THE POLYNESIAN SOCIETY, vol. 2 (New Plymouth, New Zealand, 1913), p. 87.

3. C. George Younkin, HISTORICAL AND GENEALOGICAL RECORDS OF THE FIVE CIVILIZED TRIBES AND OTHER INDIAN RECORDS, a paper read at the World Conference on Records at Salt Lake City, Utah, August 1969, p. 32.

4. Meredith B. Colket, Jr., and Frank E. Briders, GUIDE TO GENEALOGICAL RECORDS IN THE NATIONAL ARCHIVES (Washington, D. C.: Government Printing Office, 1964), p. 130.

5. From an undated letter in the files of the Research Department of the Genealogical Society, The Church of Jesus Christ of Latter-day Saints.

6. Colket and Briders, p. 131.

CHAPTER 13

SETTLEMENT PATTERNS AND MIGRATION ROUTES

A study of the history and geography of localities associated with a pedigree can actually help in gaining genealogical information about the problem. When a town's or county's records have been destroyed, or when those available do not provide the needed information, a knowledge of settlement patterns and migration routes can help determine where a particular family came from or at least can provide clues to other sources which can be investigated to locate them. Such a study can also provide valuable information about social and economic conditions which influenced the people and can explain why families and individuals were involved in certain events but not in others.

The forces influencing migration have been at work since the beginning in America; no sooner had settlers arrived in a particular locality than they felt the urge to move. New opportunities, cheaper or better land, gold, and the possibility of improving individual circumstances were strong forces. Family ties led some south and west, while political and military forces were at work with others. The depletion of the soil and overpopulation also had their effects on migration, while just plain "adventure" lured some to the frontier country.

Patterns of settlement and particular routes of travel began to emerge from all this moving. Many settlers followed paths created by wild animals and the Indians, and these have become the routes followed by many of our modern turnpikes and freeways (fig. 142).

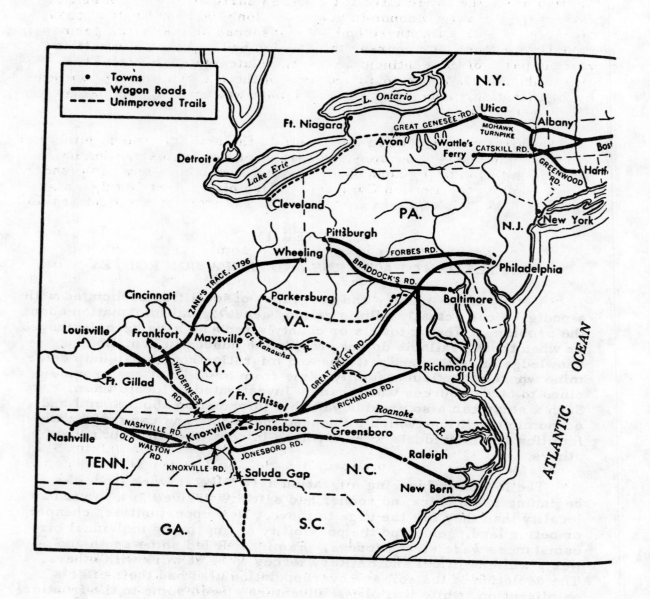

Fig. 142. Early migration routes from east coast settlements

422

Settlement and Migration in the South

Attempts to plant permanent settlements had been made by the English along the North Carolina coast as early as 1584, and settlers had engaged in some economic ventures along the New England coast as early as 1602. But these had been unsuccessful as far as permanent colonization went. Of course, the Spanish had explored and settled various parts of the continent before the sixteenth century and had established settlements south and west of the Florida-Georgia border. But the first permanent English settlement was made on the James River in 1607 (fig. 143).

The first contingent of immigrants to the new settlement numbered just over one hundred persons, primarily of English extraction but also including some French, German, and Scottish. They came under sponsorship of the London Company of Virginia. Later immigrants came in increased numbers from England and from other countries as well.

During the first few years, there was some question as to the permanence of this first settlement. But the colonists were able to conquer the strife, poor leadership, and trouble with the Indians, and by 1610 they had made up their minds to make a go of it. Their number was reduced by about half the first year, but by 1625, when the settlement became a Royal Colony, Virginia settlers numbered close to two thousand souls. By 1634, eight counties (shires) had been organized, and settlements appeared on the James, York, Rappahannock, and Potomac rivers to the west of the Chesapeake and also on the penninsula to the east (fig. 144).

The Genealogical Society Library has microfilmed and otherwise acquired an excellent collection of colonial and county records for Virginia, dating to about the Civil War period. It also maintains a progressive acquisitions program for additional material. The prime county records include marriage (primarily after 1790), birth and death (after 1852), land, probate, and other court records dating from the early 1630s.

Virginia settlers had explored the Chesapeake to the north but had not planted any settlements there prior to 1632 when the northern region was granted to Cecil Calvert, Lord Baltimore, and became Maryland. Calvert's grant was to become a Catholic haven but actually became a refuge for several other groups as well (fig. 145).

The LDS Genealogical Society has also acquired many records pertaining to Maryland, both published and microfilmed. The Hall of Records at Annapolis, Maryland, assumed responsibility for all noncurrent records in 1952, and a majority of the existing records were centralized there. Many have been microfilmed to about 1880 and filed with the Genealogical Society Library in Salt Lake City.

English and Welsh settlers from Pennsylvania moved into Maryland

423

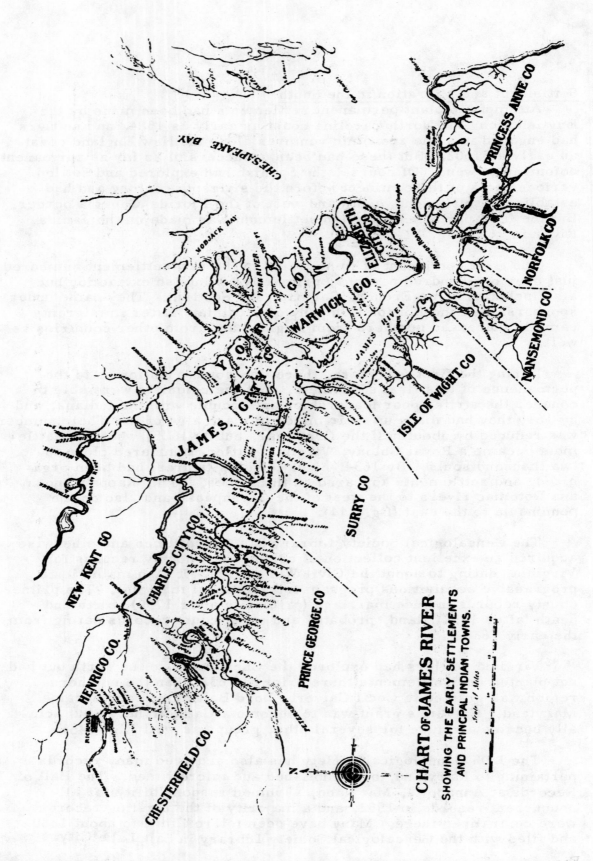

Fig. 143. Chart of James River showing early settlements

424

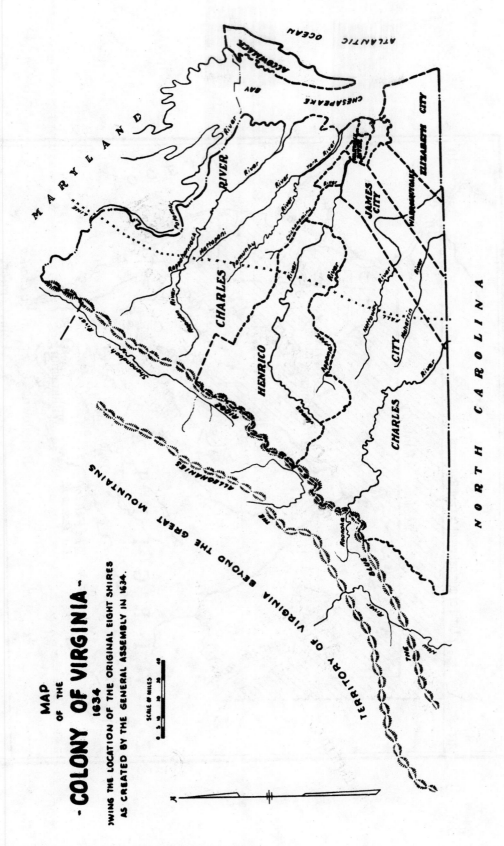

Fig. 144.　The Colony of Virginia, 1634

425

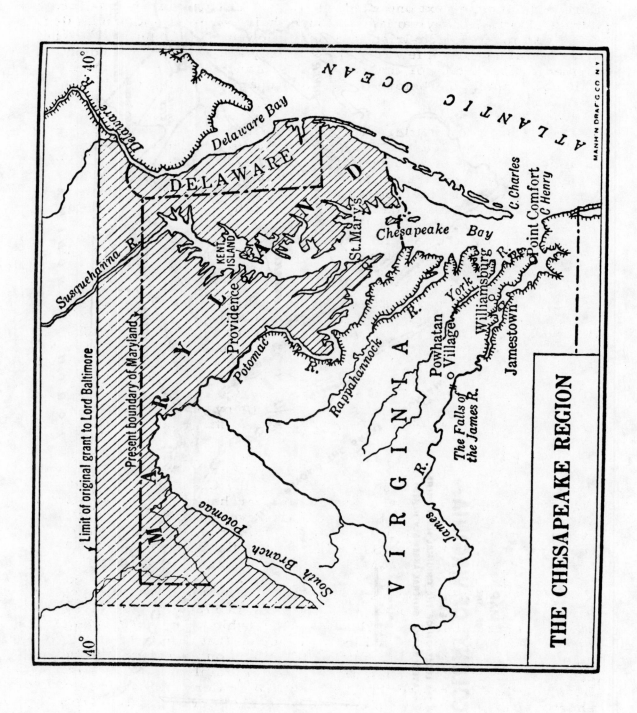

Fig. 145. The Chesapeake Region

426

and Virginia after 1682, and many came directly from England and Europe during the next one hundred years. German and Swiss-German immigrants to Pennsylvania also found their way west and south after 1700, and many Scotch-Irish families followed after about 1720. These settlers, along with a few from New Jersey and the northern colonies, formed the backbone for the great western and southern migration which took place just before the Revolutionary War and shortly after (fig. 146).

By 1680, a few settlers had moved south from the James River settlements to the Roanoke and Chowan rivers and had settled on Albemarles Sound in present North Carolina. Some had also followed the James River west through the first range of mountains into the western valleys and merged with settlers from the north. These settlers and their descendants were among those who organized the "Transylvania Company" of 1775, the "Westsylvania Company" of 1776, the "State of Franklin" in 1784, and were among those who moved into Kentucky through the Cumberland Gap between 1769 and 1792 when Kentucky became a state (fig. 147).

The Carolinas had been granted to eight English gentlemen in 1662-63. In 1670, English, French, and Scottish immigrants, via the Barbados, landed at Port Royal in present South Carolina then moved north shortly after to found "Charles Town." This colony was to be a new experiment in colonization with an aristocracy, craftsmen and artisans, slaves, and a land tenure system which smacked of feudalism. However, strong forces at work in the New World caused alteration of the land system, though the colony retained certain unusual governmental and record-keeping practices until the Revolution (fig. 148).

The first settlers were reinforced by others directly from Great Britain and Europe and also by some from the Chesapeake region to the north. A group of adventurers from Dorchester, Massachusetts, attempted a settlement on the Cape Fear River in about 1672 but evidently disliked the area and abandoned their venture only a few years after it was begun. Some returned to the Bay Colony, but a few settled in Virginia and Maryland.

By 1710, a division was taking place between the "colonists north" and those south in the Carolinas and in 1720, North Carolina separated herself from Charleston's leadership. The northern part was a "different breed," and logic suggested that a separation would take place. Virginians had settled "Edenton" on Albemarle Sound, and French Huguenots had settled "Bath" on Pamlico Sound. "New Bern" on the Neuse River had been settled by German Palatines shortly after 1700, and Welsh immigrants had arrived in the south-central part of the colony about the same time. By the time of the Revolution, Scottish Highlanders had become a strong political force along the Cape Fear region (fig. 149).

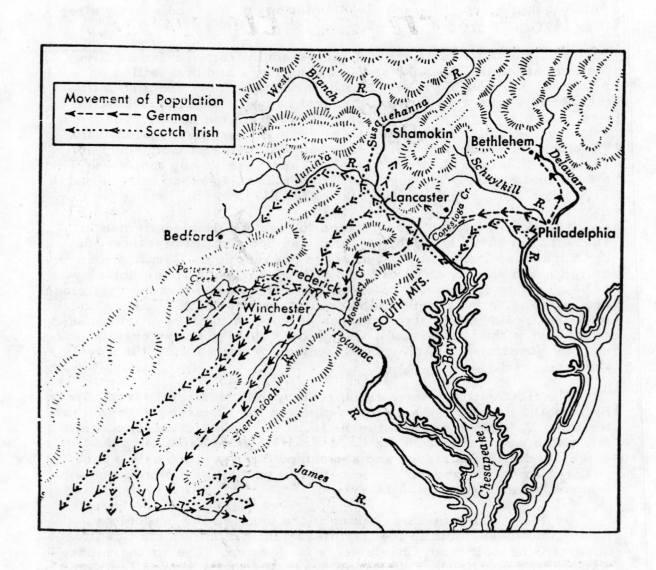

Fig. 146. Movement of German and Scotch-Irish from Pennsylvania

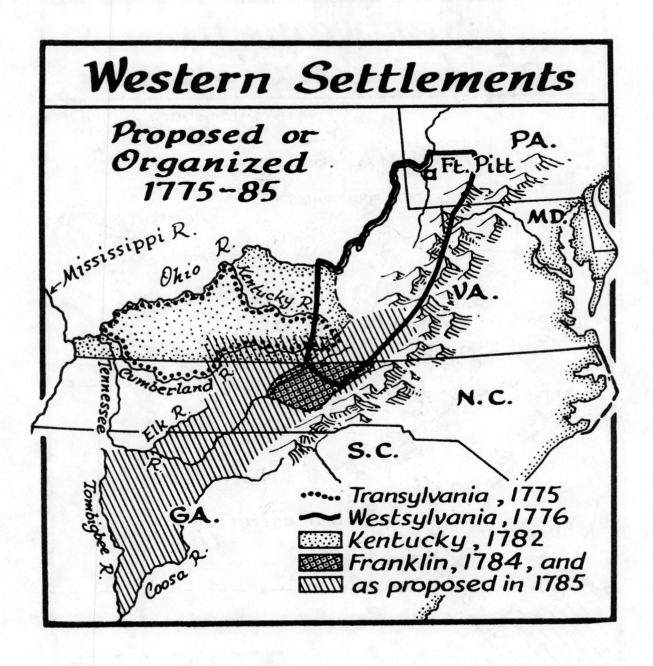

Fig. 147.   Western Settlements

429

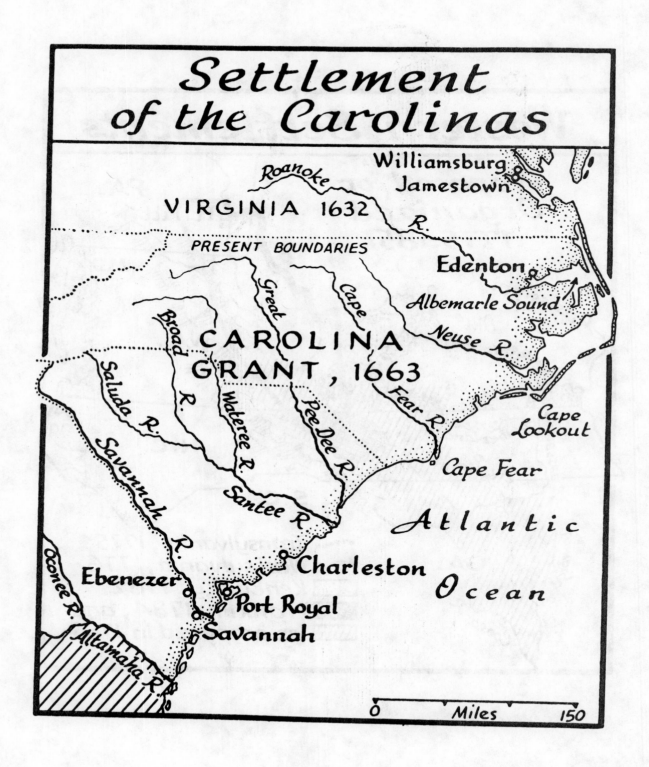

Fig. 148. Carolina Settlements

430

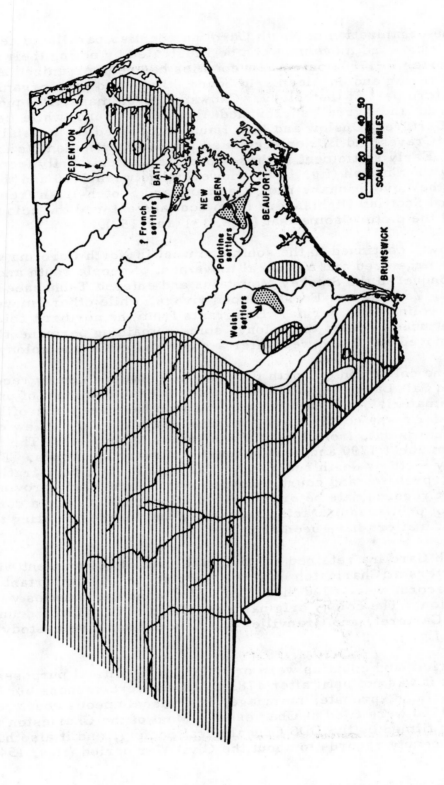

Fig. 149. North Carolina Settlements, 1730

431

The organization of North Carolina counties paralleled settlement, and the westward movement can be illustrated by noting their formation. Prior to 1750, only a few counties had been organized along the coastal region and on Albemarle Sound. None had been organized in the western part of the colony. Chowan, Perquimans, Pasquotank, Currituck, and Tyrrell surrounded Albemarle Sound while Beaufort, Hyde, Carteret, Onslow and New Hanover covered the coastal area. Bertie, Craven and Bladen accounted for such settlement as extended inland. Early settlement in these counties was primarily from Virginia by the English (fig. 150). However, between 1750 and the beginning of the Revolutionary War, Germans and Scotch-Irish from the north and Scottish Highlanders from Scotland entered the colony and changed the picture somewhat (figs. 151 and 152).

Growth continued to the south and west in North Carolina with new counties organized and a general movement of people south and west. Some conquered the Smokey Mountains and entered Tennessee via the Watauga, Yadkin, and French Broad rivers, while others moved into South Carolina and Georgia. Emigrants from the northern colonies also continued to enter the colony, some remaining permanently while others moved south and west after a short respite in the colony.

A fine collection of North Carolina colonial and county records are on file in Salt Lake City. There is a considerable amount of published colonial material, and early county records have been microfilmed. Collections for many counties are available down to 1970. A few county marriage records date from 1750 but are rather incomplete. The majority date from about 1790 and consist mostly of marriage bonds. There are no county birth or death records available until state registration in 1908, but land, probate, and court records exist. Some early provincial probate and court records date before the Revolutionary War, and a considerable number of published extracts, abstracts, and indexes relating to probate and court matters have been acquired.

South Carolina retained a provincial form of government with headquarters at Charleston until the Revolution. All important genealogical records were filed there until 1783 when the counties were given jurisdiction. The colony originally consisted of only three counties-- Craven, Carteret, and Granville--but they did not have custody of the records (fig. 153).

Districts and counties were organized for political purposes by 1769, but it was not until after 1783 that they were responsible for the records. Land, probate, marriage, and miscellaneous court records prior to 1783 were filed at Charleston. Most of the Charleston records have been filmed by the LDS Genealogical Society, and it also has copies of county records to about the Civil War period (figs. 154 and 155).

A majority of South Carolina's early settlers came directly from Great Britain and France, but after about 1750, many were attracted

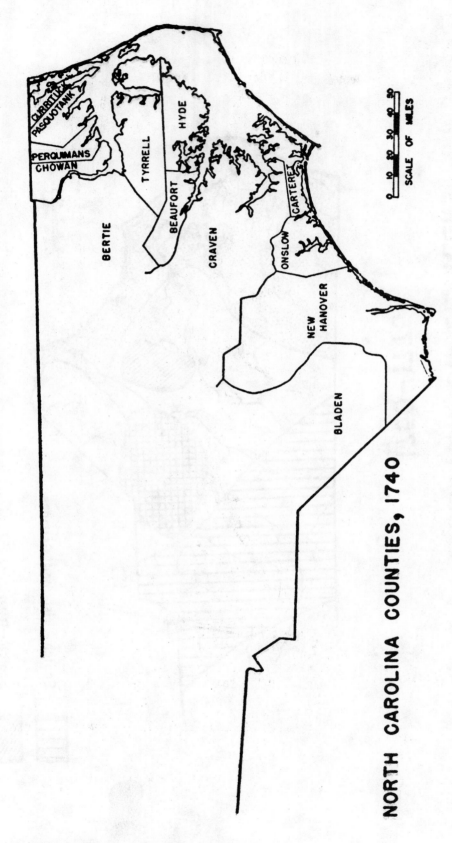

NORTH CAROLINA COUNTIES, 1740

Fig. 150. North Carolina settlements, 1740

433

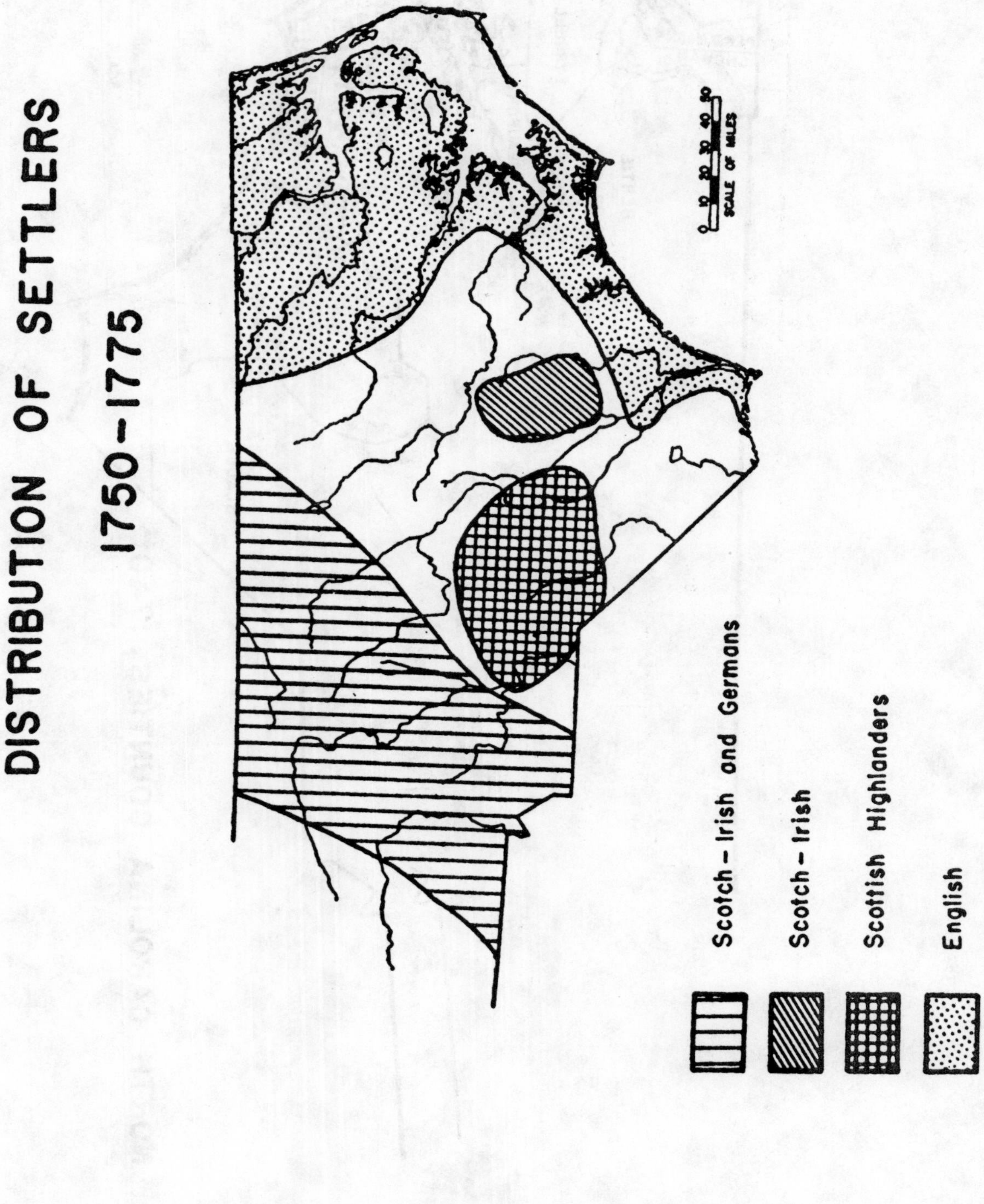
DISTRIBUTION OF SETTLERS
1750-1775
0 10 20 30 40 50
SCALE OF MILES
Scotch-Irish and Germans
Scotch-Irish
Scottish Highlanders
English

Fig. 151. Distribution of settlers, 1750-1775

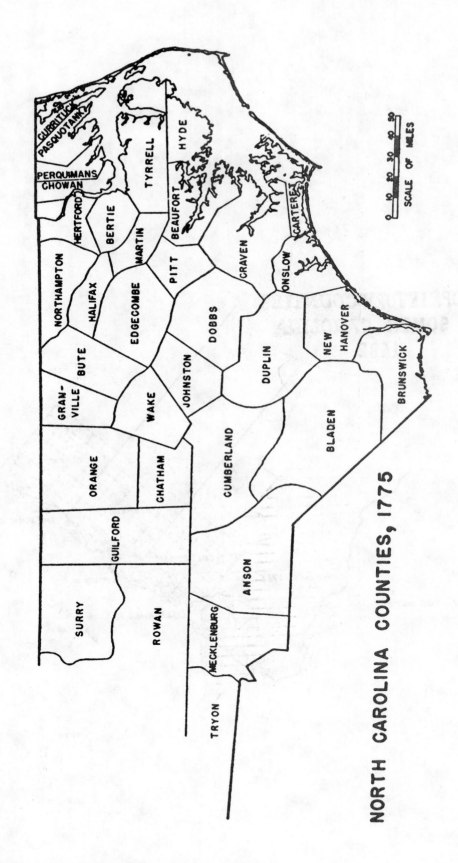

NORTH CAROLINA COUNTIES, 1775

Fig. 152. North Carolina counties, 1775

435

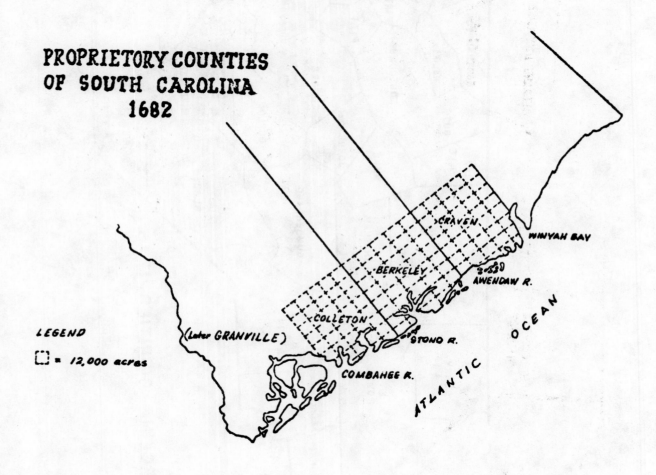

Fig. 153. The three original South Carolina counties

436

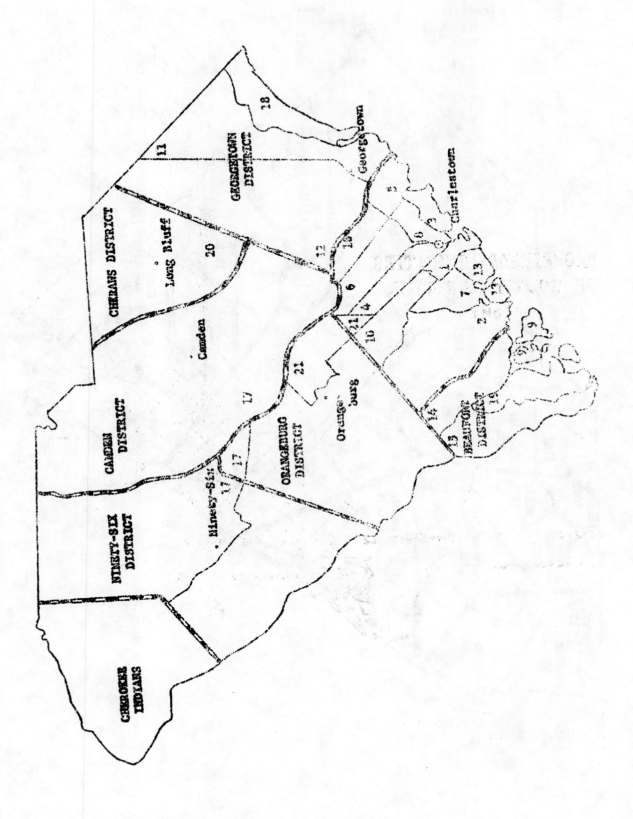

Fig. 154. South Carolina districts in 1769

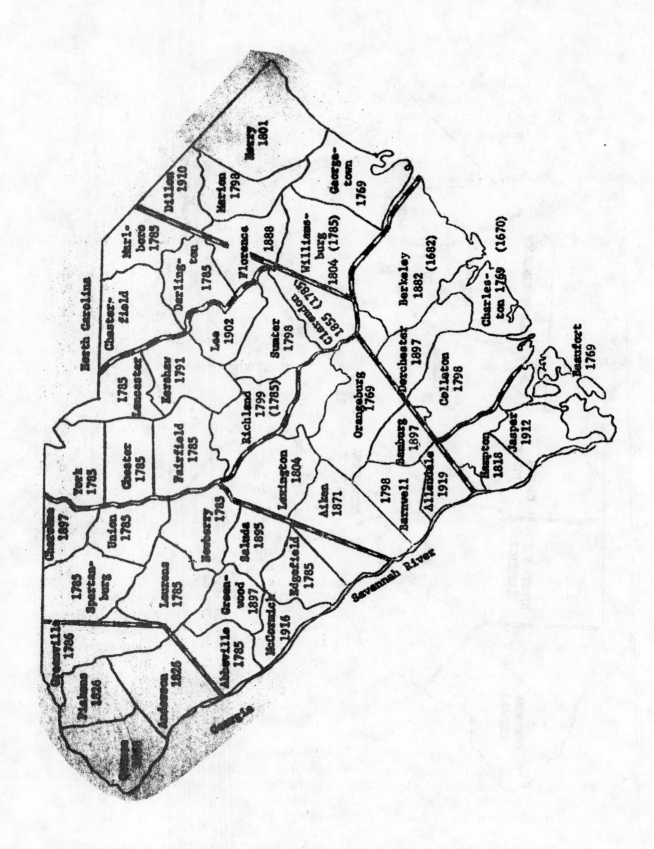

Fig. 155. South Carolina counties after 1783

438

to the colony from North Carolina, Virginia, Maryland, and points north. There was free interchange between the southern colonies, and the general movement pattern was from the "Tidewater" west to the "Piedmont" south (figs. 156 and 157).

The great Appalachian plateau with its Smokey, Blue Ridge, and Allegheny mountains formed a veritable barrier to westward migration; hence, early settlers moved from the coastal regions west to the mountains and then south along the Piedmont or the Tidewater. Movement was generally from the north to the south, but a few settlers undoubtedly reversed that pattern and moved to the northern colonies.

The movement of the Dubberly family of Accomac County, Virginia, is an example of the typical movement south. John and Grace Dubberly were Huguenot immigrants to Virginia in the early colonial period. John's estate was settled in Accomac County in 1740, and according to early court order books, his children received equal portions. Sometime before 1756, William, John, Jr., and Thomas Dubberly moved to Craven County, North Carolina, where they purchased land. They evidently remained there for several years. Shortly before the Revolutionary War, William's son Jacob (grandson to John Dubberly of Accomac County) moved from North Carolina to Beaufort District, South Carolina, then moved to Florida where descendants still remain.

The author has also documented migration from the north-central counties of North Carolina to South Carolina and Georgia during the 1750-1790 period. On the Pace problem, mentioned in earlier chapters, the family was known to be resident on the James River as early as 1630. Second and third generation family members (Virginians) migrated south to the Roanoke and Tar rivers in North Carolina, and by 1700-1750 were living in the north-central counties of Northampton, Halifax, and Edgecombe. As early as 1756, some members of the family moved to Granville County, South Carolina, on the Savannah River, where they received generous land grants. By 1790, they were up in Edgefield and Abbeville counties, and some were across the Savannah in Wilkes and Richmond counties, Georgia, during the same period. Some family members did not leave North Carolina until after 1790 and came directly to Georgia where they appear in the 1798 tax digests for Oglethorpe County. One branch of the family was documented in Oglethorpe and Clarke counties until about 1802 when they moved to Rutherford County, Tennessee.

The first English settlers on the Savannah River were brought there by James Oglethorpe from "debtor prisons" in England. They arrived in about 1732, but other settlers soon moved to the region from the north, and some German Salzburgers immigrated in 1734, founding "Ebenezer" on the Savannah (fig. 158).

The southern part of Georgia was under Spanish control until

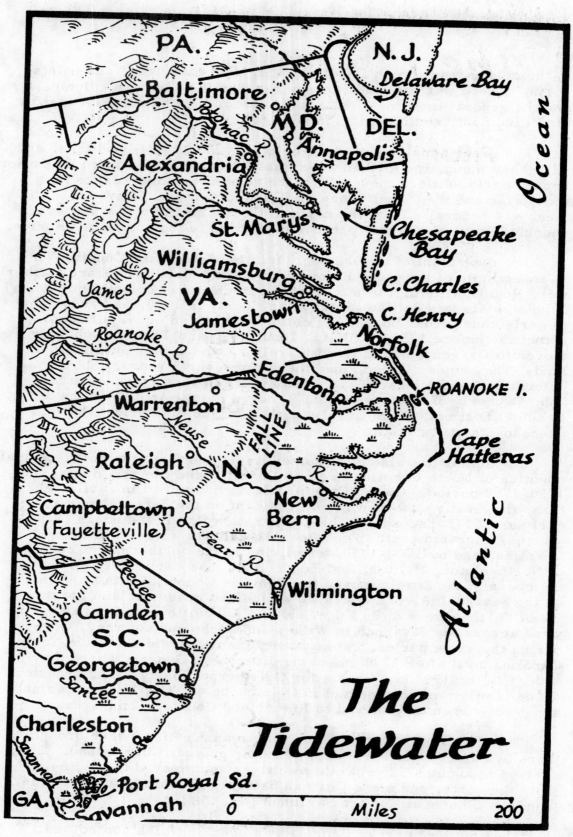

Fig. 156. The Tidewater

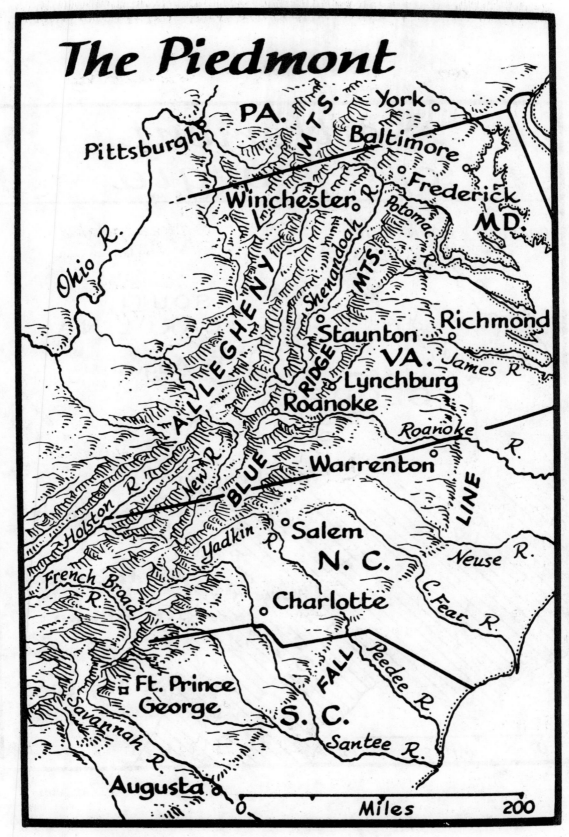

Fig. 157. The Piedmont

441

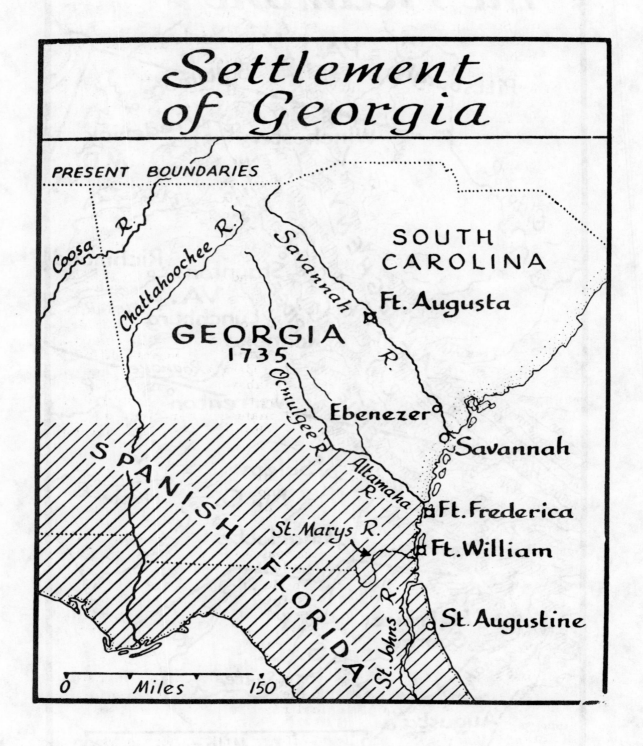

Fig. 158. Settlement of Georgia

1818, and no English settlement took place in that area until after the French and Spanish ceded their rights to it. The settlement in Georgia was first along the river counties of Chatham, Effingham, Screven, Burke, Richmond, and Wilkes, but it later moved westward and north. Beginning in 1803, seven land lotteries were held in Georgia, and settlers were attracted to the western and southern counties. After the 1832 lottery there was probably as much migration from the state into Tennessee and Alabama as there was into it. People in America were on the move, and new lands opening to the west and north began to attract them.

The most important genealogical records in Georgia were kept at the county level, and the Genealogical Society has filmed the most important well beyond the 1900 period. They include marriage records dating from about 1790, tax digests, deeds and mortgages, probate records, miscellaneous court records (including slave sales), and a good collection of military records. Unfortunately, several Georgia counties have suffered the ravages of war, and in some cases the county records are practically nonexistent.

Beginning about 1818, settlers moved from Georgia to Florida, Alabama, and Mississippi in goodly numbers, and many also moved north and west into Tennessee. North Carolinians also moved into Tennessee, which was really part of North Carolina until 1792, and followed the Tennessee River south into Alabama. Some Virginia settlers also continued to move south along the western valleys into Tennessee and south to Alabama, though many remained in East Tennessee or moved west and north through the Cumberland Gap into Kentucky (fig. 159).

Records at the Genealogical Society for Alabama are few at the present time, but the Society has just completed filming Mississippi records. Marriage, land, probate, and miscellaneous court records have been filmed.

It should be noted that French and Spanish immigrants had moved into the Gulf States region at a very early date, and records exist for them from about 1701, particularly for Mobile, Alabama, and New Orleans, Louisiana. There are also some land and estate records for Natchez, Mississippi, dating prior to the Revolution. Acadians from Canada also emigrated to this region in about 1742 and left their mark in the records.

Records pertaining to Florida are negligible at the present time in Salt Lake City, but it is presumed the Society will continue to microfilm and gather important genealogical records for the area.

Tennessee and Kentucky felt the effects of all national and ethnic groups who settled in the South, but the mainstream of migration did not enter their borders until after about 1780. Kentucky was the first to feel the influence of settlers, which began shortly after Daniel

Fig. 159. Mississippi River System, 1830

Boone found the Cumberland Gap and explored the region in 1769-1772. Western land companies were organized by Virginians and North Carolinians, beginning with the "Transylvania Company" in 1775, and the great westward movement into Kentucky was underway (fig. 160).

Settlers moved south along the western valleys of Virginia and along the Yadkin, Watauga, and French Broad rivers to the Holston. The Wilderness Road actually began at the "Block House" shown in fig. 160, but it merged with trails from the east and north, passed through the Cumberland Gap to the "Crossing of the Cumberland" and then moved north and west to the beautiful bluegrass country of central Kentucky. Boonesborough and Harrodsburg were settled before the Revolution but the great influx began after the War.

It should also be pointed out that Kentucky was also settled from the Ohio River region, particularly after 1794 when the Indians were defeated at the Battle of Fallen Timbers. The earliest settlers in Kentucky from the Ohio were from Virginia, Maryland, and Pennsylvania.

Collections of Kentucky records at the Genealogical Society in Salt Lake City are unusually good. They include marriage records dating from about 1790, birth and death records after 1851, excellent tax lists, deeds, probates, and miscellaneous court records dating from 1785. Published material relating to the state is considerable, and the Society continues to collect records from county and state repositories in Kentucky.

Tennessee received settlers from each of the colonies, but most of the early settlers came from the east and northeast. Jonesboro in Washington County was a port of entry, and records date from 1779 for that area. The region was often referred to as "that area south of the Ohio River." The whole region was Washington District, North Carolina, prior to the formation of Washington County. Then Greene, Hawkins, and Sullivan counties were organized, and settlements sprang up along the high mountain valleys extending to the south and west. Beginning in about 1820, many younger sons and adventurers moved north through Kentucky to Ohio country, while others moved west into Middle Tennessee or south into Alabama and Mississippi.

Genealogical records in Tennessee are good, consisting of marriage records dating from about 1783, some tax lists, deeds, probates, and miscellaneous court records. Tennessee county records at the Society in Salt Lake City are only fair at this writing, but new material is being acquired regularly. The Society has not yet filmed in Tennessee counties, but is purchasing microfilm or operating on an exchange program with the state.

Settlement and Migration in the North
Henry Hudson, an English naval Captain sailing for the Dutch

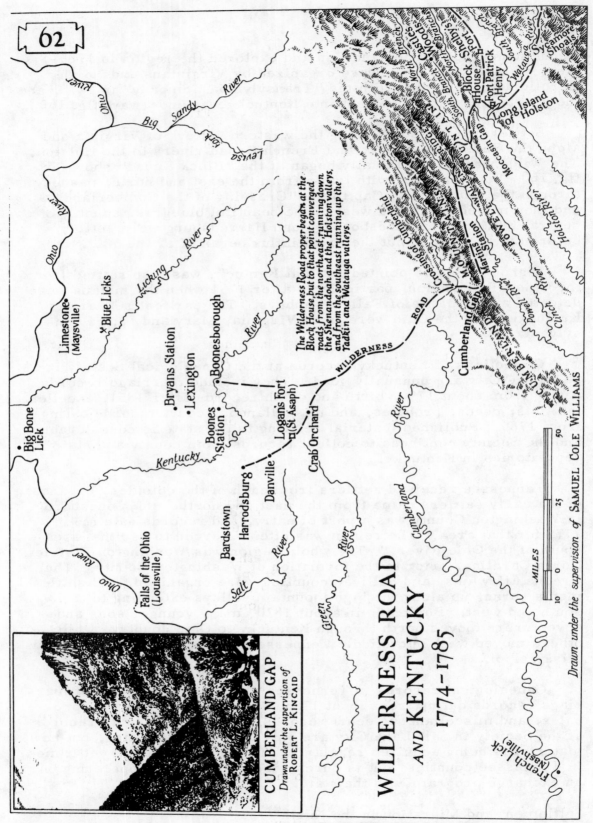

62

The Wilderness Road proper began at the Block House, but to that point converged roads from the northeast, running down the Shenandoah and the Holston valleys, and from the southeast running up the Yadkin and Watauga valleys.

CUMBERLAND GAP
Drawn under the supervision of ROBERT L. KINCAID

WILDERNESS ROAD
AND KENTUCKY
1774–1785

Drawn under the supervision of SAMUEL COLE WILLIAMS

Fig. 160. Wilderness Road

446

East India Company, explored the Hudson and Delaware regions by 1609. In 1614 there were several families from the Netherlands living on the Hudson in present New York. By 1626, the Dutch had "purchased" Manhattan Island from the Indians and Ft. Orange had been established just below present Albany. By 1638, Swedes and Finns were living on the Delaware at Ft. Christina, what is now Wilmington (fig. 161).

The Dutch followed a "patroon" system of land management which was similar to the English feudal system. Persons of substance were granted title to large tracts or patents along the Hudson River, and they became "Lords of the Manor" with the ordinary settlers working the land for a share or paying rent (fig. 162).

When the English took over New Netherland in 1664, many settlers were permitted to purchase the lands they were working, but the earlier settlers were little more than serfs.

The Dutch left vital records to the churches and kept no civil vital records. Fortunately, the records are good in content and are fairly available. There is considerable published genealogical material relating to the Dutch in New York and New Jersey and also to the Swedes and Finns on the Delaware. The Genealogical Society Library in Salt Lake City has an excellent collection of published material and also has filmed, or is now filming, many of the original records pertaining to these areas.

The first permanent settlement along the New England coast was the Plymouth Colony on Cape Cod in 1620. The Dutch had explored the region before that date but had not planted colonists east of the present New York-Connecticut border (fig. 163).

The Pilgrims who settled New Plymouth in November 1620 were mostly separatists from England who had spent a few years in Holland before emigrating to America on the Mayflower. They landed at Provincetown on Cape Cod, but within a month they had moved across the bay and established the town of Plymouth. The counties of Barnstable, Bristol, and Plymouth comprised the colony, and her first towns included Plymouth, settled in 1620; Scituate, settled in 1633; Hingham, settled in 1635; Barnstable, settled in 1638; and Yarmouth, settled in 1639. Edward Doty, an eighth great-grandfather of the author's, was buried at North Yarmouth and was among those who landed at Provincetown in 1620. He was a sixteen-year-old indentured servant to Stephan Hopkins when the Mayflower arrived and was probably born in London about 1604. We have not yet been able to locate direct evidence of his birth in English records, though we have located a marriage record for an Edward Doughtie and Elizabeth Williams in "Allhallows London Wall Parish" dated 15 February 1573, which could pertain to his parents or even grandparents. The author's descent from the Edward Doty of Massachusetts follows.

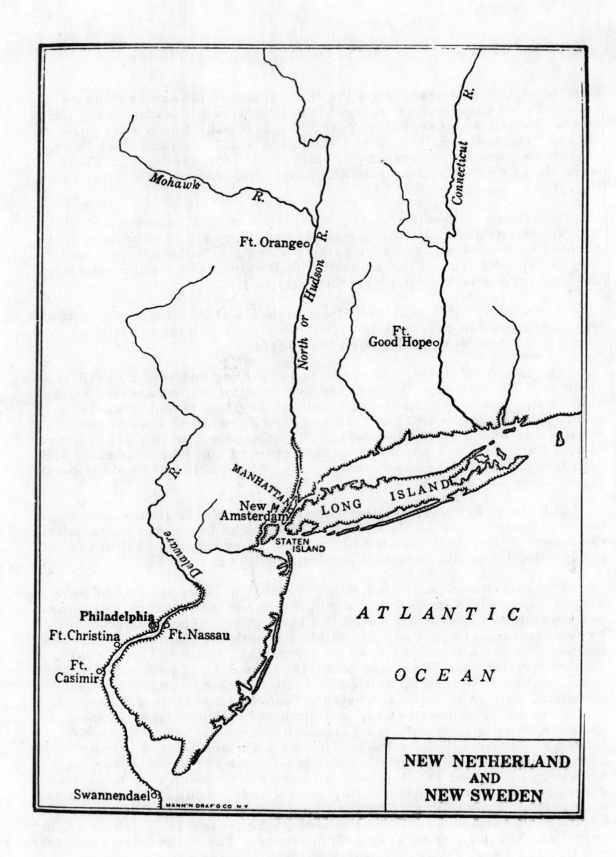

Fig. 161. New Netherland and New Sweden

448

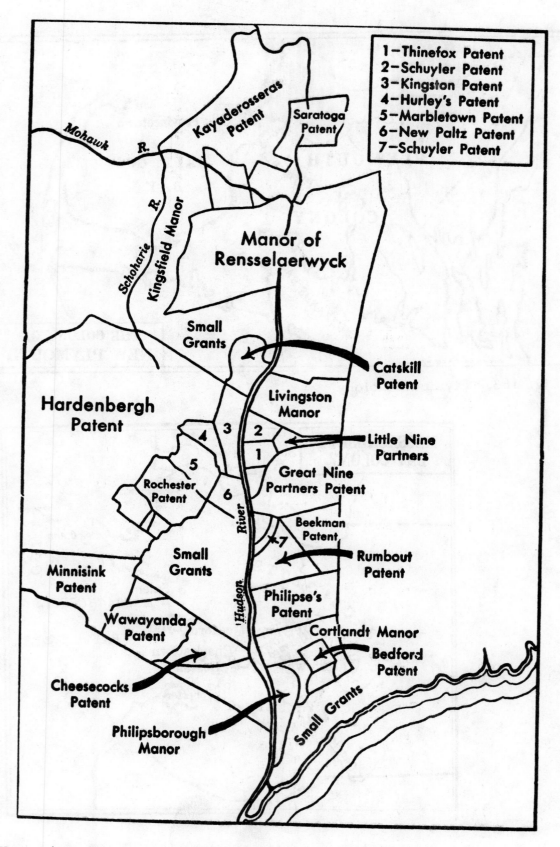

Fig. 162. Dutch patents or manors along the Hudson River

449

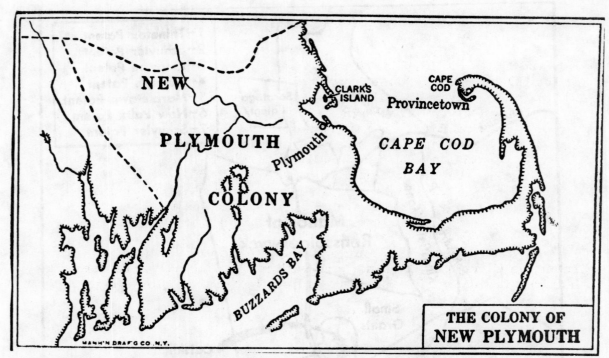

Fig. 163. Plymouth Colony

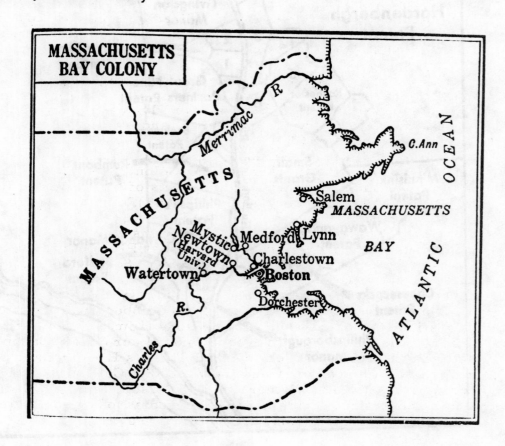

Fig. 164. Massachusetts Bay Colony

Edward Doty = Faith Clarke
  John Doty = Miss Duane
    Samuel Doty = Jean Harman
      Isaac Doty = Miss Reyno
        Azariah Doty = Sarah Tucker
          Nancy Ann Doty = Abraham Haines
            Azariah Haines = Polly Ann Newman
              Kindness Ann Haines = John C. Badger
                Kindness Ann Badger = Joseph Alma Wright
                  Cleeo Datell Wright = Mary Hill Musser
                    Norman Edgar Wright = Carolyn L. Bevan

By 1629, the Bay Colony had been settled by Puritan adherants from the Church of England, and within a few short years, several hundred families from England had settled in the colony (fig. 164).

The towns of Boston, Medford, Salem, and Watertown were all established by 1630, and by 1635, Concord, Ipswich, Marblehead, Newbury, and Weymouth were settled. The Bay Colony was at first comprised of the three counties of Essex, Middlesex, and Suffolk, but it grew to include fourteen counties, finally engulfing the entire Plymouth Colony. Settlement was directly from England in the early years, and migration took place north along the coast and southwest from Boston.

By 1633, Indians had apprised the colonists of the fertile lands along the banks of the Connecticut River, and exploration of that region soon began. Settlers from the Plymouth Colony and from the bay towns of Watertown, Dorchester, and Cambridge removed to the Connecticut Valley. By 1635, Saybrook, at the mouth of the river, and the three towns of Windsor, Hartford, and Wethersfield had been settled, constituting the Connecticut Colony. In 1638 the New Haven Colony was underway through the efforts of the Reverend John Davenport and Thophilus Eaton[1] (fig. 165).

Several of the early Connecticut towns were settled by English immigrants who had originally arrived at Plymouth or Boston and later migrated to the Connecticut Valley. Some settlers, though, came directly from England beginning in about 1640. The English counties of Devon, Dorset, and Yorkshire were important contributors to Connecticut's early settlement. In October 1635, the first general migration took place when fifty persons from New Town (Cambridge) under the leadership of John Steel moved across Massachusetts and settled at Hartford. The Reverend Thomas Hooker and his entire congregation moved overland from the Bay Colony the following spring and settled at Wethersfield, Windsor, and Hartford. By 1642, a few Connecticut people had also moved across Long Island Sound and settled Southold, Long Island[2] (fig. 166).

By 1643, the New Haven Colony included Milford, Guilford,

Fig. 165. Connecticut and New Haven colony settlement

452

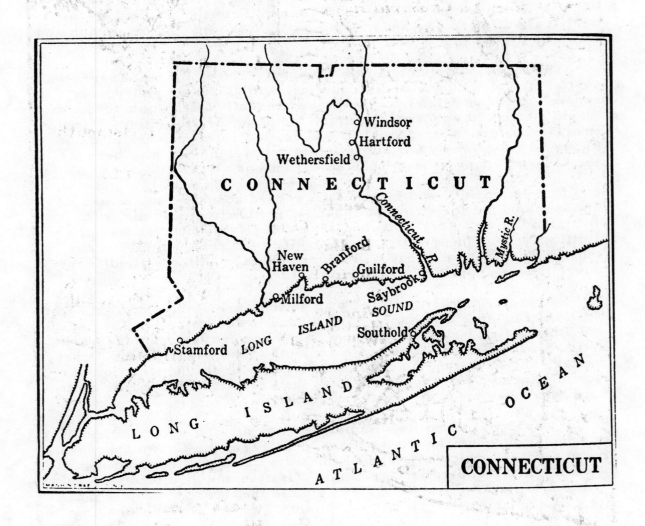

Fig. 166. Connecticut and Long Island

453

Stamford, Branford, and Southold, Long Island, and by 1665, the Connecticut Colony had absorbed the New Haven Colony to reach its full proportions with eight counties and more than 180 towns (fig. 167).

Roger Williams and other liberals were expelled from Salem, Massachusetts, in 1636 and moved south to establish the Providence Plantations. The colony proved to be a haven for the persecuted, especially for Quakers. By 1647, the towns of Providence, Portsmouth, Newport, and Warwick had united under a single charter to become Rhode Island.[3] The Quakers, or "Friends" as they are properly called, were particularly strong in the towns of Portsmouth and Newport (fig. 168).

The towns of Bristol, Little Compton, Tiverton, and Warren were part of Bristol County, Massachusetts, until 1747 when they were annexed to Rhode Island.[4] There are presently thirty-nine towns in Rhode Island and only five counties, including Bristol, Kent, Newport, Providence, and Washington. However, the relative importance of Rhode Island to westward migration far outweighs her size because she has sent many sons to open new frontiers.

New Hampshire and Maine were settled about the same time as Rhode Island but for different reasons, primarily economic. The historian Oliver Perry Chitwood says that David Thomson was at "Little Harbor" (near Portsmouth) in 1623 but returned to Boston shortly thereafter and that William and Edward Hilton settled near Dover before 1632.[5]

Hampton, New Hampshire, was settled in 1636 by emigrants from Norfolk, England, and Exeter was settled in 1638 by John Wheelwright and "thirty-five fellow heretics" who had been exiled from Massachusetts.[6] In 1641, the towns of Portsmouth (Strawberry Bank), Dover, Exeter, and Hampton, placed themselves under the jurisdiction of Norfolk County, Massachusetts, and they remained under that control until they were made a "Royal Province" in 1679.[7]

It was 1769 before New Hampshire was divided into counties and provincial government was abolished. In 1771, the Crown approved the act of 1769 which established Cheshire, Grafton, Hillsborough, Rockingham, and Strafford counties. Grafton and Strafford were annexed to Rockingham until 1773 because they were "not fully inhabited at" the time, though "the inhabitants [were] daily increasing"[8] (fig. 169).

Maine and New Hampshire had originally been granted to Sir Ferdinando Gorges and Captain John Mason by the "Council for New England," and they divided their territory in 1629, Mason taking the portion south and west of the Piscataqua (New Hampshire) and Gorges taking that between the Piscataqua and the Kennebec (Maine)[9] (fig. 170).

Fig. 167. Connecticut counties and towns

455

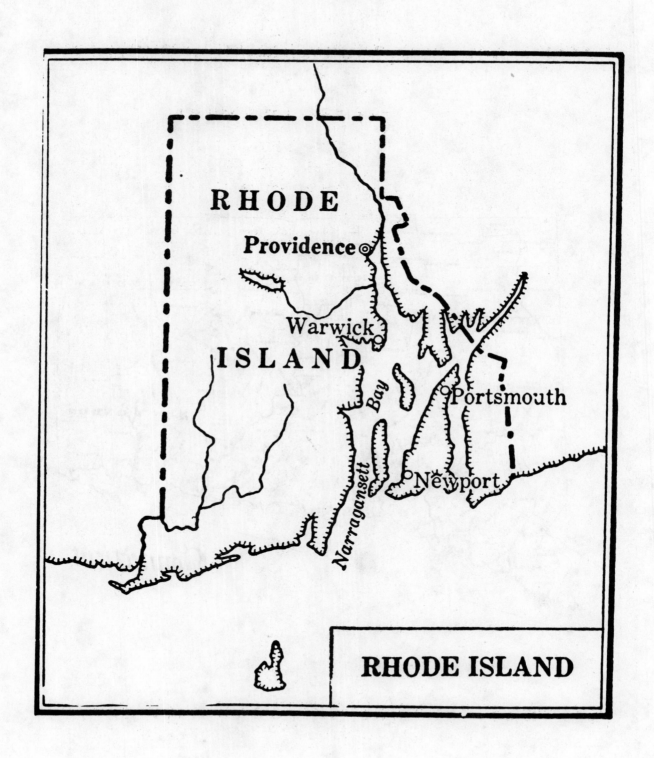

Fig. 168. Rhode Island

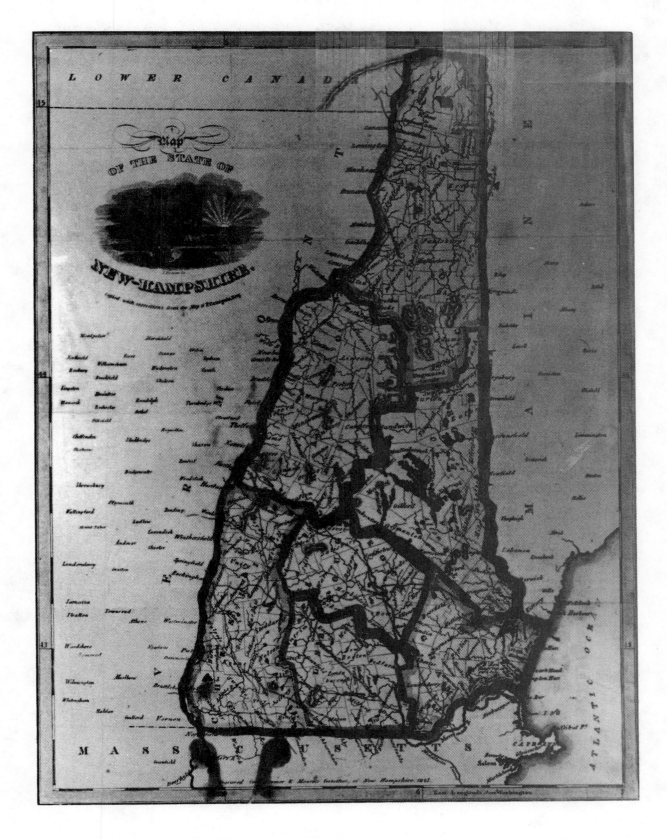

Fig. 169. New Hampshire counties and towns

457

Fig. 170. Settlements in Maine, Vermont, and New Hampshire

Maine had been settled as early as 1638, primarily from Massachusetts. In 1647, the towns of Kittery, Gorgeana, Wells, Cape Porpose, Saco, Casco, and Scarborough were annexed to Massachusetts as a "Province."[10] Kittery is generally credited with being the first organized town in Maine, though it was settled before the organization date of 1647. Agamenticus was also settled very early, before 1641, and its name was changed to Gorgeana then later to York.[11]

Settlement in Maine and New Hampshire continued from Massachusetts and directly from England until after 1700 when the same forces which brought German, French, and Scotch-Irish to the middle and southern colonies were felt in New England. Milton Rubincam says that "by the middle of the 17th century . . . Maine and New Hampshire towns were being reinforced by a stream of East Anglican Congregationalists from Massachusetts which continued to flow until after the Revolutionary War. . . . In the first quarter of the 18th century, both New Hampshire and Maine received a strong infusion of blood from the Ulster Scots. In New Hampshire, their chief settlement was the new town of Londonderry, while in Maine they are found in all of the coast towns, with particular emphasis on Wells, Falmouth, and the lower reaches of the Kennebec. Colonel Waldo's large colony of Germans from the Palatinate, with the addition of a group of French Protestants, settled farther to the eastward in the 1750's, and after the Revolution a single Pole turned up in Pownalborough"[12] (fig. 171).

The area now comprising the state of Vermont was "no man's land" prior to about 1741 but was claimed by both New York and New Hampshire. Governor Benning Wentworth of New Hampshire granted lands in present Vermont as early as 1745, and between 1761 and 1764 that region was known as the "New Hampshire Grants" (fig. 172).

In 1764, the Crown ruled that New York's boundary extended to the Connecticut River. The counties of Gloucester and Cumberland were organized by New York's taking advantage of that decision. This caused considerable strain between New York and the grantees, who were mainly from Connecticut, Massachusetts, and Rhode Island. The dispute was finally settled in 1790 when Vermont paid New York thirty thousand dollars[13] (fig. 173).

Cumberland County, organized in 1768, held jurisdiction in the southeastern part of Vermont. It was annexed to Vermont in 1791. Glocester (Gloucester) was organized in 1770 and held jurisdiction in the northeastern part of Vermont. It too was annexed to Vermont in 1791. Charlotte County held jurisdiction in the western part of Vermont and was organized from Albany County in 1772. Part of its territory was also annexed to Vermont in 1791.[14] There are presently only fourteen counties in Vermont but over 248 towns (fig. 174).

During the first years of New England's existence, settlement was primarily from England to the Plymouth and Bay colonies, and

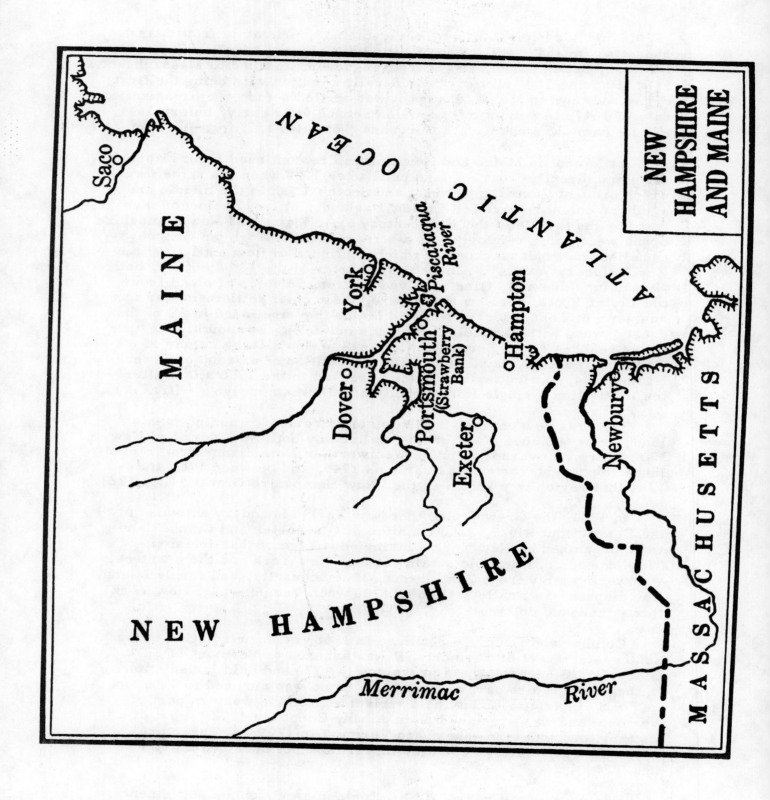

Fig. 171. New Hampshire and Maine

460

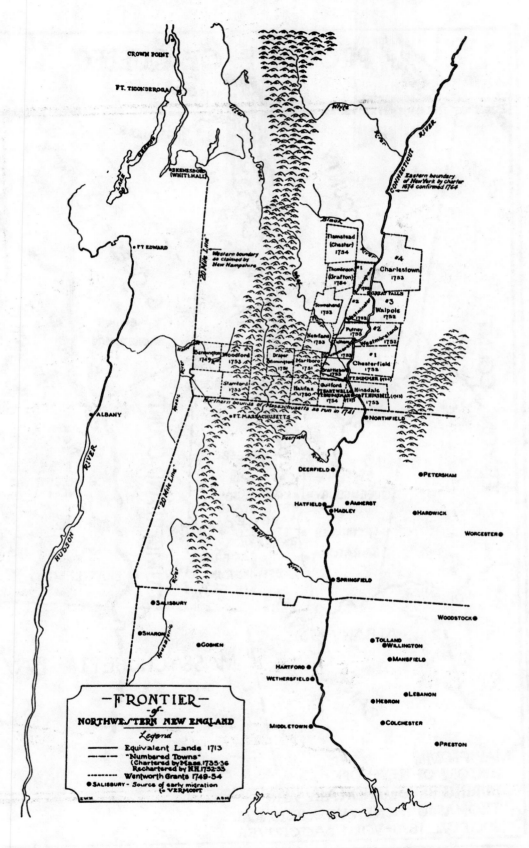

Fig. 172. Northwestern New England showing Wentworth Grants

461

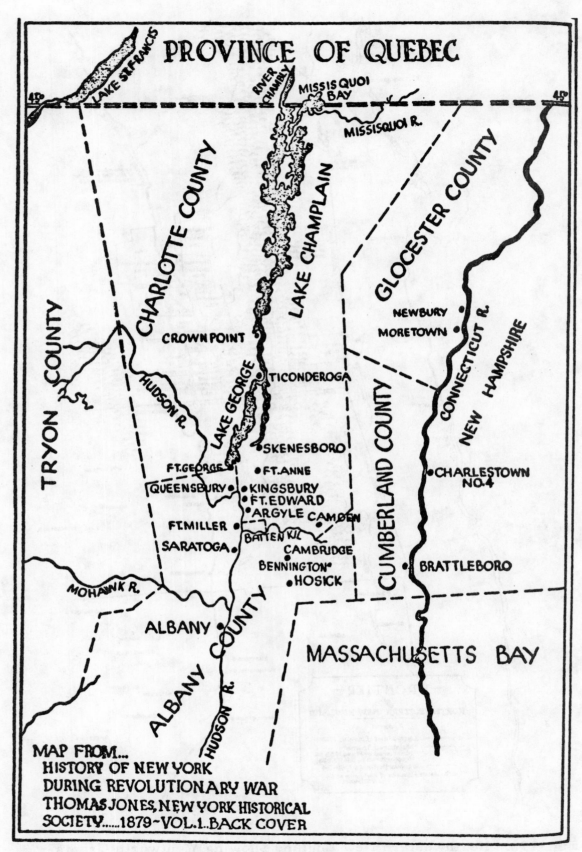

Fig. 173. New York counties in Vermont

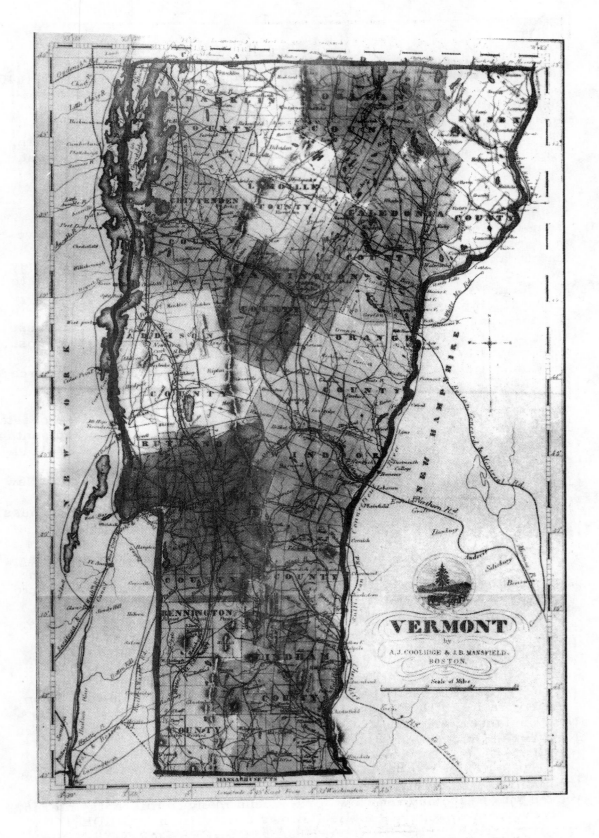

Fig. 174. Vermont counties and towns

463

those settlers provided the first inland movement. However, by 1640, immigrants were arriving at several of the coastal towns and were pushing inland. The earliest patterns of migration developed from Boston north along the coast to the Merrimac and southwest to the Providence Plantations and the Connecticut Valley. From Plymouth, the movement was both north and south and to a limited degree west to Rhode Island and Connecticut (fig. 175).

By about 1740, movement patterns were developing northwest from Boston to Vermont country, and settlers were moving north along the Connecticut River from as far south as New Jersey. Movement remained strong from Boston north to New Hampshire and Maine, and three major roads developed to the south and west. They included the "lower road" which dropped almost south from Boston to Providence and then west along the Connecticut coast, the "middle road" which pretty well followed the Great Trail to Windsor and Hartford and then dropped south along the Connecticut River and west along the coast to New York, and the "upper road" which went almost west from Boston with a little southerly movement to Springfield on the Connecticut River then south along that river joining the other roads (fig. 176).

There was constant movement by water between the various coastal towns and ports of New England and also between the middle and southern colonies. Also, after the Revolutionary War, many New England settlers pushed west to the Hudson River and settled in New York; many of these settlers became part of the great movement across New York to the Middle West in 1825 when the Erie Canal was opened. Many settlers from Connecticut moved west from Hartford to Dutchess County, New York, then northwest to Albany and along the Mohawk Valley to Utica and the Great Genesee Road to Ohio. Massachusetts settlers continued west from Springfield to the Hudson, some moving a little south and following the Catskill Road to Wattle's Ferry on the west side of the Hudson, then south along the Susquehannah River into northeastern Pennsylvania. Many of the settlers from Connecticut who pushed up the Connecticut River and followed this same route to New York and Pennsylvania, were killed in the Wyoming Valley (Pennsylvania) Massacre in 1778. [15] Some New Englanders sailed around Cape Cod through Long Island Sound to New York City and then moved north on the Hudson to Albany and the Mohawk Valley. By 1825, the Erie Canal had been built and it was possible to go from New York City to Buffalo by water at a very reasonable cost. Many New Englanders paid the going rate and followed this route to western New York, Ohio, Michigan, and points west (fig. 177).

The Dutch controlled New Netherland (New York) until 1664 when the English took over. From that date, many New England settlers moved into New York and New Jersey, and many immigrants entered directly from Europe. Rosalie Fellows Bailey, in her GUIDE TO GENEALOGICAL AND BIOGRAPHICAL SOURCES FOR NEW YORK CITY 1783-1855, says that "New York City, for a short time the

464

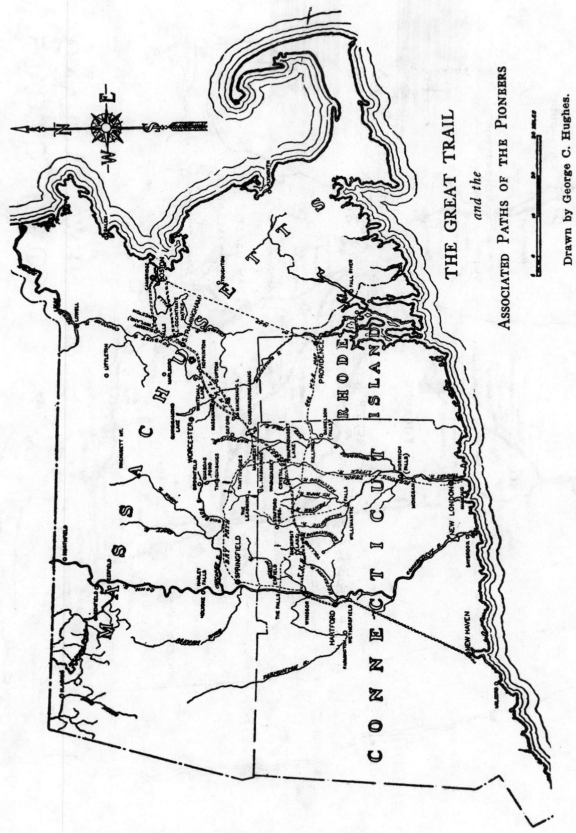

Fig. 175. The Great Trail in New England

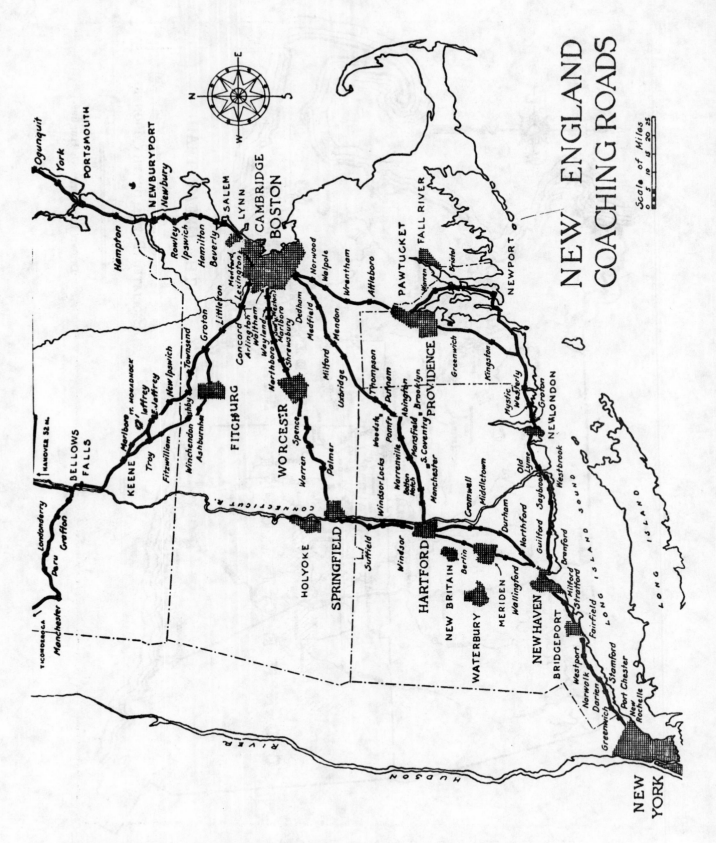

Fig. 176. New England Coaching Roads

466

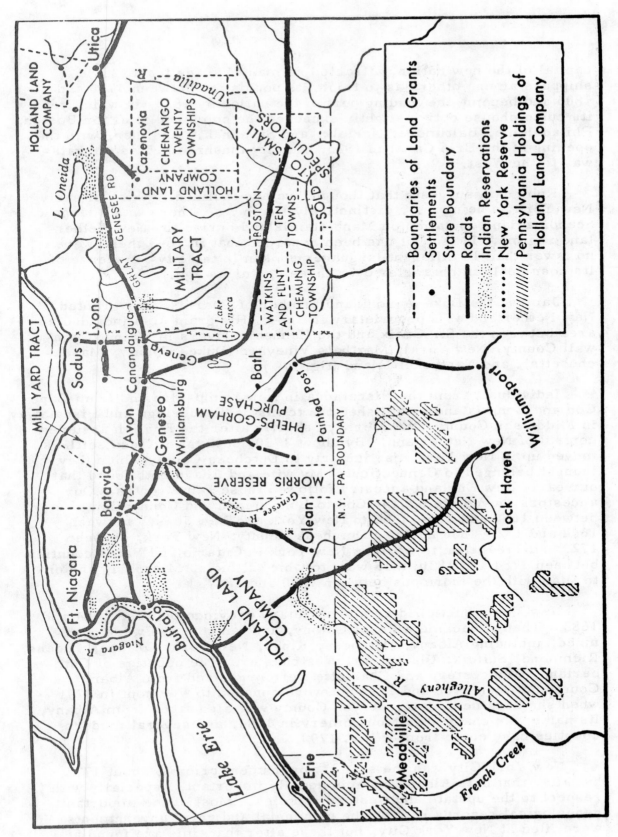

Fig. 177. New York and Pennsylvania frontier, 1790-1812

capital of the new nation, attracted so many Yankee traders and shippers among others as to triple its population between 1786 and 1805 and become the leading port of the nation by 1823, in which year its customhouse duties slightly exceeded the combined total for Boston, Philadelphia, Baltimore, Norfolk, and Savannah. And then, with the opening of the Erie Canal in 1825, the city mushroomed as the gateway to the West."[16]

Rubincam suggests that though "we are inclined to think of early New York as being . . . distinctively Dutch . . . there was a large Scandinavian population on Manhattan Island during the New Netherland regime. In fact, it has been recorded that in 1643 there were no fewer than 18 different languages spoken in the city--evidence of its cosmopolitan character over three centuries ago."[17]

James, the Duke of York and brother of Charles, was granted New Netherland as a proprietary in 1664. His grant also included an area between the St. Croix and the Kennebec rivers in Maine (Cornwall County, New York), Martha's Vineyard (Dukes County, Massachusetts), and Nantucket Island (fig. 178).

Individuals from the Piscataqua in New Hampshire and from Cape Cod and Long Island established the towns of Woodbridge and Piscataway in Middlesex County, New Jersey, shortly after the English assumed control of New Netherland. By about 1720, several of these settlers moved up to New York, particularly to Dutchess County which they thought belonged to Connecticut. My wife and I have both found that our early New England ancestry followed these same routes. Our ancestors moved from Cape Cod to Long Island and Connecticut between 1650 and 1664; then to New York and New Jersey between 1664 and 1720; then north to Dutchess County, New York, between 1720 and 1784; then to western New York in Ontario and Yates counties between 1784 and 1830; then west to Ohio, Illinois, Missouri, and on to Utah with the Mormons between 1830 and 1847.

New York functioned as a proprietary province between 1664 and 1683. Then it became a Royal Colony, and ten counties were organized, including Albany, Dutchess, Kings, New York, Orange, Queens, Richmond, Suffolk, Ulster, and Westchester. The counties of Cumberland, Gloucester, and Charlotte were organized from Albany County between 1768 and 1772 but were annexed to Vermont in 1791 when she became a state. Tryon County was also taken from Albany. Its name was changed to Montgomery in 1784, and several modern counties have come from it (fig. 179).

New York City was the seat of government prior to about 1772, but after that date Albany became equally important, especially with respect to the upstate and western counties. Most of the important genealogical records kept by the provincial and royal governments were filed at New York City, but those after that time are found at Albany or in the counties.

Fig. 178. Duke of York's Proprietary, 1664

469

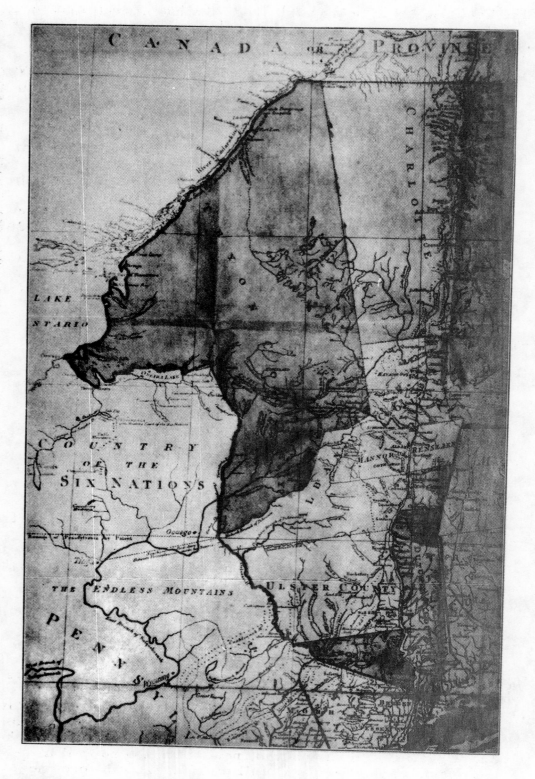

Fig. 179. New York counties, 1777

470

The Genealogical Society in Salt Lake City has microfilmed many of the more important records which have been filed at Albany and is currently filming those in the counties and at New York City. The Society has also acquired most of the important published material relating to the provincial and royal periods. Upstate and western New York counties were not keeping records until after about 1775-1780, and the Genealogical Society will have existing records for those counties filmed within a year or so.

By 1682, William Penn had been granted the area west of the Delaware River, and Europeans were emigrating to Philadelphia by the hundreds. The first settlers were primarily "Quakers" of English-Welsh birth who settled Chester and Philadelphia counties, but by 1710, German, Swiss, and Scotch-Irish were moving west along the Schuylkill River to the South Mountains and the Great Valley (fig. 180).

Shortly after the English and Welsh settlers arrived, German and Swiss immigrants came from the Continent. Thousands of Germans from the Palatinate on the Rhine River fled to England after about 1674 when their homes were laid desolate by the troops of Louis XIV. Many were sent to New York to produce naval stores and settled in Livingston Manor, but some moved to other parts of the state, and some removed to Pennsylvania where other Palatines had settled.

In Pennsylvania, many of the Swiss and German immigrants moved southwest from Philadelphia settling Lancaster and York counties, while many of the German Reformed immigrants moved north to settle Bucks, Berks, and Northampton counties. Shortly after 1700, the Scotch-Irish began to enter Pennsylvania in large numbers. Many moved west to the mountains and proceeded to settle the southwestern counties while some moved through Lancaster and York counties into Maryland and Virginia (fig. 181).

Robert E. Chaddock has described the movements of Scotch-Irish immigrants to the United States:

Driven by intolerable oppression and animated with the desire for a better opportunity, the Scotch-Irish crossed the ocean in great numbers during the 18th century. In 1718 several hundred came to Boston but were not permitted to remain. Some of them attempted to erect a church at Worcester, Massachusetts, but the Puritans destroyed it. The intolerance of the coast regions from the first forced them to the frontiers where they formed a barrier against the Indians. Many went to New York, New Jersey and the South, but the greatest numbers sought Pennsylvania, because there they hoped not only for economic freedom, but for personal and religious freedom as well . . . In 1750 the population of Virginia was reported as "growing every day more numberous by the migration of the Irish who, not succeeding so well in Pennsylvania as the Germans, sell their lands in the province and take up new ground" . . . At the close of the Revolution the

471

Fig. 180. Coastal region of the Middle Colonies

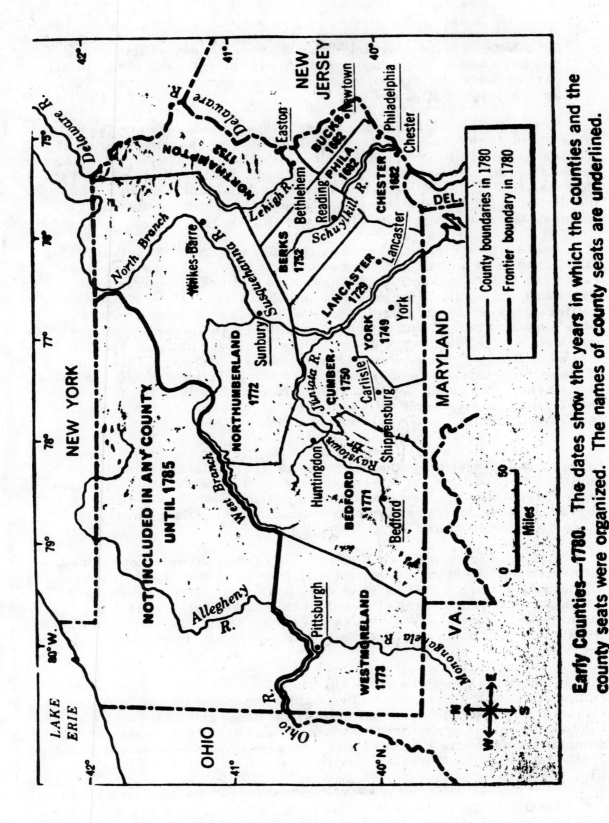

Early Counties—1780. The dates show the years in which the counties and the county seats were organized. The names of county seats are underlined.

County boundaries in 1780
Frontier boundary in 1780

Fig. 181. Early Pennsylvania colonies

473

Scotch-Irish were entering southwestern Pennsylvania in large numbers and in 1790 the population of the four counties in this part of the state was 63,000, a large majority of whom were Scotch-Irish[18] (fig. 182).

Three major migration routes developed across Pennsylvania after about 1740. One was from Philadelphia by the west branch of the Susquehannah River, reaching the Allegheny at Kittanning. Another, further south, was known as Forbes' Road. Still a third followed the Potomac to Ft. Cumberland and thence by Braddock's Road across the divide to the Youghiogheny and Monongahela Rivers. Many Virginians also came over this latter road (fig. 183).

There was a close tie between New Jersey and Pennsylvania and also between Delaware and Pennsylvania. Many settlers from the Delaware region moved into Pennsylvania and became part of the westward and southern migration from that state. Many New Jersey settlers crossed Pennsylvania to its western counties and entered Ohio country also. Stephan Jones, mentioned in an earlier chapter, was born in 1763 in Sussex County, New Jersey. In about 1780, he moved to Bucks County, Pennsylvania, where he married Keziah Straughan (of Quaker descent). He was administrator of his father-in-law's estate in Greene County, Pennsylvania, in 1801. In 1831, he was farming in west-central Ohio and east-central Indiana. He died in Quincy, Adams County, Illinois, in 1842--a Mormon.

Delaware was often referred to as the "lower counties" of Pennsylvania but chose independence in about 1701. Delaware and the southern part of New Jersey (West Jersey) were more closely allied to Pennsylvania than was the northern part of New Jersey (East Jersey). West Jersey was mostly "Quaker" while East Jersey was more "New English and Dutch" (fig. 184).

Migration from the New England and middle colonies developed into two major westward patterns with New Englanders moving west to the Hudson then crossing New York to Ohio country or moving into the northeastern part of Pennsylvania to settle. Those from the middle colonies moved across the lower part of Pennsylvania to Pittsburgh then on to the Ohio Valley or moved south into Maryland and Virginia.

In the South, settlers from Maryland and Virginia moved north and west along the Potomac to Ft. Cumberland and then to Pittsburgh and Ohio country or moved south and west along the Tidewater and Piedmont regions of the coastal plain. Many found their way through mountain passes into Kentucky and Tennessee, while some continued south and west into Georgia, Alabama, Mississippi, and Florida (fig. 185).

The Genealogical Society Library in Salt Lake City has a wonderful collection of genealogical materials pertaining to the northeastern

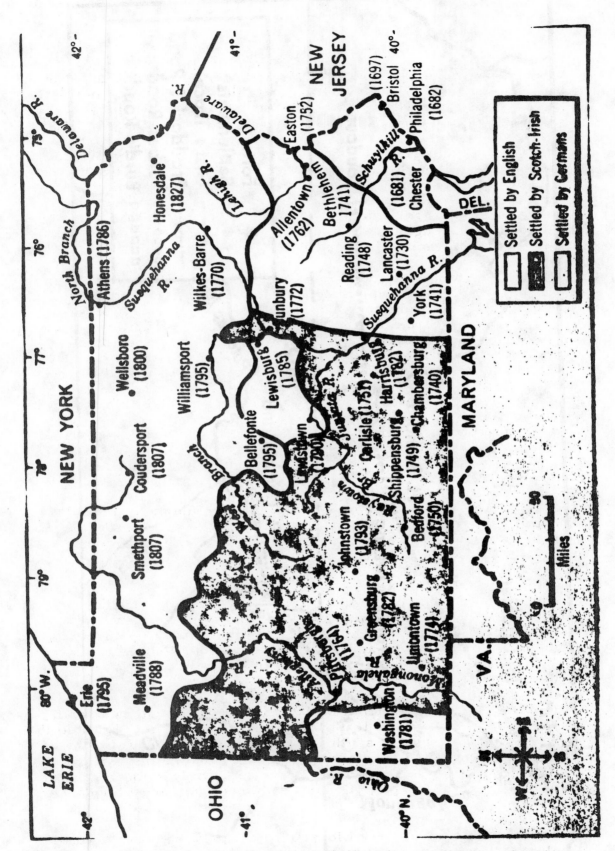

Fig. 182. Scotch-Irish settlement in southwestern Pennsylvania

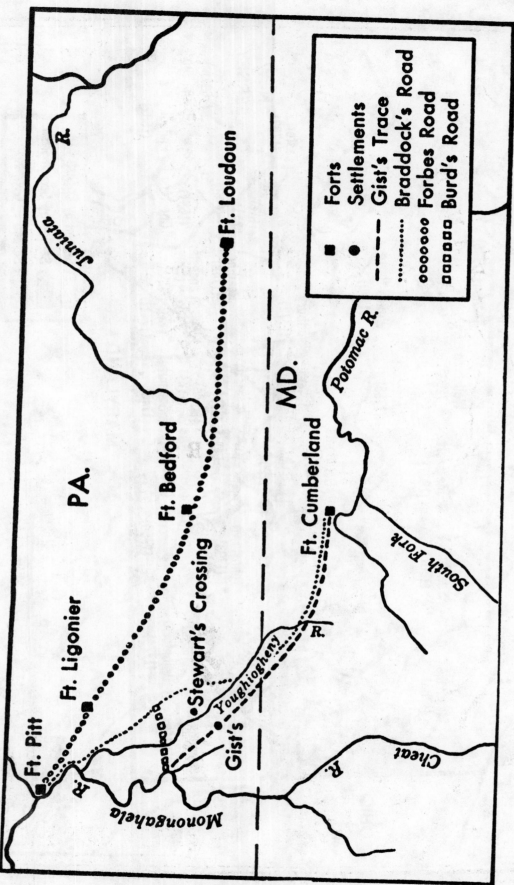

Fig. 183. Roads across Pennsylvania

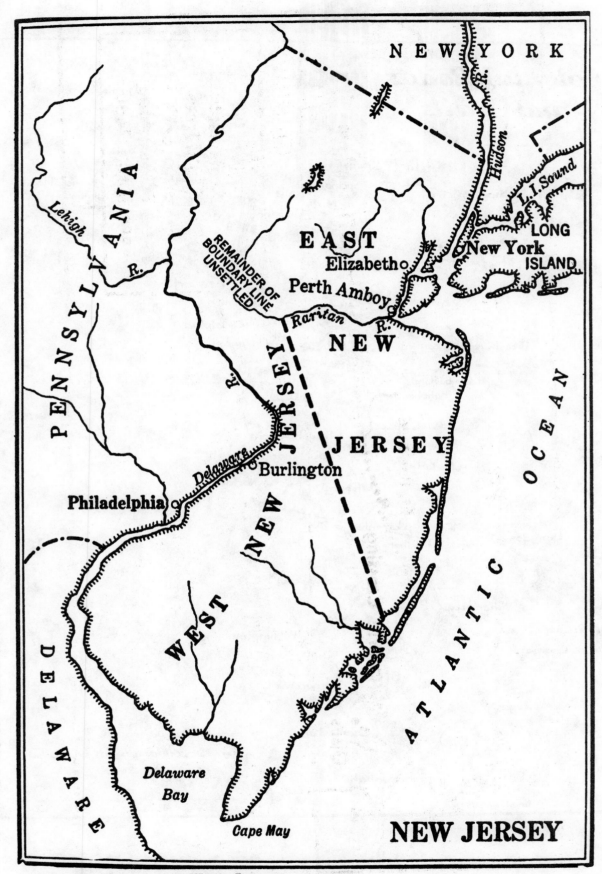

Fig. 184.   East and West Jersey

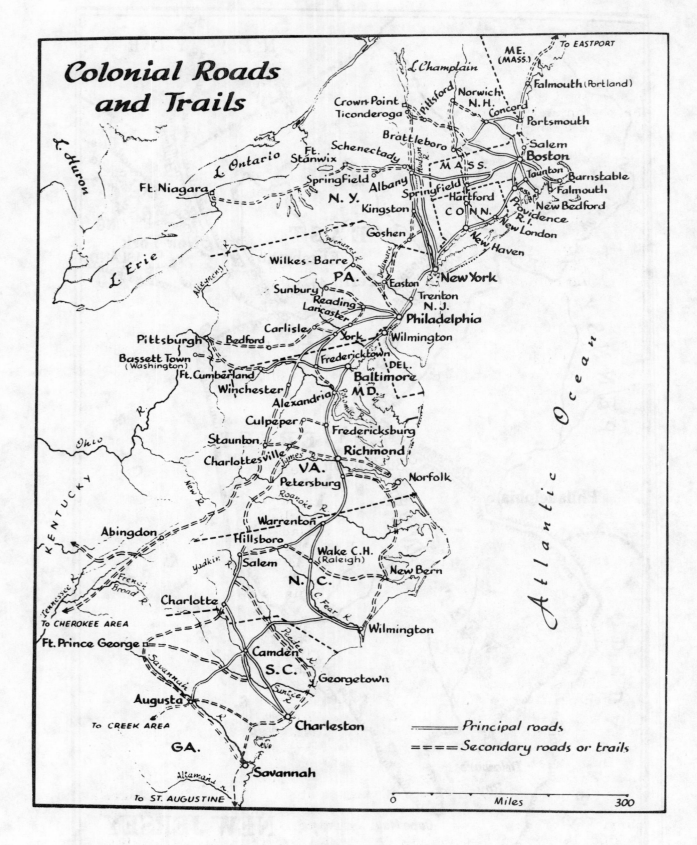

Fig. 185. Colonial roads and trails

478

United States and is constantly adding to its collection. The library has most of the important published genealogical material relating to the region and has, or is currently microfilming, most of the original town and county records of genealogical importance.

Each of the New England states has early vital record collections which have been obtained, and the Society has film copies of original town meeting books, proprietor's records, cemetery records, church records, land records, probate records, and some civil court records of the colonial period.

New York, New Jersey, and Pennsylvania did not keep vital records as early as the New England states did, but the few which were kept during the colonial period have been obtained by the Genealogical Society. A majority of the New Jersey proprietary records (about 1664-1800) have been transferred to the Department of Archives and History at the State Library, Trenton, and the Genealogical Society has recently filmed those collections. It has also filmed special genealogical and historical collections from Rutgers University and Perth Amboy. County records dating from about 1800 are now being filmed, and the Society has acquired a considerable amount of published material for the state.

County records for the eastern Pennsylvania counties have been on file in Salt Lake City for several years, and the Society has recently been filming additional county records in the state. At this writing, about one-half of the counties have been completed with orphan's court records, land records, tax lists, probates, and a few 1852-1854 vital records available. The first filming has included all of the counties across the lower half of the state from Philadelphia west to Washington and Greene counties. The Society already has most of the available published material relating to colonial Pennsylvania on its shelves.

The Genealogical Society has been filming New York county and state records for the past few years and likewise has a wonderful collection for that state. New York did not keep early vital records, except for a short span in 1847-1852, but she has good probates, land records, state census records, some tax lists, newspaper collections, and much published material. A considerable amount of colonial material has been filed at Albany, and the Society has been filming selected collections there for the past year. It also plans to film selected colonial records on file in New York City and has made arrangements to obtain materials from the Long Island Historical Society.

Both Delaware and Maryland have centralized their noncurrent public records, and the LDS Genealogical Society has microfilm copies of the early records, dating primarily to about 1850. A few miscellaneous birth and death records are available for both states, and their marriage, probate, land, and civil court records are excellent. A considerable amount of published material pertaining to both states is also available at the Society. Later county records (after about 1850-

1880) have not been microfilmed as yet, and one must correspond with county officials or agents for those.

Migration and Settlement in the West

At the close of the Revolutionary War in 1783, the United States included all of the territory between the Atlantic Ocean, west to the Mississippi River, north to the Great Lakes, and south to the lower part of Georgia. The region west of the Mississippi and south of the lower part of Georgia was held by Spain, and that north of the Great Lakes, as well as part of Maine, was claimed by Great Britain (fig. 186).

Georgia's territorial claims included most of the present states of Alabama and Mississippi while that of North and South Carolina included the present state of Tennessee and part of Alabama and Mississippi. Virginia claimed all of that territory comprising the present states of Kentucky, West Virginia, Ohio, Michigan, Indiana, Illinois, and Wisconsin. Connecticut and Massachusetts held overlapping claims with Virginia in the Northwest while Delaware, Pennsylvania, New Jersey, New York, Rhode Island, and New Hampshire each had fixed boundaries. Maine was a province of Massachusetts until 1820, and Vermont was claimed by both New York and New Hampshire until she became a state in 1791.

By 1802, the claiming states ceded their rights to these western lands, and the United States government assumed title. Kentucky was organized from part of Virginia's claim south of the Ohio River, and Tennessee was created from North Carolina's western lands. Alabama and Mississippi were organized after the treaty with Spain in 1819 which ceded Florida Territory to the United States. Ohio, Michigan, Indiana, Illinois, and Wisconsin were carved from the territory organized under the Northwest Ordinance of 1787 (fig. 187).

Migration west of the Allegheny Mountains was minimal before the French and Indian War came to a close in 1763, but it increased rapidly after the Revolution ended some ten years later. In the South, movement had been from the Tidewater west and south, with a few settlers finding their way through the mountains into Kentucky and Tennessee but with southern movement greater before about 1785. In the middle colonies, migration had been south and west across Pennsylvania to the Ohio River and south through Maryland and Virginia. In New England, settlement had proceeded throughout each of the colonies with some movement west to the Hudson River and along the Mohawk Valley as far west as Utica, New York (Oneida County). It had not gone much farther west because of the Indian problem, but after the Revolution it had continued across New York to Lake Erie and Ohio country (fig. 188).

A few settlers had moved along the Youghiogheny, the Monongahela, and Allegheny rivers in western Pennsylvania between 1740 and 1780,

Fig. 186. The United States in 1783

481

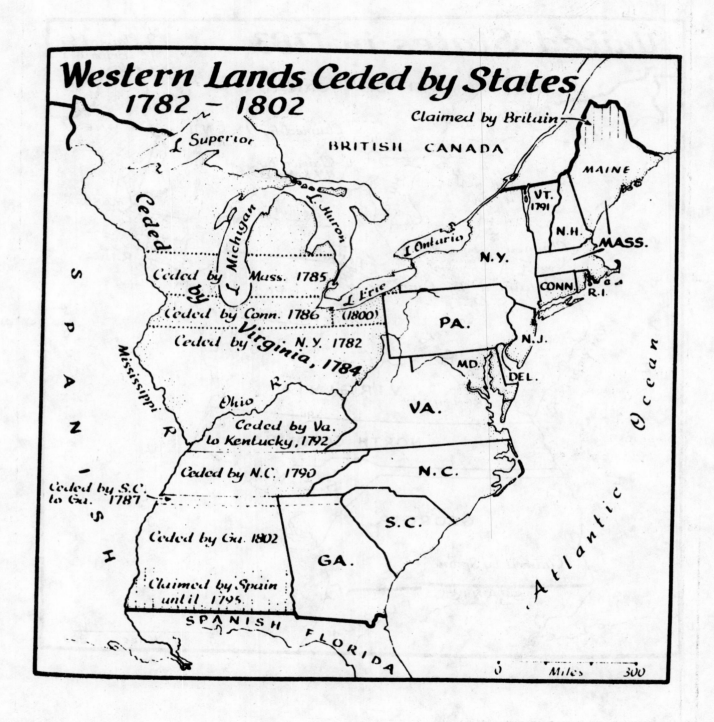

Fig. 187. Ceded lands, 1782–1802

482

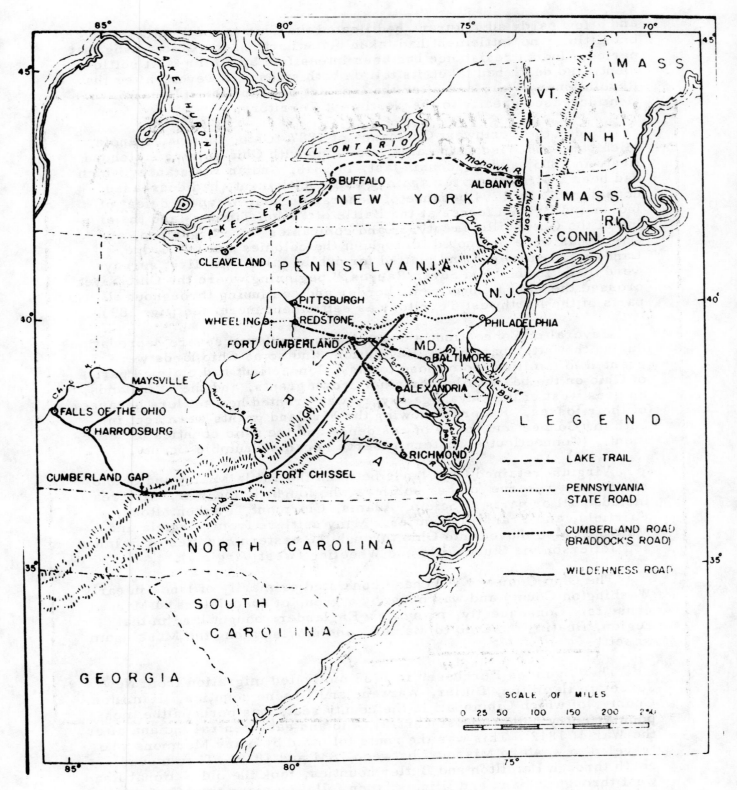

Fig. 188. Major migration routes to Ohio Country

and a few hardy adventurers had floated the Ohio to the Kentucky River, but little or no settlement had taken place north of the Ohio during that period. Indian resistance had been intensified by attempts at settlement, and death had taken its toll on both sides. However, after the Revolutionary War, and after the land act of 1785, the tide of migration increased greatly to the Northwest Territory.

Under the Northwest Ordinance of 1787, Ohio, Indiana, Illinois, Michigan, and Wisconsin came into being with Ohio gaining statehood first, in 1803, and Wisconsin last, in 1848. Indian resistance, which had been a strong barrier against white settlement, had decreased considerably by 1794 because of General Anthony Wayne's defeat of Indian and British forces at the Battle of Fallen Timbers and the signing of the Greenville Treaty. Land companies were organized, and Ohio lands were promoted throughout the colonies and in Europe. Lands were surveyed and platted for public sale. The first surveys were made in the "Old Seven Ranges," beginning where the Ohio River crossed the west Pennsylvania border and continuing throughout all parts of the Northwest Territory as settlement increased (fig. 189).

Several of Connecticut's coastal towns suffered severe depredations during the latter part of the Revolution, and some Ohio lands were granted to families from those towns. Connecticut had claimed part of Ohio on the basis of her original crown grants, and the "Firelands," an area west of the Cuyahoga River, was granted her settlers because of their losses. Records showing the Fireland grants were kept in both the Connecticut towns of residence and the Ohio counties of settlement. (Connecticut's western reserve became Trumble County.)

Virginia retained Ohio lands between the Little Miami and Scioto rivers as a reserve for her soldiers who fought in the War; this area included all or parts of Scioto, Adams, Clermont, Warren, Ross, Fairfield, and Franklin counties. Many settlers from Virginia and Maryland also moved into Ohio through the eastern counties of Belmont and Jefferson via Stubenville and Wheeling (West Virginia).

The Ohio Company Purchase consisted primarily of lands in early Washington County and was made by a group of speculators in Massachusetts. Consequently, many New Englanders bought land in that region, floating the Ohio to Marietta and moving along the Muskingum to settle.

The "Symmes Purchase" in 1788 motivated migration from New Jersey to Hamilton, Butler, Warren, and Greene counties. Hamilton County, of which Cincinnati is the county seat, was perhaps the most popular entry point to west-central Ohio and east-central Indiana after the War of 1812. This was the route followed by many Mormons who traveled to western Missouri between 1831 and 1839. They moved north through Hamilton and Butler counties, took the old National Road west through Indiana and Illinois, then followed along the Mississippi north to the Missouri River and west to Independence. Those who

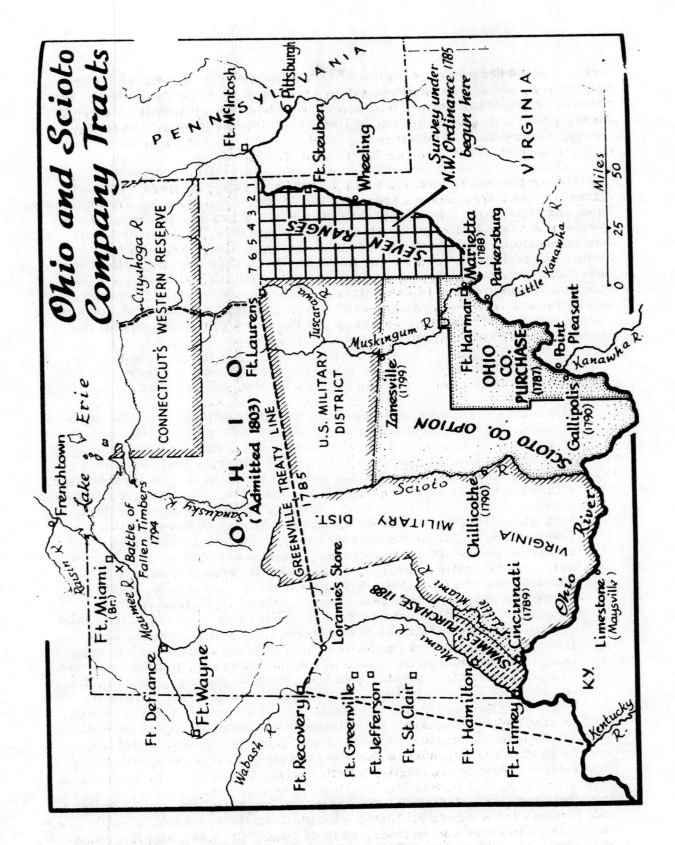

Fig. 189. Ohio and Scioto Company tracts

485

moved west from the northern part of Ohio took an overland route southwest across the upper part of Ohio to Fort Wayne, Indiana, then followed the Maumee and Wabash rivers across Indiana to Illinois and finally to St. Louis and west to the Missouri counties of Jackson, Clay, Caldwell, and Daviess.

Ohio was granted statehood in 1803, and settlers were moving across her eastern and southern borders in large numbers by that time. New Englanders were entering from New York and Pennsylvania, and settlers from the middle colonies were pouring into Columbiana, Jefferson, and Belmont counties. Maryland and Virginia settlers were entering through Jefferson and Belmont counties, and families from Kentucky and Tennessee were crossing the Ohio into all of the southern counties. Some newcomers were floating the Ohio on flat-boats and proceeding to Marietta, Gallipolis, Maysville (Kentucky), and Cincinnati. Beginning shortly after the War of 1812 and continuing to the Civil War, many settlers from North and South Carolina and Georgia were migrating to the state (fig. 190).

Shortly after 1812, the National Road and Zane's Trace became popular overland routes across Ohio. Craddock says that

the first continuous road through the state of Ohio was "Zane's Trace," passing from Wheeling, on the boundary between Virginia and Ohio, in a southwesterly direction to a point opposite Maysville, Kentucky, on the Ohio River. The Zanes had founded Wheeling in 1770, a strategic point in the valley because of its advantages for trade with the interior. Zane's road became a prime factor in Ohio's development. It determined the location of homes, taverns and villages. Where it crossed the Muskingum . . . Zanesville grew up . . . where the road crossed the Hocking, Lancaster was founded, while at the ferry over the Scioto the town of Chillicothe became the center of activity for the Virginia Military Lands . . . In like manner came the pioneers into Muskingum county. Thus also from Kentucky came the first settler into Pickaway county. Highland county received its first pioneer over the same route. The first arrivals in Fairfield county came from Kentucky but soon mingled with others coming, in ever-increasing numbers, from Virginia and Pennsylvania by this common means of approach to the interior. Family after family, coming from different regions, thus settled side by side in the country of their choice. Post-offices were soon established at Lancaster and Zanesville. The inland counties increased rapidly in wealth and population. In 1815 Ross county had 18,000 inhabitants, and was only excelled by the river county of Hamilton[19] (fig. 191).

Between 1800 and 1820, settlers also began to move into Indiana and Illinois. A majority of them floated the Ohio or took the old National Road across the lower part of Ohio, Indiana, and Illinois. Some moved north from Cincinnati to east-central Indiana, and some

Ohio county map in 1803 when the state was admitted to the Union.

Fig. 190. Ohio counties, 1803

487

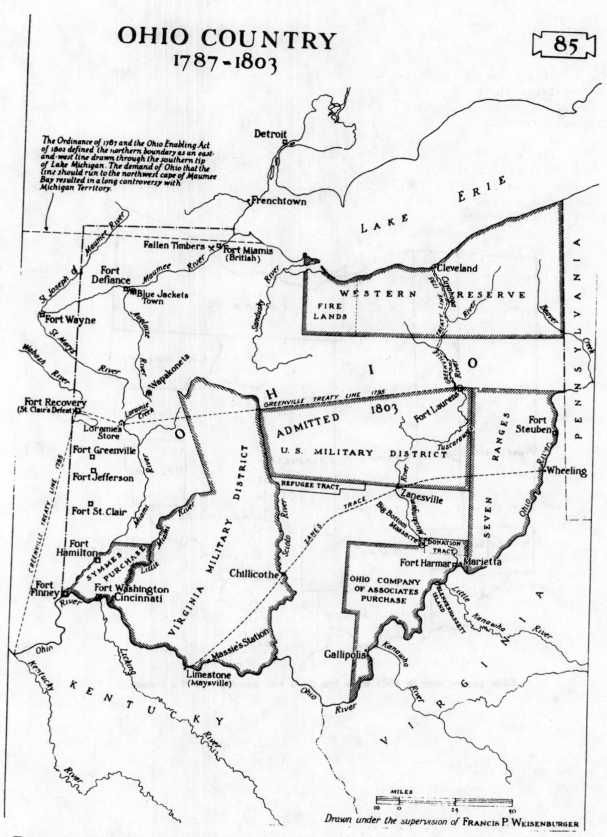

OHIO COUNTRY
1787-1803

The Ordinance of 1787 and the Ohio Enabling Act of 1802 defined the northern boundary as an east-and-west line drawn through the southern tip of Lake Michigan. The demand of Ohio that the line should run to the northwest cape of Maumee Bay resulted in a long controversy with Michigan Territory.

Detroit

LAKE ERIE

Frenchtown

Fallen Timbers × Fort Miamis (British)

Maumee River

Fort Defiance

Blue Jackets Town

St. Joseph

St. Marys

Fort Wayne

Wabash River

Auglaize River

Wapakoneta

Sandusky River

Cleveland

WESTERN RESERVE

FIRE LANDS

Cuyahoga River

GREENVILLE TREATY LINE 1795

PENNSYLVANIA

Beaver Creek

Fort Recovery (St. Clair's Defeat)

Loramie Creek

Loramies Store

GREENVILLE TREATY LINE 1795

O H I O

1803

Fort Laurens

ADMITTED

U.S. MILITARY DISTRICT

Tuscarawas River

SEVEN RANGES

Fort Steuben

Fort Greenville

Fort Jefferson

Fort St. Clair

Miami River

VIRGINIA MILITARY DISTRICT

REFUGEE TRACT

Scioto River

ZANES TRACE

Big Bottom Massacre

Muskingum River

Zanesville

DONATION TRACT

Wheeling

Ohio River

Fort Hamilton

SYMMES PURCHASE

Little Miami River

Chillicothe

OHIO COMPANY OF ASSOCIATES PURCHASE

Fort Harmar

Marietta

Blennerhassett Island

Little Kanawha River

Fort Finney

Fort Washington

Cincinnati

Massies Station

Gallipolis

Kanawha River

V I R G I N I A

Ohio River

Licking River

Limestone (Maysville)

K E N T U C K Y

Kentucky River

MILES
10 0 25 50

Drawn under the supervision of FRANCIS P. WEISENBURGER

Fig. 191. Ohio Country, 1787-1803

moved along the Ohio to the Wabash River and then traveled north to Terre Haute in the western part of the state. Those who did not move overland to Illinois were floating the Ohio to Shawneetown or Kaskaskia and were moving into the southern counties of Illinois (fig. 192).

Settlement of the northern counties in Illinois and Indiana did not increase much until after about 1820, but from that time settlers entered those counties in increased numbers and also began to settle the middle border states and Michigan. The same forces which influenced Ohio's early settlement carried over to Indiana, Illinois, Michigan, and Wisconsin, with perhaps more New England and New York settlers moving into Michigan and Wisconsin than into the other states. In his WESTWARD EXPANSION, Ray Allen Billington notes that the peopling of northern Indiana, northern and central Illinois, and southern Michigan began while Black Hawk's war still raged on the western borders of the Lake Plains. For twenty years--from 1830 to 1850--population moved steadily into the region, until the whole Northwest was filled. The source of this migratory stream was New England and the middle states. "Thrifty Yankees, driven westward by unsettled economic conditions at home and lured onward by improved transportation routes to the West, in those years filled the northern portion of the Lake Plains as solidly as their southern compatriots had the bottom lands of the Ohio Valley"[20] (fig. 193).

By 1840, a network of canals, roads, and railroads covered most of the Northwest Territory, at least to the Mississippi, and settlers continued to move west and northwest. "Some pioneers from the Middle States continued to use the old routes--the National Road, Forbes' Road, or the Catskill Turnpike--to reach the Ohio, then made their way down the river and northward to central Indiana or Illinois," Billington observes. However, "more took advantage of a newly completed all-water route between East and West. The Erie Canal, opened to traffic in 1825 from the Hudson River to Lake Erie, offered the first really satisfactory means of reaching the Lakes country from New England. Travelers might complain of the over-crowded canal boats, poor food, and swarming mosquitoes, but they were nevertheless able to travel cheaply, take their household goods with them, and be sure of reaching their destination without losing a wagon in a mudhole. Little wonder that the Erie Canal overnight became the most important route to the West, or that thousands of homeseekers made their way westward on its horse-drawn barges."[21]

After 1840, America was on its way to becoming the "melting pot" of the world, with different national and ethnic groups emigrating from the British Isles and from all quarters of the Continent. Unsettled economic conditions, religious persecution, wars, pestilence, famine, and other factors motivated emigrants to seek refuge in America, and many sought lands in the West. German, Scotch, Irish, English, Welsh, Scandinavian, Polish, Italian, and even Russian immigrants were arriving at the east-coast and gulf-coast ports. Some were finding employment and had cause to remain in the East, but more

489

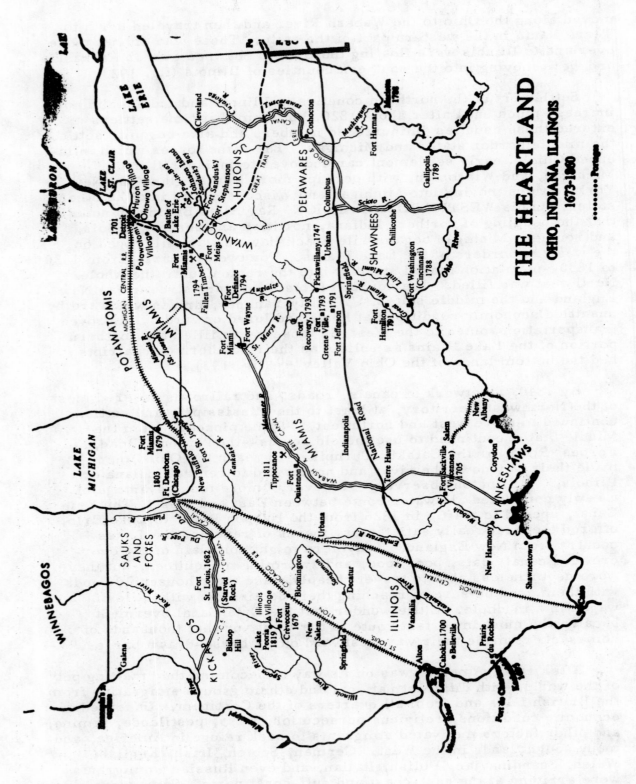

Fig. 192. The Heartland, 1673-1860

490

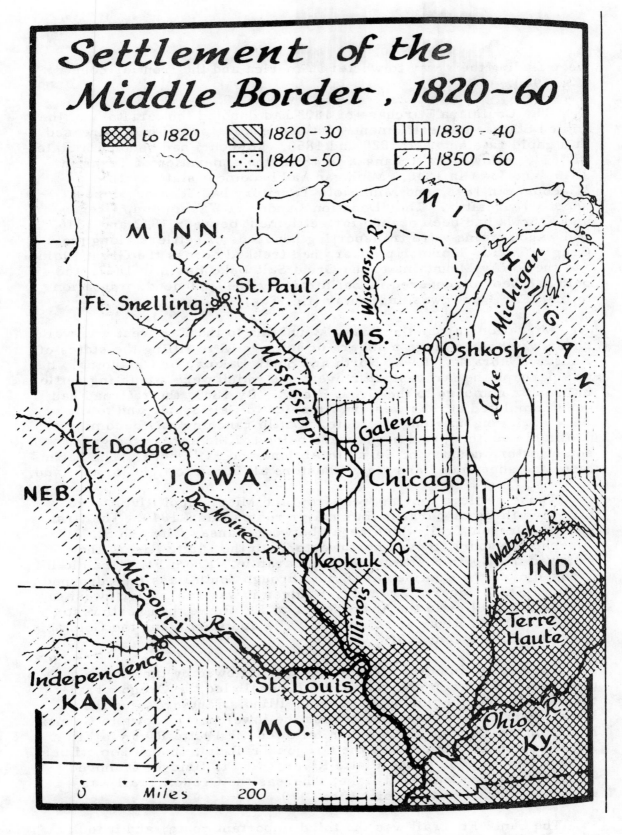

Fig. 193. Middle border settlement, 1820-1860

were finding their way to western America and the frontier country (fig. 194).

The Louisiana Purchase of 1803 had doubled the territory of the United States, and settlement west of the Mississippi had increased at a rapid rate between 1820 and 1850. Missouri had become a state in 1821, followed by Arkansas in 1836, the annexation of Texas in 1845, and Iowa in 1846. Michigan had become a state by 1837, Wisconsin in 1848, and Minnesota Territory had been organized shortly thereafter. The "Donation Lands" of Washington, Oregon, and Florida had been opened for settlement between 1842 and 1846, and wagon trains were transporting hundreds of settlers along the Oregon Trail. Mormon pioneers had trekked across the Great Plains and the Rocky Mountains to the Great Salt Lake Basin in 1847, and gold had been discovered in California by 1849. Indeed, migration to the "Far West" was under way (fig. 195).

Migration across the Rocky Mountains to the Far West was well under way before large numbers of settlers were filling the states of Kansas, Nebraska, Iowa, North and South Dakota, or Oklahoma. It was perhaps the far western movements which were attracting settlers in greater numbers to the Great Plains. By 1869, the railroad had been completed across western America to California, and towns were springing up along its route. Cattle ranching was becoming a profitable venture, and herds were being trailed across the great southwestern country of Texas to Abilene and Ft. Dodge. The cattlemen, the sheepmen, and the sodbusters all began to fight for the land.

Those settlers moving west from the Mississippi River were following three or perhaps four major routes after 1840. The first was the Oregon Trail which began between Kansas City and St. Joseph, Missouri, moved northwesterly to the Platte River, then followed the North Platte to old Ft. Laramie. From Ft. Laramie it crossed over the Continental Divide through South Pass then dropped south to Ft. Bridger. From Ft. Bridger it was routed northwest to Ft. Hall and followed the Snake River to Ft. Boise then northwest to the Columbia River at Ft. Walla Walla and west along the Columbia River to Ft. Vancouver (fig. 196).

The second important route was that followed by the Mormon pioneers and later by the railroad. It paralleled the Oregon Trail to some degree, beginning at Nauvoo, Illinois, and crossing the Mississippi River. It angled across the lower part of Iowa to Council Bluffs on the Missouri River then followed the Platte River to Ft. Laramie and Ft. Bridger as the Oregon Trail did, though sometimes on the opposite side of the Platte River. At Ft. Bridger it moved southwest to the Great Salt Lake, whereas the Oregon Trail was routed northwest at that point (fig. 197).

The Santa Fe Trail was the third important route, and it took a southwesterly course from Kansas City, Missouri, to Ft. Dodge in

492

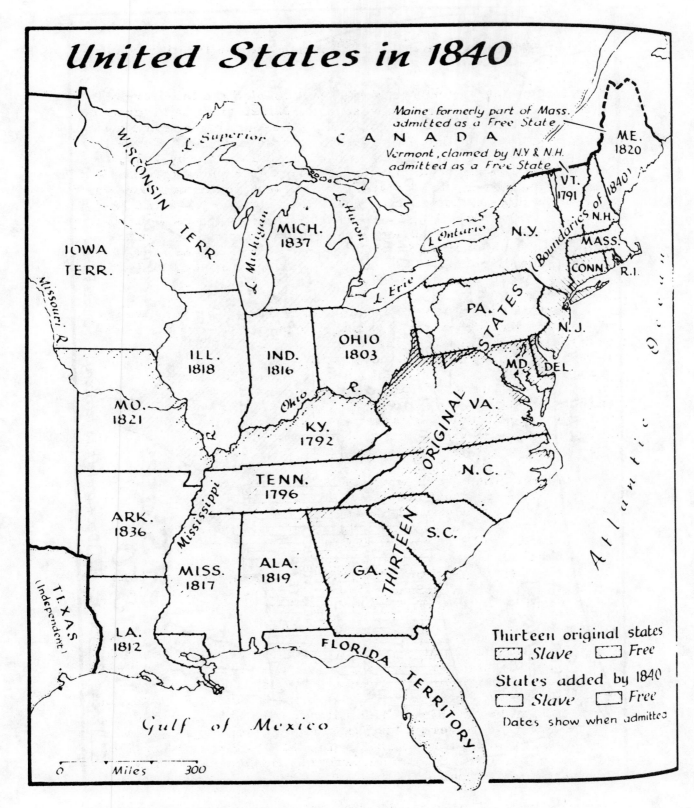

United States in 1840

Maine, formerly part of Mass. admitted as a Free State

ME. 1820

Vermont, claimed by N.Y. & N.H. admitted as a Free State

C A N A D A

WISCONSIN TERR.

L. Superior

L. Michigan

L. Huron

L. Ontario

L. Erie

VT. 1791

N.H.

(Boundaries of 1840)

IOWA TERR.

MICH. 1837

N.Y.

MASS.

CONN.

R.I.

PA.

STATES

Missouri R.

ILL. 1818

IND. 1816

OHIO 1803

Ohio R.

N.J.

MD.

DEL.

MO. 1821

KY. 1792

ORIGINAL

VA.

TENN. 1796

N.C.

ARK. 1836

Mississippi

THIRTEEN

S.C.

TEXAS (Independent)

MISS. 1817

ALA. 1819

GA.

LA. 1812

FLORIDA TERRITORY

Atlantic Ocean

Gulf of Mexico

Thirteen original states
☐ Slave   ☐ Free

States added by 1840
☐ Slave   ☐ Free

Dates show when admitted

0   Miles   300

Fig. 194.   The United States, 1840

493

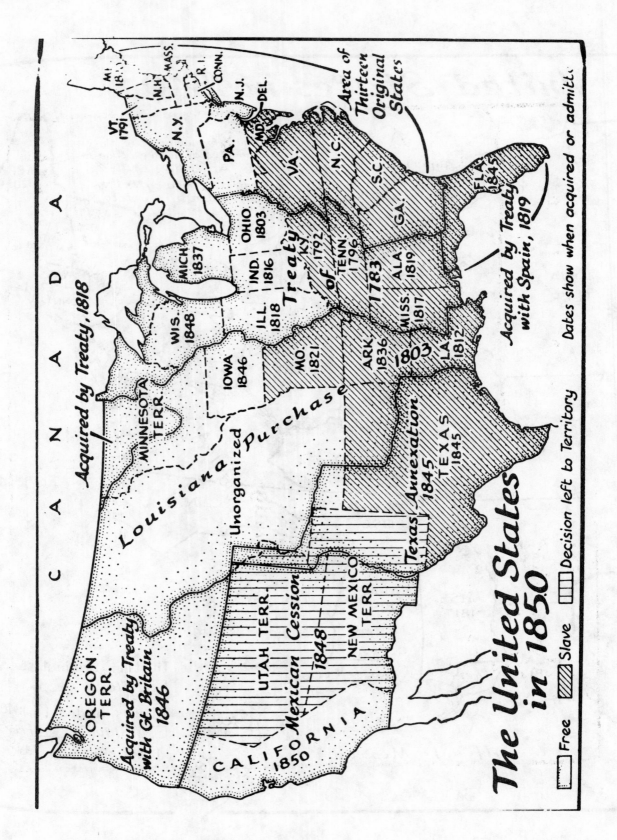

Fig. 195. The United States, 1850

494

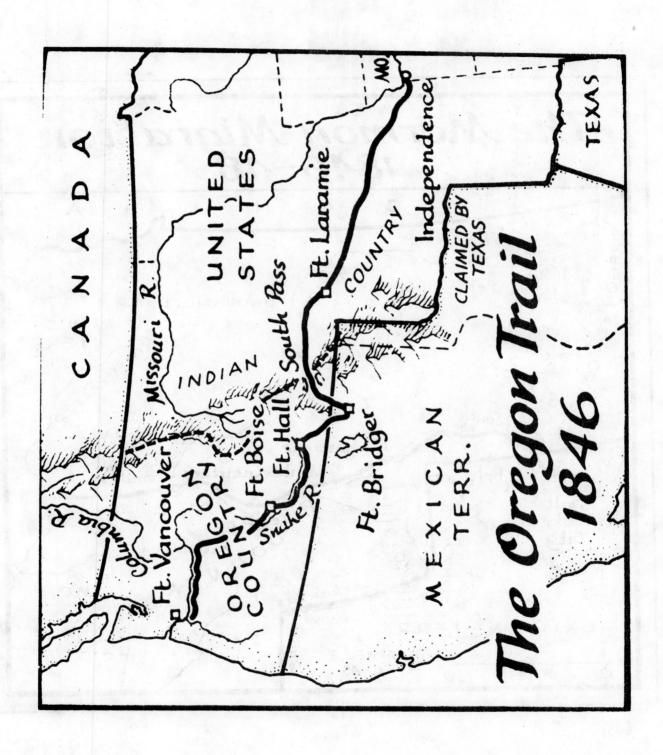

Fig. 196.   The Oregon Trail

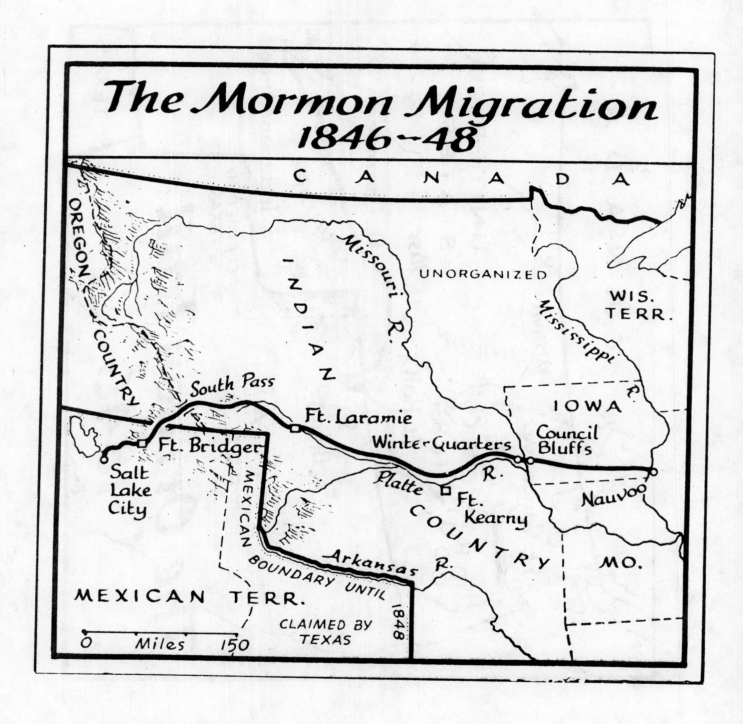

Fig. 197. The Mormon Trail

496

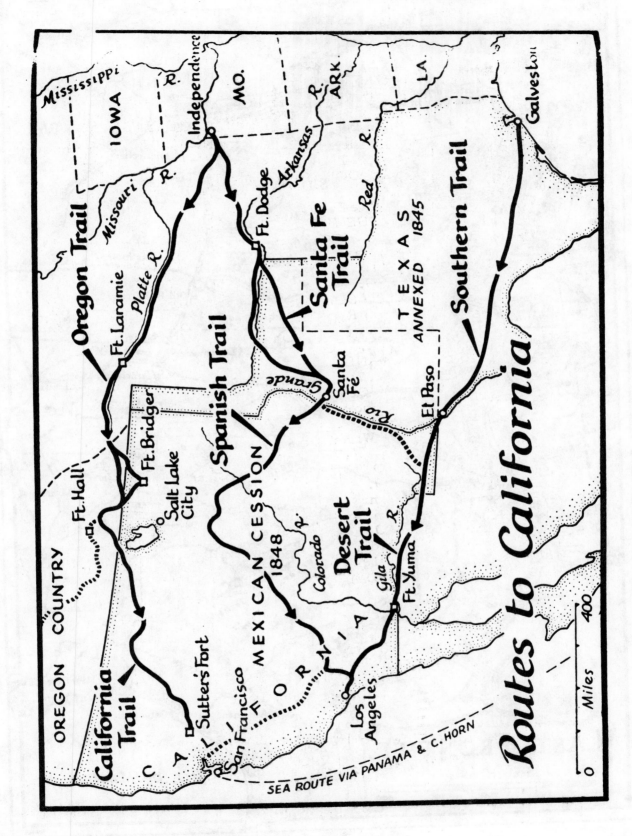

Fig. 198. Routes to California

497

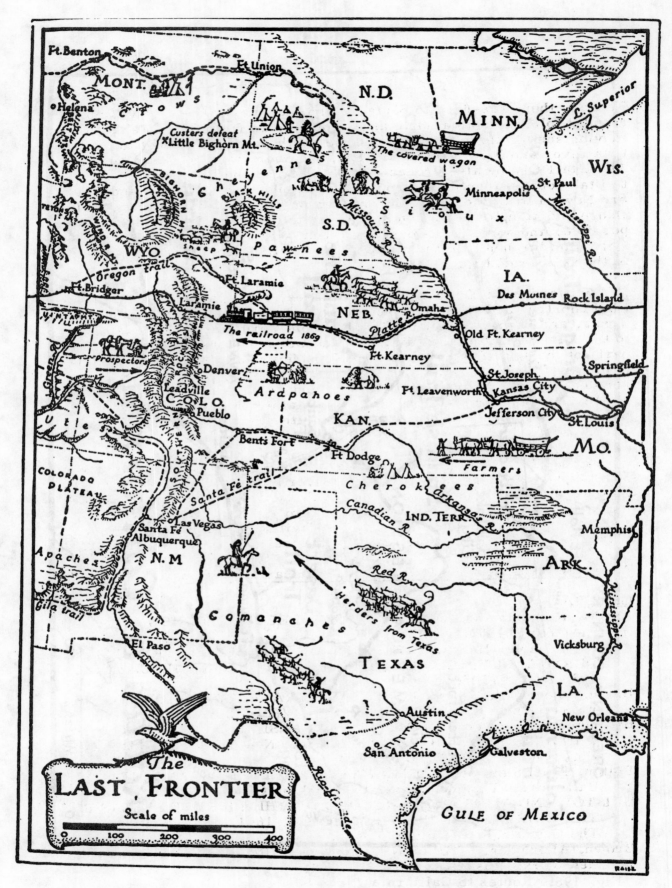

Fig. 19.9. The Last Frontier

Kansas, then proceeded to Santa Fe and the Rio Grande. Movement along it followed both a north and a south route from Santa Fe. Those moving south followed the Rio Grande south then struck west to the Gila River and Ft. Yuma in Arizona, then northwest to Los Angeles. At Santa Fe some also proceeded north across the Colorado Plateau to Utah country then moved southwest through southern Utah and southern Nevada to California. Movement along the Arkansas River to Ft. Dodge and along the Red River in Texas to the Santa Fe Trail was also possible, and some Gulf Coast migration took a southerly route from Galveston through San Antonio or Austin to El Paso, Texas, then north to the Gila Trail (fig. 198).

Settlers from Kentucky and Tennessee, from various parts of Ohio country, and from the Deep South had moved into Arkansas, Texas, and later Oklahoma. These people were among those moving to the Far West after the Civil War and were responsible for settling parts of the southwestern states of New Mexico and Arizona. Settlers from all of the southern states as well as from the Ohio country peopled Kansas, Nebraska, and Iowa, and European settlers also swelled the number of settlers in these states. Many Germanic and Slavic immigrants followed, especially after the railroad came in 1869.

Some of the Ohio country settlers, especially Scandinavians, moved north and west along the Mississippi River to Minnesota Territory, and they were instrumental in peopling North and South Dakota. The route they followed became a "northern" route to Washington and Oregon, and many settlers followed it after the Civil War. This was America's "last frontier," and she was making the most of it (fig. 199).

A Selected Bibliography Relating to American Migration

GENERAL
Abbott, Katherine M. OLD PATHS AND LEGENDS OF NEW ENGLAND. New York, 1909.

Ambler, Charles Henry. A HISTORY OF TRANSPORTATION IN THE OHIO VALLEY. Glendale, California: The Arthur H. Clark Co., 1932. (GS 973 H2ac)

Baird, Robert. THE EMIGRANTS AND TRAVELERS GUIDE TO THE WEST. 2nd ed. Philadelphia, 1834. (BYU Microcard 917.7)

Billington, Ray Allen. WESTWARD EXPANSION, A HISTORY OF THE AMERICAN FRONTIER. 2nd ed. New York: The Macmillan Co., 1963. (BYU 973 B49 1963)

Bolton, Ethel Stanwood. IMMIGRANTS TO NEW ENGLAND, 1700-1775. Baltimore: The Genealogical Publishing Co., 1967.

BRISTOL AND AMERICA: A RECORD OF THE FIRST SETTLERS IN THE COLONIES OF NORTH AMERICA, 1654-1685. Baltimore: The Genealogical Publishing Co., 1967.

Brown, Alexander. THE GENESIS OF THE UNITED STATES. 2 vols. New York: Russell & Russell, 1964.

Brown, John. THE PILGRIM FATHERS OF NEW ENGLAND AND
THEIR PURITAN SUCCESSORS. New York: Fleming H. Revell
Co., 1896. (BYU 974.4 B81)

Brown, William Garrett. THE LOWER SOUTH IN AMERICAN
HISTORY. New York: Greenwood Press, 1969. (BYU 975 B815L)

Byington, Ezra Hoyt. THE PURITAN AS A COLONIST AND
REFORMER. Boston: Little, Brown, & Co., 1899. (BYU 974
B99p)

Callins, S.R. THE EMIGRANT GUIDE TO THE UNITED STATES OF
AMERICA; INCLUDING SEVERAL AUTHORS AND HIGHLY
IMPORTANT LETTERS FROM ENGLISH EMIGRANTS NOW IN
AMERICA TO THEIR FRIENDS IN ENGLAND. 4th ed. London:
Joseph Noble, 1830.

Carter, Hodding. LOWER MISSISSIPPI. New York: Farrar &
Rinehart, 1942. (BYU 917.3 R52 V.42)

Clark, Charles E. THE EASTERN FRONTIER. New York: Alfred
A. Knopf, 1970. (BYU 974.02 C551e)

Clevinger, Woodrow R. "The Appalachian Mountaineers in the Upper
Cowlitz Basin," PACIFIC NORTHWEST QUARTERLY, 29 (1938).
(GS 979 B2pn V.29)

Coddington, John I. "Migrations from New England to New York and
New Jersey," WORLD CONFERENCE ON RECORDS AND
GENEALOGICAL SEMINAR, Area I-20 (August 1969).

Cowan, Helen I. BRITISH EMIGRATION TO BRITISH NORTH
AMERICA. THE FIRST HUNDRED YEARS. Toronto: University
of Toronto Press, 1961. (GS 942 W2ch and BYU 325.242 C838b)

Cowley, James, and Margaret Cowley. ALONG THE OLD YORK
ROAD. New Brunswick, N.J.: Rutgers University Press, 1965.
(BYU 917.4903 C317a)

Darby, William. THE EMIGRANTS' GUIDE TO THE WESTERN AND
SOUTH WESTERN STATES. New York: Kirk & Mercein, 1818.
(BYU Microcard 976)

Davis, William T., ed. BRADFORD'S HISTORY OF PLYMOUTH
PLANTATION 1606-1646. New York: Barnes & Noble, 1952.
(BYU 973.2 Or4 V.2)

Drake, Samuel G. RESULT OF SOME RESEARCHES . . . RELATIVES
TO THE FOUNDERS OF NEW ENGLAND: . . . 1858, 1859, AND
1860. Baltimore: The Genealogical Publishing Co., 1969.

Duffus, Robert Luther. THE SANTA FE TRAIL. London: Longmans
Green, 1930. (BYU 978 H2d)

Dykeman, Wilma. RIVERS OF AMERICA: THE FRENCH BROAD.
New York: Rinehart & Co., 1955.

Edwards, Agnes. THE OLD COAST ROAD FROM BOSTON TO
PLYMOUTH. Cambridge, Mass.: The Riverside Press, 1920.
(BYU 917.44 R74)

Flint, Timothy. A CONDENSED GEOGRAPHY AND HISTORY OF
THE WESTERN STATES OF THE MISSISSIPPI VALLEY.
Cincinnati: William M. Farnsworth, 1828. (BYU 917.7 F64oc)

Folsom, William Henry Carman. FIFTY YEARS IN THE NORTH-
WEST. St. Paul: Pioneer Press Co., 1888. (GS 977 H2fw)

Friis, Herman Ralph. "The Importance of Canals and Waterways in Establishing Early Paths of Migration," WORLD CONFERENCE ON RECORDS AND GENEALOGICAL SEMINAR, Area I-8-9c (August 1969).

_____. A SERIES OF POPULATION MAPS OF THE COLONIES AND THE UNITED STATES, 1625-1790. New York: The American Geographic Society, 1940.

A GENERAL MAP OF THE SOUTHERN BRITISH COLONIES IN AMERICA. (BYU Map Collection 975.8 E7u)

Giuseppi, Montague Spencer. NATURALIZATIONS OF FOREIGN PROTESTANTS IN THE AMERICAN AND WEST INDIAN COLONIES. Baltimore: The Genealogical Publishing Co., 1969.

Goff, John H. "Retracing the Old Federal Road," STUDIES IN BUSINESS AND ECONOMICS, No. 5. Emory University School of Business Administration, 1950.

Goodwin, Cardinal. A HISTORY OF ITS ACQUISITION AND SETTLE-MENT. THE TRANS-MISSISSIPPI WEST 1803-1853. New York: D. Appleton & Co., 1924. (BYU 978 G63)

Guillet, Edwin Clarence. THE GREAT MIGRATION: THE ATLANTIC CROSSING BY SAILING-SHIP SINCE 1770. 2nd ed. Toronto: University of Toronto Press, 1963. (BYU 325.242097 G945g)

Havighurst, Walter. THE HEARTLAND: OHIO, INDIANA, ILLINOIS. New York: Harper & Row, 1956.

_____. LAND OF THE LONG HORIZONS. New York: Coward-McCann, 1960.

_____. WILDERNESS FOR SALE - STORY OF THE FIRST WESTERN LAND RUSH. New York: Hastings, 1956.

Henderson, Archibald. THE CONQUEST OF THE OLD SOUTHWEST: THE ROMANTIC STORY OF THE EARLY PIONEERS INTO VIRGINIA, THE CAROLINAS, TENNESSEE, KENTUCKY 1740-1790. New York: The Century Co., c1920. (BYU 976 H2h)

Holbrook, Stewart H. THE YANKEE EXODUS, AN ACCOUNT OF MIGRATION FROM NEW ENGLAND. (GS 973 W21h)

Hulbert, Archer Butler. "The Old National Road - The Historic Highway of America," OHIO ARCHAEOLOGICAL AND HISTORICAL PUBLICATIONS 9 (May 1901): 405-510. (BYU 977.1005 Oh3)

Irwin, B. William. MIGRATION ROUTES, THE ATLANTIC TO THE MIDDLEWEST. Long Beach: Southern California Genealogical Society, n.d.

Jenkins, Stephen. THE OLD BOSTON POST ROAD. New York: G.P. Putnam's Sons, 1913. (BYU 974 J418o)

Johnson, Stanley Currie. A HISTORY OF EMIGRATION FROM THE UNITED KINGDOM TO NORTH AMERICA, 1763-1912. New York: A.M. Kelley, 1966. (BYU 325.242 J627h)

Lewis, Marcus W. THE DEVELOPMENT OF EARLY EMIGRANT TRAILS IN THE UNITED STATES. Washington, D.C.: The National Genealogical Society, 1962. (BYU 929.173 N213s #3)

Mackenzie, George Norbury. COLONIAL FAMILIES OF THE UNITED STATES OF AMERICA, vol. 5. Baltimore: The Genealogical Publishing Co., 1966.

Marlowe, George Francis. THE OLD BAY PATHS. New York: Hastings House, 1942. (BYU 917.44 M344o)

Martyn, W. Carlos. THE PILGRIM FATHERS OF NEW ENGLAND: A HISTORY. New York: The American Tract Society, 1867. (BYU 974.4 M36)

Martzolff, Clement L. "Zane's Trace," OHIO ARCHAEOLOGICAL AND HISTORICAL PUBLICATIONS 13 (April 1904): 297-331. (BYU 977.105 Oh3)

Muntz, A. Philip. "Mapping Migration Trails," WORLD CONFERENCE ON RECORDS AND GENEALOGICAL SEMINAR, Area I-8-9b (August 1969).

Myers, Richmond E. "Early Turnpikes of the Susquehanna Valley," PENNSYLVANIA HISTORY 21 (1954): 248-59. (BYU 974.8005 P38h V.21)

Patten, Jennie M. THE ARGYLE PATENT AND ACCOMPANYING DOCUMENTS. Baltimore: The Genealogical Publishing Co., 1965.

Peck, J.M., A.M. A NEW GUIDE FOR EMIGRANTS TO THE WEST. Boston: Gould, Kendal, and Lincoln, 1836. (BYU 917.7 B334n)

Perkins, Emily Ritchie. "The Perkins Family: A Sketch of Inter-Colonial Migration," PUBLICATIONS OF THE GENEALOGICAL SOCIETY OF PENNSYLVANIA 7 (1920): 163-78.

Pittman, Phillip. THE PRESENT STATE OF THE EUROPEAN SETTLEMENTS ON THE MISSISSIPPI. Cleveland: The A.H. Clark Co., 1906. (BYU Hafen 917.7 P68p)

Regan, John. THE EMIGRANTS GUIDE TO THE WESTERN STATES OF AMERICA; OR BACK WOODS AND PRAIRIES. 2nd ed. Edinburg: Boyd & Co., 1852.

Richardson, Albert E. BEYOND THE MISSISSIPPI. New York, 1867. (BYU 917.8 R39 1869)

Riegal, Robert E., and Robert G. Athearn. AMERICA MOVES WEST.

Risch, Erma. "Immigrant Aid Societies Before 1820," THE PENNSYLVANIA MAGAZINE OF HISTORY AND BIOGRAPHY 60 (1936): 15-33. (GS 974.8 B2pm V.60)

Rosenberry, Lois Kimball Mathews. THE EXPANSION OF NEW ENGLAND - THE SPREAD OF NEW ENGLAND SETTLEMENT AND INSTITUTIONS TO THE MISSISSIPPI RIVER 1620-1865. Boston: Houghton Mifflin Co., 1909. (BYU 974 M44e)

Rugg, Harold. AMERICA AND HER IMMIGRANTS. The Social Science Pamphlets, 1926. (BYU 910.7 R84a)

Savage, Henry, Jr. RIVER OF THE CAROLINAS: THE SANTEE. Chapel Hill, N.C.: The University of North Carolina Press, 1968.

Seilhamer, George O. "Old Mother Cumberland," THE PENN-SYLVANIA MAGAZINE OF HISTORY AND BIOGRAPHY 24 (1900): 17-47. (GS 974.8 B2pm V.24)

Strickland, W.P. PIONEERS OF THE WEST. New York: Carlton and Poiter, 1856. (BYU 977 St85)

Thwaites, Reuben Gold. EARLY WESTERN TRAVELS 1748-1846. 30 vols. Cleveland: The A.H. Clark Co., 1904-1907.

Tucker, W. Bowman. THE ROMANCE OF THE PALATINE MILLERS:
A TALE OF PALATINE IRISH-AMERICANS AND UNITED
EMPIRE LOYALISTS. 2nd ed. 1929. (BYU 929.2 M614t)

Wallace, W. Stewart. THE UNITED EMPIRE LOYALISTS, A
CHRONICLE OF THE GREAT MIGRATION. Toronto, 1920.

Witaker, Arthur Preston. THE SPANISH-AMERICAN FRONTIER
1783-1795. New York: Houghton Mifflin & Co., 1927. (BYU
976 W58s)

Wright, Norman E. "General Migration Patterns," WORLD
CONFERENCE ON RECORDS AND GENEALOGICAL SEMINAR,
Area I-8-9a (August 1969).

ALABAMA

Abernathy, Thomas Perkins. THE FORMATIVE PERIOD IN
ALABAMA, 1818-1828. 2nd ed. n.p.: The University of
Alabama Press, 1965. (BYU 975 So88 #8)

Kollmorgan, Walter M. THE GERMAN SETTLEMENT IN CULLMAN
COUNTY, ALABAMA. 1941. (BYU 976.1 K83)

Moore, Albert Burton. HISTORY OF ALABAMA AND HER PEOPLE.
3 vols. New York: The American Historical Society, 1927.
(BYU 976.1 M871h and GS 976.1 D2m)

CONNECTICUT

Deming, Dorothy. THE SETTLEMENT OF THE CONNECTICUT
TOWNS. New Haven: Yale University Press, 1933. (GS
974.6 H2c Ser.6)

Hinman, Royal Ralph. FIRST SETTLERS OF THE COLONY OF
CONNECTICUT. Hartford: E. Gleason, 1846. (GS 974.6 D2hr)

Koenig, Samuel. IMMIGRANT SETTLEMENTS IN CONNECTICUT,
THEIR GROWTH AND CHARACTERISTICS. Hartford: State
Department of Education, 1938. (BYU 325.746 K819i)

Mills, William Stowell. THE STORY OF THE WESTERN RESERVE
OF CONNECTICUT. New York: Brown & Wilson Press, 1900.
(BYU 974.6 M62)

Morrow, Rising Lake. CONNECTICUT INFLUENCES IN WESTERN
MASSACHUSETTS AND VERMONT. New Haven: Yale University
Press, 1936. (GS 974.6 H2c Ser.58)

Rosenberry, Lois. MIGRATIONS FROM CONNECTICUT AFTER
1800. New Haven: Yale University Press, 1936. (GS 974.6
H2c Ser.54)

_____. MIGRATIONS FROM CONNECTICUT PRIOR TO 1800.
New Haven: Yale University Press, 1934. (GS 974.6 H2c
Ser.28 and BYU 974.6 C76 #28)

DELAWARE

Bevan, Wilson Lloyd. HISTORY OF DELAWARE, PAST AND
PRESENT. 4 vols. New York: Lewis Historical Publishing
Co., 1929. (GS 975.1 H2b V.1)

Conrad, Henry Clay. HISTORY OF THE STATE OF DELAWARE,
FROM THE EARLIEST SETTLEMENTS TO THE YEAR 1907.
3 vols. Wilmington: By the Author, 1908. (GS 975.1 H2c V.1)

Ferris, Benjamin. A HISTORY OF THE ORIGINAL SETTLEMENTS
    ON THE DELAWARE. Wilmington: Wilson & Herald, 1846.
    (BYU 975.1 H2f)
Vincent, Francis. A HISTORY OF THE STATE OF DELAWARE, FROM
    ITS FIRST SETTLEMENT UNTIL THE PRESENT TIME, CON-
    TAINING A FULL ACCOUNT OF THE FIRST DUTCH AND
    SWEDISH SETTLEMENTS. (GS 975.1 H2u)
Ward, Christopher. THE DUTCH AND SWEDES ON THE DELAWARE,
    1609-1664. Philadelphia: The University of Pennsylvania Press,
    1930. (GS 975.1 F2d)

GEORGIA
Burke, Emily P. REMINISCENCES OF GEORGIA. Oberlin,
    Georgia: James M. Fitch, 1850. (BYU Microcard 975)
Coulter, E. Merton, and Albert B. Saye. A LIST OF THE EARLY
    SETTLERS OF GEORGIA. Athens: The Genealogical Publishing
    Co., 1967.
Cunningham, Thomas Mayhew. GEORGIA BEFORE PLYMOUTH
    ROCK AND AFTERWARDS. Princeton: Princeton University
    Press, 1949. (BYU 920 N43 V.9 Nos. 1-20)
Fries, Adelaide L. THE MORAVIANS IN GEORGIA, 1735-1740.
    Baltimore: The Genealogical Publishing Co., 1967.
Nicholson, Virginia. "The Settlers of Georgia," DAUGHTERS OF
    THE AMERICAN REVOLUTION MAGAZINE (1934): 217-20.
Phillips, Ulrich Bonnell. A HISTORY OF TRANSPORTATION IN
    THE EASTERN COTTON BELT TO 1860. New York: Octagon
    Books, 1968. (BYU 385.0975 P547h)
Strobel, P.A. THE SALZBURGERS AND THEIR DESCENDANTS.
    Baltimore: T. Newton Kurtz, 1855. (BYU 975.872 St87s)

ILLINOIS
Boewe, Charles. PRAIRIE ALBUM. Carbondale, Illinois: Southern
    Illinois University Press, c1962. (BYU 977.3791 B633p)
Buly, R. Carlyle. THE OLD NORTHWEST 1815-1840. 2 vols.
    Bloomington, Indiana: The Indiana University Press, 1951.
    (GS 977 H2b)
Humphrey, Grace. ILLINOIS: THE STORY OF THE PRAIRIE
    STATE. Indianapolis: The Bobbs-Merrill Co., c1917.
    (BYU 977.3 H88)
Olson, Ernest W. HISTORY OF THE SWEDES OF ILLINOIS.
    Chicago: The Engberg-Holmberg Publishing Co., 1908.
    (GS 977.3 F2so)
_____. THE SWEDISH ELEMENT IN ILLINOIS. Chicago:
    Swedish-American Biographical Association, 1917. (BYU
    325.2485 D28s)
Strand, A.E. A HISTORY OF THE NORWEGIANS OF ILLINOIS.
    Chicago: John Anderson Publishing Co., c1905. (GS 977.3
    F2ns)

INDIANA

Cox, Sanford C. RECOLLECTIONS OF EARLY SETTLEMENT OF
    THE WABASH VALLEY. Lafayette, Ind.: Courier, 1860.
Dufour, Perret. THE SWISS SETTLEMENT OF SWITZERLAND
    COUNTY, INDIANA. Indianapolis: The Indiana Historical
    Commission, 1925.
Lang, Elfrieda. "Ohioans in Northern Indiana Before 1850,"
    INDIANA MAGAZINE OF HISTORY 49 (December 1953): 391-409.
Lewis, George E. THE INDIANA COMPANY, 1763-1798. Glendale,
    California: The Arthur H. Clark Co., 1941. (GS 973 U3L)
"The National Road in Indiana," INDIANA HISTORICAL SOCIETY
    PUBLICATIONS 7 (1940): 209-37. (GS 977.2 B4)
Wilson, William E. INDIANA: A HISTORY. Bloomington, Indiana:
    The Indiana University Press, 1966. (BYU 977.2 W699i)
Woodburn, James A. THE SCOTCH-IRISH PRESBYTERIANS IN
    MONROE COUNTY, INDIANA. Indianapolis: Hecker, 1910.

IOWA

Eibsech, Joseph. THE GERMANS OF IOWA AND THEIR ACCOM-
    PLISHMENTS. Des Moines: The Iowa State Bulletin Press,
    1900. (GS 977.7 F2g)
Richman, Irving B. IOWAY TO IOWA. Iowa City: The Iowa State
    Historical Society, 1931. (BYU 977.7 R41i)
Van Der Zee, Jacob. THE BRITISH IN IOWA. Iowa City: The
    Athens Press, 1922. (BYU 977.7 Va28)
_____. THE HOLLANDERS OF IOWA. Cedar Rapids: The
    Torch Press, 1912. (BYU 977.7 Va28h)
Wick, Barthinius L. THE AMISH MENNONITES. Iowa City: The
    State Historical Society, 1894. (GS PBA #1067)

KENTUCKY

Allen, James Lane. THE BLUE-GRASS REGION OF KENTUCKY.
    New York: Harper & Brothers, 1892. (BYU 917.69 A153)
Arnold, William Erastus. A HISTORY OF METHODISM IN KENTUCKY.
    2nd ed. n.p.: Herald Press, 1935. (GS 976.9 K2a)
Bodley, Temple. HISTORY OF KENTUCKY BEFORE THE LOUISIANA
    PURCHASE IN 1803. Chicago: The S.J. Clarke Publishing Co.,
    1928. (GS 976.9 H2hr)
Cherry, Thomas Crittenden. KENTUCKY, THE PIONEER STATE OF
    THE WEST. Chicago: D.C. Heath & Co., 1923. (BYU 976.9
    C424k)
Clark, Thomas Dionysius, Ph.D. KENTUCKY: LAND OF CONTRAST.
    New York: Harper & Row, 1968.
Connelly, Thomas L. "Gateway to Kentucky: The Wilderness, 1748-
    1772," THE REGISTER OF THE KENTUCKY HISTORICAL
    SOCIETY 59 (1961): 109-32. (GS 976.9 B2k V.59)
Dupre, Huntley. "The French in Early Kentucky," FILSON CLUB
    HISTORICAL QUARTERLY, 1941.
Ely, William. THE BIG SANDY VALLEY. Cathettsburg, Kentucky,
    1887.

Hammon, Neal Owen. "Early Roads into Kentucky," THE REGISTER OF THE KENTUCKY HISTORICAL SOCIETY 68 (April 1970). (GS 976.9 B2ka V.68)

Henderson, Archibald. THE CONQUEST OF THE OLD SOUTHWEST: THE ROMANTIC STORY OF THE EARLY PIONEERS INTO VIRGINIA, THE CAROLINAS, TENNESSEE, AND KENTUCKY, 1740-1790. New York: The Century Co., 1920. (BYU 976 H38 and GS 976 H2h)

Hulbert, Archer B. HISTORIC HIGHWAYS - BOONE'S WILDERNESS ROAD. Cleveland: The Arthur H. Clark Co., 1903. (BYU 976.9 H86 V.6)

Johnson, E. Polk. HISTORY OF KENTUCKY AND KENTUCKIANS. Chicago: Lewis Publishing Co., 1912.

Kerr, Charles, ed. HISTORY OF KENTUCKY. 5 vols. Chicago: The American Historical Society, 1922. (BYU 976.9 K46h and GS 976.9 H2k)

Kincaid, Robert L. "Cumberland Gap, Gateway of an Empire," FILSON CLUB HISTORICAL QUARTERLY, 1941.

_____. THE WILDERNESS ROAD. Harrogate, Tennessee: Lincoln Memorial University Press, 1955.

O'Brien, Michael I. IRISH PIONEERS IN KENTUCKY.

Perrin, W.H., et al. KENTUCKY. Louisville: F.A. Battey & Co., 1887. (GS 976.9 H2p)

Rone, Wendell H. HISTORICAL ATLAS OF KENTUCKY. Evansville, Indiana: Walton, 1965. (GS PB #183)

Scarf, Henry P. KENTUCKY'S LAST FRONTIER. Prestonburg, Kentucky, c1966.

Shaler, Nathaniel Southgate. KENTUCKY, A PIONEER COMMON-WEALTH. Boston: Houghton Mifflin & Co., 1886. (BYU 353.9 Am351c V.4)

Smith, Zachariah Frederick. HISTORY OF KENTUCKY FROM ITS EARLIEST DISCOVERY AND SETTLEMENT. Louisville: Courier-Journal Job Printing Co., 1866. (GS 976.9 H2s)

LOUISIANA

Cable, George Washington. THE CREOLES OF LOUISIANA. New York: C. Scribner's Sons, n.d. (BYU 976.3 F2c)

Carselowry, James Manford. EARLY SETTLERS. Oklahoma: James Manford Carselowry, 1962. (BYU 976 V2c)

Davis, Andrew McFarland. CANADA AND LOUISIANA. (BYU 973 W73 V.5)

Deiler, John Hanno. THE SETTLEMENT OF THE GERMAN COAST OF LOUISIANA AND THE CREOLES OF GERMAN DESCENT. Philadelphia: Americana Germanica Press, 1909. (BYU 976.3 F2g)

DeVille, Winston. GULF COAST COLONIALS: A COMPENDIUM OF FRENCH FAMILIES IN EARLY EIGHTEENTH CENTURY LOUISIANA. Baltimore: The Genealogical Publishing Co., 1968. (BYU 976.3 W2d)

_____. LOUISIANA COLONIALS: SOLDIERS AND VAGA-
BONDS. Baltimore: The Genealogical Publishing Co., 1963.
(BYU 929.3763 D4591)

"The First French Settlement in Present-day Louisiana," THE
LOUISIANA HISTORICAL QUARTERLY 19, nos. 3-4. (GS
976.3 B2hq V.19)

King, Grace Elizabeth. CREOLE FAMILIES OF NEW ORLEANS.
New York: The Macmillan Co., 1921. (BYU 976.335/N1 F2k)

Nau, John Fredrick. THE GERMAN PEOPLE OF NEW ORLEANS
1850-1900. Leiden: E.J. Brill, 1958. (GS 976.355/N1 F2g)

Niehaus, Earl F. THE IRISH IN NEW ORLEANS 1800-1860. Baton
Rouge: The Louisiana State University, 1965. (GS 976.335/N1
F2in)

MAINE

Varney, George J. THE GAZETTEER OF MAINE. Boston: B.B.
Russell, 1881. (GS 974.1 E5v)

Williamson, William D. THE HISTORY OF THE STATE OF MAINE.
Hallowell, Maine: Glazier, Masters & Co., 1832. (BYU 974.1
W677h)

MARYLAND

Cunz, Dieter. "German Settlers in Early Colonial Maryland,"
MARYLAND HISTORICAL MAGAZINE 42 (March 1947): 101-8.

_____. THE MARYLAND GERMANS: A HISTORY. Princeton:
The Princeton University Press, 1948. (BYU 325.243 C91)

Nead, Daniel Wunderlich. "The Pennsylvania-German in the Settlement of Maryland," THE PENNSYLVANIA-GERMAN FOLKLORE
SOCIETY 22 (1914).

Newman, Harry Wright. THE FLOWERING OF THE MARYLAND
PALATINATE. Washington, 1961.

Nicklin, John Bailey Calvert. "Immigration Between Virginia and
Maryland in the Seventeenth Century," WILLIAM AND MARY
QUARTERLY 18 (1938): 440-46. (BYU Film W67)

Weishaar, J.A. THE GERMAN ELEMENT IN MARYLAND, UP TO
THE YEAR 1700.

Withgott, Margaret, et al. "The Migration from the Eastern Shore to
Ohio," MARYLAND AND DELAWARE GENEALOGIST 4 (January
1963): 14-15. (BYU 929.05 M36 V.4)

MICHIGAN

Catlin, George B. "Early Settlement in Eastern Michigan,"
MICHIGAN HISTORY MAGAZINE 26: 319-45.

Dunbar, Willis Frederick. MICHIGAN, A HISTORY OF THE
WOLVERINE STATE. Grand Rapids, Mich.: William B.
Eardmans Publishing Co., 1965. (BYU 977.4 D911m)

Jenks, William L. "Michigan Immigration," MICHIGAN HISTORY
MAGAZINE 28: 67-100.

Pieters, Aleida J. A DUTCH SETTLEMENT IN MICHIGAN. Grand
Rapids, Mich.: Eerdmans Sevensma Co., 1923. (BYU 977.4
P617)

Quaife, M., and Sidney Galzer. MICHIGAN FROM PRIMITIVE
WILDERNESS TO INDUSTRIAL COMMONWEALTH. New York:
Prentice Hall, 1948. (BYU 979.4 Q23)
Winchell, Alexander. ATLAS OF THE STATE OF MICHIGAN. (BYU
q977.4 E3w)

MINNESOTA
Burnquist, Joseph A.A. MINNESOTA AND ITS PEOPLE. Chicago:
The S.J. Clarke Publishing Co., 1924. (GS 977.6 H2b)
Castle, Henry Anson. MINNESOTA, ITS STORY AND BIOGRAPHY.
New York: The Lewis Publishing Co., 1915. (GS 977.6 H2ch)
Minnesota Governor's Interracial Commission. THE MEXICAN IN
MINNESOTA. Rev. ed. St. Paul: State of Minnesota, 1953.
(BYU 325 M66)

MISSISSIPPI
Gillis, Norman E. EARLY INHABITANTS OF THE NATCHEZ
DISTRICT. Baton Rouge, La.: Norman E. Gillis, 1963.
(BYU 929.3762 G416e)
Greenwell, Dale. TWELVE FLAGS - TRIUMPHS AND TRAGEDIES.
3 vols. Ocean Springs, Miss., 1968. (GS 976.2 H2g)
Milburn, William Henry. THE PIONEERS, PREACHERS, AND
PEOPLE OF THE MISSISSIPPI VALLEY. New York: Derby &
Jackson, 1860. (BYU 976 M59)
Monette, John Wesley. HISTORY OF THE DISCOVERY AND
SETTLEMENT OF THE VALLEY OF THE MISSISSIPPI.
New York: Harper & Brothers, 1848. (GS 973 H2mj)

MISSOURI
Barnes, C.R., ed. SWITZLER'S ILLUSTRATED HISTORY OF
MISSOURI FROM 1541-1877. St. Louis: Published by the
Editor, 1879. (BYU 977.8 Siv68)
Bryan, Wm. S., and Robert Rose. A HISTORY OF THE PIONEER
FAMILIES OF MISSOURI. St. Louis: Bryan, Brand & Co.,
1876. (GS 977.8 D2b)
Campbell, R.A. GAZETTEER OF MISSOURI. Rev. ed. St. Louis:
R.A. Campbell, 1875.
Coppage, A. Maxim III, and Dorothy Ford Wulfeck. VIRGINIA
SETTLERS IN MISSOURI. Naugatuck, Conn.: Privately
Printed, n.d.
Douglass, Robert S. HISTORY OF SOUTHWEST MISSOURI. Cape
Girardeau, Mo.: Ramfree Press, 1961.
Houck, Louis. A HISTORY OF MISSOURI FROM THE EARLIEST
EXPLORATIONS AND SETTLEMENTS UNTIL THE ADMISSION
OF THE STATE INTO THE UNION. 3 vols. Chicago: R.R.
Donnelley & Sons Co., 1908.
Kargau, E.D. "Missouri's German Immigration," MISSOURI
HISTORICAL SOCIETY COLLECTIONS 2 (1900): 23-34.
Konnyu, Leslie. "Hungarians in Missouri," MISSOURI HISTORICAL
REVIEW 46 (1952): 247-61. (BYU 977.8005 M691r V.46)

Kretzmann, P.E. "The Saxon Immigration to Missouri, 1838-1839," MISSOURI HISTORICAL REVIEW 383 (1939): 157-70. (BYU 977. 8005 M69lr V.33)

de Laureal, Edward. "Emigration from the French West Indies to St. Louis in 1848," MISSOURI HISTORICAL SOCIETY COLLECTIONS 2 (1906): 13-16.

Norton, Nell Downing. "A List of Native Kentuckians Who Settled in Ralls County, Missouri," THE REGISTER OF THE KENTUCKY HISTORICAL SOCIETY 43: 342-44. (GS 976. 9 B2k V.43)

Polack, W. Gustave, ed. "Members of the Saxon Immigration," CONCORDIA HISTORICAL INSTITUTE QUARTERLY 11 (1940): 33-47; 12 (1940): 12-14.

Rygg, A.N. "A Norwegian Settlement in Missouri," NORWEGIAN-AMERICAN STUDIES AND RECORDS 8 (1943): 108-13. (BYU 325.06 N83n V.13)

Shoemaker, Floyd Calvin, and Walter Williams. MISSOURI, MOTHER OF THE WEST. 5 vols. New York: The American Historical Society, 1930. (GS 977.85)

Todd, Lewis, and Merle Curtis. RISE OF THE AMERICAN NATION. 2nd ed. New York: Harcourt, Brace & World, 1966. (BYU 973 T366r)

Violette, E.M., et al. A HISTORY OF MISSOURI. Kansas City: Burton Publishing Co., 1954. (BYU 977.8 Vi8lh)

NEW HAMPSHIRE

Farmer, John. A GAZETTEER OF THE STATE OF NEW HAMPSHIRE. Concord, 1823.

Hayward, John. A GAZETTEER OF NEW HAMPSHIRE. Boston, 1849.

Stackpole, Everett S. HISTORY OF NEW HAMPSHIRE. vol. 2. New York, n.d.

NEW JERSEY

Chambers, Theodore Frelinghuysen. THE EARLY GERMANS OF NEW JERSEY. Dover, N.J.: Dover Printing Co., 1895. (GS 974. 9 F2gc)

Craven, Wesley Frank. NEW JERSEY AND THE ENGLISH COLONIZATION OF NORTH AMERICA. New Jersey Historical Series. Princeton: D. Van Nostrand Co., 1964.

Cunningham, John T. THIS IS NEW JERSEY. New Brunswick, N.J.: Rutgers University Press, 1968. (BYU 917.49 C917n 1968)

Leiby, Adrain C. THE EARLY DUTCH AND SWEDISH SETTLERS OF NEW JERSEY. New Jersey Historical Series. Princeton: D. Van Nostrand Co., 1964.

_____. THE HUGUENOT SETTLEMENT OF SCHRAALENBURGH. Bergenfield, N.J.: Bergenfield Free Public Library, 1964. (BYU 974. 921 L53lh)

Prince, John D. "Netherland Settlers in New Jersey," COLLECTIONS OF THE NEW JERSEY HISTORICAL SOCIETY 9.

Raum, John O. THE HISTORY OF NEW JERSEY. Philadelphia: John E. Potter & Co., 1877. (GS 974. 9 H2r)

Smith, Samuel. SMITH'S HISTORY OF NEW JERSEY. Trenton:
Wm. S. Sharp, 1877.

NEW YORK
GAZETTEER OF NEW YORK, 1824. (GS 974.7 E5s)
GAZETTEER OF NEW YORK, 1842. (GS 974.7 Etd)
HISTORICAL AND STATISTICAL GAZETTEER OF NEW YORK, 1860.
    (GS 974.7 E5f)
HISTORY OF THE MOHAWK VALLEY. 4 vols. (GS 974.7 D2mo)
Holsey, Francis Waiting. THE OLD NEW YORK FRONTIER, 1614-
    1800. New York: C. Scribner's Sons, 1901. (BYU 974.7 H16)
Ross, Peter. HISTORY OF LONG ISLAND. New York: Levin
    Publishing Co., 1902.
Wood, Silas. FIRST SETTLEMENT OF TOWNS ON LONG ISLAND.
    Brooklyn: Alden Spooner, 1828.

NORTH CAROLINA
DeMond, Robert O. THE LOYALISTS IN NORTH CAROLINA DURING
    THE REVOLUTION. Hamden, Conn., 1964. (BYU 973.314
    D3971)
Fries, Adelaide L. RECORDS OF THE MORAVIANS IN NORTH
    CAROLINA, 1752-1771. Raleigh: Edwards & Broughton
    Printing Co., 1922.
Gehrke, William H. "The Beginnings of the Pennsylvania-German
    Element in Rowan and Cabarrus Counties, North Carolina,"
    THE PENNSYLVANIA MAGAZINE OF HISTORY AND BIOGRAPHY
    58 (1934): 342-69. (GS 974.8 B2pm V.58)
Johnson, William Perry. "Migrations to and from North Carolina,
    1650-1950," THE NORTH CAROLINIAN, June 1955, pp. 35-42.
    (BYU 929.05 J826 and GS 975.6 B2j)
Merrens, Harry Roy. COLONIAL NORTH CAROLINA IN THE
    EIGHTEENTH CENTURY: A STUDY IN HISTORICAL
    GEOGRAPHY. Chapel Hill, N.C.: The University of North
    Carolina Press, 1964. (BYU 911.756 M55c)
Meyer, Duane. THE HIGHLAND SCOTS OF NORTH CAROLINA,
    1732-1776. Chapel Hill, N.C.: The University of North
    Carolina Press, 1957.
Williamson, Hugh. THE HISTORY OF NORTH CAROLINA. 2 vols.
    Philadelphia: Thomas Dobson at the Stone House, 1821.
    (BYU 975.602 W676h)

NORTH DAKOTA
Dakota Territory Centennial Commission. DAKOTA PANORAMA.
    1961. (BYU 978.3 So87d)
HISTORY OF THE RED RIVER VALLEY, PAST AND PRESENT.
    2 vols. Grand Forks: Herald Printing Co., 1909. (GS 977
    H2hr)
Robinson, Elwyn B. HISTORY OF NORTH DAKOTA. Lincoln:
    The University of Nebraska Press, 1966. (BYU 968.4 R56lh)

OHIO

Crouse, D.E. THE OHIO GATEWAY. (BYU 977 C88 1938)

Jenkins, Warren. THE OHIO GAZETTEER. Columbus: Isaac N.
    Whiting, 1837. (BYU Mormon 917.71 J419o)

Jones, William Harvey. "Welsh Settlements in Ohio," OHIO
    ARCHAEOLOGICAL AND HISTORICAL PUBLICATIONS 16 (1907):
    194-227. (BYU 977.1005 Oh3 V.16)

Mathews, Aldred. OHIO AND HER WESTERN RESERVE. New
    York: D. Appleton & Co., 1902. (BYU 977.1 M422o)

Mote, Luke Smith. EARLY SETTLEMENT OF FRIENDS IN THE
    MIAMI VALLEY. 1961. (GS PBA #017)

Orth, Samuel P. A HISTORY OF CLEVELAND, OHIO. 3 vols.
    Chicago: The S.J. Clarke Publishing Co., 1910. (GS 977.131/C1
    H2o)

Scheiber, Harry N. OHIO CANAL ERA: A CASE STUDY OF GOVERN-
    MENT AND THE ECONOMY 1820-1861. (BYU 353.9771 Sc25)

Upton, Harriet. HISTORY OF THE WESTERN RESERVE. 3 vols.
    Chicago: The Lewis Publishing Co., 1910. (GS 977.03 H2u)

Utter, William T. HISTORY OF THE STATE OF OHIO.

Wilcox, Frank N. OHIO INDIAN RAILS. Cleveland: The Gates
    Press, 1934.

PENNSYLVANIA

Birch, Edith White. "The Huguenot Settlers of Pennsylvania," THE
    HISTORICAL REVIEW OF BERKS COUNTY 6 (April 1941): 78-82.
    (GS 974.816 B2h V.6)

Browning, Charles H. WELSH SETTLEMENT OF PENNSYLVANIA.
    Baltimore: The Genealogical Publishing Co., 1967.

Cerbit, W.F. "Welsh Emigration to Pennsylvania," THE PENNSYL-
    VANIA MAGAZINE OF HISTORY AND BIOGRAPHY 1 (1877):
    330-32. (GS 974.8 B2pm V.1)

Dunaway, Wayland F. "Pennsylvania as an Early Distributing Center
    of Population," THE PENNSYLVANIA MAGAZINE OF HISTORY
    AND BIOGRAPHY 55: 134-64. (GS 974.8 B2pm V.55)

_____. THE SCOTCH-IRISH OF COLONIAL PENNSYLVANIA.
    Chapel Hill, N.C.: The University of North Carolina Press,
    1944. (GS 974.8 F2sd and BYU 325.241 D21s)

Eshleman, H. Frank. HISTORIC BACKGROUND AND ANNALS OF
    THE SWISS AND GERMAN PIONEERS OF SOUTHEASTERN
    PENNSYLVANIA. Lancaster, Pa.: By the Author, 1917.
    (BYU 974.81 F2se)

Evans, Paul Demund. "The Holland Land Company," BUFFALO
    HISTORICAL SOCIETY PUBLICATIONS 28 (1924). (BYU 974.796
    B4b V.28)

Fisher, Charles Adam. "Early Tulpehocken Settlers," THE
    HISTORICAL REVIEW OF BERKS COUNTY 4 (July 1939): 104-10.
    (GS 974.816 B2h V.4)

Fryburg, Mrs. L. Gertrude. "Huguenot Pioneers of Pennsylvania,"
    PROCEEDINGS OF THE HUGUENOT SOCIETY OF PENNSYL-
    VANIA 28 (1956): 76-130; 29 (1957): 32-125. (BYU 974.8 C4h
    V.28-29)

Glenn, Thomas Allen. WELSH FOUNDERS OF PENNSYLVANIA. 2 vols. Oxford: Fox, Jones & Co., 1911-1913. (BYU 974.8 F2wg)

Hull, William I. WILLIAM PENN AND THE DUTCH QUAKER MIGRATION TO PENNSYLVANIA. Philadelphia: Patterson & White Co., 1935. (GS 974.8 W2h)

Ingham, Joseph Washington. A SHORT HISTORY OF ASYLUM, PENNSYLVANIA, FOUNDED IN 1793 BY THE FRENCH EXILES IN AMERICA. Towanda, Pa.: Towanda Printing Co., 1916.

Jordan, John W. "Moravian Immigration to Pennsylvania, 1734-1765," THE PENNSYLVANIA MAGAZINE OF HISTORY AND BIOGRAPHY 33 (1909): 228-48. (GS 974.8 B2pm V.33)

Kuhns, Oscar. THE GERMAN AND SWISS SETTLEMENTS OF COLONIAL PENNSYLVANIA. New York: Abingdon Press, 1914. (GS 974.8 H2k)

_____. "Some Lancaster County Families from the Canton of Berne, Switzerland," NATIONAL GENEALOGICAL SOCIETY QUARTERLY 8 (October 1919): 39-41. (BYU 929.05 N21 V.8)

Laux, James B. "The Huguenot Element in Pennsylvania," PROCEEDINGS OF THE HUGUENOT SOCIETY OF PENNSYLVANIA 26 (1955): 11-27. (GS 974.8 C4h V26)

Levick, James J. "The Early Welsh Quakers and Their Emigration to Pennsylvania," THE PENNSYLVANIA MAGAZINE OF HISTORY AND BIOGRAPHY 17 (1893): 385-413. (GS 974.8 B2pm V.17)

Mattice, Paul B. "The Palatine Emigration from Schohari to the Tulpehocken," THE HISTORICAL REVIEW OF BERKS COUNTY 10 (1945): 16-21. (GS 974.816 B2h V.10)

McKenna, John J. "Early Irish in Berks County," THE HISTORICAL REVIEW OF BERKS COUNTY 17 (October-December 1951): 20-21, 25, 27, 29. (GS 974.816 B2h V.17)

_____. "Early Scotch and Scotch-Irish in Berks County," THE HISTORICAL REVIEW OF BERKS COUNTY 15 (April 1950): 212-13, 221, 223. (GS 974.816 B2h V.15)

Melchier, D. Montfort. "Connecticut Claims in the Wyoming Valley," THE PENNSYLVANIA-GERMAN FOLKLORE SOCIETY 7 (1906). (GS 974.8 B4pg V.7)

Myers, Albert Cook. QUAKER ARRIVALS AT PHILADELPHIA, 1682-1750. Baltimore: The Genealogical Publishing Co., 1969. (GS Film 56364)

Pennypacker, Samuel Whitaker. THE SETTLEMENT OF GERMANTOWN, PENNSYLVANIA, AND THE BEGINNING OF GERMAN IMMIGRATION TO NORTH AMERICA. Philadelphia: William J. Campbell, 1899.

Richards, Matthias Henry. "The German Emigration from New York Province into Pennsylvania," THE PENNSYLVANIA-GERMAN FOLKLORE SOCIETY 9 (1899). (GS 974.8 B4pg V.9)

Roberts, Charles Rhoads. "Germanic Immigrants' Names in Early Pennsylvania Ship Lists," PENNSYLVANIA GERMAN SOCIETY PROCEEDINGS AND ADDRESSES 39 (1930): 5-20.

Scheffer, J.G. de Hoop. "Mennonite Emigration to Pennsylvania,"
THE PENNSYLVANIA MAGAZINE OF HISTORY AND BIOGRAPHY
2 (1878): 117-38. (GS 974.8 B2pm V.2)

Schultz, Selina G. "The Schwenkfelders of Pennsylvania," PENNSYL-
VANIA HISTORY 24 (October 1957): 293-320. (BYU 974.8005
P38h V.24)

Sexton, John L., Jr. "Pennsylvanians in the 'Genesee Country,'"
HISTORICAL REGISTER: NOTES AND QUERIES 1 (April 1883):
86-90. (GS 974.8 B2hrl V.1)

Smith, Charles Henry. "The Mennonite Immigration to Pennsylvania
in the Eighteenth Century," THE PENNSYLVANIA-GERMAN
FOLKLORE SOCIETY 35 (1929). (GS 974.8 B4pg V.35)

Stapleton, Ammon. MEMORIALS OF THE HUGUENOTS IN AMERICA
WITH SPECIAL REFERENCE TO THEIR EMIGRATION TO
PENNSYLVANIA. Baltimore: The Genealogical Publishing Co.,
1969.

Weber, Harry F. "Migrations of the Mennonites Through Pennsylvania,"
NATIONAL GENEALOGICAL SOCIETY QUARTERLY 35 (Septem-
ber 1947): 88-89. (BYU 929.05 N21 V.35)

RHODE ISLAND

Chapin, Howard M. DOCUMENTARY HISTORY OF RHODE ISLAND.
2 vols. Providence: Preston & Rounds Co., 1916. (GS 974.5
H2ch)

Cody, John Hutchins. RHODE ISLAND BOUNDARIES 1636-1936.
Providence: The Rhode Island State Planning Board, 1936.

Greene, Welcome Arnold. THE PROVIDENCE PLANTATIONS FOR
TWO HUNDRED FIFTY YEARS. Providence: J.A. & R.A. Reid,
1886.

Loughrey, Mary Ellen. FRANCE AND RHODE ISLAND. New York:
Kings Crown Press, 1944. (BYU 974.5 L929f)

Potter, Elisha R. FRENCH SETTLEMENTS AND FRENCH SETTLERS
IN RHODE ISLAND. Providence, 1879.

_____. MEMOIR CONCERNING THE FRENCH SETTLEMENTS
AND FRENCH SETTLERS IN THE COLONY OF RHODE ISLAND.
3 vols. Chicago: J.H. Beers & Co., 1908. (GS 974.5 D2r)

SOUTH CAROLINA

Quattlebaum, Paul. THE LAND CALLED CHICARA. Gainesville:
The University of Florida Press, 1956. (BYU 975.701 Q29L)

Thomas, T. Gaillard. A CONTRIBUTION TO THE HISTORY OF THE
HUGUENOTS OF SOUTH CAROLINA. New York: The Knicker-
bocker Press, 1887. (BYU 975.7 T367c)

Wallace, David Duncan. SOUTH CAROLINA: A SHORT HISTORY.
(BYU 975.7 W15)

Woodmason, Charles. THE CAROLINA BACKCOUNTRY ON THE
EVE OF THE REVOLUTION. Edited by Richard J. Hooker.
Chapel Hill, N.C.: The University of North Carolina Press,
1953. (BYU 975.7 W859c)

SOUTH DAKOTA
Schell, Herbert S. HISTORY OF SOUTH DAKOTA. 2nd ed. Lincoln: The University of Nebraska Press, 1968. (BYU 968.3 Sc26h 1968)

TENNESSEE
Bokim, Herman. TENNESSEE HANDBOOK AND IMMIGRANTS GUIDE. Philadelphia: King & Baird, 1868.

Garrett, William Robert, and Albert Virgil Goodpasture. HISTORY OF TENNESSEE. Nashville: Brandon Publishing Co., 1900. (BYU 976.8 H2q)

Gilmore, James R. THE ADVANCE-GUARD OF WESTERN CIVILIZATION. New York: D. Appleton & Co., 1893. (BYU 976.8 G424a)

Hulbert, Archer B. "The Paths of Inland Commerce," THE CHRONICLES OF AMERICA SERIES 21 (1920). (GS 973 H2ch V.21)

TEXAS
Bender, A.B. OPENING ROUTES TO TEXAS 1848-1850. (BYU Hafen 979.1 91 #36)

Biesele, Rudolph Leopold. THE HISTORY OF THE GERMAN SETTLEMENTS IN TEXAS 1831-1861. Austin: Von Boeckmann-Jones Co., 1930. (BYU 976.4 B479h)

Biggers, Don H. GERMAN PIONEERS IN TEXAS. Fredericksburg, Texas: Fredericksburg Publishing Co., 1925. (BYU 976.465 B483g)

Carroll, H. Bailey. THE TEXAS SANTE FE TRAIL. Canyon, Texas: Panhandle-Plains Historical Society, 1951. (BYU 976.4 C23)

Connors, Seymour V. THE PETERS COLONY OF TEXAS. The Texas State Historical Association. Austin: Von Boeckmann-Jones Co., 1959. (BYU 976.404 C762p)

Dunn, John J.B. PERILOUS TRAILS OF TEXAS. Dallas: Southwest Press, 1932. (BYU 976.4 D922p)

Hogan, William Ransom. THE TEXAS REPUBLIC. Norman, Oklahoma: The University of Oklahoma Press, 1946. (BYU 976.4 H678t)

Loomis, Noel M. THE TEXAN-SANTE FE PIONEERS. Norman, Oklahoma: The University of Oklahoma Press, 1958. (BYU 976.4 L87t)

Wooten, Dudley G., M.A. A COMPLETE HISTORY OF TEXAS. Dallas: The Texas History Co., 1899. (BYU 976.4 W899c)

VERMONT
Barden, Merritt Clark. VERMONT, ONCE NO MAN'S LAND. Rutland, Vermont: The Tuttle Co., 1928. (GS 974.3 D2b)

Crockett, Walter Hill. VERMONT, THE GREEN MOUNTAIN STATE. 4 vols. New York: The Century History Co., 1921. (GS 974.3 H2c)

Hayward, John. A GAZETTEER OF VERMONT. Boston: Tappan,
    Whittemore & Mason, 1849. (BYU 917.43 H3335g)
Hemenway, Abbie Maria, ed. THE VERMONT HISTORICAL
    GAZETTEER. 6 vols. Burlington, Vermont: Miss A.M.
    Hemenway, 1868-1923. (BYU 974.3 Ve59h)
Hill, Ralph Nading. YANKEE KINGDOM. New York: Harper &
    Brothers, 1960. (BYU 974.2 H555y)
Stilwell, Lewis D. "Detailed Account of Migrations 1776-1860,
    of About Eight Thousand Vermonters to the Counties of the
    United States and Canada," PROCEEDINGS OF THE VERMONT
    HISTORICAL SOCIETY 5: 63-245. (GS 974.3 B2v V.5 No.2)
_____. MIGRATION FROM VERMONT. Montpelier, Vermont:
    The Vermont Historical Society, 1948. (BYU 974.3 W2s)

VIRGINIA
Alvord, Clarence Walworth, and Lee Bidgood. THE FIRST EXPLORA-
    TION OF THE TRANS-ALLEGHENY REGION BY THE VIRGINIANS
    1650-1674. Cleveland, Ohio: The Arthur H. Clark Co., 1912.
    (BYU 975 AL89f)
Bailey, Kenneth P. THE OHIO COMPANY OF VIRGINIA AND THE
    WESTWARD MOVEMENT 1748-1792. Glendale, California:
    The Arthur H. Clark Co., 1939. (BYU 975.5 U3b)
Brock, R.A. DOCUMENTS, CHIEFLY UNPUBLISHED, RELATING
    TO THE HUGUENOT EMIGRATION TO VIRGINIA AND THE
    SETTLEMENT AT MANAKINTOWN. Baltimore: The Genealogical
    Publishing Co., 1966.
Edward, Richard. STATISTICAL GAZETTEER OF THE STATE OF
    VIRGINIA. Richmond: Published for the Proprietor, 1855.
Kegley, Frederick Bittle. KEGLEY'S VIRGINIA FRONTIER, THE
    BEGINNING OF THE SOUTHWEST, THE ROANOKE OF COLONIAL
    DAYS, 1740-1783. Roanoke, Va.: The Southwest Virginia
    Historical Society, 1938.
Martin, Joseph, ed. A NEW AND COMPREHENSIVE GAZETTEER
    OF VIRGINIA, AND THE DISTRICT OF COLUMBIA. Charlottesville:
    J. Martin, 1835. (BYU Microcard 917)
Newton, Joseph. EMIGRATION TO AMERICA (EAST) OR THE OLD
    DOMINION STATE. 3rd ed. n.p.: The Virginia Land Agency,
    n.d. (BYU Microcard 917.55)
Nugent, Nell M. CAVALIERS AND PIONEERS. ABSTRACTS OF
    VIRGINIA LAND PATENTS AND GRANTS, 1623-1666. Baltimore:
    The Genealogical Publishing Co., 1963.
O'Brien, Michael J. EARLY IMMIGRANTS TO VIRGINIA (1623-1666).
    Baltimore: The Genealogical Publishing Co., 1965.

WEST VIRGINIA
Callahan, James Morton. HISTORY OF WEST VIRGINIA, OLD AND
    NEW. 3 vols. Chicago: The American Historical Society,
    1923. (GS 975.4 H2c)
Dayton, Ruth Woods. PIONEERS AND THEIR HOMES ON THE
    UPPER KANAWHA. Charleston, W.Va.: West Virginia Publishing
    Co., 1947. (BYU 975.43 D337p)

De Hass, Wills. HISTORY OF THE EARLY SETTLEMENT AND
    INDIAN WARS OF WESTERN VIRGINIA. Parsons, W. Va.:
    McClain Printing Co., 1960. (BYU 977 D366h)
McWhorter, Lucullus Virgil. THE BORDER SETTLERS OF
    NORTHWESTERN VIRGINIA FROM 1768 TO 1795. Hamilton,
    Ohio: The Republican Publishing Co., 1915. (GS 975.4 H2m)

CANADA
Craig, Gerald M. UPPER CANADA: THE FORMATIVE YEARS,
    1784-1841. New York: The Oxford University Press, 1963.
    (BYU 971.3 C844u)
Davin, Nicholas Flood. THE IRISHMAN IN CANADA. London:
    S. Low Marsten & Co., 1877. (GS 971 F2i)
Department of Citizenship and Immigration, Canada. Economic
    and Social Research Division. CITIZENSHIP, IMMIGRATION,
    AND ETHNIC GROUPS IN CANADA, 1962.
Dooner, Alfred James. CATHOLIC PIONEERS IN UPPER CANADA.
    Toronto: Macmillan of Canada, 1947. (BYU 971.5 D3d)
"First Settlements of Pennsylvania Mennonites in Upper Cananda,"
    ONTARIO HISTORICAL SOCIETY PAPERS AND RECORDS
    23 (1926): 8-14. (GS 971.5 B2o V.23)
Gourlay, Robert. GENERAL INTRODUCTION TO STATISTICAL
    ACCOUNT OF UPPER CANADA. New York: Johnson Reprint
    Corporation, 1966. (BYU 325.71 G743g)
Graeff, Arthur D. "The Pennsylvania Germans in Ontario, Canada:
    Eighteenth Century Settlements in Upper Canada," THE
    PENNSYLVANIA-GERMAN FOLKLORE SOCIETY 11 (1946):
    1-80. (GS 974.8 B4pg V.11)
Kaye, Vladmir Julian. EARLY UKRAINIAN SETTLEMENTS IN
    CANADA, 1895-1900. Toronto: The University of Toronto
    Press, 1964. (GS 971.2 F2k)
Kysilevsky, V.J. Kaye. SLAVIC GROUPS IN CANADA. Winnipeg:
    Ukrainian Free Academy of Science, 1951. (GS 971.46 B4s
    V.12)
Lindal, W.J. THE ICELANDERS IN CANADA. Winnipeg: National
    Publishers, 1967. (BYU 301.4513969 L64i)
Macdonald, Norman. CANADA IMMIGRATION AND COLONIZATION
    1841-1903. Toronto: Macmillan of Canada, 1966. (BYU 325.
    71 M145c)
Marunchak, Michael H. THE UKRAINIAN CANADIANS: A HISTORY.
    Yorkton, Canada: Redeemer's Voice Press, 1970. (BYU 971
    M368u)
Sack, B.G. HISTORY OF THE JEWS IN CANADA. Montreal:
    Harvest House, 1965. (GS 971 F2s)

---

1. Norman Edgar Wright, GENEALOGY IN AMERICA, vol. 1
(Salt Lake City: Deseret Book Co., 1968), p. 141.

2. Ibid., p. 140.

3. Milton Rubincam, ed., GENEALOGICAL RESEARCH METHODS AND SOURCES (Washington, D.C.: The American Society of Genealogists, 1960), p. 134.

4. Ibid., p. 136.

5. Oliver Perry Chitwood, A HISTORY OF COLONIAL AMERICA (New York: Harper & Brothers, 1948), p. 165.

6. Ibid.

7. Ibid., p. 168.

8. Historical Records Survey Commission, New Hampshire Historical Records Survey Project, "Inventory of the County Archives of New Hampshire, No. 5 - Grafton County" (Manchester, New Hampshire, Apr. 1940), p. 13.

9. Chitwood, p. 166.

10. Wright, p. 259.

11. Ibid.

12. Rubincam, pp. 99-100.

13. Historical Records Survey Commission, Writers Guide Series, VERMONT, p. 29.

14. Ibid., p. 30.

15. Richard B. Morris, ENCYCLOPEDIA OF AMERICAN HISTORY (New York: Harper & Brothers, 1953), p. 100.

16. Rosalie Fellows Bailey, GUIDE TO GENEALOGICAL AND BIOGRAPHICAL SOURCES FOR NEW YORK CITY (Manhattan) 1783-1898 (New York: Privately Published, 1954), p. 1.

17. Rubincam, p. 140.

18. Robert E. Chaddock, OHIO BEFORE 1850 (New York: Columbia University, 1908), pp. 32-33.

19. Ibid., pp. 16-18.

20. Ray Allen Billington, WESTWARD EXPANSION (New York: The Macmillan Co., 1960), p. 301.

21. Ibid.

CHAPTER 14

DETERMINING THE IMMIGRANT ANCESTRAL HOME

If the researcher is to have continued success in building his pedigree, he must, sooner or later, trace each American ancestral line to its origin in another country. For some lines, of course, this tracing may be a modern problem for which adequate records are available. But for many it will be a problem for early periods for which few pertinent sources can be found. The problem confronts every ethnic and national group which settled in America, including the American Indian, who undoubtedly had his roots elsewhere but for whom few records exist.

In the strictest sense, an "emigrant" is a person leaving one country to settle in another while an "immigrant" is one coming into a new country in order to settle there. Modern writers use the terms interchangeably, but in this chapter, emigration records will refer to those of the country from which a person departed while immigration records will refer to those of the country the person is entering for settlement. Migration will refer to movement within the country.

It is possible to gain pertinent information about some immigrants as early as 1607 in America, but very little documented movement can be established before that date. Source materials for the seventeenth and eighteenth centuries are somewhat lacking, both in content and availability, but those for the nineteenth and twentieth centuries are quite good.

Determining the immigrant ancestral home is not always easy, and some problems defy solution with present recources. Actually, the facts which are necessary to locate the ancestral home in another country can appear early as well as late in research and can come from any number of different sources, many of which have been outlined and explained in previous chapters. It is a matter first of identifying an individual as an immigrant and then of searching source materials to locate pertinent facts concerning him. Information can come from family and home sources, general LDS sources, compiled secondary materials, or from any of the major record groups already discussed. Sources of emigration, immigration, and migration should be investigated. A researcher does not reach an imaginary point where he says "now I will begin to look for information about the immigrant ancestor" but actually must be looking for it all along in his research.

Family and Home Sources

Important facts concerning the immigrant can sometimes be obtained in the home or from relatives and friends of the family. Traditions may be held by the family concerning their nativity, and associates may know of the family's previous places of residence. Certain national customs may persist with the family, or heirlooms belonging to the family might be identified with a particular time period and country. Few families are without some idea of their national origin. Of course, just knowing the country is not enough to extend a pedigree; knowing the town or village of origin is necessary to do much genealogically.

Various documents might be found with family members which can give clues to a foreign place of birth or residence. Old letters, newspaper clippings, photographs, citizenship papers, land and estate papers, as well as Bibles, diaries, journals, and related books should be considered.

One genealogy student located an article from the ST. LOUIS POST-DISPATCH of 18 November 1882 (p. 4) which gave information concerning an ancestor. It also illustrated how the testimony of a family associate can provide important genealogical information:

IDENTIFIED - The Body of the Man Who Suicided Yesterday
The Coroner held an inquest today on the body of the unknown man who was found yesterday afternoon lying on the ground in a small grove near the corner of Third and Welch streets. Peter D. Gramache testified that he lived at the corner of Third and Welch street, on the Carondelet road. Yesterday about 12 o'clock he started to walk through the grove, and as he entered a short distance into the woods he observed the body of a man lying with his face downwards. Going up to him he tried to arouse him, but in so doing he noticed a piece of rope tied around his neck. Upon further examination the witness found that the other end of the rope was tied to a limb of the tree under which the man was lying dead. The rope was small, and it appeared to the witness that the suicide had climbed into the tree, adjusted the rope and jumped off. The rope broke, but had accomplished its purposes the same. The witness could not tell how long the man had laid there. He notified the police, and the body was taken away to the Morgue. The dead man's body has been exposed to the view of the curious

who go to the Morgue every day when the doors are thrown open and unknown bodies are laid upon the slab for identification. About 12 o'clock to-day a Bohemian named Mathias Boemisch, living at No. 1715 South Tenth street, called there and when he looked at the unknown suicide immediately recognized it as a man and fellow countryman of his own whom he had known during his life and whose name was Joseph Stetina. He was fifty years old and had a wife living in Europe, and a sister and two sons living in this city, but where Doemisch did not know. Deceased had lived somewhere in Frenchtown. He had been a laborer by occupation and was a morbid-minded sort of man. He had, however, never expressed an inclination to take his own life so far as the informant had known. The Coroner rendered a verdict of death by suicide. Efforts will be made to find the relatives of the deceased.

The above article might appear rather unpleasant in its implications, especially to family members, but it certainly illustrates how an associate might have knowledge of a friend's place of birth and residence. Notice that the individual was also able to give the deceased's age and details concerning his wife and sons. He probably could also have given the name of the town of residence in Bohemia if he had been asked. Of course, Mr. Boemisch is also deceased by now and testimony from him could not be obtained; however, research could be conducted on his place of birth and residence in Bohemia, and it might turn out to be the same as that of Joseph Stetina.

Sometimes it is necessary to study the surnames and genealogy of several friends and associates of the ancestor to get the needed information. Friends and family members often emigrated together and lived together, so that the place of birth for an associate or friend might be the same as that of an ancestor. (This approach can also be used to trace families from one locality to another in America as well as from one country to another.)

The Surname and Locality
The surname itself might prove helpful in determining the country of origin, and the localities where the family has resided might also provide clues. A few years ago, a researcher at the LDS Genealogical Society was able to establish a likely German town of origin for a Kentucky "Zeigenfuz" family through his knowledge of German surname origins. Evidently the name "Zeigenfuz" (also spelled Zeigenfoot) was occupational in origin and had its beginning with a family of clock-makers in a small eastern German village. The "second hand" on the clock was the "Zeigenfuz" (swinging foot) and a particular family took that term as their surname. Of course, this approach is not possible when the surname is common and cannot be used in all countries, but it might be helpful when the name is unusual. The anglicanization of a foreign surname or other name changes by the family in America might also tend to confuse the issue. Is the surname "Black" the anglican form for the German "Schwartz" or does it have an English origin? Is "Carpenter" from the German "Zimmerman"

521

or is it English also? The answer may not be readily apparent, and some other approach might have to be taken.

In early New England, the name of the town in which an ancestor settled might provide a clue to his origin, because many early towns were named after the European home of the early settlers--Braintree, Chelsea, or Malden in Massachusetts or Londonderry in New Hampshire, for instance. It is also interesting to note that many towns and cities in the western part of America were named after their east-coast counterparts. From this it can be seen that a study of the early settlers and their places of settlement should be made, expecially when the ancestor could have been one of the original settlers.

A careful study of the history and geography of foreign places of birth and residence must also be made before successful searches can be made in the proper sources. Dr. Ottokar Israel emphasized this at the World Conference on Records when he said that "it occasionally happens that an American researcher comes to the city of Hannover with a request for help in his search for a particular ancestor who emigrated approximately 1850 to the United States from 'Hannover.' The result is that the ancestors cannot be found in today's capital of the state of Lower Saxony, because he did not come from the city of Hannover, but rather from the kingdom of the same name. This difference however was not known by his descendants in the New World. Similar mistakes are made with respect to the many ecclesiastical territories of the Holy Roman Empire of the German Nation, which were also named after their main cities. A person who came from Würzburg, Bamberg or Passau, Münster, Osnabrück or Hildesheim, might just as well come from the diocese of the same name. The origin is not always designated as it should be; 'from the Hannoverschen' or 'from the Würsburgishen.' These examples indicate how important it is for a foreign researcher to become acquainted with the territorial development of Germany in order to have a general view of the many small German states and cities of the former Holy Roman Empire."[2]

General Archival Collections
The Genealogical Society of The Church of Jesus Christ of Latter-day Saints has created some general genealogical collections which can help in determining a foreign residence or place of birth, and other libraries, societies, and archives have similar collections. Some have specialized in the history and genealogy of certain ethnic and national groups and have collected genealogical and historical materials which contain genealogy. Biographies, genealogies, family histories, regional and local histories, genealogical indexes, genealogical dictionaries, periodicals, and miscellaneous manuscript collections are among their holdings. An effort should be made to investigate these special collections for emigration-immigration information.

The Temple Records Index Bureau and the Church Records Archives of the LDS Genealogical Society, which were explained in chapter 2, should be checked just as soon as an ancestor has been identified as an immigrant. Information may be on file which refers to his place of birth in the old country, or clues to his foreign residence might be learned by investigating records of others by the same surname.

When the immigrant was known to be from England and Wales, the "Computer Print-outs" and "R-Tab" (Controlled Extraction) cards should be investigated. (These also were explained in chapter 2.) Birth and marriage information pertaining to individuals listed in early parish registers has been computerized and indexed in these collections. "Boyd's Marriage Indexes" might also prove helpful on certain English problems. They consist of several hundred volumes of English marriage records covering the period 1538-1837. The records are not complete and are arranged in three different series. Smith and Gardner's GENEALOGICAL RESEARCH IN ENGLAND AND WALES, vol. 2, pp. 200-201 gives additional information on that collection.

The Genealogical Society in Salt Lake City also has special collections of emigration records which pertain to members of The Church of Jesus Christ of Latter-day Saints who emigrated from Europe between 1849 and 1925. The records include good information on persons emigrating from Great Britain, Holland, and the Scandinavian countries. Additional information concerning these records is presented in chapter 2.

Vital Records and the Obituary

Local and state vital records should always be investigated when there is a possibility the immigrant lived to a modern period, or when his children did. Modern death records call for the "place of birth of parents" as well as that of the deceased, and many include the town or village of birth. Of course the information is no better than its source, but the facts might be correct and provide the very information needed to "cross the water." The birth record of a child might also give the foreign place of birth or residence, and records of other relatives might provide the needed facts.

Vital records of the foreign countries should also be considered, especially where the immigrant was born after national registration took place. As an example, if the immigrant was known to be from England or Wales and was born after national registration of vital statistics took place in 1837, a copy of his birth record from Somerset House in London should be obtained. National indexes exist, and copies are on file at the Genealogical Society Library in Salt Lake City. A similar approach could be taken if the individual was born in Scotland after 1854 or in Holland after 1811. Many countries did not have national registration until rather late, and in some countries the national approach is not possible. In Scandinavian countries, one must know the smaller locality and have at least the year of birth available. However, there are other excellent sources which can give the desired information, including annual extracts of parish registers, police records, emigration papers, passport journals, and certain archival collections. These are explained in detail in Carl-Erik Johansson's CRADLED IN SWEDEN (Logan, Utah: Everton Publishers, 1972).

Heinz F. Friederichs gives a brief but excellent account of sources which should be investigated on a German emigration problem in his GERMANIC RESEARCH PROBLEMS (a paper read at the World Conference on Records and Genealogical Seminar held in Salt Lake City, August 1969). Dr. Ottokar Israel's paper on Germany, cited previously, is excellent on German emigration and gives bibliographic detail on source materials. Dr. W.H. Ruoff's paper on A CENTURY OF EMIGRATION FROM THE PALATINATE TO THE USA--SWIT-ZERLAND, and several others delivered at the same conference should be consulted. Copies are on file at the Genealogical Society Library in Salt Lake City and at Brigham Young University in Provo. A few of the papers are available for purchase from the Genealogical Society at a very reasonable price.

The obituary or death notice from a local newspaper is also a good source to gain emigration-immigration information, especially in a modern period. They sometimes list the foreign place of birth or residence, next of kin, and give personal facts which might help to determine the place of birth. The family might have kept copies of older newspaper clippings, and in some cases the family may have copies of foreign newspapers which came from the "old home in Europe."

Church and cemetery records from the localities where the family has resided should be investigated. Birth, christening, baptism, marriage, and death entries in those records might include the foreign birthplace or provide clues to it.

Census-Mortality Records
Federal and state census and mortality records should also be considered on immigrant problems. The 1850 and later federal schedules list the state or country of birth, and the 1880 and later records call for the state or country of birth for parents. The 1870 schedules include a special column which is marked when the parents were of foreign birth, though the actual place is not listed. The 1900 federal schedules also include statistics on naturalization and citizenship. These records are explained in detail in chapter 4 and examples are shown.

When an immigrant lived to the 1850-1880 period, and when he died in the twelve-month period preceding the census year, he may be listed in the federal mortality schedules. They list the state or country of birth and are explained in chapter 4.

Some state and local census enumerations date much earlier than those of the federal government, and some include the place of birth. Those for Maryland, for example, date from 1772 to 1774. Many of the state schedules after 1855 contain naturalization and citizenship information, including the year naturalized and the year of immigration to the United States.

Naturalization-Citizenship Records

Naturalization-citizenship records are actually court records in America and are an excellent source of genealogical information. They include such records as oaths of allegiance, declarations of intention to become citizens, petitions to become citizens, records of aliens, and other miscellaneous affidavits and depositions. The records are public, but according to federal statute, may not be copied by xerox or photostatic processes. However, the information can be copied in longhand from the documents (fig. 200).

It should also be recognized that family members may have copies of citizenship papers in their own possession. The following document was in possession of Kenneth Zang, grandson of the immigrant Joseph Zanghi. Notice that it only gives the country of origin (Italy) and that it includes the volume and page number where the original petition is recorded, giving the county (Blair County, Pennsylvania) where the original is filed. Additional information concerning Joseph Zanghi's town or village of birth in Italy might be obtained by visiting the Blair County courthouse at Hollidaysburg, Pennsylvania (fig. 201).

A few oaths of allegiance and declarations of intention to become citizens have been published for early Pennsylvania immigrants, primarily Swiss and German, but most records remain unpublished and are filed in the various courthouses.

British subjects were seldom included in the records prior to the Revolution because they were coming to a British colony; however, modern records often include them. Early volumes in Salt Lake City include the names of many Britishers, but the records do not list the place of birth or residence in Great Britain. They simply list the name and date and indicate that the person renounced his allegiance to the king or queen of Great Britain.

Immigration records in St. Lawrence County, New York, have been inspected concerning Irish immigrants in the 1840s, and they also only list the country to which the person owes allegiance. On the other hand, records have been searched in various other states where excellent detail was given concerning towns and villages of birth or residence, but they were primarily for Germanic or Scandinavian immigrants (fig. 202).

Laws and regulations pertaining to naturalization and citizenship have varied considerably over the years, and it was not until after 1900 that the United States Department of Immigration and Naturalization

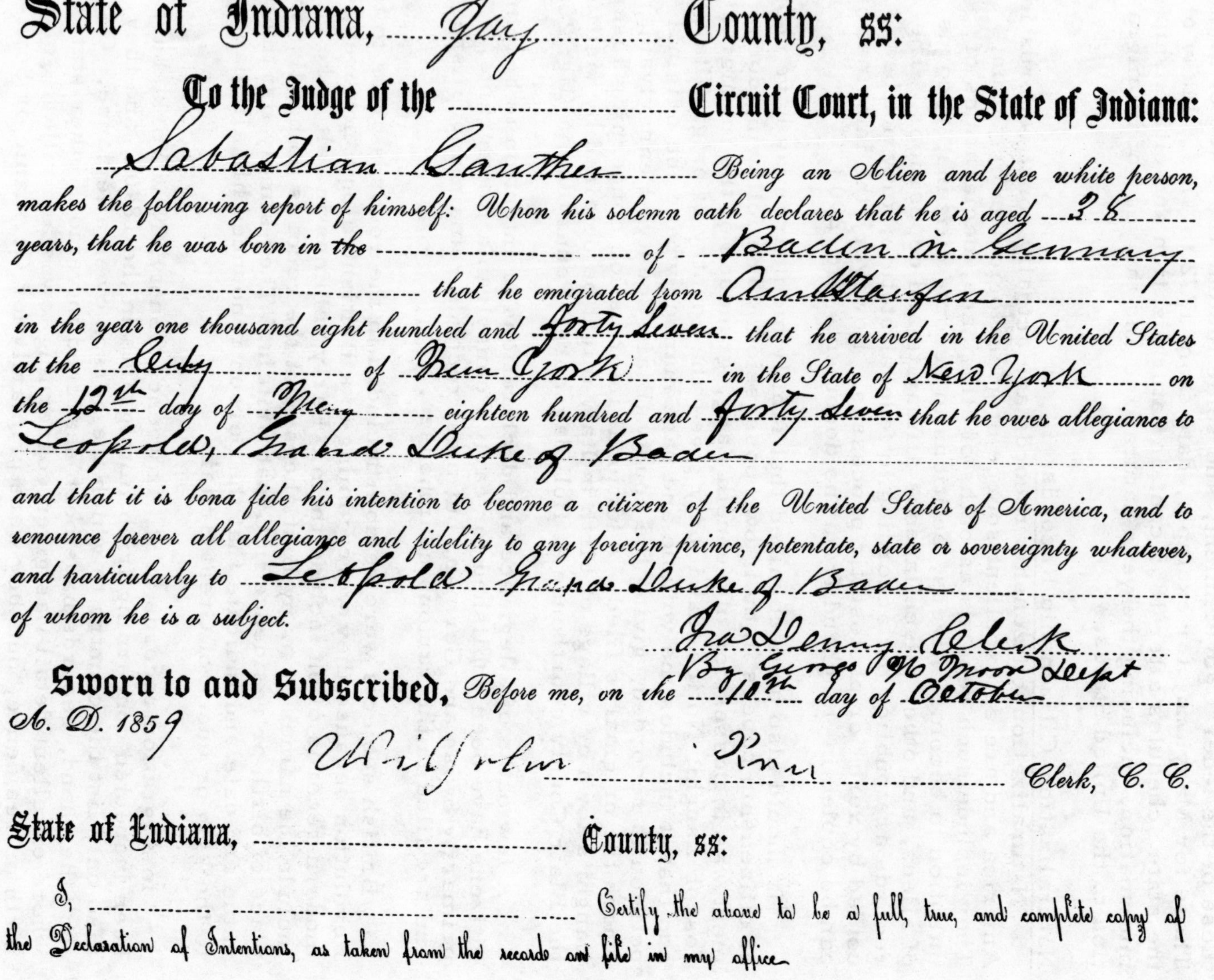

State of Indiana, Gay County, ss:

To the Judge of the ______ Circuit Court, in the State of Indiana:

Sebastian Gaunther Being an Alien and free white person, makes the following report of himself: Upon his solemn oath declares that he is aged 28 years, that he was born in the ______ of Baden in Germany ______ that he emigrated from Amsterdam in the year one thousand eight hundred and forty seven that he arrived in the United States at the City of New York in the State of New York on the 12th day of May eighteen hundred and forty seven that he owes allegiance to Leopold, Grand Duke of Baden

and that it is bona fide his intention to become a citizen of the United States of America, and to renounce forever all allegiance and fidelity to any foreign prince, potentate, state or sovereignty whatever, and particularly to Leopold Grand Duke of Baden of whom he is a subject.

Jno Denny Clerk
By George W Moor Dept

Sworn to and Subscribed, Before me, on the 10th day of October A. D. 1859

Wilhelm Rin ______ Clerk, C. C.

State of Indiana, ______ County, ss:

I, ______ Certify the above to be a full, true, and complete copy of the Declaration of Intentions, as taken from the records on file in my office

Fig. 200. Declaration of an alien to become a citizen

Fig. 201. Certificate of naturalization for Joseph Zanghi, 1917

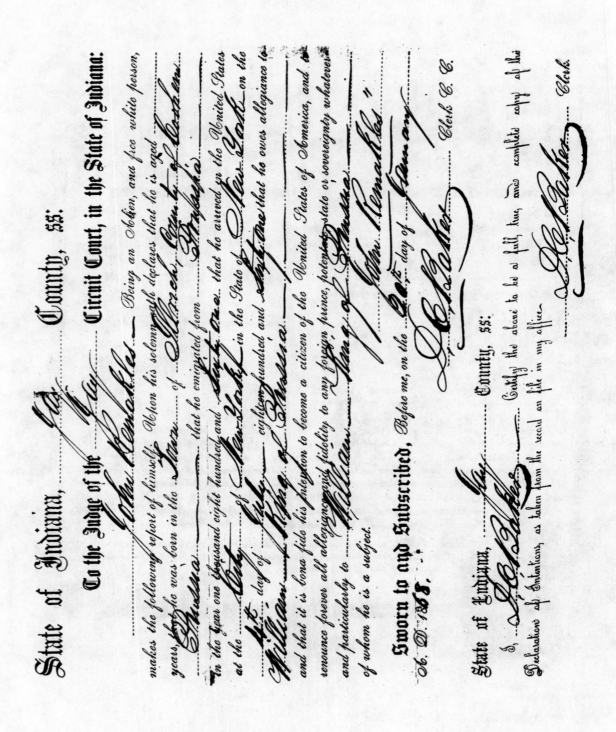

Fig. 202. Citizenship record for a German immigrant, 1861
(giving birthplace)

528

was established. A majority of the records prior to that time, and some after, are found among local court records.

IMMIGRATION LAWS OF THE UNITED STATES by Helen Silving (New York: Oceana Publications, 1948) is a good reference pertaining to laws which have directly affected citizenship, and CITIZENSHIP OF THE UNITED STATES OF AMERICA by Sidney Kansas (New York: Washington Publishing Company, 1936) is excellent in its detail. Luella Gettys's THE LAW OF CITIZENSHIP IN THE UNITED STATES (Chicago: The University of Chicago Press, 1934) is also good, and A COLLECTION OF NATIONALITY LAWS OF VARIOUS COUNTRIES, edited by Richard W. Flourney (New York: Oxford University Press, 1929) is good for information concerning other countries.

Other Court Records and Land Records

Court records other than those relating to naturalization and citizenship are also helpful in determining the foreign place of birth or residence. Some individuals changed their names through court action, and related documents and depositions often include reference to the "old country." The basement vault of the Oneida County, New York, courthouse at Utica is half filled with Italian change of name records. Many immigrants who settled in Utica and Rome, New York, changed their names (usually to a shorter English version of the European form), and records on file in the courthouse often include the individual's town or village of birth. This is probably true of other ethnic groups in other cities and counties of the United States.

An individual may also have given testimony in a civil or criminal court case, and his deposition might include his age and place of birth. Reference may only be given to his place of residence in a foreign country, but that information could be used to learn the actual place of birth (fig. 203).

Probate court and guardianship records are of special importance in this regard and can refer to an immigrant in a number of different ways. The name and place of residence of the individual could be included in the will or the petition or could be found written in other documents relating to the estate and its settlement. Many early Virginia testators left property to relatives in England and identified their places of residence right in the will. This undoubtedly happened in other colonies and was not limited to the colonial period of American history.

According to British researchers, when an individual left real or personal property to someone in America (or other countries for that matter), administration of the estate was handled in a special court, the "Prerogative Court of Canterbury," and records prior to 1859 have been microfilmed and are on file at the Genealogical Society Library in Salt Lake City. These records contain excellent genealogical information to connect families from the two worlds.

PROVINCE AND COURT RECORDS OF MAINE

VOL. I

Under Sir Ferdinando Gorges and His Councillors

From 1636 until taken away by Parliament in 1646
and by the Colony of Massachusetts Bay in 1652

Under Ferdinando Gorges the Younger ∽ ∽ ∽

Between 1661 and 1665 alternating with the Colony of Massachusetts Bay, until taken away by the Commissioners of Charles II

Under the Commissioners of Charles II ∽ ∽ ∽

✓ From 1665 to 1668 until taken away by the Colony
of Massachusetts Bay

WITH COLLATERAL PAPERS AND CITATIONS

GENEALOGICAL SOCIETY

15037

Apr. 1932.

(5 VOLS.)

PORTLAND
MAINE HISTORICAL SOCIETY
1928

Fig. 203. Deposition from a Maine court record showing a foreign residence

Judgement is given upon this verdict by the whole bench and execution by them awarded.

The declaration of John Winter and Johane his wife defendants [plaintiffs] against George Cleeve gent. plaint. [defendant]

[66] Mr. John Winter cometh into this Courte, and declareth that this defendant aboute some six yeares past, within this Province did unjustly and wrongfully slander the said plaintiffe his wife in reporting that the said plaint. his wife (who then lived in the Town of Plymouth in old England) was the veriest drunkenest whore in all that towne, with divers other such like scandalous reports not only of the said plaint. his wife, but also of the said town in generall in saying that there was not foure honest women in all that towne, by which wrongfull and unjust accusation the plaintiffes hold themselves greately prejudiced in their reputation, for which the said plaintiffes bring their action of slander into this Courte against the said defendant as high as one hundred pound starling at the least, and humbly craveth a legall proceeding according to his Majesties lawes.

The depositions of Mr. Arthur Browne, William Scadlocke and John Cosons in behalfe of the above said plaint taken at this Courte.

Mr. Arthur Browne sworne and examined saith that he hath heard the defendant say that Mris. Winter was a drunken woman, the words tending to drunken whore.

William Scadlocke sworne and examined saith that he hath heard the defendant say that Mris. Winter was a drunken whore.

John Cosons sworne and examined saith that he hath heard his wife (and others) speake the like as the aforesaid deponents, as James Cole and others.

The defendant hath liberty given him by the Courte to answeare to this action of the plaintiffes at the next Generall Courte to be holden here.

The declaration of Capt. Tho. Cammocke plaint. against Mr. John Winter defendant

Capt. Thomas Cammocke cometh into this Courte and declareth that this defendant John Winter since the last Courte holden here sent some of his servants to cutt hay in the limitts of the plaintiffes Pattent without his consent or knowledge which the plaintiffe understanding went forthwith to Spurwinke house and warned Benjamin [*sic*] and John Burridge and others being servants to the defendant that they should give knowledge to the said defendant to forbeare either to cutt any more or to make or carry away the same formerly cutt; yet notwithstanding the said defendant came himselfe and brought

Fig. 203a.

Miscellaneous documents in the probate files might also contain useful information. Petitions in New York records invariably contain the names and addresses of heirs to the estate, and letters from heirs living in foreign places are often included. This approach can also be used to trace persons from one locality to another in America.

Proprietors' records, land grants, deeds, mortgages, and other land or property records can also provide information about a foreign place of birth or residence. A few early Massachusetts proprietors' records include the English place of residence of early settlers, and land grants in some of the southern states include the previous place of residence in the "old world." Later documents of land title transfer include similar information.

Military Records

Examples of documents found in service and pension files relating to the military were identified in chapter 8. These can also be a source from which one can determine a foreign place of birth or residence. The actual enlistment or induction notices may give the needed facts, or affidavits and depositions in the files may do the job. Some immigrants joined the military as a means of getting established in this country and then retired to a more peaceful life later.

Passenger-Shipping Records

A surprising number of passenger and shipping records have been preserved, both for emigration and immigration. American lists for the period 1600-1820 are few in number and meager in genealogical content, but records after that date are fairly inclusive, though not always complete. Records of immigrants arriving at most Atlantic and Gulf Coast ports covering the period 1819-1945 are in the National Archives at Washington, and those for the ports of Boston, New York, Philadelphia, Baltimore, and New Orleans covering the period 1819-1876 are on microfilm at the Genealogical Society Library in Salt Lake City. The Genealogical Society also has a number of published lists for various ports and has many emigration records from foreign countries.

According to Colket, San Francisco passenger lists were destroyed by fires in 1851 and 1940, and lists for other Pacific coast ports, if they ever existed, were never transferred to the National Archives.[3] Lists in the National Archives include customs passenger lists, customs lists of aliens, and immigration passenger lists.

Most records relating to the colonial period that have been preserved have been published. The following selected list includes some of the more popular on file at the Genealogical Society Library and at Brigham Young University. Lancour's work is an excellent bibliography of other ship passenger lists. The works for Hotten, Stanard, and Fothergill are good for the southern colonies, and Banks' publications cover New England. Those for Knittle, Rupp, Strassburger and Westcott are particularly applicable to the middle

colonies. A majority of the early records include only the names
and ages of the passengers and do not always give reference to the
country from which they came.

A Selected Bibliography Relating to Colonial American Emigration

Ames, Azel. THE MAYFLOWER AND HER LOG: JULY 15, 1620 -
    MAY 7, 1621. Boston: Houghton, Mifflin & Co., 1901
Banks, Charles Edward. THE ENGLISH ANCESTRY AND HOMES
    OF THE PILGRIM FATHERS. Baltimore: The Genealogical
    Publishing Co., 1968
_____. THE PLANTERS OF THE COMMONWEALTH.
    Baltimore: The Genealogical Publishing Co., 1967.
_____. TOPOGRAPHICAL DICTIONARY OF 2,885 ENGLISH
    EMIGRANTS TO NEW ENGLAND, 1620-1650. Ed. E. E. Brownell.
    Baltimore: The Genealogical Publishing Co., 1963.
_____. THE WINTHROP FLEET OF 1630. Baltimore: The
    Genealogical Publishing Co., 1963.
Colket, Meredith B., and Frank E. Bridgers. GUIDE TO GENEALOG-
    ICAL RECORDS IN THE NATIONAL ARCHIVES. Washington:
    The National Archives, 1964.
Egle, William Henry, ed. NAMES OF FOREIGNERS WHO TOOK THE
    OATH OF ALLEGIANCE TO THE PROVINCE AND STATE OF
    PENNSYLVANIA, 1727-1775, WITH THE FOREIGN ARRIVALS,
    1786-1808. Baltimore: The Genealogical Publishing Co., 1967.
EMIGRANTS FROM ENGLAND, 1773-1776 and LIST OF EMIGRANTS
    TO AMERICA FROM LIVERPOOL, 1697-1707. Reprints from
    the NEW ENGLAND HISTORICAL AND GENEALOGICAL REGISTERS,
    vols. 61, 64, and 65.
Farmer, John. A GENEALOGICAL REGISTER OF THE FIRST
    FAMILIES OF NEW ENGLAND. Baltimore: The Genealogical
    Publishing Co., 1968.
Faust, Albert Bernhardt. LIST OF SWISS EMIGRANTS IN THE
    EIGHTEENTH CENTURY TO THE AMERICAN COLONIES.
    Washington: The National Genealogical Society, 1925.
Fothergill, Gerald. EMIGRANTS FROM ENGLAND, 1773-1776.
    Baltimore: The Genealogical Publishing Co., 1964.
_____. A LIST OF EMIGRANT MINISTERS TO AMERICA,
    1690-1811. Baltimore: The Genealogical Publishing Co., 1965.
French, Elizabeth. LIST OF EMIGRANTS TO AMERICA FROM
    LIVERPOOL, 1697-1707. Baltimore: The Genealogical
    Publishing Co., 1962.
Gerber, Adolph. EMIGRANTS FROM WUERTTEMBERG: THE ADOLPH
    GERBER LISTS. Ed. Donald Herbert Yoder. Baltimore:
    The Genealogical Publishing Co., n.d.
Ghirelli, Michael. LIST OF EMIGRANTS FROM ENGLAND TO
    AMERICA, 1682-1692. Baltimore: Magna Carta Book Co., 1968.
Greer, George Cabell. EARLY VIRGINIA IMMIGRANTS, 1623-1666.
    Baltimore: The Genealogical Publishing Co., 1960.
Hansen, Marcus Lee. THE ATLANTIC MIGRATION, 1607-1860.
    New York: Harper & Row, 1961.

Hoffman, William J. "Palatine Emigrants to America from the Principality of Nassau-Dillenburg," THE NATIONAL GENEALOGICAL SOCIETY QUARTERLY 30 (June 1941): 41-44.

Hotten, John Camden. THE ORIGINAL LISTS OF PERSONS OF QUALITY, 1600-1700. 2nd ed. Baltimore: The Genealogical Publishing Co., 1968.

Ireland, Gordon. "Servant of Foreign Plantations from Bristol, England 1654-1686," NEW YORK GENEALOGICAL AND BIOGRAPHICAL RECORD 79 (1948): 65-75. (GS 974 B2n V.79)

Jewson, Charles Boardman. TRANSCRIPT OF THREE REGISTERS OF PASSENGERS FROM GREAT YARMOUTH TO HOLLAND AND NEW ENGLAND, 1637-1639. Baltimore: The Genealogical Publishing Co., 1964.

Kaminkow, Jack, and Marion Kaminkow. A LIST OF EMIGRANTS FROM ENGLAND TO AMERICA, 1718-1759. Baltimore: The Genealogical Publishing Co., 1964.

Knittle, Walter Allen. EARLY EIGHTEENTH CENTURY PALATINE EMIGRATION. Baltimore: The Genealogical Publishing Co., 1965.

Krebs, Friedrich. "Emigrants from Baden-Durlach to Pennsylvania, 1749-1755," THE NATIONAL GENEALOGICAL SOCIETY QUARTERLY 45 (March 1957): 30-32.

_____. "A List of German Immigrants to the American Colonies from Zweibruecken in the Palatinate, 1750-1771," PENNSYLVANIA GERMAN FOLKLORE SOCIETY 16 (1951): 171-183.

Lancour, Harold. A BIBLIOGRAPHY OF SHIP PASSENGER LISTS, 1538-1825. 3rd ed. rev. & enl. by Richard J. Wolfe. New York: The New York Public Library, 1963.

Landis, John T. MAYFLOWER DESCENDANTS AND THEIR MARRIAGES FOR TWO GENERATIONS AFTER LANDING. Baltimore: The Genealogical Publishing Co., 1964.

Myers, Albert Cook. QUAKER ARRIVALS AT PHILADELPHIA, 1682-1750. Baltimore: The Genealogical Publishing Co., 1969.

Nicholson, Cregoe, D.P. SOME EARLY EMIGRANTS TO AMERICA. Baltimore: The Genealogical Publishing Co., 1965.

"A Partial List of the Families Who Arrived at Philadelphia Between 1682 and 1687," THE PENNSYLVANIA MAGAZINE OF HISTORY AND BIOGRAPHY 8 (1884): 328-40.

"Passenger List of the Ship 'Elizabeth' Which Arrived at Philadelphia, Pennsylvania, 1819," THE PENNSYLVANIA MAGAZINE OF HISTORY AND BIOGRAPHY 25 (1901): 255-58..

Putnam, Eben. TWO EARLY PASSENGER LISTS, 1635-1637. Baltimore: The Genealogical Publishing Co., 1964.

Revill, Janie. A COMPILATION OF THE ORIGINAL LISTS OF PROTESTANT IMMIGRANTS TO SOUTH CAROLINA, 1763-1773. Baltimore: The Genealogical Publishing Co., 1968.

Robinson, Conway. EARLY VOYAGES TO AMERICA. Richmond: Sheperd & Colin, 1848.

Rupp, Israel Daniel. A COLLECTION OF UPWARDS OF THIRTY
    THOUSAND NAMES OF GERMAN, SWISS, DUTCH, FRENCH
    AND OTHER IMMIGRANTS INTO PENNSYLVANIA FROM 1727
    TO 1776. 2nd ed. Baltimore: The Genealogical Publishing
    Co., 1965.
Sherwood, George. AMERICAN COLONISTS IN ENGLISH RECORDS.
    Baltimore: The Genealogical Publishing Co., 1969.
Stanard, William G. SOME EMIGRANTS TO VIRGINIA. 2nd ed.
    Baltimore: The Genealogical Publishing Co., 1964.
Steinemann, Ernst, ed. "A List of Eighteenth Century Emigrants
    from the Canton of Schaffhausen to the American Colonies,
    1734-1752," THE PENNSYLVANIA GERMAN FOLKLORE
    SOCIETY 16: 185-96.
Strassburger, Ralph Beaver, and William John Hinke, eds.
    PENNSYLVANIA GERMAN PIONEERS: A PUBLICATION OF
    THE ORIGINAL LISTS OF ARRIVALS IN THE PORT OF
    PHILADELPHIA FROM 1727 TO 1808. 2 vols. Baltimore:
    The Genealogical Publishing Co., 1966.
Virginia Historical Society. DOCUMENTS RELATING TO THE
    HUGUENOT EMIGRATION TO VIRGINIA. Richmond: The
    Virginia Historical Society, 1936.
Virkus, Frederick A. IMMIGRANT ANCESTORS: A LIST OF 2,500
    IMMIGRANTS TO AMERICA BEFORE 1750. Baltimore: The
    Genealogical Publishing Co., 1963.
Westcott, Thompson. NAMES OF PERSONS WHO TOOK THE OATH
    OF ALLEGIANCE TO THE STATE OF PENNSYLVANIA
    BETWEEN THE YEARS 1777 AND 1789. Baltimore: The
    Genealogical Publishing Co., 1963.

According to Colket,[3] passenger-shipping lists are on file in
the National Archives for the following ports covering the listed time
periods:

    Alexandria, Virginia: 1820-1852
    Annapolis, Maryland: 1849
    Apalachicola, Florida: 1918
    Baltimore, Maryland: 1820-1909
    Bangor, Maine: 1848
    Barnstable, Massachusetts: 1820-1826
    Bath, Maine: 1825-1832, 1867
    Beufort, North Carolina: 1865
    Belfast, Maine: 1820-1831, 1851
    Boca Grande, Florida: 1912-1935
    Boston and Charlestown, Mass.: 1820-1874; 1883-1943
    Bridgeport, Connecticut: 1870
    Bridgetown, New Jersey: 1828
    Bristol and Warren, R.I.: 1820-1828; 1843-1871
    Brunswick, Georgia: 1901-1939
    Cape May, New Jersey: 1828
    Carabelle, Florida: 1915
    Charleston, South Carolina: 1820-1829; 1906-1945

Darien, Georgia: 1823, 1825
Dighton, Mass.: 1820-1836
East River, Virginia: 1830
Edenton, North Carolina: 1820
Edgartown, Mass.: 1820-1870
Fairfield, Connecticut: 1820-1821
Fall River, Mass.: 1837-1865
Fernandina, Florida: 1904-1932
Frenchman's Bay, Maine: 1821; 1822; 1825-1827
Galveston, Texas: 1846-1871
Georgetown, District of Columbia: 1820-1821
Georgetown, South Carolina: 1923-1939
Gloucester, Mass.: 1820; 1832-1839; 1867-1870; 1906-1923;
                1930-1943
Gulfport, Mississippi: 1904-1944
Hampton, Virginia: 1821
Hartford, Connecticut: 1832; 1929-1943
Havre de Grace, Maryland: 1820
Hingham, Mass.: 1852
Jacksonville, Florida: 1904-1945
Kennebunk, Maine: 1820-1827; 1842
Key West, Florida: 1837-1868; 1898-1945
Knights Key, Florida: 1908-1912
Little Egg Harbor, New Jersey: 1831
Marblehead, Mass.: 1820-1852
Mayport, Florida: 1907-1916
Miami, Florida: 1899-1945
Millvile, Florida: 1916
Mobile, Alabama: 1820-1862; 1904-1945
Nantucket, Mass.: 1820-1862
New Bedford, Mass.: 1823-1899; 1902-1942
New Bern, North Carolina: 1820-1845; 1865
New Haven, Connecticut: 1820-1873
New London, Connecticut: 1820-1847
New Orleans, Louisiana: 1820-1945
New York, New York: 1820-1942
Newark, New Jersey: 1836
Newburyport, Mass.: 1821-1839
Newport, Rhode Island: 1820-1875
Norfolk and Portsmouth, Virginia: 1820-1857
Oswegatchie, New York: 1821-1823
Panama City, Florida: 1927-1939
Pascagoula, Mississippi: 1903-1935
Passamaquoddy, Maine: 1820-1859
Penobscot, Maine: 1851
Pensacola, Florida: 1900-1945
Perth Amboy, New Jersey: 1820; 1829-1832
Petersburg, Virginia: 1819-1822
Philadelphia, Pennsylvania: 1820-1945
Plymouth, Mass.: 1821-1843

Plymouth, North Carolina: 1820, 1823, 1825, 1840
Port Everglades, Florida: 1932-1945
Port Inglis, Florida: 1912-1913
Port Royal, South Carolina: 1865
Port St. Joe, Florida: 1923-1939
Portland and Falmouth, Maine: 1820-1868; 1873; 1893-1943
Portsmouth, New Hampshire: 1820-1861
Providence, Rhode Island: 1820-1867; 1911-1943
Richmond, Virginia: 1820-1844
Rochester, New York: 1866
Sag Harbor, New York: 1829-1834
St. Andrews, Florida: 1916-1926
St. Augustine, Florida: 1821-1827; 1870
St. Johns, Florida: 1865
St. Petersburg, Florida: 1926-1941
Salem and Beverly, Mass.: 1790-1800; 1865-1866
Sandusky, Ohio: 1820
Savannah, Georgia: 1820-1868; 1906-1945
Saybrook, Connecticut: 1820
Tampa, Florida: 1898-1945
Waldoboro, Maine: 1820-1833
Washington, North Carolina: 1820-1848
West Palm Beach, Florida: 1920-1945
Wilmington, Delaware: 1820-1848
Wiscasset, Maine: 1819; 1829
Yarmouth, Maine: 1820

As mentioned previously, passenger-shipping lists in the National Archives consist of customs passenger lists and immigration passenger lists. The records known as customs passenger lists were filed by the masters of ships with collectors of customs in compliance with congressional acts of 1819 and later. There are originals, copies, and abstracts, and State Department transcripts for the customs passenger lists. Few originals remain, but those which do are dated primarily 1820-1902 with copies and abstracts covering the period 1820-1875 and transcripts dating 1819-1832. The original lists were prepared on board ship, sworn to by the master of the ship, and filed with the collector of customs when the ship arrived at port. [4]

There are two separate card indexes to the names on the copies and abstracts of passenger lists. One of them contains entries for passengers arriving at the port of New York, 1820-1846, and the other contains entries for passengers arriving at other Atlantic and Gulf coast ports, 1820-1874, and includes a few entries for New York passengers. Both indexes are arranged alphabetically by the name of the passenger and include ages and country of citizenship. The index to passengers arriving at Atlantic and Gulf coast ports includes names for Baltimore, Mobile, New Bedford, New Orleans, and Philadelphia. [5] The index to New York lists for the period 1820-1846 is on microfilm at the Genealogical Society at Brigham Young University, but the second index has not been received by either institution at this writing.

Original lists for Boston, prior to 1883, were reportedly destroyed by fire in 1894, though copies exist for some covering an earlier period.[6] The collection at the Genealogical Society in Salt Lake City is a microfilm copy of cards which are arranged alphabetically and date after 1883.

Copies and abstracts of passenger lists were made in the offices of the collectors of customs and were sent to the Secretary of State each quarter. Some collectors prepared copies of the individual lists, while others prepared abstracts, which are consolidated lists of names of all passengers who arrived at a given port during the quarter[7] (fig. 204).

Copies and abstracts include the name of the ship, the master, the tonnage, the ports of embarkation and debarkation, the names of the passengers, their ages, their sex, their occupation, the country to which they belong, the country which they intend to inhabit, and whether they died on the voyage.

Customs collectors at New Orleans also prepared books containing abstracts covering the years 1845-1875 which they retained at the port. The National Archives has twenty-three volumes constituting that collection.[8] There are also eight volumes of transcripts for various ports covering the period 1819-1832 which were prepared from copies or abstracts in the Department of State and then sent to the Secretary of State by the collectors of customs[9] (fig. 205).

Volume 2 of the State Department Transcripts is missing, but some entries from it were printed in LETTER FROM THE SECRETARY OF STATE WITH A TRANSCRIPT OF THE LIST OF PASSENGERS WHO ARRIVED IN THE UNITED STATES FROM THE 1st OCTOBER, 1819, TO THE 30th SEPTEMBER, 1820 (16th Congress, 2nd Session, Senate Document 118, serial 45). The National Archives Library has a typescript index to the volume.[10]

The Customs Lists of Aliens pertain to Salem and Beverly, Massachusetts only and cover the period 1798-1800[11] (fig. 206). The records include the name of the ship and its master, the name of the port and the date of arrival, the names of each passenger, their ages, their places of nativity, the country from whence they have come, to what nation they belong and owe allegiance, their occupation, and a description of their person (including their complexion and height). There are no indexes to the lists, but according to Colket, they were transcribed and printed in THE NEW ENGLAND HISTORICAL AND GENEALOGICAL REGISTER vol. 106 (July 1952): 203-209.[12]

The National Archives also has negative microfilm copies of immigration passenger lists covering the period 1883-1945, which not only include the names of immigrants but also those of American citizens returning from abroad as well as visitors (fig. 207).

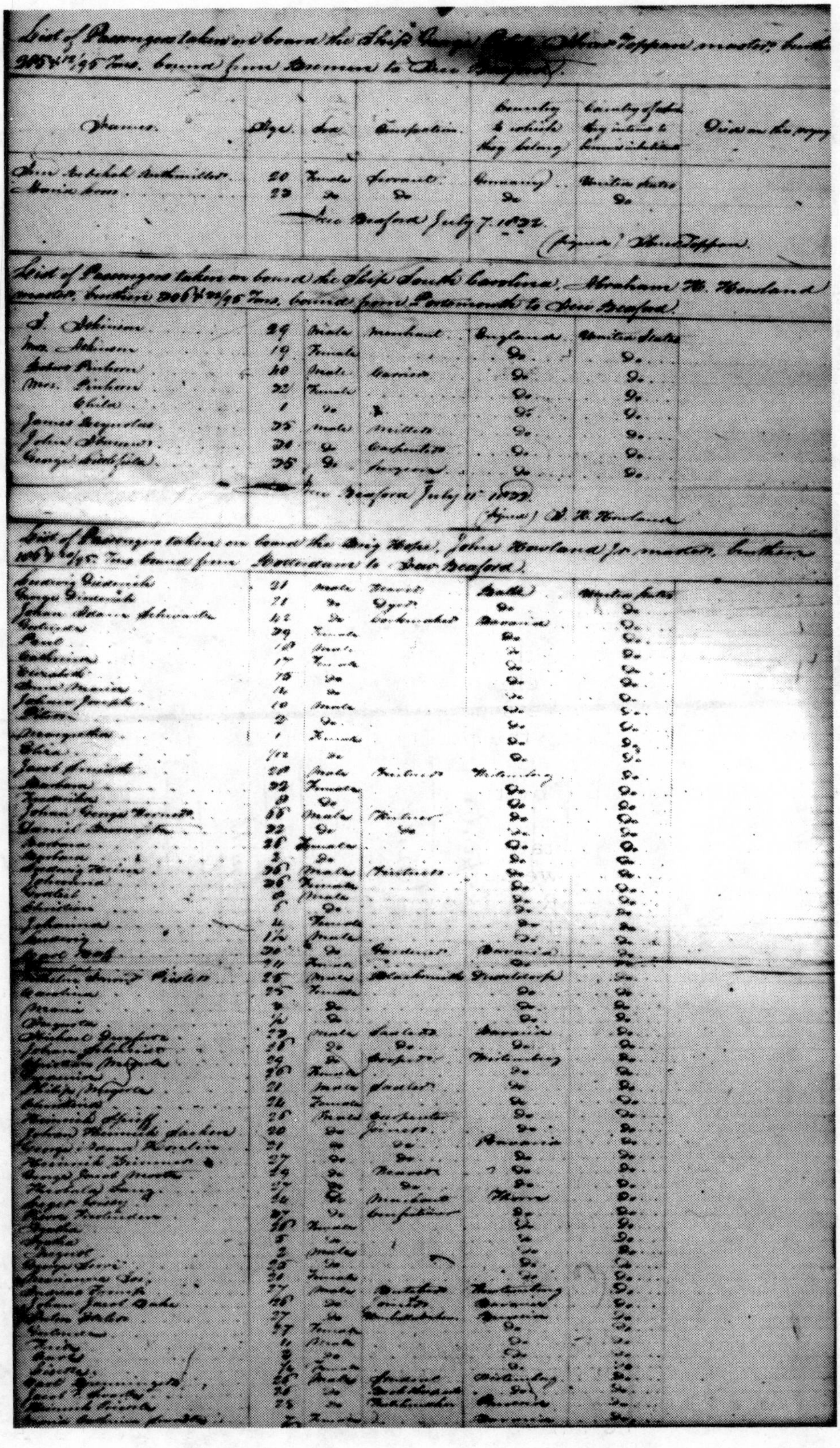

List of Passengers taken on board the Ship ... master, burthen ... Tons, bound from Bremen to New Bedford.

New Bedford July 7. 1832.

List of Passengers taken on board the Ship South Carolina, Abraham H. Howland master, burthen ... Tons, bound from Portsmouth to New Bedford

List of Passengers taken on board the Brig Hope, John Howland Jr. master, burthen ... Tons bound from Rotterdam to New Bedford.

Fig. 204. Passengers to New Bedford, Massachusetts, 1832

LIST OF PASSENGERS entered in the DISTRICT OF BALTIMORE, by vessels from Foreign Ports, from the first

of [vessel] to the 31 December 1837

NAMES OF PASSENGERS	AGE	SEX	OCCUPATION	COUNTRY TO WHICH THEY BELONG	COUNTRY OF WHICH THEY INTEND TO BECOME INHABITANTS	DIED ON THE VOYAGE
Marcus Samson	23	Male	Butcher	Germany	U. S.	None
Jenny Thurner	13	"				
Lorenz Thomas	30		Joiner			
Elizabeth	24	Female				
Anna Petry	29	"				
Saaca Jung	47	"				
Eliza Jung	14	"				
Babeth	10	"				
Anna Bates	40	"				
Bernardine	4	"				
Ludwig	1	"				
Daniel	34	Male	Carpenter			
Joseph Petry	40	"	Tanner			
Joseph Gedowake	26	Jun	"			
Fredericka	30	"				
Eva Weinrod	5	"				
Anna M	29	Male	Smith			
Hennick	3	"				
Mathias (Deidrich)	1	"				
Deidrich	30	"	Joiner			
Christian Straubinger	45	"	Farmer			
Franz Frau	29	"	Smith			
Geo (Deffenrich)	48	"	Farmer			
Lich	23	"	"			
Geo	19	"	"			
Johannes	14	"	"			
Gottlieb	12	"	"			
Geo	8	"				
Dorothea	49	Female				
Hanna	25	"				
Margeth	17	"				

Fig. 205. State department transcript for the District of Baltimore, 1837

540

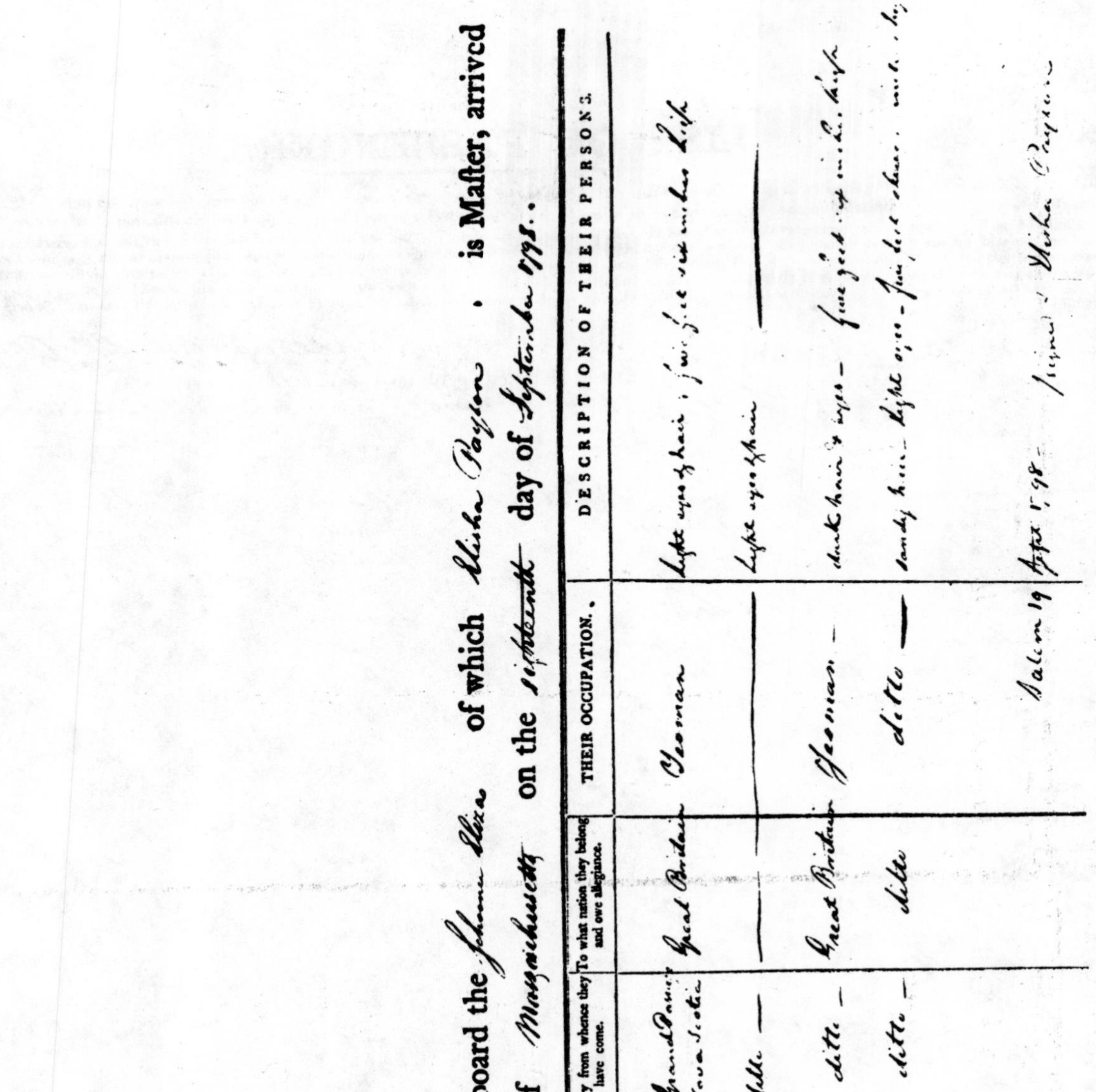

REPORT of ALIEN PASSENGERS on board the *Schooner Eliza* of which *Elisha Payson* is Master, arrived at the Port of *Salem* in the State of *Massachusetts* on the *sixteenth* day of *September* 1798.

NAMES.	AGES.	PLACES OF NATIVITY.	Country from whence they have come.	To what nation they belong and owe allegiance.	THEIR OCCUPATION.	DESCRIPTION OF THEIR PERSONS.
	forty	Beverly, Massachusetts	Grand Banks Nova Scotia	Great Britain	Yeoman	light eyes & hair, four feet seven inches high
	fifty eight		ditto			light eyes & hair
	twenty nine	Massachusetts	ditto	Great Britain	Yeoman	dark hair & eyes — five feet eight inches high
	forty	ditto	ditto	ditto	ditto	sandy hair, light eyes — five feet eleven inches high

Salem 19 Sept 1798 — Signed Elisha Payson

Fig. 206. Report of alien passengers at Salem, Massachusetts, 1798

LIST OF PASSENGERS.

I, _A. Mc Kay_ Master of the _Catalonia_ do solemnly, sincerely, and truly _Swear_ that the following List or Manifest, subscribed by me, and now delivered by me to the Collector of the Customs of the Collection District of _Boston and Charleston_ is a full and perfect List of all the passengers taken on board the said vessel at _Liverpool & Queenstown_ from which port the said vessel has now arrived; and that on the said list are truly designated the age, sex, and calling of each of the said passengers, the country of the citizenship of each, and also the destination or location intended by each; and that the said List or Manifest truly sets forth the number of the said passengers who have died on the said voyage, and the dates and causes of death, and the names and ages of those who died; also of the pieces of baggage of each; also a true statement, so far as it can be ascertained, with reference to the intention of each alien passenger as to a protracted sojourn in this country. _So help me God._

Sworn to at _Boston_ this ___ day of _____ 1887

Before me _____

List or Manifest of All the Passengers taken on board the _Catalonia_ whereof _Alex Mc Kay_ is Master, from _Liverpool & Queenstown_ burthen ___ tons.

No.	NAMES.	Years. Mth.	SEX.	CALLING.	The Country of which they are Citizens.	Intended Destination or Location.	Date and Cause of Death.	Location of compartment or space occupied.	Pieces of Baggage
1	James Spalding	19	M	Lab^r	England	Mass			1
2	Harry Wright	28		Rochester		Mass			1
3	W^m J Shields	19		Labour		Boston			1
4	Wm Lambert	40							
5	Geo Goodearl			Grocer		Boston			1
6	Edwd Stewart	24				Mass			1
7	Johnson Farrar	26		Weaver		R.			1
8	Harry Fell	11				Vt.			1
9	Fred Seale	16							1
10	John Weych					Mass			2
1	Manuel Seaver	25		Mason		Boston			1
2	John Manuer	36				Mass			1
3	James Porter	24		Clothwasher		Mass			1
4	Robt Maxwell	44		Shoemaker		Mass			1
5	Wm Lord	31		Seaver		Mass			1
6	Jane Renton	26				R.			1
7	James Carroll	30				Mass			2
8	Jacob Miller	47							
9	W^m A Kay	21							1
20	Alf Henderson	21							1
1	Luke Rice	21							
2	Wm Beasdale	23							
3	Eliza Beaton	39				Boston			
4	Mary Ellis	18		Labour		Mass			
5				Accountant		Boston			
6				Farmer					
7		47		Painter		N.Y.			
8		31		Labour		Boston			
9	Pat Actor					Mass			
30	John	9		child					
1	Tho Duncan	31		Farmer	Ireland				
2		23				Boston			
3	Allen Murray	23		Baker					
4	John Roberson			Moulder					
5	Wm Rogan	26		Laborer		Mass			1
6	Mackintosh	47		Farmer U.S.					
7	Miller	30		Clerk		Boston			
8		26							

Fig. 207. Passenger manifest from Liverpool and Queenstown to Boston and Charleston, 1887

Fig. 208. Inward passenger list from Bordeaux to New Orleans

The records include a sworn statement by the master as to the name of the ship, its tonnage, the ports of embarkation and debarkation, the date, each passenger's name, his age and sex, his occupation, his country of citizenship, his intended destination or location, date and cause of death if a passenger died at sea, and other miscellaneous information concerning housing and baggage (fig. 208).

The author had an interesting experience using New Orleans passenger lists and can vouch for their value in solving genealogical problems. My great-grandfather Joseph Wright (born 1817 in Yorkshire, England) joined the LDS Church in England in about 1839 and emigrated to America via New Orleans. From there he came through St. Louis, Missouri, and across the plains to Utah by wagon. In his journal, he said he came with his family to America on the ship ZETLAND in January 1849. Research on the line had been conducted by professionals, but they had failed to locate Joseph and his family in shipping records, though searches were made in copies of Mormon emigration records covering the period 1849-1869. When the LDS Genealogical Society obtained microfilm copies of New Orleans Customs Passenger Lists in 1962, a search located Joseph and his family on schedules for the ZETLAND which arrived at New Orleans on 3 April (not January) 1849. The entry included the following information:

Schedule A - Ship Zetland, Master Brown; Tons 1283; legal number ship can carry 333; bound to New Orleans; 276-1/2 passengers authorized; dated 24 January 1849. Ship arrived 3 April 1849 at New Orleans.

Page 7

Joseph Wright, age 34, male   Mormon Laborer Born England
Anna Maria Wright, age 34,
   female   "
Eliza Wright, age 7, female   "
William Wright, age 5, male   "
George Watson, age 66, male   "
Ann Watson, age 65, female   "
Francis Ryder, age 52, male   "

The most interesting information was that for George and Ann Watson and Francis Ryder. George and Ann were the parents of "Anna Maria Wright," wife of Joseph, and Francis Ryder was the brother of Ann Watson, wife of George. Professional researchers had been trying in vain to locate George and Ann Watson in English records. It had previously been assumed both had died in Yorkshire, England, between 1849 and 1852. But here they were in America. Joseph Wright participated in polygamy after he came to Utah and married Mary Ann Fryer as a second wife. It is interesting to note that she was also listed on the ZETLAND when it arrived in America in 1849 and was shown with her family as a young lady at that time. About eight years later, she married Joseph in Salt Lake City, but they had come to America on the same ship and probably were from the same locality in England.

---

1. The Church of Jesus Christ of Latter-day Saints accepts the BOOK OF MORMON as a history of the American Indian, and in that regard, it is a record of emigration, immigration, and migration for them.

2. Meredith B. Colket, Jr., and Frank E. Bridgers. GUIDE TO GENEALOGICAL RECORDS IN THE NATIONAL ARCHIVES (The National Archives and Records Service, General Services Administration, 1964), p. 22.

3. Dr. Ottokar Izrael. "Bridging the Atlantic--Finding the Place of Origin of Your German Ancester: Part II, Germany." Area D #1&2b. A paper read at the World Conference on Records and Genealogical Research, Salt Lake City, August 1969, p. 1.

4. Colket and Bridgers, pp. 23-30.

5. Ibid., p. 32.

6. Ibid., p. 34.

7. Ibid., p. 33.

8. Ibid.

9. Ibid.

10. Ibid., p. 35

11. Ibid.

12. Ibid., p. 36.

APPENDIX 1

PHOTOGRAPHY FOR GENEALOGISTS

Mr. George F. Tate of Provo has done extensive genealogical copywork using the camera. He presented the following paper in a BYU genealogy class:

A Practical System of Photography for

Genealogists and Historians

The purpose of this report is to describe the KISS[1] system of photography for accurately and rapidly copying genealogical and historical records on 35 mm film, developing the same and using the resulting negative roll in a regular microfilm reader for immediate viewing.

The basic requirement of the system is that it be simple to use, without complicated lights or accessories, positive in its results, and aside from the initial camera investment, very economical in operation.[2]

After careful experimentation and investigation, we have found that the most suitable instrument currently available in filling the above requirement is the Olympus Pen FT half-frame SLR camera. It is smaller, lighter, and easier to handle than a conventional full frame SLR. It easily fits into a pocket or a handbag. It takes twice as many exposures on a standard 35 mm roll of film (72-76 exposures on a regular 36 exposure roll), and the resulting format is much more suitable for the genealogical application. The SLR feature (Single Lens Reflex) provides direct viewing through the taking lens instead of through a separate finder with its attendant parallax problems. In other words, "what you see, you get." It is provided with its own light metering system for accurate exposures. It focuses to within 14" (about 4"x6" field size without attachments). Thus the basic FACE (focus, aperature (light), composition and exposure) requirements of good photography are easily achieved without supplemental equipment. It is a versatile instrument finding a full range of application other than the specified genealogical purpose.

In our investigation we first tried a regular full-frame 35 mm SLR camera (Mamiya Sekor 500 TL). With little instruction and no prior photographic experience other than the usual "snap-shot" variety, Miss Gloria Smith, a BYU genealogy student, photographed a number of deed records at the Washington County, Pennsylvania, Court House during a Christmas vacation. On her return, the film was developed as a negative roll and then projected through a conventional microfilm reader. The photographic results were fine, except that the size of the projected regular 35 mm full-frame exceeded the screen size of the conventional microfilm reading equipment, which we subsequently learned is based upon an approximate 25x25mm square format. The same situation was encountered when we attempted to make a direct record print (8"x10" positive) from a 3M Microfilm Printer-Reader (3M Filmare 400). The projected image exceeded the screen size when the widest angle lens (12.05x 36 mm focal length) available in the BYU microfilm Reading Room was used. An investigation was then made to determine if a wider angle lens could be obtained for the reader-printer. It was determined that one was commercially available, but its application would require a basic modification in the reader-printer; therefore the BYU library was not receptive to the change.

The discovery that the popular 35 mm regular full-frame format was not entirely suitable for our genealogical record copying purpose and subsequent projection on a microfilm reader came as a surprise as the microfilm is basically a 35 mm film operation.[3] Nevertheless, the 35 mm half-frame format solved our dilemma and in so doing provided a number of additional advantages aside from the film saving heretofore mentioned. For example, the format is vertical rather than horizontal. Since most documents have this format, and it is easier to handhold the camera and operate it in its normal horizontal position, the advantage thus obtained is obvious. Also, as will be seen in the format diagram below, the half-frame proportion is closer to the 8 x 10 enlargement size preferred for documentation, and therefore little cropping is required when the half-frame is enlarged thus the smaller negative size is not as disadvantageous as might first appear. In addition, it was found that the half-frame size is the same as that used in film strips for educational and similar purposes, thus enabling the use of film strip projectors as reading machines when conventional microfilm readers are not available. The half-frame pictures can likewise be projected in a regular 35 mm slide projector or viewer (with a little adaptation where rolls are used), thus readily enabling "home" viewing.

microfilm reader	half-frame	full-frame	
about 25x25 mm	18x24.5mm	36.3x24.5mm	These parts unreadable without shifting in viewer.

35mm exposed frame dimensions

x = reader-printer coverage on 35mm full-frame exposure using 12.05 wide-angle lens. (about same as 1/2 frame turned 90°).

The film used in our investigation was Tri-X Pan (Eastman) 36 Exposure with an ASA film rating of 400. This is an exceptionally fast film enabling good results at "available" light levels. While Miss Smith took along small portable lighting for auxiliary use, she found she didn't need it; nor have we in any of our experiments. While some writers[4] recommend a finer grain, slower film such as Microfile as used in commercial microfilming (ASA 32) we would not suggest this for private use as it would require 12.5 times as much light and thus require auxiliary lighting such as flood, strobe, or flash. For almost all applications in our KISS system, you will find that the fast Tri-X film will provide enough contrast for readable work. The current price of Tri-X Pan is about $1.00 per roll plus a charge of 35 to 60¢ for drug store or photo shop developing. One word of caution, however, if you have someone develop your film for you, be sure you specify that you want it returned <u>uncut - as a roll.</u> Otherwise, the processor may cut it into small strips making its use in a microfilm reader very inconvenient or difficult.

While "drug store" processing is all right initially, you will soon find that with a very small expenditure (about $3.90 for a tank and $2.00 for chemicals, clips, etc.) you can develop your own films. This will be a great convenience, especially if you buy your film in bulk and load your own magazines. In addition to saving money (a 50' roll of Tri-X would make about 800 exposures at a cost of about 1/2¢ each for the film), you can expose and develop a few frames at a time without waiting to finish a whole 40 or 72 exposure standard roll. This procedure also has the advantage of being able to change to a different type of film should technical requirements dictate.[5] The development of your film is a simple process and doesn't require the use of a darkroom (except that the film has to be loaded in the tank in the dark).

For our genealogical purpose, the film is developed as a <u>negative</u> roll and read directly on a microfilm reader using the same basic technique as that employed with commercial microfilms. Should a record copy be desired, the film is then transferred to the 3M reader printer and a <u>positive</u> obtained at a cost of about 15¢ for a 8"x10" print. Other types of reader printers are available such as the Xerox type currently being installed at the BYU Microfilm Room. This machine will be coin operated at a cost of 10¢ per print. However, the machine will be set up for positive to positive reproduction. This would mean that our negatives would be reproduced as negatives--a not very satisfying result on Xerox equipment. We accordingly recommend the use of the 3M (or similar) equipment.[6]

Genealogical records cover a wide range of materials, and, as an interesting aspect of our investigation, we copied a number of records directly from the projected images in a microfilm reader. We found the light adequate but, as it was impossible to position the camera directly above the projected image, we focused on the area of prime interest. A file folder or piece of cardboard to change the position of the projected image was also helpful. Our files contain several examples of this technique. While all items were not in equal focus the results were readable and satisfactory.[7]

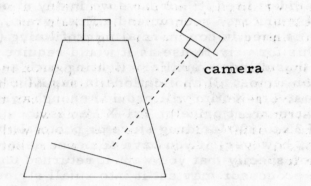

camera

1. KISS = "Keep it sweet and simple."

2. Initial camera investment with recommended f/1.8 38mm lens = $135-$160. Film and development cost, about $1.50 for 72-76 exposure roll = about 2¢ each exposure. This can be cut about in half if you use bulk film and do your own development. Positive enlargements (approx. 8x10") using microfilm printer readers (Xerox or 3M) about 10¢ to 15¢ per print.

3. The regular full frame 35mm camera <u>can</u> be used in this application. However, we suggest that the size be severely cropped so that the width does not exceed the height, or that, if convenient, two pages be taken at a time; thus, in effect obtaining half-frames from the full-frame format.

4. E. K. Kirkham, <u>Photography in Genealogy</u>, Deseret News Press, 1959, pp. 41, 43.

5. Ibid. pp. 40-43. BYU Hobby shop also has developing facilities for personal use, as does also one of the local Provo photo stores.

6. Or have a photo shop make prints from your negatives. Better yet, do your own using an enlarger such as Vivatar J-35 ($35-40), savings 50-80%. Splice your negative rolls together and store or view them from a std. microfilm reel.

7. The Pen FT has a depth-of-field preview button to help in such unusual cases.

APPENDIX 2

WRITING GENEALOGICAL REPORTS

Report writing is, and should remain, a personal matter, but a few suggestions are given which may help prevent misunderstanding and disappointment in the reporting process.

Nothing will enhance favor with a patron more than a pleasant and informative report and nothing will disappoint him like a negative or uninformative report. Some genealogists can make a report so pleasant the patron overlooks the fact nothing was actually located, while others are so brief and negative the patron withholds further orders for research. A middle ground somewhere between the two extremes should be followed.

A genealogical report should be similar to a good business letter or technical report. It should include an opening statement which gives a brief outline of the assignment given and the work completed but should not be so long that it makes the reader wonder what point is being made. The body of the report should include the bulk of the detail and should inform the patron exactly which sources were investigated and exactly what information was located. The closing should be a summary of the work completed and should give recommendations for continued research.

It is usually a good practice to refer the patron to his last request in order to refresh his memory of the problem or assignment. Many patrons need a reminder because their thoughts are with other work, while others are very much involved with research and cannot be fooled by "padded work." A brief outline of the general sources investigated and a general statement of the findings should be included in the opening of the report, but the bulk of the detail should be covered in the body. Following is a sample opening statement for a genealogical report:

Erma Pace Peterson
895 East 820 North
Provo, Utah 84601

Dear Mrs. Peterson:

In response to your request of March 25, 1972, research has been continued on your William Pace line in an effort to determine his place of birth and also to determine when he moved from Georgia to Tennessee. As you will recall, there was conflicting information in family records as to whether he was born in Virginia, North Carolina, or in South Carolina and there was also a question as to whether his older sons were born in North or South Carolina or in Georgia.

Investigation has included searches in census records, tax digests, and deeds of Rutherford County, Tennessee as well as census, land, and probate records of Clarke and Oglethorpe Counties in Georgia and Edgecombe County in North Carolina. Three research calendars and 25 pages of extract material are attached giving detail on the searches made since my last report.

The body of the report should include detail on specific searches and findings with cross reference to calendars and extracts. If the searcher has been working on several lines, he may desire to outline each one separately. Some researchers report their findings according to surname while others approach the problem on a record-source basis and indicate surname findings according to the source investigated. A sample body of a genealogical report follows:

Previous searches in St. George Temple records (see my report of 27 Feb 1971, extract #5) indicated the oldest sons of your William Pace (born abt. 1744) were William Jr., James, Wilson, Kenchon, and Jeremiah and that Drewry and Isaac were the youngest. We know that James was born in 1774, and census records have disclosed that Wilson and Jeremiah were born in North Carolina also. Isaac was also located but he was listed as born in Georgia.

Wilson Pace was located in the 1850 Federal census of Hickman County, Tennessee. He was listed as 74 years of age and born in North Carolina (see extract #4 of this report). If this information is correct, he would have been born about 1778. William Pace Jr. and Kenchon have not been located in the 1850 census but Jeremiah and Isaac were both shown in the 1850 of Perry County, Tennessee (see extract #5 of this report). Jeremiah was listed as age 61 and born in North Carolina while Isaac was shown to be age 52 and born in Georgia. This would indicate the family was in North Carolina as late as 1789 but was in Georgia by 1798 when Isaac was born.

Tax digests of Oglethorpe and Clarke Counties in Georgia show the family to be in Georgia as early as 1795 (see extract #10). Deeds and tax lists for Rutherford County, Tennessee indicate William Pace, Sr. and Jr. are both there by 1809 and evidently remove from Clarke County, Georgia shortly after 1806 (see extracts #8 and 9).

Searches were also made in North Carolina records to try and locate the family prior to 1795. We noted the names William, James, and Jeremiah Pace to be prevalent in Halifax County and also determined that the Pace family of Halifax County was from Edgecombe County earlier. Of special interest, was the fact a "William Kinchen" was prominent in that area which may account for the name Kinchen (Kenchon) appearing in your family.

A William Pace is resident early in Bertie Precinct and his estate is settled between 21 Feb 1744 and 1747. The records indicate his wife's name is Mary and that he leaves three children;

namely, William, John, and Elizabeth. The children are all minors at their father's death and William chooses Joseph John Alston his guardian while William Curlew is appointed guardian to John and Elizabeth on 21 Feb 1746 (see extracts number 7 and 10).

This could certainly be your Pace line with your William (born abt. 1745) being the young William who chooses Joseph John Alston his guardian. However, if that is the case, your approximate birth date for William might be incorrect as this William would have been born in 1732 or thereabouts. Further research should be conducted on this family as well as on that of a James Pace who is also resident there at the same time, and who could be the father of your William Pace.

When copies of extract material are to be sent to the patron, it may be better to merely refer to them in the body of the report rather than to recopy the information. Some researchers make carbon copies of extracts during research and send the original to the patron while keeping the carbon for their personal files. This helps them to better analyze the material later and preserves evidence of their work. Some patrons do not care to have copies of the raw material but want the results tabulated in family group and pedigree form. In these instances it might be necessary to copy pertinent findings in the body of the report and merely attach copies of family group records and pedigree charts which have been compiled from the findings. When very little pertinent information has been located, it might be advisable to list each source investigated and attach each calendar and extract so the patron will know the searches were actually made.

The closing of a report should include a summary of findings and should give recommendations for continued research. Sometimes the body of the report is so lengthy that it is impossible to comprehend all that was found without a summary of the material; hence, a recap of the essential facts is helpful. Specific recommendations for continued research should be made by listing the sources which might be investigated, explaining what might be found in each. A statement of the financial status of the patron's account could also be made in the closing, though some genealogists do this in the opening of their report. This would be a matter of personal taste and might vary according to the amount of money involved or the research findings. This is a sample closing section:

Time did not permit further investigation of the North Carolina records but this should certainly be done to gain further information on the family. It would be my recommendation that probates and deeds for Halifax, Edgecombe, and Northampton Counties be exhausted and all Pace entries be extracted for analysis. It might also be necessary to go into some Virginia records to determine the origin of these families in North Carolina. The Genealogical Society in Salt Lake City has a good collection of original records from these counties, and I would be happy to make further searches for you if you desire.

It would also be my recommendation that further searches be made in Oglethorpe and Clarke Counties in Georgia to determine more on the family there. Marriage records date to the early 1795 period and probates are available from a similar time period. We should extract each Pace entry from these sources and then follow through with the deeds of both the Georgia and Tennessee counties where the family was known to reside.

Your $100 deposit of March 25, 1972, was exhausted in these searches, and an additional $75 is requested to bring the account in balance. It would be my recommendation that an additional deposit of from $100 to $200 would be necessary to exhaust the records of the counties mentioned above.

Please evaluate the materials which have been included in this report and compare them with other information you have in your possession. If you have any question about the searches or the extracts, please let me know. I will be happy to reply. If you desire me to continue searches in your behalf, I will also be happy to do so.

It has been a pleasure serving you and I shall look forward to hearing from you in the near future.

Sincerely,

Truth and accuracy are of the utmost importance in a good report. If the researcher has performed his work well, he should not hesitate to ask for compensation, even though he may not have found the information requested by the patron. The genealogist performs a service and is not necessarily a producer of goods. Sometimes considerable relevant information is located in a short time while in other instances many hours of work may result in no direct findings.

APPENDIX 3

TEMPLE ORDINANCES

(From a devotional address given 12 August 1969 by Elder Howard
W. Hunter to the Fourth Annual Priesthood Genealogical Seminar.)

Ordinances for Living Persons

In order to be eligible to perform his own ordinance work, a living
person must be a baptized member of the Church and hold a current,
valid temple recommendation. This applies to all persons except children under the age of eight years who may be sealed to parents without
having been baptized. A man must have received the Melchizedek
Priesthood unless he is serving as a proxy for baptisms for the dead.
A woman whose husband is not a member of the Church may not be
recommended to the temple for her own endowment.

Following the endowment ordinance in the temple, a wife may be
sealed to her husband. If we understand the ordinance we know that a
man is not sealed to a woman--the woman is sealed to the man. We
follow the Law of Israel with respect to sealings. A man may have
only one wife at any period of his lifetime, but he may, during life,
be legally married to more than one woman; therefore, he may have
more than one wife sealed to him. Following the theory of the Law of
Israel, a woman may not be sealed to more than one man.

The next ordinance, after the sealing of wife to husband, is the
sealing of children to parents. If children are born after the sealing
of their mother to their father, they are born in the covenant of that
sealing and no specific ordinance of sealing is necessary. In the
event they are born prior to the time their parents are sealed, they
are sealed to their parents by the sealing ordinance. If a child to be
sealed is twenty-one years of age or older, or is a married daughter
even though less than twenty-one years of age, such child must be
endowed before being eligible to be sealed to the parents.

If children are born in the covenant, they cannot be sealed to any
other person as a parent. Let me give you an example. Such a
child, born in the covenant, might be adopted during lifetime by other
parents. The child has already had the benefit of the sealing covenant
and no further sealing is necessary. Another situation arises on
occasions, when after a divorce, the sealing of the wife to her husband
is cancelled because of justifiable circumstances. The cancellation of
the sealing of the wife to her husband does not cancel the sealing of the
children who had been sealed to them or born in the covenant. Such
children remain sealed to both mother and father and are not again
sealed to any other person.

We often hear the statement that under such circumstances, that is, the cancellation of a wife's sealing to her husband, the children follow the mother. This is not correct. This supposition may be based upon the fact that the husband is more often the wrongdoer, but this is not always the case. We can only assume that in the hereafter the children will follow the worthy parent as determined by the Lord. This is the reason that children sealed to parents who have subsequently been divorced are never sealed to a stepparent.

There are circumstances under which a child may be sealed to persons other than his natural parents, provided he was not born in the covenant and was not previously sealed to his natural parents. For instance, he might be sealed to a natural parent and a stepparent, or to foster parents, but he can be sealed only under one of the following circumstances: (1) if the stepparent or foster parents have legally adopted the child, or (2) if the stepparent or foster parents to whom the minor child is to be sealed have secured a written statement from the natural parent or parents consenting to the proposed sealing, or (3) if the child to be sealed is of legal age, and requests a sealing to other than his natural parents, or (4) a minor child may be sealed to a natural parent and a stepparent without the requirement of adoption in cases where the other natural parent is deceased.

For the purpose of emphasis I should repeat that children born in the covenant or sealed to their natural parents belong to their natural parents. This rule is not altered by adoption, by consent of the natural parents, by the application of the child after becoming of age, or death of the natural parents--the reason being that the child has had the benefit of the covenant of sealing and no further sealing is necessary.

Illegitimate children, of course, may be sealed to their natural mother and to the husband to whom she is sealed. This does not require the consent of the natural father because we follow the law that only the consent of the mother is necessary for anything pertaining to an illegitimate child.

I believe I have covered in general the major rules pertaining to the temple ordinances of living persons, and also the order in which these ordinances are accomplished. First, we must have been baptized; secondly, the man must have received the Melchizedek Priesthood; we are then endowed; then follows the sealing of the wife to her husband; and the sealing of the children to their parents.

Ordinances for the Dead

Let me turn from temple ordinance work for the living and discuss with you ordinance work for the dead. Your attendance at this seminar indicates your interest in research which will ultimately result in temple work for those who have preceded us, giving them the benefit of the saving ordinances of the temple even though they died without having these benefits.

From the beginning of temple work for the dead in this dispensation until the year 1942, the temple record input for ordinances was on an individual basis, but since that date we have used the family group method. This requires that we search out and identify each member of the family, group them, and follow the same sequence of doing ordinance work as we do for living persons.

Those of you engaged in research know the many problems involved in reestablishing families from inadequate records, lack of sufficient evidence, and the other handicaps that appear in this endeavor. The Genealogical Society, in its zeal to help and assist, attempted to establish the standards and rules to make the family group input acceptable for temple use, and it also engaged in research work for patrons. As time went on the volume increased and the complexity of this endeavor grew enormous. Rules, regulations, and supervision increased to the point where difficulties arose. It was finally decided that the Society should not do research or attempt to police the great volume of temple record input, but instead it should build and maintain for patrons a library facility. This objective, to a large extent, is being accomplished as we emerge as the largest genealogical library in the world.

For the past few years we have been planning and preparing for a new step forward with modern electronic equipment. It is not my purpose today to go into the ramifications of this new processing system. Most of you are aware of what this will do for us, but I do want to mention some of the procedural changes that will be compatible to the system and improve our work.

The First Presidency has ruled that after the expiration of one year from the date of death, temple ordinance work may be performed for all deceased persons without the consideration of worthiness or any other qualification. This rule eliminates investigations and decisions as to the worthiness and qualification of deceased persons whose names are submitted for temple ordinances. Under this rule we baptize all deceased persons by proxy who were not baptized during life, and endow them by proxy.

If a deceased wife was not sealed in life, we seal her by proxy to her deceased husband. If she had only one husband during her lifetime there is no problem, but if she had more than one husband, the question arises as to which husband she should be sealed. We have followed the rule in the past that she should be sealed to her first husband, everything else being equal. In many instances everything is not equal. She may have had children by subsequent marriages, but no children by her first husband. To seal her to any one of her husbands and then seal all the children of each marriage to that husband is arbitrary. The decision is not based upon any substantial evidence as to her wish or desire. It has been said that it will be left to her decision and the approval of the Lord in the hereafter.

Now comes a change in our procedure. The First Presidency has ruled that in cases where a wife has been married to more than one man in her lifetime and she and all husbands are deceased, we will seal the wife to each of her husbands. Under such circumstances the children of each marriage will be sealed to their own father and mother. This will cause the sealing lines to be the same as the blood lines and not be bent by arbitrary decisions of selection or decisions based upon weak or hearsay evidence. There is really no difference in arbitrarily sealing the wife to her first husband and leaving it to her selection with the approval of the Lord in the hereafter, than sealing her to each of her husbands and leaving it to her selection with the approval of the Lord in the hereafter. In any event she must make this decision. The latter has the greater advantage because children can be sealed to their own father and mother and the blood lines will be kept straight. This procedure, of course, is limited to ordinance work for the dead and would not apply to the living. We would assume that the adjustments will be made in the millennium. A woman in the hereafter will not be sealed to two men; but not knowing her wishes, it is felt that this is the proper course.

Valid and Effective Ordinances

Another ruling of the First Presidency will assist us in our temple work. It has been announced that the order in which the temple ordinances are performed for the dead is immaterial. In doing work for the living it is necessary that we follow the prescribed sequence. Let me explain the reason for the statement that, with respect to the dead, the order of sequence is not material. A temple ordinance performed by proxy does not become effective until it is accepted by the decedent. However, the ordinance is valid when performed if done properly by one duly authorized and it is duly recorded. There is, therefore, a distinction between a valid ordinance and an effective ordinance. If I don't make myself clear, you may wish to reread paragraphs 8 and 9 of the 128th Section of the Doctrine and Covenants where the requirements of a valid ordinance are clearly set forth. It must be performed by one having authority and a proper record made. Let me read to you just a portion of that section.

> . . . in all ages of the world, whenever the Lord has given a dispensation of the priesthood to any man by actual revelation, or any set of men, this power (that is, the power to bind on earth and consequently bind in heaven) has always been given. Hence, whatsoever those men did in authority, in the name of the Lord, and did it truly and faithfully, and kept a proper and faithful record of the same, it became a law on earth and in heaven, and could not be annulled, according to the decrees of the great Jehovah. . . . (D&C 128:9.)

This is the basis for doing a valid temple ordinance. A valid temple ordinance, therefore, consists of proper authority and a faithful and true record. It does not become effective, however, until accepted by the principal who is dead. He might accept of it quickly; it may take a long time; it may never be accepted; this we don't know. We might assume that the ordinance would be accepted immediately by the person for whom it was performed because of his expanded understanding but reason would dictate to us that in many instances it would take a long time before being accepted by one who is dead. Under such circumstances the ordinance would be ready when the time comes for acceptance. It is on that basis that we do ordinance work for the dead. We do the ordinance work only once, knowing it will be effective when the time comes for acceptance. This being true, what difference would it make as to the order of doing ordinance work for the dead? If they are all accomplished, regardless of the order, they will be validly performed and waiting to be accepted in the proper order and time when the one for whom they were done qualifies himself and accepts of them.

I hope that I have made this procedural matter clear because it will become important to us in our ordinance work for the dead as we move forward. This was never necessary when we were processing input from family group sheets, because we had assembled the family, and we did the ordinance work in the same order as for the living. Under our new input system on an individual entry basis, we will have more latitude in processing the input for temple work.

This new procedure will now permit us to take the original birth, or christening record, and perform the baptism, the endowment, and the sealing to parents. We may not have come to the marriage record of the parents, but from the birth record we are able to seal the child to the parents. From the marriage records, wives may be sealed to husbands. In each instance the persons are positively identified. The work will be properly done and it will not depend upon the judgment of those who were assembling family groups. We know as we do research that sometimes there is no positive identification and we conjecture as we assemble families, and later discover that some were not members of the same family. About 95 percent of the ordinance work for the dead will be done in the same order as for living persons even though the order is not material.

A Great New Era

We are looking forward to a great new era of increased research and temple work. Modern methods and faster electronic equipment will aid us. Roadblocks will be removed and simplification will lighten the burden. Although temple record input may be by individual record rather than by the family group, nevertheless, each of us will have the responsibility of making certain that all of the ordinances have been or will be performed for those in our family lines.

I know we are engaged in the work of the Lord. Our testimony of this fact brings us together that we might learn more of our responsibility and the ways to perform it so that the saving ordinances may

559

redeem those of our families who have preceded us.   May the Lord
bless us in this endeavor, I humbly pray in the name of Jesus Christ.
Amen.

APPENDIX 4

OBTAINING VITAL RECORDS

The Genealogy Department at Brigham Young University recently conducted a survey of vital statistics offices in the United States and gained some very useful information. Each state office and over one hundred metropolitan city offices were included in the study, and nearly a 98 percent return was received from the questionnaires sent. The states of Idaho and Wisconsin were the only two which did not respond to our questionnaire. Idaho did return the forms but refused to complete any part of them. Each office was asked to provide current information on the following items:

1. Their present mailing address for vital statistics.

2. The time periods covered by their records of birth, marriage, and death.

3. Current fees required for searches and for copies of documents located.

4. Whether their records were confidential or whether a person other than the individual of concern could obtain copies.

5. Whether or not their office would make a general search of their files when only an approximate date of an event was known.

6. Whether or not they would refund the fee when a specified record was not located.

Current mailing addresses were usually the state boards of health or city offices called by a similar name, such as "Department of Health" or "Department of Health and Welfare." The offices were generally located in the city hall, city-county building, state house, or state capitol building.

The periods covered by the various types of records differed considerably with each office. There seemed to be no uniformity between state, county, or city registration. A majority of the states did not register vital statistics until after 1880. Massachusetts began recording the earliest (1841) and West Virginia the latest (1917).

Many cities and counties registered vital statistics earlier than their respective states did, and many New England towns registered births, marriages, and deaths from the date the town was organized. Marriages were usually recorded in the counties or towns from the date of organization, but births and deaths were not recorded until 1850 to 1880. By 1890, most counties in the South and West had some form of vital statistics registration, but the states did not begin until after 1900 as a rule.

There was a time when some offices would allow genealogists to copy vital statistics without restriction or fee, but that is no longer the case. Every office questioned and every office with which the writer has had experience requires some fee for searching the records or for certified copies. And many offices have begun to restrict searching in their records by professionals, as well as amateurs. In 1960, the Illinois State Legislature passed laws to restrict Illinois county and state vital records, and a fee is required, not only for the search, but also for the record copy. Genealogists usually do not object to the fee, but they often would like to search the records in order to reach other conclusions than they can from simply receiving a copy of the record. As it is now, the genealogist must provide more facts to get the record than he can hope to receive from it.

Five years ago, most state offices were charging $1.00 for a certified copy of a birth or death record, but now most are charging $2.00 or more. Fees will undoubtedly continue to increase, and the records will probably continue to become more confidential as protests about "human rights" continue.

A majority of the offices contacted will make a general search of their files when an approximate date for a particular event is given, but some refuse to make a search unless the exact date is provided. Most offices considered the initial fee a "search fee" as well as a certificate fee; however, a few require special hourly fees. Most offices will make a two- or three-year search without a special fee, but some have special rates for five- and ten-year periods.

Birth records are considered confidential with most offices, and one must have proper authorization to obtain copies. This is particularly true where the individual could still be living or where the information might be unfavorable, indicating the birth was illegitimate for instance. Usually, such records are restricted to the person himself, to his parents, or to his legal guardian. Records showing illegitimacy can usually only be copied after one has obtained a court order from a county or district judge.

Death and marriage records were not restricted as often as birth records but some offices do require special authorization from the appropriate party before copies can be obtained.

Document fees are not generally refunded, and most offices consider the fee a search fee as well as a copy fee. Only one or two states indicated they refunded the fee when a specified record was not located, but several county and city offices indicated they refunded the fee on a negative search. A few offices refunded half of the specified fee when a negative search was made and considered half to be the search fee. A few offices also required a special application form be completed before a search would be made of their files.

562

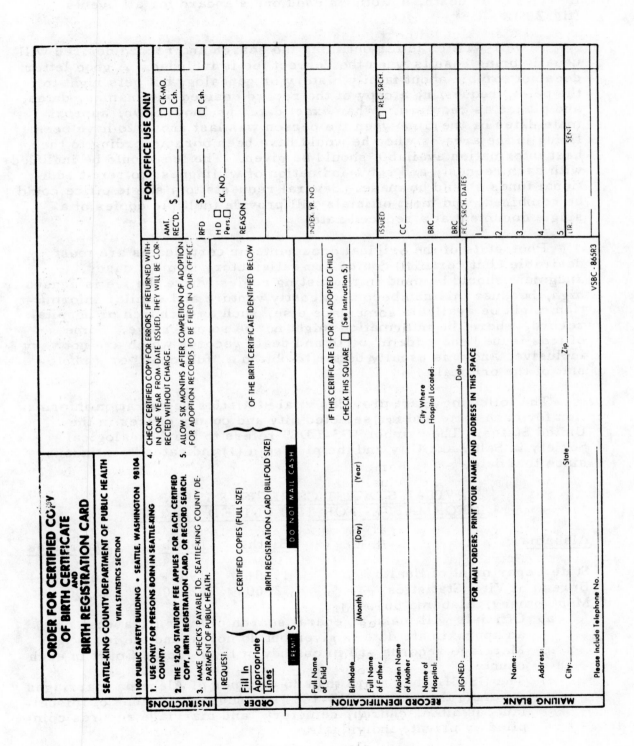

Fig. 209.   Application for vital record

563

Some offices require different forms for each event, such as birth, marriage, or death, but others used one standard for all events (fig. 209).

A well-written letter outlining the search and record desired will usually bring results when the correct fee is included. A good letter does not ramble about family history or genealogy but gets right to the point, requesting a copy of the record desired with names, dates, and places as required. When exact dates are not known, approximate dates or the time when the person was last known to have been living in the area or when he would have been born according to the best information available should be given. The fee should be included with each request, and some indication of willingness to remit additional funds should be made. Several requests to a single office could be combined, and most officials will provide multiple copies of a single document at a reduced rate.

Photostats of the original documents or certificates are most desirable, but certified copies are satisfactory in most cases. Judgment should be used in requesting copies where the fee is unusually high, because this can become a costly venture and similar information might be available someplace else, such as a church or hospital record, where the information might not be so expensive. Some offices issue "short form" birth and death records which are not very inclusive, and it is usually better to obtain a "full copy" or a photostat of the original.

The following chart provides vital statistics registration information for each state and for selected city and county offices in the United States. The symbol "GS-LDS" refers to the Genealogical Society in Salt Lake City and the plus sign (+) indicates "continuous since that date."

VITAL STATISTICS REGISTRATION
INFORMATION FOR THE UNITED STATES

Alabama	Births	Deaths	Marriages
State Department of Health	1908+	1908+	Aug-1936+
Bureau of Vital Statistics	$2.00	$2.00	$2.00
Montgomery, Alabama 36104			

   a. Officials will make a general search of their files when only an approximate date is given but do not refund the fee.

   b. Marriage records are in custody of the Probate Court in each county.

   c. The GS-SLC has more than 26 volumes of Alabama marriages covering the period 1818-1881 and several volumes of miscellaneous bible, church, cemetery, and marriage records compiled by private individuals.

564

Alabama (continued)	Births	Deaths	Marriages
Mobile County Board of Health	1871+	1820+	none
P. O. Box 4533	$1.00	$1.00	
Mobile, Alabama 36604			

    a. Officials will make a general search of their files when only an approximate date is given but do not refund the fee.

    b. Death records 1820-1876 consist only of an index and certificates exist only after 1875.

    c. Marriage records are in custody of the Probate Court Office, County Courthouse, Mobile, Alabama 36604.

Alaska

	Births	Deaths	Marriages
State Dept. of Health & Welfare	1913+	1913+	1913+
Bureau of Vital Statistics	$2.00	$2.00	$2.00
State Office Building			
Juneau, Alaska 99801			

    a. Officials will make a general search of their files when only an approximate date is given but do not refund the fee.

    b. The state office has a few marriage records dating prior to 1913 but they are incomplete.

    c. The GS-SLC currently has no official vital records pertaining to Alaska and has only a few cemetery compilations which were copied by LDS Church members.

American Samoa

	Births	Deaths	Marriages
Registrar of Vital Statistics	1900+	1900+	1900+
Government of American Samoa	$1.00	$1.00	$1.00
Pago Pago, American Samoa 96920			

    a. Officials will make a general search of their files when only an approximate date is given but do not refund the fee.

    b. The GS-SLC currently has no vital record collections pertaining to Samoa.

Arizona

	Births	Deaths	Marriages
State Board of Health	July-1909+	July-1909+	July-1909+
Bureau of Vital Statistics			
Phoenix, Arizona 85007	$2.00	$2.00	$2.00

    a. Officials will make a general search of their files when only an approximate date is given but do not refund the fee.

    b. Marriage records are in custody of the Clerk of the Superior Court in each county.

    c. The GS-SLC currently has only two volumes listed in their catalog which pertain to Arizona vital records and they are cemetery records.

Arkansas	Births	Deaths	Marriages
State Department of Health	1914+	1914+	1917+
Bureau of Vital Statistics	$2.00	$2.00	$2.00
4815 West Markham Street			
Little Rock, Arkansas 72201			

a. Officials will make a general search of their files when only an approximate date is given but do not refund the fee.
b. Marriage records are in custody of the County Clerk in each county.
c. The GS-SLC currently has no official vital records pertaining to Arkansas but does have a few privately compiled cemetery and county marriage collections.

California

	Births	Deaths	Marriages
State Dept. of Public Health	July-	July-	July-
Bureau of Vital Statistics and	1905+	1905+	1905+
Data Processing, 631 J Street	$2.00	$2.00	$2.00
Sacramento, California 95814			

a. State records are computerized and officials must have the name of the person and the date of event before a search can be made. The fee is not refunded.
b. Marriage records are in custody of each County Clerk.
c. The GS-SLC currently has a few volumes of privately compiled church and cemetery records for the state, mainly pertaining to southern California.

	Births	Deaths	Marriages
Alameda County Health Dept.	1870+	1870+	none
499 - 5th Street	$2.00	$2.00	
Oakland, California 94607			

a. Records on file pertain to Oakland and Alameda cities only.
b. Officials will make a general search of their files when only an approximate date is given but charge $2.00 for the first 5 year period search then $2.00 per hour thereafter.
c. Marriage records are in custody of the County Recorder at Oakland.

	Births	Deaths	Marriages
Berkeley City Health Department	1890+	1890+	none
Bureau of Vital Statistics	$2.00	$2.00	
2121 McKinley Avenue			
Berkeley, California 94703			

a. Officials will make no more than a five-year search in their files when only an approximate date is given and do not refund the fee.
b. Marriage records are in custody of the Alameda County Recorder.

California (continued)	Births	Deaths	Marriages
Long Beach City Health Dept.	1895+	1895+	none
Vital Statistics Office	$2.00	$2.00	

P. O. Box 6157
Long Beach, California 90806

    a. Officials will make a general search of their files when only an approximate date is given but refund the fee only when an exact date is given and the record cannot be found.

    b. Marriage records are in custody of the Los Angeles County Recorder and copies are $2.00 each.

	Births	Deaths	Marriages
Los Angeles County Health Dept.	1905+	1905+	1905+
Room 900	$2.00	$2.00	$2.00

220 North Broadway
Los Angeles, California 90012

    a. Officials will make a general search of their files when only an approximate date is given and charge $2.00 per hour, or fraction thereof, for their time.

    b. Records are retained for only a short time and are then transferred to the State Office at Sacramento.

    c. Marriage records are in custody of the County Recorder.

	Births	Deaths	Marriages
Pasadena City Health Department	1890+	1890+	none
Division of Vital Statistics	$2.00	$2.00	

100 North Garfield Avenue
Pasadena, California 91109

    a. Records from 1890-1905 are in a handwritten index book and show the name, date of birth, and parents' names (birth records only).

    b. Officials will make a general search of their files when only an approximate date is given and also refund the fee if the record cannot be located.

    c. Marriage records are in custody of the Los Angeles County Recorder.

	Births	Deaths	Marriages
San Francisco Dept. of Public Health	1905+	1865+	none
101 Grove Street	$2.00	$2.00	

San Francisco, California 94102

    a. Birth records prior to 18 April 1906 were destroyed, except those from 1 July 1905 to 31 March 1906 which have been filed with the State Office at Sacramento.

    b. Death records dating from 8 November 1865 to 31 January 1905 have been preserved, some with indexes and some not.

    c. All original birth and death certificates since 1 July 1905 have been filed monthly with the State Office at Sacramento.

    d. Officials will make a general search of their files when only an approximate date is given but do not refund the fee.

    e. Marriage records covering part of 1904-1906 and from 17 September 1906 to the present time are in custody of the County Recorder, City Hall, San Francisco 94102. Earlier records were destroyed.

Canal Zone	Births	Deaths	Marriages
Canal Zone Government Registrar of Vital Statistics Health Director's Office Box M Balboa Heights, Canal Zone	1905+ $1.00	1905+ $1.00	none

    a. Records are incomplete for the period 1904-1910, and a short form only is issued for births.

    b. Officials will make a general search of their files when only an approximate date is given and also refund the fee when a specified record cannot be located.

    c. Marriage records are in custody of the U. S. District Court, Drawer 2006, Balboa Heights, Canal Zone.

    d. The GS-SLC currently has no vital record collections listed for the Canal Zone.

Colorado

	Births	Deaths	Marriages
State Department of Health Records and Statistics Section 4210 East 11th Avenue Denver, Colorado 80220	1910+ $2.00	1910+ $2.00	to 1940; 1968+ $2.00

    a. Delayed birth and death records have been filed with the State office dating to the early 1860s.

    b. Some marriage records early to 1904 and those after 1968 have been filed with the State office but are also recorded with the County Clerk in each county.

    c. Some early Colorado marriages for the period 1849-1878 have been published in THE COLORADO GENEALOGIST, a quarterly magazine.

    d. Officials will make a general search of their files when only an approximate date is given and will also refund the fee if the search only takes a few minutes.

    e. The GS-SLC currently has only a few privately compiled church, cemetery, and marriage records pertaining to Colorado.

Connecticut

	Births	Deaths	Marriages
State Department of Health Public Health Statistics Section 79 Elm Street Hartford, Connecticut 06115	1897+ $2.00	1897+ $2.00	none

    a. Birth records are held strictly confidential and only the individual, his parent, or his legal representative may obtain copies.

    b. Birth, marriage, and death records have been recorded with each town clerk and date from the organization of the town, or before.

    c. Officials will make a general search of their files for an authorized person when only an approximate date is given but do not refund the fee.

    d.   The GS-SLC has an excellent collection of vital records per-
taining to Connecticut, including
- (1) The Barbour collection of Connecticut vital records which is an alphabetical index to over one million entries from town records (GS #02,887-02,966).
- (2) Microfilm copies of many original town and vital records.
- (3) Over 600 Connecticut church records, mostly Congregational.
- (4) The Charles R. Hale collection of early Connecticut cemetery and newspaper records with over 2000 cemeteries included and newspapers to the Civil War period covered (350 microfilm rolls).
- (5) Seven volumes of early marriage records taken from ancient Connecticut church records and dating early to 1800, compiled by Frederic Bailey.

Delaware

	Births	Deaths	Marriages
State Board of Health	1860+	1860+	1847+
Bureau of Vital Statistics	$2.50	$2.50	$2.00

P. O. Box 637
Dover, Delaware 19901

    a.   Birth and death records are only complete 1860-1863 and after 1880.

    b.   Marriage records are only complete 1847-1863 and after 1880.

    c.   Officials will make a general search of their files for a $1.00 search fee and any amount in excess of that will be refunded on an unproductive search.

    d.   Marriage records, and some birth and death records, date earlier than those shown above but are in custody of the Clerk of the Peace in each county.

    e.   The GS-SLC has an excellent collection of early Delaware vital records, including
- (1) Microfilm copies of index cards showing Delaware births, marriages, and deaths for the period 1680-1913. The records are not complete and have been compiled from many different sources.
- (2) Several compiled collections of church and cemetery records and a few DAR compilations of family bible and cemetery records.
- (3) Microfilm copies of genealogical collections filed with the Hall of Records at Dover, Delaware.

District of Columbia (see Washington, D.C.)

Florida	Births	Deaths	Marriages
State Department of Health	1865+	1877+	1927+
Bureau of Vital Statistics	$2.00	$2.00	$2.00
P. O. Box 210			
Jacksonville, Florida 32201			

a. Birth and death records prior to 1914 are incomplete.
b. Officials will make a general search of their files when only an approximate date is given but charge $1.00 for each year searched.
c. Marriage records are in custody of the County Judge's Office in each county.
d. The GS-SLC currently has only a few privately compiled church and cemetery records pertaining to Florida and has only one roll of microfilm listed which contains DAR family and bible records.

Hillsborough County Health Dept.	1875+	1910+	none
Division of Vital Statistics	$2.00	$2.00	
P. O. Box 1731			
Tampa, Florida 33601			

a. Birth records are held strictly confidential and only a short form will be provided authorized persons.
b. Officials will make a general search of their files when only an approximate date is given but do not refund the fee.
c. Marriage records are in custody of the County Judge's Office.

Georgia

State Dept. of Public Health	1919+	1919+	1953+
Vital Records Service	$3.00	$3.00	$1.00
47 Trinity Avenue, S. W.			
Atlanta, Georgia 30334			

a. Birth records are held strictly confidential and copies will only be provided authorized persons.
b. Officials will make a limited search of a year or two in their files for the $1.00 fee but a $10.00 fee is required for an unlimited search. No refund is made.
c. Marriage records are in custody of the Court of Ordinary in each county and often date from the organization of the county.
d. The GS-SLC has a good collection of records pertaining to Georgia, including
   (1) Microfilm copies of county marriage records which often date to the 1795-1800 period. No birth and death records were kept early in Georgia counties.
   (2) Several privately compiled vital, church, cemetery, and marriage record collections.
   (3) Several published DAR vital record collections.

Georgia (continued)	Births	Deaths	Marriages
Chatham County Health Dept.	1890+	1803+	none
Division of Vital Records	$1.00	$1.00	

Intermediate at Meridian Road
P. O. Box 6648
Savannah, Georgia 31405

   a. Officials will make a general search of their files when only an approximate date is given but do not refund the fee.

   b. Marriage records are in custody of the Court of Ordinary, P. O. Box 2206, Savannah.

Guam

	Births	Deaths	Marriages
Department of Public Health &	Oct-	Oct-	1899+
Social Services	1901+	1901+	$1.00
Government of Guam	$1.00	$1.00	

P. O. Box 2816
Agana, Guam 96910

   a. Officials will make a general search of their files when only an approximate date is given and will also refund the fee when a specified record cannot be located.

   b. The GS-SLC currently has no vital records pertaining to Guam listed in their card catalog.

Hawaii

	Births	Deaths	Marriages
State Department of Health	1850+	1861+	1849+
Research and Statistics Office	$2.00	$2.00	$2.00

P. O. Box 3378
Honolulu, Hawaii 96801

   a. Birth records are held strictly confidential and normally certified copies are released to the registrants only.

   b. Officials will not accept orders unless the requestor can furnish specific and detailed identifying information, including full names, date of the event, and place of the event.

   c. When the request is made by a person other than the registrant, the reason and fee must be included.

   d. The fee is not refunded on a negative search.

   e. The GS-SLC currently has no vital record collections pertaining to Hawaii, other than LDS Church records; but it does have an excellent historical collection pertaining to the Islands and also has an excellent collection of family group records pertaining to Polynesians.

Idaho

	Births	Deaths	Marriages
State Department of Health	1911+	1911+	1911+
Bureau of Vital Statistics	$2.00	$2.00	$2.00

Boise, Idaho 83707

   a. All records are held strictly confidential and are released only to authorized persons.

b. Records are filed alphabetically by each year so the date of an event must be given to locate a desired record. No refund is made.
c. Idaho officials have something against genealogists so it is well not to indicate genealogy as a purpose for which records are requested.
d. Marriage records are in custody of the County Recorder in each county and they are much more cooperative than State officials.
e. The GS-SLC currently has a poor collection of vital records for Idaho consisting primarily of a few privately compiled cemetery records.

Illinois

	Births	Deaths	Marriages
Department of Public Health	1916+	1916+	1962+
Bureau of Vital Records	$2.00	$2.00	$2.00

525 West Jefferson Street
Springfield, Illinois 62706

a. Legislation in 1960 rendered all state and county vital records confidential though copies may be provided interested persons for a fee.
b. Officials will make a general search of their files when only an approximate date is given but do not refund the fee.
c. Birth and death records were kept in many counties as early as 1850-1870 and copies may be obtained from the County Clerk for a fee.
d. Marriage records are in custody of each County Clerk and date from the organization of the county.
e. The GS-SLC currently has a poor collection of Illinois vital records, consisting mainly of a few privately compiled cemetery and newspaper collections with a few DAR compilations.

	Births	Deaths	Marriages
Chicago Board of Health	1955+	1955+	none
Room CL - 111 Civic Center	$2.00	$2.00	

Chicago, Illinois 60602

a. Birth and death records are held confidential but officials will provide copies to interested persons for the fee.
b. Marriage records are in custody of the Cook County Clerk.

	Births	Deaths	Marriages
Peoria City Health Department	1878+	1872+	none
2116 North Sheridan Road	$2.00	$2.00	

Peoria, Illinois 61604

a. Officials will make a general search of their files when only an approximate date is given but do not refund the fee. $2.00 is charged for the first copy and $1.00 for each additional copy.
b. Marriage records are in custody of the Peoria County Clerk at the Courthouse, Peoria.

Indiana	Births	Deaths	Marriages
State Board of Health	Oct-	Oct-	none
Division of Vital Records	1907+	1907+	
1330 W. Michigan Street	$3.00	$3.00	
Indianapolis, Indiana 46207			

    a. Officials will make a general search of their files when only an approximate date is given and will also refund the fee when a specified record is not located.

    b. Birth and death records for the period 1882-1908 exist for most counties and typed copies are filed with each County Clerk and with the State Library at Indianapolis.

    c. Marriage records are in custody of each County Clerk and often date from the organization of the county.

    d. The State Library, 126 North Senate Avenue, Indianapolis 46200 has an excellent collection of Indiana county birth, marriage, and death records but an interested person must employ an agent or go there himself to make use of the records.

    e. The GS-SLC has a poor collection of Indiana vital records; consisting of a few published county birth and death records (1882-1908) and a few privately compiled church and cemetery records. The Society is now purchasing microfilm copies of county records and plans soon to film records at the State Library.

    f. County and City Board of Health officials are very cooperative in Indiana and often will search their files for existing birth, marriage, and death records for a very reasonable fee.

	Births	Deaths	Marriages
Gary City Board of Health	1908+	1908+	none
Vital Records Department	$1.00	$1.00	
1429 Virginia Street			
Gary, Indiana 46407			

    a. Officials will make a general search of their files when only an approximate date is given and also refund the fee when a specified record cannot be located.

    b. Marriage records are in custody of the Lake County Clerk, Gary.

    c. The Lake County Clerk also has copies of birth and death records for the period 1882-1908.

	Births	Deaths	Marriages
Marion County Health Department	1882+	1882+	none
1841 City-County Building	$1.00	$1.00	
Indianapolis, Indiana 46204			

    a. Officials will make a general search of their files when only an approximate date is given and also refund the fee when a specified record cannot be located.

    b. Marriage records are in custody of the County Clerk, Suite 122, City-County Building, Indianapolis.

Iowa	Births	Deaths	Marriages
State Department of Health	July-	July-	July-
Records & Statistics Division	1880+	1880+	1880+
Des Moines, Iowa 50319	$2.00	$2.00	$1.00

  a. Indexes for births begin 1880, for deaths in 1896, and for marriages in 1916 and officials will make a general search of the files only after those dates. The fee is not refunded.
  b. Marriage records are in custody of the Probate Court in each county and often date from the organization of the county.
  c. The GS-SLC currently has a poor collection of vital records pertaining to Iowa, consisting only of a few volumes of privately compiled cemetery, church, and newspaper collections.

Kansas

	Births	Deaths	Marriages
State Department of Health	July-	July-	May-
Division of Vital Statistics	1911+	1911+	1913+
Records Section	$2.00	$2.00	$2.00
Topeka, Kansas 66612			

  a. Illegitimacy indicated in any record renders it confidential, but otherwise birth, marriage, and death records may be copied.
  b. Officials will make a general search of their files for a $1.00 fee and also refund the fee when a specified record cannot be located.
  c. Kansas City, Kansas, has a few birth and death records dating from 1892 which are in custody of the City Clerk, City Hall, 6th and Ann, Kansas City, Kansas 66101.
  d. Marriage records are in custody of the Probate Judge in each county and often date from the organization of the county.
  e. The Kansas State Historical Society at Topeka has an excellent collection of marriage, church, and cemetery records pertaining to the state.
  f. The GS-SLC currently has a poor collection of vital records pertaining to Kansas, consisting of a few Catholic church records and privately compiled cemetery records.

Kentucky

	Births	Deaths	Marriages
State Department of Health	1911+	1911+	July-
Office of Vital Statistics	$2.00	$2.00	1958+
275 East Main Street			$2.00
Frankfort, Kentucky 40601			

  a. Officials will make a general search of their files when only an approximate date is given but do not refund the fee.
  b. Marriage records are in custody of each County Clerk and date from the organization of the county.
  c. The GS-SLC has an excellent collection of Kentucky vital records including

Kentucky (continued)	Births	Deaths	Marriages

(1) Births, deaths, and marriages for the period 1852-1910 on 29 rolls of microfilm.

(2) Births, deaths, and marriages for the period 1911-1954 on 91 rolls of microfilm.

(3) Several volumes of county marriage records covering the period 1790-1850; also many original records on film.

(4) THE KENTUCKY GENEALOGICAL REGISTER, a quarterly magazine which contains county vital record information.

(5) Several volumes of privately compiled church, cemetery, marriage, and family bible records.

Louisiana

	Births	Deaths	Marriages
State Department of Health	1914+	1914+	none
Bureau of Vital Records	$2.00	$2.00	
P. O. Box 60631			
New Orleans, Louisiana 70630			

a. Records are restricted to members of the family or persons who have a tangible interest therein.

b. Officials will make a general search of their files when only an approximate date is given but do not refund the fee. Records are filed alphabetically by year.

c. Marriage records are in custody of the Clerk of Court in each parish (county).

d. The GS-SLC has a good collection of Louisiana parish (county) records and is currently microfilming there. No birth and death records were kept early on a county basis but marriage records were and some date from the 1700s. Vital information is also recorded in other parish (county) records, including land and court records.

	Births	Deaths	Marriages
New Orleans City Health Dept.	1790+	1804+	1831
Bureau of Vital Records	$2.00	$2.00	$2.00
City Hall - Civic Center			
New Orleans, Louisiana 70112			

a. Records are confidential by a recent act of the State Legislature but copies may be provided authorized persons for a fee.

b. Officials will make a three-year search for the $2.00 fee when an exact date is not given but do not refund the fee when a specified record is not found.

c. The GS-SLC currently has a few early Catholic church records for New Orleans and a few privately compiled cemetery records for different parts of Louisiana.

575

Louisiana (continued)	Births	Deaths	Marriages
Caddo-Shreveport Health Unit	1875+	1875+	none
P. O. Box 3008	$2.00	$2.00	
Shreveport, Louisiana 71103			

    a. Officials will make a general search of their files when an approximate date is given but do not refund the fee.

    b. Marriage records are in custody of the Clerk of Court for Caddo County.

Maine

State Dept. of Health & Welfare	1892+	1892+	1892+
Office of Vital Statistics	$1.00	$1.00	$1.00
State House			
Augusta, Maine 04330			

    a. Officials will make a general search of their files when only an approximate date is given but do not refund the fee.

    b. Birth, marriage, and death information prior to 1892 is recorded in town and vital records and in custody of each Town Clerk.

    c. Town Clerks will also make searches in their records for vital information.

    d. The GS-SLC has an excellent collection of vital records pertaining to Maine including

        (1) An alphabetical index to vital records of over 80 Maine towns covering the period 1640-1892 on 141 rolls of microfilm.

        (2) An alphabetical index to vital records in the Secretary of State office covering the period 1892-1907 on 184 rolls of microfilm.

        (3) Brides index to marriages for the period 1895-1953 on 111 rolls of microfilm.

        (4) Microfilm copies of several early church records.

        (5) Several volumes of privately compiled church, cemetery, and marriage records.

        (6) Several private genealogical collections in manuscript form and also on microfilm.

        (7) THE NEW ENGLAND HISTORICAL AND GENEALOGICAL REGISTER which carries many early Maine church and vital records.

Maryland

State Department of Health	1898+	1898+	June-1951+
Division of Vital Records	$2.00	$2.00	$2.00
301 West Preston Street			
Baltimore, Maryland 21201			

    a. All records are held to be confidential but officials will make a general search of their files for an authorized person but the fee is not refunded.

   b.   Marriage records were kept on a county basis but early records have been transferred to the Hall of Records at Annapolis.

   c.   The GS-SLC has a good collection of Maryland vital records including

     (1) All important genealogical records in custody of the Hall of Records at Annapolis.

     (2) Miscellaneous birth records for the period 1801-1877.

     (3) Miscellaneous death records for the period 1865-1880.

     (4) Miscellaneous marriage records for the period 1777-1850.

     (5) Privately compiled marriage records for the period 1700-1800.

     (6) An excellent collection of Maryland church records on film and in book form.

     (7) A good collection of DAR compilations.

     (8) Several volumes of privately compiled cemetery records.

	Births	Deaths	Marriages
Baltimore City Health Dept.	1875+	1875+	none
Bureau of Vital Records	$2.00	$2.00	
Municipal Office Building			
Baltimore, Maryland 21202			

   a.   Officials will make a general search of their files when only an approximate date is given but do not refund the fee. A search fee of $2.00 is required for the first three consecutive calendar years of search and $1.00 is charged for each three years thereafter.

   b.   Marriage records were kept on a county basis and the GS-SLC has Baltimore County marriage records dating from the late 1700s. Originals are at the Hall of Records at Annapolis.

Massachusetts

	Births	Deaths	Marriages
Office of the Secretary of State	1841+	1841+	1841+
Division of Vital Statistics	$1.00	$1.00	$1.00
Room 272 State House			
Boston, Massachusetts 02133			

   a.   Officials will make a five-year search in their files for the prescribed fee and will also refund the fee if a specified record cannot be located.

   b.   Birth, marriage, and death statistics are recorded in town, proprietor, and vital records on a town basis and Town Clerks may also be called upon to provide vital statistics.

   c.   About 60 percent of the early Massachusetts towns have published vital records pertaining to their respective towns and have also included facts from church, cemetery, and family records.

   d.   The GS-SLC has an excellent collection of vital records pertaining to Massachusetts and is presently filming additional records on a town, county, and state basis. Current collections include

Massachusetts (continued)	Births	Deaths	Marriages

(1) Original town and vital records on microfilm.
(2) Over 200 volumes of compiled vital statistics.
(3) A good collection of original church records.
(4) An excellent collection of private genealogical material.
(5) Several volumes of privately compiled family and cemetery records.
(6) State vital records dating from 1841.

	Births	Deaths	Marriages
Cambridge City Clerks Office	1635+	1638+	1648+
City Hall	$1.00	$1.00	$1.00
Cambridge, Massachusetts 02139			

a. Officials will make a general search of their files when only an approximate date is given and will also refund the fee when a specified record cannot be located.
b. The GS-SLC is currently filming Massachusetts town records and is about 90 percent finished.

	Births	Deaths	Marriages
Worcester City Clerks Office	1714+	1714+	1714+
Room 206 - City Hall	$1.00	$1.00	$1.00
Worcester, Massachusetts 01608			

Officials will make a general search of their files when only an approximate date is given and will also refund the fee when a specified record cannot be located.

Michigan

	Births	Deaths	Marriages
State Dept. of Public Health	1867+	1867+	1868+
Division of Vital Statistics	$2.00	$2.00	$2.00
3500 North Logan Street			
Lansing, Michigan 48914			

a. Officials will make a general search of their files charging $2.00 for the first year (includes certified copy when found) and 50 cents for each additional year to be searched.
b. Marriage records, and a few birth and death records, are available from the county offices prior to state registration. They are in custody of the Clerk of the Circuit Court at the county seat.
c. The GS-SLC currently has a poor collection of Michigan vital records consisting of a few privately compiled church, cemetery, and marriage records.
d. Records 1867-1906 are incomplete in the State office.

	Births	Deaths	Marriages
Kent County Clerk's Office	1867+	1867+	1845+
300 Monroe Avenue N.W.	$2.00	$2.00	$2.00
Grand Rapids, Michigan 49502			

Officials will make a general search of their files for the prescribed fee and charge 50¢ for duplicate copies of certificates when they are ordered at the same time.

Michigan (continued)	Births	Deaths	Marriages
Flint City Department of Health	1886+	1879+	none
Vital Records Section	$2.00	$2.00	
121 East Seventh Street			
Flint, Michigan 48502			

    a.   Birth and death records are incomplete.

    b.   A $2.00 fee is charged for each year searched and the fee is refunded when a specified record cannot be located.

    c.   The City and County Health Departments are expected to merge in the near future.

Minnesota

	Births	Deaths	Marriages
State Department of Health	1900+	1900+	1958+
Section of Vital Statistics	$2.00	$2.00	free
717 Delaware S.E.			
Minneapolis, Minnesota 55440			

    a.   Officials will make a general search of their files when only an approximate date is given but do not refund the fee.

    b.   State marriage records consist of an index only and the original marriage records are in custody of the Clerk of the District Court in each county.

    c.   Some city health departments have records which date prior to that of the state.

    d.   The GS-SLC currently has a poor collection of vital records pertaining to Minnesota, consisting of one volume of church records, two volumes of cemetery records, and three volumes of DAR family and bible records.

	Births	Deaths	Marriages
St. Louis County	1870+	1870+	1870+
Clerk of the District Court	$2.00	$2.00	$1.00
320 Court House			
Duluth, Minnesota 55802			

    a.   Officials will make a general search of their files and charge $1.00 for each five-year period searched when the exact date is not given.

    b.   Birth and death records are somewhat incomplete in the earlier period but marriage records are quite complete.

	Births	Deaths	Marriages
Minneapolis City Health Dept.	1885+	1903+	none
Public Health Center			
250 South 4th Street			
Minneapolis, Minnesota 55415			

    a.   Officials will make a general search of their files when only an approximate date is given but do not refund the fee.

    b.   Marriage records are in custody of the Clerk of the District Court for Hennepin County, Room 302, City Hall, Minneapolis, Minnesota 55415.

Minnesota (continued)	Births	Deaths	Marriages
St. Paul City Bureau of Health	1857+	1870+	none
Public Health Center	$2.00	$2.00	
555 Cedar Street			
St. Paul, Minnesota 55101			

    a. Officials will make a general search of their files when only an approximate date is given but do not refund the fee.

    b. Marriage records are in custody of the Ramsey County Clerk of the District Court.

Mississippi

State Board of Health	Nov-1912+	Nov-1912+	1926+
Vital Records Registration	$2.00	$2.00	$1.00
P. O. Box 1700			
Jackson, Mississippi 39205			

    a. All records are considered confidential but officials will search their files for an authorized person. A three-year search will be made for the regular fee but no refund is made when a specified record is not located.

    b. Marriage records are in custody of the Clerk of the Circuit Court in each county.

    c. The Department of Archives and History at Jackson, Mississippi, has copies of many marriage records dating to 1826.

    d. The GS-SLC currently has a poor collection of vital records pertaining to Mississippi, consisting of only a few privately compiled church, cemetery, and marriage records. However, they are now filming original county records which include probate, court, and land records.

Missouri

State Division of Health	1910+	1910+	July-1948+
Vital Records	$1.00	$1.00	$1.00
Jefferson City, Missouri 65101			

    a. Officials will make a general search of their files when only an approximate date is given but do not refund the fee.

    b. Marriage records are in custody of the Recorder of Deeds in each county and many date from the organization of the county.

    c. The GS-SLC currently has a poor collection of vital records pertaining to Missouri, consisting primarily of two or three counties' marriage records, a few volumes of DAR records, and a few volumes of privately compiled cemetery and marriage records.

Missouri (continued)	Births	Deaths	Marriages
Kansas City Health Department	1874+	1874+	none
10th Floor - City Hall	$2.00	$2.00	
Kansas City, Missouri 64106			

    a. Officials will make a general search of their files when only an approximate date is given and will also refund the fee when a prescribed record cannot be located, unless a great deal of time has gone into the search.

    b. Marriage records are in custody of the Jackson County Recorder of Deeds.

	Births	Deaths	Marriages
St. Louis Department of Health	1870+	1850+	none
Bureau of Vital Statistics	$2.00	$2.00	
Room 10 Municipal Courts Building			
1320 Market Street			
St. Louis, Missouri 63103			

    a. Birth and death records are incomplete prior to February 1910 when registration became mandatory.

    b. Records indicating illegitimacy are confidential but otherwise officials will make a search of their files charging $1.00 for each three-year period searched. Half of the fee ($1.00) is refunded when a specified record cannot be located in the files.

    c. The GS-SLC has a few early LDS branch records on microfilm which pertain to St. Louis.

Montana

	Births	Deaths	Marriages
State Department of Health	1907+	1907+	1943+
Records and Statistics	$2.00	$2.00	$2.00
Helena, Montana 59601			

    a. Officials will make a five-year search of their files without a special search fee but charge $2.50 per hour or fraction thereof if a wider search is required.

    b. The fee is refunded in a majority of the cases when a specified record cannot be located.

    c. Marriage records are in custody of the Clerk of Court in each county and most of them date from the organization of the county.

    d. The GS-SLC currently has a poor collection of vital records pertaining to Montana consisting of only one volume of cemetery records.

Nebraska

	Births	Deaths	Marriages
State Department of Health	1904+	1904+	1909+
Vital Statistics	$2.00	$2.00	$2.00
Box 94757			
Lincoln, Nebraska 68509			

    a. Officials will make a general search of their files when only an approximate date is given but do not refund the fee.

b.   Marriage records are in custody of the County Judge in each
     county.
c.   The GS-SLC currently has a poor collection of vital records
     pertaining to Nebraska, consisting of two or three volumes
     of privately compiled cemetery records.

Omaha-Douglas County Health Dept.   1873+   1873+   none
Division of Vital Statistics $2.00 $2.00
1602 South 50th Street
Omaha, Nebraska 68106
   a.   Records are considered confidential and officials decide the
        merit of each request individually. They will make a general
        search of their files when sufficient identifying information
        is provided and also refund the fee when a specified record
        cannot be located.
   b.   Marriage records are in custody of the Douglas County Court
        and date from 1856.

Nevada

State Department of Health   July-   July-   1968+
Welfare and Rehabilitation   1911+   1911+ $2.00
Section of Vital Statistics $2.00 $2.00
Carson City, Nevada 89701
   a.   Officials will make a general search of their files when only
        an approximate date is given but do not refund the fee.
   b.   Some counties have birth and death records dating from 1887
        to 1911.
   c.   Marriage records are in custody of the County Recorder in
        each county.
   d.   The GS-SLC currently has only a fair collection of vital
        records pertaining to Nevada, consisting of a few volumes
        of cemetery-sextons' records, a few volumes of morticians'
        records, and a few volumes of privately compiled church
        records.

New Hampshire

State Dept. of Health & Welfare   1640+   1640+   1640+
Bureau of Vital Statistics $1.00 $1.00 $1.00
61 South Spring Street
Concord, New Hampshire 03301
   a.   Officials will make a general search of their files when only
        an approximate date is given but do not refund the fee.
   b.   Birth, marriage, and death records were a matter of town
        record and Town Clerks are able to provide vital statistics
        also.
   c.   The GS-SLC has an excellent collection of vital records per-
        taining to New Hampshire including

(1) An alphabetical index to all names listed in existing town records on 111 rolls of microfilm (GS #3663 pts 1-111).
(2) Microfilm copies of many original and copied town records on over 320 rolls of microfilm (GS #3663 pts 112-432).
(3) New Hampshire vital records contained in the HAZELTINE PAPERS covering the period 1719-1900.
(4) Several church records on microfilm.
(5) Several volumes of privately compiled church and cemetery records.
(6) An excellent collection of published local history books, many of which contain vital statistics.
(7) A few vital record collections taken from newspapers.

New Jersey

	Births	Deaths	Marriages
State Department of Health	June-	June-	June-
Bureau of Vital Statistics	1878+	1878+	1878+
P. O. Box 1540	$2.00	$2.00	$2.00
Trenton, New Jersey 08625			

a. Birth, marriage, and death records from May 1848 through May 1878 are in custody of the Archives and History Bureau, State Library Division, Trenton, New Jersey.
b. Officials will make a search of their files charging $2.00 for the first year and fifty cents for each year thereafter and do not refund the fee when a specified record cannot be located.
c. Marriage records were not kept on a county or a state basis in any uniform manner until 1848 but many marriages from a variety of sources have been published in volume 22 of the New Jersey Archives, Series 1 which cover the period 1665-1800.
d. The GS-SLC has a fair collection of vital records pertaining to New Jersey including
   (1) Microfilmed copies of early state records 1848-1878.
   (2) Special WPA indexes to records dating early to 1900.
   (3) Marriages 1665-1800 compiled by Wm Nelson (N.J. Archives).
   (4) Marriage bonds 1670-1800 filed at the State Library.
   (5) Miscellaneous birth, marriage, and death records filed at the State Library, on 290 rolls of microfilm.
   (6) Several volumes of DAR record compilations.
   (7) Several volumes of privately compiled church and cemetery records.

	Births	Deaths	Marriages
Camden City Dept. of Health	1924+	1924+	1924+
Bureau of Vital Statistics	$1.00	$1.00	$1.00
Room 103, City Hall			
Camden, New Jersey 08100			

a. Officials will make a one-year search before and after the specified date for the prescribed fee and will also refund the fee when a record is not located.

New Jersey (continued)	Births	Deaths	Marriages
Elizabeth City Dept. of Health Bureau of Vital Statistics City Hall Elizabeth, New Jersey 07201	1848+ $2.00	1848+ $2.00	1848+ $2.00

    a.   Birth records are considered confidential and only a short form is issued to authorized persons.

    b.   Officials will search their files only when an exact date is given but do refund the fee when a record cannot be located.

	Births	Deaths	Marriages
Newark City Division of Health Bureau of Vital Statistics City Hall Newark, New Jersey 07102	1850+ $2.00	1850+ $2.00	1850+ $2.00

    Officials will make a general search of their files for the prescribed fee but do not refund it when a specified record cannot be located.

	Births	Deaths	Marriages
Paterson City Board of Health 25 Mill Street Paterson, New Jersey 07501	1902+ $2.00	1910+ $2.00	1910+ $2.00

    a.   Records are considered strictly confidential.

    b.   Officials will make a three-year search for the prescribed fee and charge fifty cents for each year thereafter but do not refund the fee when a record cannot be located.

New Mexico

	Births	Deaths	Marriages
State Department of Health & Social Services P. O. Box 2348 Santa Fe, New Mexico 87501	1920+ $1.00	1920+ $1.00	none

    a.   Officials will make a general search of their files when only an approximate date is given but do not refund the fee.

    b.   Marriage records are in custody of the County Clerk in each county.

    c.   The GS-SLC currently has a poor collection of vital records pertaining to New Mexico consisting of only two or three volumes of privately compiled cemetery and family bible records.

New York

	Births	Deaths	Marriages
State Department of Health Office of Vital Records 84 Holland Avenue Albany, New York 12208	1880+ $2.50	1880+ $2.50	1880+ $2.00

    a.   State office does not have records 1880-1914 for Albany, Buffalo, nor Yonkers, q.v.

b.   For New York City records, see the respective boroughs of Bronx, Brooklyn, Manhattan, Queens, or Richmond.

c.   Officials will search a two consecutive year period for the initial $2.00 fee but the fee is not refunded when a record cannot be found. Duplicate copies of records requested are $1.00 each.

d.   The GS-SLC has a good collection of vital records pertaining to New York and is presently microfilming extensively in the state. Records on file at Salt Lake City include

    (1)   County birth, marriage, and death records 1847-1852.

    (2)   One volume of marriages recorded with the Secretary of State 1664-1784 (GS #974.7 V25m).

    (3)   An excellent collection of Quaker (Friends) records on 152 rolls of microfilm.

    (4)   An excellent collection of Reformed Church records known as the "Vosburgh Collection" on 61 rolls of micro-film (GS #4025 pts 1-61).

    (5)   Several volumes of newspaper clippings containing vital records.

    (6)   Several volumes of privately compiled church and cemetery records.

    (7)   Several volumes of DAR records.

	Births	Deaths	Marriages
Albany City Health Department	Sept-	Sept-	none
Registrar of Vital Statistics	1870+	1870+	
City Hall	$2.00	$2.00	
Albany, New York 12207			

a.   Officials will make a two consecutive year search for the $2.00 fee and charge $1.00 each for duplicate copies but they do not refund the fee when a record is not located.

b.   Marriage records are in custody of the City Clerk, Room 202, City Hall, Albany.

	Births	Deaths	Marriages
Buffalo City Health Department	1878+	1852+	none
Registrar of Vital Statistics	$2.50	$2.50	$2.00
Room 613, City Hall			
Buffalo, New York 14202			

a.   Birth records are considered strictly confidential but officials will search their files for authorized persons but the fee is not refunded when a specified record is not located.

b.   Marriage records are in custody of the Marriage License Bureau, 1301 City Hall, Buffalo.

	Births	Deaths	Marriages
Bronx District Health Center	1898+	1898+	none
1826 Arthur Avenue	$2.50	$2.50	
Bronx, New York 10457			

a.   Records for the period 1866-1897 are filed with the Manhattan Health Center, q.v.

b.   Birth records are considered strictly confidential but officials

will search their files for authorized persons. The fee is not
refunded.

c. Marriage records are in custody of the City Clerk, 1780
    Grand Concourse, New York, New York 10457 and the fee
    is $2.05 for a copy.

Brooklyn District Health Center	1866+	1866+	none
295 Flatbush Avenue Ext.	$2.50	$2.50	
Brooklyn, New York 11201			

a. Records registered prior to 1866 for Old City of Brooklyn
    are filed with the Kings County Clerk's Office, Historical
    Division, 360 Adams Street, Brooklyn, New York 11201.
b. Birth records are considered strictly confidential but offi-
    cials will search their files for authorized persons. The
    fee is not refunded.
c. Marriage records are in custody of the City Clerk, Municipal
    Building, Brooklyn, New York 11201 and the fee is $2.05.

Manhattan District Health Center	1866+	1866+	none
125 Worth Street	$2.50	$2.50	
New York, New York 10013			

a. Death records prior to 1866 are in custody of the Municipal
    Archives and Records Retention Center of the New York
    Public Library, 238 William Street, New York, New York 10038.
b. Birth records are considered strictly confidential but offi-
    cials will search their files for authorized persons. The fee
    is not refunded.
c. Marriage records are in custody of the City Clerk, Municipal
    Building, New York, New York 10007 and the fee is $2.05.

Queens District Health Center	1898+	1898+	none
90-37 Parsons Boulevard	$2.50	$2.50	
Jamaica, New York 11432			

a. Records prior to 1898 are in custody of the State Department
    of Health at Albany.
b. Birth records are considered strictly confidential but offi-
    cials will search their files for authorized persons. The
    fee is not refunded.
c. Marriage records are in custody of the City Clerk, 88-11
    Sutphin Boulevard, Jamaica, New York 11435 and the fee is
    $2.05.

Richmond District Health Center	1898+	1898+	none
55-61 Stuyvesant Place, St. George	$2.50	$2.50	
Staten Island, New York 10301			

a. Records prior to 1898 are filed with the State Department
    of Health at Albany.
b. Birth records are considered strictly confidential but offi-
    cials will search their files for authorized persons. The
    fee is not refunded.

   c.   Marriage records are in custody of the City Clerk, Borough
        Hall, Staten Island, New York 10301 and the fee is $2.05.

| Monroe County Health Department | 1875+ | 1875+ | 1886-1907 |
| Office of Vital Statistics | $2.00 | $2.00 | $2.00 |

111 Westfall Road
Rochester, New York 14602

   a.   Birth and death records from 1875 are for Rochester City
        only and are incomplete.
   b.   Marriage records after 1907 are in custody of the City Clerk,
        City Hall, Rochester, New York 14614.
   c.   Officials will make a general search of their files and charge
        $2.50 per hour but the initial fee is not refunded.

| Syracuse City Health Department | 1873+ | 1873+ | 1873-1914 |
| Bureau of Vital Statistics | $2.00 | $2.00 | $2.00 |

300 S. Geddes Street
Box 1325
Syracuse, New York 13201

   a.   Birth and death records on file are for Onondaga County.
   b.   Marriage records 1873-1914 on file pertain to Syracuse
        City only and records after 1914 are in custody of the City
        Clerk at the City Hall in Syracuse.
   c.   Birth records are held strictly confidential but officials will
        search their files for authorized persons. The fee is not
        refunded.

| Utica City Health Department | 1873+ | 1865+ | none |
| Bureau of Vital Statistics | $2.00 | $2.00 | |

406 Elizabeth Street
Utica, New York 13501

   a.   Officials will make a search of their files only when the month
        and year of the event is given and will refund the initial $2.00
        fee when a specified record cannot be located.
   b.   Marriage records are in custody of the City Clerk, City Hall.

| Yonkers City Dept. of Public Health | 1875+ | 1875+ | none |
| Bureau of Vital Statistics | $2.00 | $2.00 | |

Yonkers, New York 10701

   a.   For records after 1914, write to the State Department of
        Health at Albany.
   b.   Marriage records are in custody of the City Clerk, City Hall.
   c.   Officials will make a general search of their files when only
        an approximate date is given but do not refund the fee.

NOTE: Many township and county historians in New York have special
        vital record collections pertaining to their respective areas.
        They are often very cooperative with genealogists and can pro-
        vide excellent help in many instances.

North Carolina	Births	Deaths	Marriages
State Board of Health	Oct-	1906+	1962+
Office of Vital Statistics	1913+	$2.00	$2.00
P. O. Box 2091	$2.00		
Raleigh, North Carolina 27602			

    a. Officials will make a three-year search of their files for the $2.00 fee but do not refund it when a record cannot be located.

    b. Marriage records are in custody of the Register of Deeds in each county. Marriage bonds covering the period 1760-1968 have been published and are on file at Salt Lake City.

    c. The GS-SLC has a good collection of existing vital records pertaining to North Carolina including

        (1) County marriage bonds, early to 1968.

        (2) Microfilm copies of original county marriage records.

        (3) Several volumes of privately compiled vital, church, and cemetery records.

        (4) Several volumes of DAR records.

        (5) Several private genealogical collections.

        (6) A few vital record collections taken from local newspapers.

North Dakota			
State Department of Health	1893+	1893+	July-1925+
Division of Vital Statistics	$2.00	$2.00	$1.00
17th Floor, State Capitol			
Bismarck, North Dakota 58501			

    a. Birth records are held strictly confidential and certificates are issued only to authorized persons or agencies.

    b. Officials will search their statewide alphabetical index but without specific identifying facts, it is difficult for them to locate a particular record.

    c. Marriage records are in custody of the County Judge in each county.

Ohio			
State Department of Health	Dec-	Dec-	Sept-
Division of Vital Statistics	1908+	1908+	1949+
65 South Front Street Room G-20	$1.00	$1.00	$2.00
Ohio Departments Building			
Columbus, Ohio 43215			

    a. Officials will make a general search of their files and charge $2.00 per hour or fraction thereof. They can search a ten-year period in one hour for one name and charge $1.00 for a certified or photostat copy, which is in addition to the $2.00 search fee when a general search is necessary.

    b. Marriage records are in custody of the Probate Court in each county.

    c. Many Ohio county marriage records have been copied and filed at the Western Reserve Historical Society Library in Cleveland.

    d. The GS-SLC has a good collection of existing vital records pertaining to Ohio and has recently completed filming about 75 percent of Ohio county records. The Society's collection includes

        (1) Ohio marriage records from the State Library at Columbus on 228 rolls of microfilm (GS #41094 pts 1-228).

        (2) An excellent collection of soldiers' grave registrations on 92 rolls of microfilm (GS #25116 pts 1-92).

        (3) Several volumes of DAR records.

        (4) Several volumes of privately compiled church, cemetery, and marriage records.

	Births	Deaths	Marriages
Cleveland City Health Department	1878+	1878+	1880+
Bureau of Vital Statistics	$1.00	$1.00	$.50
Room 18, City Hall			
Cleveland, Ohio 44114			

    a. Officials request an exact date of an event to search their files and will refund the fee when a specified record is not located.

    b. Marriage records prior to 1880 are in custody of the Probate Court, 1230 Ontario Street, Cleveland, Ohio.

	Births	Deaths	Marriages
Dayton City Health Department	June-	June-	none
Bureau of Vital Statistics	1867+	1867+	
Room 409, Municipal Building	$1.00	$1.00	
101 West Third Street			
Dayton, Ohio 45402			

    a. Officials must have the exact date of an event to locate a record prior to 1909 but from that date they have an alphabetical file and can check for a record with only an approximate date. The fee is refunded when a specified record is not found.

    b. Marriage records are in custody of the Probate Court at the Montgomery County courthouse.

	Births	Deaths	Marriages
Toledo City Board of Health	1883+	1890+	none
Bureau of Vital Statistics	$1.00	$1.00	
635 North Erie			
Toledo, Ohio 43624			

    a. Records prior to 1908 are incomplete.

    b. Officials will search their files for a fee of $2.00 per hour and require an additional fee of $1.00 for certificate copies when a general search is made. The certificate fee is refunded when a specified record is not located.

    c. Marriage records are in custody of the Probate Court at the Lucas County Court House, Erie and Adams Street, Toledo.

Ohio (continued)	Births	Deaths	Marriages
Youngstown City Health Department City Hall Building Youngstown, Ohio 44503	1892+	1892+	none

a. Officials will search their files for the prescribed fee with only an approximate date and will also refund the fee when a record is not located.

b. Some marriage records prior to 1864 are filed at the Probate Court, Warren, Ohio, but after 1864 are located at the Mahoning County Court House, Youngstown, Ohio.

Oklahoma

	Births	Deaths	Marriages
State Department of Health Bureau of Vital Statistics 3400 North Eastern Oklahoma City, Oklahoma 73105	Oct- 1908+ $2.00	Oct- 1908+ $2.00	none

a. Copies of birth records may be obtained only if one is an authorized agent working in the interest of the individual.

b. Officials will search their files when an approximate date is given and charge $2.00 per hour for their time. The fee is not refunded.

c. Marriage records are filed at the Court House in each county.

d. The GS-SLC currently has a poor collection of vital records pertaining to Oklahoma, consisting of two or three volumes of privately compiled cemetery records.

Oregon

	Births	Deaths	Marriages
State Board of Health Vital Statistics Section P. O. Box 231 Portland, Oregon 97207	1903+ $3.00	1903+ $3.00	1907+ $2.00

a. The State office has some early birth and death records for the City of Portland covering the period early to 1880 which are incomplete and not indexed.

b. Birth records are held strictly confidential.

c. Officials will make a reasonable search of their files for a short period before and after the date provided, but will not make a general search of their entire file. $1.00 is retained as a search fee.

d. Marriage records are in custody of the County Clerk of each county and records date from 1845 or the date the county was organized.

e. The GS-SLC currently has a poor collection of vital records pertaining to Oregon, consisting of only a few volumes of privately compiled cemetery records.

f. Oregon Donation Land Claims, in three volumes, contains some good marriage information on early settlers and it is on file at Salt Lake City and BYU.

Pennsylvania	Births	Deaths	Marriages
State Department of Health	1906+	1906+	none
Division of Vital Statistics	$2.00	$2.00	

P. O. Box 90
Harrisburg, Pennsylvania 17120

    a.   Birth records are held strictly confidential and a special application form is required for birth and death records.

    b.   Birth and death records for the period 1852-1854 and birth, marriage, and death records after about 1895 are in custody of the Register of Wills in each county. These records are open to the public and may be copied by interested persons.

    c.   The GS-SLC is presently microfilming Pennsylvania county records and currently has a fair collection of vital records pertaining to the state including

        (1)   Miscellaneous vital records from the Pennsylvania Historical Society on 162 rolls of microfilm.

        (2)   Pennsylvania Marriages Prior to 1790 published 1890 in vol. 2 of the PENNSYLVANIA ARCHIVES, Second Series and recently reprinted by the Genealogical Publishing Company, Baltimore.

        (3)   County birth, death, and marriage records, now coming in on microfilm.

        (4)   An excellent collection of Quaker (Friends) church records, including the Swarthmore and Orthodox collections.

        (5)   An excellent collection of Lutheran and German Reformed church records.

        (6)   Hundreds of individual church records, various denominations, and many volumes of privately compiled church and cemetery records.

Allegheny County Health Dept.	1870-	1870-	1875-
Division of Vital Statistics	1905	1905	1905
Room 637 City-County Building	$1.00	$1.00	$1.00

Pittsburgh, Pennsylvania 15219

    a.   Birth records are held strictly confidential.

    b.   The $1.00 fee is considered a search fee and is not refunded.

    c.   For records after 1905, write to the State Health Department at Harrisburg.

Reading Bureau of Health	1876-	1873-	1876-
City Hall	1905	1905	1909
8th and Washington Streets	$1.00	$1.00	$1.00

Reading, Pennsylvania 19601

    a.   Birth records on file cover the period 1 July 1876 to 31 December 1905.

    b.   Death records on file cover the period 1 July 1873 to 31 December 1905.

    c.   Marriage records cover the period 1 July 1876 to 31 December 1909.

    d.   The Register of Wills Office at the Berks County Court House, 6th and Court Street, Reading, has death records for the period 1 January 1894 to 31 December 1905, marriage records

Pennsylvania (continued)	Births	Deaths	Marriages

1 April 1885 to the present time and birth records from May
1893 to July 1906.
   e. Officials will search their files for the stated fee.

Rhode Island

	Births	Deaths	Marriages
State Department of Health	1853+	1853+	1853+
Division of Vital Statistics	$1.00	$1.00	$1.00

Room 351 State Office Building
Providence, Rhode Island 02903
   a. Birth records are held strictly confidential.
   b. Officials will make a three-year search of their files for the
$1.00 fee but do not refund it when a record is not located.
   c. Birth, marriage, and death records, dating from the earliest
times (1636) have been published as the JAMES N. ARNOLD
COLLECTION OF RHODE ISLAND VITAL RECORDS. They
are arranged alphabetically by town and event.
   d. The GS-SLC recently received permission to film original
Rhode Island town and state records and has begun the work.
Currently, the Society has a fair collection of vital records
pertaining to Rhode Island consisting of
   (1) Published volumes of the Arnold vital records, early to
1900.
   (2) The Arnold collection of vital records on film 1636-1850
on 42 rolls of microfilm.
   (3) The Anthony Tarbox Briggs collection of family and cemetery records on 25 rolls of microfilm.
   (4) Several other private genealogical collections filed with
the State Historical Society at Providence.
   (5) An excellent collection of Quaker (Friends) records on
eleven rolls of microfilm.
   (6) Several volumes of privately compiled church and cemetery records pertaining to various towns and churches.

South Carolina

	Births	Deaths	Marriages
State Board of Health	1915+	1915+	July-1950+
Dept. of Vital Records	$2.00	$2.00	$1.00

J. Marion Sims Building
Columbia, South Carolina 29201
   a. Officials will make a general search of their files when only
an approximate date is given but do not refund the fee.
   b. Birth and death records were not kept in South Carolina by
civil authorities prior to state registration.
   c. Marriage records, primarily bonds, have been kept on a
county basis but they are few until after the Civil War period.

   d.   The GS-SLC has copies of most existing early South Carolina
        vital records including
        (1)   Several volumes of marriage bonds.
        (2)   Marriage settlements on ten rolls of microfilm.
        (3)   A good collection of Baptist, Methodist, Lutheran, and
              Presbyterian church records.
        (4)   A few volumes of DAR records.
        (5)   Several volumes of privately compiled cemetery records.
        (6)   A few volumes of vital records taken from newspapers.

South Dakota

	Births	Deaths	Marriages
State Department of Health	1906+	1906+	1906+
Division of Public Health Statistics	$2.00	$2.00	$2.00
Pierre, South Dakota 57501			

   a.   Officials will make a general search of their files as time
        permits but do not refund the fee when a record is not located.
        The $2.00 fee pays for the certificate and the search.
   b.   Marriage records prior to 1906 are in custody of the Clerk of
        the Circuit Court at the county seat and many date from the
        organization of the county.
   c.   The GS-SLC currently has a poor collection of vital records
        pertaining to South Dakota, consisting of one or two volumes
        of privately compiled cemetery records.

Tennessee

	Births	Deaths	Marriages
State Dept. of Public Health	1914+	1914+	1945+
Division of Vital Records	$2.00	$2.00	$2.00
Cordell Hull Building			
Nashville, Tennessee 37219			

   a.   Birth records are held strictly confidential.
   b.   Officials will search a three-year period for the prescribed
        fee and do not refund it.
   c.   Marriage records are in custody of the County Clerk in each
        county and date from the organization of the county.
   d.   The GS-SLC currently has only a fair collection of vital re-
        cords pertaining to Tennessee including
        (1)   A few county marriage records on microfilm.
        (2)   A few church records, mainly Baptist and Methodist.
        (3)   Several DAR record collections.
        (4)   A few privately compiled church and cemetery records.
        (5)   Several newspaper collections on microfilm.

Texas	Births	Deaths	Marriages
State Department of Health	1903+	1903+	1966+
Bureau of Vital Statistics	$2.00	$2.00	$1.50
410 East 5th Street			
Austin, Texas 78701			

   a. Birth records are held confidential but officials will issue copies if the purpose is stated in the request.

   b. Officials will make a general search of their files for the prescribed fee but do not refund it when a record is not found.

   c. Marriage records are in custody of the County Clerk in the county where the license was issued.

   d. The GS-SLC currently has a poor collection of vital records pertaining to Texas including

      (1) A few privately compiled marriage collections.

      (2) A few privately compiled cemetery and church collections.

	Births	Deaths	Marriages
San Antonio Metropolitan	1897+	1873+	none
Health Dist.	$1.50	$1.50	
131 West Nueva Street			
San Antonio, Texas 78204			

   a. Birth and death records are held strictly confidential and records indicating illegitimacy may only be had upon a court order.

   b. Officials must have the exact date of the event to search their files and do not refund the fee.

   c. Marriage records are in custody of the County Clerk, Bexar County Court House, San Antonio.

Utah

	Births	Deaths	Marriages
State Department of Health	1905+	1905+	1954+
44 Medical Drive	$2.00	$2.00	$2.00
Division of Vital Statistics			
Salt Lake City, Utah 84113			

   a. Birth records are held strictly confidential.

   b. Officials will make a general search of their files for the prescribed fee but do not refund it.

   c. Birth, death, and marriage records have been kept in most counties antidating state registration and records may be obtained from city and county health offices.

   d. Marriage records prior to 1878 are missing for Salt Lake County.

   e. Birth records dating from 1898 and death records dating from 1848 are on microfilm at the GS-SLC for the City of Salt Lake.

   f. The GS-SLC has a fair collection of vital records pertaining to Utah but they primarily relate to Salt Lake City. See chapter 5 for specific details.

Virgin Islands	Births	Deaths	Marriages
V. I. Department of Health	1906+	1906+	1954+
Bureau of Vital Records	$1.00	$1.00	$1.00
Charlotte Amalie			
St. Thomas, Virgin Islands 00801			

    a. Officials will make a general search of their files and will also refund the fee when a record is not located.

    b. Marriage records are in custody of the Clerk of the District Court at St. Thomas.

	Births	Deaths	Marriages
Charles Harwood Memorial Hospital	1893+	1893+	1890+
Local Registrar Box 520	$1.00	$1.00	$1.50
Christianated, St. Croix, V. I. 00820			

    a. Officials will make a general search of their files and also refund the fee when a record is not located.

    b. Marriage records are in custody of the Clerk of the District Court at St. Thomas.

    c. The GS-SLC currently has no vital records pertaining to the Virgin Islands.

Virginia

	Births	Deaths	Marriages
State Department of Health	1912+	1912+	1853+
Bureau of Vital Records	$2.00	$2.00	$1.00
James Madison Building			
P. O. Box 1000			
Richmond, Virginia 23208			

    a. State office also has birth and death records for the period 1853-1896 but none between 1896-1912.

    b. Marriage records prior to 1853 are in custody of the County Clerk in each county.

    c. Officials will make a general search of their files but do not refund the fee when a record is not located.

    d. The GS-SLC has a good collection of existing Virginia vital records including

        (1) Microfilm copies of original county marriage records for about 75 percent of Virginia's early counties.

        (2) Microfilm copies of the early county birth and death records dating from 1853.

        (3) Several volumes of early Anglican parish registers.

        (4) Several church record collections on microfilm.

        (5) Several volumes of privately compiled church, cemetery, and marriage records.

        (6) Many private genealogical collections on microfilm and in book form.

NOTE: The following Virginia cities had vital statistics registration prior to state registration and inquiries may be sent to the respective City Board of Health for document copies: Roanoke-1891; Norfolk-1892; Newport News-1896; Portsmouth-

Virginia (continued)	Births	Deaths	Marriages

1900; Richmond-1900; Lynchburg-1910; Petersburg-1900;
and Elizabeth City County-1900.

Vermont

	Births	Deaths	Marriages
Secretary of State	1760+	1857+	1780+
Division of Vital Records	$2.00	$2.00	$1.50
Montpelier, Vermont 05602			

    a. Officials will make a general search of their files for the prescribed fee but do not refund it.

    b. Birth, marriage, and death records were kept on a town basis and information may also be obtained from the Town Clerk.

    c. The GS-SLC has an excellent collection of Vermont vital records including

        (1) A microfilm copy of the Secretary of State's index to Vermont vital records 1770-1870 on 287 rolls of microfilm and his index 1871-1908 on 120 rolls of film.

        (2) Microfilm copies of existing town and vital records.

        (3) Several volumes of privately compiled church, cemetery, and family Bible records.

        (4) Several church records on microfilm.

        (5) A few private genealogical collections.

Washington (State)

	Births	Deaths	Marriages
State Department of Health	July-	July-	1968+
Bureau of Vital Statistics	1907+	1907+	$2.00
Public Health Buildings	$3.00	$3.00	
Olympia, Washington 98501			

    a. Officials will make a general search of their files for the prescribed fee but do not refund it when a record is not found.

    b. Marriage records are in custody of the County Auditor in each county and many date from the organization of the county.

    c. The GS-SLC has microfilm copies of Washington State's birth and death records on 164 rolls of microfilm covering the period 1907-1945. It has no other vital records with exception of LDS Church records and a few cemetery collections.

	Births	Deaths	Marriages
Spokane City Health Department	July-	July-	1890+
Vital Statistics	1891+	1891+	$2.00
Room 551 City Hall	$2.00	$2.00	
Spokane, Washington 99201			

    a. Officials will make a general search of their files for the prescribed fee and also refund it when a record is not found.

    b.   Marriage records prior to 1890, as well as after, are in custody of the County Auditor.

	Births	Deaths	Marriages
Tacoma-Pierce County Health Dept.	1887+	1887+	1861+
Room 654 County-City Building	$2.00	$2.00	$2.00
Tacoma, Washington 98402			

    a.   Officials will make a general search of their files for the prescribed fee and also refund it when a record is not found.
    b.   The early records cover Tacoma city only.
    c.   Marriage records are in custody of the County Auditor, Room 140, County-City Building, Tacoma.

Washington, D. C.

	Births	Deaths	Marriages
D. C. Department of Public Health	1871+	1855+	1811+
Vital Records Division, Room 1025	$1.00	$1.00	$2.00
300 Indiana Avenue			
Washington, D. C. 20001			

    a.   Officials will make a five-year search for the prescribed fee but do not refund it.
    b.   No records were kept during the Civil War (1862-1865).
    c.   Marriage records are in custody of the Marriage License Bureau, U. S. District Court, Washington, D. C.

West Virginia

	Births	Deaths	Marriages
State Department of Health	1917+	1917+	1921+
Division of Vital Statistics	$1.00	$1.00	$1.00
State Capitol Building			
Charleston, West Virginia 25305			

    a.   Officials will make a general search of their files for the prescribed fee but do not refund it.
    b.   Birth records are held strictly confidential.
    c.   Marriage records, and some birth and death records prior to state registration, are in custody of the County Clerks in each county.
    d.   The GS-SLC has a good collection of existing West Virginia vital records including
        (1) Miscellaneous county records, including marriages, on 256 rolls of microfilm.
        (2) Miscellaneous WPA-HRS record collections on 78 rolls of microfilm.
        (3) Several church record collections on microfilm.
        (4) Several volumes of privately compiled church and cemetery records.

Wisconsin	Births	Deaths	Marriages
State Board of Health	1876+	1876+	1840+
Bureau of Vital Statistics	$2.00	$2.00	$2.00
State Office Building			
Madison, Wisconsin 53702			

a. Records are incomplete until 1907 and are indexed by county up to that date.

b. Officials will search the early records only when an exact date and county is given but will search records after 1907 with only an approximate date. The fee is not refunded.

c. Marriage records are in custody of the County Clerks and Recorders of Deeds in some counties.

d. The GS-SLC currently has a poor collection of Wisconsin vital records, consisting of only two or three volumes of privately compiled church and cemetery records.

Wyoming			
State Department of Health	1909+	1909+	1914+
State Office Building	$2.00	$2.00	$2.00
Cheyenne, Wyoming 82001			

a. Officials will check their alphabetical index for a record when only an approximate date is given but charge $2.00 per hour for a more intensive search.

b. Marriage records are in custody of the County Clerk in each county.

c. The GS-SLC currently has a poor collection of Wyoming vital records consisting primarily of a few early marriage records and a few privately compiled cemetery records.

APPENDIX 5

PROBATE RESPONSIBILITY BY STATE WITH
CURRENT LDS GENEALOGICAL SOCIETY HOLDINGS

The following list shows probate jurisdictional responsibility by state and also includes information on probate holdings at the LDS Genealogical Society in Salt Lake City. It is quite impossible to include an inventory of all probate records at the Society (hereafter referred to as GS), but the following includes a general picture of their holdings and the direction they are taking in probate records acquisition. In some cases, early probate collections are identified in detail.

A surprising number of probates have been published, and many have been microfilmed for genealogical use. The GS has followed a general practice of microfilming will books and indexes, where they exist, but have not filmed the "files" or "probate packets." Their early filming policy also included a cut-off date of about the Civil War period (1850-65), but later policy includes filming important records down to a modern period. The GS has purchased and continues to purchase probate extracts, abstracts, and compilations containing court record information from whatever sources are available, and many of these records date after 1865.

ALABAMA
The PROBATE COURT in each county has been and remains responsible for administration of estates and the CLERK OF THE COURT has custody of the records.[1]

The GS plans to film Alabama probate records in the near future, but to date its collection consists only of a few published records. An INDEX TO ALABAMA WILLS 1808-1870, compiled by the Alabama Chapter, Daughters of the American Revolution, 1955 (GS #976.1 S2d) is on file, and over one hundred volumes of ALABAMA RECORDS are available for research. Kathleen Paul Jones and Mildred Jones Gandrud of Tuscaloosa, Alabama, have been responsible for the Alabama Record collection which includes probate information.

ALASKA
The UNITED STATES DISTRICT COURT with divisions in Juneau, Nome, Anchorage, and Fairbanks has been responsible for probate action in the state. The CLERK OF THE COURT has custody of the records.[2]

The GS has done no microfilming of probate records for the state and presently has no published material cataloged.

ARIZONA
The SUPERIOR COURT in each county holds probate responsibility

and the CLERK OF THE COURT has custody of the records.[3]

The GS has done no microfilming in the state and presently has only one published collection--PIMA COUNTY WILL BOOKS 1 and 2 (GS F#844,408).

ARKANSAS

The PROBATE COURT in each county holds probate responsibility, and the CLERK OF THE COURT has custody of the records.[4]

The GS plans to film records in the state in the near future but presently has but two published collections cataloged. They include CLARK COUNTY PROBATES (GS F#844,407) and PULASKI COUNTY ABSTRACTS OF EARLY WILLS, dating from 1818.

CALIFORNIA

The COUNTY COURT in each county holds probate responsibility, and the COUNTY CLERK has custody of the records.[5]

The GS has done no filming in the state and only has one published collection on file--WILLS OF INYO COUNTY 1868-1900 (GS F#564,337).

COLORADO

The COUNTY COURT in each county holds probate responsibility, and the COUNTY CLERK has custody of the records.[6]

The GS has done no microfilming in the state and presently has no published probate material cataloged. However, the COLORADO GENEALOGIST, a genealogical quarterly, includes some court records.

CONNECTICUT

The GENERAL COURT held probate responsibility until 1 May 1666, when the Connecticut and New Haven colonies were combined. Some probate action was also taken by the PARTICULAR COURT during that period. After 1666, the counties of Hartford, New Haven, Fairfield, and New London had separate probate jurisdiction with judges appointed who presided over joint COUNTY and PROBATE COURTS.[7] Towns are grouped in probate districts with some of the larger towns constituting a single district.[8] Many of the early probate records, particularly the "files" have been deposited with the State Library at Hartford, except for the districts of Hartford, New London, and New Haven which retained theirs. New London probate district record volumes and files covering the period 1666-1700 have been destroyed by fire.

The GS did some microfilming in Connecticut during 1948-1952 and microfilmed district probate record volumes but did not film the "files." They filmed records dating from the earliest period to about 1865, though some cover a later period. In many cases, the indexes cover a wider period than the microfilmed records.

Arrangements have just been completed which will allow the GS to return and film the remaining probate record volumes as well as other sources for the state. Officials of the GS indicate they will not film the "files," however, which is certainly unfortunate for the genealogist. Many difficult Connecticut genealogical problems can only be solved through the use of these records. Fortunately the State Library at Hartford realizes the value of these records and will provide copies at a reasonable charge.

The GS has the INDEX TO CONNECTICUT PROBATES (all districts) 1641-1948 (GS F#22786 pts 1-67) and has A DIGEST OF EARLY CONNECTICUT PROBATES 1635-1750, 3 vols., by Charles William Manwaring (GS #973.6 S2m). These two collections are indispensable for researchers working Connecticut probates. The general index includes reference to the files as well as probate volume entries, and Manwaring's Digest lists each probate district and its origin. For the colonial period, the PUBLIC RECORDS OF THE COLONY OF CONNECTICUT 1636-1776 (GS #974.6 N2c) is useful.

DELAWARE
The ORPHANS COURT in each county has been responsible for probate action since 1681/2, and prior to that time Delaware was part of New Sweden and came under control of the Dutch from New Netherland (New York). Noncurrent probate records for the three counties have been deposited with the Public Archives Commission at the Hall of Records (Dover, Delaware) and have been microfilmed by the GS.

KENT COUNTY WILLS on film cover the period 1680-1860 (GS F#2255 pts 1-9) with an index covering the period 1680-1948. KENT COUNTY GUARDIANSHIP ACCOUNTS for the period 1750-1850 are also on film (GS F#2259 pts. 1-12).
NEW CASTLE COUNTY WILLS on film cover the period 1682-1854 (GS F#2265 pts 1-7).
SUSSEX COUNTY WILLS on film cover the period 1682-1851 (GS F#2273 pts 1-5).

Other judicial records at the Hall of Records include PAPERS AND DOCKETS OF THE COLONIAL COURTS 1676-1776, CHANCERY COURT RECORDS 1776-1873 and 1914-1947, ORPHANS COURT RECORDS 1776-1873, including a series of Guardian Accounts, COURT OF OYER AND TERMINER RECORDS 1776-1868, records of the COURTS OF GENERAL SESSIONS 1776-1873, QUARTER SESSIONS 1776-1850, COMMON PLEAS 1726-1860 and 1917-1952, SUPREME COURT WRITS AND EXECUTIONS 1798-1831, and SUPERIOR COURT WRITS 1832-1890. [9]

A CALENDAR OF DELAWARE WILLS 1682-1800 was published

several years ago by the Colonial Dames of Delaware, and in 1944 the Public Archives Commission produced A CALENDAR OF KENT COUNTY DELAWARE PROBATE RECORDS 1689-1800, edited by Leon deValinger, Jr., then State Archivist. In 1964, Mr. deValinger published A CALENDAR OF SUSSEX COUNTY DELAWARE PROBATE RECORDS 1680-1800 for the Commission. [10] Copies of each of the published collections are on file at the GS in Salt Lake City.

DISTRICT OF COLUMBIA

The UNITED STATES DISTRICT COURT, Washington, D.C., and the PROBATE COURT have held probate responsibility in the District of Columbia with the REGISTER OF WILLS and the CLERK OF THE PROBATE COURT in custody of records. [11]

The National Archives has certain court records relating to the part of the District of Columbia that was not retroceded to Virginia, including naturalization records, transcripts of wills, administration papers relating to the estates of decedents, guardianship papers, and indentures of apprenticeship. [12] Transcripts of wills probated in the District of Columbia, 1801-1888, are arranged in twenty-five volumes and indexed. A second series of transcripts, 1801-1919, and the original wills are deposited with the Register of Wills and Clerk of the Probate Court, U.S. Courthouse, Washington, D.C. [13] The National Archives also has ADMINISTRATION PAPERS dating 1801-1878, GUARDIAN RECORDS dating 1801-1878, and indexes to the records. [14]

The GS in Salt Lake City has done no filming of Probates in the District of Columbia but does have DISTRICT OF COLUMBIA WILLS (abstracts) copied, typed, and indexed in 1945-46 by Mrs. Alexander H. Bell from records in the Office of the Register of Wills, Washington, D.C.--vol. 1 1776-1808, vol. 2 1808-1815. A microfilm copy of records for the period 1808-1845 is on film purchased by the GS in 1960 (GS F#28010).

FLORIDA

The COUNTY COURT and the CIRCUIT COURT have both held probate responsibility, and the COUNTY CLERK has custody of probate records. [15] The GS has done no filming of Florida probates, and the only published probates on file is an INDEX TO PROBATE BOOKS B-C for Levy County, 1858-1878 (SOUTHERN GENEALOGIST EXCHANGE 1, no. 2: 19-20).

GEORGIA

The ORDINARY COURT holds probate responsibility in each county, and the CLERK OF COURTS has custody of the records. SUPERIOR and INFERIOR COURTS also include some probate information.

The GS has filmed existing probate records for each county dating from the earliest period to about 1900 and has cataloged them under each county. Listings include estate records, annual returns of estates, guardianship records, wills, administrations, inventories, petitions, and dismissions.

EARLY COLONIAL RECORDS OF GEORGIA, which include wills and administrations, have been published under authority of the Georgia Legislature and were edited by Allen D. Candler. Volumes 1-26 (except vol. 20) are at the GS in book form. Volumes 20 and 27-39 have been transcribed, typed, and indexed but have not been published, though they are available on microfilm at the GS (GS F#158, 964; F#158,967; F#158,969; F#158,975; F#158,986; F#158,987; and F#158,992).[16]

ABSTRACTS OF THE COLONIAL WILLS OF THE STATE OF GEORGIA 1733-1777 was published in 1962 by the Colonial Dames of America, and HISTORICAL COLLECTIONS OF THE JOSEPH HABERSHAM CHAPTER, Daughters of the American Revolution carries over four hundred colonial wills of Georgia (vol. 3: 161-72. 1734-1779). The GS has copies of the above two items and also has over fifteen volumes of county court and probate extracts and abstracts. EARLY RECORDS OF WILKES COUNTY, GEORGIA, in two volumes (GS #975.6) and EARLY COURT RECORDS OF COLUMBIA COUNTY, by Mrs. F.F. Baker (GS #975.8635 P2b) are examples.

HAWAII
The CIRCUIT COURT holds probate responsibility in the Hawaiian Islands, and the CLERK OF THE COURT has custody of the records.[17] The GS has an excellent collection of historical material relating to the islands but currently has no court records on file.

IDAHO
The PROBATE COURT in each county holds probate responsibility, and the CLERK OF THE COURT has custody of the records.[18] The GS presently has no court records on file for the state.

ILLINOIS
PROBATE COURTS are organized in counties with a population of fifty thousand or over, and the COUNTY COURT holds probate responsibility in other counties. The COUNTY CLERK in each county has custody of the records.

The GS recently arranged to function in an exchange program with the state but presently does not have probate records of any consequence for the state. CHAMPAIGN COUNTY EARLY SETTLER'S RECORDS (GS #977.366 S2c), which includes wills, administrations, bonds, and letters, is the only publication currently cataloged.

INDIANA
The CIRCUIT COURT handled probates until 1829, and from then until 1873 various courts, including COURTS OF COMMON PLEAS and regular PROBATE COURTS, held responsibility. After 1873, CIRCUIT COURTS again held probate responsibility on a county basis,

and records are in custody of the CLERK OF THE CIRCUIT COURT in each county. The State Library at Indianapolis has acquired county records from commercial microfilming organizations in the state, and the GS is currently participating in an exchange program with them. Probates covering the period from county formation to about 1850-1880 have been filed for about 50 percent of Indiana's counties, and a few compiled extracts (by the D.A.R.) are available.

IOWA

The COUNTY CLERK has custody of probate records in each county, but probate jurisdiction has varied. From 1837 until about 1873, DISTRICT COURTS were responsible, but from 1873 until 1887 CIRCUIT COURTS handled such matters. In 1887, the circuit courts were abolished and district courts again took over.

The GS currently has no original probate material filed and has but two probate compilations which were produced by local chapters of the D.A.R.

KANSAS

PROBATE COURTS were established by the first Territorial Congress in 1855, and records are in custody of the PROBATE JUDGE in each county. The GS presently has no Kansas probates cataloged.

KENTUCKY

The COUNTY COURT has been responsible for probates since Kentucky was set off from Virginia, and the COUNTY CLERK has custody of the records. Probate records pertaining to the earliest settlers (1769-1784) may be found in certain Virginia county records, particularly those of Augusta, Fincastle, and Orange.

The GS has done extensive microfilming of Kentucky records and has acquired several compiled probate collections. Will books and indexes for over 75 percent of the counties are on file and cover the period from county formation to 1935. Over fifty volumes of county will extracts and abstracts have been copied by Annie Walker Burns Bell and filed at the Society.

KENTUCKY RECORDS and KENTUCKY COURT AND OTHER RECORDS, both compiled by Mrs. William B. Ardery of Paris, Kentucky, are on file at the GS and include early probate information. KENTUCKY PIONEER AND COURT RECORDS by Mrs. H.K. McAdams of Lexington, Kentucky, and ABSTRACTS OF EARLY KENTUCKY WILLS AND INVENTORIES, copied by J. Estelle Stewart King and published in 1933, fall under the same category. OLD KENTUCKY ENTRIES AND DEEDS, by Willard Rouse Jillson (The Standard Printing Co., Louisville, Kentucky, 1926) also contains probate information. It is "A Complete Index to All of the Earliest Land Entries, Military Warrants, Deeds and Wills of the Commonwealth of Kentucky."

LOUISIANA

DISTRICT COURTS sitting on a parish basis have been responsible for probate matters, and the CLERK OF COURTS has custody of the records in each parish (county). Probate records are often referred to as "successions," and documents called "tutorships" and "curatorships" are common.

The GS is currently microfilming Louisiana probate and related records, and NOTORIAL ACTS as well as FAMILY MEETINGS TO DECIDE CURATORSHIP AND TUTORSHIP are cataloged at the Library. An excellent collection of Baton Rouge probates is also on file. LOUISIANA SUCCESSIONS (GS #976.3 B4a) is the only compiled probate collection cataloged at the present time.

MAINE

The COUNTY COURT holds probate responsibility, and the REGISTER OF PROBATE has custody of the records in each county. The state was a "province" of Massachusetts until 1820 and was comprised of only one county (York) until 1760, when Cumberland and Lincoln counties were established.

Wills proved in Maine during the period 1640-1760 have been published by William Mitchell Sargent as MAINE WILLS 1640-1760 (Portland, Maine, 1887). The GS has Sargent's work in book form (GS #974.1 S2sw) and also on microfilm (GS F#599,180). LINCOLN PROBATES 1760-1800 by William Davis Patterson are also in print, and PROVINCE AND COURT RECORDS OF MAINE, in four volumes, also include some early probate information (GS #974.1 N2m).

The GS has done considerable microfilming in Maine and has existing probate records on microfilm covering the period 1640 to about 1850-1865. York, Maine, probates for the colonial period (1640-1760) are also on film at the GS and are in excellent form. General indexes exist for county probate records, and the various probate documents pertaining to a particular estate are identified in the indexes and included in the microfilm copies.

MARYLAND

Prior to 1777, a central probate agency existed in Maryland with the PREROGATIVE COURT handling probate and the COMMISSARIAT responsible for the records. Deputy "commissariats" received and filed probate papers in the counties but forwarded them to the central agency for recording. Deputies kept docket books in the counties but retained no probate documents.[19] When the first constitution was adopted in February 1777, the prerogative court was abolished, and ORPHANS COURTS were established in each county with a REGISTER OF WILLS responsible for the records.[20]

The HALL OF RECORDS at Annapolis, Maryland, has been the repository for noncurrent records, and existing probates for the provincial period as well as those from the counties are in its custody.

The provincial records date primarily for the period 1635-1777, and those from the counties date from 1777. All county probates to 1850 are on file, and many to 1949 have been centralized.

The GS has done extensive microfilming at the Hall of Records, and probates have been among the records copied. The following probates pertaining to the colonial period are on file at Salt Lake:

COLONIAL WILLS 1635-1777 (GS F#3296 pts 1-19).
TESTAMENT PROCEEDINGS 1657-1777 (GS F#3302 pts 1-11).
INVENTORIES OF ESTATES 1674-1718 (GS F#3301 pts 1-12).
INVENTORIES OF ESTATES 1718-1777 (GS F#3299 pts 1-37).
PREROGATIVE COURT ACCOUNTS 1718-1777 (GS F#3300 pts 1-19).
BALANCE BOOKS OF ESTATES 1751-1776 (GS F#3298 pts 1-7).

The following published probate collections pertaining to the state are also on file:

INDEX OF MARYLAND COLONIAL WILLS, 1634-1777, in three volumes by James M. Magruder, rpt. Baltimore, 1967, in one volume (GS #975.2 S2m).
MARYLAND CALENDAR OF WILLS, 1635-1743, in eight volumes by Jane Baldwin Cotton, rpt. Baltimore, 1967 (GS #3297 pt 19).
MARYLAND COLONIAL ABSTRACTS, 1772-1777, in five volumes by James M. Magruder, rpt. Baltimore, 1968 (GS #975.2 S2mj).
INDEX AND ABSTRACTS OF MARYLAND WILLS, 1686-1772, in fourteen volumes by Annie Walker Burns Bell (GS #975.2 S2b).
LAND OFFICE AND PREROGATIVE COURT RECORDS OF COLONIAL MARYLAND, by Elizabeth Hartsook and Gust Skordas (GS #975.2 B2ms #4).

MASSACHUSETTS
The GENERAL COURT held legislative and judicial power over the entire colony until 1639 when COUNTY COURTS (also known as "Quarter Courts in the Lawes and Libertyes") were established to handle probate and administration of estates.[21] A "Judge of Probate" and a "Register of Probate" were appointed in each county, with jurisdiction over probate, administration of estates, guardianship and adoption, and matters relating to insane or incompetent persons. The SUPREME JUDICIAL COURT was made "Supreme Judge of Probate" with appellate jurisdiction from the county courts.[22] The county courts could be held by one or more "magistrates" or "assistants" residing in a county, and clerks were "ex officio recorders" and could grant letters of administration and probate wills with two of the magistrates when court was not in session.[23]

According to Rubincam, probate includes divorce as well as

change of name since 1888, and records are in custody of the REGISTRY OF PROBATE in each shiretown (county seat).[24] Holman says that "in 1653, the Bay Colony was divided into four counties, Middlesex, Suffolk, Essex and Norfolk. This last named was the 'old' Norfolk, set up to include the towns of Dover, Exeter, Portsmouth, Salisbury, and Hampton (in New Hampshire). Its deeds and estates, 1649-1714, in 4 volumes, separately indexed, are at Salem, county seat of Essex."[25]

Old Plymouth records, including probates, were almost totally destroyed in a fire on 7 November 1881, but extant loose papers from those old files were published in the PLYMOUTH COLONY SCRAP BOOK 1636-1693, by Charles Henry Pope (Boston: Goodspeed Co., 1918). Some have also been published in the MAYFLOWER DESCENDANT, a genealogical magazine.

The GS is presently microfilming Massachusetts county and state records. Several hundred rolls of microfilm have been cataloged at this writing. Some of the Massachusetts probate indexes refer to "docket numbers" rather than to book and page numbers, and one must keep this in mind when searching the records.

MICHIGAN
The PROBATE COURT is responsible for wills and administration of estates, and the CLERK OF THE COURT has custody of the records in each county.[26] CIRCUIT COURTS also hold forth on a quarterly basis in each county, and some probate work is handled by them. The GS is currently filming Michigan county records and several have already been cataloged at this writing.

MINNESOTA
The PROBATE COURT holds probate responsibility, and the CLERK OF THE COURT has custody of the records.[27] The GS has done no microfilming in the state, as yet, and no published probate collections are presently on file.

MISSISSIPPI
The CHANCERY COURT in each county has been responsible for wills and administration of estates, and the CLERK OF THE COURT has custody of the records.[28] The GS has recently completed filming in Mississippi counties, though few have been cataloged at this writing. MISSISSIPPI COURT RECORDS 1799-1835 by June Estelle King (GS #976.2 S2k) and PROBATE RECORDS OF MARION COUNTY 1812-1959 by E. Williams (GS #929.376221 W67lo) are the only published probate collections cataloged.

MISSOURI
The PROBATE COURT in each county holds probate responsibility, and the CLERK OF THE COURT has custody of the records.[29] The GS is now in the process of filming Missouri county records, and the following published probate collections are presently cataloged at the Library:

WILLS OF MISSOURI NORTH CENTRAL COUNTIES 1853-1894
(GS #P.B. 1086).

BOONE COUNTY WILLS AND ADMINISTRATIONS 1821-1870
(GS #977.829 S2e)

CARROLL COUNTY WILLS AND ADMINISTRATIONS 1834-1879
(GS #P.B. 1091).

JASPER COUNTY ABSTRACTS OF WILLS PROVED 1881-1890
(GS #973 D4dar, vol. 14, pp. 153-83).

JASPER COUNTY WILL BOOK A; ABSTRACTS 1842-1881
(GS #977.8 V2d, vol. 2, pp. 47-94).

CLINTON COUNTY WILLS AND ADMINISTRATIONS 1833-1870
(GS #977.8155 S2c).

MACON COUNTY LETTERS OF ADMINISTRATION 1839-1855
(GS F#3617).

MACON COUNTY WILL RECORDS 1838-1880 (GS #977.827
V25e).

NEW MADRID COUNTY WILLS 1791-1804 (GS #977.8 ASh).

RANDOLPH COUNTY WILLS AND ESTATES 1836+ (GS #973
B2dar, vol. 78).

SHELBY COUNTY WILL RECORDS 1845-1876 (GS #977.832
S2e).

MONTANA
The DISTRICT COURT holds probate responsibility, and the
CLERK OF THE COURT in each county has custody of the records.[30]
The GS has done no filming in the state and has no published probate
collections cataloged.

NEBRASKA
The COUNTY COURT holds probate responsibility, and the
COUNTY CLERK has custody of the records.[31] The GS has done
no filming in the state and has no published probate collections
cataloged.

NEVADA
The COUNTY COURT has probate responsibility, and the COUNTY
CLERK has custody of the records.[32] The GS has done no microfilming in the state and currently has no published probate material on
file for the state.

NEW HAMPSHIRE
New Hampshire was not divided into counties until 29 April 1769,
when Rockingham, Strafford, Hillsborough, Cheshire, and Grafton
were organized, and all land and probate business was transacted at
the PROVINCIAL capital before that date.[33] The early towns of
Exeter, Portsmouth, Dover, and Hampton were under jurisdiction of
"Old Norfolk" County, Massachusetts, for a short time beginning in

1641, and some early probates may be in custody of the REGISTRY
OF PROBATE at Salem, Essex, Massachusetts.[34] During the
Edmond Andros Administration (1686-1690) the governor "or such
person as he might commission" granted probate of wills, but by
1767 PROBATE JUDGES were appointed.[35]

Most probate records dating from about 1635 to 1771, including
wills, administration, inventories, and related papers, are printed
in volumes 31-39 of PROVINCIAL, TOWN AND STATE PAPERS,
NEW HAMPSHIRE (GS #974. 2 N2np). The collection is also on film
at the Society (GS F#3666 pts 1-11). The original probate and
court material from which these volumes were transcribed are
filed at the library of the New Hampshire Historical Society in
Concord.[36]

An INDEX TO NEW HAMPSHIRE PROBATES OF FIVE
ORIGINAL COUNTIES 1769-1800, covering Cheshire, Grafton,
Hillsborough, Strafford, and Rockingham counties is on file at
the GS (GS F#22827), and an INDEX TO EARLY NEW HAMPSHIRE
PROBATES 1655-1701, in four volumes, is in print (GS #974. 2
S2n).

In 1951 the GS filmed New Hampshire county probates to about
1850-1870 and the following are cataloged at the library:

BELKNAP COUNTY PROBATES 1841-1865 (GS F#3674
pts 1-3).
CARROLL COUNTY PROBATES 1840-1870 (GS F#3683
pts 1-4).
CHESHIRE COUNTY PROBATES, wills and inventories 1771-
1815 (GS F#3677 pts 1-6, wills 1799-1869 (GS F#3678 pts 1-3),
administrations 1823-1869 (GS F#3681 pts 1-2), dow claims 1814-
1886 (GS F#3680 pts 1-2), and guardianship papers 1824-1853 (GS
F#3679).
COOS COUNTY PROBATES (not currently on file).
GRAFTON COUNTY PROBATES 1773-1854 with the index
1773-1900 (GS F#3695 pts 1-16).
HILLSBOROUGH COUNTY PROBATES 1771-1859 (GS F#3700
pts 1-30) and WILLS AND ADMINISTRATIONS 1771-1755 by Jessie
M. Higbee (GS #P.B. 322).
MERRIMACK COUNTY PROBATES 1823-1875 (GS F#3708 pts
1-12).
ROCKINGHAM COUNTY PROBATES 1771-1862, with the index
1660-1894 (GS F#3718 pts 1-34).

There may be some overlap between the "provincial" records and the "county" records, so both collections should be searched.

It should also be noted that "Inventories of Estates" have been cataloged at the GS for several New Hampshire towns and are not listed in the catalog under the counties.

NEW JERSEY

The PREROGATIVE COURT, held by the ordinary (governor) had jurisdiction of probate during colonial times, and the SURROGATE in each county was responsible for initiating the papers. ORPHANS COURTS were later established with the "surrogate" retaining record responsibility, but some wills and inventories have been placed in custody of the CLERK OF THE SUPERIOR COURT for a more modern period.[37]

The SECRETARY OF STATE received copies of wills and inventories probated in the various New Jersey courts and copies have been placed in the NEW JERSEY STATE LIBRARY, Archives and History Bureau, 185 West State Street, Trenton, New Jersey 08625. Wills and inventories covering the period 1663-1900 have been filed with the Bureau and have been indexed.[38] An INDEX TO NEW JERSEY WILLS AND INVENTORIES ON FILE IN THE OFFICE OF THE SECRETARY OF STATE PRIOR TO 1901, in three volumes, is on file at the GS (GS #974.9 S2n). The early records (prior to 1831) are indexed by the name of each testator, regardless of county, while those after 1831 are indexed on a county basis. The New Jersey State Library will search the indexes and provide Xerox or photostat copies at a reasonable charge or copies may be made from the microfilm copies at Salt Lake City.

The State Library at Trenton has an INDEX OF WILLS 1670-1830, in two volumes (volume 1 covers 1670-1804, and volume 2 covers 1804-1830), with the name of each testator indexed. It also has an INDEX OF WILLS 1705-1900 with Atlantic to Essex counties in volume 1, Gloucester to Monmouth counties in volume 2, and Morris to Warren counties in volume 3. The last three volumes are indexed by the name of each testator in each county.[39]

Wills covering the period 1670-1817 have been published in volumes 23 and 30-42 of the NEW JERSEY ARCHIVES, 1st series. The GS recently microfilmed probate collections at the State Library in Trenton and has the following general collections cataloged:

NEW JERSEY PROBATES 1600-1900 on thirty-three rolls of microfilm.
NEW JERSEY PROBATES ON FILE AT RUTGERS UNIVERSITY on four rolls of microfilm.
UNRECORDED WILLS AND PREROGATIVE COURT WILLS 1786-1905 on thirteen microfilm rolls.

NEW JERSEY WILLS 1705-1805 on twenty-seven rolls of microfilm.

MISCELLANEOUS NEW JERSEY WILLS 1600-1900 from Rutgers University on sixteen rolls of film.

Probate records after 1804 have been kept in the SURROGATE'S OFFICES in each county, and the GS is currently filming them and should have a majority of them cataloged within two years. Copies of wills filed since 1901 are in custody of the CLERK OF THE SUPERIOR COURT (Probate Section, State House Annex, Trenton, New Jersey 08625), and officials will search their files and send copies of documents found at a reasonable cost. [40]

NEW MEXICO
The PROBATE COURT is responsible for probate and the CLERK OF THE COURT in each county has custody of the records. [41] The GS has filmed no probate records for the state and no published material is presently cataloged for the state.

NEW YORK
Different courts and jurisdictions have held probate responsibility in New York since it was first settled. During the Dutch rule (1609-1664), the GOVERNOR GENERAL AND COUNCIL, the MAGISTRATES, and the COURTS OF THE PATROONS were responsible for most court action. After 1653, a court of the SCHOUT, BURGOMASTERS AND SCHEPENS was established, and the "burgomasters" were ORPHAN MASTERS until 1655 when an ORPHANS COURT was created. [42]

After the English gained control of New Netherland in 1664, the COURTS OF SESSIONS held probate responsibility and were held in each riding (district) three times a year. Amendments of 1666 reduced the number of sittings to two per year at New York City and Albany, but after 1683 they were held in each county four times a year. [43] From 1683 until 1778, probate was essentially a "provincial system" with the governor acting as "ordinary" of the PREROGATIVE COURT and SURROGATES acting in each county. An act in 1778 created a state JUDGE OF PROBATE and SURROGATES in the several counties. [44] The COURT OF COMMON PLEAS and the OLD SUPREME COURT (1683-1847) also held some probate jurisdiction, and several legislative acts have changed and amended probate procedure since that time. [45]

Probates prior to 1778 must be found in New York County or Albany County records. Rosalie Fellows Bailey says that the "Surrogate's Office of New York County has complete sets of libers, except for the missing volume 1 of letters of administration (covering a few years before Feb. 14, 1784). As to papers, many of the early laws including the Revised Laws of 1813 specified that the will might be returned to executor or family after recording. The New York Surrogate's files of papers are full and complete only after about 1845, despite an 1829 law specifying that the Surrogate had to keep on file affidavits, petitions, etc. Of these, the most important to the genealogist is usually the petition or citation listing all the next of kin, often giving the exact relationship and sometimes exact addresses."[46] She lists the following published materials which apply to New York, a few of which are on file at the GS:

SURROGATES COURTS AND RECORDS IN THE COLONY AND STATE OF NEW YORK, 1664-1847, by Royden W. Vosburgh, in N.Y. HISTORICAL ASSOCIATE QUARTERLY JOURNAL, April 1922, pp. 105-16.

EARLY NEW YORK PROBATE RECORDS AT THE HALL OF RECORDS, CHAMBERS ST., MANHATTAN, by Rosalie Fellows Bailey, in the NEW YORK GENEALOGICAL AND BIOGRAPHICAL RECORD 81: 44-47.

INDEX OF WILLS FOR NEW YORK COUNTY 1662-1850, 1851-1875, by Ray C. Sawyer (Manuscript).

INDEX OF LETTERS OF ADMINISTRATION FILED IN NEW YORK COUNTY 1743-1875, by Gertrude Barber (Manuscript).

ABSTRACTS OF WILLS in the NEW YORK HISTORICAL SOCIETY COLLECTIONS 25-39 (1892-1908), covering wills and administrations for 1665-1800.

ABSTRACTS OF WILLS FOR NEW YORK COUNTY 1801-1855 by Sawyer and Barber (Manuscript); copies filed at the New York Public Library and the Long Island Historical Society.

REPORTS OF CASES ARGUED AND DETERMINED IN THE SURROGATE'S COURT OF THE COUNTY OF NEW YORK, 2 vols. (1851 and 1854), by Alexander W. Bradford.

RECORDS IN THE NEW YORK COUNTY SURROGATE'S OFFICE, HALL OF RECORDS, CHAMBERS STREET, primarily administration bonds 1742-1828, 1835-1926; letters of administration 1743-1927; guardianship bond books 1802-1927; guardians accounts 1837-1898; record of dower 1831-1857; inventories of property 1776-1786, 1793-1865; wills 1665-1927; letters testamentary 1830-1927; renunciation of executors 1831-1914; orders for citation 1851-1872; proceedings in the sale of real estate 1800-1927; proceedings to probate wills of real estate 1830-1874 (files for each estate may include other items).

NEW YORK COUNTY SURROGATE'S OFFICE first fifty-six libers of wills 1665-1823, lithographed 1870-71; sheets for about forty of these libers are filed with the NEW YORK HISTORICAL SOCIETY with a manuscript index for 1801-1823.

INVENTORIES OF ESTATES IN THE SOUTHERN DISTRICT OF NEW YORK, 610 original papers, 1717-1844, at the New York Historical Society, including seventy-nine after 1800; for lists before 1800 see NYHS QUARTERLY BULLETIN 6 and 8.

INTESTATE ESTATES 1831 to date, settled by the Public Administrator for New York County, Department of Finance, Room 309, Hall of Records, Chambers Street, New York, New York.

INDEX TO WILLS PROVED IN SUPREME COURT (at N.Y.C. and Albany), Court of Common Pleas, County Court and Court of Probates, and on file in Office of Clerk of Court of Appeals, John J. Post, 1899, at Long Island Historical Society and New York Historical Society (concerns wills affecting real estate in Greater N.Y.C. not on record in Surrogate's Offices of the counties of Greater N.Y.C.).

ABSTRACTS OF WILLS PROBATED AT COMMON PLEAS COURT, N.Y.C. 1819-1892 and at Supreme Court for New York County 1821-1829, 1847-1870, by Ray C. Sawyer 1938 (a Manuscript at NYGB and LIHS).

WILLS RECORDED IN SUPREME COURT 1787-1829, 1847-1883 and in Court of Common Pleas 1805-1829, 1886-1892; in seven libers with card index at New York County Clerk's Office, Room 703, Hall of Records, Chambers Street, New York, New York.

INDEX TO WILLS OF NEW YORK STATE 1653-1815 copied by Wm. A.D. Eardely dec'd and typed 1941, MS at LIHS and NYGB (includes Court of Chancery wills and Court of Probates files and wills and also some of its administrations 1787-1815, but not volume 1 1778-1797).

CALENDAR OF WILLS ON FILE AND RECORDED IN THE OFFICES OF THE CLERK OF THE COURT OF APPEALS, OF THE COUNTY CLERK AT ALBANY, and of the Secretary of State, 1626-1836, Berthold Fernow, 1896.

COURT OF PROBATES RECORDS 1778-1823, now in custody of Clerk of the Court of Appeals, Eagle St., Albany, New York (Letters of Administration, vol. 1 for 1778-1797, 215 pages, and volume for 1815-1823 are nowhere else available by abstract or index).

COURT OF CHANCERY RECORDS, 1700-1847, registers, minute books (seventy volumes in Albany and sixty-eight volumes in N.Y.C.), order books, decrees, pleadings, depositions, and other papers mostly indexed by chief plaintiff; partly with the Clerk of the Court of Appeals, Eagle St., Albany, and partly with the New York County Clerk, Chambers St., New York.[47]

For several years, the GS had only a few abstracts from selected counties of New York, but for the past two years has been engaged in an extensive microfilming program in the state. Microfilmers are currently working in New York county records, and a considerable amount of material has already been filmed at Albany. The filming of county records, including will books and indexes, but not the files, should be complete within a two-year period, but work has not yet started in New York City. The GS recently arranged to film special genealogical material on file at the LONG ISLAND HISTORICAL SOCIETY which should be in Salt Lake also within two years.

The GS currently has eight rolls of microfilm covering early court records of the Dutch period (1650-1895) and has one volume of WILLS OF EARLY NEW YORK JEWS (1704-1799) by Leo Hershkowits (GS #973 B4s). ABSTRACTS OF NEW YORK WILLS 1665-1801 carried in the New York Historical Society Collections (vols. 25-41) are also on file (GS #974. 7 B4n). EARLY WILLS OF WESTCHESTER COUNTY 1664-1784, by William Smith Pelletreau (GS #974. 727 S2p) are on file, and a few miscellaneous published collections for New York City are cataloged. Eighty-eight rolls of microfilm presently constitute the New York City will collection which covers the period 1662-1927. There are also six rolls of film constituting the Queens College Collection of Probates covering wills 1664-1683 from the Surrogates office and probates for the period 1730-1786.

County probates in the surrogates' offices are well kept and open to the public during reasonable hours. Most offices have separate indexes for testate and intestate estates, and files are referenced in the general indexes. The probate files in the counties are usually numbered and are quite easy to locate and investigate. A variety of documents can be found in the packets, and the "petition" is probably most valuable, often including the names and addresses of conceivable heirs to the estate. Some petitions have copies of obituary notices from local papers attached which are often very helpful to the genealogist. The will books and other volumes containing inventory and administration information are also filed in the surrogates' offices and are referenced in the general indexes.

NORTH CAROLINA

Prior to 1760, the administration of estates and the proving of wills was evidently the responsibility of a "SUPREME OR GENERAL COURT," consisting of a chief justice and three associate justices commissioned by the governor.[48] In 1760, that responsibility was assigned to the SUPERIOR COURT and COURT OF PLEAS AND QUARTER SESSIONS, and in 1777, an act for establishing courts of law divided the state into six districts with a SUPERIOR COURT in each district made up of three judges learned in the law. One judge could hold court. These courts were given jurisdiction of all actions at law, administration of estates, and criminal prosecutions. By 1868, the Court of Pleas and Quarter Sessions was abolished, and probate responsibility rested with the SUPERIOR COURT, and the CLERK OF

THE COURT in each county has custody of the records, some dating from 1760.[49] Dr. H.G. Jones, North Carolina State Archivist in 1966, said that "until 1760 original wills were filed in the Office of Secretary of State, and those that have survived are now alphabetically arranged in the Archives."[50]

The GS has done extensive microfilming in North Carolina counties and also in records at the Historical Commission at Raleigh. The following general collections are on file at Salt Lake City:

NORTH CAROLINA WILLS 1663-1789, in thirty-five volumes at the Historical Commission (GS F#4546 pts 1-12).

INDEX TO NORTH CAROLINA WILLS 1663-1900, compiled by William Perry Johnson (GS #975.6 S2j).

INDEX TO MISCELLANEOUS WILLS AT THE HISTORICAL COMMISSION, Raleigh, North Carolina (GS F#4564).

NORTH CAROLINA WILLS AND COURT RECORDS 1679-1773, filed with the Secretary of State (GS F#4547 pts 1-5).

J. Bryan Grimes published an ABSTRACT OF NORTH CAROLINA WILLS in 1906 covering the period 1690-1760 and taken from wills in the Office of the Secretary of State (GS F#481,061 and book number 975.6 S2gr; also 975.6 S2nh).

Fred A. Olds compiled AN ABSTRACT OF NORTH CAROLINA WILLS from about 1760 to about 1800 which supplements Grimes Abstract (GS #975.6 S2o).

Stephenson has said that

. . . with respect to wills, the situation at first glance seems to be good. Grimes' North Carolina Wills, and North Carolina Wills and Inventories contain abstracts of the majority of the wills prior to 1760 and are well indexed. Olds' North Carolina Wills, 1760-1800 give brief abstracts; the volume is arranged by counties, but is not indexed. Wills of the earliest eastern counties are to be found in the NORTH CAROLINA HISTORICAL AND GENEALOGICAL REGISTER, generally known as 'Hathaway'. This is not indexed, but a partial index was issued by Worth S. Ray in 1945. The D.A.R. Library has a typescript index.

However, none of these compilations of abstracts is wholly satisfactory. Grimes so abbreviated his notes, to lessen the bulk of the book, that there are important omissions; also, some wills found in the counties were not included and others have been discovered since publication. Olds' is full of errors and omissions. Much of it was based on notes made for Colonel Olds by the county clerks who hastily went through their will books, jotting down pertinent facts. Hathaway is probably more accurate than either of the others. But the fact remains that none of them can be considered as complete, either in the list of testators or the abstracts.[51]

In addition to the above listed publications, the GS also has an excellent collection of North Carolina county probate records dating from 1760 (some to 1968). The majority are on microfilm, but some abstracts and extracts are in book form and date after 1760.

NORTH DAKOTA

The COUNTY COURT holds probate responsibility, and the COUNTY CLERK has custody of the records.[52] The GS has done no microfilming in the state, and no compiled probate collections are currently cataloged at Salt Lake.

OHIO

A PROBATE COURT was first established under an ordinance of the Northwest Territory in 1788, but when Ohio became a state in 1803, probate courts were abolished and the COURT OF COMMON PLEAS was given probate jurisdiction. A new state constitution in 1851 restored the probate court to handle administration of estate but also retained the Court of Common Pleas. Probate court matters included wills and administrations, testaments, administrations, guardianships, inventories, naturalization papers, vital records (births, marriages, and deaths). The Court of Common Pleas retained custody of trial dockets, journal and executor books and other civil court actions.[53]

During the past three years, the GS has microfilmed about 75 percent of Ohio's county records, including probates, but has stopped work in the state for a time. It is estimated that filming will continue within the next two years and be completed by 1975; however, this hinges on several variable factors. Less than half a dozen published probate extracts and abstracts pertaining to Ohio are currently cataloged at the GS.

OKLAHOMA

The COUNTY COURT holds probate responsibility, and the COUNTY CLERK has custody of the records.[54] The GS has done no microfilming in the state and has no published probate records on file.

OREGON

The COUNTY COURT holds probate responsibility, and the COUNTY CLERK has custody of the records.[55] Some estates between 1841 and 1845 have been filed at the State Archives in Portland.[56] The GS has done no microfilming in the state, and no published probate material is currently on file at the library in Salt Lake City.

PENNSYLVANIA

Prior to 1682, wills and administrations were recorded in NEW YORK "att the COURT OF ASSIZES OR SESSIONS," but after that date an ORPHANS' COURT was established, and the REGISTER OF WILLS, being Clerk of the Orphans Court, had custody of the records.[57] By 1776, orphans' courts were sitting quarterly in each city and county, and the COURTS OF COMMON PLEAS were given some probate jurisdiction, including jurisdiction of cases where property outside the state was involved and in guardianship of defectives.[58]

Records in the offices of the Registers of Wills consist of original wills which have been probated, unrecorded wills, will books (containing recorded copies), indexes to will books, executors' and administrators' papers and bonds, inventories and appraisements, inheritance taxes, and vital statistics for the period 1852-1855.[59]

The office of the "prothonotary," in some counties, has been combined with the "Register of Wills." So have some of their records. In Beaver, Washington, Greene, and Westmoreland counties, matters pertaining to "intestate estates" are often recorded in civil court docket books and record volumes. Rubincam says that since 1707, "Prothonotary" has been the title held by the clerk of the "court of common pleas," and that his function is to keep records pertaining to all civil cases and to establish dockets and books for the maintenance of such records.[60]

The GS microfilmed early records of several of the southeastern counties, including Philadelphia, Chester, and Lancaster, several years ago and has had excellent land and probate collections of those counties for some time. The Society recently initiated a program to film selected records in the remainder of Pennsylvania's counties and has filmed about 75 percent of the records to date. It is estimated the project will be completed within about three years. Unfortunately, the GS is not filming all county records but is being quite selective. It is giving priority to general probate indexes, will books, and land records, but is not filming civil court records from the courts of common pleas. Less than half a dozen published probate abstracts or extracts are currently cataloged at the GS library, but several hundred rolls of microfilm constitute its microfilm collection of county probates.

RHODE ISLAND

In Rhode Island, each town has kept its own deeds, probate, town council and town meeting records, and as new towns were organized, the same procedures have been followed.[61] The COUNTY COURTS may also have some probate information on file, but they have been responsible primarily for other civil and criminal court matters.

The GS is currently microfilming Rhode Island records, including probates, and will likely have the filming completed within a year. Previously, the Society has only had a few published probate extracts and no original materials.

Pertinent information about Rhode Island counties, including the location of county court offices follows.[62]

BRISTOL COUNTY - Incorporated 17 Feb 1746/7 with county limits as at present. Originally the county consisted of two towns, Bristol and Warren. In June 1770, Warren was divided and Barrington was incorporated. The County Offices are at BRISTOL.

KENT COUNTY - Incorporated 11 June 1750 and taken from Providence County. Incorporated with the same county limits as at present with the same towns, except that West Warwick was formed from Warwick in 1913. The County Offices are at EAST GREENWICH.

NEWPORT COUNTY - Incorporated 22 June 1703 as Rhode Island County. On 16 June 1729 it was incorporated as Newport County and included then Newport, Portsmouth, Jamestown and New Shoreham. New Shoreham (Block Island) joined Washington County in 1963. The County Offices are at NEWPORT.

PROVIDENCE COUNTY - Originally incorporated 22 June 1703 as County of Providence Plantations, and included the present territory of Providence, Kent and Washington counties, excepting the present towns of Cumberland, Pawtucket and East Providence. The name was changed to Providence County 16 June 1729. The Providence County Courthouse is at PROVIDENCE.

WASHINGTON COUNTY - Originally called Narragansett County. Name King's Province 20 March 1654. Boundaries established 21 May 1669. Incorporated June 1729 as King's County, with three towns of South Kingstown, North Kingstown and Westerly, the same territory as at present. Name changed to Washington County 29 Oct 1791. The town of New Shoreham was added on 17 Sept 1963. The County Offices are at WAKEFIELD, with county court sessions held in WEST KINGSTON.

SOUTH CAROLINA

Prior to 1769, probate responsibility rested with certain proprietary and crown courts at "Charles Town," and the proving of wills and administration of estates was handled by them and records were filed at Charleston.[63] In 1769, a CIRCUIT COURT system was approved with DISTRICTS established which were more convenient to the growing population. Probate as well as other court matters were handled in the districts but the records were still sent to Charleston for recording.[64]

Janie Revill notes that "all public records of the Provincial or Colonial period, 1672-1780, were kept in Charles Town (now Charleston). Some of these records have been removed to Columbia and are now kept in the office of the Secretary of State and in the archives of the Historical Commission of South Carolina. In searching out the genealogical history of any family who resided in any part of the Province prior to 1780 it is always necessary to cover these records in Charleston and Columbia."[65]

The districts established in 1769 were Beaufort, Camden, Charles

Town, Cheraws, George Town, Ninety-Six, and Orangeburgh. The towns of the same names were the district seats where court was held and where cases were tried. However, the records were sent to Charleston for filing.[66] Counties were later established in the several districts, and after 1780 probate and land records were kept in their respective courthouses. The early wills of Beaufort, Chesterfield, Colleton, Georgetown, Lancaster, Lexington, and Orangeburg have been destroyed but records of the other twenty-one counties remain intact.[67]

The GS has done extensive microfilming in South Carolina, including the filming of records at Charleston, Columbia, and in counties whose records date prior to about 1850. Most of the filming was done during 1950-1952, and the Society evidently does not plan to film additional records there in the near future.

The following entries include bibliographic information on probate publications which are general to the state and on microfilm collections from Charleston and Columbia:

INDEX TO WILLS OF SOUTH CAROLINA BEFORE 1853, by Mrs. John D. Rogers, 1959 (GS #975.7 S2rj).

ABSTRACTS OF THE OLDEST WILLS OF SOUTH CAROLINA 1672-1730, by Janie Revill, 1939 (GS #975.7 S2r).

ABSTRACTS OF WILLS OF SOUTH CAROLINA 1670-1740, by Caroline T. Moore and Agatha A. Simmons (GS #975.7 S2m).

SOUTH CAROLINA WILLS AND OTHER COURT RECORDS, by the DAR (GS #975.7 N2d).

INDEXES TO SOUTH CAROLINA WILLS COMPILED BY MARTHA LOU HOUSTON (GS #975.7 S2wp).

GENEALOGICAL COLLECTION OF SOUTH CAROLINA WILLS, by Pauline Young, 1955 (GS #975.7 S2y).

ABSTRACTS FROM COURT OF ORDINARY (Wills, Administration of estates, etc., 1679-1711, 1764-1771), carried in the SOUTH CAROLINA HISTORICAL AND GENEALOGICAL MAGAZINE 8-13 (GS #975.7 N2h).

WILLS 1694-1799 PROVED IN THE PREROGATIVE COURT OF CANTERBURY, ENGLAND OF TESTATORS BELONGING TO CAROLINA, SOUTH CAROLINA HISTORICAL AND GENEALOGICAL MAGAZINE 12: 215-18 (GS #975.7 N2h and also #975.7 B2s).

INDEX TO WILLS OF CHARLESTON COUNTY, SOUTH CAROLINA 1671-1868 (GS #975.791 S2L).

WILLS AND MISCELLANEOUS RECORDS 1687-1754 IN THE PROBATE COURT OF CHARLESTON COUNTY, SOUTH CAROLINA, transcribed by the WPA, typewritten and indexed (GS F#5435 pts 1-22).

WILLS, INVENTORIES AND OTHER MISCELLANEOUS PROBATE RECORDS 1711-1927 OF CHARLESTON COUNTY, SOUTH CAROLINA, handwritten and indexed (GS F#26430 pts 1-84).

OLD WILLS AND MISCELLANEOUS RECORDS OF SOUTH CAROLINA 1692-1868 (GS F#5431 pts 14-17).

WILLS 1671-1868 OF CHARLESTOWN COUNTY, SOUTH CAROLINA, typewritten and indexed (GS F#5432 pts 1-25; pt 25 is the general index).

CHARLESTON COUNTY, SOUTH CAROLINA COURT RECORDS CONTAINING RENUNCIATION OF DOWERS, LAND, PROBATE, AND MISCELLANEOUS COURT ACTIONS 1740-1787, typewritten (GS F#46623 pts 1-3).

RECORDS OF THE SECRETARY OF THE PROVINCE AND THE REGISTER OF THE PROVINCE OF SOUTH CAROLINA 1671-1754, from the Historical Commission, 1951 (GS F#5349 pts 1-5).

MISCELLANEOUS RECORDS (Bonds, Mortgages, Bills of Sale, Powers of Attorney, etc.) 1771-1787, Columbia, South Carolina, 1950 (GS F#5338 pts 1-3).

MISCELLANEOUS RECORDS 1774-1868 FROM ORIGINAL RECORDS AT CHARLESTON, SOUTH CAROLINA, 1951 (GS F#5348 pts 1-6).

SOUTH DAKOTA

The COUNTY COURT holds probate responsibility, and the COUNTY CLERK has custody of the records.[68] The GS has done no microfilming in the state and currently has no published probate material on file in its library.

TENNESSEE

The COUNTY COURT holds probate responsibility, and the COUNTY CLERK has custody of the records.[69] The GS has filmed a few county probate records for the state and is participating in an exchange program to acquire additional records, but at present, less than 30 percent of the counties have any probates cataloged at the GS library. A few recent acquisitions (1970-71) indicate the exchange program is still operating but evidently quite slowly. Less than half a dozen published probate collections are presently cataloged and most of the microfilm holdings are incomplete WPA copies.

TEXAS

The COUNTY COURT holds probate responsibility, and the COUNTY CLERK has custody of the records.[70] The GS has done no microfilming of Texas probates and presently has no published probate collections cataloged in its library.

UTAH

The COUNTY COURT holds probate responsibility in most counties, with a PROBATE court or the CIRCUIT court holding jurisdiction in some. The COUNTY CLERK or the PROBATE JUDGE have custody of the records, but some noncurrent records are in custody of the State Archivist at the State Capitol in Salt Lake City.

The GS has done extensive microfilming of county probate records but no published probate collections for Utah counties are presently on file at the Society.

VERMONT

Legislation in 1778 and 1779 established county courts in Vermont "to handle matters of justice," and PROBATE COURTS were established shortly thereafter and given responsibility for the proving of wills and administration of estates.[71] The REGISTER of the Probate Court is responsible for the records in each of the state's twenty probate districts. Each county comprises one or more probate districts with Caledonia, Chittenden, Essex, Franklin, Grand Isle, Lamoille, Orleans, and Washington constituting single districts[72] (fig. 210).

The following list includes details about each of Vermont's twenty probate districts and shows which probate records are at the GS library in Salt Lake City:

ADDISON COUNTY - formed 17 Oct 1785 from Rutland
Addison District: Probates begin 1852; none at the GS.
New Haven District: Probates 1824-1857 at the GS.

BENNINGTON COUNTY - formed 11 Feb 1779 from Cumberland (N. Y.)
Bennington District: Probates 1778-1851 at the GS.
Manchester District: Probates 1779-1850 at the GS.

CALEDONIA COUNTY - formed 27 Feb 1787 from Orange
Caledonia District: Probates 1796-1859 at the GS.

CHITTENDEN COUNTY - formed 22 Oct 1787 from Charlotte (N. Y.)
Chittenden District: Probates 1795-1857 at the GS.

ESSEX COUNTY - formed 5 Nov 1792 from Gloucester (N. Y.)
Essex District: Probates 1791-1855 at the GS.

FRANKLIN COUNTY - formed 5 Nov 1792 from Chittenden
Franklin District: Probates 1796-1858 at the GS.

GRAND ISLE COUNTY - formed 9 Nov 1802 from Franklin
Grand Isle District: Probates 1796-1854 at the GS.

LAMOILLE COUNTY - formed 26 Oct 1835 from Franklin, Orleans, and Washington.
Lamoille District: Probates 1837-1859 at the GS.

ORANGE COUNTY - formed 22 Feb 1781 from Cumberland (N. Y.)
Bradford District: Probates 1781-1852 at the GS.
Randolph District: Probates 1792-1850 at the GS.

ORLEANS COUNTY - formed 5 Nov 1792 from Gloucester (N. Y.)
Orleans District: Probates 1796-1855 at the GS.

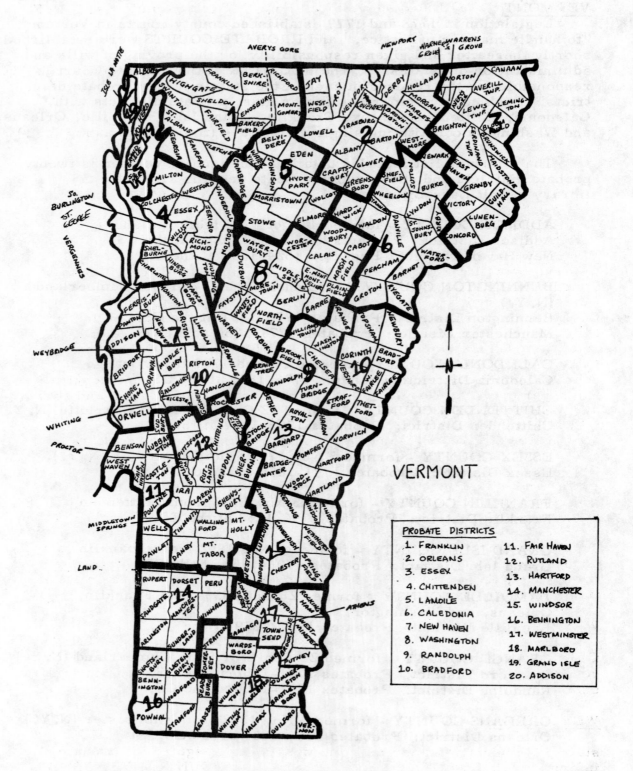

VERMONT

PROBATE DISTRICTS
1. FRANKLIN
2. ORLEANS
3. ESSEX
4. CHITTENDEN
5. LAMOILE
6. CALEDONIA
7. NEW HAVEN
8. WASHINGTON
9. RANDOLPH
10. BRADFORD
11. FAIR HAVEN
12. RUTLAND
13. HARTFORD
14. MANCHESTER
15. WINDSOR
16. BENNINGTON
17. WESTMINSTER
18. MARLBORO
19. GRAND ISLE
20. ADDISON

Fig. 210.   Vermont probate districts

622

RUTLAND COUNTY - formed 22 Feb 1781 from Cumberland (N.Y.)
Fairhaven District: Probates 1797-1823 at the GS.
Rutland District: Probates 1784-1850 at the GS.

WASHINGTON COUNTY - formed 1 Dec 1811 from Caledonia and Orange.
Washington District: Probates 1815-1857 at the GS.

WINDHAM COUNTY - formed 22 Feb 1781 from Cumberland (N.Y.)
Marlboro District: Probates 1781-1851 at the GS.
Westminster District: Probates 1781-1851 at the GS.

WINDSOR COUNTY - formed 22 Feb 1781 from Cumberland (N.Y.)
Windsor District: Probates 1787-1850 at the GS.
Hartford District: Probates 1787-1850 at the GS.

VIRGINIA

The GENERAL ASSEMBLY and the HOUSE OF BURGESSES held jurisdiction in all court matters until 1623 when MONTHLY COURTS were established. In 1642 their name was changed to COUNTY COURTS, and they were given jurisdiction in all cases at law and in equity and in probate and administration.[73] The COUNTY court has retained primary probate responsibility since that time, and the COUNTY CLERK has retained custody of the records. However, courts of common pleas and common law as well as chancery courts and superior courts have also held some probate jurisdiction and some probate information may be found among their records. Probate information is known to be of record in civil court order books, and some wills are actually recorded in deed books and vice-versa.

The GS has done considerable microfilming in Virginia, both in county and state records, and has acquired an extensive collection of published materials relating to the state. The Society filmed probate, land, and other court records for about 65 percent of Virginia's counties several years ago, and the collection covers the period "early" to about 1865. Over 150 volumes of county records, including probate indexes, extracts, and abstracts have also been acquired by the Society, and additional publications are being added to their collection monthly.

WASHINGTON

The COUNTY COURT holds probate jurisdiction, and the COUNTY CLERK has custody of the records.[74] The GS has filmed no probate records for the state and currently has no published probate material cataloged in its library.

WEST VIRGINIA

Prior to the Civil War (1862), West Virginia was part of the state of Virginia, and her records must be investigated for probate information before that date. After 1862, the COUNTY COURT held probate jurisdiction, and the COUNTY CLERK has custody of the records.[75] The GS has done some microfilming of West Virginia records and has a fair collection of WPA record collections which include probates. The Society also has a few volumes of county record extracts and abstracts which include wills and inventories.

WISCONSIN

The COUNTY COURT holds probate jurisdiction, and the COUNTY CLERK has custody of the records.[76] The GS has no probate records on file for Wisconsin at the present time.

WYOMING

The COUNTY COURT holds probate jurisdiction, and the COUNTY CLERK has custody of the records.[77] The GS has no probate records on file for Wyoming at the present time.

---

1. Noel C. Stevenson, SEARCH AND RESEARCH (Salt Lake City: Deseret Book Co., 1964), p. 66.

2. Ibid., p. 68.

3. Ibid., p. 70.

4. Ibid., p. 74.

5. Ibid., p. 78.

6. Ibid., p. 81.

7. Norman E. Wright, GENEALOGY IN AMERICA, vol. 1 (Salt Lake City: Deseret Book Co., 1968), p. 196.

8. Ibid., pp. 198, 213.

9. Public Archives Commission, State of Delaware, DELAWARE'S PUBLIC RECORDS, rev. 1964 (Dover, Delaware), n.d.

10. Milton Rubincam, PENNSYLVANIA AND DELAWARE, A paper delivered at the World Conference on Records, Salt Lake City, Utah (August 1969), p. 23.

11. Stevenson, p. 98.

12. Meredith B. Colket, Jr. and Frank E. Bridgers, GUIDE TO GENEALOGICAL RECORDS IN THE NATIONAL ARCHIVES (Washington: The National Archives, 1964), p. 142.

13. Ibid., p. 143.

14. Ibid.

15. Stevenson, p. 98.

16. Georgia Department of Archives and History, GENEALOGICAL
RESEARCH IN GEORGIA, A pamphlet prepared by Ben W.
Fortson, Jr.

17. Stevenson, p. 105.

18. Ibid., p. 107.

19. Norman E. Wright, "Midatlantic States and Canada," NORTH
AMERICAN GENEALOGICAL SOURCES (Provo, Utah: BYU
Press, 1968), p. 96.

20. Ibid.

21. Roscoe Pound, ORGANIZATION OF COURTS, (Boston: Little,
Brown & Co., 1940), p. 29.

22. Ibid., p. 137.

23. Ibid., p. 30.

24. Milton Rubincam, ed., GENEALOGICAL RESEARCH
METHODS AND SOURCES, (Washington: The American Society
of Genealogists, 1960), p. 113.

25. Ibid., p. 114.

26. Stevenson, p. 161.

27. Ibid., p. 165.

28. Ibid., p. 171.

29. Ibid., p. 175.

30. Ibid., p. 177.

31. Ibid., p. 181.

32. Ibid., p. 184.

33. Rubincam, METHODS AND SOURCES, p. 100.

34. Ibid., p. 113.

35. Pound, p. 79.

36. Rubincam, METHODS AND SOURCES, p. 100.

37. Pound, p. 79.

38. State of New Jersey, Department of Education, New Jersey State Library, Archives and History Bureau, "Genealogical Research, A Guide to Source Materials in the Archives and History Bureau of the New Jersey State Library and Other State Agencies" (July 1966), p. 15.

39. Ibid.

40. Ibid.

41. Stevenson, p. 198.

42. Pound, pp. 36, 37.

43. Ibid., p. 41.

44. Ibid.

45. Rosalie Fellows Bailey, GUIDE TO GENEALOGICAL AND BIOGRAPHICAL SOURCES FOR NEW YORK CITY (Manhattan 1783-1898) (New York: Published by the Author, 1954), p. 4.

46. Ibid., pp. 5, 6.

47. Ibid., pp. 6, 7.

48. Pound, p. 71.

49. Ibid.

50. H. G. Jones (State Archivist), "Genealogical Research in North Carolina," GEORGIA GENEALOGICAL QUARTERLY (June-July 1966).

51. Rubincam, pp. 224, 225.

52. Stevenson, p. 225.

53. Mrs. Florence Main, A LETTER TO THE LDS GENEALOG-ICAL SOCIETY, 15 December 1962, copy in possession of the author.

54. Stevenson, p. 233.

55. Ibid., p. 237.

56. David C. Duniway (Oregon State Archivist), HAVE YOU AN OREGON ANCESTOR? Bulletin no. 5, pub. no. 26, Oregon State Archives (October 1962), p. 4.

57. Rubincam, PENNSYLVANIA AND DELAWARE, p. 9.

58. Pound, p. 97.

59. Rubincam, p. 9.

60. Ibid., p. 11.

61. Charles W. Farnham, RHODE ISLAND COLONIAL RECORDS, A paper delivered at the World Conference on Records, Salt Lake City, Utah (August 1969), p. 2.

62. Ibid.

63. Pound, p. 56.

64. Mrs. Charles G. Young, RESEARCH IN SOUTH CAROLINA, A paper read at a meeting of the Memphis, Tennessee, Genealogical Society (October 1961), p. 9.

65. Janie Revill, SOUTH CAROLINA COUNTIES, DISTRICTS, PARISHES AND OLD RECORDS (GS #PB 900).

66. Ibid.

67. Young, p. 9.

68. Stevenson, p. 264.

69. Ibid., p. 270.

70. Ibid., p. 273.

71. Pound, p. 143.

72. Stevenson, p. 281.

73. Pound, p. 54.

74. Stevenson, p. 293.

75. Ibid., p. 297.

76. Ibid., p. 301.

77. Ibid., p. 304.

BIBLIOGRAPHY

American Association for State and Local History. GENEALOGICAL
RESEARCH: A BASIC GUIDE. Technical Leaflet #14, 1969.

Austin, John Osborn. GENEALOGICAL DICTIONARY OF RHODE
ISLAND IN 1887.

Ayer, N.W. & Sons. DIRECTORY, NEWSPAPERS AND PERIODICALS.
Philadelphia: N.W. Ayer & Sons, 1880+.

Bailey, Rosalie Fellows. GUIDE TO GENEALOGICAL AND
BIOGRAPHICAL SOURCES. Published by the author in New
York, 1954.

Bennett, Archibald F. A GUIDE FOR GENEALOGICAL RESEARCH.
2nd ed. Salt Lake City: Genealogical Society, 1960.

_____. ADVANCED GENEALOGICAL RESEARCH. Salt
Lake City: Bookcraft, 1959.

_____. FAMILY EXALTATION. Salt Lake City: Deseret
Book Co., 1957.

_____. FINDING YOUR FOREFATHERS IN AMERICA.
Salt Lake City: Bookcraft, 1957.

_____. PROVING YOUR PEDIGREE.

_____. SEARCHING WITH SUCCESS. Salt Lake City:
Deseret Book Co., 1962.

_____, ed. THE UTAH GENEALOGICAL AND HISTORICAL
MAGAZINE. 31 vols. Salt Lake City: The Genealogical
Society of Utah, 1910-1940.

Bennion, Howard S. GENEALOGICAL RESEARCH: A PRACTICAL
MISSION. Salt Lake City: Deseret News Press, 1964.

Bidlack, Russell E. FIRST STEPS IN CLIMBING THE FAMILY
TREE. Detroit: Detroit Society for Genealogical Research,
1962.

Boykin, Phyllis M., and Donna J. Porter. THE WELDING LINK:
A TRAINING COURSE IN GENEALOGY. Denver: Boykin-
Porter, 1967.

Brigham, Clarence S. HISTORY AND BIBLIOGRAPHY OF
AMERICAN NEWSPAPERS 1690-1820. 2 vols. Worcester,
Massachusetts: American Antiquarian Society, 1947.

Brigham Young University. GENEALOGICAL DEVOTIONAL ADDRESSES. Address by Howard W. Hunter. FOURTH ANNUAL PRIESTHOOD GENEALOGICAL RESEARCH SEMINAR (12 August 1969). Provo, Utah: BYU Press, 1969.

BULLINGER'S POSTAL GUIDE.

Bushby, Gladys and Evelyn Fish. PRACTICAL RESEARCH IN GENEALOGY: A COMPILATION OF GENEALOGICAL RESEARCH DATA. Mesa, Arizona: Arizona Temple District Genealogical Library, 1955.

Cache Genealogical Library. HANDBOOK FOR GENEALOGICAL CORRESPONDENCE. Salt Lake City: Bookcraft, 1963.

Canada Public Archives. TRACING YOUR ANCESTORS IN CANADA. Ottawa: The Dominion Archives, 1966.

Cappon, Lester J. AMERICAN GENEALOGICAL PERIODICALS: A BIBLIOGRAPHY WITH A CHRONOLOGICAL FINDING-LIST. New York: The New York Public Library, 1964.

_____. "Genealogy: Handmaid of History." NATIONAL GENEALOGICAL SOCIETY QUARTERLY 45, 1957.

Cardner, Robert W. INDEX TO GENEALOGICAL PERIODICALS. Madison, Connecticut: n.p., 1953-1967.

Carter, Kate B. HEART THROBS OF THE WEST. 12 vols. Salt Lake City: Daughters of Utah Pioneers, 1939-1951.

_____. TREASURES OF PIONEER HISTORY. 5 vols. Salt Lake City: Daughters of Utah Pioneers, 1947-1950.

Child, Sargent B. and Dorothy P. Holmes. CHECK LIST OF HISTORICAL RECORDS SURVEY PUBLICATIONS. Bibliography of Research Projects Reports. Baltimore: The Genealogical Publishing Co., 1969.

The Church of Jesus Christ of Latter-day Saints. A CONTINUING PRIESTHOOD PROGRAM FOR FAMILY EXALTATION. 1970.

Clough, Wilson O. ANCESTORS ALL: A SIMPLE, SCIENTIFIC METHOD FOR RECORDING ANCESTORS. Laramie, Wyoming: n.p. 1960.

Colket, Meredith B., Jr. "Creating a Worthwhile Family Genealogy." NATIONAL GENEALOGICAL SOCIETY QUARTERLY 506, no. 4 (December 1968).

_____. GUIDE TO GENEALOGICAL RECORDS IN NATIONAL ARCHIVES. 1964.

Crozier, William Armstrong. A KEY TO SOUTHERN PEDIGREES. 2d ed. Baltimore: Southern Book Co., 1953.

Daughters of the American Revolution. IS THAT LINEAGE RIGHT?: A TRAINING MANUAL. Washington: National Society of DAR, 1958.

Doane, Gilbert H. SEARCHING FOR YOUR ANCESTORS. Minnepolis, Minnesota: University Press, 1960.

Dragsted, Ove. "The Marstrand System of Filing Genealogical Material." GENEALOGISTS MAGAZINE 11 (1952).

Esshom, Frank. PIONEERS AND PROMINENT MEN OF UTAH. Salt Lake City: Utah Pioneers Book Publishing Co., 1913.

Evans, Charles, and Shaw-Shoemaker. AMERICAN BIBLIOGRAPHY.

Everton, George B., Sr., ed. THE HANDY BOOK FOR GENEALO-GISTS. 6th ed. rev. & enl. Logan, Utah: The Everton Publishers, 1971.

_____. THE HOW BOOK FOR GENEALOGISTS.

Farmer, John. A GENEALOGICAL REGISTER OF THE FIRST SETTLERS OF NEW ENGLAND. Lancaster, Massachusetts: Carter-Andrews, 1829.

Filby, P. William. AMERICAN & BRITISH GENEALOGY & HERALDRY: A SELECTED LIST OF BOOKS. Chicago: American Library Association, 1968.

Fotheringham, Ila J. GENEALOGICAL SOURCES FOR UTAH AND LDS CHURCH SURVEY AND RESEARCH. n.p. 1968.

Gardner, David E., et al. A BASIC COURSE IN GENEALOGY, VOLUME I: INTRODUCTION TO RECORD KEEPING AND RESEARCH. Salt Lake City: Bookcraft, 1958.

Genealogical Associates. GENEALOGY AND LOCAL HISTORY: AN ARCHIVAL AND BIBLIOGRAPHICAL GUIDE. Evanston, Illinois: n.p. 1958. In progress.

Genealogical Society. PAPERS PRESENTED AT THE WORLD CONFERENCE ON RECORDS. Several vols. Salt Lake City: 1969.

THE GENEALOGISTS REFERENCE JOURNAL. Leicester: n.p., 1925.

Glenn, Thomas Allen. LIST OF SOME AMERICAN GENEALOGIES WHICH HAVE BEEN PRINTED IN BOOK FORM IN 1896. Baltimore: Genealogical Publishing Co., n.d.

Gobble, John R. WHAT TO SAY IN YOUR GENEALOGICAL LETTERS: DO'S AND DONT'S IN GENEALOGICAL CORRESPONDENCE. Idaho Falls, Idaho, n.p., 1967.

_____. WHO'S WHERE IN YOUR GENEALOGICAL RECORDS: A FILING AND FINDING SYSTEM. Idaho Falls, Idaho: n.p., 1963.

Gooch, Roe Ann. THE NOTE KEEPER: GENEALOGICAL RESEARCH, SCIENTIFICALLY SYSTEMATIZED. Salt Lake City: Litho Graphics, 1966.

Greenwood, Val D. THE RESEARCHER'S GUIDE TO AMERICAN GENEALOGY. Baltimore: The Genealogical Publishing Co., 1973.

Gregory, Winifred. AMERICAN NEWSPAPERS 1821-1936: A UNION LIST OF FILES AVAILABLE IN THE UNITED STATES AND CANADA. New York: The H.W. Wilson Co., 1937.

Harland, Derek. GENEALOGICAL RESEARCH STANDARDS. Salt Lake City: Bookcraft, 1963.

Highland Stake. A TO Z IN GENEALOGY: SOME BASIC SUGGESTIONS ON RECORD MAKING. Salt Lake City: n.p., 1958.

Historical Records Survey Projects of the Works Progress Administration. GUIDES TO MANUSCRIPT COLLECTIONS AND INVENTORIES.

Holben, Richard E. RESEARCHING THE FAMILY HISTORY FOR BEGINNERS. Albuquerque, New Mexico: Family History, 1968.

Hopkins, Garland E. YOUR FAMILY TREE: A HOBBY HANDBOOK. Richmond: Deitz Press, 1949.

Ireland, David. YOUR FAMILY TREE: A HANDBOOK ON TRACING YOUR ANCESTORS AND COMPILING ONE'S OWN PEDIGREE. Tring, Herts.: Shire Publications, 1970.

Jacobus, Donald Lines. GENEALOGY AS PASTIME AND PROFESSION. 2nd ed. rev. Baltimore: The Genealogical Publishing Co., 1968.

_____. INDEX TO GENEALOGICAL PERIODICALS, vol. 1 (1932).

_____. "Is Genealogy an Exact Science: Methods of Research." AMERICAN GENEALOGIST 10 (1934).

_____. "The Value of Searching Original Records." THE AMERICAN GENEALOGIST 40 (July 1964).

Jaussi, Laureen R., and Gloria D. Chaston. FUNDAMENTALS OF A GENEALOGICAL RESEARCH. 2nd ed. rev. & enl. Salt Lake City: Deseret Book Co., 1972.

_____. REGISTER OF LDS CHURCH RECORDS. Salt Lake City: Deseret Book Co., 1968.

Jenson, Andrew. DAY BY DAY WITH THE UTAH PIONEERS. 1847.

_____. ENCYCLOPEDIC HISTORY OF THE CHURCH OF JESUS CHRIST OF LATTER-DAY SAINTS. Salt Lake City: Deseret News Publishing Co., 1941.

_____. HISTORICAL RECORD AND CHURCH CHRONOLOGY.

_____. LATTER-DAY SAINT BIOGRAPHICAL ENCYCLOPEDIA. 4 vols. Salt Lake City: The Andrew Jenson History Co., 1901-1936.

Jones, Milton J. GENEALOGICAL RESEARCH WORK BOOK. Salt Lake City: LDS Aids, 1965.

Jones, Vincent L. "Effective Ways to Prepare and Preserve Research Notes." INSTRUCTOR, October 1963.

_____, et al. GENEALOGICAL RESEARCH: A JURISDICTIONAL APPROACH. Rev. ed. Salt Lake Publishers Press, 1972.

_____. "Make a Preliminary Survey." INSTRUCTOR 94 (1960).

_____. STAMP OUT CHAOS, ELIMINATE CONFUSION. Transcript of lecture given 20 April 1963. Mt. Hood Genealogical Forum, Oregon City, Oregon.

Jordan, D.S., and S.L. Kimball. YOUR FAMILY TREE: BEING A GLANCE AT SCIENTIFIC ASPECTS OF GENEALOGY. New York: n.p., 1929.

Jeustrich, Max N. FAMILY HISTORY. West New York, New Jersey: n.p., 1936.

Kaminkow, Marion J., ed. GENEALOGIES IN THE LIBRARY OF CONGRESS: A BIBLIOGRAPHY. 2 vols. Baltimore: Magna Carta Book Co., 1972.

Kent, D.B.G. "The Study of Ancestry." THE VERMONTER 20 (1915).

Kirkham, E. Kay. THE ABC'S OF AMERICAN GENEALOGICAL RESEARCH. Salt Lake City: Deseret Book Co., 1954.

_____. A SURVEY OF AMERICAN CHURCH RECORDS, vol. 1. 3rd ed. enl. Logan, Utah: Everton Publishers, 1971.

_____. THE COUNTIES OF THE UNITED STATES. Salt Lake City: Kay Publishing Co., 1961.

_____. THE COUNTIES OF THE UNITED STATES AND THEIR GENEALOGICAL VALUE. Salt Lake City: Deseret Book Co., 1965.

_____. HOW TO READ THE HANDWRITING AND RECORDS OF EARLY AMERICA. Salt Lake City: Kay Publishing Co., 1961.

_____. THE LAND RECORDS OF AMERICA AND THEIR GENEALOGICAL VALUE. Washington: n.p., 1963.

_____. MAKING THE GENEALOGICAL RECORD: AN EXPLANATION OF THE O-KAY SYSTEM OF RECORD-KEEPING. Salt Lake City: Deseret Book Co., 1959.

_____. PHOTOGRAPHY IN GENEALOGY: AN EXPLANATION OF THE O-KAY SYSTEM OF RECORD-KEEPING. Salt Lake City: n.p., 1951.

_____. RESEARCH IN AMERICAN GENEALOGY. Salt Lake City: Deseret Book Co., 1956.

_____. SIMPLIFIED GENEALOGY FOR AMERICANS. Salt Lake City: Deseret Book Co., 1968.

_____. SOME OF THE MILITARY RECORDS OF AMERICA BEFORE 1900: THEIR USE AND VALUE IN GENEALOGICAL AND HISTORICAL RESEARCH. Washington: n.p., 1963.

_____. A SURVEY OF AMERICAN CENSUS SCHEDULES: AN EXPLANATION AND DESCRIPTION OF OUR FEDERAL CENSUS ENUMERATIONS 1790 TO 1950. Salt Lake City: Deseret Book Co., 1959.

_____. A SURVEY OF AMERICAN CHURCH RECORDS; FOR THE PERIOD BEFORE THE CIVIL WAR, EAST OF THE MISSISSIPPI RIVER. 2 vols. Salt Lake City: Deseret Book Co., 1959-1960.

Komaiko, Jean and Kate Rosenthal. YOUR FAMILY TREE. New York: Parents Magazine Press, 1963.

Langton, D. "Records and Record Searching in Jersey." GENEALOGISTS MAGAZINE 5 (1931).

Libby, Charles T. GENEALOGICAL DICTIONARY OF MAINE AND NEW HAMPSHIRE. 1928-1939.

Long Island Historical Society. A CATALOG OF AMERICAN GENEALOGIES IN THE LONG ISLAND HISTORICAL SOCIETY. New York: n.p., 1935.

Lundgren, Victor. INDEXING NAMES TO SAVE DUPLICATIONS WHEN RESEARCHING. Provo, Utah: J. Grant Stevenson, n.d.

Macko, George W. "The Generations of Men Shall Be Numbered," ARIZONA LIBRARIAN 22, no. 3 (Summer 1965).

MacLachen, John D. FAMILY RECORD BOOK. New York: n.p., 1936.

Meads, Dorothy M. "Searching Local Records," REVIEW OF ENGLISH STUDIES 4 (1928).

Mears, Neal F. WHAT IS UP IN YOUR FAMILY TREE? Chicago: n.p., 1928.

Mesa Tenth Ward. PRIMARY SOURCES FOR GENEALOGICAL RESEARCH. Mesa, Arizona: East Mesa Stake, 1965.

Michael, Prudence G. DON'T CRY TIMBER. n.p., 1970.

Mills, William S. FOUNDATIONS OF GENEALOGY. New York: Monographs Publishing Co., 1899.

Moore, Russell F. THE FAMILY HISTORY BOOK: A GENEALOGICAL RECORD. New York: Simmons-Boardman Publishing Corp., 1961.

Morris, Louise E.B. PRIMER IN GENEALOGICAL RESEARCH. Dallas: B. & W. Printing and Letter Service, 1965.

Munsell, Joel's Sons. INDEX TO AMERICAN GENEALOGIES. 4th and 5th editions, 1895 and 1900.

_____. SUPPLEMENT TO THE INDEX TO GENEALOGIES 1900-1908.

Newberry Library. GENEALOGICAL INDEX. 4 vols. Boston: G.K. Hall, 1960.

_____. GENEALOGY BEGINNERS MANUAL. Chicago: Newberry Library, 1965.

Nerney, Mary C. "Excursion into Genealogy: Immortality in Reverse." VERMONT HISTORY 16 (1948).

Nichols, Elizabeth L. THE GENESIS OF YOUR GENEALOGY: A SIMPLIFIED STEP-BY-STEP INSTRUCTION BOOK FOR THE BEGINNER IN GENEALOGY. Providence, New Jersey for the author, 1969.

Oates, Addison F. THE ART OF COLLECTING GENEALOGY AND HISTORY. n.p., 1971.

O'Connell, Basil M. (Articles on Genealogy Reprinted from Various Periodicals), 1955-.

Owen, Joyce D. LET'S CLIMB A FAMILY TREE. n.p., 1967.

Oyler, Beth. INDEX TO HEART THROBS OF THE WEST. Salt Lake City: Free Public Library, 1948.

Peterson, Clarence Stewart. CONSOLIDATED BIBLIOGRAPHY OF COUNTY HISTORIES IN FIFTY STATES IN 1961. 2nd ed. Baltimore: The Genealogical Publishing Co., 1963.

Phillimore, W.P.W. HOW TO WRITE THE HISTORY OF THE FAMILY: A GUIDE FOR THE GENEALOGIST. Boston: Cupples & Hurd, 1888. (2nd ed. 1900. 3rd ed. London: 1905 under title, THE FAMILY HISTORIAN: A SHORT GUIDE FOR WRITING AND PRINTING THE HISTORY OF A FAMILY.)

Pine, Leslie G. AMERICAN ORIGINS. Garden City: Doubleday, 1960. (Reissued, Baltimore: Genealogical Book Co., 1967).

_____. THE GENEALOGISTS ENCYCLOPEDIA. Newton-Abbott: David & Charles, 1969.

Pitoni, Venanzio P. GUIDEX: GENEALOGICAL RESEARCH: A GUIDE TO PRINCIPAL SOURCES AND INDEXES. 2nd ed. Annapolis: n.p., 1946.

Powell, Thomas. DIRECTION FOR THE SEARCH OF RECORDS. 1622. Reissued as Repertoire of Records, 1631.

Preece, Florence S. and Phyllis P. PRELIMINARY SURVEY WORK-BOOK. n.p. 1966.

Public Archives of Canada. TRACING YOUR ANCESTORS IN CANADA. Ottawa: Public Archives, 1966. Reprinted, GENEALOGISTS MAGAZINE 15 (1966).

RAND MCNALLY COMMERCIAL ATLAS AND MARKETING GUIDE.

Reed, Evan L. WAYS AND MEANS OF IDENTIFYING ANCESTORS. Chicago: Ancestral Publishing & Supply Co., 1947.

_____. WHENCE CAME YOU AND HOW TO PROVIDE THE ANSWER. Chicago: Ancestral Publishing & Supply Co., 1947.

Rider, Fremont. AMERICAN GENEALOGICAL INDEX. 48 vols. Middletown, Connecticut: The Godfrey Memorial Library, 1952-1953.

_____. AMERICAN GENEALOGICAL-BIOGRAPHICAL INDEX. 74 vols. Middletown, Connecticut: The Godfrey Memorial Library, 1952+. (Alphabet covered from 'A-H' only.)

Rogers, Ellen Stanley, ed., vols. 1-4. GENEALOGICAL PERIODICAL ANNUAL INDEX. Bladensburg, Maryland: The Genealogical Recorders, 1963-1967.

Rubincam, Milton, ed. GENEALOGICAL RESEARCH: METHODS AND SOURCES. Washington, D.C.: American Society of Genealogists, 1960.

Russell, George Ely, ed. vols. 5-8. GENEALOGICAL PERIODICAL ANNUAL INDEX. Bowie, Maryland: The Genealogical Recorders, 1968-1970.

Shephard, Charles. "Genealogical Bibliographies and Handbooks." NATIONAL GENEALOGICAL SOCIETY QUARTERLY 12 (1923).

Stetson, Oscar F. THE ART OF ANCESTRAL HUNTING: A GUIDE TO ANCESTRAL RESEARCH AND GENEALOGY. Brattleboro, Vermont: n.p., 1936. 3rd ed. New York: Stephen Daye Press, 1956.

Stevenson, J. Grant. A GENEALOGICAL CHECKLIST. Provo, Utah: Stevenson Supply, 1964.

_____. A GENEALOGICAL STUDY GUIDE. Provo, Utah: Stevenson Supply, 1962.

Stevenson, Noel C., ed. THE GENEALOGICAL READER. Salt Lake City: Deseret Book Co., 1958.

_____. SEARCH AND RESEARCH: THE RESEARCHERS HANDBOOK. Salt Lake City: Deseret Book Co., 1951. 2nd ed. 1959.

Stewart, Robert Armistead. INDEX TO PRINTED VIRGINIA GENEAL-
OGIES. Baltimore: The Genealogical Publishing Co., 1965.

Stiles, Henry E. A HANDBOOK OF PRACTICAL SUGGESTIONS FOR
THE USE OF THE STUDENT OF GENEALOGY. Albany: Joel
Munsell & Sons, 1899.

Swem, Earl G. VIRGINIA HISTORICAL INDEX. Gloucester, Massachusetts: Peter Smith, 1965.

Tate, George F. A PRACTICAL SYSTEM OF PHOTOGRAPHY FOR
GENEALOGISTS AND HISTORIANS, Provo, Utah: n.p., n.d.

Tolman, William O. AN INTRODUCTION TO RECORD-KEEPING
AND RESEARCH. Provo, Utah: n.p., n.d.

United States Library of Congress. A CHECK LIST OF AMERICAN
EIGHTEENTH CENTURY NEWSPAPERS IN THE LIBRARY OF
CONGRESS. New ed. Washington: United States Government
Printing Office, 1936.

United States Library of Congress. A CHECK LIST OF FOREIGN
NEWSPAPERS IN THE LIBRARY OF CONGRESS. Washington:
United States Government Printing Office, 1929.

United States Library of Congress. CATALOG OF PRINTED CARDS.

United States Library of Congress. GUIDE TO GENEALOGICAL
RESEARCH: A SELECT LIST. Washington, D.C.: n.d.

United States Library of Congress. Union Catalog Division.
NEWSPAPERS ON MICROFILM. 6th ed. Washington:
Government Printing Office, 1967.

UNITED STATES OFFICIAL POSTAL GUIDE.

Vallentine, John R., ed. HANDBOOK FOR GENEALOGICAL
CORRESPONDENCE. (Sponsored by Cache Genealogical Library,
Logan, Utah.) Salt Lake City, Utah: Bookcraft, 1963.

Virkus, Frederick A. THE ABRIDGED COMPENDIUM OF AMERICAN
GENEALOGY. 7 vols. Chicago: A.N. Marquis & Co., 1952.

Wadham, Rex A., and Evan H. Memmott. CREATIVE GENEALOGY.
Provo, Utah: Offset Copy Co., 1965.

Waldermaier, Inez. GENEALOGICAL NEWSLETTER.

Wall, Alexander J. "American Genealogical Research," PAPERS
OF THE BIBLIOGRAPHIC SOCIETY OF AMERICA 36 (1942).

Wallace, Arthur, and Shirley Bousfield. RECORD-KEEPING IN GENEALOGICAL RESEARCH. Los Angeles: Los Angeles Temple Genealogical Library, 1964.

White, David. REFERENCE MANUAL FOR GENEALOGICAL RESEARCH. Penelyn, Pennsylvania: n.p., 1954.

Williams, Ethel W. KNOW YOUR ANCESTORS: A GUIDE TO GENEALOGICAL RESEARCH. Rutland, Vermont: C.E. Tuttle Co., 1961.

Wolf, J.C. "Tools and Techniques of Genealogical Research." INDIANA MAGAZINE OF HISTORY 38 (1942).

Wright, Norman E. GENEALOGY IN AMERICA, VOLUME I: MASSACHUSETTS, CONNECTICUT AND MAINE. Salt Lake City: Deseret Book Co., 1968.

_____. KEY TO GENEALOGICAL RESEARCH ESSENTIALS. Provo, Utah: Brigham Young University Press, 1966. (Reissued Salt Lake City: Bookcraft, 1967.)

_____. MIGRATION SOURCES OF GREAT BRITAIN AND NORTH AMERICA. Provo, Utah: Brigham Young University Press, 1968.

_____. "Orderly Preservation of Research Notes." INSTRUCTOR 99 (1964).

Zabriskie, George O. CLIMBING OUR FAMILY TREE SYSTEMAT-ICALLY. Salt Lake City: Parliament Press, 1969.